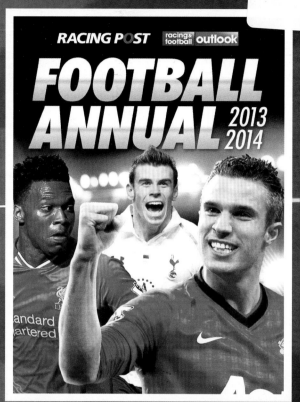

RACING POST racing&football outlook

FOOTBALL ANNUAL 2013 2014

Edited by Paul Charlton and Dan Sait

Contributors Paul Charlton, Dan Childs, Alex Deacon, Andy Dietz, Derek Guldberg, Dylan Hill, Glenn Jeffreys, Chris Mann, Kevin Pullein, Dan Sait, Danny Hayes, Nigel Speight, Ian Wilkerson

Published in 2013 by Raceform Ltd

High Street, Compton, Newbury, Berkshire, RG20 6NL

A catalogue record for this book is available from the British Library.

ISBN 978-1-908216-91-5

Printed and bound in Great Britain by the Buxton Press

After the hangover, it's time to cut loose

Trailing in the wake of an all-time classic campaign, 2012-13 always had a lot to live up to. And, in truth, it didn't come close to matching the last-minute drama of the 2011-12 domestic season or a dizzy summer in which we were spoilt by the heady thrills of Euro 2012 and the London Olympics.

Certainly the top tiers of the English and Scottish domestic leagues failed to deliver much in the way of twists and turns.

Man United might have had to wait until April before officially cracking open the bubbly, but the title was bound for Old Trafford from the moment that the Red Devils won the Manchester derby in early December. There was a distinct lack of squeaky bum time as United's pursuers never came within four points of a side who were 15 points clear going into April, but what better way for Sir Alex Ferguson to bow out than by steamrollering the opposition with yet another of his newly constructed teams? A true great signed off in fitting fashion.

But United's cruise looked a roller-coaster ride compared to an SPL campaign that was decided before a ball had been kicked. After Rangers had suffered demotion to the fourth tier, Celtic were granted a free pass to silverware and the 1-100 shots never looked like embarrassing themselves.

With Rangers marching to the Division Three title by 24 points, the only real intrigue north of the border lay in what happened behind the scenes, with the SPL and SFL finally merging as Scottish football took the first small, and relatively uninspiring, steps towards fixing a struggling system. Developments over the next few years will hopefully be far more interesting.

Looking further afield, and while one season is too small a sample from which to draw firm conclusions, there seemed something seismic about events on the European front.

Britain's performance in the Champions League was mixed. Celtic delivered, beating Barcelona during a fantastic run to the last 16, but the English sides did not.

Both Man United and Arsenal bemoaned their luck in the knockout stages, but the truth was that they were outclassed. At least they escaped the group stage, however, in contrast to the disappointing displays offered by first-round casualties Man City and Chelsea. That the Blues went on to celebrate Europa League success says more about the flawed structure of Uefa's tournaments than it does about the level of the Blues' achievement in claiming a consolation prize.

But while the Premier League stalled in European competition, the Bundesliga went through the gears in impressive style to put Spanish domestic dominance on the back burner.

A Champions League final of exceptional quality between Bayern Munich and Borussia Dortmund capped a season in which all seven German sides escaped the group stage of the two Uefa competitions. Time will tell if it will prove an isolated spike or a solid trend but any 'best league in the world' claims from the Premier League are sounding ever more like wishful thinking.

But after suffering a hangover campaign in 2012-13, all the signs point to a thriller for the year ahead.

Sir Alex may be gone but Jose Mourinho is back, and with new faces in the dugouts of the Premier League's top three sides the title race has a truly open feel to it.

And, on the international stage, we have been treated to a tantalising taster with this summer's thrilling Confederations Cup, won in fine style by the hosts of the 2014 World Cup. If England and Ireland can make it to Brazil next summer we could be in for a treat.

You'll find the best football betting coverage on the market in the Racing & Football Outlook every Tuesday and in the Racing Post every day of the week, with unique stats, form and ratings along with tipping and analysis from some fine betting brains. And don't forget to point your browser at soccerbase.com, where you'll find a range of tools to help you pick winners.

It's going to be a brilliant year of football – we hope you'll join us for it!

A summer of change means London clubs can set the title pace

t has to be London's turn. After three years of Manchester domination, Chelsea can reclaim the crown they last won in 2010, writes Figaro.

There are many things I could add to the points made about both **Chelsea** and **Arsenal** in our Analysis feature on page 124. Even Fernando Torres was putting in good shifts as Rafa Benitez gave him a prolonged run in the side. The Spanish striker then capped that by scoring five times to take the Golden Boot in the Confederations Cup, where David Luiz played a blinder in the final.

I first tipped Chelsea for the title at 13-5 in the Racing & Football Outlook back in the spring. Since then, their price has continued to shrink and rightly so. Major signings by the Manchester clubs and Chelsea may or may not come nearer the end of the transfer window when the new managers will have had time to assess more accurately the value of the sides they have inherited.

By selling Carlos Tevez to Juventus though, Man City made it quite clear that they are keeping an eye on the Uefa Financial Fair Play rules that are poised to apply and they will miss the dressing room experience of Kolo Toure as well, while Man United are now bossed by a man whose personality and experience are very different to Sir Alex Ferguson's – when Fergie picked up the reins at Old Trafford, he had already won 11 titles in Scotland and in Europe.

As regards Arsenal, it's pleasing that no-one else seems to be considering them. Everyone has concentrated on the value of the managerial merry-go-round to Chelsea, without considering how Arsenal (and Tottenham – and Liverpool if they can keep Luis Suarez) stand to benefit as well.

The extent to which things have changed at The Emirates was evident from the gossip linking them with a £20m move for Wayne Rooney or the actual £23m purchase of Gonzalo Higuain from Real Madrid. A year ago no-one would have dreamt that Arsenal would sanction a £20m move for anyone.

What about lower down? For once we have big favourites in all three of the other English Leagues – QPR, Wolves and Portsmouth, all of whom were relegated last term.

As I write, Harry Redknapp has been clearing the decks at Loftus Road with Chris Samba, Jay Bothroyd, Rob Hulse, DJ Campbell and Djibril Cisse among the rejects. There have been clearouts at Wolves and Pompey too and until the identities of any replacements are known, all three are worth taking on.

Instead, three longshots have caught my eye. How about Corals' offer of 18-1 about **Leeds**? The evidence of the Johnstone's Paint Trophy final is that Crewe's skipper Luke Murphy could be as big a hit at Elland Road as his namesake Danny was at Anfield after leaving Alex. Brian McDermott is certainly up to the challenge of organising a relatively starless squad into a promotion package at this level as he proved with Reading two years ago.

Then should **Charlton** be out at 40-1 as they are with Hills? They ended the season in stellar form, the best away defence and equal lowest away defeats (six), plus a run of one defeat in 11 which included draws at Cardiff and Brighton and wins over Leeds and Bolton.

Boss Chris Powell tends to rotate his squad heavily for cup ties as well as he concentrates on the league.

Portsmouth kick off the season against **Oxford**, whose squad has remained settled. They flirted with relegation a little before Christmas, but their poor run coincided with

Jose Mourinho knows how to win titles

a horrendous injury list. When that cleared up they made progress and three straight wins at the end left them only four points off the play-offs.

Manager Chris Wilder has caught his main summer target, striker Dave Kitson, and the big lad with Premier League experience looks sure to cut the mustard at this level.

Scotland? Three markets look sorted. Celtic and Rangers will dot up, while Hearts, with a 15-point deduction and all of their players up for sale look destined for Division One.

Otherwise Dundee United's summer business looks to have weakened them, Aberdeen have recruited some interesting replacements having released almost a team's worth of players, while Inverness have brought in eight new boys from the likes of Kidderminster, Hereford, Kendall Town, Maidstone and Coleraine, a reflection of the levels to which the SPL has sunk.

Ross County have imported three Dutch players but let a useful pair in Iain Vigurs and Paul Lawson go to **Motherwell**, who look nailed-on to retain second place.

We got Peterhead right in the betting without Rangers in Division Three last term, and this year, with money behind them, **East Fife** at a bigger price look promising to follow the Gers home.

Recommended bets
10 points on Chelsea, 5 points each-way on Arsenal, 3 points each-way on Charlton, 3 points each-way Leeds, 5 points each-way on Oxford, 10 points on Motherwell without Celtic, 5 points on East Fife without Rangers

Accumulator any two, any three and all six of Chelsea, Charlton, Oxford, Motherwell without Celtic, Telford and Ebbsfleet = 36 bets

Premier League winner

	b365	BtFrd	BtVic	Coral	Hills	Lads	Power
Man Utd	9-4	9-4	9-4	2	2	2	11-5
Man City	9-4	9-4	9-4	12-5	2	11-5	23-10
Chelsea	9-4	9-4	2	9-4	2	11-5	23-10
Arsenal	10	10	10	10	10	12	10
Liverpool	33	33	33	16	16	20	28
Tottenham	33	33	33	40	25	33	25
Everton	250	250	200	750	250	350	250
Newcastle	1000	750	1000	1250	1000	1250	1000
Aston Villa	2000	1000	2000	2000	1500	1500	2000
West Brom	1500	1000	1500	2000	1500	1500	1500
Southampton	2000	1000	1500	2000	1500	2000	2500
Swansea	1500	1500	2000	2500	1500	1500	1500
Fulham	2000	2000	3000	2500	1500	3000	2000
Sunderland	2500	2000	2000	3000	2500	3000	2500
West Ham	2000	2000	3000	2000	1500	1500	2500
Stoke	3000	2000	4000	3000	2500	4000	4000
Cardiff	5000	5000	5000	5000	5000	5000	4000
Norwich	4000	2500	4000	5000	2500	3500	5000
Hull	7500	5000	7500	7500	5000	7500	5000
C Palace	10000	7500	10000	10000	5000	10000	10000

Win or each-way. See bookmakers for terms

Premier League relegation

	b365	BtFrd	BtVic	Coral	Hills	Lads	Power
C Palace	4-9	8-15	8-15	4-7	8-15	8-15	8-15
Hull	4-6	4-6	4-7	8-13	4-6	7-10	4-6
Cardiff	7-4	6-4	6-4	13-8	11-8	13-10	6-4
Norwich	5-2	5-2	13-5	12-5	5-2	11-4	12-5
Stoke	3	10-3	11-4	10-3	3	10-3	3
Sunderland	9-2	5	11-2	9-2	5	10-3	5
Fulham	13-2	5	7	6	6	4	7
Swansea	13-2	6	7	13-2	7	7	7
Aston Villa	15-2	6	7	8	7	8	5
West Brom	7	7	8	6	7	13-2	5
West Ham	8	6	7	9	8	7	6
Southampton	7	7	8	8	6	11-2	6
Newcastle	10	10	8	12	10	11	10
Everton	28	28	25	22	25	33	20
Liverpool	500	150	100	300	250	500	250
Tottenham	500	250	350	250	250	300	250
Arsenal	1000	1000	2000	750	750	1500	1000
Chelsea	2500	2000	2000	2500	2000	2500	1000
Man Utd	5000	2000	2000	5000	2500	3000	1000
Man City	5000	2000	2000	5000	2500	2500	1000

Win only

Scottish Premier League winner

	b365	BtFrd	BtVic	Coral	Hills	Lads	Power
Celtic	1-100	1-50	1-66	1-50	1-40	1-40	1-66
Motherwell	50	50	66	28	25	25	66
Aberdeen	50	66	50	66	40	66	66
Dundee Utd	125	125	125	100	125	100	150
Hibernian	200	125	150	125	125	125	200
Inverness	200	250	250	150	200	125	400
St Johnstone	200	200	200	200	200	150	400
Hearts	500	400	500	300	200	350	500
Kilmarnock	300	250	300	250	250	250	500
Ross County	250	250	300	200	250	200	500
St Mirren	500	500	400	300	500	350	500
Partick	750	400	400	500	500	400	500

Win only

Scottish Division One winner

	b365	BtFrd	BtVic	Coral	Hills	Lads	Power
Dundee	13-8	15-8	6-4	15-8	13-8	6-4	11-8
Falkirk	11-2	5	9-2	11-2	9-2	5	4
Queen of Sth	8	5	6	4	11-2	6	8
Morton	11-2	7	8	13-2	11-2	6	15-2
Livingston	8	8	8	11	13-2	7	11
Hamilton	11	7	10	8	8	9	11
Raith	12	12	14	12	14	12	8
Dumbarton	25	25	20	25	20	22	25
Alloa	33	33	33	33	33	25	25
Cowdenbeath	33	33	33	33	33	33	33

Win or each-way. See bookmakers for terms

Scottish Division Two winner

	b365	BtFrd	BtVic	Coral	Hills	Lads	Power
Rangers	1-20	1-10	1-10	1-14	1-14	1-10	1-20
Brechin	33	20	14	16	16	20	25
Airdrie	33	25	33	28	25	20	40
Ayr	40	25	20	20	20	22	40
Dunfermline	33	33	33	33	25	33	40
East Fife	40	25	16	33	16	12	40
Arbroath	66	50	66	66	40	33	66
Forfar	50	40	50	33	33	33	66
Stenhousemuir	80	66	80	80	50	33	80
Stranraer	100	80	100	50	66	66	100

Win only

Scottish Division Three winner

	b365	BtFrd	BtVic	Coral	Hills	Lads	Power
Peterhead	7-4	7-4	7-4	15-8	7-4	7-4	6-4
Albion	11-2	5	4	9-2	5	9-2	4
Queen's Park	6	9-2	11-2	13-2	9-2	5	6
Berwick	9	8	9	7	8	7	10
Stirling	8	9	9	15-2	8	8	7
Elgin	9	9	10	12	8	8	11
Annan	14	14	14	12	14	14	14
Montrose	14	10	14	12	10	14	14
Clyde	33	16	20	25	16	20	33
E Stirling	33	50	25	33	50	40	40

Others available. Win or each-way. See bookmakers for terms

Championship winner

	b365	BtFrd	BtVic	Coral	Hills	Lads	Power
QPR	6	6	6	6	5	5	9-2
Reading	8	8	8	9	9	8	9
Bolton	10	8	10	8	9	9	10
Leicester	11	11	10	11	9	9	10
Wigan	12	11	12	12	12	12	9
Nottm Forest	10	10	10	10	10	10	9
Watford	12	12	12	14	12	12	12
Brighton	14	14	12	16	16	14	14
Leeds	16	18	16	18	14	16	14
Blackburn	20	16	20	20	14	20	16
Bournemouth	20	20	20	20	16	18	16
Ipswich	20	20	16	16	20	18	16
Derby	25	28	20	25	20	33	25
Middlesbrough	33	25	25	28	25	28	33
Birmingham	28	28	25	28	25	20	16
Charlton	33	40	33	33	40	33	20
Blackpool	40	50	50	50	40	33	33
Burnley	50	50	66	50	33	50	50
Sheffield Weds	40	50	66	40	40	40	33
Huddersfield	66	100	100	50	50	50	66
Millwall	80	66	66	80	80	66	66
Barnsley	100	125	125	80	66	100	66
Doncaster	150	150	150	100	66	66	66
Yeovil	250	200	200	125	100	100	100

Win or each-way. See bookmakers for terms

League 1 winner

	b365	BtFrd	BtVic	Coral	Hills	Lads	Power
Wolves	4	4	4	7-2	7-2	4	4
Peterborough	7	7	7	9	8	8	7
Sheffield Utd	10	10	10	9	10	10	9
Bristol City	10	9	8	11	9	10	10
Brentford	10	14	8	10	12	10	12
MK Dons	12	12	10	14	12	11	10
Preston	16	14	14	14	12	14	16
Rotherham	16	20	16	20	20	14	16
Swindon	25	25	25	28	16	18	14
Bradford	25	25	25	22	20	25	20
Coventry	33	33	33	22	16	20	20
Notts Co	33	25	33	33	20	25	25
Leyton Orient	33	25	33	33	33	28	25
Gillingham	33	33	33	33	20	25	25
Tranmere	40	33	40	33	40	33	25
Crewe	40	33	40	33	33	33	33
Crawley	40	25	50	33	33	28	25
Port Vale	40	33	40	40	33	33	40
Walsall	50	25	50	40	33	33	25
Oldham	66	50	66	50	66	50	50
Carlisle	50	40	50	50	66	40	40
Colchester	80	50	66	80	80	50	50
Stevenage	50	66	66	50	66	50	50
Shrewsbury	80	66	66	80	80	66	50

Win or each-way. See bookmakers for terms

League 2 winner

	b365	BtFrd	BtVic	Coral	Hills	Lads	Power
Portsmouth	4	4	9-2	9-2	4	4	4
Chesterfield	8	8	7	15-2	7	7	8
Fleetwood	8	8	8	9	7	8	15-2
Bristol Rovers	14	12	12	11	11	11	11
Scunthorpe	16	14	14	11	14	12	14
Northampton	16	16	16	18	16	16	16
Oxford	16	16	16	20	16	16	16
Cheltenham	20	20	16	16	16	16	18
Hartlepool	20	20	20	20	20	20	20
Rochdale	25	20	25	16	20	16	13
Burton	20	20	25	25	20	20	22
Southend	25	20	20	20	25	22	20
Mansfield	28	25	33	22	20	25	25
Plymouth	33	33	25	25	25	25	25
Wycombe	33	33	25	33	25	25	25
Bury	20	25	33	40	25	28	25
York	33	33	33	33	20	33	35
Exeter	40	25	33	33	25	25	25
Newport Co	40	40	40	40	33	40	35
Torquay	40	33	40	40	50	40	35
Wimbledon	50	66	40	80	50	66	55
Accrington	100	66	66	80	66	40	55
Dag & Red	100	66	66	100	66	66	55
Morecambe	100	40	66	80	66	66	55

Win or each-way. See bookmakers for terms

Conference winner

	b365	BtFrd	BtVic	Coral	Hills	Lads	Power
Luton	4	9-2	7-2	9-2	4	9-2	9-2
Forest Green	4	4	7-2	9-2	3	4	4
Kidderminster	7	6	8	7	7	6	6
Grimsby	9	8	7	8	9	7	8
Wrexham	9	7	9	9	8	8	15-2
Cambridge	11	8	12	9	10	12	10
Chester	14	12	12	12	12	12	11
Barnet	10	14	14	18	16	12	12
Macclesfield	33	33	33	25	14	16	16
Hereford	33	20	25	25	25	22	20
Halifax	33	40	40	33	25	33	33
Lincoln	33	50	40	40	33	40	40
Gateshead	33	33	25	33	40	40	50
Braintree	100	100	100	80	100	100	100
Dartford	100	80	100	80	100	80	80
Welling	150	100	100	80	150	80	100
Woking	150	100	100	80	80	80	100
Hyde	150	150	200	125	150	150	150
Southport	200	150	150	100	150	125	150
Alfreton	200	100	150	100	150	125	100
Salisbury	200	100	100	125	200	100	100
Aldershot	125	80	250	100	40	50	22
Nuneaton	250	200	200	125	200	150	200
Tamworth	250	150	200	150	150	150	200

Win or each-way. See bookmakers for terms

Cromwell and Keynes can make you a more profitable punter

Soccer boffin Kevin Pullein reveals his five golden rules for better betting

If you do what others do, you will get what others get. Trust me, you don't want what others get.

Almost everyone who bets loses. Every year bookmakers announce enormous profits. Where do those profits come from? Their customers' losses.

So if you want to give yourself a reasonable hope of winning money by betting, don't be like everyone else…

Be yourself

John Maynard Keynes was the most influential economist of the 20th century. He was also a company director. Unusually for an economist – influential or otherwise – he was something else as well: a profitable stock market investor.

Keynes wrote: "Investing is the one sphere of life and activity were victory, security and success is always to the minority and never to the majority. When you find anyone agreeing with you, change your mind. When I can persuade the Board of my Insurance Company to buy a share, that, I am learning from experience, is the right moment for selling it."

Investing, in anything, is just a fancy word for betting. And the bets that are most likely to prove profitable for you over time are those bookmakers find hardest to sell.

Go to a shop, any shop. On what product could you get the best deal? The one that everyone else is falling over themselves to buy – the one the shop can sell as fast as they can replenish the shelf? Or the one that is almost unnoticed gathering dust in the corner? The questions should answer themselves.

Play the percentages

What I really mean by this is think probabilistically – but probabilistically is not a word that is in everyday use, and it has a lot of syllables, so I didn't want to put it in bold type.

Stop thinking in terms of what will or will not happen. Anything can happen. In a football match, every outcome is possible in every market.

As Dan Gardner put it in Future Babble, a brilliant book about forecasting: "The most that we can ever hope to do is distinguish between degrees of probability with reasonable accuracy."

In other words, assess the chance – in percentage terms – of each outcome happening.

Your best hope of winning money over time by betting is to identify outcomes that are more likely than bookmakers' odds imply. And to be able to do that you must…

Compile your own odds

At first you will find that your odds for nearly every match differ wildly from those offered by bookmakers. This is bad. It means that at least one set of prices must be wrong. Believe me, it will be yours.

Don't give up, though. With practice you will find that your odds for most markets become very similar to those available from bookmakers. This is good. It means that where a bookmaker is still quoting a price that is bigger than yours there is now a possibility that yours is right and theirs is wrong.

But at this stage it is only a possibility, so…

Proceed with caution

Oliver Cromwell, ruler of England after the 17th century Civil War, wrote to his opponents in Scotland: "I beseech you, in the bowels of Christ, think it possible you may be mistaken."

It is a famous quote. Most people who use it direct it at others. Direct it at yourself.

Ask yourself why a bookmaker is offering those odds. Bookmakers sometimes make mistakes – otherwise I would be discouraging you from betting altogether – but it doesn't happen very often. Have they noticed a potential influence on the outcome that you have missed? Do they perhaps know something that you have not yet learned?

Start by assuming your odds are wrong. Only if you are unable to prove that they are wrong should you accept the possibility that they might be right. Like bookmakers, you will sometimes make mistakes.

Whenever possible, discover them before you have parted with your money rather than afterwards.

Keep records

Make a note of every bet – what it was, the odds, your stake, whether it won or lost. It is the only way you will be able to avoid deceiving yourself. Ask someone else how their betting is going. If they say they are breaking even, they are probably losing a bit. If they say they are losing a little, they are probably losing a lot.

Keeping records will force you to confront reality. And it is only by accepting reality as it is that you will be able to recognise the changes that might become necessary as you go along to improve your betting. How do your odds compare with actual outcomes? Are you doing less well in some markets than in others? If you keep records, you will know – really know.

Important dates 2013-14

July 2013

Tuesday 2-3	Champions League first qualifying round, first leg
Thursday 4	Europa League first qualifying round, first leg
Tuesday 9-10	Champions League first qualifying round, second leg
Thursday 11	Europa League first qualifying round, second leg
Tuesday 16-17	Champions League second qualifying round, first leg
Thursday 18	Europa League second qualifying round, first leg
Friday 19	Champions League third qualifying round draw
	Europa League third qualifying round draw
Tuesday 23-24	Champions League second qualifying round, second leg
Thursday 25	Europa League second qualifying round, second leg
Saturday 27	Scottish Challenge Cup first round
Tuesday 30-31	Champions League third qualifying round, first leg

August 2013

Thursday 1	Europa League third qualifying round, first leg
Friday 2	Start of Dutch Eredivisie season
Saturday 3	Start of Football League season
	Start of Scottish Premier League season
	Scottish League Cup first round
Monday 5 (week of)	League Cup first round
Tuesday 6-7	Champions League third qualifying round, second leg
Thursday 8	Europa League third qualifying round, second leg
Friday 9	Champions League play-off round draw
	Europa League play-off round draw
	Start of German Bundesliga season
Saturday 10	Start of Scottish Football League season
	Start of Conference Premier season
	Start of French Ligue 1 season
Sunday 11	FA Community Shield
	Wigan v Man United
Wednesday 14	International friendlies
	England v Scotland
	Wales v Republic of Ireland
	World Cup 2014 qualifier
	Northern Ireland v Russia
Saturday 17	Start of Premier League season
	Start of Conference North/South season
	FA Cup extra preliminary round
	Scottish Cup preliminary round
	Start of Spanish Primera Liga season
Sunday 18	Start of Portuguese Primeira Liga season
Tuesday 20-21	Champions League play-off round, first leg
	Scottish Challenge Cup second round
Thursday 22	Europa League play-off round, first leg
Saturday 24	Start of Italian Serie A season
Monday 26 (week of)	League Cup second round
Tuesday 27-28	Champions League play-off round, second leg
	Scottish League Cup second round
Thursday 29	Champions League group stage draw
	Europa League play-off round, second leg
Friday 30	Europa League group stage draw
	Uefa Super Cup, Prague
	Bayern Munich v Chelsea
Saturday 31	FA Cup preliminary round

September 2013

Monday 2 (week of)	Football League Trophy first round
Friday 6	World Cup 2014 qualifiers
	Scotland v Belgium
	England v Moldova
	Macedonia v Wales
	Republic of Ireland v Sweden
	Northern Ireland v Portugal
Saturday 7	FA Trophy preliminary round
	FA Vase first qualifying round
	Scottish Challenge Cup quarter-finals
Tuesday 10	World Cup 2014 qualifiers
	Macedonia v Scotland
	Ukraine v England
	Wales v Serbia
	Austria v Republic of Ireland
	Luxembourg v Northern Ireland
Saturday 14	FA Cup first qualifying round
	Scottish Cup first round
Tuesday 17-18	Champions League group stage, matchday one
Thursday 19	Europa League group stage, matchday one
Saturday 21	FA Vase second qualifying round
Monday 23 (week of)	League Cup third round
Tuesday 24-25	Scottish League Cup third round
Saturday 28	FA Cup second qualifying round

October 2013

Tuesday 1-2	Champions League group stage, matchday two
Thursday 3	Europa League group stage, matchday two
Saturday 5	FA Trophy first qualifying round
	Scottish Cup second round
Monday 7 (week of)	Football League Trophy second round
Friday 11	World Cup 2014 qualifiers
	England v Montenegro
	Wales v Macedonia
	Germany v Republic of Ireland
	Azerbaijan v Northern Ireland
Saturday 12	FA Cup third qualifying round
Sunday 13	Scottish Challenge Cup semi-finals
Tuesday 15	World Cup 2014 qualifiers
	Scotland v Croatia
	England v Poland
	Belgium v Wales
	Republic of Ireland v Kazakhstan
	Israel v Northern Ireland
Saturday 19	FA Trophy second qualifying round
	FA Vase first round
Tuesday 22-23	Champions League group stage, matchday three
Thursday 24	Europa League group stage, matchday three
Saturday 26	FA Cup fourth qualifying round
Monday 28 (week of)	League Cup fourth round
Tuesday 29-30	Scottish League Cup quarter-finals

November 2013

Saturday 2	FA Trophy third qualifying round
	Scottish Cup third round
Tuesday 5-6	Champions League group stage, matchday four
Thursday 7	Europa League group stage, matchday four
Saturday 9	FA Cup first round
Monday 11 (week of)	Football League Trophy area quarter-finals
Friday 15	World Cup 2014 play-offs (Uefa & intercontinental), first leg

Saturday 16	FA Vase second round
Tuesday 19	World Cup 2014 play-offs (Uefa & intercontinental), second leg
Saturday 23	FA Trophy first round
Tuesday 26-27	Champions League group stage, matchday five
Thursday 28	Europa League group stage, matchday five
Saturday 30	Scottish Cup fourth round

December 2013

Friday 6	World Cup 2014 final draw
Saturday 7	FA Cup second round
	FA Vase third round
Monday 9 (week of)	Football League Trophy area semi-finals
Tuesday 10-11	Champions League group stage, matchday six
Wednesday 11	Fifa Club World Cup begins, Morocco
Thursday 12	Europa League group stage, matchday six
Friday 13	Champions League last 16 draw
	Europa League last 32/last 16 draw
Saturday 14	FA Trophy second round
Monday 16 (week of)	League Cup fifth round
Saturday 21	Fifa Club World Cup final, Marrakesh

January 2014

Saturday 4	FA Cup third round
Monday 6 (week of)	League Cup semi-finals, first leg
Saturday 11	FA Trophy third round
Saturday 18	FA Vase fourth round
Monday 20 (week of)	League Cup semi-finals, second leg
Saturday 25	FA Cup fourth round

February 2014

Saturday 1-2	FA Trophy fourth round
	Scottish League Cup semi-finals
Monday 3 (week of)	Football League Trophy area finals, first leg (subject to change)
Saturday 8	Scottish Cup fifth round
Saturday 15	FA Cup fifth round
	FA Trophy semi-finals, first leg
	FA Vase fifth round
Monday 17 (week of)	Football League Trophy area finals, second leg (subject to change)
Tuesday 18-19	Champions League last 16, first leg
Thursday 20	Europa League last 32, first leg
Saturday 22	FA Trophy semi-finals, second leg
Tuesday 25-26	Champions League last 16, first leg
Thursday 27	Europa League last 32, second leg

March 2014

Sunday 2	League Cup final
Wednesday 5	International friendly date
Saturday 8	FA Cup sixth round
	FA Vase sixth round
	Scottish Cup quarter-finals
Sunday 9	Euro 2016 qualifying draw
Tuesday 11-12	Champions League last 16, second leg
Thursday 13	Europa League last 16, first leg
Sunday 16	Scottish League Cup final
Tuesday 18-19	Champions League last 16, second leg
Thursday 20	Europa League last 16, second leg
Friday 21	Champions League quarter-final draw
	Europa League quarter-final draw
Sunday 23	FA Trophy final
Saturday 29	FA Vase semi-finals, first leg
Sunday 30	Football League Trophy final

April 2014

Tuesday 1-2	Champions League quarter-finals, first leg
Thursday 3	Europa League quarter-finals, first leg
Saturday 5	FA Vase semi-finals, second leg
Sunday 6	Scottish Challenge Cup final
Tuesday 8-9	Champions League quarter-finals, second leg
Thursday 10	Europa League quarter-finals, second leg
Friday 11	Champions League semi-final draw
	Europa League semi-final draw
Saturday 12-13	FA Cup semi-finals
	Scottish Cup semi-finals
Tuesday 22-23	Champions League semi-finals, first leg
Thursday 24	Europa League semi-finals, first leg
Tuesday 29-30	Champions League semi-finals, second leg

May 2014

Thursday 1	Europa League semi-finals, second leg
Wednesday 7	Scottish Football League play-off semi-finals, first leg
Saturday 10	FA Vase final
	Scottish Football League play-off semi-finals, second leg
Wednesday 14	Europa League final, Turin
	Scottish Football League play-off finals, first leg
Saturday 17	FA Cup final
	Scottish Cup final
Sunday 18	Scottish Football League play-off finals, second leg
	Conference play-off final
Saturday 24	Champions League final, Lisbon
	Championship play-off final
Sunday 25	League 1 play-off final
Monday 26	League 2 play-off final

June 2014

Wednesday 12	World Cup 2014 begins, Brazil
Saturday 28-1	World Cup 2014 round of 16

July 2014

Friday 4-5	World Cup 2014 quarter-finals
Tuesday 8-9	World Cup 2014 semi-finals
Sunday 13	World Cup 2014 final, Rio de Janeiro

The revamped Estadio do Maracana, venue for July's World Cup final

Moyes to keep a steady hand on the tiller

Three of the top four in the Premier League have changed manager and while that's been par for the course over the last decade and beyond as far as Chelsea and Man City are concerned, Sir Alex Ferguson's retirement after 26 years at Old Trafford really does mark the end of an era, writes Paul Charlton.

Although that brings uncertainty it still seems remarkable that last season's champions, who won the league by 11 points and have won the title in five of the last seven years, can be backed at bigger than 2-1.

Ferguson was a giant of the modern game but David Moyes deserves his reputation as one of the best in the business. It will be fascinating to see how he gets on.

With very little between the top three in terms of price it's not hard to make a case for any of them. Moyes transformed Everton into regular contenders for the European places on a relative shoestring and is taking over one of the richest and best run clubs in the world. Manuel Pellegrini looks a very solid appointment at Man City, where he is being backed with plenty of cash. And we know what happened last time Jose Mourinho took up residence at Stamford Bridge.

And that's before you mention Arsenal, who came on strong over the second half of the season to finish just two points behind the Blues. They have money to spend and stability, with an excellent manager in Arsene Wenger still in the dugout.

Waiting and seeing is an option – there will be plenty of opportunities to bet or trade once the season is underway – but there's some appeal to the **Man United/Chelsea**

dual forecast at 13-5, with Paddy Power or Ladbrokes, on the basis that Mourinho can unlock Chelsea's potential and Moyes can hold steady at United.

I also like the look of **Romelu Lukaku** in the top scorer betting. It may be that he has to wait his turn at Chelsea. But it may be that his direct style is tailor-made for Mourinho and 17 goals at West Brom when 15 of his 35 appearances came as a substitute is seriously good going. At 25-1 with BetVictor I'm happy to take a chance.

If it will be interesting to see how Moyes gets on at United, it will be just as interesting watching Roberto Martinez in action at Everton. No team in the Premier League conceded more goals than Wigan last term and it's very easy to imagine the battle for European football becoming a scrap to stay in the top ten. This is one to wait and see on but there might well be trading potential (lay to back) in exchange odds that were 1.27 at the time of writing.

The relegation market is as interesting as usual. Play-off winners Crystal Palace look set to struggle with 30-goal Glenn Murray in-

Key to the data

The table next to every team profile shows head-to-head data for every side they have to play in the league this season.

It's been a summer of change at the top of the Premier League

	2012-13		Last six seasons at home							
	H	A	P	W	D	L	OV	UN	BS	CS
Man United	L	L	6	0	3	3	3	3	4	1
Man City	L	L	6	2	2	2	1	5	3	1
Chelsea	L	L	6	2	1	3	3	3	3	2
Arsenal	D	L	6	0	3	3	4	2	4	2
Tottenham	L	L	6	1	2	3	4	2	5	0
Everton	L	D	6	2	3	1	3	3	4	2
Liverpool	L	W	6	1	1	4	2	4	2	2
West Brom	D	D	4	2	1	1	3	1	4	0
Swansea	W	D	2	1	0	1	0	2	0	1
West Ham	W	L	5	3	2	0	2	3	2	3
Norwich	D	W	2	1	1	0	1	1	2	0
Fulham	D	L	6	3	3	0	2	4	3	3
Stoke	D	W	5	1	4	0	1	4	3	2
Southampton	L	L	1	0	0	1	0	1	0	0
Aston Villa										
Newcastle	L	D	5	3	1	1	2	3	3	2
Sunderland	W	W	6	2	2	2	2	4	3	1
Cardiff			-	-	-	-	-	-	-	-
Hull			2	2	0	0	1	1	0	2
Crystal Palace			-	-	-	-	-	-	-	-

Season	Division	Pos	P	W	D	L	F	A	GD	Pts
2012-13	Premier League	15	38	10	11	17	47	69	-22	41
2011-12	Premier League	16	38	7	17	14	37	53	-16	38
2010-11	Premier League	9	38	12	12	14	48	59	-11	48

Over/Under 61%/39% 7th   Both score 61%/39% 4th

1 Every team that the club will have to face this season in the order they finished last season

2 Results of last season's league meetings

W is a win, **D** is a draw, **L** is a loss, colour-coded green, amber and red. Where there was more than one meeting in the league, the latest is at the right. Regular season only

3 Head-to-head results over the last six seasons at the club's own ground

P games played **W** games won **D** games drawn **L** games lost **OV** number of games finishing with over 2.5 goals **UN** number of games with under 2.5 goals **BS** number of games in which both teams scored **CS** games in which the home team kept a clean sheet

4 Promoted and relegated teams are shown in fawn in the order in which they finished in their previous division

5 League table over the last three seasons

6 Over and under 2.5 goals and both sides to score stats, including rank in club's division last season. The bar chart shows, horizontally, from top to bottom, and rounded to the nearest 5%, the division high, the profiled club, and the division low

Leading scorers Numbers in brackets show first goals followed by 'anytime' goals

jured and Wilfried Zaha now at Man United.

And with Cardiff having won the Championship with just 87 points, the division was either quite weak or exceptionally competitive last season.

Four of the last ten Championship winners went straight back down again but the last time all three promoted teams were relegated was in 1997-98 when, coincidentally, Palace won promotion via the play-offs. I'd rather look for somebody else who might struggle, however.

The impact Paolo Di Canio made in his brief time in charge at **Sunderland** might have been overrated a little. The bottom half of the Premier League is very tight and although the Black Cats finished just three points behind 13th-placed Stoke, they were also three points above the relegation zone.

Di Canio has had a good clearout over the summer and brought in plenty of new faces, but 11-2 about a team who took fewer than 40 points and whose W2, D2, L3 record under a relatively unproven new manager includes a 6-1 hiding against Aston Villa is big enough to tempt me in.

Arsenal

Nickname: The Gunners
Colours: Red and white

Ground: Emirates Stadium
Tel: 020 7704 4000
Capacity: 60,362
Web: www.arsenal.com

For a second season running the Gunners lost their star man at the eleventh hour, with Robin van Persie, the league's top scorer in 2011-12, joining Man United on the eve of the new campaign.

But Theo Walcott got 14 goals and three of Arsene Wenger's summer signings, Lukas Podolski, Olivier Giroud and Santi Cazorla, all broached double figures. Arsenal conceded fewer than 40 goals the first time in three seasons, with Laurent Koscielny superb at the back.

Overall, the Gunners scored just two goals fewer in the league, finished the season with a goal difference ten goals superior to 2012 and took three more points as they wrapped up a top-four finish for the 17th season in a row. It looked touch and go halfway through, though – Arsenal were tenth in December and looking more likely to finish in mid-table than in the Champions League places.

Longest run without a loss: 10
Longest run without a win: 3
Highest/lowest league position: 5/10
Clean sheets: 14
Yellow cards: 42 **Red cards:** 4
Average attendance: 60,079 **Players used:** 25
Leading scorer: T Walcott 14 (4,12)

	2012-13		Last six seasons at home							
	H	A	P	W	D	L	OV	UN	BS	CS
Man United	D	L	6	2	2	2	4	2	5	1
Man City	L	D	6	3	2	1	0	6	0	5
Chelsea	L	L	6	2	1	3	4	2	3	2
Arsenal										
Tottenham	W	L	6	4	1	1	6	0	5	1
Everton	D	D	6	4	2	0	3	3	3	3
Liverpool	D	W	6	1	4	1	1	5	4	1
West Brom	W	W	4	3	0	1	2	2	1	3
Swansea	L	W	2	1	0	1	0	2	0	1
West Ham	W	W	5	4	1	0	1	4	1	4
Norwich	W	L	2	1	1	0	2	0	2	0
Fulham	D	W	6	3	3	0	4	2	4	2
Stoke	W	D	5	5	0	0	2	3	2	3
Southampton	W	D	1	1	0	0	1	0	1	0
Aston Villa	W	D	6	3	1	2	4	2	3	2
Newcastle	W	W	5	4	0	1	4	1	2	2
Sunderland	D	W	6	3	3	0	2	4	2	4
Cardiff	-	-	-	-	-	-	-	-	-	-
Hull			2	1	0	1	2	0	1	1
Crystal Palace	-	-	-	-	-	-	-	-	-	-

Season	Division	Pos	P	W	D	L	F	A	GD	Pts
2012-13	Premier League	4	38	21	10	7	72	37	+35	73
2011-12	Premier League	3	38	21	7	10	74	49	+25	70
2010-11	Premier League	4	38	19	11	8	72	43	+29	68

Over/Under 45%/55% 18th   **Both score** 55%/45% 11th

Key stat: Arsenal kept clean sheets in nine of their 19 away games – a division high 47 per cent. In 2011-12 they kept just five clean sheets on the road

Premier League appearances 2012-13

	P	G	Y	R
A Arshavin	0 (7)	0	1	0
M Arteta	34	6	6	0
S Cazorla	37 (1)	12	1	0
F Coquelin	3 (8)	0	0	0
A Diaby	10 (1)	0	1	0
L Fabianski	4	0	0	0
Gervinho	12 (6)	5	1	0
K Gibbs	23 (4)	0	2	0
O Giroud	24 (10)	11	3	1
S Gnabry	0 (1)	0	0	0
C Jenkinson	14	0	1	1
L Koscielny	20 (5)	2	1	1
V Mannone	9	0	0	0
P Mertesacker	33 (1)	3	3	1
I Miquel	0 (1)	0	0	0
N Monreal	9 (1)	1	2	0
A O-Chamberlain	11 (14)	1	1	0
L Podolski	25 (8)	11	1	0
A Ramsey	21 (15)	1	5	0
T Rosicky	7 (3)	2	2	0

	P	G	Y	R
B Sagna	25	0	2	0
A Santos	3 (5)	0	0	0
W Szczesny	25	0	1	0
T Vermaelen	25 (4)	0	3	0
T Walcott	24 (8)	14	3	0
J Wilshere	20 (5)	0	4	1

Arsenal's leading scorer Theo Walcott on the ball

Aston Villa

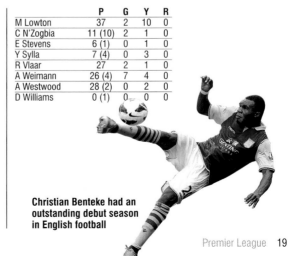

Nickname: The Villans
Colours: Claret and blue

Ground: Villa Park   **Capacity:** 42,785
Tel: 0121 327 2299   **Web:** www.avfc.co.uk

Aston Villa's first season under Paul Lambert was a bit of a curate's egg, with a few high points offset by some real lows – the worst of which was probably either the Capital One Cup semi-final defeat to League 2 Bradford or the 8-0 rout at Stamford Bridge – and a long fight against relegation.

But the Villans finished the season strongly, only losing to Liverpool, Man United and Chelsea in their final ten games, and improved their showing in the league by one place and three points on what they had achieved under Alex McLeish the previous season.

Their 19-goal summer signing Christian Benteke stole the headlines but Brad Guzan won plenty of plaudits in goal and Andreas Weimann continued to improve – when the Austrian started, Villa's win percentage rose from 20 per cent to 39 per cent.

Longest run without a loss: 5
Longest run without a win: 8
Highest/lowest league position: 13/19
Clean sheets: 5
Yellow cards: 74 **Red cards:** 3
Average attendance: 35,059 **Players used:** 28
Leading scorer: C Benteke 19 (8,15)

	2012-13 H	2012-13 A	Last six seasons at home P	W	D	L	OV	UN	BS	CS
Man United	L	L	6	0	3	3	3	3	4	1
Man City	L	L	6	2	2	2	1	5	3	1
Chelsea	L	L	6	2	1	3	3	3	3	2
Arsenal	D	L	6	0	3	3	4	2	4	2
Tottenham	L	L	6	1	2	3	4	2	5	0
Everton	L	D	6	2	3	1	3	3	4	2
Liverpool	L	W	6	1	1	4	2	4	2	2
West Brom	D	D	4	2	1	1	3	1	4	0
Swansea	W	D	2	1	0	1	0	2	0	1
West Ham	W	L	5	3	2	0	2	3	2	3
Norwich	D	W	2	1	1	0	1	1	2	0
Fulham	D	L	6	3	3	0	2	4	3	3
Stoke	D	W	5	1	4	0	1	4	3	2
Southampton	L	L	1	0	0	1	0	1	0	0
Aston Villa										
Newcastle	L	D	5	3	1	1	2	3	3	2
Sunderland	W	W	6	2	2	2	2	4	3	1
Cardiff	-	-	-	-	-	-	-	-	-	-
Hull			2	2	0	0	1	1	0	2
Crystal Palace	-	-	-	-	-	-	-	-	-	-

Season	Division	Pos	P	W	D	L	F	A	GD	Pts
2012-13	Premier League	15	38	10	11	17	47	69	-22	41
2011-12	Premier League	16	38	7	17	14	37	53	-16	38
2010-11	Premier League	9	38	12	12	14	48	59	-11	48

Over/Under 61%/39% 7th   **Both score** 61%/39% 4th

Key stat: Villa's record against the teams who finished in the final top six was a dreadful P12, W0, D2, L10, F8, A36

Premier League appearances 2012-13

	P	G	Y	R		P	G	Y	R
G Agbonlahor	24 (4)	9	4	0	M Lowton	37	2	10	0
M Albrighton	4 (5)	0	0	0	C N'Zogbia	11 (10)	2	1	0
N Baker	25 (1)	0	4	0	E Stevens	6 (1)	0	1	0
B Bannan	18 (6)	0	3	0	Y Sylla	7 (4)	0	3	0
J Bennett	21 (4)	0	3	1	R Vlaar	27	2	1	0
D Bent	8 (8)	3	1	0	A Weimann	26 (4)	7	4	0
C Benteke	32 (2)	19	8	1	A Westwood	28 (2)	0	2	0
J Bowery	3 (7)	0	0	0	D Williams	0 (1)	0	0	0
C Clark	28 (1)	1	6	1					
S Dawkins	0 (4)	0	0	0					
N Delfouneso	1	0	1	0					
F Delph	19 (5)	0	7	0					
K El Ahmadi	12 (8)	1	5	0					
G Gardner	0 (2)	0	0	0					
S Given	2	0	0	0					
B Guzan	36	0	2	0					
C Herd	9	0	1	0					
B Holman	16 (11)	1	1	0					
S Ireland	9 (4)	0	1	0					
E Lichaj	9 (8)	0	6	0					

Christian Benteke had an outstanding debut season in English football

Cardiff City

Nickname: The Bluebirds
Colours: Red

Ground: Cardiff City Stadium
Tel: 02920 221 001

Capacity: 26,847
Web: www.cardiffcityfc.co.uk

After missing out in the play-offs three years running, the Bluebirds returned to the top flight for the first time since 1962.

Malky Mackay took them up in his second year at the helm, but it will be as hard to stay in the top flight as it was to get there – three of the last four Championship winners, Reading, QPR and Wolves, have been relegated since, although only the Royals went straight back down.

Only Brighton had a tighter defence and only Watford and Crystal Palace scored more goals as Cardiff led for almost the entire season, kicking off with ten straight home wins.

Frazier Campbell scored seven goals from 12 appearances after joining at the end of January, and Craig Bellamy, who laid on eight assists, provides more Premier League experience. But it's classy South Korean midfielder Kim Bo-Kyung who provides the creativity in the side.

Longest run without a loss: 9
Longest run without a win: 4
Highest/lowest league position: 1/7
Clean sheets: 18 **Yellow cards:** 76 **Red cards:** 3
Average attendance: 22,998 **Players used:** 27
Leading scorer: H Helguson 8 (4,7)
P Whittingham 8 (1, 6) A Gunnarson 8 (2, 8)

	2012-13 H	A	P	W	D	L	OV	UN	BS	CS
Man United	-	-	-	-	-	-	-	-	-	-
Man City	-	-	-	-	-	-	-	-	-	-
Chelsea	-	-	-	-	-	-	-	-	-	-
Arsenal	-	-	-	-	-	-	-	-	-	-
Tottenham	-	-	-	-	-	-	-	-	-	-
Everton	-	-	-	-	-	-	-	-	-	-
Liverpool	-	-	-	-	-	-	-	-	-	-
West Brom			2	0	2	0	0	2	1	1
Swansea			3	1	1	1	2	1	2	0
West Ham			1	0	0	1	0	1	0	0
Norwich			3	1	1	1	3	0	3	0
Fulham	-	-	-	-	-	-	-	-	-	-
Stoke			1	0	0	1	0	1	0	0
Southampton			3	3	0	0	2	1	2	1
Aston Villa	-	-	-	-	-	-	-	-	-	-
Newcastle			1	0	0	1	0	1	0	0
Sunderland	-	-	-	-	-	-	-	-	-	-
Cardiff										
Hull	W	D	4	3	0	1	2	2	1	2
Crystal Palace	W	L	6	3	3	0	2	4	4	2

Season	Division	Pos	P	W	D	L	F	A	GD	Pts
2012-13	Championship	1	46	25	12	9	72	45	+27	87
2011-12	Championship	6	46	19	18	9	66	53	+13	75
2010-11	Championship	4	46	23	11	12	76	54	+22	80

Over/Under 54%/46% 8th   **Both score** 59%/41% 11th

Key stat: Since 1996, only one team – West Brom in 2008 – has won the Championship with fewer points than Cardiff's total of 87

Championship appearances 2012-13

	P	G	Y	R
L Barnett	8	0	2	0
C Bellamy	28 (5)	4	4	0
K Bo-Kyung	20 (8)	2	3	0
F Campbell	9 (3)	7	0	0
M Connolly	36	5	5	0
C Conway	21 (6)	2	1	0
D Cowie	15 (10)	2	3	0
K Frei	1 (2)	0	0	0
R Gestede	5 (22)	5	0	0
A Gunnarsson	35 (10)	8	7	0
H Helguson	27 (11)	8	5	0
M Hudson	33	4	8	0
F Kiss	0 (2)	0	0	0
S Lappin	2	0	1	1
D Marshall	46	0	3	0
J Mason	12 (16)	6	1	0
N Maynard	3 (1)	1	0	0
K McNaughton	24 (3)	0	2	0
J Mutch	18 (4)	0	7	0
C Noone	25 (7)	7	4	1

	P	G	Y	R
B Nugent	7 (5)	1	4	0
J Ralls	1 (3)	0	0	0
T Smith	19 (5)	1	3	0
A Taylor	43	0	3	1
B Turner	30 (1)	1	5	0
E Velikonja	1 (2)	0	1	0
P Whittingham	37 (3)	8	5	0

Peter Whittingham was one of three players to score eight goals last season

Chelsea

Nickname: The Blues
Colours: Blue

Ground: Stamford Bridge
Tel: 0871 984 1955

Capacity: 41,798
Web: www.chelseafc.com

Despite some real stars arriving last summer, with Eden Hazard and Oscar the pick, Chelsea's season was all about the manager again – as it will be this term.

With their defence of the Champions League all but over after a 3-0 group-stage defeat to Juventus, Roberto Di Matteo was sacked in November and Rafa Benitez was the unpopular replacement.

In the end, Di Matteo and Benitez ended their spells at Chelsea with similar records – win rates of 57 and 58 per cent respectively, qualification for the Champions League (albeit by different routes) and a European trophy in the cabinet.

Under Benitez, Fernando Torres sometimes looked like the striker of old, especially in Europe, and David Luiz flourished after a switch to midfield. Frank Lampard became the club's record goalscorer but John Terry had to get used to being rotated, starting just 11 league games.

Longest run without a loss: 8
Longest run without a win: 7
Highest/lowest league position: 1/4
Clean sheets: 14
Yellow cards: 53 **Red cards:** 3
Average attendance: 41,462 **Players used:** 26
Leading scorer: F Lampard 15 (2,13)

	2012-13		Last six seasons at home							
	H	A	P	W	D	L	OV	UN	BS	CS
Man United	L	W	6	3	2	1	4	2	5	1
Man City	D	L	6	4	1	1	3	3	2	4
Chelsea										
Arsenal	W	W	6	4	0	2	4	2	4	2
Tottenham	D	W	6	3	3	0	3	3	3	3
Everton	W	W	6	2	4	0	3	3	5	1
Liverpool	D	D	6	1	2	3	1	5	2	2
West Brom	W	L	4	4	0	0	2	2	1	3
Swansea	W	D	2	2	0	0	1	1	1	1
West Ham	W	L	5	4	1	0	2	3	2	3
Norwich	W	W	2	2	0	0	2	0	2	0
Fulham	D	W	6	3	3	0	2	4	3	3
Stoke	W	W	5	5	0	0	2	3	1	4
Southampton	D	L	1	0	1	0	1	0	1	0
Aston Villa	W	W	6	3	2	1	5	1	4	2
Newcastle	W	L	5	2	2	1	2	3	2	2
Sunderland	W	W	6	5	0	1	4	2	2	3
Cardiff	-	-	-	-	-	-	-	-	-	-
Hull			2	1	1	0	1	1	1	1
Crystal Palace	-	-	-	-	-	-	-	-	-	-

Season	Division	Pos	P	W	D	L	F	A	GD	Pts
2012-13	Premier League	3	38	22	9	7	75	39	+36	75
2011-12	Premier League	6	38	18	10	10	65	46	+19	64
2010-11	Premier League	2	38	21	8	9	69	33	+36	71

Over/Under 61%/39% 7th   **Both score** 58%/42% 7th

Key stat: Chelsea won 124 of their 185 games during Jose Mourinho's first spell in charge, a strike-rate of 67 per cent

Premier League appearances 2012-13

	P	G	Y	R		P	G	Y	R
N Ake	1 (2)	0	0	0	Raul Meireles	1 (2)	0	0	0
C Azpilicueta	24 (3)	0	4	0	O Romeu	4 (2)	0	1	0
D Ba	11 (3)	2	0	0	D Sturridge	1 (6)	1	0	0
Y Benayoun	0 (6)	0	0	0	J Terry	11 (3)	4	1	0
R Bertrand	14 (5)	0	1	0	F Torres	28 (8)	8	5	1
G Cahill	24 (2)	2	1	0	R Turnbull	2 (1)	0	0	0
P Cech	36	0	2	0					
A Cole	31	1	3	0					
P Ferreira	0 (2)	0	0	0					
E Hazard	31 (3)	9	2	0					
B Ivanovic	33 (1)	5	4	1					
F Lampard	21 (8)	15	2	0					
L Piazon	0 (1)	0	0	0					
D Luiz	29 (1)	2	8	0					
M Marin	2 (4)	1	2	0					
J Mata	31 (4)	12	3	0					
J Mikel	19 (3)	0	3	0					
V Moses	12 (11)	1	0	0					
Oscar	24 (10)	4	2	0					
Ramires	28 (7)	5	9	1					

Frank Lampard lifts the Europa League trophy

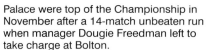

Crystal Palace

Nickname: The Eagles
Colours: Red and blue

Ground: Selhurst Park
Tel: 020 8768 6000

Capacity: 26,225
Web: www.cpfc.co.uk

Palace were top of the Championship in November after a 14-match unbeaten run when manager Dougie Freedman left to take charge at Bolton.

It was left to Ian Holloway to complete the job and he took Palace up via the play-offs for a second crack at the Premier League – his previous season as a top-flight manager saw Blackpool go down on the final day of 2010-11 after losing 4-2 at Old Trafford.

Only Watford scored more than the Eagles and Glenn Murray's 30 goals made him the Championship's top scorer last season but a long-term knee injury sustained in the play-off semi-final means he may miss much of 2013-14.

In his absence, Wilfried Zaha was the difference in the play-off final. He's gone too, but for a club who were just 100-30 in the ante-post relegation market, just being in the Premier League is a bonus.

Longest run without a loss: 14
Longest run without a win: 9
Highest/lowest league position: 1/15
Clean sheets: 11
Yellow cards: 65 **Red cards:** 2
Average attendance: 17,280 **Players used:** 30
Leading scorer: G Murray 30 (11, 17)

	2012-13		Last six seasons at home							
---	H	A	P	W	D	L	OV	UN	BS	CS
Man United	-	-	-	-	-	-	-	-	-	-
Man City	-	-	-	-	-	-	-	-	-	-
Chelsea	-	-	-	-	-	-	-	-	-	-
Arsenal	-	-	-	-	-	-	-	-	-	-
Tottenham	-	-	-	-	-	-	-	-	-	-
Everton	-	-	-	-	-	-	-	-	-	-
Liverpool	-	-	-	-	-	-	-	-	-	-
West Brom			2	0	2	0	0	2	2	0
Swansea			3	1	0	2	1	2	0	1
West Ham			1	0	1	0	1	0	1	0
Norwich			3	1	2	0	1	2	2	1
Fulham	-	-	-	-	-	-	-	-	-	-
Stoke			1	0	0	1	1	0	1	0
Southampton			3	1	1	1	1	2	1	1
Aston Villa	-	-	-	-	-	-	-	-	-	-
Newcastle			1	0	0	1	0	1	0	0
Sunderland	-	-	-	-	-	-	-	-	-	-
Cardiff	W	L	6	2	1	3	3	3	3	2
Hull	W	D	4	1	3	0	1	3	2	2
Crystal Palace										

Season	Division	Pos	P	W	D	L	F	A	GD	Pts
2012-13	Championship	5	46	19	15	12	73	62	+11	72
2011-12	Championship	17	46	13	17	16	46	51	-5	56
2010-11	Championship	20	46	12	12	22	44	69	-25	48

Over/Under 65%/35% 2nd   **Both score** 61%/39% 8th

Key stat: Since going down in the first season of the Premier League era, Palace have been promoted three teams and gone straight back down every time

Championship appearances 2012-13

	P	G	Y	R
K Appiah	0 (2)	0	0	0
D Blake	9 (1)	0	1	0
Y Bolasie	38 (4)	3	6	0
J Butterfield	4 (5)	0	0	0
K De Silva	0 (1)	0	0	0
D Delaney	40	3	9	1
K Dikgacoi	39	4	7	0
S Dobbie	8 (7)	3	0	0
J Easter	2 (6)	1	1	0
D Gabbidon	8 (2)	1	0	0
O Garvan	23 (4)	4	0	0
D Goodwillie	0 (1)	0	0	0
M Jedinak	41	3	9	0
A Marrow	3 (1)	0	1	0
A Martin	3 (1)	0	1	0
A Moritz	12 (15)	5	0	0
D Moxey	20 (10)	0	6	1
G Murray	42	30	9	0
A Nimely	1 (1)	0	0	0
S O'Keefe	2 (3)	0	0	0

	P	G	Y	R
J Parr	33 (5)	0	3	0
K Phillips	2 (11)	6	0	0
P Ramage	39 (1)	4	0	0
A Richards	10 (1)	0	0	0
J Speroni	46	0	0	0
J Ward	22 (3)	0	2	0
A Wilbraham	4 (17)	0	0	0
J Williams	11 (18)	0	1	0
D Wright	0 (1)	0	0	0
W Zaha	43	6	8	0

30-goal Glenn Murray could miss much of the season

Everton

Nickname: The Toffees
Colours: Blue and white

Ground: Goodison Park **Capacity:** 39,571
Tel: 0870 442 1878 **Web:** www.evertonfc.com

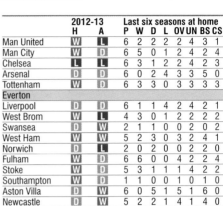

As usual, Everton averaged more points over the second half of the season – but only just, taking an average 1.67 points a game in 2013 compared to 1.65 in 2012.

It was far from the usual slow start as the season kicked off with a 1-0 win over Man United, Marouane Fellaini scoring the first of his 11 league goals, and Everton finished strongly too, ending the campaign in sixth place and ahead of Liverpool for the second season running.

The final day of the campaign saw the Toffees beaten by Chelsea – they didn't win a game away to a top-eight team – as David Moyes bowed out after 11 full seasons in charge, during which time he transformed the club from a bottom-half side to regular contenders for Europe.

It's a hard act for Roberto Martinez to follow but there is real quality at the club, especially at the back, where Leighton Baines and Phil Jagielka were superb.

Longest run without a loss: 8
Longest run without a win: 4
Highest/lowest league position: 4/7
Clean sheets: 11
Yellow cards: 61 **Red cards:** 3
Average attendance: 36,355 **Players used:** 23
Leading scorer: M Fellaini 11 (3,9)

	2012-13		Last six seasons at home							
	H	A	P	W	D	L	OV	UN	BS	CS
Man United	W	L	6	2	2	2	4	3	1	
Man City	W	D	6	5	0	1	2	4	2	4
Chelsea	L	L	6	3	1	2	2	4	2	3
Arsenal	D	D	6	0	2	4	3	3	5	0
Tottenham	W	D	6	3	3	0	3	3	3	3
Everton										
Liverpool	D	D	6	1	1	4	2	4	2	1
West Brom	W	L	4	3	0	1	2	2	2	2
Swansea	D	W	2	1	1	0	0	2	0	2
West Ham	W	W	5	2	3	0	3	2	4	1
Norwich	D	L	2	0	2	0	0	2	2	0
Fulham	D	D	6	6	0	0	4	2	2	4
Stoke	W	D	5	3	1	1	1	4	2	2
Southampton	W	D	1	1	0	0	1	0	1	0
Aston Villa	D	W	6	0	5	1	5	1	6	0
Newcastle	D	W	5	2	2	1	4	1	4	0
Sunderland	W	L	6	6	0	0	4	2	2	4
Cardiff	-	-	-	-	-	-	-	-	-	-
Hull			2	2	0	0	1	1	1	1
Crystal Palace	-	-	-	-	-	-	-	-	-	-

Season	Division	Pos	P	W	D	L	F	A	GD	Pts
2012-13	Premier League	6	38	16	15	7	55	40	+15	63
2011-12	Premier League	7	38	15	11	12	50	40	+10	56
2010-11	Premier League	7	38	13	15	10	51	45	+6	54

Over/Under 53%/47% 11th **Both score** 63%/37% 3rd

Key stat: Everton's average finishing position in 11 seasons under David Moyes was 7.5. In the ten seasons before he arrived it was 14.1

Premier League appearances 2012-13

	P	G	Y	R
V Anichebe	19 (7)	6	2	0
L Baines	38	5	4	0
R Barkley	2 (5)	0	2	0
S Coleman	24 (2)	0	4	0
S Distin	31 (3)	0	2	0
S Duffy	0 (1)	0	0	0
M Fellaini	31	11	8	0
D Gibson	22 (1)	1	4	1
M Gueye	0 (2)	0	0	0
J Heitinga	17 (9)	0	5	0
T Hibbert	4 (2)	0	1	0
T Hitzlsperger	4 (3)	0	0	0
T Howard	36	0	0	0
P Jagielka	36	2	1	0
N Jelavic	26 (11)	7	4	0
K Mirallas	23 (4)	6	3	0
J Mucha	2	0	0	0
S Naismith	13 (18)	4	0	0
P Neville	18	0	4	0
L Osman	36	5	9	0

	P	G	Y	R
B Oviedo	1 (14)	0	1	0
S Pienaar	35	6	7	2
A Vellios	0 (6)	0	0	0

Marouane Fellaini was the first Everton player to get into double figures since Louis Saha in 2010

Fulham

Nickname: The Cottagers
Colours: White and black

Ground: Craven Cottage **Capacity:** 25,700
Tel: 0870 442 1222 **Web:** www.fulhamfc.com

The summer of 2012 wasn't great for the Cottagers, with 17-goal Clint Dempsey and Mousa Dembele both leaving for Tottenham late in the day, but the arrival of Dimitar Berbatov softened the blow.

The Bulgarian weighed in with 15 league goals but no other Fulham player came close, with Bryan Ruiz and Mladen Petric next best on five apiece.

Martin Jol's second season in charge saw Fulham finish outside the top ten for the first time since 2010, nine points off their 2011-12 total, and 60 goals against was their joint-worst total since promotion to the top flight. The last time they shipped that many they finished 17th.

Jol has boosted his defensive options with Venezuelan hardman Fernando Amorebieta from Athletic Bilbao – he was shown 11 red cards in eight seasons in Spain's Primera Liga – and Dutch international keeper Maarten Stekelenburg.

Longest run without a loss: 5
Longest run without a win: 7
Highest/lowest league position: 7/15
Clean sheets: 8
Yellow cards: 48 **Red cards:** 3
Average attendance: 25,394 **Players used:** 29
Leading scorer: D Berbatov 15 (9,12)

	2012-13		Last six seasons at home							
	H	A	P	W	D	L	OV	UN	BS	CS
Man United	L	L	6	2	1	3	4	2	1	2
Man City	L	L	6	0	3	3	5	1	6	0
Chelsea	L	D	6	0	3	3	3	3	3	1
Arsenal	L	D	6	2	1	3	3	3	2	1
Tottenham	L	W	6	1	2	3	5	1	4	1
Everton	D	L	6	2	2	2	3	3	3	2
Liverpool	L	L	6	2	0	4	3	3	3	1
West Brom	W	W	4	3	1	0	2	2	1	3
Swansea	L	W	2	0	0	2	2	0	1	0
West Ham	W	L	5	2	0	3	4	1	4	0
Norwich	W	D	2	2	0	0	2	0	1	1
Fulham										
Stoke	W	L	5	4	0	1	1	4	1	3
Southampton	D	D	1	0	1	0	0	1	1	0
Aston Villa	W	D	6	3	2	1	2	4	3	2
Newcastle	W	L	5	4	0	1	3	2	3	1
Sunderland	L	D	6	2	2	2	3	3	3	3
Cardiff	-	-	-	-	-	-	-	-	-	-
Hull			2	1	0	1	0	2	0	1
Crystal Palace	-	-	-	-	-	-	-	-	-	-

Season	Division	Pos	P	W	D	L	F	A	GD	Pts
2012-13	Premier League	12	38	11	10	17	50	60	-10	43
2011-12	Premier League	9	38	14	10	14	48	51	-3	52
2010-11	Premier League	8	38	11	16	11	49	43	+6	49

Over/Under 63%/37% 4th **Both score** 53%/47% 16th

Key stat: With four wins and seven draws on the road, Fulham's away points haul was their best since 2003-04

Premier League appearances 2012-13

	P	G	Y	R		P	G	Y	R
C Baird	14 (5)	2	5	0	S Riether	35	1	4	0
D Berbatov	32 (1)	15	1	0	J Riise	29 (2)	0	4	0
M Briggs	3 (2)	0	0	0	H Rodallega	14 (15)	3	0	0
A Dejagah	13 (8)	0	3	0	B Ruiz	26 (3)	5	2	0
M Dembele	2	0	0	0	M Schwarzer	36	0	0	0
M Diarra	7 (1)	0	1	0	P Senderos	18 (3)	0	6	0
D Duff	27 (4)	3	0	0	S Sidwell	24 (4)	4	7	2
U Emanuelson	5 (8)	1	1	0	A Smith	0 (1)	0	0	0
E Enoh	8 (1)	0	3	0	D Stockdale	2	0	2	0
K Frei	2 (5)	0	0	0					
E Frimpong	2 (4)	0	1	0					
B Hangeland	35	0	2	1					
A Hughes	23 (1)	0	1	0					
A Kacaniklic	16 (4)	4	0	0					
G Karagounis	20 (5)	1	3	0					
P Kasami	0 (2)	0	0	0					
S Kelly	0 (2)	0	0	0					
S Manolev	4 (1)	0	2	0					
M Petric	9 (14)	5	0	0					
K Richardson	12 (2)	1	2	0					

Dimitar Berbatov volleys home the only goal of the game against Stoke

Hull City

Nickname: The Tigers
Colours: Amber and black

Ground: The KC Stadium
Tel: 0870 837 0003

Capacity: 25,404
Web: www.hullcityafc.net

Three years since their two seasons in the top flight Hull won promotion as Championship runners-up after a nail-biting final day. A 2-2 draw with champions Cardiff meant the Tigers were left waiting on Watford's result which, because of an injury to Hornets keeper Jonathan Bond, was delayed by 16 minutes. Victory for Leeds at Vicarage Road sent Hull up.

Steve Bruce, appointed the previous summer, has now won promotion to the top flight three times as a manager and it was a proud day for owner Assem Allam too, who bought the club in 2010 when they were battling to stay out of administration in the wake of their relegation.

A number of players were released but Bruce will have experience in the ranks, with Abdoulaye Faye, now 35, in the defence, and Robert Koren, top scorer last season, having played in the top flight for West Brom.

Longest run without a loss: 8
Longest run without a win: 4
Highest/lowest league position: 2/10
Clean sheets: 16
Yellow cards: 59 **Red cards:** 0
Average attendance: 17,368 **Players used:** 30
Leading scorer: R Koren 9 (4,9)

	2012-13 H	A	Last six seasons at home P	W	D	L	OV	UN	BS	CS
Man United	2	0	0	2	1	1	1	0		
Man City	2	1	1	0	2	0	2	0		
Chelsea	2	0	1	1	1	1	1	0		
Arsenal	2	0	0	2	2	0	2	0		
Tottenham	2	0	0	2	2	0	2	0		
Everton	2	1	1	0	2	0	2	0		
Liverpool	2	0	1	1	1	1	1	1		
West Brom	2	0	1	1	2	0	2	0		
Swansea	1	1	0	0	0	1	0	1		
West Ham	3	1	1	1	1	2	1	1		
Norwich	2	1	1	0	1	1	2	0		
Fulham	2	2	0	0	1	1	1	1		
Stoke	3	1	1	1	2	1	3	0		
Southampton	2	1	0	1	1	0	1	0		
Aston Villa	2	0	0	2	0	2	0	0		
Newcastle	1	0	1	0	0	1	1	0		
Sunderland	2	0	0	2	1	1	1	0		
Cardiff	D	L	4	1	2	1	3	1	3	0
Hull										
Crystal Palace	D	L	4	1	2	1	1	3	2	1

Season	Division	Pos	P	W	D	L	F	A	GD	Pts
2012-13	Championship	2	46	24	7	15	61	52	+9	79
2011-12	Championship	8	46	19	11	16	47	44	+3	68
2010-11	Championship	11	46	16	17	13	52	51	+1	65

Over/Under 48%/52% 16th   **Both score** 50%/50% 20th

Key stat: Hull won just one of their ten games when midfielder Ahmed Elmohamady – now permanently signed – wasn't in the starting line-up

Championship appearances 2012-13

	P	G	Y	R		P	G	Y	R
S Aluko	22 (1)	8	1	0	P McShane	20 (5)	2	1	0
B Amos	17	0	1	0	D Meyler	25 (3)	5	10	0
G Boyd	12 (1)	4	1	0	S Olofinjana	9 (3)	0	1	0
R Brady	28 (4)	4	7	0	M Oxley	0 (1)	0	0	0
A Bruce	29 (3)	0	2	0	N Proschwitz	5 (22)	3	1	0
T Cairney	0 (10)	0	0	0	S Quinn	41 (1)	3	2	0
J Chester	43 (1)	1	2	0	L Rosenior	15 (17)	0	3	0
A Dawson	3 (1)	0	0	0	J Simpson	27 (16)	6	2	0
J Dudgeon	9	0	0	0	C Stewart	1 (1)	0	0	0
A Elmohamady	41	3	4	0	D Stockdale	24	0	2	0
C Evans	23 (9)	1	10	0					
A Fathi	1 (6)	0	1	0					
A Faye	28 (3)	4	2	0					
M Fryatt	2 (2)	0	0	0					
Gedo	10 (2)	5	2	0					
J Hobbs	20 (2)	0	1	0					
E Jakupovic	5	0	0	0					
R Koren	37 (3)	9	0	0					
P McKenna	6 (3)	0	2	0					
A McLean	3 (11)	1	1	0					

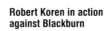

Robert Koren in action against Blackburn

Liverpool

Nickname: The Reds
Colours: Red

Ground: Anfield
Tel: 0151 263 2361

Capacity: 45,276
Web: www.liverpoolfc.tv

The season started with Brendan Rodgers doing his best David Brent impression in the Being Liverpool documentary but under the new manager, the Reds did make progress and finished with over 60 points for the first time since Rafa Benitez left the club at the end of 2009-10.

It was Luis Suarez who dominated their year, scoring 23 goals – more than double his tally of the previous season – but also serving a ten-match ban for biting Chelsea's Branislav Ivanovic, with the suspension covering the first six games of the coming season.

Daniel Sturridge made hay in Suarez's absence with five goals in Liverpool's final four games, but another January buy, Philippe Coutinho, could be the star this term. In the eight games Coutinho and Sturridge started together, Liverpool's win rate stood at 63 per cent, compared to 43 per cent over the season as a whole.

Longest run without a loss: 8
Longest run without a win: 5
Highest/lowest league position: 5/14
Clean sheets: 16
Yellow cards: 54 **Red cards:** 2
Average attendance: 44,748 **Players used:** 28
Leading scorer: L Suarez 23 (5,16)

| | 2012-13 | | Last six seasons at home | | | | | | | |
	H	A	P	W	D	L	OV	UN	BS	CS
Man United	L	L	6	3	1	2	3	3	4	1
Man City	D	D	6	2	4	0	3	3	4	2
Chelsea	D	D	6	3	2	1	2	4	3	2
Arsenal	L	L	6	0	3	3	3	3	5	0
Tottenham	W	L	6	3	2	1	3	3	3	2
Everton	D	D	6	3	3	0	2	4	2	4
Liverpool										
West Brom	L	L	4	2	0	2	1	3	0	2
Swansea	W	D	2	1	1	0	1	1	0	2
West Ham	D	W	5	3	2	0	3	2	0	5
Norwich	W	W	2	1	1	0	1	1	1	1
Fulham	W	W	6	3	2	1	1	5	0	5
Stoke	D	L	5	2	3	0	1	4	0	5
Southampton	W	L	1	1	0	0	0	1	0	1
Aston Villa	L	W	6	2	2	2	5	1	4	2
Newcastle	D	W	5	4	1	0	4	1	2	3
Sunderland	W	D	6	4	2	0	4	2	2	4
Cardiff	-	-	-	-	-	-	-	-	-	-
Hull			2	1	1	0	2	0	2	0
Crystal Palace	-	-	-	-	-	-	-	-	-	-

Season	Division	Pos	P	W	D	L	F	A	GD	Pts
2012-13	Premier League	7	38	16	13	9	71	43	+28	61
2011-12	Premier League	8	38	14	10	14	47	40	+7	52
2010-11	Premier League	6	38	17	7	14	59	44	+15	58

Over/Under 66%/34% 2nd   **Both score** 50%/50% 17th

Key stat: A whopping 79 per cent of Liverpool's Premier League away games ended with over 2.5 goals – the highest in the division

Premier League appearances 2012-13

	P	G	Y	R
D Agger	35	3	3	1
J Allen	21 (6)	0	2	0
O Assaidi	0 (4)	0	0	0
F Borini	5 (8)	1	1	0
J Carragher	16 (8)	0	4	0
A Carroll	0 (2)	0	1	0
C Coady	0 (1)	0	0	0
S Coates	2 (3)	0	0	0
J Cole	0 (6)	1	0	0
P Coutinho	12 (1)	3	0	0
S Downing	25 (4)	3	0	0
J Enrique	25 (4)	2	1	0
S Gerrard	36	9	5	0
J Henderson	16 (14)	5	3	0
J Ibe	1	0	0	0
G Johnson	36	1	7	0
B Jones	7	0	0	0
M Kelly	4	0	0	0
Lucas	24 (2)	0	6	0
J Reina	31	0	1	0

	P	G	Y	R
N Sahin	7	1	0	0
J Shelvey	9 (10)	1	3	1
M Skrtel	23 (2)	2	4	0
R Sterling	19 (5)	2	1	0
D Sturridge	11 (3)	10	2	0
L Suarez	33	23	10	0
Suso	8 (6)	0	0	0
A Wisdom	12	0	0	0

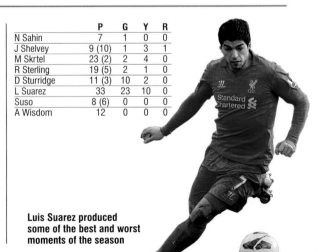

Luis Suarez produced some of the best and worst moments of the season

Manchester City

Nickname: The Citizens
Colours: Sky blue and white

Ground: Etihad Stadium   **Capacity:** 47,405
Tel: 0870 062 1894   **Web:** www.mcfc.co.uk

It shows how far City have come that finishing second as beaten FA Cup finalists cost the manager his job.

There was more to it than that – the limp exit from the Champions League without winning a game and a squad who no longer seemed to respond to Roberto Mancini – and new manager Manuel Pellegrini has been given an ambitious brief to take the club forward while playing attractive football by the former Barcelona pair of chief executive Ferran Soriano and director of football Txiki Begiristain.

Perhaps the best performances of last season came at the back where Pablo Zabaleta was superb and Matija Nastasic, 20, showed bags of promise. There have been some exciting summer buys, with Fernandinho and Jesus Navas arriving from Shakhtar Donetsk and Sevilla respectively before Pellegrini's appointment was even confirmed.

Longest run without a loss: 15
Longest run without a win: 3
Highest/lowest league position: 1/3
Clean sheets: 18
Yellow cards: 63 **Red cards:** 3
Average attendance: 46,074 **Players used:** 25
Leading scorer: E Dzeko 14 (3,12)

	2012-13 H	2012-13 A	Last six seasons at home P	W	D	L	OV	UN	BS	CS
Man United	L	W	6	2	1	3	1	5	1	3
Man City										
Chelsea	W	D	6	4	0	2	3	3	3	2
Arsenal	D	W	6	3	1	2	4	2	3	2
Tottenham	W	L	6	4	0	2	4	2	4	1
Everton	D	L	6	1	1	4	1	5	2	1
Liverpool	D	D	6	2	3	1	4	2	2	4
West Brom	W	W	4	4	0	0	3	1	1	3
Swansea	W	D	2	2	0	0	1	1	0	2
West Ham	W	D	5	4	1	0	4	1	4	1
Norwich	L	W	2	1	0	1	2	0	2	0
Fulham	W	W	6	2	2	2	4	2	4	2
Stoke	W	D	5	5	0	0	4	1	0	5
Southampton	W	L	1	1	0	0	1	0	1	0
Aston Villa	W	W	6	6	0	0	4	2	2	4
Newcastle	W	W	5	5	0	0	5	0	4	1
Sunderland	W	L	6	5	1	0	4	2	2	4
Cardiff	-	-	-	-	-	-	-	-	-	-
Hull			2	1	1	0	1	1	2	0
Crystal Palace	-	-	-	-	-	-	-	-	-	-

Season	Division	Pos	P	W	D	L	F	A	GD	Pts
2012-13	Premier League	2	38	23	9	6	66	34	+32	78
2011-12	Premier League	1	38	28	5	5	93	29	+64	89
2010-11	Premier League	3	38	21	8	9	60	33	+27	71

Over/Under 50%/50% 15th   **Both score** 47%/53% 18th

Key stat: City took fewer points than they had the previous season for the first time since 2008-09 and their goal difference was half that of 2011-12

Premier League appearances 2012-13

	P	G	Y	R
S Aguero	22 (8)	12	2	0
M Balotelli	7 (7)	1	2	0
G Barry	27 (4)	1	6	0
G Clichy	26 (2)	0	3	0
E Dzeko	16 (16)	14	4	0
J Hart	38	0	1	0
J Garcia	17 (7)	2	5	0
A Kolarov	11 (9)	1	5	0
V Kompany	26	1	3	1
J Lescott	17 (9)	1	3	0
Maicon	4 (5)	0	0	0
J Milner	19 (7)	4	1	1
S Nasri	22 (6)	2	3	1
M Nastasic	21	0	1	0
A Razak	0 (3)	0	0	0
K Rekik	1	0	2	0
M Richards	7	0	2	0
J Rodwell	6 (5)	2	2	0
D Silva	29 (3)	4	2	0
S Sinclair	2 (9)	0	0	0

	P	G	Y	R
C Tevez	28 (6)	11	3	0
Y Toure	32	6	6	0
K Toure	10 (5)	0	2	0
P Zabaleta	29 (1)	2	7	0
N de Jong	1	0	0	0

Edin Dzeko made the most of limited opportunities and grabbed 16 goals

Manchester United

Nickname: The Red Devils
Colours: Red and white

Ground: Old Trafford **Capacity:** 75,765
Tel: 0161 868 8000 **Web:** www.manutd.com

Sir Alex Ferguson's final season in charge at Old Trafford didn't end in the repeat of 1999's treble that looked like it might be on the cards at one point but they won the title at a canter, the 11-point margin of victory United's biggest since 2000.

United had a handy lead by the turn of the year but it was a sequence of seven wins, the last six all to nil, that stretched their lead from seven points at the end of January to 15 points before the run ended in a 2-1 home defeat to Man City at the beginning of April. It highlighted the depth of United's squad that golden boot winner Robin van Persie only scored in one of those seven victories. Indeed, United had 20 different goalscorers in the league last season.

They finished on 89 points, the same as when pipped to the post in 2012, and it is that consistency that David Moyes will want to maintain.

Longest run without a loss: 18
Longest run without a win: 2
Highest/lowest league position: 1/2
Clean sheets: 13
Yellow cards: 57 **Red cards:** 1
Average attendance: 75,529 **Players used:** 25
Leading scorer: R Van Persie 26 (6,21)

	2012-13 H	A	Last six seasons at home P	W	D	L	OV	UN	BS	CS
Man United										
Man City	L	W	6	3	0	3	5	1	5	1
Chelsea	L	W	6	4	0	2	4	2	3	2
Arsenal	W	D	6	5	1	0	4	2	4	2
Tottenham	L	D	6	5	0	1	4	2	3	3
Everton	W	L	6	5	1	0	3	3	2	4
Liverpool	W	W	6	5	0	1	6	0	5	1
West Brom	W	D	4	3	1	0	2	2	1	3
Swansea	W	D	2	2	0	0	1	1	1	1
West Ham	W	D	5	5	0	0	3	2	1	4
Norwich	W	L	2	2	0	0	1	1	0	2
Fulham	W	W	6	6	0	0	3	3	1	5
Stoke	W	W	5	5	0	0	4	1	2	3
Southampton	W	W	1	1	0	0	1	0	1	0
Aston Villa	W	W	6	5	0	1	5	1	2	3
Newcastle	W	W	5	3	2	0	3	2	3	2
Sunderland	W	W	6	5	1	0	2	4	2	4
Cardiff	-	-	-	-	-	-	-	-	-	-
Hull			2	2	0	0	2	0	1	1
Crystal Palace	-	-	-	-	-	-	-	-	-	-

Season	Division	Pos	P	W	D	L	F	A	GD	Pts
2012-13	Premier League	1	38	28	5	5	86	43	+43	89
2011-12	Premier League	2	38	28	5	5	89	33	+56	89
2010-11	Premier League	1	38	23	11	4	78	37	+41	80

Over/Under 63%/37% 4th **Both score** 58%/42% 7th

Key stat: Under Sir Alex Ferguson, United averaged 83.4 points in the Premier League era, and 86.7 points in the last six seasons

Premier League appearances 2012-13

	P	G	Y	R		P	G	Y	R
Anderson	9 (8)	1	1	0	N Vidic	18 (1)	1	2	0
A Buttner	4 (1)	2	1	0	D Welbeck	13 (14)	1	1	0
M Carrick	34 (2)	1	3	0	A Young	17 (2)	0	1	0
T Cleverley	18 (4)	2	1	0	D de Gea	28	0	0	0
J Evans	21 (2)	3	2	0	R van Persie	35 (3)	26	6	0
P Evra	34	4	3	0					
R Ferdinand	26 (2)	1	2	0					
D Fletcher	2 (1)	1	0	0					
R Giggs	12 (10)	2	0	0					
J Hernandez	9 (13)	10	1	0					
P Jones	13 (4)	0	4	0					
S Kagawa	17 (3)	6	1	0					
A Lindegaard	10	0	0	0					
Nani	7 (4)	1	1	0					
N Powell	0 (2)	1	0	0					
Rafael Da Silva	27 (1)	3	6	1					
W Rooney	22 (5)	12	7	0					
P Scholes	8 (8)	1	7	0					
C Smalling	10 (5)	0	1	0					
L Valencia	24 (6)	1	6	0					

Robin van Persie volleys one of the goals of the season against Aston Villa

Newcastle United

Nickname: The Magpies
Colours: Black and white

Ground: St James' Park
Tel: 0191 201 8400

Capacity: 52,405
Web: www.nufc.co.uk

After finishing fifth in 2012 and winning the Premier League's manager of the year award, Alan Pardew signed an eight-year contract last September.

But, after Newcastle finished 16th in a season that included a 6-0 thrashing by Liverpool at St James' Park – their worst top-flight home defeat since 1925 – plus the arrival of Joe Kinnear as director of football and the departure of managing director Derek Llambias, Pardew was the sack race favourite as we went to press.

Demba Ba finished as top scorer, despite leaving in January, and the Magpies finished with their worst goal difference since they finished bottom of the old Division One in 1988-89.

It wasn't all bad – they reached the Europa League quarter-finals and Moussa Sissoko was an impressive January signing from Toulouse – but it was a massive return to earth after the highs of 2011-12.

Longest run without a loss: 4
Longest run without a win: 5
Highest/lowest league position: 10/17
Clean sheets: 6
Yellow cards: 73 **Red cards:** 4
Average attendance: 50,517 **Players used:** 32
Leading scorer: D Ba 13 (4,9)

	2012-13		Last six seasons at home							
	H	A	P	W	D	L	OV	UN	BS	CS
Man United	L	L	5	1	1	3	4	1	2	2
Man City	L	L	5	0	1	4	3	2	3	0
Chelsea	W	L	5	1	1	3	2	3	2	0
Arsenal	L	L	5	0	3	2	2	3	3	1
Tottenham	W	L	5	3	2	0	4	1	5	0
Everton	L	D	5	2	1	2	4	1	4	1
Liverpool	L	D	5	2	0	3	4	1	2	1
West Brom	W	D	5	2	2	1	5	0	5	0
Swansea	L	L	3	1	1	1	2	1	1	2
West Ham	L	D	4	2	1	1	3	1	2	1
Norwich	W	D	2	2	0	0	2	0	2	0
Fulham	W	L	5	3	1	1	1	4	1	3
Stoke	W	L	4	2	1	1	4	0	3	1
Southampton	W	L	1	1	0	0	1	0	1	0
Aston Villa	D	W	5	3	2	0	2	3	2	3
Newcastle										
Sunderland	L	D	5	2	2	1	2	3	3	1
Cardiff			1	1	0	0	1	0	1	0
Hull			1	0	0	1	1	0	1	0
Crystal Palace			1	1	0	0	0	1	0	1

Season	Division	Pos	P	W	D	L	F	A	GD	Pts
2012-13	Premier League	16	38	11	8	19	45	68	-23	41
2011-12	Premier League	5	38	19	8	11	56	51	+5	65
2010-11	Premier League	12	38	11	13	14	56	57	-1	46

Over/Under 63%/37% 4th

Both score 61%/39% 4th

Key stat: No team won fewer road games – they won twice on the road and took one more away point than in their 2008-09 relegation season

Premier League appearances 2012-13

	P	G	Y	R
Sammy Ameobi	1 (7)	0	1	0
Shola Ameobi	4 (19)	1	5	0
V Anita	17 (8)	0	2	0
D Ba	19 (1)	13	0	0
H Ben Arfa	16 (3)	4	1	0
G Bigirimana	3 (10)	1	1	0
Y Cabaye	25 (1)	6	8	0
A Campbell	0 (3)	0	0	0
P Cisse	35 (1)	8	6	0
F Coloccini	22	0	1	1
M Debuchy	14	0	3	1
R Elliot	9 (1)	0	1	1
S Ferguson	4 (5)	0	0	0
D Gosling	0 (3)	0	0	0
Y Gouffran	14 (1)	3	1	0
J Gutierrez	34	4	8	0
M Haidara	2 (2)	0	0	0
S Harper	5 (1)	0	0	0
T Krul	24	0	0	0
S Marveaux	10 (12)	1	0	0

	P	G	Y	R
G Obertan	4 (10)	0	0	0
J Perch	19 (8)	1	9	0
N Ranger	0 (2)	0	0	0
D Santon	31	1	4	0
D Simpson	18 (1)	0	3	0
M Sissoko	12	3	2	0
J Tavernier	0 (2)	0	0	0
R Taylor	0 (1)	0	0	0
S Taylor	24 (1)	0	2	0
C Tiote	22 (2)	0	7	1
M Williamson	19	0	8	0
M Yanga-Mbiwa	11 (3)	0	0	0

Papiss Cisse weighed in with eight goals but the departed Demba Ba was top scorer

Norwich City

Nickname: The Canaries
Colours: Yellow and green

Ground: Carrow Road   **Capacity:** 27,224
Tel: 01603 760 760   **Web:** www.canaries.co.uk

Paul Lambert's summer departure left the Canaries looking vulnerable to second season syndrome and, despite only missing out on the top ten on goal difference in 2011-12, they were among the relegation favourites as last season kicked off.

Chris Hughton steered them to 11th place but for long periods Norwich's top-flight status looked far from certain.

A slow start didn't help. The Canaries were beaten 5-0 by Fulham in Hughton's first match in charge and didn't get their first league win until October, eight games in, with a 1-0 victory over Arsenal.

Although they tightened up a little defensively compared to the previous season, only Stoke scored fewer goals and stayed up. Grant Holt remained in yellow and green to finish as the club's top scorer again, but with eight league goals compared to 15 in their first season back in the Premier League.

Longest run without a loss: 10
Longest run without a win: 9
Highest/lowest league position: 8/19
Clean sheets: 10
Yellow cards: 60 **Red cards:** 1
Average attendance: 26,671 **Players used:** 27
Leading scorer: G Holt 8 (2,8)

	2012-13 H	A	Last six seasons at home P	W	D	L	OV	UN	BS	CS
Man United	W	L	2	1	0	1	1	1	1	1
Man City	L	W	2	0	0	2	2	0	2	0
Chelsea	L	L	2	0	1	1	0	2	0	1
Arsenal	W	L	2	1	0	1	1	1	1	1
Tottenham	D	D	2	0	1	1	0	2	1	0
Everton	W	D	2	1	1	0	2	0	2	0
Liverpool	L	L	2	0	0	2	2	0	1	0
West Brom	W	L	3	1	0	2	2	1	1	1
Swansea	D	W	4	2	1	1	3	1	3	1
West Ham	D	L	1	0	1	0	0	1	0	1
Norwich										
Fulham	D	L	2	0	2	0	0	2	1	1
Stoke	W	L	3	1	1	1	0	3	1	1
Southampton	D	D	4	1	2	1	2	2	2	1
Aston Villa	L	D	2	1	0	1	1	1	1	1
Newcastle	D	L	2	1	1	0	1	1	1	1
Sunderland	W	D	2	2	0	0	2	0	2	0
Cardiff			3	1	1	1	1	2	2	1
Hull			2	0	1	1	0	2	1	0
Crystal Palace			3	1	0	2	2	1	2	1

Season	Division	Pos	P	W	D	L	F	A	GD	Pts
2012-13	Premier League	11	38	10	14	14	41	58	-17	44
2011-12	Premier League	12	38	12	11	15	52	66	-14	47
2010-11	Championship	2	46	23	15	8	83	58	+25	84

Over/Under 47%/53% 17th   **Both score** 55%/45% 11th

Key stat: Norwich didn't win a single Premier League game when Grant Holt wasn't in the starting XI

Premier League appearances 2012-13

	P	G	Y	R
L Barnett	6 (2)	0	1	0
S Bassong	34	3	3	0
L Becchio	2 (6)	0	0	0
E Bennett	9 (15)	1	3	0
R Bennett	10 (5)	1	2	0
M Bunn	22 (1)	0	2	1
L Camp	1 (2)	0	1	0
D Fox	0 (2)	0	0	0
J Garrido	34	0	4	0
G Holt	28 (6)	8	8	0
W Hoolahan	28 (5)	3	3	0
J Howson	22 (8)	2	2	0
S Jackson	5 (8)	1	0	0
B Johnson	37	1	10	0
K Kamara	7 (4)	1	0	0
H Kane	1 (2)	0	0	0
C Martin	0 (1)	0	0	0
R Martin	30 (1)	3	1	0
S Morison	4 (15)	1	0	0
A Pilkington	25 (5)	5	2	0

	P	G	Y	R
J Ruddy	15	0	0	0
R Snodgrass	35 (2)	6	8	0
A Surman	4	0	0	0
A Tettey	21 (6)	0	4	0
M Tierney	1	0	0	0
M Turner	25 (1)	3	6	0
S Whittaker	12 (1)	1	0	0

Grant Holt in action in the final day win over Man City at Eastlands

Southampton

Nickname: The Saints
Colours: Red and white

Ground: St Mary's Stadium
Tel: 0845 688 9448

Capacity: 32,689
Web: www.saintsfc.co.uk

Southampton's season started badly – after ten games, they were bottom with eight defeats and 28 goals conceded – but just as they seemed to have turned a corner under Nigel Adkins, the Saints sacked the man who led them from League 1 to the top flight.

Adkins' dismissal came on the back of a battling 2-2 draw against Chelsea but his replacement, former Espanyol manager Mauricio Pochettino, did well in the face of a sceptical reception from the press. However, while the Saints played nice possession football under the new man, their 25 per cent win-rate under Pochettino wasn't much better than the 23 per cent they had achieved under Adkins.

In the end, though, their survival was fairly comfortable. Rickie Lambert showed he could do it in the Premier League while Luke Shaw, 17, got plenty of games and looks like the real deal.

Longest run without a loss: 6
Longest run without a win: 6
Highest/lowest league position: 11/20
Clean sheets: 7
Yellow cards: 43 **Red cards:** 2
Average attendance: 30,873 **Players used:** 25
Leading scorer: R Lambert 15 (5,14)

	2012-13		Last six seasons at home							
	H	A	P	W	D	L	OV	UN	BS	CS
Man United	L	L	1	0	0	1	1	0	1	0
Man City	W	L	1	1	0	0	1	0	1	0
Chelsea	W	D	1	1	0	0	1	0	1	0
Arsenal	D	L	1	0	1	0	0	1	1	0
Tottenham	L	L	1	0	0	1	1	0	1	0
Everton	D	L	1	0	1	0	0	1	0	1
Liverpool	W	L	1	1	0	0	1	0	1	0
West Brom	L	L	2	1	0	1	2	0	1	0
Swansea	D	D	2	0	2	0	1	1	2	0
West Ham	D	L	2	1	1	0	0	2	1	1
Norwich	D	D	4	1	2	1	3	2	1	
Fulham	D	D	1	0	1	0	1	0	1	0
Stoke	D	D	2	1	1	0	1	1	2	0
Southampton										
Aston Villa	W	W	1	1	0	0	1	0	1	0
Newcastle	W	L	1	1	0	0	0	1	0	1
Sunderland	L	D	1	0	0	1	0	1	0	0
Cardiff			3	2	1	0	0	3	1	2
Hull			2	2	0	0	2	0	1	1
Crystal Palace			3	2	0	1	1	2	1	2

Season	Division	Pos	P	W	D	L	F	A	GD	Pts
2012-13	Premier League	14	38	9	14	15	49	60	-11	41
2011-12	Championship	2	46	26	10	10	85	46	+39	88
2010-11	League 1	2	46	28	8	10	86	38	+48	92

Over/Under 50%/50% 15th   **Both score** 66%/34% 2nd

Key stat: Aston Villa were the only team to match Southampton's total of five Premier League own goals last season and stay up

Premier League appearances 2012-13

	P	G	Y	R			P	G	Y	R
A Boruc	20	0	1	0		M Schneiderlin	36	5	9	0
R Chaplow	0 (3)	0	0	0		B Sharp	0 (2)	0	0	0
N Clyne	34	1	2	0		L Shaw	22 (3)	0	2	0
J Cork	28	0	1	0		J Ward-Prowse	4 (11)	0	0	0
K Davis	9 (1)	0	0	0		M Yoshida	31 (1)	0	2	0
S Davis	22 (10)	2	1	0						
S De Ridder	0 (4)	0	1	0						
G Do Prado	8 (10)	0	0	0						
J Fonte	25 (2)	2	5	0						
D Fox	14 (6)	1	3	1						
P Gazzaniga	9	0	0	0						
J Hooiveld	23 (2)	0	5	0						
A Lallana	26 (4)	3	2	0						
R Lambert	35 (3)	15	2	0						
E Mayuka	1 (10)	0	0	0						
J Puncheon	25 (7)	6	1	0						
G Ramirez	20 (6)	5	2	1						
B Reeves	0 (3)	0	0	0						
F Richardson	2 (3)	0	0	0						
J Rodriguez	24 (11)	6	4	0						

Rickie Lambert scored against all of the top three last term

Stoke City

Nickname: The Potters
Colours: Red and white

Ground: Britannia Stadium
Tel: 0871 663 2008

Capacity: 27,740
Web: www.stokecityfc.com

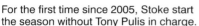

For the first time since 2005, Stoke start the season without Tony Pulis in charge.

Since Pulis took the Potters into the Premier League as Championship runners-up in 2008, eight of the other 14 promoted teams have gone back down and for a while last season it looked like Stoke might join them.

A ten-game unbeaten run that included a 3-1 win at home to Liverpool on Boxing Day ended on New Year's Day. After that, the Potters' only league victories came against the final bottom two, Reading and QPR, and at home to a Norwich side who, like Stoke, ended the season with just two away wins against their name.

Stoke were hard to beat, though – 15 stalemates – and they finished 13th.

Pulis had drawn up a plan for the club's future before he left but Mark Hughes is the man charged with taking the Potters forward.

Longest run without a loss: 10
Longest run without a win: 7
Highest/lowest league position: 8/16
Clean sheets: 12
Yellow cards: 81 **Red cards:** 4
Average attendance: 26,919 **Players used:** 24
Leading scorer: J Walters 8 (3,7)

2012-13	H	A	P	W	D	L	OV	UN	BS	CS
			Last six seasons at home							
Man United	L	L	5	0	1	4	1	4	2	0
Man City	D	L	5	1	4	0	0	5	4	1
Chelsea	L	L	5	0	2	3	2	3	2	1
Arsenal	D	L	5	2	2	1	3	2	4	1
Tottenham	L	D	5	2	0	3	5	0	5	0
Everton	D	L	5	1	3	1	1	4	3	2
Liverpool	W	D	5	3	2	0	1	4	2	3
West Brom	D	W	5	2	2	1	2	3	3	2
Swansea	W	L	2	2	0	0	0	2	0	2
West Ham	L	D	4	1	1	2	1	3	2	0
Norwich	W	L	3	3	0	0	1	2	1	2
Fulham	W	L	5	3	1	1	1	4	1	3
Stoke										
Southampton	D	D	2	1	1	0	2	0	2	0
Aston Villa	L	D	5	2	2	1	3	2	3	2
Newcastle	W	L	4	2	1	1	3	1	3	1
Sunderland	D	D	5	3	1	1	1	4	1	3
Cardiff			1	1	0	0	1	0	1	0
Hull			3	1	2	0	0	3	2	1
Crystal Palace			1	0	0	1	1	0	1	0

Season	Division	Pos	P	W	D	L	F	A	GD	Pts
2012-13	Premier League	13	38	9	15	14	34	45	-11	42
2011-12	Premier League	14	38	11	12	15	36	53	-17	45
2010-11	Premier League	13	38	13	7	18	46	48	-2	46

Over/Under 34%/66% 20th   **Both score** 45%/55% 20th

Key stat: Only five of the Potters' 19 away days ended with over 2.5 goals (26 per cent) as their road games averaged a total of just 1.89 goals

Premier League appearances 2012-13

	P	G	Y	R
C Adam	22 (5)	3	8	1
A Begovic	38	0	3	0
G Cameron	29 (6)	0	5	0
P Crouch	28 (6)	7	2	0
R Delap	0 (1)	0	0	0
M Edu	0 (1)	0	0	0
M Etherington	21 (10)	0	3	0
R Huth	35	1	5	0
C Jerome	8 (18)	3	3	0
K Jones	10 (16)	3	0	0
M Kightly	14 (8)	3	2	0
S Nzonzi	35	1	9	1
M Owen	0 (8)	1	0	0
W Palacios	0 (4)	0	0	0
J Pennant	1	0	0	0
R Shawcross	37	1	9	0
B Shea	0 (2)	0	0	0
R Shotton	20 (3)	0	5	1
M Upson	1	1	0	0
J Walters	38	8	4	0

	P	G	Y	R
G Whelan	31 (1)	0	4	0
D Whitehead	12 (14)	1	10	1
A Wilkinson	19 (5)	0	6	0
M Wilson	19	0	3	0

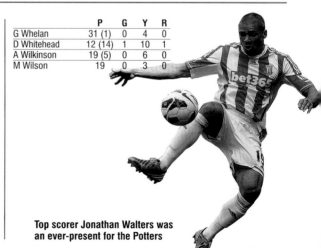

Top scorer Jonathan Walters was an ever-present for the Potters

Sunderland

Nickname: Mackems/The Black Cats
Colours: Red and white

Ground: Stadium of Light
Tel: 0191 551 5000

Capacity: 48,707
Web: www.safc.com

For the second season running, Sunderland changed manager when they found themselves in trouble and the new man made an instant impact.

In December 2011, it was Martin O'Neill who came in to replace Steve Bruce with the Black Cats 16th in the table. Last season they left it later, with O'Neill being shown the door at the end of March, hours after a 1-0 defeat to Man United, their eighth game without a win, had left them 16th, a point above the drop zone.

The appointment of Paolo Di Canio as his successor was controversial but a W2, D2, L3 record in his seven games in charge was enough to keep them up in 17th place – the last four teams to finish there, Hull, West Ham, Wolves and QPR, were all relegated the following season.

It was a lack of creativity and attacking threat that nearly cost the Mackems with only Stoke and QPR scoring fewer goals.

Longest run without a loss: 5
Longest run without a win: 9
Highest/lowest league position: 11/17
Clean sheets: 11
Yellow cards: 60 **Red cards:** 3
Average attendance: 40,544 **Players used:** 29
Leading scorer: S Fletcher 11 (7,9)

	2012-13 H	A	Last six seasons at home P	W	D	L	OV	UN	BS	CS
Man United	L	L	6	0	1	5	2	4	1	1
Man City	W	L	6	3	1	2	2	4	2	3
Chelsea	L	L	6	0	0	6	5	1	5	0
Arsenal	L	D	6	1	2	3	1	5	3	1
Tottenham	L	L	6	2	2	2	3	3	4	2
Everton	W	L	6	1	3	2	1	5	3	1
Liverpool	D	L	6	2	1	3	0	6	1	2
West Brom	L	L	4	1	1	2	4	0	3	1
Swansea	D	D	2	1	1	0	0	2	0	2
West Ham	W	D	5	3	1	1	3	2	2	2
Norwich	D	L	2	1	1	0	1	1	1	1
Fulham	D	W	6	1	4	1	2	4	2	3
Stoke	D	D	5	3	2	0	1	4	1	4
Southampton	D	W	1	0	1	0	0	1	1	0
Aston Villa	L	L	6	1	2	3	2	4	3	1
Newcastle	D	W	5	1	3	1	1	4	4	0
Sunderland										
Cardiff	-	-	-	-	-	-	-	-	-	-
Hull			2	2	0	0	1	1	1	1
Crystal Palace	-	-	-	-	-	-	-	-	-	-

Season	Division	Pos	P	W	D	L	F	A	GD	Pts
2012-13	Premier League	17	38	9	12	17	41	54	-13	39
2011-12	Premier League	13	38	11	12	15	45	46	-1	45
2010-11	Premier League	10	38	12	11	15	45	56	-11	47

Over/Under 53%/47% 11th   **Both score** 55%/45% 11th

Key stat: Just six (32 per cent) of Sunderland's home games finished with over 2.5 goals – the fewest in the Premier League

Premier League appearances 2012-13

	P	G	Y	R		P	G	Y	R
P Bardsley	11 (7)	1	5	0	A Mitchell	0 (1)	0	0	0
T Bramble	12 (4)	0	3	0	A N'Diaye	15 (1)	0	3	0
F Campbell	1 (11)	1	0	0	J O'Shea	34	2	3	0
L Cattermole	10	0	2	0	K Richardson	1	0	0	0
J Colback	30 (5)	0	4	0	D Rose	25 (2)	1	6	0
C Cuellar	26	1	5	0	L Saha	0 (11)	0	0	0
A Elmohamady	0 (2)	0	0	0	S Sessegnon	34 (1)	7	1	1
S Fletcher	28	11	3	0	D Vaughan	6 (18)	1	2	1
C Gardner	32 (1)	6	10	1	C Wickham	3 (9)	0	0	0
D Graham	11 (2)	0	0	0					
A Johnson	35	5	3	0					
M Kilgallon	6	0	1	0					
B Knott	0 (1)	0	0	0					
S Larsson	36 (2)	1	6	0					
M Mandron	0 (2)	0	1	0					
A Mangane	0 (2)	0	0	0					
J McClean	24 (12)	2	4	0					
J McFadden	0 (3)	0	0	0					
D Meyler	0 (3)	0	0	0					
S Mignolet	38	0	1	0					

Steven Fletcher was the only Sunderland player to hit double figures for Sunderland

Swansea City

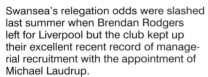

Nickname: The Swans
Colours: White

Ground: Liberty Stadium
Tel: 01792 616 600

Capacity: 20,745
Web: www.swanseacity.net

Swansea's relegation odds were slashed last summer when Brendan Rodgers left for Liverpool but the club kept up their excellent recent record of managerial recruitment with the appointment of Michael Laudrup.

The new manager put his knowledge of Spanish football to good use with Chico Flores – who played under Laudrup at Real Mallorca – Pablo Hernandez and Michu – a £2m bargain from Rayo Vallecano who had scored 15 goals in La Liga the previous season – all signing last summer.

Michu took eight minutes to open his account and finished the season with 18 league goals as the Swans did enough to earn a top-half finish and secure a place in Europe after winning the League Cup.

Their season tailed off though, with two wins from 11 games after their Wembley triumph.

Longest run without a loss: 7
Longest run without a win: 7
Highest/lowest league position: 6/12
Clean sheets: 10
Yellow cards: 59 **Red cards:** 2
Average attendance: 20,370 **Players used:** 25
Leading scorer: Michu 18 (6,14)

	2012-13 H	2012-13 A	P	W	D	L	OV	UN	BS	CS
			Last six seasons at home							
Man United	D	L	2	0	1	1	0	2	1	0
Man City	D	L	2	1	1	0	0	2	0	2
Chelsea	D	L	2	0	2	0	0	2	2	0
Arsenal	L	W	2	1	0	1	1	1	1	0
Tottenham	L	L	2	0	1	1	1	1	2	0
Everton	L	D	2	0	0	2	1	1	0	0
Liverpool	D	L	2	1	1	0	0	2	0	2
West Brom	W	L	3	2	0	1	2	1	1	1
Swansea										
West Ham	W	L	1	1	0	0	1	0	0	1
Norwich	L	D	4	2	0	2	4	0	3	1
Fulham	L	W	2	1	0	1	1	0	1	1
Stoke	W	L	2	2	0	0	1	1	1	1
Southampton	D	D	2	1	1	0	1	1	0	2
Aston Villa	D	L	2	0	2	0	1	1	1	1
Newcastle	W	W	3	1	1	1	0	3	1	1
Sunderland	D	D	2	0	2	0	1	1	1	1
Cardiff			3	1	1	1	2	1	2	0
Hull			1	0	1	0	0	1	1	0
Crystal Palace			3	1	1	1	2	1	1	2

Season	Division	Pos	P	W	D	L	F	A	GD	Pts
2012-13	Premier League	9	38	11	13	14	47	51	-4	46
2011-12	Premier League	11	38	12	11	15	44	51	-7	47
2010-11	Championship	3	46	24	8	14	69	42	+27	80

Over/Under 53%/47% 11th

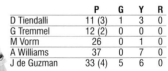

Both score 47%/53% 18th

Key stat: Swansea were one of four teams to record a division-high six goalless draws and won just four times when they kept a clean sheet

Premier League appearances 2012-13

	P	G	Y	R
G Agustien	4 (14)	0	2	0
K Bartley	1 (1)	0	0	0
L Britton	30 (3)	0	4	0
Chico	26	0	5	1
B Davies	33 (4)	1	5	0
N Dyer	25 (12)	3	4	1
M Gower	0 (1)	0	0	0
D Graham	10 (8)	3	0	0
P Hernandez	27 (3)	3	3	0
S Ki	20 (9)	0	3	0
R Lamah	1 (4)	0	0	0
Michu	35	18	6	0
G Monk	10 (1)	0	0	0
L Moore	4 (13)	3	0	0
A Rangel	30 (3)	3	7	0
W Routledge	30 (6)	5	0	0
E Shechter	7 (11)	1	3	0
S Sinclair	0 (1)	1	0	0
A Tate	2 (1)	0	0	0
N Taylor	4 (2)	0	0	0

	P	G	Y	R
D Tiendalli	11 (3)	1	3	0
G Tremmel	12 (2)	0	0	0
M Vorm	26	0	1	0
A Williams	37	0	7	0
J de Guzman	33 (4)	5	6	0

Michu was an absolute steal at £2 million

Tottenham Hotspur

Nickname: Spurs
Colours: White and navy blue

Ground: White Hart Lane **Capacity:** 36,284
Tel: 0870 420 5000 **Web:** www.tottenhamhotspur.com

After Spurs were fourth twice and fifth once under Harry Redknapp the pressure was on for Andre Villas-Boas, who was looking to restore his reputation following an unhappy spell in charge of Chelsea.

And while Spurs finished outside the top four, their haul of 72 points would have been enough for the runners-up spot in 2011 and represented their highest tally since 1984-85, when there were 22 teams in the the old First Division.

But while Villas-Boas impressed, and it is good news for the club that PSG failed to tempt their manager onto the Eurostar to replace Carlo Ancelotti, the star of the show was Gareth Bale.

It's hard to believe now that last summer he was a best price of 6-1 to be Tottenham's top scorer.

The big disappointment was Emmanuel Adebayor, who followed up his 17 goals in 2011-12 with five last season.

Longest run without a loss: 12
Longest run without a win: 3
Highest/lowest league position: 3/8
Clean sheets: 9
Yellow cards: 55 **Red cards:** 2
Average attendance: 36,029 **Players used:** 28
Leading scorer: G Bale 21 (8,17)

	2012-13 H	2012-13 A	P	W	D	L	OV	UN	BS	CS
Man United	D	W	6	0	4	2	2	4	4	2
Man City	W	L	6	4	1	1	5	1	4	2
Chelsea	L	D	6	2	3	1	3	3	5	1
Arsenal	W	L	6	3	2	1	5	1	5	1
Tottenham										
Everton	D	L	6	2	2	2	3	3	4	1
Liverpool	W	L	6	5	0	1	5	1	4	1
West Brom	D	W	4	2	2	0	1	3	2	2
Swansea	W	W	2	2	0	0	1	1	1	1
West Ham	W	W	5	4	1	0	2	3	1	4
Norwich	D	D	2	0	1	1	1	1	2	0
Fulham	L	W	6	4	1	1	1	5	1	4
Stoke	D	W	5	2	2	1	2	3	3	1
Southampton	W	W	1	1	0	0	0	1	0	1
Aston Villa	W	W	6	3	2	1	3	3	3	3
Newcastle	W	L	5	4	0	1	3	2	2	3
Sunderland	W	W	6	4	1	1	1	5	2	4
Cardiff	-	-	-	-	-	-	-	-	-	-
Hull			2	0	1	1	0	2	0	1
Crystal Palace	-	-	-	-	-	-	-	-	-	-

Season	Division	Pos	P	W	D	L	F	A	GD	Pts
2012-13	Premier League	5	38	21	9	8	66	46	+20	72
2011-12	Premier League	4	38	20	9	9	66	41	+25	69
2010-11	Premier League	5	38	16	14	8	55	46	+9	62

Over/Under 66%/34% 2nd **Both score** 71%/29% 1st

Key stat: Only three of Tottenham's away games ended with under 2.5 goals last season – overs was up at 84 per cent

Premier League appearances 2012-13

	P	G	Y	R		P	G	Y	R
M Adebayor	18 (7)	5	3	1	K Naughton	13 (1)	0	0	0
B Assou-Ekotto	12 (3)	1	2	0	S Parker	15 (6)	0	1	0
G Bale	33	21	6	0	Sandro	22	1	4	0
T Carroll	0 (7)	0	0	0	G Sigurdsson	12 (21)	3	0	0
S Caulker	17 (1)	2	1	0	A Townsend	0 (5)	0	0	0
M Dawson	23 (4)	1	4	0	J Vertonghen	34	4	7	0
J Defoe	27 (7)	11	4	0	K Walker	36	0	5	0
M Dembele	26 (4)	1	4	0	R van der Vaart	1 (1)	0	0	0
C Dempsey	22 (7)	7	4	0					
I Falque	0 (1)	0	0	0					
B Friedel	11	0	0	0					
W Gallas	16 (3)	1	2	0					
L Holtby	4 (7)	0	2	0					
T Huddlestone	11 (9)	0	3	1					
J Jenas	0 (1)	0	0	0					
Y Kaboul	1	0	0	0					
H Kane	0 (1)	0	0	0					
A Lennon	33 (1)	4	1	0					
J Livermore	4 (7)	0	3	0					
H Lloris	27	0	0	0					

Gareth Bale's stellar season made him one of the most coveted players in world football

West Brom

WEST BROMWICH ALBION

Nickname: The Baggies/Throstles/Albion
Colours: Navy blue and white

Ground: The Hawthorns   **Capacity:** 26,445
Tel: 0871 271 1100   **Web:** www.wba.co.uk

Steve Clarke showed in his first season as a manager why he has been in such demand as a number two, especially in the first half of the season when the Baggies looked like challengers for the European places – on Boxing Day, West Brom were sixth, just two points behind Chelsea in third.

Results tailed off in the second half of the campaign – the Baggies only won four more games – but in the end they finished eighth, and the season must go down as a success.

Romelu Lukaku, on loan from Chelsea, had an outstanding season scoring 17 league goals, with Shane Long next best on eight.

But it was Gareth McAuley who was voted player of the season after an excellent season at the centre of West Brom's defence and the 33-year-old has signed a new two-year deal.

Longest run without a loss: 4
Longest run without a win: 6
Highest/lowest league position: 4/9
Clean sheets: 8
Yellow cards: 63 **Red cards:** 4
Average attendance: 25,359 **Players used:** 25
Leading scorer: R Lukaku 17 (3,13)

	2012-13		Last six seasons at home							
	H	A	P	W	D	L	OV	UN	BS	CS
Man United	D	L	4	0	1	3	4	0	3	0
Man City	L	L	4	1	1	2	2	2	2	1
Chelsea	W	L	4	2	0	2	3	1	2	1
Arsenal	L	L	4	0	1	3	4	0	4	0
Tottenham	L	L	4	1	1	2	1	3	2	1
Everton	W	L	4	2	0	2	1	3	1	2
Liverpool	W	W	4	2	0	2	2	2	1	1
West Brom										
Swansea	W	L	3	1	0	2	2	1	2	0
West Ham	D	L	3	1	2	0	2	1	2	1
Norwich	W	L	3	2	0	1	2	1	2	1
Fulham	L	L	4	2	1	1	2	2	2	2
Stoke	L	D	5	0	1	4	1	4	1	0
Southampton	W	W	2	1	1	0	0	2	1	1
Aston Villa	D	D	4	1	2	1	3	1	3	1
Newcastle	D	L	5	1	2	2	3	2	5	0
Sunderland	W	W	4	4	0	0	3	1	1	3
Cardiff			2	0	1	1	1	1	1	0
Hull			2	0	0	2	2	0	1	0
Crystal Palace			2	0	1	1	0	2	1	0

Season	Division	Pos	P	W	D	L	F	A	GD	Pts
2012-13	Premier League	8	38	14	7	17	53	57	-4	49
2011-12	Premier League	10	38	13	8	17	45	52	-7	47
2010-11	Premier League	11	38	12	11	15	56	71	-15	47

Over/Under 61%/39% 7th   **Both score** 58%/42% 7th

Key stat: West Brom only lost four of the 14 matches in which they were drawing at half time and won eight of the nine that they were winning at the break

Premier League appearances 2012-13

	P	G	Y	R
I Brown	0 (1)	0	1	0
C Brunt	23 (8)	2	4	0
C Dawson	1	0	0	0
G Dorrans	21 (5)	1	3	0
M Fortune	9 (12)	2	2	1
B Foster	30	0	0	0
Z Gera	14 (2)	4	1	0
G Jara	0 (1)	0	0	0
B Jones	24 (3)	1	8	0
S Long	25 (9)	8	3	0
R Lukaku	20 (15)	17	3	0
G McAuley	36	3	3	0
J Morrison	33 (2)	5	4	0
Y Mulumbu	28	2	4	1
B Myhill	8	0	0	0
P Odemwingie	13 (12)	5	1	1
J Olsson	36	0	5	0
G Popov	10 (2)	0	1	1
S Reid	11	0	4	0
L Ridgewell	28 (2)	0	6	0

	P	G	Y	R
M Rosenberg	5 (19)	0	0	0
G Tamas	7 (4)	0	3	0
J Thomas	4 (6)	0	0	0
G Thorne	3 (2)	0	0	0
C Yacob	29 (1)	0	7	0

The pressure is on Shane Long to fill the void left by Romelu Lukaku

West Ham United

Nickname: The Hammers/Irons
Colours: Claret and blue

Ground: Boleyn Ground   **Capacity:** 35,016
Tel: 020 8548 2748   **Web:** www.whufc.com

It's hard to believe after the Hammers' top-ten finish in their first season back in the top flight that Sam Allardyce was 7-1 favourite for the sack race last summer.

Although they won promotion with the best away record in the Championship, only Norwich, QPR and Reading were worse on the road in the Premier League last season – they took just two points away to the teams above them.

But the flipside is that West Ham finished with the best home record outside the top six.

Andy Carroll, who made last season's loan from Liverpool a permanent move in the summer, only started 22 games in an injury hit season. But most of his seven goals came in the second half of the campaign and in the games he started the Hammers' win-rate stood at 36 per cent compared to 25 per cent when he was left out.

Longest run without a loss: 5
Longest run without a win: 4
Highest/lowest league position: 6/14
Clean sheets: 11
Yellow cards: 74 **Red cards:** 1
Average attendance: 34,719 **Players used:** 26
Leading scorer: K Nolan 10 (4,8)

	2012-13		Last six seasons at home							
	H	A	P	W	D	L	OV	UN	BS	CS
Man United	D	L	5	1	1	3	4	1	3	0
Man City	D	L	5	1	2	2	1	4	2	2
Chelsea	W	L	5	1	1	3	3	2	3	0
Arsenal	L	L	5	0	1	4	3	2	2	0
Tottenham	L	L	5	1	1	3	2	3	3	1
Everton	L	L	5	0	1	4	3	2	4	0
Liverpool	L	D	5	2	0	3	4	1	3	1
West Brom	W	D	3	1	2	0	2	1	2	1
Swansea	W	L	1	1	0	0	0	1	0	1
West Ham										
Norwich	W	D	1	1	0	0	1	0	1	0
Fulham	W	L	5	3	2	0	4	1	4	1
Stoke	D	W	4	2	1	1	2	2	2	1
Southampton	W	D	2	1	1	0	1	1	2	0
Aston Villa	W	L	5	2	1	2	3	2	3	1
Newcastle	D	W	4	1	2	1	3	1	3	1
Sunderland	D	L	5	3	1	1	2	3	2	2
Cardiff			1	0	0	1	0	1	0	0
Hull			3	3	0	0	2	1	1	2
Crystal Palace			1	0	1	0	0	1	0	1

Season	Division	Pos	P	W	D	L	F	A	GD	Pts
2012-13	Premier League	10	38	12	10	16	45	53	-8	46
2011-12	Championship	3	46	24	14	8	81	48	+33	86
2010-11	Premier League	20	38	7	12	19	43	70	-27	33

Over/Under 53%/47% 11th   **Both score** 55%/45% 11th

Key stat: West Ham were the only team in the top flight not to win successive league matches last season

Premier League appearances 2012-13

	P	G	Y	R		P	G	Y	R
Y Benayoun	4 (2)	0	1	0	D Potts	1 (1)	0	0	0
A Carroll	22 (2)	7	5	0	W Reid	36	1	8	0
M Chamakh	2 (1)	0	0	0	J Spence	0 (4)	0	0	0
J Cole	7 (4)	2	2	0	M Taylor	14 (14)	1	2	0
C Cole	14 (13)	2	2	1	J Tomkins	18 (8)	1	5	0
J Collins	29	0	9	0	R Vaz Te	18 (6)	3	3	0
J Collison	5 (12)	2	2	0					
G Demel	28 (3)	0	2	0					
M Diame	31 (2)	3	3	0					
A Diarra	1 (2)	0	1	0					
R Hall	0 (1)	0	0	0					
J Jaaskelainen	38	0	2	0					
M Jarvis	29 (3)	2	0	0					
M Maiga	2 (15)	2	2	0					
G McCartney	9 (3)	0	2	0					
M Noble	25 (3)	4	7	0					
K Nolan	35	10	6	0					
J O'Brien	32 (1)	2	6	0					
G O'Neil	17 (7)	1	2	0					
E Pogatetz	1 (5)	0	2	0					

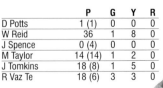

Kevin Nolan was West Ham's top scorer last season

Premier League stats 2012-13

Key Points do not include any deductions imposed by the league. **GFA** Goals For Average per match, **GAA** Goals Against Average per match, **PGA** Average Points Gained per match, **CS** Clean Sheet, **FS** First to Score, **Ov** Over 2.5 total goals, **Un** Under 2.5 total goals, **BS** Both teams Score

Top scorers 2012-13

		P	W	D	L	F	GFA	PGA	Pts
1	Man Utd	38	28	5	5	86	2.26	2.3	89
2	Chelsea	38	22	9	7	75	1.97	2.0	75
3	Arsenal	38	21	10	7	72	1.89	1.9	73
4	Liverpool	38	16	13	9	71	1.87	1.6	61
5	Man City	38	23	9	6	66	1.74	2.1	78
	Tottenham	38	21	9	8	66	1.74	1.9	72
7	Everton	38	16	15	7	55	1.45	1.7	63
8	West Brom	38	14	7	17	53	1.39	1.3	49
9	Fulham	38	11	10	17	50	1.32	1.1	43
10	Southampton	38	9	14	15	49	1.29	1.1	41
11	Swansea	38	11	13	14	47	1.24	1.2	46
	Aston Villa	38	10	11	17	47	1.24	1.1	41
	Wigan	38	9	9	20	47	1.24	0.9	36
14	West Ham	38	12	10	16	45	1.18	1.2	46
	Newcastle	38	11	8	19	45	1.18	1.1	41
16	Reading	38	6	10	22	43	1.13	0.7	28
17	Norwich	38	10	14	14	41	1.08	1.2	44
	Sunderland	38	9	12	17	41	1.08	1.0	39
19	Stoke	38	9	15	14	34	0.89	1.1	42
20	QPR	38	4	13	21	30	0.79	0.7	25

Best defences 2012-13

		P	W	D	L	A	GAA	PGA	Pts
1	Man City	38	23	9	6	34	0.89	2.1	78
2	Arsenal	38	21	10	7	37	0.97	1.9	73
3	Chelsea	38	22	9	7	39	1.03	2.0	75
4	Everton	38	16	15	7	40	1.05	1.7	63
5	Man Utd	38	28	5	5	43	1.13	2.3	89
	Liverpool	38	16	13	9	43	1.13	1.6	61
7	Stoke	38	9	15	14	45	1.18	1.1	42
8	Tottenham	38	21	9	8	46	1.21	1.9	72
9	Swansea	38	11	13	14	51	1.34	1.2	46
10	West Ham	38	12	10	16	53	1.39	1.2	46
11	Sunderland	38	9	12	17	54	1.42	1.0	39
12	West Brom	38	14	7	17	57	1.50	1.3	49
13	Norwich	38	10	14	14	58	1.53	1.2	44
14	Fulham	38	11	10	17	60	1.58	1.1	43
	Southampton	38	9	14	15	60	1.58	1.1	41
	QPR	38	4	13	21	60	1.58	0.7	25
17	Newcastle	38	11	8	19	68	1.79	1.1	41
18	Aston Villa	38	10	11	17	69	1.82	1.1	41
19	Wigan	38	9	9	20	73	1.92	0.9	36
	Reading	38	6	10	22	73	1.92	0.7	28

Record when keeping a clean sheet 2012-13

		P	W	D	L	F	GFA	PGA	Pts
1	Man Utd	13	13	0	0	30	2.31	3.0	39
	Wigan	5	5	0	0	10	2.00	3.0	15
3	Man City	18	14	4	0	30	1.67	2.6	46
	Chelsea	14	11	3	0	27	1.93	2.6	36
	Tottenham	9	7	2	0	13	1.44	2.6	23
6	Fulham	8	6	2	0	14	1.75	2.5	20
	West Brom	8	6	2	0	13	1.63	2.5	20
8	Liverpool	16	11	5	0	36	2.25	2.4	38
	Arsenal	14	10	4	0	13	0.93	2.4	34
10	Everton	11	7	4	0	12	1.09	2.3	25
	Sunderland	11	7	4	0	13	1.18	2.3	25
	Newcastle	6	4	2	0	6	1.00	2.3	14
13	Aston Villa	5	3	2	0	4	0.80	2.2	11
14	West Ham	11	6	5	0	9	0.82	2.1	23
	Southampton	7	4	3	0	6	0.86	2.1	15
16	Stoke	12	6	6	0	8	0.67	2.0	24
17	Norwich	10	4	6	0	7	0.70	1.8	18
	Swansea	10	4	6	0	11	1.10	1.8	18
19	Reading	5	1	4	0	1	0.20	1.4	7
20	QPR	7	1	6	0	1	0.14	1.3	9

Record when first to score 2012-13

		P	W	D	L	F	A	PGA	Pts
1	Man Utd	22	19	3	0	52	15	2.7	60
2	Arsenal	20	17	3	0	48	15	2.7	54
3	Man City	23	20	2	1	51	15	2.7	62
4	Swansea	13	10	2	1	32	12	2.5	32
5	Chelsea	26	19	6	1	61	23	2.4	63
	Liverpool	19	14	3	2	55	17	2.4	45
7	West Brom	16	12	1	3	34	17	2.3	37
	West Ham	15	11	1	3	29	18	2.3	34
	Tottenham	23	16	4	3	45	26	2.3	52
10	Fulham	18	11	4	3	36	20	2.1	37
	Everton	18	11	4	3	30	15	2.1	37
12	Norwich	14	8	3	3	23	18	1.9	27
	Wigan	13	7	4	2	26	16	1.9	25
	Sunderland	15	8	4	3	24	13	1.9	28
15	Newcastle	15	8	3	4	24	18	1.8	27
16	Stoke	16	7	6	3	21	16	1.7	27
	Southampton	18	8	6	4	32	25	1.7	30
18	Aston Villa	19	8	7	4	36	27	1.6	31
19	Reading	10	3	3	4	20	21	1.2	12
	QPR	10	3	3	4	13	15	1.2	12

Over 2.5 goals top ten 2012-13

		H	A	Ov%
1	Wigan	15	12	71.1
2	Liverpool	10	15	65.8
	Tottenham	9	16	65.8
4	Fulham	13	11	63.2
	Man Utd	14	10	63.2
	Newcastle	13	11	63.2
7	Aston Villa	10	13	60.5
	Chelsea	10	13	60.5
	Reading	11	12	60.5
	West Brom	12	11	60.5

Under 2.5 goals top ten 2012-13

		H	A	Un%
1	Stoke	8	5	65.8
2	Arsenal	11	6	55.3
	QPR	8	9	55.3
4	Norwich	9	9	52.6
5	Man City	11	8	50.0
	Southampton	9	10	50.0
7	Everton	10	10	47.4
	Sunderland	6	14	47.4
	Swansea	12	8	47.4
	West Ham	11	9	47.4

Both to score top ten 2012-13

		H	A	BS%
1	Tottenham	12	15	71.1
2	Southampton	13	12	65.8
3	Everton	12	12	63.2
4	Aston Villa	11	12	60.5
	Newcastle	10	13	60.5
	Reading	11	12	60.5
7	Chelsea	10	12	57.9
	Man United	11	11	57.9
	West Brom	12	10	57.9
	Wigan	13	9	57.9

Clean sheets 2012-13		P	CS	CS%
1	Man City	38	18	**47.4**
2	Liverpool	38	16	**42.1**
3	Arsenal	38	14	**36.8**
	Chelsea	38	**14**	**36.8**
5	Man Utd	38	13	**34.2**
6	Stoke	38	12	**31.6**
7	Everton	38	11	**28.9**
	West Ham	38	**11**	**28.9**
	Sunderland	38	**11**	**28.9**
10	Norwich	38	10	**26.3**
	Swansea	38	**10**	**26.3**
12	Tottenham	38	9	**23.7**
13	Fulham	38	8	**21.1**
	West Brom	38	**8**	**21.1**
15	QPR	38	7	**18.4**
	Southampton	38	**7**	**18.4**
17	Newcastle	38	6	**15.8**
18	Wigan	38	5	**13.2**
	Reading	38	**5**	**13.2**
	Aston Villa	38	**5**	**13.2**

First to score 2012-13		P	FS	FS%
1	Chelsea	38	26	**68.4**
2	Man City	38	23	**60.5**
3	Tottenham	38	23	**60.5**
4	Man Utd	38	22	**57.8**
5	Arsenal	38	20	**52.6**
6	Aston Villa	38	19	**50.0**
7	Liverpool	38	19	**50.0**
8	Everton	38	18	**47.3**
9	Fulham	38	18	**47.3**
10	Southampton	38	18	**47.3**
11	Stoke	38	16	**42.1**
12	West Brom	38	16	**42.1**
13	Newcastle	38	15	**39.4**
14	Sunderland	38	15	**39.4**
15	West Ham	38	15	**39.4**
16	Norwich	38	14	**36.8**
17	Swansea	38	13	**34.2**
18	Wigan	38	13	**34.2**
19	QPR	38	10	**26.3**
20	Reading	38	10	**26.3**

Top scorers 2012-13	Goals
R van Persie (Man Utd)	26
L Suarez (Liverpool)	23
G Bale (Tottenham)	21
C Benteke (Aston Villa)	19
Michu (Swansea)	18
R Lukaku (West Brom)	17
D Ba (Chelsea*)	15
D Berbatov (Fulham)	15
R Lambert (Southampton)	15
F Lampard (Chelsea)	15
E Dzeko (Man City)	14
T Walcott (Arsenal)	14
S Aguero (Man City)	12
S Cazorla (Arsenal)	12
A Le Fondre (Reading)	12
J Mata (Chelsea)	12
W Rooney (Man Utd)	12
J Defoe (Tottenham)	11
M Fellaini (Everton)	11
S Fletcher (Sunderland)	11

Gareth Bale's 21 league goals helped make Spurs a standing dish for both teams to score backers

Improving Trotters to scupper favourite backers

Leicester were the latest side to let down backers of second-tier favourites last term, going off as short as 11-2 to win the Championship but finishing 19 points behind winners Cardiff, writes Dan Sait.

That should serve as a warning to those thinking of backing QPR at 5-1, as very few clubs reward such short favouritism in this division. Newcastle are the only side to do so in recent years and while there are some parallels between the 2008-09 Newcastle side and QPR – both were unexpectedly relegated and both were in disarray but had significant financial clout – the R's also bear similarities to the likes of Wolves and Blackburn last term, and countless other clubs before them, who were underpriced to go back up despite all the evidence of a shambolic relegation campaign.

It's also worth remembering that QPR had superior spending power to their fellow relegated teams last term but still finished below them, a huge 14 points from safety.

Even after Harry Redknapp took charge the R's collected just 0.84 points per game which would have lifted them just one place over the course of the season. Redknapp is a good manager but the support he enjoys from the media tends to outweigh his actual achievements.

The other relegated sides, Wigan and Reading, look more sensibly priced.

Reading didn't overspend last season, made their managerial change early enough to blood Nigel Adkins in the Madejski dugout and effectively treated their year in the top flight as a strengthening exercise.

However, they still finished eight points behind Wigan, who look tempting at 12-1.

The Latics built firm foundations during their eight-year stay in the top flight and there's a danger of treating the departure of Roberto Martinez as too serious a negative.

Yes, he produced some attractive football but Martinez had a dire defensive record at Wigan and the club struggled against the drop in each of the four years under him. Prior to the Spaniard's arrival, Wigan had finished tenth, 17th, 14th and 11th in the top flight, only seriously flirting with relegation in 2006-07.

The squad is sure to look very different by September 1 but owner Dave Whelan has promised to reinvest profits made from player sales and has also made it clear that the Latics' European campaign is of secondary importance to their push for promotion.

The nagging concern, though, is how the squad will take to incoming manager Owen Coyle. The Scot offers a very different style to his predecessor and while he achieved promotion with Burnley, his time at Bolton can only be judged as a failure. After relegation from the top flight, Coyle was sacked last October with the Trotters languishing in 18th place and with rumours abound of player unrest.

Wigan look too strong to fail to put in a serious title challenge, but that slight doubt makes 4-1 for promotion look a better option than backing the Latics for the title.

It's Coyle's former employers, **Bolton**, who look the real deal and 10-1 for a Trotters title looks more than fair.

The club bounced hard following relegation in the summer of 2012 but the swift squad trimming and financial prudence is paying off. And in landing Dougie Freedman, Bolton chairman Phil Gartside may just have landed a masterstroke.

Freedman's fledgling managerial career has shown great promise, with the Scot setting up Crystal Palace's promotion campaign in the early part of 2012-13 before heading to the Reebok Stadium and lifting the Trotters from 18th place to seventh.

He hasn't won anything yet, of course, but players seem to want to play for Freedman and his early summer business looked encouraging, adding further strength to an already solid Championship squad.

Watford would also be worth serious

consideration for the title if it wasn't for the uncertainty about their transfers and loans.

While the suspicion is that a mountain has been made out of a molehill regarding the impact on Watford that the loan rule changes will have – surely they simply sign the best loanees on favourable terms given both Watford and Udinese are owned by the same family – it may be worth waiting until the transfer window closes before backing them for the title. For now, backing Gianfranco Zola's men at 9-2 for promotion looks an appealing alternative.

At the other end of the table, it's very hard to see how **Yeovil** will cope at this level.

While backing promoted League 1 sides to drop straight back down at short prices can be a recipe for disaster, it seems too big a step for the Glovers, who lost a third of their League 1 games last season. But a shade of odds-on doesn't set the pulse racing, so for the other two drop slots consider two bigger-priced sides.

Millwall have been steadily slipping in recent seasons and only finished two points above relegation last May, yet they're 4-1 to drop in 2013-14. That looks too big.

But even bigger to go down are **Middlesbrough**, at a huge 10-1, and I'm tempted to back that even if it's with a view to trading.

Boro have suffered two morale-sapping collapses in two seasons, plummeting from third to 16th in 2013, and Tony Mowbray's men have a tricky start this season, too. They don't look the daftest shout to become the latest big-priced former Premier League side to drop into the third tier.

On a more positive note, two sides who improved markedly following a change of manager last season are **Barnsley** and **Ipswich**, with both appealing to outperform expectations this season.

Barnsley picked up points at the rate of a top-six side after David Flitcroft replaced Keith Hill at Oakwell, taking an average of 1.7 points from their final 20 games. While it would be a huge surprise to see them maintain that form over the course of a full season, the 5-1 about Barnsley finishing in the top half is big enough to tempt.

Similarly, Ipswich improved dramatically after Mick McCarthy arrived in November, taking their points-per-game average up from 0.53 to 1.61 – again, enough for a top-six finish. McCarthy knows this division inside out and the Tractor Boys have the additional benefit of starting from a healthier financial footing than the Tykes, so prices of 5-2 about a top-six finish look big enough to warrant an interest.

Marvin Sordell gets on the scoresheet for Bolton

Barnsley

Nickname: Tykes
Colours: Red and white
Ground: Oakwell (23,287)
Tel: 01226 211 211   www.barnsleyfc.co.uk

David Flitcroft has made an extremely promising start to his managerial career, with the former assistant stepping up after Keith Hill was dismissed in late December for taking just 21 points from Barnsley's first 25 games of the season.

The Tykes rallied superbly under Flitcroft, taking 34 points from their final 21 games to dodge the drop by a point.

It's doubtful that a limited squad can continue picking up points at that rate in 2013-14 but their survival prospects look far brighter after workaholic Flitcroft extended his contract over the summer.

Longest run without win/loss: 11/6
High/low league position: 12/24
Clean sheets: 11 **Yellow cards:** 68 **Red cards:** 3
Average attendance: 10,207 **Players used:** 34
Leading scorer: C Davies 8 (2,5)
Key stat: Flitcroft's points-per-game average of 1.62 would have equated to 75 points over the course of a full season

	2012-13 H	2012-13 A	Last six seasons at home P	W	D	L	OV	UN	BS	CS
Wigan			-	-	-	-	-	-	-	-
Reading			4	0	0	4	2	2	1	0
QPR			4	1	1	2	1	3	1	1
Watford	W	L	6	4	2	0	2	4	3	3
Brighton	W	L	2	1	1	0	1	1	1	1
Leicester	W	D	5	2	1	2	0	5	1	2
Bolton	L	D	1	0	0	1	1	0	1	0
Nottm Forest	L	D	5	2	2	1	3	2	5	0
Charlton	L	W	3	1	1	1	2	1	0	2
Derby	D	L	5	2	3	0	1	4	3	2
Burnley	D	D	5	2	2	1	2	3	4	1
Birmingham	L	W	3	0	1	2	2	1	3	0
Leeds	W	L	3	3	0	0	2	1	2	1
Ipswich	D	D	6	2	2	2	4	2	6	0
Blackpool	D	W	5	2	1	2	2	3	3	1
Middlesbrough	W	W	4	3	0	1	2	2	2	2
Blackburn	L	L	1	0	0	1	1	0	1	0
Sheffield Weds	L	L	4	1	1	2	2	2	2	1
Huddersfield	L	D	1	0	0	1	0	1	0	0
Millwall	W	W	3	2	0	1	1	2	1	2
Barnsley										
Doncaster			4	2	1	1	2	2	2	1
Bournemouth			-	-	-	-	-	-	-	-
Yeovil			-	-	-	-	-	-	-	-

Season	Division	Pos	P	W	D	L	F	A	GD	Pts
2012-13	Championship	21	46	14	13	19	56	70	-14	55
2011-12	Championship	21	46	13	9	24	49	74	-25	48
2010-11	Championship	17	46	14	14	18	55	66	-11	56

Over/Under 46%/54% 20th   **Both score** 61%/39% 8th

Birmingham City

Nickname: Blues
Colours: Blue
Ground: St Andrews (29,409)
Tel: 0844 557 1875   www.bcfc.com

Following relegation from the top flight in 2010-11 and play-off heartbreak in 2011-12, a season of mid-table stability was far from the worst that Birmingham fans have had to endure in recent times.

However, there were no cup runs to keep fans entertained and no European adventures. It's hard to envisage much in the way of fireworks for Blues in 2013-14 either, after Wolves' relegation removed the remaining derby fixture.

Hopes of promotion have also been undermined following a reduction in the budget available for squad strengthening.

Longest run without win/loss: 4/5
High/low league position: 10/21
Clean sheets: 10 **Yellow cards:** 63 **Red cards:** 3
Average attendance: 16,702 **Players used:** 31
Leading scorer: M King 13 (0,10)
Key stat: Only two sides secured more draws than Birmingham's 16 in last season's Championship

	2012-13 H	2012-13 A	Last six seasons at home P	W	D	L	OV	UN	BS	CS
Wigan			3	2	1	0	1	2	1	2
Reading			3	1	1	1	1	2	2	1
QPR			1	1	0	0	0	1	0	1
Watford	L	L	3	2	0	1	3	0	1	1
Brighton	D	W	2	0	2	0	1	1	1	1
Leicester	D	D	2	1	1	0	0	2	1	1
Bolton	W	L	4	3	0	1	3	1	3	1
Nottm Forest	W	D	3	2	0	1	2	1	2	1
Charlton	D	D	2	1	1	0	1	1	2	0
Derby	W	L	4	2	2	0	2	2	3	1
Burnley	D	L	4	2	2	0	3	1	4	0
Birmingham										
Leeds	W	W	2	2	0	0	0	2	0	2
Ipswich	L	L	3	2	0	1	2	1	2	0
Blackpool	D	D	4	2	1	1	1	3	1	2
Middlesbrough	W	W	3	3	0	0	3	0	1	2
Blackburn	D	D	4	3	1	0	3	1	4	0
Sheffield Weds	D	L	2	1	1	0	1	1	1	1
Huddersfield	L	D	1	0	0	1	0	1	0	0
Millwall	D	D	2	1	1	0	1	1	2	1
Barnsley	L	W	3	1	1	1	1	2	1	1
Doncaster			2	2	0	0	1	1	1	1
Bournemouth			-	-	-	-	-	-	-	-
Yeovil			-	-	-	-	-	-	-	-

Season	Division	Pos	P	W	D	L	F	A	GD	Pts
2012-13	Championship	12	46	15	16	15	63	69	-6	61
2011-12	Championship	4	46	20	16	10	78	51	+27	76
2010-11	Premier League	18	38	8	15	15	37	58	-21	39

Over/Under 50%/50% 14th   **Both score** 63%/37% 3rd

Blackburn Rovers

Nickname: Rovers
Colours: Blue and white
Ground: Ewood Park (31,154)
Tel: 0871 702 1875   www.rovers.co.uk

At least Rovers didn't emulate Wolves' feat of suffering back-to-back relegations, but that's probably the pinnacle of Venky's achievements at Ewood Park.

They came close enough to a drop into League 1 though, falling into the bottom three as late as April, but that sort of performance is no great surprise given the chaotic leadership of the club.

Rovers had five managers and caretaker-managers over the course of the season and a decent squad continues to be hampered by inept performances in the boardroom.

Longest run without win/loss: 10/6
High/low league position: 3/22
Clean sheets: 10 **Yellow cards:** 75 **Red cards:** 1
Average attendance: 14,974 **Players used:** 38
Leading scorer: J Rhodes 27 (10,23)
Key stat: Blackburn didn't win a single game away to a side outside the Championship's bottom five last season

| | 2012-13 | | Last six seasons at home | | | | | | | |
	H	A	P	W	D	L	OV	UN	BS	CS
Wigan			5	4	0	1	3	2	3	1
Reading			1	1	0	0	1	0	1	0
QPR			1	1	0	0	1	0	1	0
Watford	W	L	1	1	0	0	0	1	0	1
Brighton	D	D	1	0	1	0	0	1	1	0
Leicester	W	L	1	1	0	0	0	1	0	1
Bolton	L	L	6	3	1	2	5	1	4	2
Nottm Forest	W	D	1	1	0	0	1	0	0	1
Charlton	L	D	1	0	0	1	1	0	1	0
Derby	W	D	2	2	0	0	1	1	1	1
Burnley	D	D	2	1	1	0	1	1	0	2
Birmingham	D	D	4	2	2	0	2	2	4	0
Leeds	D	D	1	0	1	0	0	1	0	1
Ipswich	W	D	1	1	0	0	0	1	0	1
Blackpool	D	L	2	0	2	0	1	1	2	0
Middlesbrough	L	L	3	0	2	1	1	2	3	0
Blackburn										
Sheffield Weds	W	L	1	1	0	0	0	1	0	1
Huddersfield	W	D	1	1	0	0	0	1	0	1
Millwall	L	W	1	0	0	1	0	1	0	0
Barnsley	W	W	1	1	0	0	1	0	1	0
Doncaster	-	-	-	-	-	-	-	-	-	-
Bournemouth	-	-	-	-	-	-	-	-	-	-
Yeovil	-	-	-	-	-	-	-	-	-	-

Season	Division	Pos	P	W	D	L	F	A	GD	Pts
2012-13	Championship	17	46	14	16	16	55	62	-7	58
2011-12	Premier League	19	38	8	7	23	48	78	-30	31
2010-11	Premier League	15	38	11	10	17	46	59	-13	43

Over/Under 39%/61% 23rd   **Both score** 57%/43% 15th

Blackpool

Nickname: The Seasiders/Tangerines
Colours: Tangerine and white
Ground: Bloomfield Road (16,007)
Tel: 0870 443 1953   www.blackpoolfc.co.uk

Is was no great surprise that Ian Holloway left for pastures new last season given how little financial assistance he was receiving from owner Karl Oyston.

Oyston has been slow to reinvest the riches that Holloway earned by taking Blackpool up into the top tier in 2010 and the Seasiders won't progress unless he does start to back his managers.

The facilities are an embarrassment, the pitch is a disgrace and successive new managers are realising how tough an act Holloway is to follow – Paul Ince is the latest to test tight purse-strings.

Longest run without win/loss: 6/8
High/low league position: 4/18
Clean sheets: 10 **Yellow cards:** 64 **Red cards:** 3
Average attendance: 13,916 **Players used:** 31
Leading scorer: T Ince 18 (3,14)
Key stat: In last season's Championship, only relegated Peterborough had a smaller capacity ground than Blackpool's Bloomfield Road

| | 2012-13 | | Last six seasons at home | | | | | | | |
	H	A	P	W	D	L	OV	UN	BS	CS
Wigan			1	0	0	1	1	0	1	0
Reading			3	2	1	0	1	2	1	2
QPR			3	1	1	2	1	1	1	
Watford	D	W	5	1	3	1	2	3	3	1
Brighton	D	L	2	1	1	0	1	1	2	0
Leicester	D	L	4	1	2	1	3	1	3	1
Bolton	D	D	2	1	1	0	2	0	2	0
Nottm Forest	D	D	4	1	2	1	3	1	4	0
Charlton	L	L	3	2	0	1	1	2	1	1
Derby	W	L	4	2	1	1	2	2	2	1
Burnley	W	L	4	3	0	1	2	2	0	3
Birmingham	D	D	4	1	2	1	2	2	3	1
Leeds	W	L	2	2	0	0	1	1	1	1
Ipswich	W	L	5	3	1	1	1	4	1	3
Blackpool										
Middlesbrough	W	L	3	3	0	0	2	1	1	2
Blackburn	W	D	2	1	0	1	1	1	1	1
Sheffield Weds	D	W	4	1	1	2	2	2	2	1
Huddersfield	L	D	1	0	0	1	0	1	0	0
Millwall	W	W	2	2	0	0	1	1	1	1
Barnsley	L	D	5	1	2	2	2	3	4	1
Doncaster			3	2	0	1	2	1	2	1
Bournemouth	-	-	-	-	-	-	-	-	-	-
Yeovil	-	-	-	-	-	-	-	-	-	-

Season	Division	Pos	P	W	D	L	F	A	GD	Pts
2012-13	Championship	15	46	14	17	15	62	63	-1	59
2011-12	Championship	5	46	20	15	11	79	59	+20	75
2010-11	Premier League	19	38	10	9	19	55	78	-23	39

Over/Under 50%/50% 14th   **Both score** 63%/37% 3rd

Bolton Wanderers

Nickname: The Trotters
Colours: White and blue
Ground: The Reebok Stadium (28,100)
Tel: 01204 673 673   www.bwfc.co.uk

Phil Gartside can be pleased with the way in which he managed Bolton's drop from the top flight last summer. The Bolton chairman slashed the wage bill without dismantling the squad and his decision to put Dougie Freedman in the dugout in place of Owen Coyle looks inspired.

Freedman was responsible for Crystal Palace's stunning start to 2012-13 and it's noticable how dramatically Palace's form tailed off and Bolton's form improved after he switched from Selhurst Park to the Reebok – Wanderers rose from 18th to seventh under the Scot.

Longest run without win/loss: 4/8
High/low league position: 6/20
Clean sheets: 9 **Yellow cards:** 85 **Red cards:** 4
Average attendance: 18,103 **Players used:** 32
Leading scorer: C Eagles 12 (5,12)
Key stat: Bolton had the second-best home record in the Championship last season

	2012-13 H	A	Last six seasons at home P	W	D	L	OV	UN	BS	CS
Wigan			5	2	1	2	3	2	3	1
Reading			1	1	0	0	1	0	0	1
QPR			1	1	0	0	1	0	1	0
Watford	W	L	1	1	0	0	1	0	1	0
Brighton	W	D	1	1	0	0	0	1	0	1
Leicester	D	L	1	0	1	0	0	1	0	1
Bolton										
Nottm Forest	D	D	1	0	1	0	1	0	1	0
Charlton	W	L	1	1	0	0	0	1	0	1
Derby	W	D	2	2	0	0	0	2	0	2
Burnley	W	D	2	2	0	0	1	1	1	1
Birmingham	W	L	4	3	1	0	4	0	3	1
Leeds	D	L	1	0	1	0	1	0	1	0
Ipswich	L	L	1	0	0	1	1	0	1	0
Blackpool	D	D	2	0	2	0	2	0	2	0
Middlesbrough	W	L	3	2	1	0	2	1	2	1
Blackburn	W	W	6	3	1	2	3	3	3	2
Sheffield Weds	L	W	1	0	0	1	0	1	0	0
Huddersfield	W	D	1	1	0	0	0	1	0	1
Millwall	D	L	1	0	1	0	0	1	1	0
Barnsley	D	W	1	0	1	0	0	1	1	0
Doncaster			-	-	-	-	-	-	-	-
Bournemouth			-	-	-	-	-	-	-	-
Yeovil			-	-	-	-	-	-	-	-

Season	Division	Pos	P	W	D	L	F	A	GD	Pts
2012-13	Championship	7	46	18	14	14	69	61	+8	68
2011-12	Premier League	18	38	10	6	22	46	77	-31	36
2010-11	Premier League	14	38	12	10	16	52	56	-4	46

Over/Under 57%/43% 5th   **Both score** 70%/30% 1st

Bournemouth

Nickname: The Cherries
Colours: Red and black
Ground: Goldsands Stadium (9,287)
Tel: 01202 726 300   www.afcb.co.uk

Eddie Howe and Bournemouth seem to be a match made in heaven. In 2008-09, 31-year-old Howe overcame a 17-point deduction to rescue the club from relegation out of the Football League. And by the time he left for Burnley in January 2011 he'd gained promotion and led the Cherries to second place in League 1.

The club struggled in his absence and were one point and one place above the relegation places when he returned in October last season. Howe again worked wonders, carving through the third tier to automatic promotion. Truly extraordinary.

Longest run without win/loss: 6/15
High/low league position: 1/21
Clean sheets: 15 **Yellow cards:** 63 **Red cards:** 1
Average attendance: 6,852 **Players used:** 32
Leading scorer: B Pitman 19 (8,15)
Key stat: Bournemouth's league record under Howe last term was W22, D6, L6 – a 65 per cent win rate and an average of 2.12 points per game

	2012-13 H	A	Last six seasons at home P	W	D	L	OV	UN	BS	CS
Wigan			-	-	-	-	-	-	-	-
Reading			-	-	-	-	-	-	-	-
QPR			-	-	-	-	-	-	-	-
Watford			-	-	-	-	-	-	-	-
Brighton			2	1	0	1	0	2	0	1
Leicester			-	-	-	-	-	-	-	-
Bolton			-	-	-	-	-	-	-	-
Nottm Forest			1	1	0	0	0	1	0	1
Charlton			2	0	1	1	1	1	1	0
Derby			-	-	-	-	-	-	-	-
Burnley			-	-	-	-	-	-	-	-
Birmingham			-	-	-	-	-	-	-	-
Leeds			1	0	0	1	1	0	1	0
Ipswich			-	-	-	-	-	-	-	-
Blackpool			-	-	-	-	-	-	-	-
Middlesbrough			-	-	-	-	-	-	-	-
Blackburn			-	-	-	-	-	-	-	-
Sheffield Weds			2	1	1	0	0	2	0	2
Huddersfield			3	1	1	1	0	3	1	1
Millwall			1	1	0	0	0	1	0	1
Barnsley			-	-	-	-	-	-	-	-
Doncaster	L	W	2	0	0	2	1	1	1	0
Bournemouth			-	-	-	-	-	-	-	-
Yeovil	W	W	4	3	1	0	1	3	0	4

Season	Division	Pos	P	W	D	L	F	A	GD	Pts
2012-13	League 1	2	46	24	11	11	76	53	+23	83
2011-12	League 1	11	46	15	13	18	48	52	-4	58
2010-11	League 1	6	46	19	14	13	75	54	+21	71

Over/Under 54%/46% 4th   **Both score** 57%/43% 5th

Brighton & Hove A

Nickname: The Seagulls
Colours: Blue and white
Ground: AmEx Community Stadium (27,500)
Tel: 01273 695 400   www.seagulls.co.uk

Brighton's rise from a League 1 relegation scrap in 2009-10 to fourth place in the Championship last term may owe as much to Tony Bloom's money than Gus Poyet's management but Poyet's summer departure still comes as a blow.

The Seagulls' league positions improved dramatically in each of Poyet's four seasons in charge and while his side was admired for its attractive passing football, they were also the tightest defensive unit in the division.

He'll be a tough act to follow for his replacement, attack-minded Oscar Garcia.

Longest run without win/loss: 7/9
High/low league position: 1/10
Clean sheets: 17 **Yellow cards:** 67 **Red cards:** 4
Average attendance: 26,236 **Players used:** 30
Leading scorer: C Mackail-Smith 11 (3,8)
Key stat: No side lost fewer games than Brighton in the Championship last season

| | 2012-13 | | Last six seasons at home | | | | | | | |
	H	A	P	W	D	L	OV	UN	BS	CS
Wigan			-	-	-	-	-	-	-	-
Reading			1	0	0	1	0	1	0	0
QPR			-	-	-	-	-	-	-	-
Watford	L	W	2	0	1	1	2	0	2	0
Brighton										
Leicester	D	L	3	2	1	0	1	2	2	1
Bolton	D	L	1	0	1	0	0	1	1	0
Nottm Forest	D	D	3	1	1	1	0	3	0	2
Charlton	D	D	3	0	2	1	0	3	1	1
Derby	W	D	2	2	0	0	1	1	1	1
Burnley	W	W	2	1	0	1	0	2	0	1
Birmingham	L	D	2	0	1	1	0	2	1	0
Leeds	D	W	5	0	2	3	3	2	2	0
Ipswich	D	W	2	1	1	0	1	1	1	1
Blackpool	W	D	2	1	1	0	2	0	2	0
Middlesbrough	L	W	2	0	1	1	0	2	1	0
Blackburn	D	D	1	0	1	0	0	1	1	0
Sheffield Weds	W	L	2	2	0	0	1	1	0	2
Huddersfield	W	W	5	1	2	2	2	3	3	1
Millwall	D	W	5	2	2	1	4	1	3	1
Barnsley	W	L	2	2	0	0	1	1	1	1
Doncaster			2	2	0	0	1	1	1	1
Bournemouth			2	1	1	0	1	1	2	0
Yeovil			4	3	0	1	2	2	1	3

Season	Division	Pos	P	W	D	L	F	A	GD	Pts
2012-13	Championship	4	46	19	18	9	69	43	+26	75
2011-12	Championship	10	46	17	15	14	52	52	0	66
2010-11	League 1	1	46	28	11	7	85	40	+45	95

Over/Under 46%/54% 20th   **Both score** 50%/50% 20th

Burnley

Nickname: The Clarets
Colours: Claret and blue
Ground: Turf Moor (21,940)
Tel: 0871 221 1882 www.burnleyfootballclub.com

Eddie Howe's tenure never really took off at Turf Moor and while it was far from a disastrous partnership it suited both that they went their separate ways in October.

Replacement Sean Dyche has done a steady job since coming in, guiding the club to a comfortable 11th-placed finish.

But the worry for this season is that Burnley's parachute payments have ended and the club's financial position means they are struggling to hold onto their better players. Losing Charlie Austin would be a real blow and would make 2013-14 a bit of a struggle for the Clarets.

Longest run without win/loss: 6/4
High/low league position: 7/17
Clean sheets: 12 **Yellow cards:** 88 **Red cards:** 4
Average attendance: 12,928 **Players used:** 26
Leading scorer: C Austin 25 (11,18)
Key stat: Charlie Austin scored 40 per cent of Burnley's Championship goals in 2012-13

| | 2012-13 | | Last six seasons at home | | | | | | | |
	H	A	P	W	D	L	OV	UN	BS	CS
Wigan			1	0	0	1	1	0	1	0
Reading			3	1	0	2	1	2	0	1
QPR			3	1	1	0	3	0	2	0
Watford	D	D	5	2	3	0	4	1	5	0
Brighton	L	L	2	1	0	1	1	1	1	1
Leicester	L	L	4	1	1	2	2	2	2	1
Bolton	W	L	2	1	1	0	0	2	1	1
Nottm Forest	D	L	4	3	1	0	2	2	2	2
Charlton	L	W	3	2	0	1	2	1	1	
Derby	W	W	4	3	1	0	2	2	1	3
Burnley										
Birmingham	L	D	4	1	1	2	3	1	4	0
Leeds	W	L	3	1	0	2	2	1	2	1
Ipswich	W	L	5	2	1	2	4	1	2	2
Blackpool	W	L	4	3	1	0	2	2	2	2
Middlesbrough	D	L	3	1	1	1	2	1	1	1
Blackburn	D	D	2	0	1	1	0	2	1	0
Sheffield Weds	D	W	3	0	2	1	2	1	3	0
Huddersfield	L	L	1	0	0	1	0	1	0	0
Millwall	D	W	3	0	1	2	3	0	2	0
Barnsley	D	D	5	3	1	1	3	2	3	2
Doncaster			3	1	2	0	1	2	1	2
Bournemouth			-	-	-	-	-	-	-	-
Yeovil			-	-	-	-	-	-	-	-

Season	Division	Pos	P	W	D	L	F	A	GD	Pts
2012-13	Championship	11	46	16	13	17	62	60	+2	61
2011-12	Championship	13	46	17	11	18	61	58	+3	62
2010-11	Championship	8	46	18	14	14	65	61	+4	68

Over/Under 39%/61% 23rd   **Both score** 52%/48% 18th

Charlton Athletic

Nickname: Addicks
Colours: Red and white
Ground: The Valley (27,111)
Tel: 020 8333 4000   www.cafc.co.uk

That Chris Powell managed to build a League 1 side on shoestring budget in the summer of 2011, led them to the third-tier title the following season and then took them to within three points of a play-off place in the Championship stands testament to the excellent work he is doing in his first managerial post.

The Addicks can't begin to match the financial clout of some of the bigger hitters in the second tier but there is a positive air about the Valley and Powell is well on the way to his goal of making Charlton a stable Championship side once again.

Longest run without win/loss: 6/8
High/low league position: 9/20
Clean sheets: 10 **Yellow cards:** 60 **Red cards:** 2
Average attendance: 18,449 **Players used:** 32
Leading scorer: Jackson 12 (4,11) Kermorgant 12 (3,10) **Key stat:** Charlton were the joint fifth-worst home side in the Championship last season but were fourth-best on the road

	2012-13 H	A	Last six seasons at home P	W	D	L	OV	UN	BS	CS
Wigan	-	-	-	-	-	-	-	-	-	-
Reading			1	1	0	0	1	0	1	0
QPR			2	0	1	1	1	1	1	0
Watford	L	W	3	0	1	2	3	0	3	0
Brighton	D	D	3	0	1	2	3	0	2	0
Leicester	W	W	2	2	0	0	1	1	1	1
Bolton	W	L	1	1	0	0	1	0	1	0
Nottm Forest	L	L	2	0	0	2	0	2	0	0
Charlton										
Derby	D	L	2	0	2	0	1	1	2	0
Burnley	L	W	3	0	1	2	1	2	2	0
Birmingham	D	D	2	0	2	0	0	2	1	1
Leeds	W	D	2	2	0	0	1	1	1	1
Ipswich	L	W	3	2	0	1	3	0	3	0
Blackpool	W	W	3	2	1	0	3	0	3	0
Middlesbrough	L	D	1	0	0	1	0	1	0	0
Blackburn	D	W	1	0	1	0	0	1	1	0
Sheffield Weds	L	L	5	2	1	2	3	2	4	1
Huddersfield	D	W	4	2	1	1	1	3	2	1
Millwall	L	D	2	0	1	1	1	1	1	0
Barnsley	L	W	3	0	1	2	1	2	2	0
Doncaster			1	0	0	1	1	0	1	0
Bournemouth			2	2	0	0	1	1	0	2
Yeovil			3	3	0	0	2	1	1	2

Season	Division	Pos	P	W	D	L	F	A	GD	Pts
2012-13	Championship	9	46	17	14	15	65	59	+6	65
2011-12	League 1	1	46	30	11	5	82	36	+46	101
2010-11	League 1	13	46	15	14	17	62	66	-4	59

Over/Under 48%/52% 16th   **Both score** 61%/39% 8th

Derby County

Nickname: The Rams
Colours: White and black
Ground: Pride Park Stadium (33,502)
Tel: 0871 472 1884   www.dcfc.co.uk

In a Championship season memorable for its twists, turns and remarkably tight nature, Derby gave their fans a disappointingly dull ride – from late September the Rams never dropped lower than 16th or rose higher than eighth and they made no impression on either cup competition.

But Derby are a stable, well-run club and tenth place represented their best league finish since dropping from the top tier five seasons ago. Nigel Clough might be right in thinking a couple of good attacking signings could turn Derby into serious promotion contenders.

Longest run without win/loss: 8/5
High/low league position: 9/17
Clean sheets: 8 **Yellow cards:** 61 **Red cards:** 3
Average attendance: 23,228 **Players used:** 25
Leading scorer: J Ward 12 (2,11)
Key stat: Derby were the joint-fourth strongest home side in last season's Championship but were third worst on their travels

	2012-13 H	A	Last six seasons at home P	W	D	L	OV	UN	BS	CS
Wigan			1	0	0	1	0	1	0	0
Reading			5	1	0	4	3	2	2	0
QPR			3	0	1	2	2	1	2	0
Watford	W	L	5	4	0	1	3	2	3	2
Brighton	D	L	2	0	1	1	0	2	0	1
Leicester	W	L	4	2	0	2	1	3	1	1
Bolton	D	L	2	0	2	0	0	2	0	0
Nottm Forest	D	W	5	2	2	1	0	5	2	2
Charlton	W	D	2	2	0	0	1	1	1	1
Derby										
Burnley	L	L	4	0	1	3	3	1	4	0
Birmingham	W	L	4	2	1	1	3	1	4	0
Leeds	W	W	3	3	0	0	2	1	2	1
Ipswich	L	W	5	0	1	4	2	3	2	1
Blackpool	W	L	4	3	0	1	3	1	3	0
Middlesbrough	W	D	5	2	1	2	3	2	3	0
Blackburn	D	L	2	0	1	1	1	1	2	0
Sheffield Weds	D	D	3	2	1	0	3	0	1	2
Huddersfield	W	L	1	1	0	0	1	0	0	1
Millwall	W	L	3	2	1	0	2	1	0	3
Barnsley	W	D	5	1	3	1	1	4	2	3
Doncaster			4	1	0	3	2	2	1	1
Bournemouth	-	-	-	-	-	-	-	-	-	-
Yeovil	-	-	-	-	-	-	-	-	-	-

Season	Division	Pos	P	W	D	L	F	A	GD	Pts
2012-13	Championship	10	46	16	13	17	65	62	+3	61
2011-12	Championship	12	46	18	10	18	50	58	-8	64
2010-11	Championship	19	46	13	10	23	58	71	-13	49

Over/Under 57%/43% 5th   **Both score** 65%/35% 2nd

Doncaster Rovers

Nickname: Rovers
Colours: Red and white
Ground: Keepmoat Stadium (15,231)
Tel: 01302 764 664 www.doncasterroversfc.co.uk

Doncaster's promotion was a dramatic affair, conceding a 94th-minute penalty on the final day of 2012-13 that, if scored, would have sent them into the play-offs. Instead, Brentford's Marcello Trotta hit the bar and Doncaster raced up the other end to score and secure promotion.

Their prospects back in the second tier are hard to assess for bettors as Dean Saunders had the team flying but left in January, leaving Brian Flynn to guide them to promotion. Flynn's move upstairs gives Paul Dickov a chance to improve on a hit-and-miss record at Oldham.

Longest run without win/loss: 5/6
High/low league position: 1/12
Clean sheets: 16 **Yellow cards:** 72 **Red cards:** 2
Average attendance: 7,238 **Players used:** 26
Leading scorer: B Paynter 13 (4,12)
Key stat: Doncaster earned 15 away wins last season – more than any other English or Scottish league side

	2012-13 H	A	Last six seasons at home P	W	D	L	OV	UN	BS	CS
Wigan			-	-	-	-	-	-	-	-
Reading			4	0	1	3	2	2	2	0
QPR			3	2	0	1	0	3	0	2
Watford			4	1	2	1	2	2	3	1
Brighton			2	0	2	0	0	2	1	1
Leicester			3	1	1	1	1	2	2	0
Bolton			-	-	-	-	-	-	-	-
Nottm Forest			5	2	2	1	0	5	1	3
Charlton			1	0	0	1	0	1	0	0
Derby			4	2	0	2	4	0	4	0
Burnley			3	2	0	1	2	1	2	1
Birmingham			2	0	0	2	1	1	1	0
Leeds			3	0	1	2	1	2	0	1
Ipswich			4	1	1	2	3	1	2	1
Blackpool			3	0	2	1	2	1	2	1
Middlesbrough			3	1	0	2	3	0	3	0
Blackburn			-	-	-	-	-	-	-	-
Sheffield Weds			2	2	0	0	0	2	0	2
Huddersfield			1	1	0	0	0	1	0	1
Millwall			3	1	1	1	2	1	1	1
Barnsley			4	1	0	3	0	4	0	1
Doncaster										
Bournemouth	L	W	2	0	0	2	1	1	1	0
Yeovil	D	L	2	0	1	1	1	1	2	0

Season	Division	Pos	P	W	D	L	F	A	GD	Pts
2012-13	League 1	1	46	25	9	12	62	44	+18	84
2011-12	Championship	24	46	8	12	26	43	80	-37	36
2010-11	Championship	21	46	11	15	20	55	81	-26	48

Over/Under 46%/54% 11th   **Both score** 48%/52% 17th

Huddersfield Town

Nickname: The Terriers
Colours: Blue and white
Ground: John Smith's Stadium (24,554)
Tel: 01484 484 100   www.htafc.com

Despite guiding the club to promotion from League 1, Simon Grayson survived less than a year at Huddersfield after a run of 12 Championship games without a win spooked chairman Dean Hoyle.

Incoming manager Mark Robins kept the Terriers up but was solid rather than spectacular and his side finished one place lower in the league than they had been when Grayson departed in January.

Goals remain the concern following last summer's departure of Jordan Rhodes, with only two Championship sides scoring fewer in 2012-13.

Longest run without win/loss: 12/6
High/low league position: 2/22
Clean sheets: 11 **Yellow cards:** 92 **Red cards:** 4
Average attendance: 15,113 **Players used:** 29
Leading scorer: J Vaughan 14 (5,12)
Key stat: Huddersfield's top two scorers from last season were both loanees, now departed – no other player scored more than four goals

	2012-13 H	A	Last six seasons at home P	W	D	L	OV	UN	BS	CS
Wigan			-	-	-	-	-	-	-	-
Reading			-	-	-	-	-	-	-	-
QPR			-	-	-	-	-	-	-	-
Watford	L	L	1	0	0	1	1	0	1	0
Brighton	L	L	5	3	1	1	5	0	5	0
Leicester	L	L	2	0	0	2	1	1	1	0
Bolton	D	L	1	0	1	0	1	0	1	0
Nottm Forest	D	L	2	0	2	0	0	2	2	0
Charlton	L	D	4	2	1	1	1	3	2	1
Derby	W	L	1	1	0	0	0	1	0	1
Burnley	W	W	1	1	0	0	0	1	0	1
Birmingham	D	W	1	0	1	0	0	1	1	0
Leeds	L	W	4	2	1	1	2	2	2	2
Ipswich	D	D	1	0	1	0	0	1	0	1
Blackpool	L	W	1	0	1	0	0	1	1	0
Middlesbrough	W	L	1	1	0	0	1	0	1	0
Blackburn	D	L	1	0	1	0	1	0	1	0
Sheffield Weds	D	W	3	1	1	1	0	3	0	2
Huddersfield										
Millwall	W	L	4	3	0	1	2	2	1	3
Barnsley	D	W	1	0	1	0	1	0	1	0
Doncaster			1	0	1	0	1	0	1	0
Bournemouth			3	1	1	1	1	2	1	1
Yeovil			5	4	1	0	2	3	2	3

Season	Division	Pos	P	W	D	L	F	A	GD	Pts
2012-13	Championship	19	46	15	13	18	53	73	-20	58
2011-12	League 1	4	46	21	18	7	79	47	+32	81
2010-11	League 1	3	46	25	12	9	77	48	+29	87

Over/Under 52%/48% 10th   **Both score** 52%/48% 18th

Ipswich Town

Nickname: Town/Tractor Boys
Colours: Blue and white
Ground: Portman Road (30,311)
Tel: 01473 400 500   www.itfc.co.uk

Mick McCarthy looks a wise appointment for long-suffering Ipswich owner Marcus Evans, as the Yorkshireman has led all three of his former club sides to the top six of the second tier, gaining promotion with both Sunderland and Wolves.

He arrived at Portman Road to replace Paul Jewell after Town had taken just seven points from their first 12 games. But McCarthy worked wonders, winning his first game in charge and lifting the club from the foot of the table to as high as 11th in the penultimate weekend of the season.

Longest run without win/loss: 11/5
High/low league position: 11/24
Clean sheets: 15 **Yellow cards:** 54 **Red cards:** 2
Average attendance: 17,526 **Players used:** 39
Leading scorer: D Campbell 10 (5,9)
Key stat: McCarthy raised Ipswich's points-per-game average from 0.53 to 1.61 – enough for a play-off place over the course of a season

	2012-13 H	A	Last six seasons at home P	W	D	L	OV	UN	BS	CS
Wigan	-	-	-	-	-	-	-	-	-	-
Reading			4	2	0	2	3	1	3	1
QPR			4	2	1	1	2	2	0	3
Watford	L	W	6	0	2	4	3	3	3	1
Brighton	L	D	2	1	0	1	2	0	1	0
Leicester	W	L	5	3	1	1	3	2	2	3
Bolton	W	W	1	1	0	0	0	1	0	1
Nottm Forest	W	L	5	2	1	2	3	2	4	0
Charlton	L	L	3	1	1	1	1	2	2	1
Derby	L	W	5	3	0	2	1	4	1	3
Burnley	W	L	5	2	3	0	1	4	3	2
Birmingham	W	W	3	1	1	1	1	2	2	0
Leeds	W	L	3	3	0	0	3	0	2	1
Ipswich										
Blackpool	W	L	5	3	2	0	3	2	4	1
Middlesbrough	W	L	4	1	3	0	2	2	3	1
Blackburn	D	L	1	0	1	0	0	1	1	0
Sheffield Weds	L	D	4	1	2	1	2	2	1	1
Huddersfield	D	D	1	0	1	0	1	0	1	0
Millwall	W	D	3	2	0	1	2	1	0	2
Barnsley	D	D	6	3	2	1	2	4	2	4
Doncaster			4	1	1	2	3	1	4	0
Bournemouth	-	-	-	-	-	-	-	-	-	-
Yeovil	-	-	-	-	-	-	-	-	-	-

Season	Division	Pos	P	W	D	L	F	A	GD	Pts
2012-13	Championship	14	46	16	12	18	48	61	-13	60
2011-12	Championship	15	46	17	10	19	69	77	-8	61
2010-11	Championship	13	46	18	8	20	62	68	-6	62

Over/Under 46%/54% 20th   **Both score** 41%/59% 24th

Leeds United

Nickname: United
Colours: White
Ground: Elland Road (37,914)
Tel: 0113 367 6000   www.leedsunited.com

With promotion looking deeply unlikely, Neil Warnock left Leeds on amicable terms in April. But United fans weren't too distraught following an uninspiring season in which a team short on pace, goals and youth plodded along in mid-table.

This season looks brighter. It remains to be seen whether Brian McDermott, who took over for the final five games, can replicate his Reading success at Elland Road but he started brightly and the noises made by new owners GFH Capital hint at positive, albeit perhaps unspectacular, progress for the club.

Longest run without win/loss: 7/6
High/low league position: 7/19
Clean sheets: 10 **Yellow cards:** 70 **Red cards:** 5
Average attendance: 21,572 **Players used:** 28
Leading scorer: L Becchio 15 (8,12)
Key stat: With three victories, Brian McDermott won more games in his five matches than Leeds had managed in the previous 14

	2012-13 H	A	Last six seasons at home P	W	D	L	OV	UN	BS	CS
Wigan	-	-	-	-	-	-	-	-	-	-
Reading			2	0	1	1	0	2	0	1
QPR			1	1	0	0	0	1	0	1
Watford	L	W	3	0	1	2	2	1	2	0
Brighton	L	D	5	1	2	2	3	2	4	1
Leicester	W	D	4	1	1	2	2	2	3	1
Bolton	W	D	1	1	0	0	0	1	0	1
Nottm Forest	W	L	4	2	1	1	3	1	4	0
Charlton	D	L	2	0	2	0	0	2	1	1
Derby	L	L	3	0	0	3	2	1	0	0
Burnley	W	W	3	3	0	0	1	2	1	2
Birmingham	L	L	2	0	0	2	1	1	1	0
Leeds										
Ipswich	W	L	3	2	1	0	1	1	1	2
Blackpool	W	L	2	1	0	1	1	1	0	1
Middlesbrough	W	L	3	1	1	1	1	2	2	0
Blackburn	D	D	1	0	1	0	1	0	1	0
Sheffield Weds	W	D	1	1	0	0	1	0	1	0
Huddersfield	L	W	4	1	1	2	4	0	3	1
Millwall	W	L	6	5	0	1	2	4	2	3
Barnsley	W	L	3	1	1	1	2	1	2	1
Doncaster			3	2	0	1	2	1	2	0
Bournemouth			1	1	0	0	0	1	0	1
Yeovil			3	3	0	0	2	1	0	3

Season	Division	Pos	P	W	D	L	F	A	GD	Pts
2012-13	Championship	13	46	17	10	19	57	66	-9	61
2011-12	Championship	15	46	17	10	19	65	68	-3	61
2010-11	Championship	7	46	19	15	12	81	70	+11	72

Over/Under 52%/48% 10th   **Both score** 59%/41% 11th

Leicester City

Nickname: The Foxes
Colours: Blue
Ground: King Power Stadium (32,312)
Tel: 0844 815 6000   www.lcfc.co.uk

Leicester rarely looked like justifying their 11-2 title favourites tag last season.

They twice occupied the automatic promotion places after enjoying a pair of five-match winning runs in early autumn and January, but those two spurts accounted for over half of their wins in a campaign that fizzled out horribly and ended in a play-off semi-final defeat.

The club enjoys significant financial backing but Nigel Pearson would be expected to get more out of a very decent squad than the 68 points and sixth-place finished that 2012-13 returned.

Longest run without win/loss: 9/7
High/low league position: 1/8
Clean sheets: 14 **Yellow cards:** 52 **Red cards:** 2
Average attendance: 22,054 **Players used:** 26
Leading scorer: D Nugent 14 (5,10)
Key stat: Only one side scored more goals at home than Leicester in 2012-13 and no team conceded fewer than the Foxes on their travels

	2012-13 H	A	Last six seasons at home P	W	D	L	OV	UN	BS	CS
Wigan			-	-	-	-	-	-	-	-
Reading			3	0	0	3	2	1	2	0
QPR			3	1	1	1	1	2	1	1
Watford	L	L	5	4	0	1	4	1	4	1
Brighton	W	D	3	2	1	0	0	3	0	3
Leicester										
Bolton	W	D	1	1	0	0	1	0	1	0
Nottm Forest	D	W	4	2	2	0	2	2	1	3
Charlton	L	L	2	0	1	1	1	2	2	0
Derby	W	L	4	3	1	0	2	2	1	3
Burnley	W	W	4	2	1	1	2	2	1	2
Birmingham	D	D	2	1	1	0	2	0	2	0
Leeds	D	L	4	1	2	1	1	3	2	1
Ipswich	W	L	5	3	2	0	2	3	3	2
Blackpool	W	D	4	3	0	1	1	3	1	2
Middlesbrough	W	W	4	2	2	0	1	3	1	3
Blackburn	W	L	1	1	0	0	1	0	0	1
Sheffield Weds	L	W	3	1	0	2	2	1	1	1
Huddersfield	W	W	2	2	0	0	2	0	2	0
Millwall	L	L	4	1	0	3	2	2	1	0
Barnsley	D	L	5	3	1	1	3	2	3	2
Doncaster			3	2	1	0	2	1	1	2
Bournemouth			-	-	-	-	-	-	-	-
Yeovil			1	1	0	0	0	1	0	1

Season	Division	Pos	P	W	D	L	F	A	GD	Pts
2012-13	Championship	6	46	19	11	16	71	48	+23	68
2011-12	Championship	9	46	18	12	16	66	55	+11	66
2010-11	Championship	10	46	19	10	17	76	71	+5	67

Over/Under 52%/48% 10th   **Both score** 54%/46% 17th

Middlesbrough

Nickname: Boro
Colours: Red and white
Ground: Riverside Stadium (34,998)
Tel: 0844 499 6789   www.mfc.co.uk

Boro endured a dramatically contrasting season of two halves. A point off an automatic promotion place at the turn of the year, a dismal 2013 saw them plummet down to finish just five points above relegation in 16th place.

Tony Mowbray blamed injuries and bad luck for the stark reversal of form but while the Middlesbrough manager may have a some reason to bemoan his fortunes last term, Boro fans could be running out of patience after two late slumps have now seen their side miss out on promotion in consecutive seasons.

Longest run without win/loss: 7/8
High/low league position: 2/16
Clean sheets: 11 **Yellow cards:** 58 **Red cards:** 2
Average attendance: 16,794 **Players used:** 32
Leading scorer: S Mcdonald 12 (2,10)
Key stat: Middlesbrough's league record in 2013 was W3, D3, L15, having been W15, D2, L8 in the first half of the season

	2012-13 H	A	Last six seasons at home P	W	D	L	OV	UN	BS	CS
Wigan			2	1	1	0	0	2	0	2
Reading			4	1	1	2	1	3	2	0
QPR			2	1	0	1	1	1	0	1
Watford	L	W	4	2	0	2	2	2	2	1
Brighton	L	W	2	1	0	1	0	2	0	1
Leicester	L	L	4	0	2	2	2	2	2	1
Bolton	W	L	3	1	0	2	2	1	2	0
Nottm Forest	W	D	4	2	2	0	1	3	3	1
Charlton	D	W	1	0	1	0	1	0	1	0
Derby	D	L	5	4	1	0	2	3	2	3
Burnley	W	D	3	2	0	1	2	1	2	0
Birmingham	L	L	3	2	0	1	1	2	1	1
Leeds	W	L	3	1	0	2	1	2	1	1
Ipswich	W	L	4	2	1	1	2	2	2	2
Blackpool	W	L	3	1	1	1	3	0	2	0
Middlesbrough										
Blackburn	W	W	3	1	1	1	1	2	1	2
Sheffield Weds	W	L	2	2	0	0	1	1	1	1
Huddersfield	W	L	1	1	0	0	1	0	0	1
Millwall	L	L	3	0	1	2	1	2	2	0
Barnsley	L	L	4	2	1	1	2	2	3	1
Doncaster			3	2	1	0	1	2	0	3
Bournemouth			-	-	-	-	-	-	-	-
Yeovil			-	-	-	-	-	-	-	-

Season	Division	Pos	P	W	D	L	F	A	GD	Pts
2012-13	Championship	16	46	18	5	23	61	70	-9	59
2011-12	Championship	7	46	18	12	16	52	51	+1	70
2010-11	Championship	12	46	17	11	18	68	68	0	70

Over/Under 61%/39% 3rd   **Both score** 57%/43% 15th

Millwall

Nickname: The Lions
Colours: Blue and white
Ground: The Den (19,734)
Tel: 020 7232 1222   www.millwallfc.co.uk

Kenny Jackett's resignation at the end of a slightly disappointing season makes Millwall a wait-and-see side for bettors.

The former Lions manager had led the side with calm authority for six relatively successful years, taking the reins with the club in League 1, guiding them to promotion and steering them to three seasons of second-tier safety.

However, Millwall's league placings have been steadily slipping in recent years and, after a late season collapse in 2012-13, perhaps it was the right time for club and manager to part ways.

Longest run without win/loss: 6/13
High/low league position: 5/22
Clean sheets: 12 **Yellow cards:** 93 **Red cards:** 3
Average attendance: 10,559 **Players used:** 33
Leading scorer: C Wood 11 (5,8)
Key stat: Millwall lost just six of their first 23 games of the season but 14 of their final 23

	2012-13 H	A	Last six seasons at home P	W	D	L	OV	UN	BS	CS
Wigan			-	-	-	-	-	-	-	-
Reading			2	0	1	1	1	1	1	1
QPR			1	1	0	0	0	1	0	1
Watford	W	D	3	1	0	2	1	2	1	1
Brighton	L	D	5	1	2	2	2	3	3	1
Leicester	W	W	4	3	0	1	1	3	1	2
Bolton	W	D	1	1	0	0	1	0	1	0
Nottm Forest	L	W	4	1	2	1	1	3	1	2
Charlton	D	W	2	1	1	0	1	1	0	2
Derby	W	L	3	2	1	0	1	2	1	2
Burnley	L	D	3	0	1	2	0	3	1	0
Birmingham	D	D	2	0	1	1	2	0	1	0
Leeds	W	L	6	4	0	2	3	3	3	1
Ipswich	D	L	3	2	1	0	2	1	2	1
Blackpool	L	L	2	0	1	1	1	1	1	0
Middlesbrough	W	W	3	1	0	2	3	0	3	0
Blackburn	L	W	1	0	0	1	1	0	1	0
Sheffield Weds	L	L	1	0	0	1	1	0	1	0
Huddersfield	W	L	4	3	0	1	4	0	3	1
Millwall										
Barnsley	L	L	3	1	1	1	1	2	1	2
Doncaster			3	2	0	1	2	1	1	1
Bournemouth			1	1	0	0	1	0	1	0
Yeovil			3	1	2	0	1	2	2	1

Season	Division	Pos	P	W	D	L	F	A	GD	Pts
2012-13	Championship	20	46	15	11	20	51	62	-11	56
2011-12	Championship	16	46	15	12	19	55	57	-2	57
2010-11	Championship	9	46	18	13	15	62	48	+14	67

Over/Under 48%/52% 16th   **Both score** 48%/52% 23rd

Nottingham Forest

Nickname: Forest
Colours: Red and white
Ground: City Ground (30,540)
Tel: 0115 982 4444   www.nottinghamforest.co.uk

Forest choked at the death last season, missing out on the play-offs by one point after losing three of their final five games of the campaign.

However, that shouldn't mask the fact that the club looks firmly back on track after a troubling period, even if their wealthy new owners, the Al-Hasawi family, seem a little trigger happy having hired three new managers in the space of eight months. Still, Forest fans will hope the return to the dugout of popular and successful boss Billy Davies will end a run of managerial comings and goings.

Longest run without win/loss: 6/10
High/low league position: 5/16
Clean sheets: 12 **Yellow cards:** 81 **Red cards:** 5
Average attendance: 23,082 **Players used:** 28
Leading scorer: B Sharp 10 (1,9)
Key stat: Forest earned 1.73 points per game under Davies – enough for second place in 2012-13 had it stayed at that rate over the whole season

	2012-13 H	A	Last six seasons at home P	W	D	L	OV	UN	BS	CS
Wigan			-	-	-	-	-	-	-	-
Reading			4	2	1	1	2	2	2	2
QPR			3	1	2	0	2	1	1	2
Watford	L	L	5	2	1	2	3	2	3	1
Brighton	D	D	3	0	3	0	1	2	2	1
Leicester	L	D	4	2	1	1	4	0	4	0
Bolton	D	D	1	0	1	0	0	1	1	0
Nottm Forest										
Charlton	W	W	2	1	1	0	1	1	1	1
Derby	L	D	5	2	0	3	4	1	4	0
Burnley	W	D	4	2	0	2	1	3	1	2
Birmingham	D	L	3	0	2	1	2	1	3	0
Leeds	W	L	4	1	1	2	3	1	3	0
Ipswich	W	L	5	4	1	0	2	3	2	3
Blackpool	D	D	4	0	3	1	0	4	1	2
Middlesbrough	D	L	4	3	1	0	0	4	0	4
Blackburn	D	L	1	0	1	0	0	1	0	1
Sheffield Weds	W	W	3	3	0	0	2	1	2	1
Huddersfield	D	D	2	2	0	0	2	0	2	0
Millwall	L	W	4	2	1	1	2	2	3	1
Barnsley	D	W	5	2	3	0	1	4	1	4
Doncaster			5	1	2	2	3	2	3	2
Bournemouth			1	0	1	0	0	1	0	1
Yeovil			1	1	0	0	1	0	1	0

Season	Division	Pos	P	W	D	L	F	A	GD	Pts
2012-13	Championship	8	46	17	16	13	63	59	+4	67
2011-12	Championship	19	46	14	8	24	48	63	-15	50
2010-11	Championship	6	46	20	15	11	69	50	+19	75

Over/Under 52%/48% 10th   **Both score** 59%/41% 11th

QPR

Nickname: The R's
Colours: Blue and white
Ground: Loftus Road (18,439)
Tel: 020 8743 0262   www.qpr.co.uk

QPR were consistently overrated by the bookies last term despite showing very little to merit that faith.

There is money at the club but owner Tony Fernandes has taken a scattergun approach to signings, exemplified by the purchase of goalkeeper Julio Cesar a week after Rob Green made his debut.

Spending big on the likes of Loic Remy and Christopher Samba in January failed to save QPR and even the appointment of Harry Redknapp following Mark Hughes' sacking couldn't keep the team from finishing rock bottom.

Longest run without win/loss: 16/5
High/low league position: 19/20
Clean sheets: 7 **Yellow cards:** 60 **Red cards:** 3
Average attendance: 17,779 **Players used:** 30
Leading scorer: L Remy 6 (4,6)
Key stat: QPR averaged 0.84 points per game under Redknapp, which equates to just 32 points and relegation over the course of a full season

	2012-13		Last six seasons at home							
	H	A	P	W	D	L	OV	UN	BS	CS
Wigan	D	D	2	1	1	0	1	1	2	0
Reading	D	D	4	2	2	0	2	2	3	1
QPR										
Watford			4	1	2	1	1	3	2	2
Brighton			-	-	-	-	-	-	-	-
Leicester			3	2	0	1	2	1	2	1
Bolton			1	0	0	1	1	0	0	0
Nottm Forest			3	1	2	0	1	2	3	0
Charlton			2	2	0	0	1	1	1	1
Derby			3	0	2	1	0	3	1	1
Burnley			3	0	1	2	2	1	3	0
Birmingham			1	1	0	0	0	1	0	1
Leeds			1	0	0	1	1	0	1	0
Ipswich			4	1	1	2	2	2	3	1
Blackpool			3	1	2	0	1	2	3	0
Middlesbrough			2	1	0	1	2	0	1	1
Blackburn			1	0	1	0	0	1	1	0
Sheffield Weds			3	1	2	0	1	2	2	1
Huddersfield			-	-	-	-	-	-	-	-
Millwall			1	0	1	0	0	1	0	1
Barnsley			4	4	0	0	3	1	2	2
Doncaster			3	3	0	0	2	1	1	2
Bournemouth			-	-	-	-	-	-	-	-
Yeovil			-	-	-	-	-	-	-	-

Season	Division	Pos	P	W	D	L	F	A	GD	Pts
2012-13	Premier League	20	38	4	13	21	30	60	-30	25
2011-12	Premier League	17	38	10	7	21	43	66	-23	37
2010-11	Championship	1	46	24	16	6	71	32	+39	88

Over/Under 45%/55% 18th   **Both score** 55%/45% 11th

Reading

Nickname: The Royals
Colours: Blue and white
Ground: Madejski Stadium (24,197)
Tel: 0118 968-1100   www.readingfc.co.uk

By Premier League standards Reading spent nothing following their promotion, so it was no surprise that a Championship side failed in the top tier.

But while the Royals dropped straight back down and lost manager Brian McDermott in the process, Reading's season was far from disastrous.

The appointment of Nigel Adkins is sensible enough given his experience in winning promotions, the club's finances are in good order under Anton Zingarevich and the squad is made up of high-quality Championship players.

Longest run without win/loss: 10/4
High/low league position: 17/20
Clean sheets: 5 **Yellow cards:** 45 **Red cards:** 1
Average attendance: 23,862 **Players used:** 28
Leading scorer: A Le Fondre 12 (0,9)
Key stat: In 2011-12, Reading finished 13 points clear of Birmingham – the nearest challenger still in the division in 2013-14

	2012-13		Last six seasons at home							
	H	A	P	W	D	L	OV	UN	BS	CS
Wigan	L	L	2	1	0	1	2	0	1	0
Reading										
QPR	D	D	4	1	2	1	0	4	0	3
Watford			4	1	2	1	1	3	2	1
Brighton			1	1	0	0	1	0	0	1
Leicester			3	2	0	1	2	1	2	0
Bolton			1	0	0	1	0	1	0	0
Nottm Forest			4	1	2	1	0	4	1	2
Charlton			1	0	1	0	1	0	1	0
Derby			5	4	1	0	4	1	3	2
Burnley			3	3	0	0	2	1	2	1
Birmingham			3	2	0	1	2	1	2	1
Leeds			2	1	1	0	0	2	0	2
Ipswich			4	2	1	1	0	4	1	2
Blackpool			3	3	0	0	2	1	2	1
Middlesbrough			4	1	2	1	1	3	2	1
Blackburn			1	0	1	0	0	1	0	1
Sheffield Weds			2	2	0	0	2	0	0	2
Huddersfield			-	-	-	-	-	-	-	-
Millwall			2	1	1	0	2	0	2	0
Barnsley			4	2	1	1	2	2	1	3
Doncaster			4	3	1	0	2	2	2	2
Bournemouth			-	-	-	-	-	-	-	-
Yeovil			-	-	-	-	-	-	-	-

Season	Division	Pos	P	W	D	L	F	A	GD	Pts
2012-13	Premier League	19	38	6	10	22	43	73	-30	28
2011-12	Championship	1	46	27	8	11	69	41	+28	89
2010-11	Championship	5	46	20	17	9	77	51	+26	77

Over/Under 61%/39% 7th   **Both score** 61%/39% 4th

Sheff Wednesday

Nickname: The Owls
Colours: Blue and white
Ground: Hillsborough (39,732)
Tel: 0870 999 1867   www.swfc.co.uk

Patience paid off for Sheffield Wednesday last season as Dave Jones, the man who got the Owls promoted from League 1 in the summer of 2012, kept his place in the dugout despite his side occupying a bottom-three spot at the turn of the year.

By taking 33 points from the final 60 available Jones eventually kept the side in the second tier, but he should enjoy a more comfortable ride this time around.

To do so, however, he needs to work on Wednesday's performance in the final third as no Owls player scored more than eight league goals last term.

Longest run without win/loss: 9/7
High/low league position: 14/23
Clean sheets: 11 **Yellow cards:** 96 **Red cards:** 2
Average attendance: 24,078 **Players used:** 34
Leading scorer: M Antonio 8 (2,8)
Key stat: Wednesday had the joint-ninth best defensive record last term but only two sides scored fewer goals than the Owls

	2012-13		Last six seasons at home							
	H	A	P	W	D	L	OV	UN	BS	CS
Wigan			-	-	-	-	-	-	-	-
Reading			2	0	0	2	1	1	1	0
QPR			3	2	0	1	2	1	2	1
Watford	L	L	4	2	0	2	2	2	2	1
Brighton	W	L	2	2	0	0	1	1	1	1
Leicester	L	W	3	1	0	2	0	3	0	1
Bolton	L	W	1	0	0	1	0	1	0	0
Nottm Forest	L	L	3	1	1	1	0	3	1	1
Charlton	W	W	5	2	2	1	2	3	2	2
Derby	D	D	3	0	2	1	1	2	1	1
Burnley	L	D	3	1	0	2	1	2	1	0
Birmingham	W	D	2	1	1	0	1	1	2	0
Leeds	D	L	1	0	1	0	0	1	1	0
Ipswich	D	W	4	0	2	2	1	3	2	1
Blackpool	L	D	4	2	1	1	1	3	2	1
Middlesbrough	W	L	2	1	0	1	1	1	1	1
Blackburn	W	L	1	1	0	0	1	0	1	0
Sheffield Weds										
Huddersfield	L	D	3	0	1	2	2	1	2	0
Millwall	W	W	1	1	0	0	1	0	1	0
Barnsley	W	W	4	2	1	1	2	2	2	1
Doncaster			2	1	0	1	0	2	0	1
Bournemouth			2	1	1	0	1	1	0	0
Yeovil			2	1	1	0	2	0	2	0

Season	Division	Pos	P	W	D	L	F	A	GD	Pts
2012-13	Championship	18	46	16	10	20	53	61	-8	58
2011-12	League 1	2	46	28	9	9	81	48	+33	93
2010-11	League 1	15	46	16	10	20	67	67	0	58

Over/Under 48%/52% 16th   **Both score** 50%/50% 20th

Watford

Nickname: The Hornets
Colours: Yellow and red
Ground: Vicarage Road (17,477)
Tel: 0845 442 1881   www.watfordfc.co.uk

Watford suffered play-off final heartbreak but will hope to emulate Reading, who followed their 2010-11 play-off final defeat by winning the title the following season.

It is possible. High player turnover and the summer appointment of Gianfranco Zola contributed to a slow start but Watford soon emerged as one of the best passing sides in the league and they came very close to automatic promotion.

The impact of the changes to the loan system rule seem exaggerated, too, as Watford's better loanees from last season look likely to sign on a permanent basis.

Longest run without win/loss: 4/7
High/low league position: 2/20
Clean sheets: 11 **Yellow cards:** 82 **Red cards:** 6
Average attendance: 13,453 **Players used:** 36
Leading scorer: M Vydra 20 (6,14)
Key stat: With 44 goals, Watford scored more away from home than any other side in the top five English divisions last season

	2012-13		Last six seasons at home							
	H	A	P	W	D	L	OV	UN	BS	CS
Wigan			-	-	-	-	-	-	-	-
Reading			4	1	2	1	3	1	3	1
QPR			4	2	0	2	3	1	2	1
Watford										
Brighton	L	W	2	1	0	1	0	2	0	1
Leicester	W	W	5	4	1	0	4	1	4	1
Bolton	W	L	1	1	0	0	1	0	1	0
Nottm Forest	W	W	5	2	2	1	1	4	2	2
Charlton	L	W	3	1	1	1	1	2	2	1
Derby	W	L	5	3	0	2	3	2	2	1
Burnley	D	D	5	2	1	2	5	0	4	1
Birmingham	W	W	3	1	1	1	2	1	1	0
Leeds	L	W	3	0	1	2	1	2	2	0
Ipswich	L	W	6	5	0	1	4	2	4	1
Blackpool	L	D	5	0	2	3	3	2	4	0
Middlesbrough	L	W	4	2	1	1	3	1	4	0
Blackburn	W	L	1	1	0	0	1	0	0	1
Sheffield Weds	W	W	4	3	1	0	4	0	4	0
Huddersfield	W	W	1	1	0	0	1	0	1	0
Millwall	D	L	3	2	1	0	1	2	1	2
Barnsley	W	L	6	4	1	1	3	3	3	2
Doncaster			4	1	3	0	2	2	4	0
Bournemouth			-	-	-	-	-	-	-	-
Yeovil			-	-	-	-	-	-	-	-

Season	Division	Pos	P	W	D	L	F	A	GD	Pts
2012-13	Championship	3	46	23	8	15	85	58	+27	77
2011-12	Championship	11	46	16	16	14	56	64	-8	64
2010-11	Championship	14	46	16	13	17	77	71	+6	61

Over/Under 67%/33% 1st   **Both score** 63%/37% 3rd

Wigan Athletic

Nickname: The Latics
Colours: Blue and white
Ground: DW Stadium (25,133)
Tel: 01942 774 000   www.wiganlatics.co.uk

After the great escapes of 2011 and 2012, it was third time unlucky for Wigan as an eight-year stay in the top flight ended.

FA Cup joy was dampened by the club's relegation and subsequent loss of manager Roberto Martinez, but bettors would be wise to avoid getting caught up in Martinez hype – he offered attractive football but received a kinder press than some of the stats suggest he deserved.

The Latics will lose some star men but should attract decent replacements given the club's financial health and their participation in the Europa League.

Longest run without win/loss: 6/3
High/low league position: 13/19
Clean sheets: 5 **Yellow cards:** 66 **Red cards:** 2
Average attendance: 19,375 **Players used:** 28
Leading scorer: A Kone 11 (3,10)
Key stat: Wigan's Premier League goals conceded per season rose from an average of 52 before Martinez took over to 69 under him

	2012-13 H	A	Last six seasons at home P	W	D	L	OV	UN	BS	CS
Wigan										
Reading	W	W	2	1	1	0	1	1	1	1
QPR	D	D	2	1	1	0	1	1	1	1
Watford			-	-	-	-	-	-	-	-
Brighton			-	-	-	-	-	-	-	-
Leicester			-	-	-	-	-	-	-	-
Bolton			5	1	3	1	1	4	2	3
Nottm Forest			-	-	-	-	-	-	-	-
Charlton			-	-	-	-	-	-	-	-
Derby			1	1	0	0	1	0	1	
Burnley			1	1	0	0	0	1	0	1
Birmingham			3	2	0	1	2	1	2	1
Leeds			-	-	-	-	-	-	-	-
Ipswich			-	-	-	-	-	-	-	-
Blackpool			1	0	0	1	1	0	0	0
Middlesbrough			2	1	0	1	0	2	0	1
Blackburn			5	3	2	0	4	1	4	1
Sheffield Weds			-	-	-	-	-	-	-	-
Huddersfield			-	-	-	-	-	-	-	-
Millwall			-	-	-	-	-	-	-	-
Barnsley			-	-	-	-	-	-	-	-
Doncaster			-	-	-	-	-	-	-	-
Bournemouth			-	-	-	-	-	-	-	-
Yeovil			-	-	-	-	-	-	-	-

Season	Division	Pos	P	W	D	L	F	A	GD	Pts
2012-13	Premier League	18	38	9	9	20	47	73	-26	36
2011-12	Premier League	15	38	11	10	17	42	62	-20	43
2010-11	Premier League	16	38	9	15	14	40	61	-21	42

Over/Under 71%/29% 1st   **Both score** 58%/42% 7th

Yeovil Town

Nickname: The Glovers
Colours: Green and white
Ground: Huish Park (9,565)
Tel: 01935 423 662   www.ytfc.net

Yeovil were rewarded for sticking by Gary Johnson last term, as a run of six consecutive defeats in September would have had any owner fretting about relegation.

Johnston soon steadied the ship, though, and a run of eight consecutive victories at the turn of the year set up Yeovil's promotion via the play-offs.

Their first taste of second-tier life looks likely to be short lived, however. The club is a real minnow at this level with a tiny average attendance of just 4,071 last term and a playing budget to match. Survival would be a stunning achievement.

Longest run without win/loss: 6/9
High/low league position: 4/16
Clean sheets: 15 **Yellow cards:** 72 **Red cards:** 3
Average attendance: 4,071 **Players used:** 31
Leading scorer: P Madden 22 (10,17)
Key stat: Yeovil lost a third of their League 1 games last season

	2012-13 H	A	Last six seasons at home P	W	D	L	OV	UN	BS	CS
Wigan			-	-	-	-	-	-	-	-
Reading			-	-	-	-	-	-	-	-
QPR			-	-	-	-	-	-	-	-
Watford			-	-	-	-	-	-	-	-
Brighton			4	1	2	1	2	2	3	0
Leicester			1	0	0	1	0	1	0	0
Bolton			-	-	-	-	-	-	-	-
Nottm Forest			1	0	0	1	1	0	0	0
Charlton			3	0	1	2	1	2	2	0
Derby			-	-	-	-	-	-	-	-
Burnley			-	-	-	-	-	-	-	-
Birmingham			-	-	-	-	-	-	-	-
Leeds			3	0	1	2	1	2	2	0
Ipswich			-	-	-	-	-	-	-	-
Blackpool			-	-	-	-	-	-	-	-
Middlesbrough			-	-	-	-	-	-	-	-
Blackburn			-	-	-	-	-	-	-	-
Sheffield Weds			2	0	0	2	1	1	1	0
Huddersfield			5	1	1	3	0	5	1	1
Millwall			3	1	1	1	0	3	1	1
Barnsley			-	-	-	-	-	-	-	-
Doncaster	W	D	2	2	0	0	2	0	2	0
Bournemouth	L	L	4	1	1	2	3	1	3	0
Yeovil										

Season	Division	Pos	P	W	D	L	F	A	GD	Pts
2012-13	League 1	4	46	23	8	15	71	56	+15	77
2011-12	League 1	17	46	14	12	20	59	80	-21	54
2010-11	League 1	14	46	16	11	19	56	66	-10	59

Over/Under 59%/41% 2nd   **Both score** 52%/48% 12th

Championship stats 2012-13

Key Points do not include any deductions imposed by the league. **GFA** Goals For Average per match, **GAA** Goals Against Average per match, **PGA** Average Points Gained per match, **CS** Clean Sheet, **FS** First to Score, **Ov** Over 2.5 total goals, **Un** Under 2.5 total goals, **BS** Both teams Score

Top scorers 2012-13

		P	W	D	L	F	GFA	PGA	Pts
1	Watford	46	23	8	15	85	1.85	**1.7**	77
2	C Palace	46	19	15	12	73	1.59	**1.6**	72
3	Cardiff	46	25	12	9	72	1.57	**1.9**	87
4	Leicester	46	19	11	16	71	1.54	**1.5**	68
5	Brighton	46	19	18	9	69	1.50	**1.6**	75
	Bolton	46	18	14	14	69	1.50	**1.5**	68
7	Peterborough	46	15	9	22	66	1.43	**1.2**	54
8	Charlton	46	17	14	15	65	1.41	**1.4**	65
	Derby	46	16	13	17	65	1.41	**1.3**	61
10	Nottm Forest	46	17	16	13	63	1.37	**1.5**	67
	Birmingham	46	15	16	15	63	1.37	**1.3**	61
12	Burnley	46	16	13	17	62	1.35	**1.3**	61
	Blackpool	46	14	17	15	62	1.35	**1.3**	59
14	Hull	46	24	7	15	61	1.33	**1.7**	79
	Middlesbro	46	18	5	23	61	1.33	**1.3**	59
16	Bristol City	46	11	8	27	59	1.28	**0.9**	41
17	Leeds	46	17	10	19	57	1.24	**1.3**	61
18	Barnsley	46	14	13	19	56	1.22	**1.2**	55
19	Blackburn	46	14	16	16	55	1.20	**1.3**	58
	Wolves	46	14	9	23	55	1.20	**1.1**	51
21	Sheff Wed	46	16	10	20	53	1.15	**1.3**	58
	Huddersfield	46	15	13	18	53	1.15	**1.3**	58
23	Millwall	46	15	11	20	51	1.11	**1.2**	56
24	Ipswich	46	16	12	18	48	1.04	**1.3**	60

Best defence 2012-13

		P	W	D	L	A	GAA	PGA	Pts
1	Brighton	46	19	18	9	43	0.93	**1.6**	75
2	Cardiff	46	25	12	9	45	0.98	**1.9**	87
3	Leicester	46	19	11	16	48	1.04	**1.5**	68
4	Hull	46	24	7	15	52	1.13	**1.7**	79
5	Watford	46	23	8	15	58	1.26	**1.7**	77
6	Nottm Forest	46	17	16	13	59	1.28	**1.5**	67
	Charlton	46	17	14	15	59	1.28	**1.4**	65
8	Burnley	46	16	13	17	60	1.30	**1.3**	61
9	Bolton	46	18	14	14	61	1.33	**1.5**	68
	Ipswich	46	16	12	18	61	1.33	**1.3**	60
	Sheff Wed	46	16	10	20	61	1.33	**1.3**	58
12	C Palace	46	19	15	12	62	1.35	**1.6**	72
	Derby	46	16	13	17	62	1.35	**1.3**	61
	Blackburn	46	14	16	16	62	1.35	**1.3**	58
	Millwall	46	15	11	20	62	1.35	**1.2**	56
16	Blackpool	46	14	17	15	63	1.37	**1.3**	59
17	Leeds	46	17	10	19	66	1.43	**1.3**	61
18	Birmingham	46	15	16	15	69	1.50	**1.3**	61
	Wolves	46	14	9	23	69	1.50	**1.1**	51
20	Middlesbro	46	18	5	23	70	1.52	**1.3**	59
	Barnsley	46	14	13	19	70	1.52	**1.2**	55
22	Huddersfield	46	15	13	18	73	1.59	**1.3**	58
23	Peterborough	46	15	9	22	75	1.63	**1.2**	54
24	Bristol C	46	11	8	27	84	1.83	**0.9**	41

Watford's Matej Vydra celebrates his first goal of the season, a late winner against Crystal Palace

Clean sheets 2012-13

		P	CS	CS%
1	Cardiff	46	18	39.1
2	Brighton	46	17	37.0
3	Hull	46	16	34.8
4	Ipswich	46	15	32.6
5	Leicester	46	14	30.4
6	Burnley	46	12	26.1
	Millwall	46	12	26.1
	Nottm Forest	46	12	26.1
9	Watford	46	11	23.9
	C Palace	46	11	23.9
	Barnsley	46	11	23.9
	Sheff Wed	46	11	23.9
	Middlesbro	46	11	23.9
	Huddersfield	46	11	23.9
15	Leeds	46	10	21.7
	Charlton	46	10	21.7
	Blackburn	46	10	21.7
	Blackpool	46	10	21.7
	Birmingham	46	10	21.7
20	Bolton	46	9	19.6
	Wolves	46	9	19.6
22	Derby	46	8	17.4
	Peterborough	46	8	17.4
24	Bristol C	46	6	13.0

First to score 2012-13

		P	FS	FS%
1	Cardiff	46	29	63.0
2	Watford	46	27	58.6
3	Bolton	46	26	56.5
4	Burnley	46	25	54.3
5	C Palace	46	24	52.1
6	Brighton	46	23	50.0
	Charlton	46	23	50.0
	Hull	46	23	50.0
	Ipswich	46	23	50.0
	Wolves	46	23	50.0
11	Birmingham	46	22	47.8
12	Blackburn	46	21	45.6
	Huddersfield	46	21	45.6
	Leicester	46	21	45.6
	Millwall	46	21	45.6
16	Derby	46	20	43.4
	Leeds	46	20	43.4
18	Peterborough	46	19	41.3
	Sheff Wed	46	19	41.3
20	Barnsley	46	18	39.1
	Middlesbro	46	18	39.1
	Nottm Forest	46	18	39.1
23	Bristol C	46	16	34.7
24	Blackpool	46	15	32.6

Top goalscorers 2012-13

	Goals
G Murray (C Palace)	30
J Rhodes (Blackburn)	29
C Austin (Burnley)	25
M Vydra (Watford)	20
C Wood (Leicester)	20
T Deeney (Watford)	19
T Ince (Blackpool)	18
L Becchio (Leeds)	15
S Ebanks-Blake (Wolves)	14
D Nugent (Leicester)	14
J Vaughan (Huddersfield)	14

Glenn Murray of Crystal Palace

Record when keeping a clean sheet 2012-13

		P	W	D	L	F	GFA	PGA	Pts
1	Burnley	12	11	1	0	17	1.42	2.8	34
2	Leeds	10	9	1	0	11	1.10	2.8	28
	Birmingham	10	9	1	0	14	1.40	2.8	28
4	Leicester	14	11	3	0	25	1.79	2.6	36
5	Watford	11	9	2	0	23	2.09	2.6	29
	Barnsley	11	9	2	0	17	1.55	2.6	29
7	Blackburn	10	8	2	0	12	1.20	2.6	26
8	Bolton	9	7	2	0	10	1.11	2.6	23
	Wolves	9	7	2	0	10	1.11	2.6	23
10	Ipswich	15	11	4	0	21	1.40	2.5	37
11	Middlesbro	11	8	3	0	13	1.18	2.5	27
	Huddersfield	11	8	3	0	11	1.00	2.5	27
13	Derby	8	6	2	0	12	1.50	2.5	20
14	Cardiff	18	13	5	0	24	1.33	2.4	44
15	Hull	16	11	5	0	14	0.88	2.4	38
16	Brighton	17	11	6	0	21	1.24	2.3	39
17	Millwall	12	8	4	0	13	1.08	2.3	28
	Nottm Forest	12	8	4	0	10	0.83	2.3	28
19	C Palace	11	7	4	0	16	1.45	2.3	25
	Sheff Wed	11	7	4	0	11	1.00	2.3	25
21	Peterborough	8	5	3	0	10	1.25	2.3	18
22	Charlton	10	6	4	0	14	1.40	2.2	22
	Blackpool	10	6	4	0	14	1.40	2.2	22
24	Bristol C	6	3	3	0	6	1.00	2.0	12

Record when first to score 2012-13

		P	W	D	L	F	A	PGA	Pts
1	Hull City	23	21	1	1	42	15	2.8	64
2	Brighton	23	19	4	0	53	14	2.7	61
3	Leicester	21	15	5	1	49	14	2.4	50
4	Middlesbro	18	14	0	4	34	17	2.3	42
	Barnsley	18	13	3	2	32	15	2.3	42
	Blackpool	15	10	5	0	34	12	2.3	35
	Cardiff	29	21	4	4	55	25	2.3	67
	Derby	20	14	4	2	47	22	2.3	46
	Nottm Forest	18	12	5	1	29	14	2.3	41
10	Peterborough	19	13	3	3	44	24	2.2	42
	Leeds	20	14	2	4	30	19	2.2	44
	Millwall	21	14	4	3	39	20	2.2	46
	Watford	27	18	5	4	62	27	2.2	59
	Sheff Wed	19	13	2	4	34	21	2.2	41
15	Birmingham	22	13	8	1	34	18	2.1	47
	Ipswich	23	15	4	4	39	16	2.1	49
	Huddersfield	21	13	5	3	38	27	2.1	44
	Charlton	23	14	6	3	43	24	2.1	48
19	C Palace	24	13	9	2	50	26	2.0	48
	Blackburn	21	11	9	1	34	17	2.0	42
	Burnley	25	14	7	4	47	29	2.0	49
22	Bristol City	16	9	3	4	38	26	1.9	30
	Wolves	23	13	4	6	40	29	1.9	43
24	Bolton	26	14	6	6	44	32	1.8	48

Over 2.5 goals 2012-13

		H	A	Ov%
1	Watford	16	15	67.4
2	Crystal Palace	18	12	65.2
3	Middlesbrough	14	14	60.9
	Peterborough	16	12	60.9
5	Bolton	11	15	56.5
	Derby	13	13	56.5
	Wolves	14	12	56.5
8	Bristol C, Cardiff			54.3

Under 2.5 goals 2012-13

		H	A	Un%
1	Blackburn	8	10	60.9
	Burnley	6	12	60.9
3	Barnsley	8	13	54.3
	Brighton	9	12	54.3
	Ipswich	14	7	54.3
6	Charlton, Hull, Millwall, Sheffield Wednesday			52.2

Both to score 2012-13

		H	A	BS%
1	Bolton	13	19	69.6
2	Derby	15	15	65.2
3	Birmingham	14	15	63.0
	Blackpool	13	16	63.0
	Peterborough	16	13	63.0
	Watford	14	15	63.0
	Wolves	17	12	63.0
8	Barnsley, Charlton, Palace			60.9

Posh have the class to bounce back from relegation

F ew teams as good as Wolves and Peterborough have ever been relegated from the second tier and they could well set the standard in League 1 this season, writes Dylan Hill.

Only Leicester have gone down with a comparable points total in recent times, when their total of 52 points wasn't good enough to survive six seasons ago, and the Foxes duly went straight back up as champions.

Wolves are 4-1 favourites to do the same, but **Peterborough**, at 9-1, were arguably even stronger last season and should find it easier to adjust to the third tier.

Plenty of clubs as big as Wolves have struggled to get out of this division, which is shown by the fact that no outright favourites have won in 19 years.

Opposition teams are likely to find added motivation at the prospect of turning over Wolves, whose new boss Kenny Jackett, after his move from Millwall, doesn't know the division as well as Darren Ferguson, who has already taken Peterborough up to the Championship twice.

Unfortunately for Posh, Ferguson didn't have his team ready for the start of last season as they lost their first seven matches and picked up just 13 points from the first 21. But they finished in the sort of form that would have had them in the thick of the hunt for promotion to the Premier League over a full season.

Dwight Gayle has left for Crystal Palace and the likes of Lee Tomlin are in demand, but a certain level of change was inevitable

– Wolves have lost a host of key men – and both players have already shown Posh's strength in depth and Ferguson's eye for forward talent as they stepped up to atone for the January loss of George Boyd.

Peterborough are also worth backing at 11-5 to finish as the top relegated club, because the third team in the mix, Bristol City, have a mountain to climb after finishing 13 points behind them.

Brentford and Sheffield United both came close to promotion last season but make only limited appeal this time.

Having lost in the play-off final in 2012, Sheffield United rebuilt last season and unearthed another young gem in goalkeeper George Long to add to improving teenage centre-back Harry Maguire.

The problem could still be a lack of goals as the Blades are yet to adequately replace jailed goal machine Ched Evans and the club's long and ultimately humiliating search for a new manager, during which prospective candidate Graham Arnold was fiercely critical of the process, suggests a lack of direction at the top.

Brentford have just as much quality but over the last nine years only two beaten play-off finalists have gone up the following season from the bottom two divisions and the blow of their Wembley defeat to Yeovil is exacerbated by the way they were also denied automatic promotion on the final day of the regular season.

MK Dons and Preston are two who should improve enough to enter the promotion picture, with narrow preference at the prices for **Preston**, who look a decent each-way bet for the title at 16-1.

They pulled off a major coup when getting Simon Grayson as their new manager given he has achieved promotion from this division with all three of his previous clubs, most recently Huddersfield in 2012.

It would have been reasonable to expect significant improvement anyway, as the squad was hastily put together by former boss Graham Westley last summer and was always likely to need longer to gel.

Those of a more cautious nature can take the safer route of backing **Preston** for a top-six finish at 13-8 with BetVictor.

MK Dons never really got going last season but were let down by injuries, notably key man Stephen Gleeson. And, having been prone to defensive howlers for much

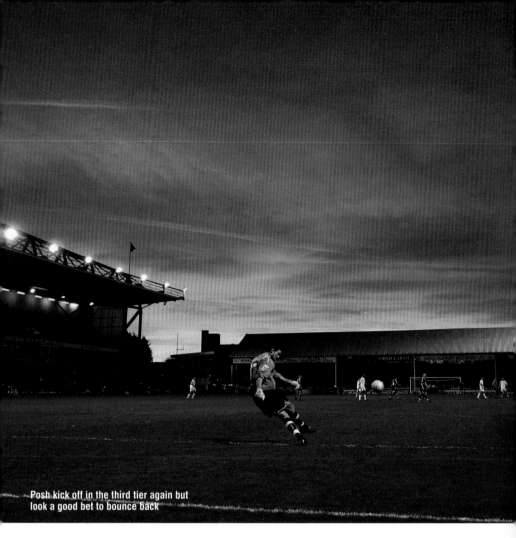

Posh kick off in the third tier again but look a good bet to bounce back

of the season, the rearguard improved markedly as players returned towards the end of the campaign.

They should be set for a better campaign in 2013-14 and 6-4 (BetFred) about a top-six finish is worth taking.

The division looks to have a lot of strength in depth this season with all four promoted clubs capable of doing well.

That means those who were close to the drop last season will probably have to improve just to avoid falling through the trap door, while it would be no surprise to see some teams plummet down the standings.

Colchester certainly look justifiably short for the drop despite showing signs of progress under Joe Dunne, while Carlisle have also been fairly identified among the most likely candidates.

However, at a more appealing price of 7-1 with Ladbrokes, it would be no surprise to see **Swindon** find themselves in trouble and they look the best value bet for relegation.

Despite reaching the play-offs and only losing to Brentford on penalties, they were already in decline at the end of last season, picking up 19 points from their final 15 matches after losing manager Paolo Di Canio and star man Matt Ritchie.

And, with their new owner announcing plans to halve the wage bill, the departures have kept on coming, including that of captain Alan McCormack, who refused a new deal to join Brentford, and key defender Aden Flint, who has signed for Bristol City.

Bradford City

Nickname: The Bantams
Colours: Claret and amber
Ground: Coral Windows Stadium (25,136)
Tel: 01274 773 355   www.bradfordcityfc.co.uk

Bradford won the League 2 play-offs despite finishing the regular season only seventh, but they were certainly well worth their place in the third tier.

In fact, Bradford proved their ability to compete at a higher level when knocking out Arsenal, Aston Villa and Wigan in a sensational run to the League Cup final.

And, despite understandably taking their eye off the ball with a run of two wins in 14 around that time, they did well to get back in the promotion mix before a 3-0 win over Northampton at Wembley secured their return to League 1.

Longest run without win/loss: 6/6
High/low league position: 4/12
Clean sheets: 18 **Yellow cards:** 42 **Red cards:** 3
Average attendance: 10,322 **Players used:** 28
Leading scorer: N Wells 18 (8,14)
Key stat: Bradford won just five out of 22 matches against top-half opposition last season

	2012-13		Last six seasons at home							
	H	A	P	W	D	L	OV	UN	BS	CS
Peterborough			1	1	0	0	0	1	0	1
Wolves	-	-	-	-	-	-	-	-	-	-
Bristol City	-	-	-	-	-	-	-	-	-	-
Brentford			2	0	1	1	1	1	2	0
Sheffield United	-	-	-	-	-	-	-	-	-	-
Swindon			1	0	1	0	0	1	0	1
Leyton Orient	-	-	-	-	-	-	-	-	-	-
MK Dons			1	0	0	1	1	0	1	0
Walsall	-	-	-	-	-	-	-	-	-	-
Crawley Town			1	0	0	1	1	0	1	0
Tranmere	-	-	-	-	-	-	-	-	-	-
Notts County			3	2	1	0	2	1	1	2
Crewe			3	1	0	2	3	0	2	1
Preston	-	-	-	-	-	-	-	-	-	-
Coventry	-	-	-	-	-	-	-	-	-	-
Shrewsbury			5	2	1	2	4	1	4	1
Carlisle	-	-	-	-	-	-	-	-	-	-
Stevenage			1	1	0	0	0	1	0	1
Oldham	-	-	-	-	-	-	-	-	-	-
Colchester	-	-	-	-	-	-	-	-	-	-
Gillingham	L	L	4	1	2	1	2	2	2	1
Rotherham	L	L	6	3	0	3	5	1	4	1
Port Vale	L	D	5	0	2	3	0	5	1	1
Bradford										

Season	Division	Pos	P	W	D	L	F	A	GD	Pts
2012-13	League 2	7	46	18	15	13	63	52	+11	69
2011-12	League 2	18	46	12	14	20	54	59	-5	50
2010-11	League 2	18	46	15	17	24	43	68	-25	52

Over/Under 43%/57% 17th   **Both score** 46%/54% 15th

Brentford

Nickname: The Bees
Colours: Red
Ground: Griffin Park (12,763)
Tel: 0845 3456 442   www.brentfordfc.co.uk

No team in the Football League endured such a heartbreaking end to the season as Brentford, who were a missed stoppage-time penalty away from automatic promotion and then blew their chance of redemption when losing to Yeovil in the play-off final.

In the running for promotion all season, only a modest late run of form denied the Bees as they perhaps paid the price for a fixture backlog caused by playing four FA Cup matches from January onwards.

However, that run did show their quality as Brentford held Chelsea at Griffin Park.

Longest run without win/loss: 4/13
High/low league position: 2/12
Clean sheets: 15 **Yellow cards:** 75 **Red cards:** 5
Average attendance: 6,302 **Players used:** 29
Leading scorer: C Donaldson 18 (6,14)
Key stat: Brentford won 15 matches by a single goal last season

	2012-13		Last six seasons at home							
	H	A	P	W	D	L	OV	UN	BS	CS
Peterborough			2	1	0	1	2	0	2	0
Wolves	-	-	-	-	-	-	-	-	-	-
Bristol City	-	-	-	-	-	-	-	-	-	-
Brentford										
Sheffield United	W	D	2	1	0	1	0	2	0	1
Swindon	W	W	3	1	0	2	2	1	2	0
Leyton Orient	D	L	4	3	1	0	3	1	2	2
MK Dons	W	L	5	1	2	2	4	1	3	0
Walsall	D	D	4	0	3	1	1	3	2	2
Crawley Town	W	W	1	1	0	0	1	0	1	0
Tranmere	L	D	4	2	0	2	3	1	3	0
Notts County	W	W	5	1	4	0	1	4	3	2
Crewe	W	W	1	1	0	0	1	0	1	0
Preston	W	D	2	1	0	1	1	1	1	1
Coventry	W	D	1	1	0	0	1	0	1	0
Shrewsbury	D	D	3	0	3	0	0	3	2	1
Carlisle	W	L	4	4	0	0	4	0	3	1
Stevenage	W	L	2	1	0	1	0	2	0	1
Oldham	W	W	4	2	1	1	3	2	2	2
Colchester	W	W	4	2	2	0	0	4	2	2
Gillingham			2	1	1	0	1	1	1	1
Rotherham			2	0	2	0	0	2	1	1
Port Vale			1	1	0	0	0	1	0	1
Bradford			2	1	1	0	2	0	2	0

Season	Division	Pos	P	W	D	L	F	A	GD	Pts
2012-13	League 1	3	46	21	16	9	62	47	+15	79
2011-12	League 1	9	46	18	13	15	63	52	+11	67
2010-11	League 1	11	46	17	10	19	55	62	-7	61

Over/Under 46%/54% 11th   **Both score** 54%/46% 9th

Bristol City

In such a tight division as last season's Championship, it doesn't bode well for Bristol City that they were the only team cut adrift at the bottom.

The Robins went down with a whimper, winning just one of their last 12 games to be relegated with 41 points (ten behind second-bottom Wolves), despite a brief improvement when Sean O'Driscoll replaced Derek McInnes in January.

Losses of £41m over the last four years will make things particularly tough for City, with managing director Jon Lansdown promising departures.

Longest run without win/loss: 11/4
High/low league position: 10/24
Clean sheets: 6 **Yellow cards:** 50 **Red cards:** 0
Average attendance: 13,348 **Players used:** 35
Leading scorer: S Davies 13 (4,12)
Key stat: Bristol City didn't record a single 1-0 win all season in 2012-13

	2012-13 H	A	P	W	D	L	OV	UN	BS	CS
Peterborough	W	W	3	1	1	1	2	1	3	0
Wolves	L	L	3	0	2	1	2	1	2	1
Bristol City										
Brentford			-	-	-	-	-	-	-	-
Sheffield United			4	2	1	1	2	2	1	3
Swindon			-	-	-	-	-	-	-	-
Leyton Orient			-	-	-	-	-	-	-	-
MK Dons			-	-	-	-	-	-	-	-
Walsall			-	-	-	-	-	-	-	-
Crawley Town			-	-	-	-	-	-	-	-
Tranmere			-	-	-	-	-	-	-	-
Notts County			-	-	-	-	-	-	-	-
Crewe			-	-	-	-	-	-	-	-
Preston			4	2	2	0	2	2	3	1
Coventry			5	3	1	1	3	2	4	1
Shrewsbury			-	-	-	-	-	-	-	-
Carlisle			-	-	-	-	-	-	-	-
Stevenage			-	-	-	-	-	-	-	-
Oldham			-	-	-	-	-	-	-	-
Colchester			1	0	1	0	0	1	1	0
Gillingham			-	-	-	-	-	-	-	-
Rotherham			-	-	-	-	-	-	-	-
Port Vale			-	-	-	-	-	-	-	-
Bradford			-	-	-	-	-	-	-	-

Season	Division	Pos	P	W	D	L	F	A	GD	Pts
2012-13	Championship	24	46	11	8	27	59	84	-25	41
2011-12	Championship	20	46	12	13	21	44	68	-24	49
2010-11	Championship	15	46	17	9	20	62	65	-3	60

Over/Under 54%/46% 8th   **Both score** 59%/41% 11th

Carlisle United

Brunton Park was the place for entertainment last season, as there were 75 goals there – but the home fans won't have enjoyed many of them.

Carlisle finished the campaign with the worst defensive record in the division as they fell well short of the level reached in the previous three seasons which had seen them twice reach the Johnstone's Paint Trophy final.

Things at least picked up slightly in the spring as they lost just two of their last eight matches to finish seven points clear of the drop zone.

Longest run without win/loss: 6/6
High/low league position: 10/19
Clean sheets: 7 **Yellow cards:** 61 **Red cards:** 3
Average attendance: 4,302 **Players used:** 31
Leading scorer: L Miller 9 (1,7)
Key stat: Carlisle hit the woodwork 23 times last season – the most in League 1

	2012-13 H	A	P	W	D	L	OV	UN	BS	CS
Peterborough			2	0	1	1	1	1	1	0
Wolves			-	-	-	-	-	-	-	-
Bristol City										
Brentford	W	L	4	2	1	1	2	2	2	2
Sheffield United	L	D	2	1	0	1	2	0	2	0
Swindon	D	L	5	1	3	1	2	3	2	2
Leyton Orient	L	L	5	3	1	1	4	1	4	1
MK Dons	D	L	5	3	1	1	4	1	4	1
Walsall	L	W	6	1	3	2	3	3	5	0
Crawley Town	L	D	1	0	0	1	0	1	0	0
Tranmere	L	W	6	2	1	3	3	3	1	3
Notts County	L	L	3	1	0	2	2	1	0	1
Crewe	D	L	3	2	1	0	1	2	1	2
Preston	D	D	2	0	2	0	0	2	1	1
Coventry	W	W	1	1	0	0	0	1	0	1
Shrewsbury	W	L	1	0	1	0	1	0	1	0
Carlisle										
Stevenage	W	D	2	2	0	0	1	1	1	1
Oldham	W	W	6	2	3	1	4	2	5	1
Colchester	L	L	5	3	0	2	2	3	2	1
Gillingham			2	2	0	0	0	2	0	2
Rotherham			-	-	-	-	-	-	-	-
Port Vale			1	1	0	0	1	0	1	0
Bradford			-	-	-	-	-	-	-	-

Season	Division	Pos	P	W	D	L	F	A	GD	Pts
2012-13	League 1	17	46	14	13	19	56	77	-21	55
2011-12	League 1	8	46	18	15	13	65	66	-1	69
2010-11	League 1	12	46	16	11	19	60	62	-2	59

Over/Under 57%/43% 3rd   **Both score** 63%/37% 1st

Colchester United

Nickname: The U's
Colours: Blue and white
Ground: Weston Homes Stadium (10,105)
Tel: 01206 508 800   www.cu-fc.com

After a miserable start to 2012-13, survival was a considerable achievement for Colchester last season.

It was always likely the U's would slide towards trouble after repeatedly being forced to slash their playing budget in recent years, and their average attendance stayed the fifth-lowest in League 1.

However, after John Ward was sacked in September, with just four points taken from their first eight matches, Colchester improved enough under his former assistant Joe Dunne to secure their safety with a final-day 2-0 success at Carlisle.

Longest run without win/loss: 9/4
High/low league position: 12/22
Clean sheets: 13 **Yellow cards:** 75 **Red cards:** 4
Average attendance: 3,529 **Players used:** 37
Leading scorer: J Ibehre 8 (2,6)
Key stat: Colchester lost 14 of the 15 matches in which they trailed at half-time

| | 2012-13 | | Last six seasons at home | | | | | | | |
	H	A	P	W	D	L	OV	UN	BS	CS
Peterborough			2	1	0	1	1	1	1	0
Wolves			1	0	0	1	0	1	0	0
Bristol City			1	0	0	1	1	0	1	0
Brentford	L	L	4	1	1	2	3	1	3	0
Sheffield United	D	L	3	0	3	0	1	2	3	0
Swindon	L	W	4	3	0	1	3	1	2	1
Leyton Orient	W	W	5	4	1	0	2	3	3	2
MK Dons	L	L	5	1	0	4	3	2	2	1
Walsall	W	L	5	4	0	1	1	4	1	3
Crawley Town	D	L	1	0	1	0	0	1	1	0
Tranmere	L	L	5	2	1	2	3	2	4	0
Notts County	L	L	3	2	0	1	2	1	2	0
Crewe	L	L	2	0	0	2	1	1	1	0
Preston	W	D	3	3	0	0	2	1	1	2
Coventry	L	D	2	0	0	2	2	0	2	0
Shrewsbury	D	D	1	0	1	0	0	1	0	1
Carlisle	W	W	5	3	2	0	2	3	3	2
Stevenage	W	W	2	1	0	1	1	1	1	1
Oldham	L	D	5	3	1	1	2	3	2	2
Colchester										
Gillingham			1	1	0	0	1	0	1	0
Rotherham			-	-	-	-	-	-	-	-
Port Vale			-	-	-	-	-	-	-	-
Bradford			-	-	-	-	-	-	-	-

Season	Division	Pos	P	W	D	L	F	A	GD	Pts
2012-13	League 1	20	46	14	9	23	47	68	-21	51
2011-12	League 1	10	46	13	20	13	61	66	-5	59
2010-11	League 1	10	46	16	14	16	57	63	-6	62

Over/Under 43%/57% 15th   **Both score** 43%/57% 19th

Coventry City

Nickname: The Sky Blues
Colours: Sky blue
Ground: Ricoh Arena (32,604)
Tel: 0870 421 1987   www.ccfc.co.uk

Perhaps you'd be better off asking a finance expert rather than a football writer to assess Coventry's prospects.

For what it's worth, their performance on the pitch was pretty good last season – without a ten-point deduction, and despite taking two points from their last five games once that punishment ended their play-off hopes, Coventry would have been just nine points off the top six.

However they lost gaffer Mark Robins halfway through the season and his replacement, Steven Pressley, spent the start of the summer trimming his squad.

Longest run without win/loss: 8/8
High/low league position: 8/24
Clean sheets: 9 **Yellow cards:** 72 **Red cards:** 1
Average attendance: 10,948 **Players used:** 37
Leading scorer: D Mcgoldrick 16 (5,12)
Key stat: Coventry lost 33 points from winning positions last season

| | 2012-13 | | Last six seasons at home | | | | | | | |
	H	A	P	W	D	L	OV	UN	BS	CS
Peterborough			2	1	1	0	2	0	2	0
Wolves			2	1	1	0	1	1	2	0
Bristol City			5	1	1	3	3	2	2	1
Brentford	D	L	1	0	1	0	0	1	1	0
Sheffield United	D	W	5	1	2	2	2	3	3	1
Swindon	L	D	1	0	0	1	1	0	1	0
Leyton Orient	L	W	1	0	0	1	0	1	0	0
MK Dons	D	W	1	0	1	0	0	1	1	0
Walsall	W	L	1	1	0	0	1	0	1	0
Crawley Town	W	L	1	1	0	0	1	0	1	0
Tranmere	W	L	1	1	0	0	0	1	0	1
Notts County	L	D	1	0	0	1	1	0	1	0
Crewe	L	L	1	0	0	1	1	0	1	0
Preston	D	D	5	1	3	1	2	3	4	1
Coventry										
Shrewsbury	L	L	1	0	0	1	0	1	0	0
Carlisle	L	L	1	0	0	1	1	0	1	0
Stevenage	L	W	1	0	0	1	1	0	1	0
Oldham	W	W	1	1	0	0	1	0	1	0
Colchester	D	W	2	1	1	0	1	1	1	1
Gillingham			-	-	-	-	-	-	-	-
Rotherham			-	-	-	-	-	-	-	-
Port Vale			-	-	-	-	-	-	-	-
Bradford			-	-	-	-	-	-	-	-

Season	Division	Pos	P	W	D	L	F	A	GD	Pts
2012-13	League 1	15	46	18	11	17	66	59	+7	55
2011-12	Championship	23	46	9	13	24	41	65	-24	40
2010-11	Championship	18	46	14	13	19	54	58	-4	55

Over/Under 52%/48% 5th   **Both score** 61%/39% 2nd

Crawley Town

Nickname: The Red Devils
Colours: Red and white
Ground: Broadfield Stadium (5,973)
Tel: 01293 410002   www.crawleytownfc.com

Crawley's recent rise has been meteoric, with the Red Devils achieving back-to-back promotions to reach League 1, but last season was much more tricky.

At least they were never in danger of an immediate return to League 2, which was no mean feat after a troubled summer which saw Sean O'Driscoll last less than two months as manager.

However, they were put up for sale in March after Crawley's owners realised they didn't have the funds to take the club to the next level and things will be tough with such a low average attendance.

Longest run without win/loss: 7/7
High/low league position: 3/15
Clean sheets: 15 **Yellow cards:** 58 **Red cards:** 5
Average attendance: 3,408 **Players used:** 30
Leading scorer: B Clarke 10 (5,9)
Key stat: Crawley won ten of the 11 matches in which they led at half-time

	2012-13 H	2012-13 A	P	W	D	L	OV	UN	BS	CS
Peterborough			-	-	-	-	-	-	-	-
Wolves			-	-	-	-	-	-	-	-
Bristol City			-	-	-	-	-	-	-	-
Brentford	L	L	1	0	0	1	1	0	1	0
Sheffield United	L	W	1	0	0	1	0	1	0	0
Swindon	D	L	2	0	1	1	1	1	1	0
Leyton Orient	W	W	1	1	0	0	0	1	0	1
MK Dons	W	D	1	1	0	0	0	1	0	1
Walsall	D	D	1	0	1	0	1	0	1	0
Crawley Town										
Tranmere	L	L	1	0	0	1	1	0	1	0
Notts County	D	D	1	0	1	0	0	1	0	1
Crewe	W	L	2	1	1	0	0	2	1	1
Preston	W	W	1	1	0	0	0	1	0	1
Coventry	W	L	1	1	0	0	0	1	0	1
Shrewsbury	D	L	2	1	1	0	2	0	2	0
Carlisle	D	W	1	0	1	0	0	1	1	0
Stevenage	D	W	4	1	1	2	2	2	2	0
Oldham	D	L	1	0	1	0	1	0	1	0
Colchester	W	D	1	1	0	0	1	0	0	1
Gillingham			1	0	0	1	1	0	1	0
Rotherham			1	1	0	0	1	0	0	1
Port Vale			1	1	0	0	1	0	1	0
Bradford			1	1	0	0	1	0	1	0

Season	Division	Pos	P	W	D	L	F	A	GD	Pts
2012-13	League 1	10	46	18	14	14	59	58	+1	68
2010-11	Conference	1	46	31	12	3	93	30	+63	105

Over/Under 48%/52% 10th   **Both score** 50%/50% 13th

Crewe Alexandra

Nickname: The Railwaymen
Colours: Red and white
Ground: The Alexandra Stadium (10,109)
Tel: 01270 213 014   www.crewealex.net

It was a fairytale campaign for Crewe – they did well to finish in mid-table after going up via the play-offs and enjoyed another amazing day at Wembley when lifting the Johnstone's Paint Trophy.

Steve Davis has carried on the work of his legendary predecessor Dario Gradi and their final-day win when fielding a team of 11 academy graduates (at an average age of 21) typified their approach.

The Railwaymen relied heavily on their home form but should improve on the road as their young squad grows in stature and experience.

Longest run without win/loss: 6/5
High/low league position: 10/19
Clean sheets: 11 **Yellow cards:** 40 **Red cards:** 1
Average attendance: 4,903 **Players used:** 29
Leading scorer: M Pogba 12 (1,11)
Key stat: Crewe won five times after falling behind last season

	2012-13 H	2012-13 A	P	W	D	L	OV	UN	BS	CS
Peterborough			1	0	1	0	0	1	1	0
Wolves			-	-	-	-	-	-	-	-
Bristol City			-	-	-	-	-	-	-	-
Brentford	L	L	1	0	0	1	0	1	0	0
Sheffield United	W	D	1	1	0	0	0	1	0	1
Swindon	W	L	4	3	1	0	1	3	1	3
Leyton Orient	D	D	3	0	1	0	1	3	1	3
MK Dons	W	L	2	1	1	0	2	0	2	0
Walsall	W	D	3	2	1	0	1	2	1	2
Crawley Town	W	L	2	1	1	0	0	2	1	1
Tranmere	D	L	3	2	1	0	2	1	2	1
Notts County	L	D	2	0	0	2	1	1	1	0
Crewe										
Preston	W	W	1	1	0	0	0	1	0	1
Coventry	W	W	1	1	0	0	0	1	0	1
Shrewsbury	D	L	4	0	2	2	2	2	3	0
Carlisle	W	D	3	1	0	2	1	2	1	1
Stevenage	L	D	2	0	0	2	1	1	1	0
Oldham	L	W	3	0	0	3	2	1	1	0
Colchester	W	W	2	2	0	0	1	1	1	1
Gillingham			3	0	1	2	2	1	3	0
Rotherham			3	0	0	3	2	1	2	0
Port Vale			4	1	1	2	2	2	3	0
Bradford			3	2	0	1	2	1	2	1

Season	Division	Pos	P	W	D	L	F	A	GD	Pts
2012-13	League 1	13	46	18	10	18	54	62	-8	64
2011-12	League 2	7	46	20	12	14	67	59	+8	72
2010-11	League 2	10	46	18	11	17	87	65	+22	65

Over/Under 50%/50% 8th   **Both score** 57%/43% 5th

Gillingham

Nickname: The Gills
Colours: Blue and white
Ground: Priestfield Stadium (11,440)
Tel: 01634 300000 www.gillinghamfootballclub.com

Having just missed out on the play-offs in each of the previous two seasons, Gillingham left no margin for error last term and wrapped up promotion on the first weekend in April.

It was a magnificent achievement in Martin Allen's first season at the helm, and the Gills went on to amass 83 points.

League 2 champions have gone on to finish in the top half of League 1 the following year for eight of the last 12 seasons, which bodes well. However, the fact that Allen tends to have only a short-term impact as a manager is a slight concern.

Longest run without win/loss: 3/9
High/low league position: 1/2
Clean sheets: 18 **Yellow cards:** 57 **Red cards:** 6
Average attendance: 6,601 **Players used:** 36
Leading scorer: D Kedwell 14 (5,12)
Key stat: It's 67 matches since Gillingham last lost a league match by more than a single goal

	2012-13 H	A	Last six seasons at home P	W	D	L	OV	UN	BS	CS
Peterborough	-	-	-	-	-	-	-	-	-	-
Wolves	-	-	-	-	-	-	-	-	-	-
Bristol City	-	-	-	-	-	-	-	-	-	-
Brentford			2	0	1	1	0	2	1	0
Sheffield United	-	-	-	-	-	-	-	-	-	-
Swindon			3	2	1	0	2	1	2	1
Leyton Orient			2	1	1	0	1	1	2	0
MK Dons			1	0	1	0	1	0	1	0
Walsall			2	1	1	0	1	1	1	1
Crawley Town			1	0	0	1	0	1	0	0
Tranmere			2	0	0	2	0	2	0	0
Notts County			1	0	1	0	1	0	1	0
Crewe			3	0	0	3	3	0	2	0
Preston	-	-	-	-	-	-	-	-	-	-
Coventry	-	-	-	-	-	-	-	-	-	-
Shrewsbury			3	1	1	1	1	2	1	1
Carlisle			2	0	2	0	0	2	0	2
Stevenage			1	1	0	0	0	1	0	1
Oldham			2	1	1	0	0	1	0	1
Colchester			1	0	1	0	0	1	0	1
Gillingham										
Rotherham	W	W	4	3	1	0	2	2	1	3
Port Vale	L	W	5	2	1	2	3	2	3	2
Bradford	W	W	4	2	1	1	1	3	1	2

Season	Division	Pos	P	W	D	L	F	A	GD	Pts
2012-13	League 2	1	46	23	14	9	66	39	+27	83
2011-12	League 2	8	46	20	10	16	79	62	+17	70
2010-11	League 2	8	46	17	17	12	67	57	+10	68

Over/Under 43%/57% 17th   **Both score** 52%/48% 7th

Leyton Orient

Nickname: The O's
Colours: Red
Ground: Matchroom Stadium (9,311)
Tel: 0871 310 1881   www.leytonorient.com

Orient chairman Barry Hearn spent much of the last campaign warning of the dire consequences for his club when West Ham move into the Olympic Stadium.

However, the O's went from strength to strength on the pitch as a strong late run – 24 points from their final 12 matches – took them close to the play-offs.

It's now two seventh-place finishes in three seasons for Leyton Orient, but they plummeted to 20th in between and will be lucky to repeat last season's haul of 12 single-goal victories compared to just eight draws.

Longest run without win/loss: 4/7
High/low league position: 7/20
Clean sheets: 14 **Yellow cards:** 73 **Red cards:** 1
Average attendance: 4,001 **Players used:** 29
Leading scorer: K Lisbie 16 (3,13)
Key stat: Leyton Orient picked up just three points from losing positions last season

	2012-13 H	A	Last six seasons at home P	W	D	L	OV	UN	BS	CS
Peterborough			2	1	0	1	2	0	2	0
Wolves	-	-	-	-	-	-	-	-	-	-
Bristol City	-	-	-	-	-	-	-	-	-	-
Brentford	W	D	4	4	0	0	1	3	1	3
Sheffield United	L	D	2	0	1	1	0	2	1	0
Swindon	D	W	5	2	2	1	3	2	2	3
Leyton Orient										
MK Dons	W	L	5	1	1	3	4	1	3	1
Walsall	W	W	6	3	2	1	1	5	2	3
Crawley Town	L	L	1	0	0	1	0	1	0	0
Tranmere	W	W	6	3	0	3	4	2	2	1
Notts County	W	D	3	2	0	1	2	1	1	1
Crewe	D	D	3	1	1	1	0	3	1	1
Preston	W	D	2	2	0	0	1	1	1	1
Coventry	L	W	1	0	0	1	0	1	0	0
Shrewsbury	W	W	1	1	0	0	1	0	1	0
Carlisle	W	W	6	1	3	2	4	2	3	2
Stevenage	L	W	2	0	1	1	0	2	0	1
Oldham	D	L	6	3	1	2	3	3	4	2
Colchester	L	L	5	2	0	3	2	3	2	0
Gillingham			2	1	1	0	1	1	1	1
Rotherham	-	-	-	-	-	-	-	-	-	-
Port Vale			1	1	0	0	1	0	1	0
Bradford	-	-	-	-	-	-	-	-	-	-

Season	Division	Pos	P	W	D	L	F	A	GD	Pts
2012-13	League 1	7	46	21	8	17	55	48	+7	71
2011-12	League 1	20	46	13	11	22	48	75	-27	50
2010-11	League 1	7	46	19	13	14	71	62	+9	70

Over/Under 37%/63% 20th   **Both score** 43%/57% 19th

MK Dons

Nickname: The Dons
Colours: White
Ground: stadium:mk (22,233)
Tel: 01908 622 922   www.mkdons.co.uk

The Dons began 2012-13 hoping to take the next step after reaching the play-offs in the previous two seasons, but instead suffered a disappointing drop backwards.

Ultimately they were just four points off another top-six finish, but MK Dons were never seriously in the promotion running and only got close after a decent end to the campaign in which they picked up 19 points from their final ten matches.

Injuries and indiscipline played their part and highly rated boss Karl Robinson has stuck around for another crack after turning down talks at Sheffield United.

Longest run without win/loss: 8/7
High/low league position: 3/13
Clean sheets: 20 **Yellow cards:** 62 **Red cards:** 6
Average attendance: 8,611 **Players used:** 32
Leading scorer: R Lowe 11 (4,10)
Key stat: MK Dons failed to win a single match after falling behind last season

	2012-13 H	2012-13 A	P	W	D	L	OV	UN	BS	CS
Peterborough			3	1	1	1	1	2	2	1
Wolves			-	-	-	-	-	-	-	-
Bristol City			-	-	-	-	-	-	-	-
Brentford	W	L	5	1	2	2	1	4	3	1
Sheffield United	W	D	2	2	0	0	2	0	0	2
Swindon	W	L	4	3	0	1	3	1	3	1
Leyton Orient	W	L	5	3	0	2	3	2	3	2
MK Dons										
Walsall	L	L	5	1	1	3	1	4	2	1
Crawley Town	D	L	1	0	1	0	0	1	0	1
Tranmere	W	W	5	5	0	0	2	3	0	5
Notts County	D	W	4	3	1	0	3	1	2	2
Crewe	W	L	2	1	1	0	1	1	1	1
Preston	D	D	2	0	1	1	0	2	1	0
Coventry	L	D	1	0	0	1	1	0	1	0
Shrewsbury	L	D	2	1	0	1	2	0	1	1
Carlisle	W	D	5	3	0	2	4	1	4	1
Stevenage	L	W	2	1	0	1	0	2	0	1
Oldham	W	L	5	3	2	0	2	3	1	4
Colchester	W	W	5	3	2	0	2	3	4	1
Gillingham			1	1	0	0	0	1	0	1
Rotherham			1	0	1	0	0	1	1	0
Port Vale			-	-	-	-	-	-	-	-
Bradford			1	1	0	0	1	0	1	0

Season	Division	Pos	P	W	D	L	F	A	GD	Pts
2012-13	League 1	8	46	19	13	14	62	45	+17	70
2011-12	League 1	5	46	22	14	10	84	47	+37	80
2010-11	League 1	5	46	23	8	15	67	60	+7	77

Over/Under 35%/65% 23rd   **Both score** 41%/59% 21st

Notts County

Nickname: The Magpies
Colours: Black and white
Ground: Meadow Lane (20,280)
Tel: 0115 952 9000   www.nottscountyfc.co.uk

Much was expected of Notts County last season and Keith Curle was perhaps a victim of high expectations when he was sacked in February with the club just five points outside the play-offs.

Chairman Ray Trew expressed his concern at dwindling attendances but should perhaps look more at a lack of stability as Chris Kiwomya became the club's eighth permanent manager since October 2009.

Kiwomya sought to make County hard to beat and under him the team conceded more than two goals just twice in 13 games against sides outside the top four.

Longest run without win/loss: 5/7
High/low league position: 2/14
Clean sheets: 15 **Yellow cards:** 81 **Red cards:** 7
Average attendance: 5,521 **Players used:** 34
Leading scorer: J Campbell-Ryce 8 (1,8) A Judge 8 (2,8)
Key stat: County won just two of 22 games against teams who finished in the top half

	2012-13 H	2012-13 A	P	W	D	L	OV	UN	BS	CS
Peterborough			2	0	0	2	0	2	0	0
Wolves			-	-	-	-	-	-	-	-
Bristol City			-	-	-	-	-	-	-	-
Brentford	L	L	5	0	4	1	1	4	5	0
Sheffield United	D	D	2	0	1	1	1	1	2	0
Swindon	W	D	2	2	0	0	2	0	2	0
Leyton Orient	D	L	3	1	1	1	2	1	3	0
MK Dons	L	D	4	1	1	2	2	2	3	1
Walsall	L	D	3	1	1	1	1	2	2	0
Crawley Town	D	D	1	0	1	0	0	1	1	0
Tranmere	L	D	3	1	0	2	1	2	1	0
Notts County										
Crewe	D	W	2	1	1	0	0	2	1	1
Preston	L	D	2	0	1	1	0	2	0	1
Coventry	W	W	1	0	1	0	1	0	1	0
Shrewsbury	W	D	4	2	2	0	3	1	4	0
Carlisle	W	W	3	2	0	1	0	3	0	2
Stevenage	L	L	2	1	0	1	1	1	1	1
Oldham	W	D	3	2	0	1	0	3	0	2
Colchester	W	W	3	3	0	0	2	1	2	1
Gillingham			1	0	0	1	0	1	0	0
Rotherham			3	1	0	2	1	2	0	1
Port Vale			2	2	0	0	2	0	0	0
Bradford			3	2	0	1	3	0	2	1

Season	Division	Pos	P	W	D	L	F	A	GD	Pts
2012-13	League 1	12	46	16	17	13	61	49	+12	65
2011-12	League 1	7	46	21	10	15	75	63	+12	73
2010-11	League 1	19	46	14	8	24	46	60	-14	50

Over/Under 43%/57% 15th   **Both score** 57%/43% 5th

Oldham Athletic

Nickname: The Latics
Colours: Blue
Ground: Boundary Park (10,850)
Tel: 08712 262 235   www.oldhamathletic.co.uk

Paul Dickov was subject to one of the harsher sackings of last season, though Oldham will feel justified at the move as his replacement, Lee Johnson, kept the Latics up following a relegation scare.

Dickov would probably have achieved the same as the club's league form had only really suffered during the FA Cup heroics that saw them knock out Liverpool and draw with Everton.

The mission for Johnson – 32-year-old son of Yeovil boss Gary – is to try and match Dickov's success on what remains a shoestring budget at Boundary Park.

Longest run without win/loss: 9/4
High/low league position: 16/21
Clean sheets: 9 **Yellow cards:** 92 **Red cards:** 5
Average attendance: 4,128 **Players used:** 34
Leading scorer: J Baxter 13 (5,12)
Key stat: Oldham lost 14 matches by a single goal

	2012-13 H	A	Last six seasons at home P	W	D	L	OV	UN	BS	CS
Peterborough			2	0	0	2	2	0	1	0
Wolves			-	-	-	-	-	-	-	-
Bristol City			-	-	-	-	-	-	-	-
Brentford	L	L	4	1	0	3	2	2	2	0
Sheffield United	L	D	2	0	0	2	0	2	0	0
Swindon	L	D	5	1	3	1	2	3	2	2
Leyton Orient	W	D	6	3	2	1	0	6	2	3
MK Dons	W	L	5	4	0	1	4	1	4	1
Walsall	D	L	6	3	2	1	2	4	4	1
Crawley Town	W	D	1	1	0	0	1	0	1	0
Tranmere	L	L	6	2	2	2	1	5	1	3
Notts County	D	L	3	2	1	0	3	0	2	1
Crewe	L	W	3	1	1	1	2	1	3	0
Preston	W	L	2	1	1	0	1	1	2	0
Coventry	L	L	1	0	0	1	0	1	0	0
Shrewsbury	L	L	1	1	0	0	0	1	0	1
Carlisle	L	L	6	3	1	2	2	4	2	3
Stevenage	L	W	2	0	1	1	0	2	1	0
Oldham										
Colchester	D	W	5	0	4	1	1	4	3	1
Gillingham			2	2	0	0	1	1	1	1
Rotherham			-	-	-	-	-	-	-	-
Port Vale			1	0	1	0	0	1	1	0
Bradford			-	-	-	-	-	-	-	-

Season	Division	Pos	P	W	D	L	F	A	GD	Pts
2012-13	League 1	19	46	14	9	23	46	59	-13	51
2011-12	League 1	16	46	14	12	20	50	66	-16	54
2010-11	League 1	17	46	13	17	16	53	60	-7	56

Over/Under 37%/63% 20th   **Both score** 50%/50% 13th

Peterborough Utd

Nickname: The Posh
Colours: Blue
Ground: London Road (11,494)
Tel: 01733 563 947   www.theposh.com

It seems incredible that Peterborough start this season in League 1 when their form in the second half of 2012-13 would have seen them firmly in the hunt for promotion to the Premier League.

The Posh paid for a rotten start that saw them collect just 13 points from their first 21 matches, though even then their eventual haul of 54 was more than every other team relegated from the Championship in the last 20 years.

Darren Ferguson has twice led Peterborough to promotion from this division and they are among the favourites again.

Longest run without win/loss: 8/10
High/low league position: 20/24
Clean sheets: 8 **Yellow cards:** 56 **Red cards:** 1
Average attendance: 8,215 **Players used:** 31
Leading scorer: D Gayle 13 (2,10)
Key stat: Peterborough averaged 1.64 points over last 25 matches – enough for 75 points over the full course of a season

	2012-13 H	A	Last six seasons at home P	W	D	L	OV	UN	BS	CS
Peterborough										
Wolves	L	W	1	0	0	1	0	1	0	0
Bristol City	L	L	3	1	0	2	2	1	1	1
Brentford			2	2	0	0	2	0	1	1
Sheffield United			1	1	0	0	0	1	0	1
Swindon			2	1	1	0	2	0	2	0
Leyton Orient			2	1	1	0	2	0	1	1
MK Dons			3	1	1	1	2	1	2	1
Walsall			2	2	0	0	1	1	1	1
Crawley Town			-	-	-	-	-	-	-	-
Tranmere			2	1	1	0	2	0	2	0
Notts County			2	0	1	1	1	1	1	1
Crewe			1	1	0	0	1	0	1	0
Preston			1	0	0	1	0	1	0	0
Coventry			2	1	0	1	0	2	0	1
Shrewsbury			1	1	0	0	1	0	1	0
Carlisle			2	2	0	0	1	1	0	2
Stevenage			-	-	-	-	-	-	-	-
Oldham			2	1	1	0	2	0	2	0
Colchester			2	1	1	0	1	1	2	0
Gillingham			-	-	-	-	-	-	-	-
Rotherham			1	1	0	0	1	0	1	0
Port Vale			-	-	-	-	-	-	-	-
Bradford			1	1	0	0	1	0	1	0

Season	Division	Pos	P	W	D	L	F	A	GD	Pts
2012-13	Championship	22	46	15	9	22	66	75	-9	54
2011-12	Championship	18	46	13	11	22	67	77	-10	50
2010-11	League 1	4	46	23	10	13	106	75	+31	79

Over/Under 61%/39% 3rd   **Both score** 63%/37% 3rd

Port Vale

Nickname: The Valiants
Colours: White and black
Ground: Vale Park (19,148)
Tel: 01782 655 800   www.port-vale.co.uk

Promotion in May completed an incredible turnaround for Vale, who had entered administration the previous March and had just three players under contract at the end of June.

A £1.25m takeover by Paul Wildes was behind their resurrection, so his summer resignation is a worry, but fans have been assured the club is still in safe hands.

On the pitch Micky Adams deserves huge credit for rebuilding his squad so adeptly. Vale's promotion charge was led by Tom Pope's 31 goals and they should improve with more time together.

Longest run without win/loss: 5/8
High/low league position: 1/3
Clean sheets: 13 **Yellow cards:** 79 **Red cards:** 3
Average attendance: 5,727 **Players used:** 28
Leading scorer: T Pope 31 (9,19)
Key stat: Port Vale conceded just 21 second-half goals last season, the fewest in League 2

	2012-13		Last six seasons at home							
	H	A	P	W	D	L	OV	UN	BS	CS
Peterborough			-	-	-	-	-	-	-	-
Wolves			-	-	-	-	-	-	-	-
Bristol City			-	-	-	-	-	-	-	-
Brentford			1	0	0	1	1	0	0	0
Sheffield United			-	-	-	-	-	-	-	-
Swindon			2	1	0	1	1	1	1	0
Leyton Orient			1	1	0	0	1	0	1	0
MK Dons			-	-	-	-	-	-	-	-
Walsall			1	0	1	0	0	1	1	0
Crawley Town			1	0	1	0	1	0	1	0
Tranmere			1	0	1	0	0	1	0	1
Notts County			2	1	0	1	2	0	2	0
Crewe			4	1	1	2	1	3	2	0
Preston			-	-	-	-	-	-	-	-
Coventry			-	-	-	-	-	-	-	-
Shrewsbury			4	1	2	1	1	3	3	1
Carlisle			1	0	1	0	0	1	1	0
Stevenage			1	0	0	1	1	0	1	0
Oldham			1	0	0	1	1	0	0	0
Colchester			-	-	-	-	-	-	-	-
Gillingham	L	W	5	2	1	2	3	2	3	1
Rotherham	W	W	5	3	1	1	2	3	2	3
Port Vale										
Bradford	D	W	5	3	1	1	3	2	3	1

Season	Division	Pos	P	W	D	L	F	A	GD	Pts
2012-13	League 2	3	46	21	15	10	87	52	+35	78
2011-12	League 2	12	46	20	9	17	68	60	+8	59
2010-11	League 2	11	46	17	14	15	54	49	+5	65

Over/Under 54%/46% 4th   **Both score** 54%/46% 4th

Preston North End

Nickname: The Lilywhites/North End
Colours: White and navy blue
Ground: Deepdale (23,404)
Tel: 0870 442 1964   www.pnefc.co.uk

It was a strange season at Deepdale that began with Graham Westley overhauling the squad to such an extent that only three players have now been at the club for more than a year.

Considering there were so many new faces Preston started remarkably well, but a mid-season slump of just one win in 14 league matches cost Westley his job.

However, Simon Grayson instilled some solidity as they battled to safety with a run of 24 points from their final 15 matches, remarkably not conceding more than one goal in a single match.

Longest run without win/loss: 8/6
High/low league position: 5/18
Clean sheets: 15 **Yellow cards:** 83 **Red cards:** 3
Average attendance: 9,214 **Players used:** 31
Leading scorer: N Wroe 8 (2,6)
Key stat: The draw/draw half-time/full-time double result was landed 14 times in Preston's 46 league matches last term

	2012-13		Last six seasons at home							
	H	A	P	W	D	L	OV	UN	BS	CS
Peterborough			1	1	0	0	0	1	0	1
Wolves			2	1	0	1	2	0	2	0
Bristol City			4	1	2	1	2	2	1	2
Brentford	D	L	2	0	1	1	1	1	2	0
Sheffield United	L	D	6	3	1	2	4	2	4	1
Swindon	W	D	1	1	0	0	1	0	1	0
Leyton Orient	D	L	2	0	1	1	0	2	0	1
MK Dons	D	D	2	0	2	0	0	2	1	1
Walsall	L	L	2	0	1	1	1	1	1	1
Crawley Town	L	L	1	0	0	1	1	0	1	0
Tranmere	W	D	2	2	0	0	1	1	1	1
Notts County	D	W	2	1	1	0	0	2	0	2
Crewe	L	L	1	0	0	1	1	0	1	0
Preston										
Coventry	D	D	5	4	1	0	4	1	4	1
Shrewsbury	L	L	1	0	0	1	1	0	1	0
Carlisle	D	D	2	0	2	0	1	1	2	0
Stevenage	W	W	2	1	1	0	0	2	0	2
Oldham	W	L	2	1	1	0	1	1	1	1
Colchester	D	L	3	0	1	2	2	1	1	1
Gillingham			-	-	-	-	-	-	-	-
Rotherham			-	-	-	-	-	-	-	-
Port Vale			-	-	-	-	-	-	-	-
Bradford			-	-	-	-	-	-	-	-

Season	Division	Pos	P	W	D	L	F	A	GD	Pts
2012-13	League 1	14	46	14	17	15	54	49	+5	59
2011-12	League 1	15	46	13	15	18	54	68	-14	54
2010-11	Championship	22	46	10	12	24	54	79	-25	42

Over/Under 37%/63% 20th   **Both score** 50%/50% 13th

Rotherham United

Nickname: The Millers
Colours: Red and white
Ground: New York Stadium (12,009)
Tel: 08444 140733   www.themillers.co.uk

Having been among the top clubs in League 2 for some time, the only real surprise about Rotherham's promotion last term was that it hadn't happened sooner.

After three successive top-ten finishes, including a play-off final defeat, the Millers finally went up in manager Steve Evans's first full season after finishing with 79 points, even sneaking ahead of Port Vale to claim second.

Consolidation would normally be the aim, but Rotherham have made it clear they want successive promotions and have the funds to make it possible.

Longest run without win/loss: 3/6
High/low league position: 2/13
Clean sheets: 15 **Yellow cards:** 67 **Red cards:** 7
Average attendance: 7,954 **Players used:** 36
Leading scorer: D Nardiello 18 (4,13)
Key stat: Rotherham led at half-time in just ten matches last season

	2012-13 H	A	P	W	D	L	OV	UN	BS	CS
Peterborough			1	1	0	0	1	0	1	0
Wolves	-	-	-	-	-	-	-	-	-	-
Bristol City	-	-	-	-	-	-	-	-	-	-
Brentford			2	0	1	1	1	1	1	1
Sheffield United	-	-	-	-	-	-	-	-	-	-
Swindon			1	0	0	1	1	0	1	0
Leyton Orient	-	-	-	-	-	-	-	-	-	-
MK Dons			1	0	0	1	0	1	0	0
Walsall	-	-	-	-	-	-	-	-	-	-
Crawley Town			1	0	0	1	1	0	1	0
Tranmere	-	-	-	-	-	-	-	-	-	-
Notts County			3	1	2	0	1	2	2	1
Crewe			3	1	2	0	1	2	2	1
Preston	-	-	-	-	-	-	-	-	-	-
Coventry	-	-	-	-	-	-	-	-	-	-
Shrewsbury			5	1	2	2	2	3	4	1
Carlisle	-	-	-	-	-	-	-	-	-	-
Stevenage			1	0	1	0	0	1	1	0
Oldham	-	-	-	-	-	-	-	-	-	-
Colchester	-	-	-	-	-	-	-	-	-	-
Gillingham	L	L	4	2	0	2	2	2	1	2
Rotherham										
Port Vale	L	L	5	2	0	3	3	2	2	2
Bradford	W	W	6	2	2	2	3	3	2	3

Season	Division	Pos	P	W	D	L	F	A	GD	Pts
2012-13	League 2	2	46	24	7	15	74	59	+15	79
2011-12	League 2	10	46	18	13	15	67	63	+4	67
2010-11	League 2	9	46	17	15	14	75	60	+15	66

Over/Under 61%/39% 2nd   **Both score** 54%/46% 4th

Sheffield United

Nickname: The Blades
Colours: Red and white
Ground: Bramall Lane (32,609)
Tel: 0871 222 1899   www.sufc.co.uk

It's normally harder second time around when teams fail to go straight back up to the Championship and so it proved for last term's title favourites Sheffield United.

Danny Wilson had to rebuild his squad and they were just found wanting in the home stretch, winning just two of their last 11 matches of the campaign – during which time Wilson was sacked – before losing to Yeovil in the play-offs.

David Weir is the new man entrusted with masterminding a promotion bid, although only after several other contenders turned down the Bramall Lane post.

Longest run without win/loss: 5/16
High/low league position: 1/6
Clean sheets: 21 **Yellow cards:** 72 **Red cards:** 3
Average attendance: 18,611 **Players used:** 32
Leading scorer: D Kitson 11 (3,11) N Blackman 11 (5,11)
Key stat: Sheffield United kept the most clean sheets in League 1 last season, with 21

	2012-13 H	A	P	W	D	L	OV	UN	BS	CS
Peterborough			1	1	0	0	0	1	0	1
Wolves			2	1	0	1	2	0	2	0
Bristol City			4	4	0	0	3	1	2	2
Brentford	D	L	2	1	1	0	1	1	1	1
Sheffield United										
Swindon	W	D	1	1	0	0	0	1	0	1
Leyton Orient	D	W	2	1	1	0	1	1	1	1
MK Dons	D	L	2	1	1	0	1	1	1	1
Walsall	W	D	2	2	0	0	1	1	1	1
Crawley Town	L	W	1	0	0	1	0	1	0	0
Tranmere	D	W	2	0	2	0	0	2	1	1
Notts County	D	D	2	1	1	0	1	1	2	0
Crewe	D	L	1	0	1	0	1	0	1	0
Preston	D	W	6	4	2	0	1	5	2	4
Coventry	L	D	5	2	1	2	2	3	3	1
Shrewsbury	W	W	1	1	0	0	1	0	0	1
Carlisle	D	W	2	1	1	0	0	2	0	2
Stevenage	W	L	2	1	1	0	2	0	2	0
Oldham	D	W	2	0	1	1	1	1	2	0
Colchester	W	D	3	2	1	0	3	0	1	2
Gillingham	-	-	-	-	-	-	-	-	-	-
Rotherham	-	-	-	-	-	-	-	-	-	-
Port Vale	-	-	-	-	-	-	-	-	-	-
Bradford	-	-	-	-	-	-	-	-	-	-

Season	Division	Pos	P	W	D	L	F	A	GD	Pts
2012-13	League 1	5	46	19	18	9	56	42	+14	75
2011-12	League 1	3	46	27	9	10	92	51	+41	90
2010-11	Championship	23	46	11	9	26	44	79	-35	42

Over/Under 30%/70% 24th   **Both score** 39%/61% 23rd

Shrewsbury Town

Nickname: The Shrews
Colours: Blue and amber
Ground: Greenhous Meadow (9,875)
Tel: 0871 811 8800   www.shrewsburytown.com

It took the Shrews several years of knocking on the door before they finally won promotion in 2012 and they refused to give up their League 1 status lightly, battling hard against the drop all season.

Veteran boss Graham Turner oversaw a steady improvement in his team as they took 24 points from their last 16 games, eventually creeping up towards mid-table with two wins to finish the season.

Shrewsbury don't appear to have the means to progress beyond that, however, and they are again among the favourites for the drop this season.

Longest run without win/loss: 5/8
High/low league position: 15/23
Clean sheets: 12 **Yellow cards:** 39 **Red cards:** 1
Average attendance: 5,735 **Players used:** 35
Leading scorer: M Richards 7 (1,7) M Morgan 7 (2,6)
Key stat: Shrewsbury conceded at least two goals 21 times

	2012-13 H	2012-13 A	Last six seasons at home P	W	D	L	OV	UN	BS	CS
Peterborough			1	0	0	1	0	1	0	0
Wolves			-	-	-	-	-	-	-	-
Bristol City			-	-	-	-	-	-	-	-
Brentford	D	D	3	0	1	2	1	2	1	1
Sheffield United	L	L	1	0	0	1	0	1	1	0
Swindon	L	L	2	1	0	1	1	1	1	0
Leyton Orient	L	L	1	0	0	1	0	1	0	0
MK Dons	D	W	2	0	2	0	2	0	2	0
Walsall	W	L	1	1	0	0	0	1	0	1
Crawley Town	W	D	2	2	0	0	2	0	1	1
Tranmere	D	W	1	0	1	0	0	1	1	0
Notts County	D	L	4	1	2	1	2	2	2	1
Crewe	W	D	4	3	0	1	0	4	0	3
Preston	W	W	1	1	0	0	1	0	1	0
Coventry	W	W	1	1	0	0	1	0	1	0
Shrewsbury										
Carlisle	W	D	1	1	0	0	1	0	1	0
Stevenage	W	D	2	2	0	0	1	1	1	1
Oldham	W	L	1	1	0	0	0	1	0	1
Colchester	D	D	1	0	1	0	1	0	1	0
Gillingham			3	2	1	0	1	2	0	3
Rotherham			5	4	1	0	1	4	2	3
Port Vale			4	1	1	2	2	2	2	1
Bradford			5	4	0	1	2	3	2	3

Season	Division	Pos	P	W	D	L	F	A	GD	Pts
2012-13	League 1	16	46	13	16	17	54	60	-6	55
2011-12	League 2	2	46	26	10	10	66	41	+25	88
2010-11	League 2	4	46	22	13	11	72	49	+23	79

Over/Under 52%/48% 5th   **Both score** 57%/43% 5th

Stevenage

Nickname: The Boro
Colours: White and red
Ground: Lamex Stadium (6,722)
Tel: 01438 223 223   www.stevenagefc.com

Survival should really be the aim for a club with the second-lowest attendance in the division and it was achieved with plenty to spare last season – but that still wasn't enough to satisfy the chairman.

Gary Smith led the club to a flying start that ultimately secured the Boro's safety, but a run of 14 defeats in 18 matches saw him sacked in March.

The fact that former manager Graham Westley had recently left Preston may have had something to do with it and Westley is now back at the helm for his third spell in charge.

Longest run without win/loss: 6/11
High/low league position: 2/18
Clean sheets: 10 **Yellow cards:** 62 **Red cards:** 5
Average attendance: 3,169 **Players used:** 31
Leading scorer: L Akins 10 (4,10)
Key stat: Stevenage had the fewest shots in League 1 last season, averaging just 8.24 per match

	2012-13 H	2012-13 A	Last six seasons at home P	W	D	L	OV	UN	BS	CS
Peterborough			-	-	-	-	-	-	-	-
Wolves			-	-	-	-	-	-	-	-
Bristol City			-	-	-	-	-	-	-	-
Brentford	W	L	2	2	0	0	1	1	1	1
Sheffield United	W	L	2	2	0	0	2	0	1	1
Swindon	L	L	1	0	0	1	1	0	0	0
Leyton Orient	L	W	2	0	0	2	0	0	0	0
MK Dons	L	W	2	1	0	1	1	1	1	0
Walsall	W	L	2	1	1	0	1	1	1	1
Crawley Town	L	D	4	2	1	1	2	2	3	1
Tranmere	D	L	2	1	1	0	1	1	2	0
Notts County	W	W	2	1	0	1	0	2	0	1
Crewe	D	D	2	0	2	0	1	1	2	0
Preston	L	L	2	0	1	1	1	1	2	0
Coventry	L	W	1	0	0	1	0	1	0	0
Shrewsbury	D	L	2	0	2	0	0	2	2	0
Carlisle	D	L	2	1	1	0	0	2	1	1
Stevenage										
Oldham	L	W	2	1	0	1	1	1	1	1
Colchester	L	L	2	0	1	1	0	2	0	1
Gillingham			1	0	1	0	1	0	1	0
Rotherham			1	1	0	0	1	0	0	1
Port Vale			1	1	0	0	1	0	1	0
Bradford			1	1	0	0	1	0	1	0

Season	Division	Pos	P	W	D	L	F	A	GD	Pts
2012-13	League 1	18	46	15	9	22	47	64	-17	54
2011-12	League 1	6	46	18	15	13	62	45	+17	69
2010-11	League 2	6	46	18	15	13	62	45	+17	69

Over/Under 43%/57% 15th   **Both score** 50%/50% 13th

Swindon Town

Nickname: The Robins
Colours: Red and white
Ground: County Ground (14,983)
Tel: 0871 423 6433   www.swindontownfc.co.uk

Swindon haven't had many more dramatic seasons than the last one, but ultimately it fizzled out with defeat to Brentford in the play-off semi-finals.

The resignation of Paolo Di Canio proved the turning point as Swindon took just 19 points in their final 15 matches without the inspirational Italian, having looked likely to go up automatically.

Swindon were hit with a transfer embargo for spending beyond their means and were sold by Andrew Black, who tired of covering their losses. Things could be tough for new boss Kevin MacDonald.

Longest run without win/loss: 5/13
High/low league position: 1/8
Clean sheets: 19 **Yellow cards:** 69 **Red cards:** 1
Average attendance: 8,528 **Players used:** 32
Leading scorer: J Collins 15 (6,11)
Key stat: Swindon scored four goals or more seven times during the 2012-13 campaign

	2012-13 H	A	Last six seasons at home P	W	D	L	OV	UN	BS	CS
Peterborough			2	0	2	0	1	1	2	0
Wolves			-	-	-	-	-	-	-	-
Bristol City			-	-	-	-	-	-	-	-
Brentford	L	L	3	1	1	1	1	2	2	0
Sheffield United	D	L	1	0	1	0	0	1	0	1
Swindon										
Leyton Orient	L	D	5	1	2	2	2	3	3	0
MK Dons	W	L	4	1	2	1	0	4	1	2
Walsall	D	W	5	1	3	1	3	2	3	1
Crawley Town	W	D	2	2	0	0	2	0	0	2
Tranmere	W	W	5	4	1	0	3	2	1	4
Notts County	D	L	2	0	1	1	1	1	1	1
Crewe	W	L	4	2	2	0	2	2	2	2
Preston	D	L	1	0	1	0	0	1	1	0
Coventry	D	W	1	0	1	0	1	0	1	0
Shrewsbury	W	W	2	2	0	0	1	1	1	1
Carlisle	W	D	5	2	2	1	2	3	2	2
Stevenage	W	W	1	1	0	0	1	0	0	1
Oldham	D	W	5	3	1	1	3	2	2	1
Colchester	L	W	4	1	1	2	2	2	3	0
Gillingham			3	3	0	0	2	1	1	2
Rotherham			1	1	0	0	1	0	1	0
Port Vale			2	2	0	0	2	0	0	2
Bradford			1	0	1	0	0	1	0	1

Season	Division	Pos	P	W	D	L	F	A	GD	Pts
2012-13	League 1	6	46	20	14	12	72	39	+33	74
2011-12	League 2	1	46	29	6	11	75	32	+43	93
2010-11	League 1	24	46	9	14	23	50	72	-22	41

Over/Under 41%/59% 18th   **Both score** 41%/59% 21st

Tranmere Rovers

Nickname: Rovers
Colours: White
Ground: Prenton Park (16,151)
Tel: 0871 221 2001   www.tranmererovers.co.uk

Mid-table was the expectation at the start of the season, but 11th place turned out to be a massive disappointment for Tranmere.

Rovers were top of the table for much of the campaign but a disastrous run of 12 defeats in their last 17 matches – with no goals in their last six – then saw them plummet down the standings.

Injuries played a key part in Tranmere's plight – especially with 21-year-old captain James Wallace ruled out for the season at the start of December – as their lack of depth was exposed.

Longest run without win/loss: 6/12
High/low league position: 1/11
Clean sheets: 15 **Yellow cards:** 52 **Red cards:** 2
Average attendance: 6,172 **Players used:** 30
Leading scorer: J Cassidy 11 (3,8)
Key stat: Tranmere failed to score in 17 of their league games last season

	2012-13 H	A	Last six seasons at home P	W	D	L	OV	UN	BS	CS
Peterborough			2	1	1	0	0	2	1	1
Wolves			-	-	-	-	-	-	-	-
Bristol City			-	-	-	-	-	-	-	-
Brentford	D	W	4	1	2	1	2	2	2	1
Sheffield United	L	D	2	0	1	1	0	2	1	0
Swindon	L	L	5	2	0	3	3	2	3	1
Leyton Orient	W	L	6	3	2	1	3	3	4	2
MK Dons	L	L	5	1	1	3	1	4	2	0
Walsall	D	L	6	2	3	1	4	2	4	2
Crawley Town	W	W	1	1	0	0	0	1	0	1
Tranmere										
Notts County	D	W	3	0	2	1	0	3	2	0
Crewe	W	D	3	2	1	0	1	2	2	1
Preston	D	L	2	1	1	0	1	1	2	0
Coventry	W	L	1	1	0	0	1	0	1	0
Shrewsbury	L	D	1	0	0	1	0	1	0	0
Carlisle	L	D	6	3	1	2	3	3	3	2
Stevenage	W	D	2	2	0	0	2	0	1	1
Oldham	W	W	6	2	0	4	1	5	1	2
Colchester	W	W	5	2	2	1	2	3	2	3
Gillingham			2	2	0	0	1	1	1	1
Rotherham			-	-	-	-	-	-	-	-
Port Vale			1	1	0	0	0	1	0	1
Bradford			-	-	-	-	-	-	-	-

Season	Division	Pos	P	W	D	L	F	A	GD	Pts
2012-13	League 1	11	46	19	10	17	58	48	+10	67
2011-12	League 1	12	46	14	14	18	49	53	-4	56
2010-11	League 1	18	46	15	11	20	53	60	-7	56

Over/Under 39%/61% 19th   **Both score** 39%/61% 23rd

Walsall

Nickname: The Saddlers
Colours: Red and white
Ground: Banks's Stadium (10,989)
Tel: 0871 221 0442   www.saddlers.co.uk

Walsall were one of the surprise packages in League 1 last term, coming within six points of a play-off place despite finishing the previous campaign in 19th.

Held to 20 draws that season, Walsall placed more emphasis on their attacking game as they rattled in 65 goals – the fifth-best tally – and rightly earned praise for their slick passing football.

Unfortunately for the Saddlers, that put their players in the shop window and several have moved on in the summer, so survival will be the sole aim now for manager Dean Smith.

Longest run without win/loss: 13/15
High/low league position: 7/19
Clean sheets: 12 **Yellow cards:** 49 **Red cards:** 3
Average attendance: 4,234 **Players used:** 28
Leading scorer: W Grigg 19 (6,14)
Key stat: Walsall picked up just two points out of 33 when trailing at half-time

	2012-13 H	A	Last six seasons at home P	W	D	L	OV	UN	BS	CS
Peterborough			2	0	0	2	2	0	2	0
Wolves			-	-	-	-	-	-	-	-
Bristol City			-	-	-	-	-	-	-	-
Brentford	D	D	4	2	1	1	3	1	3	0
Sheffield United	D	L	2	1	1	0	1	1	2	0
Swindon	L	D	5	1	2	2	3	2	4	0
Leyton Orient	L	L	6	1	2	3	2	4	2	2
MK Dons	W	W	5	2	0	3	3	2	2	1
Walsall										
Crawley Town	D	D	1	0	1	0	1	0	1	0
Tranmere	W	D	6	3	0	3	3	3	3	1
Notts County	D	W	3	0	1	2	1	2	1	0
Crewe	D	L	3	0	3	0	1	2	3	0
Preston	W	W	2	2	0	0	1	1	1	1
Coventry	W	L	1	1	0	0	1	0	0	1
Shrewsbury	W	L	1	1	0	0	1	0	1	0
Carlisle	L	W	6	2	3	1	4	2	6	0
Stevenage	W	L	2	1	1	0	0	2	1	1
Oldham	W	D	6	2	1	3	4	2	3	1
Colchester	W	L	5	4	0	1	1	4	1	3
Gillingham			2	1	1	0	1	1	1	1
Rotherham			-	-	-	-	-	-	-	-
Port Vale			1	0	1	0	0	1	0	1
Bradford			-	-	-	-	-	-	-	-

Season	Division	Pos	P	W	D	L	F	A	GD	Pts
2012-13	League 1	9	46	17	17	12	65	58	+7	68
2011-12	League 1	19	46	10	20	16	51	57	-6	50
2010-11	League 1	20	46	12	12	22	56	75	-19	48

Over/Under 52%/48% 5th   **Both score** 61%/39% 2nd

Wolverhampton W

Nickname: Wolves
Colours: Gold and black
Ground: Molineux Stadium (30,852)
Tel: 0871 880 8442   www.wolves.co.uk

Relegation from the Premier League was bad enough, but falling straight through the Championship last season was a bitter blow for Wolves.

The club paid a massive price for the disastrous appointments of Terry Connor and Stale Solbakken, which ultimately left them with too much to do in a hugely competitive division.

Dean Saunders followed the pair to the exit, despite a run of five wins in his final 11 games suggesting he was finding his feet. Kenny Jackett, dropping a division from Millwall, must pick up the pieces.

Longest run without win/loss: 12/4
High/low league position: 3/23
Clean sheets: 9 **Yellow cards:** 59 **Red cards:** 5
Average attendance: 21,662 **Players used:** 35
Leading scorer: S Ebanks-Blake 14 (6,12)
Key stat: Wolves lost six matches in which they took the lead last season

	2012-13 H	A	Last six seasons at home P	W	D	L	OV	UN	BS	CS
Peterborough	L	W	1	0	0	1	1	0	0	0
Wolves			-	-	-	-	-	-	-	-
Bristol City	W	W	3	2	1	0	1	2	2	1
Brentford			-	-	-	-	-	-	-	-
Sheffield United			2	0	2	0	0	2	1	1
Swindon			-	-	-	-	-	-	-	-
Leyton Orient			-	-	-	-	-	-	-	-
MK Dons			-	-	-	-	-	-	-	-
Walsall			-	-	-	-	-	-	-	-
Crawley Town			-	-	-	-	-	-	-	-
Tranmere			-	-	-	-	-	-	-	-
Notts County			-	-	-	-	-	-	-	-
Crewe			-	-	-	-	-	-	-	-
Preston			2	1	0	1	1	1	1	1
Coventry			2	2	0	0	1	1	1	1
Shrewsbury			-	-	-	-	-	-	-	-
Carlisle			-	-	-	-	-	-	-	-
Stevenage			-	-	-	-	-	-	-	-
Oldham			-	-	-	-	-	-	-	-
Colchester			1	1	0	0	0	1	0	1
Gillingham			-	-	-	-	-	-	-	-
Rotherham			-	-	-	-	-	-	-	-
Port Vale			-	-	-	-	-	-	-	-
Bradford			-	-	-	-	-	-	-	-

Season	Division	Pos	P	W	D	L	F	A	GD	Pts
2012-13	Championship	23	46	14	9	23	55	69	-14	51
2011-12	Premier League	20	38	5	10	23	40	82	-42	25
2010-11	Premier League	17	38	11	7	20	46	66	-20	40

Over/Under 57%/43% 5th   **Both score** 63%/37% 3rd

Key Points do not include any deductions imposed by the league. **GFA** Goals For Average per match, **GAA** Goals Against Average per match, **PGA** Average Points Gained per match, **CS** Clean Sheet, **FS** First to Score, **Ov** Over 2.5 total goals, **Un** Under 2.5 total goals, **BS** Both teams Score

Top scorers 2012-13

		P	W	D	L	F	GFA	PGA	Pts
1	Bournemouth	46	24	11	11	76	1.65	**1.8**	83
2	Swindon	46	20	14	12	72	1.57	**1.6**	74
3	Yeovil	46	23	8	15	71	1.54	**1.7**	77
4	Coventry	46	18	11	17	66	1.43	**1.4**	65
5	Walsall	46	17	17	12	65	1.41	**1.5**	68
6	Doncaster	46	25	9	12	62	1.35	**1.8**	84
	Brentford	46	21	16	9	62	1.35	**1.7**	79
	MK Dons	46	19	13	14	62	1.35	**1.5**	70
9	Notts Co	46	16	17	13	61	1.33	**1.4**	65
10	Crawley	46	18	14	14	59	1.28	**1.5**	68
11	Tranmere	46	19	10	17	58	1.26	**1.5**	67
12	Sheff Utd	46	19	18	9	56	1.22	**1.6**	75
	Carlisle	46	14	13	19	56	1.22	**1.2**	55
14	Leyton Orient	46	21	8	17	55	1.20	**1.5**	71
15	Crewe	46	18	10	18	54	1.17	**1.4**	64
	Preston	46	14	17	15	54	1.17	**1.3**	59
	Shrewsbury	46	13	16	17	54	1.17	**1.2**	55
18	Portsmouth	46	10	12	24	51	1.11	**0.9**	42
19	Scunthorpe	46	13	9	24	49	1.07	**1.0**	48
20	Stevenage	46	15	9	22	47	1.02	**1.2**	54
	Colchester	46	14	9	23	47	1.02	**1.1**	51
22	Oldham	46	14	9	23	46	1.00	**1.1**	51
23	Bury	46	9	14	23	45	0.98	**0.9**	41
24	Hartlepool	46	9	14	23	39	0.85	**0.9**	41

Best defence 2012-13

		P	W	D	L	A	GAA	PGA	Pts
1	Swindon	46	20	14	12	39	0.85	**1.6**	74
2	Sheff Utd	46	19	18	9	42	0.91	**1.6**	75
3	Doncaster	46	25	9	12	44	0.96	**1.8**	84
4	MK Dons	46	19	13	14	45	0.98	**1.5**	70
5	Brentford	46	21	16	9	47	1.02	**1.7**	79
6	Leyton Orient	46	21	8	17	48	1.04	**1.5**	71
	Tranmere	46	19	10	17	48	1.04	**1.5**	67
8	Notts Co	46	16	17	13	49	1.07	**1.4**	65
	Preston	46	14	17	15	49	1.07	**1.3**	59
10	Bournemouth	46	24	11	11	53	1.15	**1.8**	83
11	Yeovil	46	23	8	15	56	1.22	**1.7**	77
12	Crawley	46	18	14	14	58	1.26	**1.5**	68
	Walsall	46	17	17	12	58	1.26	**1.5**	68
14	Coventry	46	18	11	17	59	1.28	**1.4**	65
	Oldham	46	14	9	23	59	1.28	**1.1**	51
16	Shrewsbury	46	13	16	17	60	1.30	**1.2**	55
17	Crewe	46	18	10	18	62	1.35	**1.4**	64
18	Stevenage	46	15	9	22	64	1.39	**1.2**	54
19	Hartlepool	46	9	14	23	67	1.46	**0.9**	41
20	Colchester	46	14	9	23	68	1.48	**1.1**	51
21	Portsmouth	46	10	12	24	69	1.50	**0.9**	42
22	Scunthorpe	46	13	9	24	73	1.59	**1.0**	48
23	Bury	46	9	14	23	73	1.59	**0.9**	41
24	Carlisle	46	14	13	19	77	1.67	**1.2**	55

When Brett Pitman blanked against Tranmere on the final day it was the end of an eight-game scoring streak – can he do it in the Championship?

Clean sheets 2012-13

		P	CS	CS%
1	Sheff Utd	46	21	**45.7**
2	MK Dons	46	20	**43.5**
3	Swindon	46	19	41.3
4	Doncaster	46	16	34.8
5	Yeovil	46	15	32.6
	Crawley	46	15	32.6
	Preston	46	15	32.6
	Brentford	46	15	32.6
	Notts Co	46	15	32.6
	Tranmere	46	15	32.6
	Bournemouth	46	15	32.6
12	Leyton Orient	46	14	30.4
13	Colchester	46	13	28.3
14	Walsall	46	12	26.1
	Shrewsbury	46	12	26.1
16	Crewe	46	11	23.9
17	Stevenage	46	10	21.7
18	Oldham	46	9	19.6
	Coventry	46	9	19.6
	Hartlepool	46	9	19.6
	Portsmouth	46	9	19.6
22	Bury	46	7	15.2
	Carlisle	46	7	15.2
24	Scunthorpe	46	5	10.9

First to score 2012-13

		P	FS	FS%
1	Coventry	46	27	58.6
	MK Dons	46	27	58.6
3	Bournemouth	46	26	56.5
	Swindon	46	26	56.5
	Yeovil	46	26	56.5
6	Leyton Orient	46	25	54.3
	Walsall	46	25	54.3
8	Notts Co	46	24	52.1
	Sheff Ut	46	24	52.1
10	Brentford	46	23	50.0
	Crawley	46	23	50.0
	Doncaster	46	23	50.0
13	Crewe	46	21	45.6
	Preston	46	21	45.6
	Tranmere	46	21	45.6
16	Stevenage	46	20	43.4
17	Scunthorpe	46	19	41.3
18	Oldham	46	18	39.1
19	Carlisle	46	17	36.9
	Shrewsbury	46	17	36.9
21	Colchester	46	16	34.7
	Hartlepool	46	16	34.7
23	Portsmouth	46	15	32.6
24	Bury	46	14	30.4

Top goalscorers 2012-13

	Goals
P Madden (Yeovil)	23
L Clarke (Coventry)	19
W Grigg (Walsall)	19
B Pitman (Bournemouth)	19
C Donaldson (Brentford)	18
K Lisbie (Leyton Orient)	16
D McGoldrick (Coventry)	16
J Collins (Swindon)	15
J Hayter (Yeovil)	14
J Baxter (Oldham)	13
L Grabban (Bournemouth)	13
B Paynter (Doncaster)	13

League 1 top dog Paddy Madden

Record when keeping a clean sheet 2012-13

		P	W	D	L	F	GFA	PGA	Pts
1	Oldham	9	9	0	0	14	1.56	**3.0**	27
	Coventry	9	9	0	0	15	1.67	**3.0**	27
3	Doncaster	16	14	2	0	26	1.63	**2.8**	44
	Stevenage	10	9	1	0	14	1.40	**2.8**	28
5	Crawley	15	13	2	0	23	1.53	**2.7**	41
	Bournemouth	15	13	2	0	23	1.53	**2.7**	41
7	MK Dons	20	16	4	0	29	1.45	**2.6**	52
	Swindon	19	15	4	0	40	2.11	**2.6**	49
	Yeovil	15	12	3	0	23	1.53	**2.6**	39
	Leyton Orient	14	11	3	0	16	1.14	**2.6**	36
	Crewe	11	9	2	0	12	1.09	**2.6**	29
	Scunthorpe	5	4	1	0	4	0.80	**2.6**	13
13	Notts Co	15	11	4	0	20	1.33	**2.5**	37
	Tranmere	15	11	4	0	21	1.40	**2.5**	37
	Colchester	13	10	3	0	17	1.31	**2.5**	33
16	Carlisle	7	5	2	0	9	1.29	**2.4**	17
17	Sheff Utd	21	14	7	0	22	1.05	**2.3**	49
	Brentford	15	10	5	0	14	0.93	**2.3**	35
	Walsall	12	8	4	0	15	1.25	**2.3**	28
	Portsmouth	9	6	3	0	13	1.44	**2.3**	21
21	Shrewsbury	12	7	5	0	10	0.83	**2.2**	26
22	Preston	15	8	7	0	17	1.13	**2.1**	31
	Bury	7	4	3	0	7	1.00	**2.1**	15
24	Hartlepool	9	4	5	0	8	0.89	**1.9**	17

Record when first to score 2012-13

		P	W	D	L	F	A	PGA	Pts
1	Doncaster	23	21	2	0	45	11	**2.8**	65
2	Bournemouth	26	22	3	1	55	18	**2.7**	69
3	Leyton Orient	25	21	3	1	49	17	**2.6**	66
4	Yeovil	26	21	3	2	54	21	**2.5**	66
	Sheff Utd	24	18	6	0	41	12	**2.5**	60
	Tranmere	21	16	4	1	45	14	**2.5**	52
7	Colchester	16	12	3	1	29	11	**2.4**	39
	Brentford	23	17	5	1	43	19	**2.4**	56
	Carlisle	17	12	5	0	33	14	**2.4**	41
10	Crawley	23	16	6	1	41	15	**2.3**	54
	Swindon	26	19	4	3	61	16	**2.3**	61
	Oldham	18	13	3	2	29	14	**2.3**	42
	Shrewsbury	17	11	6	0	31	15	**2.3**	39
	MK Dons	27	19	4	4	52	20	**2.3**	61
15	Portsmouth	15	9	5	1	28	12	**2.1**	32
	Notts Co	24	15	6	3	43	22	**2.1**	51
	Preston	21	13	5	3	42	20	**2.1**	44
	Crewe	21	13	5	3	31	17	**2.1**	44
19	Walsall	25	14	9	2	45	26	**2.0**	51
	Stevenage	20	12	3	5	30	17	**2.0**	39
21	Bury	14	8	3	3	24	18	**1.9**	27
	Coventry	27	14	8	5	44	25	**1.9**	50
23	Scunthorpe	19	10	5	4	31	22	**1.8**	35
	Hartlepool	16	8	5	3	27	18	**1.8**	29

Over 2.5 goals 2012-13

	H	A	Ov%
Scunthorpe	17	11	61
Yeovil	14	13	59
Carlisle	15	11	57
Bournemouth	12	13	54
Coventry	11	13	52
Shrewsbury	12	12	52
Walsall	13	11	52
Crewe	9	14	50
Portsmouth	10	13	50

Under 2.5 goals 2012-13

	H	A	Un%
Sheff Utd	15	17	70
MK Dons	15	15	65
Leyton Orient	15	14	63
Oldham	14	15	63
Preston	13	16	63
Tranmere	14	14	61
Swindon	13	14	59
Colchester, Notts County, Stevenage			57

Both to score 2012-13

	H	A	BS%
Carlisle	14	15	63
Coventry	16	12	61
Walsall	15	13	61
Scunthorpe	18	9	59
Bournemouth	15	11	57
Crewe	11	15	57
Notts County	13	13	57
Shrewsbury	12	14	57

Spireites can dent Pompey's promotion prospects

Despite suffering a second consecutive relegation last season, Portsmouth fans have been celebrating in recent months and the bookmakers are expecting a promotion party at Fratton Park come May, writes Andy Dietz.

The 2008 FA Cup winners are as short as 4-5 to go up and 4-1 to do so as table-toppers after falling from the top tier to the bottom in just four seasons.

Why so short? And why the celebrations? Portsmouth's rapid decline was caused by financial mismanagement placing the club in administration twice in three years. But now, after a complex 14-month legal battle, the Pompey Supporters' Trust have finally taken control of the club, delivering it from the hands of less loving custodians.

The slate has been wiped clean as the club escaped carrying a ten-point penalty over into the new season and the rebuilding process has begun in earnest with Portsmouth among the Football League's most active clubs in the transfer market during the early summer exchanges.

But while the narrative could rival a soap opera there isn't much value in their outright price and, as Rotherham proved again last season, the recent record of ante-post favourites in the basement is poor with only one obliging in the last 12 seasons.

There's no doubt Pompey are a huge club at this level but Guy Whittingham has his work cut out constructing an almost entirely new squad and, with the players needing time to gel, punters are best advised to leave Portsmouth alone.

Next in the betting are 9-1 joint-second favourites Fleetwood and **Chesterfield**, and it is the Spireites who appeal most to clinch the title.

Chesterfield were flagged up as title contenders here 12 months ago but a slow start undermined their chances. They are a few points shorter this time around but their credentials look rock solid.

Only champions Gillingham had a better defensive record last season, with goalkeeper Tommy Lee continuing to excel and defenders Liam Cooper and Nathan Smith developing well.

They have bolstered their attacking options with some key signings and the goals should flow with a strike-force consisting of Eoin Doyle and Marc Richards feeding off the likes of Jay O'Shea, Jimmy Ryan and Gary Roberts. It's also worth noting that in five of the past nine seasons the team that finished in Chesterfield's eighth-place position has gone on to achieve promotion the following campaign.

Further down the list, despite their back-to-back appearances in the play-offs, **Cheltenham** are unfancied by the layers and 2-1 for a top-seven finish is an attractive price that warrants interest.

Robins manager Mark Yates has done a sterling job to transform the side into a consistent outfit and the acquisition of experienced striker Jamie Cureton, scorer of 21 goals for mid-table Exeter last term, could be the best bit of business done in the close season.

Handicap bettors and spreads traders should consider looking for ways to get behind 25-1 **Rochdale**, particularly now that Keith Hill is back in the dugout. Hill has a knack for getting the best out of his players and although money is tight at Spotland it was the same story back in 2009-10 when they gained promotion – and you can bet it won't stop well-connected shrewdy Hill unearthing a gem or two.

The most appealing ante-post wager in this section centres on the relegation market where **Dagenham & Redbridge** look a fantastic bet at 9-2 to go down.

The Daggers struggled to come to terms with the departure of long-serving manager John Still last season and only avoided the drop on goal difference after a woeful run of just two wins in 12 games under interim boss Wayne Burnett.

Burnett has been set a mammoth task in his first crack at management as he bids to revive a side who have finished 19th and 22nd in the last two campaigns. There is a strong trend in the basement for regressive teams falling through the trapdoor and the Essex club are in a precarious position.

Another team placing their trust in a rookie manager producing results are **Accrington Stanley** and they could join Dagenham in returning to the Conference.

Former England striker James Beattie takes his place in the hot seat for the first time and while the Lancastrian's local knowl-edge will be valuable he will have to cope with a meagre budget. Like Dagenham, Stanley are pulling in average crowds well below 2,000 and their limited resources are a major disadvantage. Throw in the fact that former boss Leam Richardson sacrificed his job to become assistant manager at Chesterfield and the signs are ominous.

Of the competition, Wimbledon, York and Plymouth all struggled last season but can be expected to improve, and while Morecambe have to deal with budget cuts, they should have just enough about them to scrap their way to survival.

Chesterfield could be partying again in May

Accrington Stanley

Nickname: Stanley
Colours: Red
Ground: Crown Ground (5,070)
Tel: 01254 356 950 www.accringtonstanley.co.uk

James Beattie faces a baptism of fire in his first managerial role as Accrington have regressed in the last two seasons and now rate as relegation candidates.

Low attendances mean cash is always tight and Beattie's decision to hang up his boots to concentrate on his day job leaves Stanley short on firepower, particularly as his goals were crucial in the club avoiding relegation last term.

Beattie got the job after Leam Richardson left to rejoin Paul Cook, the man he succeeded at the Crown Ground, in an assistant capacity at Chesterfield.

Longest run without win/loss: 7/5
High/low league position: 6/24
Clean sheets: 14 **Yellow cards:** 64 **Red cards:** 5
Average attendance: 1,674 **Players used:** 36
Leading scorer: R Boco 10 (2,9)
Key stat: Accrington failed to win in the league last season when the opposition scored first, drawing five and losing 19

	2012-13 H	A	Last six seasons at home P	W	D	L	OV	UN	BS	CS
Scunthorpe			-	-	-	-	-	-	-	-
Bury			4	1	0	3	2	2	2	1
Hartlepool			-	-	-	-	-	-	-	-
Portsmouth			-	-	-	-	-	-	-	-
Burton	D	L	4	2	1	1	3	1	3	0
Cheltenham	D	W	4	1	1	2	3	1	2	1
Northampton	L	L	4	2	0	2	4	0	3	0
Chesterfield	W	L	5	4	1	0	2	3	2	3
Oxford	L	L	3	0	1	2	1	2	0	1
Exeter	L	L	2	1	0	1	2	0	1	0
Southend	D	W	3	1	1	1	2	1	3	0
Rochdale	L	W	4	0	0	4	4	0	4	0
Fleetwood Town	L	W	1	0	0	1	1	0	0	0
Bristol Rovers	W	W	2	2	0	0	1	1	1	1
Wycombe	L	W	4	0	1	3	0	4	1	0
Morecambe	W	D	6	4	2	0	2	4	4	2
York	L	D	1	0	0	1	0	1	0	0
Accrington										
Torquay	D	L	4	3	1	0	2	2	2	2
AFC Wimbledon	W	W	2	2	0	0	2	0	1	1
Plymouth	D	D	2	0	1	1	1	1	1	0
Dag & Red	L	D	5	2	1	2	1	4	0	3
Mansfield			1	1	0	0	0	1	0	1
Newport County										

Season	Division	Pos	P	W	D	L	F	A	GD	Pts
2012-13	League 2	18	46	14	12	20	51	68	-17	54
2011-12	League 2	14	46	14	15	17	54	66	-12	57
2010-11	League 2	5	46	18	19	9	73	55	+18	73

Over/Under 43%/57% 17th **Both score** 41%/59% 23rd

AFC Wimbledon

Nickname: The Dons
Colours: Blue and yellow
Ground: The Cherry Red Records Stadium (5,339)
Tel: 020 8547 3528 www.afcwimbledon.co.uk

Wimbledon's 2012-13 campaign went right down to the wire before they secured their survival and the Dons need to strengthen to avoid a similar struggle this season.

It was tough going for Neil Ardley during his first taste of management but he got his side over the line with a dramatic final-day success against Fleetwood.

Following a rocky start, seven victories in the last 16 games show that Ardley's methods were working and with a couple of marquee signings, Wimbledon should be able to keep out of bother.

Longest run without win/loss: 6/5
High/low league position: 16/24
Clean sheets: 7 **Yellow cards:** 59 **Red cards:** 3
Average attendance: 4,060 **Players used:** 45
Leading scorer: J Midson 13 (3,12)
Key stat: The Dons had the leakiest defence is League 2 last term, conceding 76 goals and finishing with the worst goal difference

	2012-13 H	A	Last six seasons at home P	W	D	L	OV	UN	BS	CS
Scunthorpe			-	-	-	-	-	-	-	-
Bury			-	-	-	-	-	-	-	-
Hartlepool			-	-	-	-	-	-	-	-
Portsmouth			-	-	-	-	-	-	-	-
Burton	D	L	2	1	1	0	1	1	1	1
Cheltenham	L	L	2	1	0	1	2	0	2	0
Northampton	D	L	2	0	1	1	1	1	1	0
Chesterfield	W	L	1	1	0	0	0	1	0	1
Oxford	L	L	3	0	0	3	1	2	0	0
Exeter	D	L	1	0	1	0	1	0	1	0
Southend	L	W	2	0	0	2	2	0	1	0
Rochdale	L	W	1	0	0	1	1	0	1	0
Fleetwood Town	W	D	2	2	0	0	1	1	1	1
Bristol Rovers	W	L	2	1	0	1	2	0	2	0
Wycombe	D	W	1	0	1	0	1	0	1	0
Morecambe	W	W	2	1	1	0	0	2	1	1
York	W	W	3	2	0	1	2	1	1	1
Accrington	L	L	2	0	0	2	1	1	1	0
Torquay	L	W	2	1	0	1	0	2	0	1
AFC Wimbledon										
Plymouth	D	W	2	0	1	1	1	1	2	0
Dag & Red	D	W	2	1	1	0	2	0	2	0
Mansfield			2	2	0	0	1	1	1	1
Newport County			1	0	1	0	1	0	1	0

Season	Division	Pos	P	W	D	L	F	A	GD	Pts
2012-13	League 2	20	46	14	11	21	54	76	-22	53
2011-12	League 2	16	46	15	9	22	62	78	-16	54
2010-11	Conference	2	46	27	9	10	83	47	+36	90

Over/Under 54%/46% 4th **Both score** 57%/43% 3rd

Bristol Rovers

Nickname: The Pirates/The Gas
Colours: Blue and white
Ground: Memorial Stadium (11,626)
Tel: 01179 096 648   www.bristolrovers.co.uk

Having orchestrated an incredible turnaround last season, John Ward will aim to keep the Gas cooking and they could be one of the division's big improvers.

Ward returned for a second spell at the club in December and took Rovers from rock-bottom at Christmas to a comfortable mid-table finish.

He revamped the squad with loan and short-term signings and if the majority of the players can be kept then they should be able to maintain their progress.

They aren't eye-popping value at 12-1 but are worth considering for promotion.

Longest run without win/loss: 7/6
High/low league position: 11/24
Clean sheets: 10 **Yellow cards:** 72 **Red cards:** 6
Average attendance: 6,308 **Players used:** 36
Leading scorer: T Eaves 7 (2,6)
Key stat: John Ward's record since taking over at Bristol Rovers reads W12, D6, L6

	2012-13		Last six seasons at home							
	H	A	P	W	D	L	OV	UN	BS	CS
Scunthorpe			1	0	0	1	1	0	1	0
Bury	-	-	-	-	-	-	-	-	-	
Hartlepool			4	2	2	0	1	3	1	3
Portsmouth	-	-	-	-	-	-	-	-	-	
Burton	W	D	2	2	0	0	2	0	1	1
Cheltenham	L	D	4	2	0	2	2	2	2	1
Northampton	W	L	4	3	1	0	2	2	3	1
Chesterfield	W	L	1	1	0	0	1	0	1	0
Oxford	L	W	2	0	1	1	0	2	0	1
Exeter	W	W	3	2	0	1	0	3	0	2
Southend	L	D	5	3	1	1	3	2	4	1
Rochdale	W	L	2	2	0	0	2	0	2	0
Fleetwood Town	D	W	1	0	1	0	0	1	0	1
Bristol Rovers										
Wycombe	W	L	2	1	0	1	1	1	1	1
Morecambe	L	D	2	1	0	1	2	0	1	0
York	D	L	1	0	1	0	0	1	0	1
Accrington	L	L	2	1	0	1	1	1	1	0
Torquay	W	D	2	1	0	1	2	0	2	0
AFC Wimbledon	W	L	2	2	0	0	0	2	0	2
Plymouth	W	D	3	1	0	2	3	0	3	0
Dag & Red	L	W	3	1	0	2	0	3	0	1
Mansfield	-	-	-	-	-	-	-	-	-	
Newport County	-	-	-	-	-	-	-	-	-	

Season	Division	Pos	P	W	D	L	F	A	GD	Pts
2012-13	League 2	14	46	16	12	18	60	69	-9	60
2011-12	League 2	13	46	15	12	19	60	70	-10	57
2010-11	League 1	22	46	11	12	23	48	82	-34	45

Over/Under 52%/48% 7th   **Both score** 52%/48% 7th

Burton Albion

Nickname: The Brewers
Colours: Yellow and black
Ground: Pirelli Stadium (6,912)
Tel: 01283 565938   www.burtonalbionfc.co.uk

The Brewers might have been beaten in the play-offs but everyone connected with the club should raise a pint to a season of major overachievement.

Juggling one of the smaller budgets in the division, Gary Rowett made an excellent fist of his first full season as a manager.

His attacking style resulted in high entertainment – 15 of their games in all competitions featured five goals or more – and although key players will move on there is no reason why last season's bold show should be a one-off.

Longest run without win/loss: 4/8
High/low league position: 2/12
Clean sheets: 12 **Yellow cards:** 58 **Red cards:** 5
Average attendance: 2,859 **Players used:** 34
Leading scorer: J Maghoma 15 (6,12)
Key stat: Burton's home record of W17, D3, L3 was the best in the Football League last season

	2012-13		Last six seasons at home							
	H	A	P	W	D	L	OV	UN	BS	CS
Scunthorpe	-	-	-	-	-	-	-	-	-	
Bury			2	0	1	1	1	1	1	1
Hartlepool	-	-	-	-	-	-	-	-	-	
Portsmouth	-	-	-	-	-	-	-	-	-	
Burton										
Cheltenham	W	L	4	2	0	2	2	2	2	1
Northampton	D	L	4	1	2	1	2	2	3	0
Chesterfield	L	D	3	1	1	1	1	2	1	1
Oxford	W	D	5	1	2	2	2	3	2	2
Exeter	W	L	2	1	1	0	2	0	2	0
Southend	W	W	3	2	0	1	1	2	1	1
Rochdale	W	W	2	2	0	0	1	1	1	1
Fleetwood Town	L	W	1	0	0	1	0	1	0	0
Bristol Rovers	D	L	2	1	1	0	1	1	2	0
Wycombe	W	L	2	1	0	1	1	1	1	1
Morecambe	W	D	4	4	0	0	4	0	4	0
York	W	L	3	3	0	0	3	0	3	0
Accrington	W	D	4	1	1	2	0	4	1	1
Torquay	W	D	6	2	1	3	4	2	4	0
AFC Wimbledon	W	D	2	2	0	0	2	0	2	0
Plymouth	W	W	2	2	0	0	1	1	1	1
Dag & Red	W	D	3	1	1	1	1	2	2	0
Mansfield			1	1	0	0	0	1	0	1
Newport County	-	-	-	-	-	-	-	-	-	

Season	Division	Pos	P	W	D	L	F	A	GD	Pts
2012-13	League 2	4	46	22	10	14	71	65	+6	76
2011-12	League 2	17	46	14	12	20	54	81	-27	54
2010-11	League 2	19	46	12	15	19	56	70	-14	51

Over/Under 50%/50% 10th   **Both score** 50%/50% 11th

Bury

Nickname: The Shakers
Colours: White and blue
Ground: Gigg Lane (11,313)
Tel: 0161 764 4881   www.buryfc.co.uk

The arrival of a new board signals a fresh start for the Shakers as the club adjusts to life back in the fourth tier.

Serious financial problems not only contributed to last season's relegation but put the club's whole future in jeopardy, with Bury's previous owners going public with a plea for £1m to save the club.

Kevin Blackwell remains in charge of the threadbare squad – they released 16 players after their relegation – but with the transfer embargo lifted, Bury new owners look set to back their manager.

Longest run without win/loss: 13/4
High/low league position: 21/24
Clean sheets: 7 **Yellow cards:** 64 **Red cards:** 3
Average attendance: 2,749 **Players used:** 38
Leading scorer: S Schumacher 8 (3,8)
Key stat: The shot-shy Shakers averaged less than a goal a game in League 1 last term

	2012-13 H	2012-13 A	Last six seasons at home P	W	D	L	OV	UN	BS	CS
Scunthorpe	W	W	2	1	1	0	1	1	1	1
Bury										
Hartlepool	W	L	2	1	0	1	2	0	2	0
Portsmouth	W	L	1	1	0	0	0	1	0	1
Burton			2	2	0	0	1	1	0	2
Cheltenham			2	0	0	2	1	1	1	0
Northampton			2	0	2	0	1	1	2	0
Chesterfield			5	1	2	2	2	3	4	0
Oxford			1	1	0	0	1	0	0	1
Exeter			2	1	0	1	0	2	0	1
Southend			1	1	0	0	0	1	0	1
Rochdale			4	2	1	1	2	2	3	1
Fleetwood Town			-	-	-	-	-	-	-	-
Bristol Rovers			-	-	-	-	-	-	-	-
Wycombe			4	0	2	2	3	1	3	1
Morecambe			4	3	1	0	2	2	2	2
York			-	-	-	-	-	-	-	-
Accrington			4	3	0	1	2	2	1	2
Torquay			2	0	0	2	2	0	1	0
AFC Wimbledon			-	-	-	-	-	-	-	-
Plymouth			-	-	-	-	-	-	-	-
Dag & Red			3	0	2	1	1	2	1	1
Mansfield			1	1	0	0	0	1	0	1
Newport County			-	-	-	-	-	-	-	-

Season	Division	Pos	P	W	D	L	F	A	GD	Pts
2012-13	League 1	22	46	9	14	23	45	73	-28	41
2011-12	League 1	14	46	15	11	20	60	79	-19	56
2010-11	League 2	2	46	23	12	11	82	50	+32	81

Over/Under 46%/54% 11th   **Both score** 54%/46% 9th

Cheltenham Town

Nickname: The Robins
Colours: Red and white
Ground: The Abbey Business Stadium (7,133)
Tel: 01242 573 558   www.ctfc.com

CHELTENHAM TOWN FC

Back-to-back play-off finishes mark Cheltenham out as one of League 2's most consistent sides and they should be capable of fighting for promotion again.

The Robins went into the final game still in touching distance of third place but the goals dried up at a crucial time and the season finished with a whimper.

Only scoring three times in their final seven games (including both legs of the play-off semi-final) will have disappointed Mark Yates and, despite having proven performers at this level, his forward line is an obvious area for improvement.

Longest run without win/loss: 4/6
High/low league position: 3/11
Clean sheets: 19 **Yellow cards:** 68 **Red cards:** 1
Average attendance: 3,252 **Players used:** 27
Leading scorer: S Harrad 8 (5,8)
Key stat: Cheltenham kept the most clean sheets in League 2 last term with 19 shutouts

	2012-13 H	2012-13 A	Last six seasons at home P	W	D	L	OV	UN	BS	CS
Scunthorpe			1	0	0	1	1	0	1	0
Bury			2	1	0	1	1	1	1	0
Hartlepool			2	1	1	0	0	2	1	1
Portsmouth			-	-	-	-	-	-	-	-
Burton	W	L	4	3	0	1	1	3	1	2
Cheltenham										
Northampton	W	W	6	2	3	1	2	4	3	2
Chesterfield	W	L	3	1	0	2	1	2	0	1
Oxford	W	L	3	1	2	0	1	2	2	1
Exeter	W	W	1	1	0	0	1	0	0	1
Southend	L	W	5	1	2	2	2	3	2	2
Rochdale	D	L	2	0	1	1	1	1	1	1
Fleetwood Town	D	D	1	0	1	0	1	0	1	0
Bristol Rovers	D	W	4	2	1	1	1	3	2	1
Wycombe	W	D	2	1	0	1	2	0	1	1
Morecambe	W	D	4	2	1	1	1	3	2	2
York	D	D	1	0	1	0	0	1	1	0
Accrington	L	D	4	1	1	2	3	1	3	0
Torquay	W	D	4	1	2	1	2	2	3	0
AFC Wimbledon	W	W	2	1	1	0	1	1	1	1
Plymouth	W	L	2	2	0	0	2	0	2	0
Dag & Red	W	L	3	2	1	0	1	2	2	1
Mansfield			-	-	-	-	-	-	-	-
Newport County			-	-	-	-	-	-	-	-

Season	Division	Pos	P	W	D	L	F	A	GD	Pts
2012-13	League 2	5	46	20	15	11	58	51	+7	75
2011-12	League 2	6	46	23	8	15	66	50	+16	77
2010-11	League 2	17	46	13	13	20	56	77	-21	52

Over/Under 46%/54% 15th   **Both score** 50%/50% 11th

Chesterfield

Nickname: Spireites
Colours: Blue and white
Ground: The Proact Stadium (10,300)
Tel: 01246 209 765   www.chesterfield-fc.co.uk

It's been a frustrating couple of years but the 2010-11 champions are showing signs of getting their act together.

Hopes were high for an immediate return to League 1 last term but a poor start cost John Sheridan his job and the Spireites only got going under new boss Paul Cook towards the end of the season.

Cook has bolstered his attacking options following the retirement of Football League legend Jack Lester and he's also persuaded Leam Richardson to give up a managerial job at Accrington to be his assistant.

Longest run without win/loss: 5/8
High/low league position: 8/18
Clean sheets: 16 **Yellow cards:** 64 **Red cards:** 3
Average attendance: 5,431 **Players used:** 32
Leading scorer: M Richards 12 (2,9)
Key stat: Chesterfield's miserly defensive record of 45 league goals conceded last season was only bettered by champions Gillingham

	2012-13 H	A	Last six seasons at home P	W	D	L	OV	UN	BS	CS
Scunthorpe			1	0	0	1	1	0	1	0
Bury			5	3	0	2	3	2	3	2
Hartlepool			1	0	0	1	1	0	1	0
Portsmouth			-	-	-	-	-	-	-	-
Burton	D	W	3	1	1	1	2	1	3	0
Cheltenham	W	L	3	3	0	0	2	1	1	2
Northampton	W	D	3	3	0	0	2	1	1	2
Chesterfield										
Oxford	W	W	2	1	0	1	2	0	2	0
Exeter	W	W	3	2	0	1	2	1	1	1
Southend	L	L	2	1	0	1	1	1	1	0
Rochdale	D	D	5	3	1	1	3	2	3	2
Fleetwood Town	L	W	1	0	0	1	1	0	1	0
Bristol Rovers	W	L	1	1	0	0	0	1	0	1
Wycombe	W	L	5	4	0	1	3	2	2	2
Morecambe	D	L	5	0	3	2	2	3	4	0
York	W	D	1	1	0	0	1	0	0	1
Accrington	W	L	5	4	1	0	3	2	4	1
Torquay	D	L	3	2	1	0	0	3	1	2
AFC Wimbledon	W	L	1	1	0	0	0	1	0	1
Plymouth	L	W	1	0	0	1	1	0	1	0
Dag & Red	L	W	4	0	3	1	2	2	4	0
Mansfield			1	1	0	0	0	1	0	1
Newport County			-	-	-	-	-	-	-	-

Season	Division	Pos	P	W	D	L	F	A	GD	Pts
2012-13	League 2	8	46	18	13	15	60	45	+15	67
2011-12	League 1	22	46	10	12	24	56	81	-25	42
2010-11	League 2	1	46	24	14	8	85	51	+34	66

Over/Under 39%/61% 23rd   **Both score** 46%/54% 15th

Dagenham & R

Nickname: Daggers
Colours: Red and white
Ground: LB Barking & Dagenham Stadium (6,070)
Tel: 020 8592 1549   www.daggers.co.uk

After coming so close to relegation last term, the Daggers are a strong fancy to fall. Losing long-serving manager John Still to Luton sent shockwaves through the club and they only avoided falling out of the Football League on goal difference after ending the season poorly.

Interim boss Wayne Burnett has taken over full time but his record of two wins in 12 games doesn't inspire confidence.

In the last 18 seasons, six of the teams who finished a place above the League 2 drop zone – 33 per cent – went down the following year.

Longest run without win/loss: 8/5
High/low league position: 12/22
Clean sheets: 12 **Yellow cards:** 52 **Red cards:** 2
Average attendance: 1,903 **Players used:** 30
Leading scorer: L Howell 9 (4,8)
Key stat: The Daggers have only gained one win at home in their last nine games

	2012-13 H	A	Last six seasons at home P	W	D	L	OV	UN	BS	CS
Scunthorpe			-	-	-	-	-	-	-	-
Bury			3	1	1	1	2	1	3	0
Hartlepool			1	0	1	0	0	1	1	0
Portsmouth			-	-	-	-	-	-	-	-
Burton	D	L	3	1	2	0	1	2	3	0
Cheltenham	W	L	3	1	0	2	1	2	0	1
Northampton	L	L	3	0	0	3	0	3	0	0
Chesterfield	L	W	4	2	0	2	3	1	1	1
Oxford	L	W	2	0	0	2	0	2	0	0
Exeter	D	W	3	0	2	1	1	2	3	0
Southend	L	L	2	0	0	2	2	0	1	0
Rochdale	W	D	5	2	1	2	3	2	4	0
Fleetwood Town	W	L	1	1	0	0	0	1	0	1
Bristol Rovers	L	W	3	1	0	2	3	0	1	1
Wycombe	W	L	3	1	1	1	2	1	1	1
Morecambe	L	L	5	1	1	3	2	3	3	1
York	L	W	1	0	0	1	0	1	0	0
Accrington	D	W	5	2	2	1	3	2	4	1
Torquay	D	L	3	1	2	0	2	1	3	0
AFC Wimbledon	L	D	2	0	0	2	0	2	0	0
Plymouth	D	D	3	0	1	2	1	2	1	1
Dag & Red										
Mansfield			1	1	0	0	0	1	0	1
Newport County			-	-	-	-	-	-	-	-

Season	Division	Pos	P	W	D	L	F	A	GD	Pts
2012-13	League 2	22	46	13	12	21	55	62	-7	51
2011-12	League 2	19	46	14	8	24	50	72	-22	50
2010-11	League 1	21	46	12	11	23	52	70	-18	47

Over/Under 50%/50% 10th   **Both score** 54%/46% 4th

Exeter City

Nickname: The Grecians
Colours: Black and white
Ground: St James' Park (8,830)
Tel: 0871 855 1904   www.exetercityfc.co.uk

On a good day Exeter remain one of the best sides in League 2 but any promotion ambitions are likely to be restricted by the tight finances at the club.

Money is at such premium that supporters are paying the wages of young striker Elliott Chamberlain and 21-goal hitman Jamie Cureton has left the club.

It won't be just Cureton's goals that will be missed as he struck up a potent understanding with Alan Gow and Liam Sercombe before injuries to the latter pair extinguished any promotion ambitions as the side's form tailed off drastically.

Longest run without win/loss: 7/6
High/low league position: 3/11
Clean sheets: 13 **Yellow cards:** 56 **Red cards:** 2
Average attendance: 4,141 **Players used:** 29
Leading scorer: J Cureton 21 (9,16)
Key stat: Exeter finished the season as the most out of form side in the league after gaining one point out of a possible 21

	2012-13 H	A	Last six seasons at home P	W	D	L	OV	UN	BS	CS
Scunthorpe			1	0	1	0	0	1	0	1
Bury			2	1	1	0	1	1	1	1
Hartlepool			3	1	1	1	2	1	2	1
Portsmouth			-	-	-	-	-	-	-	-
Burton	W	L	2	1	0	1	2	0	1	1
Cheltenham	L	L	1	0	0	1	0	1	0	0
Northampton	W	L	1	1	0	0	1	0	0	1
Chesterfield	L	L	3	1	0	2	2	1	2	0
Oxford	L	W	2	1	0	1	1	1	1	1
Exeter										
Southend	W	L	2	2	0	0	1	1	0	2
Rochdale	L	W	4	3	0	1	3	1	3	1
Fleetwood Town	D	D	1	0	1	0	1	0	1	0
Bristol Rovers	L	L	3	1	1	1	2	1	2	1
Wycombe	W	W	4	2	1	1	2	2	3	1
Morecambe	L	W	2	0	1	1	2	0	1	0
York	D	W	2	0	2	0	0	2	2	0
Accrington	W	W	2	2	0	0	1	1	1	1
Torquay	L	D	2	1	0	1	1	1	1	0
AFC Wimbledon	W	D	1	1	0	0	0	1	0	1
Plymouth	D	L	2	1	1	0	0	2	1	1
Dag & Red	L	D	3	2	0	1	2	1	2	0
Mansfield			-	-	-	-	-	-	-	-
Newport County			-	-	-	-	-	-	-	-

Season	Division	Pos	P	W	D	L	F	A	GD	Pts
2012-13	League 2	10	46	18	10	18	63	62	+1	64
2011-12	League 1	23	46	10	12	24	46	75	-29	42
2010-11	League 1	8	46	20	10	16	66	73	-7	70

Over/Under 57%/43% 3rd   **Both score** 46%/54% 15th

Fleetwood Town

Nickname: The Cod Army
Colours: Red and white
Ground: Highbury Stadium (5,092)
Tel: 01253 770702   www.fleetwoodtownfc.com

Big-spending Fleetwood Town flopped badly in the 2012-13 campaign.

Much was expected of the Cod Army as they embarked on their first season in the Football League but when results didn't go to plan Micky Mellon was shown the door, with Fleetwood sitting in the play-off places.

The appointment of Graham Alexander didn't improve matters – they were seventh when he took charge but finished the season in mid-table – and the rookie boss has the pressure of delivering promotion in his first full-time post.

Longest run without win/loss: 6/6
High/low league position: 3/13
Clean sheets: 16 **Yellow cards:** 90 **Red cards:** 7
Average attendance: 2,855 **Players used:** 38
Leading scorers: Parkin 10 (3,6) Brown 10 (3,9)
Key stat: Fleetwood finished last season out of sorts, with four straight defeats and nine losses in their last 15 games

	2012-13 H	A	Last six seasons at home P	W	D	L	OV	UN	BS	CS
Scunthorpe			-	-	-	-	-	-	-	-
Bury			-	-	-	-	-	-	-	-
Hartlepool			-	-	-	-	-	-	-	-
Portsmouth			-	-	-	-	-	-	-	-
Burton	L	W	1	0	0	1	1	0	0	0
Cheltenham	D	D	1	0	1	0	0	1	1	0
Northampton	W	L	1	1	0	0	1	0	1	0
Chesterfield	L	W	1	0	0	1	1	0	1	0
Oxford	L	W	1	1	0	0	1	0	0	1
Exeter	D	D	1	0	1	0	0	1	0	1
Southend	L	D	1	0	1	0	0	1	0	1
Rochdale	L	D	1	0	0	1	1	0	0	0
Fleetwood Town										
Bristol Rovers	L	D	1	0	0	1	1	0	1	0
Wycombe	L	L	1	0	0	1	0	1	0	0
Morecambe	W	W	1	1	0	0	0	1	0	1
York	D	W	3	1	2	0	1	2	1	2
Accrington	L	W	1	0	0	1	1	0	1	0
Torquay	D	W	1	0	1	0	0	1	0	1
AFC Wimbledon	D	L	2	0	2	0	0	2	2	0
Plymouth	W	L	1	1	0	0	1	0	0	1
Dag & Red	W	L	1	1	0	0	1	0	0	1
Mansfield			2	2	0	0	1	1	0	2
Newport County			2	0	1	1	1	1	2	0

Season	Division	Pos	P	W	D	L	F	A	GD	Pts
2012-13	League 2	13	46	15	15	16	55	57	-2	60
2011-12	Conference	1	46	31	10	5	102	48	+54	103
2010-11	Conference	5	46	22	12	12	68	42	+26	78

Over/Under 52%/48% 7th   **Both score** 46%/54% 15th

Hartlepool United

Nickname: Pools
Colours: White and blue
Ground: Victoria Park (7,856)
Tel: 01429 272 584   www.hartlepoolunited.co.uk

Hartlepool are back in League 2 for the first time since 2007 and their chances of an immediate return to the third tier are not strikingly obvious.

Despite having four different managers in just two years, the playing and back-room staff remained pretty constant before a major shake-up was instigated by the board following their relegation.

New boss Colin Cooper, who will be assisted by former Middlesbrough team-mate Craig Hignett, has described the job as a "big task" and it's hard to get too excited about their prospects.

Longest run without win/loss: 20/7
High/low league position: 20/24
Clean sheets: 9 **Yellow cards:** 62 **Red cards:** 3
Average attendance: 3,612 **Players used:** 24
Leading scorer: A Monkhouse 7 (1,5)
Key stat: Hartlepool were the least prolific scorers in the Football League last term with a meagre 39 goals

| | 2012-13 | | Last six seasons at home | | | | | | | |
	H	A	P	W	D	L	OV	UN	BS	CS
Scunthorpe	W	W	3	1	0	2	2	1	2	1
Bury	W	L	2	2	0	0	1	1	0	2
Hartlepool										
Portsmouth	D	W	1	0	1	0	0	1	0	1
Burton										
Cheltenham			2	1	0	1	1	1	1	0
Northampton			2	1	0	1	0	2	0	1
Chesterfield			1	0	0	1	1	0	1	0
Oxford			-	-	-	-	-	-	-	-
Exeter			3	1	1	1	1	2	2	1
Southend			3	3	0	0	3	0	1	2
Rochdale			2	1	0	1	0	2	0	1
Fleetwood Town			-	-	-	-	-	-	-	-
Bristol Rovers			4	1	2	1	2	2	3	1
Wycombe			2	0	1	1	1	1	2	0
Morecambe			-	-	-	-	-	-	-	-
York			-	-	-	-	-	-	-	-
Accrington			-	-	-	-	-	-	-	-
Torquay			-	-	-	-	-	-	-	-
AFC Wimbledon			-	-	-	-	-	-	-	-
Plymouth			1	1	0	0	0	1	0	1
Dag & Red			1	0	0	1	0	1	0	0
Mansfield			-	-	-	-	-	-	-	-
Newport County			-	-	-	-	-	-	-	-

Season	Division	Pos	P	W	D	L	F	A	GD	Pts
2012-13	League 1	23	46	9	14	23	39	67	-28	41
2011-12	League 1	13	46	14	14	18	50	55	-5	56
2010-11	League 1	16	46	15	12	19	47	65	-18	57

Over/Under 46%/54% 11th   **Both score** 46%/54% 18th

Mansfield Town

Nickname: The Stags
Colours: Yellow and blue
Ground: One Call Stadium (8,186)
Tel: 01623 482 482   www.mansfieldtown.net

The Conference champions appear well equipped to maintain a phenomenal run of form on their return to the Football League following a six-year exodus.

The Stags took 60 points in the second half of last season – after a third-round FA Cup loss to Liverpool, a match decided by Luis Suarez's hand, they won 20 of their last 24 games in a run that included a string of 12 victories on the bounce.

Chairman John Radford and manager Paul Cox seem to have a strong rapport and the club could make an impact in the top half of the table.

Longest run without win/loss: 4/12
High/low league position: 1/14
Clean sheets: 18 **Yellow cards:** 90 **Red cards:** 3
Average attendance: 2,209 **Players used:** 33
Leading scorer: M Green 25 (11,21)
Key stat: Mansfield scored first in over 71 per cent of their Conference Premier games last season

| | 2012-13 | | Last six seasons at home | | | | | | | |
	H	A	P	W	D	L	OV	UN	BS	CS
Scunthorpe			-	-	-	-	-	-	-	-
Bury			1	0	1	0	0	1	1	0
Hartlepool			-	-	-	-	-	-	-	-
Portsmouth			-	-	-	-	-	-	-	-
Burton			1	0	0	1	0	1	0	0
Cheltenham			-	-	-	-	-	-	-	-
Northampton			-	-	-	-	-	-	-	-
Chesterfield			1	0	0	1	1	0	1	0
Oxford			2	1	0	1	2	0	2	0
Exeter			-	-	-	-	-	-	-	-
Southend			-	-	-	-	-	-	-	-
Rochdale			1	0	0	1	1	0	0	0
Fleetwood Town			2	0	1	1	1	1	2	0
Bristol Rovers			-	-	-	-	-	-	-	-
Wycombe			1	0	0	1	1	0	0	0
Morecambe			1	0	0	1	1	0	1	0
York			4	2	1	1	1	3	1	2
Accrington			1	0	0	1	1	0	1	0
Torquay			1	0	1	0	0	1	0	0
AFC Wimbledon			2	0	0	2	1	1	1	0
Plymouth			-	-	-	-	-	-	-	-
Dag & Red			1	0	0	1	0	1	0	0
Mansfield										
Newport County	L	L	3	1	1	1	3	0	2	1

Season	Division	Pos	P	W	D	L	F	A	GD	Pts
2012-13	Conference	1	46	30	5	11	92	52	+40	95
2011-12	Conference	3	46	25	14	7	87	48	+39	89
2010-11	Conference	13	46	17	10	19	73	75	-2	61

Over/Under 61%/39% 5th   **Both score** 54%/46% 17th

Morecambe

Nickname: The Shrimps
Colours: Red and white
Ground: The Globe Arena (6,400)
Tel: 01524 411 797   www.morecambefc.com

Cutbacks continue to threaten Morecambe's League 2 status and it's hard to see anything other than a tough season ahead for the Shrimps.

Having bettered their 2011-12 points haul with a last-game victory, manager Jim Bentley described his team's 16th-place finish as a "massive achievement" and will be under no illusions as to the size of his task this season.

Key players have left and more are expected to follow in what is forecast to be a difficult summer as budgetary constraints at the Globe Arena begin to bite.

Longest run without win/loss: 6/4
High/low league position: 10/18
Clean sheets: 12 **Yellow cards:** 58 **Red cards:** 6
Average attendance: 1,954 **Players used:** 26
Leading scorer: J Redshaw 15 (7,13)
Key stat: The Shrimps raised their game against teams in the top half last season with a record of W8, D8, L8

	2012-13		Last six seasons at home							
	H	A	P	W	D	L	OV	UN	BS	CS
Scunthorpe			-	-	-	-	-	-	-	-
Bury			4	2	1	1	3	1	2	2
Hartlepool			-	-	-	-	-	-	-	-
Portsmouth			-	-	-	-	-	-	-	-
Burton	D	L	4	2	2	0	3	1	3	1
Cheltenham	D	L	4	2	2	0	1	3	2	2
Northampton	D	L	4	0	1	3	3	1	4	0
Chesterfield	W	D	5	1	3	1	1	4	3	1
Oxford	D	D	3	0	2	1	1	2	1	1
Exeter	L		2	0	1	1	1	1	1	0
Southend	W	W	3	3	0	0	1	2	1	2
Rochdale	W	W	4	1	3	0	2	2	3	1
Fleetwood Town	L	L	1	0	0	1	1	0	0	0
Bristol Rovers	D	W	2	0	1	1	1	1	2	0
Wycombe	L	D	4	0	1	3	1	3	0	1
Morecambe										
York	D	W	1	0	1	0	1	0	1	0
Accrington	D	L	6	0	2	4	3	3	4	1
Torquay	L	L	4	2	0	2	2	2	2	1
AFC Wimbledon	W	L	2	1	0	1	2	0	2	0
Plymouth	L	L	2	0	1	1	2	0	2	0
Dag & Red	W	W	5	3	0	2	3	2	3	2
Mansfield			1	1	0	0	1	0	1	0
Newport County			-	-	-	-	-	-	-	-

Season	Division	Pos	P	W	D	L	F	A	GD	Pts
2012-13	League 2	16	46	15	13	18	55	61	-6	58
2011-12	League 2	15	46	14	14	18	63	57	+6	56
2010-11	League 2	20	46	13	12	21	54	73	-19	51

Over/Under 52%/48% 7th   **Both score** 52%/48% 7th

Newport County

Nickname: The Exiles
Colours: Yellow and black
Ground: Rodney Parade (5,511)
Tel: 01633 670 690   www.newport-county.co.uk

Having risen from the ashes, new boys Newport County will be doing everything in their power to flourish in the league.

Relegated from the Football League in 1988, County reformed a year later and started off the long journey back in the ninth tier of English football.

While promoted Conference sides historically hold their own, York diced with relegation last season. But shrewd boss Justin Edinburgh, backed by a board that includes a EuroMillions winner, has said he will stick with the core of the team that won promotion.

Longest run without win/loss: 3/9
High/low league position: 1/5
Clean sheets: 14 **Yellow cards:** 60 **Red cards:** 0
Average attendance: 1,753 **Players used:** 28
Leading scorer: A O'connor 18 (5,13)
Key stat: Exiles manager Justin Edinburgh has a 44 per cent career win ratio since starting out in 2009

	2012-13		Last six seasons at home							
	H	A	P	W	D	L	OV	UN	BS	CS
Scunthorpe			-	-	-	-	-	-	-	-
Bury			-	-	-	-	-	-	-	-
Hartlepool			-	-	-	-	-	-	-	-
Portsmouth			-	-	-	-	-	-	-	-
Burton			-	-	-	-	-	-	-	-
Cheltenham			-	-	-	-	-	-	-	-
Northampton			-	-	-	-	-	-	-	-
Chesterfield			-	-	-	-	-	-	-	-
Oxford			-	-	-	-	-	-	-	-
Exeter			-	-	-	-	-	-	-	-
Southend			-	-	-	-	-	-	-	-
Rochdale			-	-	-	-	-	-	-	-
Fleetwood Town			2	0	0	2	1	1	1	0
Bristol Rovers			-	-	-	-	-	-	-	-
Wycombe			-	-	-	-	-	-	-	-
Morecambe			-	-	-	-	-	-	-	-
York			2	2	0	0	2	0	1	1
Accrington			-	-	-	-	-	-	-	-
Torquay			-	-	-	-	-	-	-	-
AFC Wimbledon			1	0	1	0	1	0	1	0
Plymouth			-	-	-	-	-	-	-	-
Dag & Red			-	-	-	-	-	-	-	-
Mansfield	W	W	3	3	0	0	3	0	3	0
Newport County										

Season	Division	Pos	P	W	D	L	F	A	GD	Pts
2012-13	Conference	3	46	25	10	11	85	60	+25	85
2011-12	Conference	19	46	11	14	21	53	65	-12	47
2010-11	Conference	9	46	18	15	13	78	60	+18	69

Over/Under 61%/39% 5th   **Both score** 59%/41% 9th

Northampton Town

Nickname: The Cobblers
Colours: Claret and white
Ground: Sixfields Stadium (7,300)
Tel: 01604 683 700   www.ntfc.co.uk

DEFEAT in the play-off final will have been hard for the Cobblers to stomach but it shouldn't mask a season of great progress for Northampton.

In his two-year tenure, Aidy Boothroyd has galvanised the club and all eyes at Sixfields will be fixed on cracking promotion this time after last term's near-miss.

Even with the loss of experienced duo Clarke Carlisle and Adebayo Akinfenwa, Northampton look one of the sides best equipped to make their presence felt at the top of the division – if Boothroyd can lift their dreadful away form.

Longest run without win/loss: 5/5
High/low league position: 3/17
Clean sheets: 16 **Yellow cards:** 81 **Red cards:** 4
Average attendance: 4,785 **Players used:** 29
Leading scorer: A Akinfenwa 16 (7,13)
Key stat: Only relegated Barnet had a worse away record than Northampton in League 2

	2012-13 H	A	Last six seasons at home P	W	D	L	OV	UN	BS	CS
Scunthorpe	1	0	1	0	1	0	1	0		
Bury	2	0	1	1	1	1	2	0		
Hartlepool	2	1	1	0	0	2	1	1		
Portsmouth	-	-	-	-	-	-	-	-		
Burton	W	D	4	1	1	2	2	2	3	1
Cheltenham	L	L	6	3	1	2	5	1	6	0
Northampton										
Chesterfield	D	L	3	0	2	1	1	2	1	2
Oxford	W	L	3	3	0	0	2	1	2	1
Exeter	W	L	1	1	0	0	1	0	0	1
Southend	D	W	5	1	1	3	4	1	4	0
Rochdale	W	D	2	1	0	1	2	0	2	0
Fleetwood Town	W	L	1	1	0	0	1	0	1	0
Bristol Rovers	W	L	4	2	1	1	3	1	2	
Wycombe	W	D	2	1	1	0	1	1	2	0
Morecambe	W	D	4	2	1	1	2	2	1	2
York	L	D	1	0	0	1	0	1	0	0
Accrington	W	W	4	2	2	0	3	0	4	
Torquay	W	D	4	1	3	0	1	3	1	3
AFC Wimbledon	W	D	2	2	0	0	2	0	2	
Plymouth	W	L	2	1	1	0	0	2	0	2
Dag & Red	W	W	3	3	0	0	2	1	2	1
Mansfield	-	-	-	-	-	-	-	-		
Newport County	-	-	-	-	-	-	-	-		

Season	Division	Pos	P	W	D	L	F	A	GD	Pts
2012-13	League 2	6	46	21	10	15	64	55	+9	73
2011-12	League 2	20	46	12	12	22	56	79	-23	48
2010-11	League 2	16	46	11	16	19	63	71	-8	52

Over/Under 48%/52% 13th   **Both score** 46%/54% 15th

Oxford United

Nickname: The U's
Colours: Yellow
Ground: The Kassam Stadium (12,500)
Tel: 01865 337533   www.oufc.co.uk

It's crunch time for Chris Wilder after the Oxford United manager signed a new one-year contract despite some supporters calling for his head.

While credit goes to the board for sticking by the man who led the club back to the Football League three years ago, there was widespread frustration at another failed play-off attempt.

Wilder knows he has to improve on back-to-back ninth-placed finishes but the board's request that he does it with a squad made up of 25 per cent youth system products may make life harder.

Longest run without win/loss: 6/8
High/low league position: 9/19
Clean sheets: 14 **Yellow cards:** 61 **Red cards:** 4
Average attendance: 5,954 **Players used:** 33
Leading scorer: Craddock 10 (2,5) Potter 10 (4,10)
Key stat: Oxford United won ten and drew one of the 11 league games in which they were leading at half-time

	2012-13 H	A	Last six seasons at home P	W	D	L	OV	UN	BS	CS
Scunthorpe	-	-	-	-	-	-	-	-		
Bury	1	0	0	1	1	0	1	0		
Hartlepool	-	-	-	-	-	-	-	-		
Portsmouth	-	-	-	-	-	-	-	-		
Burton	D	L	5	2	2	1	4	1	3	1
Cheltenham	W	L	3	1	1	1	1	2	2	1
Northampton	W	L	3	3	0	0	2	1	2	1
Chesterfield	L	L	2	0	1	1	0	2	0	1
Oxford										
Exeter	L	W	2	0	1	1	2	0	2	0
Southend	W	L	3	1	0	2	0	3	0	1
Rochdale	W	L	1	1	0	0	1	0	0	1
Fleetwood Town	L	L	1	0	0	1	1	0	1	0
Bristol Rovers	L	W	2	1	0	1	1	0	1	0
Wycombe	W	L	2	0	1	1	1	1	1	0
Morecambe	D	D	3	1	1	1	2	1	2	1
York	D	L	4	2	2	0	1	3	2	2
Accrington	W	W	3	1	2	0	1	2	1	2
Torquay	D	W	5	0	3	2	2	3	2	1
AFC Wimbledon	W	W	3	3	0	0	1	2	1	2
Plymouth	W	W	2	2	0	0	2	0	2	0
Dag & Red	L	W	2	1	0	1	2	0	2	0
Mansfield			2	2	0	0	2	0	2	
Newport County	-	-	-	-	-	-	-	-		

Season	Division	Pos	P	W	D	L	F	A	GD	Pts
2012-13	League 2	9	46	19	8	19	60	61	-1	65
2011-12	League 2	9	46	17	17	12	59	48	+11	63
2010-11	League 2	12	46	17	17	12	58	60	-2	63

Over/Under 54%/46% 4th   **Both score** 46%/54% 15th

Plymouth Argyle

Nickname: The Pilgrims
Colours: Green and white
Ground: Home Park (16,388)
Tel: 01752 562 561   www.pafc.co.uk

Plymouth will glad to see the back of another wretched campaign and they'll be setting their sights higher up the table.

The main problem is obvious with a desperate lack of goals continuing to undermine their progress.

On-loan Jason Banton was top scorer with six goals last term and only rock-bottom Aldershot scored fewer overall.

John Sheridan, who took charge in January, has a promotion from this league with Chesterfield on his cv but the Pilgrims finished the season just a point ahead of relegated Barnet.

Longest run without win/loss: 7/4
High/low league position: 15/24
Clean sheets: 9 **Yellow cards:** 70 **Red cards:** 4
Average attendance: 7,095 **Players used:** 35
Leading scorer: J Banton 6 (3,5)
Key stat: Plymouth have scored 93 goals in the last two seasons – just over a goal a game

	2012-13 H	A	Last six seasons at home P	W	D	L	OV	UN	BS	CS
Scunthorpe			2	2	0	0	2	0	1	1
Bury	-	-	-	-	-	-	-	-		
Hartlepool			1	0	0	1	0	1	0	0
Portsmouth	-	-	-	-	-	-	-	-		
Burton	L	L	2	1	0	1	2	0	2	0
Cheltenham	W	L	2	1	0	1	1	1	1	1
Northampton	W	L	2	2	0	0	2	0	2	0
Chesterfield	L	W	1	0	0	1	0	1	0	0
Oxford	L	L	2	0	1	1	0	2	1	0
Exeter	W	D	2	2	0	0	2	0	2	0
Southend	D	W	2	0	2	0	1	1	2	0
Rochdale	W	L	2	1	0	1	1	1	1	0
Fleetwood Town	W	L	1	1	0	0	1	0	1	0
Bristol Rovers	D	L	3	1	2	0	1	2	3	0
Wycombe	L	D	1	0	0	1	0	1	0	0
Morecambe	W	W	2	1	1	0	1	1	2	0
York	W	L	1	1	0	0	0	1	0	1
Accrington	D	D	2	0	2	0	1	1	1	1
Torquay	D	D	2	0	1	1	1	1	2	0
AFC Wimbledon	L	D	2	0	0	2	1	1	1	0
Plymouth										
Dag & Red	D	D	3	1	2	0	1	2	1	2
Mansfield	-	-	-	-	-	-	-	-		
Newport County	-	-	-	-	-	-	-	-		

Season	Division	Pos	P	W	D	L	F	A	GD	Pts
2012-13	League 2	21	46	13	13	20	46	55	-9	52
2011-12	League 2	21	46	10	16	20	47	64	-17	46
2010-11	League 1	23	46	15	7	24	51	74	-23	42

Over/Under 41%/59% 21st   **Both score** 52%/48% 7th

Portsmouth

Nickname: Pompey
Colours: Blue and white
Ground: Fratton Park (21,178)
Tel: 023 9273 1204   www.portsmouthfc.co.uk

Rarely has the fourth tier welcomed a club of Portsmouth's stature and the layers feel size matters as they were immediately chalked up as 5-1 favourites.

Having been bought by a supporters' trust in April, Portsmouth's ten-point deduction took effect last term, leaving them with a clean slate as they start out on the road to recovery from financial strife.

Pompey would have been relegated from League 1 even without the points deduction, but the survival of the club was their real achievement.

Longest run without win/loss: 22/5
High/low league position: 14/24
Clean sheets: 9 **Yellow cards:** 64 **Red cards:** 3
Average attendance: 12,232 **Players used:** 46
Leading scorer: I Mcleod 10 (3,9)
Key stat: Portsmouth finished last season in good form, winning five out of their last 11 games

	2012-13 H	A	Last six seasons at home P	W	D	L	OV	UN	BS	CS
Scunthorpe	W	L	2	2	0	0	1	1	1	1
Bury	W	L	1	1	0	0	0	1	0	1
Hartlepool	L	D	1	0	0	1	1	0	1	0
Portsmouth										
Burton	-	-	-	-	-	-	-	-		
Cheltenham	-	-	-	-	-	-	-	-		
Northampton	-	-	-	-	-	-	-	-		
Chesterfield	-	-	-	-	-	-	-	-		
Oxford	-	-	-	-	-	-	-	-		
Exeter	-	-	-	-	-	-	-	-		
Southend	-	-	-	-	-	-	-	-		
Rochdale	-	-	-	-	-	-	-	-		
Fleetwood Town	-	-	-	-	-	-	-	-		
Bristol Rovers	-	-	-	-	-	-	-	-		
Wycombe	-	-	-	-	-	-	-	-		
Morecambe	-	-	-	-	-	-	-	-		
York	-	-	-	-	-	-	-	-		
Accrington	-	-	-	-	-	-	-	-		
Torquay	-	-	-	-	-	-	-	-		
AFC Wimbledon	-	-	-	-	-	-	-	-		
Plymouth	-	-	-	-	-	-	-	-		
Dag & Red	-	-	-	-	-	-	-	-		
Mansfield	-	-	-	-	-	-	-	-		
Newport County	-	-	-	-	-	-	-	-		

Season	Division	Pos	P	W	D	L	F	A	GD	Pts
2012-13	League 1	24	46	10	12	24	51	69	-18	32
2011-12	Championship	22	46	13	11	22	50	59	-9	40
2010-11	Championship	16	46	15	13	18	53	60	-7	58

Over/Under 50%/50% 8th   **Both score** 54%/46% 9th

Rochdale

Nickname: The Dale
Colours: Blue and black
Ground: Spotland Stadium (10,037)
Tel: 0870 822 1907   www.rochdaleafc.co.uk

With Keith Hill back in the Spotland hotseat, Rochdale could be set for a decent season.

The return of the club's most successful manager in January was widely celebrated and despite a slow start to his second spell in charge, he got a strong finish out of his side with 15 points gained from the last eight games.

Hill is a shrewd operator – he took Dale up into League 1 in his first spell in the dugout – and with some talented players already at his disposal, a place in the top seven is a realistic target.

Longest run without win/loss: 6/6
High/low league position: 5/18
Clean sheets: 11 **Yellow cards:** 67 **Red cards:** 5
Average attendance: 2,439 **Players used:** 33
Leading scorer: R Grant 15 (1,14)
Key stat: Dale sacrificed 22 points from a winning position last season

	2012-13 H	2012-13 A	P	W	D	L	OV	UN	BS	CS
Scunthorpe			1	1	0	0	0	1	0	1
Bury			4	2	1	1	3	1	2	2
Hartlepool			2	0	1	1	1	1	1	1
Portsmouth			-	-	-	-	-	-	-	-
Burton	L	L	2	0	0	2	1	1	0	0
Cheltenham	W	D	2	1	0	1	1	1	1	0
Northampton	D	L	2	1	1	0	0	2	0	2
Chesterfield	D	D	5	1	2	2	2	3	4	0
Oxford	W	L	1	1	0	0	0	1	0	1
Exeter	L	W	4	1	1	2	3	1	3	0
Southend	W	L	1	1	0	0	1	0	1	0
Rochdale										
Fleetwood Town	D	W	1	0	1	0	0	1	0	1
Bristol Rovers	W	L	2	2	0	0	2	0	2	0
Wycombe	W	W	4	2	0	2	2	2	2	0
Morecambe	L	L	4	2	1	1	2	2	3	1
York	L	D	1	0	0	1	1	0	1	0
Accrington	L	W	4	2	0	2	4	0	3	0
Torquay	W	L	2	2	0	0	1	1	1	1
AFC Wimbledon	L	W	1	0	0	1	0	1	0	0
Plymouth	W	L	2	1	1	0	0	2	1	1
Dag & Red	D	L	5	3	1	1	3	2	3	1
Mansfield			1	1	0	0	0	1	0	1
Newport County			-	-	-	-	-	-	-	-

Season	Division	Pos	P	W	D	L	F	A	GD	Pts
2012-13	League 2	12	46	16	13	17	68	70	-2	61
2011-12	League 1	24	46	8	14	24	47	81	-34	38
2010-11	League 1	9	46	18	14	14	63	55	+8	68

Over/Under 65%/35% 1st   **Both score** 65%/35% 1st

Scunthorpe United

Nickname: The Iron
Colours: Claret and blue
Ground: Glanford Park (9,144)
Tel: 01724 848 077 www.scunthorpe-united.co.uk

Brian Laws will be targeting a third bottom-tier promotion as Scunthorpe boss, having achieved the feat in 1999 and 2005.

After ending a three-year break from management, Laws returned for a third spell last October, breathing new life into his struggling side but not doing enough to save them from relegation.

He will need to chop and change his squad but Scunthorpe are a well run club with strong form at this level and they should be battling it out at the upper echelons of the table.

Longest run without win/loss: 7/4
High/low league position: 18/23
Clean sheets: 5 **Yellow cards:** 62 **Red cards:** 5
Average attendance: 3,348 **Players used:** 35
Leading scorer: Hawley 11 (4,11) Clarke 11 (5,10)
Key stat: Scunthorpe shipped 73 league goals last season, an average of 1.58 per game

	2012-13 H	2012-13 A	P	W	D	L	OV	UN	BS	CS
Scunthorpe										
Bury	L	L	2	0	0	2	2	0	2	0
Hartlepool	L	L	3	1	0	2	2	1	1	1
Portsmouth	W	L	2	1	1	0	1	1	2	0
Burton			-	-	-	-	-	-	-	-
Cheltenham			1	1	0	0	1	0	0	1
Northampton			1	0	1	0	1	0	1	0
Chesterfield			1	0	1	0	1	0	1	0
Oxford			-	-	-	-	-	-	-	-
Exeter			1	1	0	0	1	0	1	0
Southend			1	0	1	0	0	1	1	0
Rochdale			1	1	0	0	0	1	0	1
Fleetwood Town			-	-	-	-	-	-	-	-
Bristol Rovers			1	0	0	1	0	1	0	0
Wycombe			1	1	0	0	1	0	1	0
Morecambe			-	-	-	-	-	-	-	-
York			-	-	-	-	-	-	-	-
Accrington			-	-	-	-	-	-	-	-
Torquay			-	-	-	-	-	-	-	-
AFC Wimbledon			-	-	-	-	-	-	-	-
Plymouth			2	2	0	0	1	1	1	1
Dag & Red			-	-	-	-	-	-	-	-
Mansfield			-	-	-	-	-	-	-	-
Newport County			-	-	-	-	-	-	-	-

Season	Division	Pos	P	W	D	L	F	A	GD	Pts
2012-13	League 1	21	46	13	9	24	49	73	-24	48
2011-12	League 1	18	46	10	22	14	55	59	-4	52
2010-11	Championship	24	46	12	6	28	43	87	-44	42

Over/Under 61%/39% 1st   **Both score** 59%/41% 4th

Southend United

Nickname: The Shrimpers
Colours: Blue
Ground: Roots Hall (11,927)
Tel: 01702 304 050   www.southendunited.co.uk

With off-the-field activities providing an unwelcome distraction it would be no surprise to see Southend slip this season.

Plans for a new stadium, which have been in the pipeline for 15 years, remain unrealised and in May the club were issued with an winding-up petition for the sixth time in four years – they again paid the arrears, but none of this will help Phil Brown's pre-season planning.

Brown took over from Paul Sturrock towards the end of a topsy-turvy season but his record of one win in eight needs improving.

Longest run without win/loss: 7/10
High/low league position: 4/14
Clean sheets: 12 **Yellow cards:** 47 **Red cards:** 5
Average attendance: 5,034 **Players used:** 36
Leading scorer: B Assombalonga 15 (4,12)
Key stat: Southend accumulated nine more points on the road than they did at home last season

	2012-13 H	A	Last six seasons at home P	W	D	L	OV	UN	BS	CS
Scunthorpe			1	1	0	0	0	1	0	1
Bury			1	0	1	0	0	1	1	0
Hartlepool			3	3	0	0	3	0	3	0
Portsmouth	-	-	-	-	-	-	-	-	-	-
Burton	L	L	3	0	1	2	0	3	1	0
Cheltenham	L	W	5	2	1	2	4	1	3	2
Northampton	L	D	5	1	3	1	2	3	4	1
Chesterfield	W	W	2	1	0	1	2	0	1	1
Oxford	W	L	3	3	0	0	2	1	2	1
Exeter	W	L	2	1	1	0	1	1	1	1
Southend										
Rochdale	W	L	1	1	0	0	1	0	1	0
Fleetwood Town	D	D	1	0	1	0	0	1	1	0
Bristol Rovers	D	W	5	2	2	1	1	4	2	2
Wycombe	W	W	3	2	1	0	1	2	2	1
Morecambe	L	L	3	0	1	2	1	2	2	0
York	D	L	1	0	1	0	0	1	0	1
Accrington	L	D	3	0	2	1	1	2	2	0
Torquay	D	W	3	2	1	0	2	1	3	0
AFC Wimbledon	L	W	2	1	0	1	1	1	1	1
Plymouth	L	D	2	1	0	1	0	2	0	1
Dag & Red	W	W	2	1	1	0	1	1	2	0
Mansfield	-	-	-	-	-	-	-	-	-	-
Newport County	-	-	-	-	-	-	-	-	-	-

Season	Division	Pos	P	W	D	L	F	A	GD	Pts
2012-13	League 2	11	46	16	13	17	61	55	+6	61
2011-12	League 2	4	46	25	8	13	77	48	+29	83
2010-11	League 2	13	46	16	13	17	62	56	+6	61

Over/Under 50%/50% 10th   **Both score** 50%/50% 11th

Torquay United

Nickname: The Gulls
Colours: Yellow and blue
Ground: Plainmoor (6,145)
Tel: 01803 328 666   www.torquayunited.com

The Gulls suffered an alarming decline last season but things should pick up with a new regime in place.

Losing play-off semi-finalists in 2011-12, Torquay became embroiled in a relegation scrap and were rudderless for a key part of the season with Martin Ling absent on sick leave.

Alan Knill came in for nine weeks as interim boss to steer the side to safety and he has been rewarded for his efforts by getting the gig permanently.

He worked wonders in this league with Bury and should oversee a turnaround.

Longest run without win/loss: 11/5
High/low league position: 7/22
Clean sheets: 9 **Yellow cards:** 65 **Red cards:** 5
Average attendance: 2,709 **Players used:** 26
Leading scorer: R Howe 16 (5,15)
Key stat: Backing Torquay blindly would have returned -£11.13 (to a £1 level stake) throughout the course of the league season

	2012-13 H	A	Last six seasons at home P	W	D	L	OV	UN	BS	CS
Scunthorpe	-	-	-	-	-	-	-	-	-	-
Bury			2	0	1	1	1	1	2	0
Hartlepool	-	-	-	-	-	-	-	-	-	-
Portsmouth	-	-	-	-	-	-	-	-	-	-
Burton	D	L	6	2	2	2	4	2	5	1
Cheltenham	D	L	4	2	2	0	4	0	3	1
Northampton	D	L	4	3	1	0	1	3	1	3
Chesterfield	W	D	3	2	1	0	1	2	1	2
Oxford	L	D	5	1	2	2	3	2	4	1
Exeter	D	W	2	1	1	0	0	2	1	1
Southend	L	D	3	0	2	1	1	2	2	1
Rochdale	W	L	2	2	0	0	2	0	1	1
Fleetwood Town	L	D	1	0	0	1	0	1	0	0
Bristol Rovers	D	L	2	0	2	0	2	0	2	0
Wycombe	L	L	2	0	1	1	1	1	1	1
Morecambe	W	W	4	2	2	0	2	2	3	1
York	W	W	3	1	2	0	1	2	2	1
Accrington	W	D	4	3	1	0	2	2	2	2
Torquay										
AFC Wimbledon	L	W	2	1	0	1	2	0	1	1
Plymouth	D	D	2	1	1	0	1	1	1	1
Dag & Red	W	D	3	2	1	0	1	2	1	2
Mansfield			1	1	0	0	0	1	0	1
Newport County	-	-	-	-	-	-	-	-	-	-

Season	Division	Pos	P	W	D	L	F	A	GD	Pts
2012-13	League 2	19	46	13	14	19	55	62	-7	53
2011-12	League 2	5	46	23	12	11	63	50	+13	81
2010-11	League 2	7	46	17	18	11	74	53	+21	68

Over/Under 46%/54% 15th   **Both score** 61%/39% 2nd

Wycombe Wanderers

Nickname: The Chairboys
Colours: Sky and navy blue
Ground: Adams Park (10,000)
Tel: 01494 472 100   www.wwfc.com

Is there anything Wycombe's Gareth Ainsworth can't do? A Premier League performer in his heyday, the 40-year-old player-manager was still pulling the strings on the pitch last season as well as taking his side from bottom of League 2 in November to mid-table security.

Not only has he hung up his boots to concentrate on management but he has also quit his lead role in rock 'n' roll band Road To Eden.

With that type of dedication he should keep the momentum going, although he may be restricted by a lack of funds.

Longest run without win/loss: 8/5
High/low league position: 13/23
Clean sheets: 14 **Yellow cards:** 72 **Red cards:** 4
Average attendance: 3,720 **Players used:** 36
Leading scorer: M Mcclure 11 (5,9)
Key stat: The layers underestimated Wycombe last season as they returned a total profit of £13.28 (to a £1 level stake)

	2012-13 H	2012-13 A	P	W	D	L	OV	UN	BS	CS
Scunthorpe			1	0	1	0	0	1	1	0
Bury			4	3	0	1	1	3	1	2
Hartlepool			2	2	0	0	1	1	0	2
Portsmouth			-	-	-	-	-	-	-	-
Burton	W	L	2	2	0	0	2	0	1	1
Cheltenham	D	L	2	1	1	0	1	1	2	0
Northampton	D	L	2	0	2	0	1	1	1	1
Chesterfield	W	L	5	3	1	1	3	2	4	1
Oxford	L	W	2	0	1	1	1	1	1	1
Exeter	L	L	4	1	2	1	2	2	3	0
Southend	L	L	3	1	1	1	2	1	3	0
Rochdale	L	L	4	1	0	3	2	2	1	1
Fleetwood Town	W	W	1	1	0	0	0	1	0	1
Bristol Rovers	W	L	2	2	0	0	1	1	1	1
Wycombe										
Morecambe	D	W	4	2	2	0	1	3	2	2
York	W	W	1	1	0	0	1	0	0	1
Accrington	L	W	4	1	0	3	2	2	2	0
Torquay	W	W	2	1	0	1	2	0	2	0
AFC Wimbledon	L	D	1	0	0	1	0	1	0	0
Plymouth	D	W	1	0	1	0	0	1	1	0
Dag & Red	W	L	3	2	0	1	1	2	1	1
Mansfield			1	0	0	1	1	0	1	0
Newport County			-	-	-	-	-	-	-	-

Season	Division	Pos	P	W	D	L	F	A	GD	Pts
2012-13	League 2	15	46	17	9	20	50	60	-10	60
2011-12	League 1	21	46	11	10	25	65	88	-23	43
2010-11	League 2	3	46	22	14	10	69	50	+19	80

Over/Under 48%/52% 13th   **Both score** 43%/57% 22nd

York City

Nickname: Minstermen
Colours: Red, white and blue
Ground: Bootham Crescent (8,105)
Tel: 01904 624447 www.yorkcityfootballclub.co.uk

A fantastic finish saw York City avoid an instant return to the Conference but they will have to guard against a similar scenario occurring this time.

Four wins and two draws in the last six games not only resulted in an April manager of the month award for Nigel Worthington but, crucially, guaranteed their Football League survival.

Before that the Minstermen were praying for three points after a shocking 16-match winless stretch and there's plenty of work to do, starting with finding a solution to their poor home form.

Longest run without win/loss: 16/6
High/low league position: 9/23
Clean sheets: 15 **Yellow cards:** 50 **Red cards:** 0
Average attendance: 3,878 **Players used:** 36
Leading scorer: A Chambers 10 (4,8)
Key stat: Only rock-bottom Aldershot took fewer League 2 home points than York

	2012-13 H	2012-13 A	P	W	D	L	OV	UN	BS	CS
Scunthorpe			-	-	-	-	-	-	-	-
Bury			-	-	-	-	-	-	-	-
Hartlepool			-	-	-	-	-	-	-	-
Portsmouth			-	-	-	-	-	-	-	-
Burton	W	L	3	1	1	1	2	1	1	2
Cheltenham	D	D	1	0	1	0	0	1	0	1
Northampton	D	W	1	0	1	0	0	1	1	0
Chesterfield	D	L	1	0	1	0	1	0	1	0
Oxford	W	D	4	1	2	1	1	3	2	1
Exeter	L	D	2	1	0	1	2	0	2	0
Southend	W	D	1	1	0	0	1	0	1	0
Rochdale	D	W	1	0	1	0	0	1	0	1
Fleetwood Town	L	D	3	1	0	2	0	3	0	1
Bristol Rovers	W	D	1	1	0	0	1	0	1	0
Wycombe	L	L	1	0	0	1	1	0	1	0
Morecambe	W	D	1	0	1	0	0	1	0	1
York										
Accrington	D	W	1	0	1	0	0	1	1	0
Torquay	L	L	3	0	0	3	1	2	1	0
AFC Wimbledon	L	L	3	2	0	1	3	0	1	1
Plymouth	W	L	1	1	0	0	1	0	1	0
Dag & Red	W	W	1	1	0	0	1	0	1	0
Mansfield			4	2	2	0	3	1	3	1
Newport County			2	1	0	1	1		2	0

Season	Division	Pos	P	W	D	L	F	A	GD	Pts
2012-13	League 2	17	46	12	19	15	50	60	-10	55
2011-12	Conference	4	46	23	14	9	81	45	+36	83
2010-11	Conference	8	46	19	14	13	55	50	+5	71

Over/Under 43%/57% 17th   **Both score** 50%/50% 11th

League 2 stats 2012-13
Key Points do not include any deductions imposed by the league. **GFA** Goals For Average per match, **GAA** Goals Against Average per match, **PGA** Average Points Gained per match, **CS** Clean Sheet, **FS** First to Score, **Ov** Over 2.5 total goals, **Un** Under 2.5 total goals, **BS** Both teams Score

Top scorers 2012-13

		P	W	D	L	F	GFA	PGA	Pts
1	Port Vale	46	21	15	10	87	1.89	**1.7**	78
2	Rotherham	46	24	7	15	74	1.61	**1.7**	79
3	Burton	46	22	10	14	71	1.54	**1.7**	76
4	Rochdale	46	16	13	17	68	1.48	**1.3**	61
5	Gillingham	46	23	14	9	66	1.43	**1.8**	83
6	Northampton	46	21	10	15	64	1.39	**1.6**	73
7	Bradford	46	18	15	13	63	1.37	**1.5**	69
	Exeter	46	18	10	18	63	1.37	**1.4**	64
9	Southend	46	16	13	17	61	1.33	**1.3**	61
10	Chesterfield	46	18	13	15	60	1.30	**1.5**	67
	Oxford	46	19	8	19	60	1.30	**1.4**	65
	Bristol Rovers	46	16	12	18	60	1.30	**1.3**	60
13	Cheltenham	46	20	15	11	58	1.26	**1.6**	75
14	Fleetwood	46	15	15	16	55	1.20	**1.3**	60
	Morecambe	46	15	13	18	55	1.20	**1.3**	58
	Torquay	46	13	14	19	55	1.20	**1.2**	53
	Dag & Red	46	13	12	21	55	1.20	**1.1**	51
18	Wimbledon	46	14	11	21	54	1.17	**1.2**	53
19	Accrington	46	14	12	20	51	1.11	**1.2**	54
20	Wycombe	46	17	9	20	50	1.09	**1.3**	60
	York	46	12	19	15	50	1.09	**1.2**	55
22	Barnet	46	13	12	21	47	1.02	**1.1**	51
23	Plymouth	46	13	13	20	46	1.00	**1.1**	52
24	Aldershot	46	11	15	20	42	0.91	**1.0**	48

Best defence 2012-13

		P	W	D	L	A	GAA	PGA	Pts
1	Gillingham	46	23	14	9	39	0.85	**1.8**	83
2	Chesterfield	46	18	13	15	45	0.98	**1.5**	67
3	Cheltenham	46	20	15	11	51	1.11	**1.6**	75
4	Port Vale	46	21	15	10	52	1.13	**1.7**	78
	Bradford	46	18	15	13	52	1.13	**1.5**	69
6	Northampton	46	21	10	15	55	1.20	**1.6**	73
	Southend	46	16	13	17	55	1.20	**1.3**	61
	Plymouth	46	13	13	20	55	1.20	**1.1**	52
9	Fleetwood	46	15	15	16	57	1.24	**1.3**	60
10	Rotherham	46	24	7	15	59	1.28	**1.7**	79
	Barnet	46	13	12	21	59	1.28	**1.1**	51
12	Wycombe	46	17	9	20	60	1.30	**1.3**	60
	York	46	12	19	15	60	1.30	**1.2**	55
	Aldershot	46	11	15	20	60	1.30	**1.0**	48
15	Oxford	46	19	8	19	61	1.33	**1.4**	65
	Morecambe	46	15	13	18	61	1.33	**1.3**	58
17	Exeter	46	18	10	18	62	1.35	**1.4**	64
	Torquay	46	13	14	19	62	1.35	**1.2**	53
	Dag & Red	46	13	12	21	62	1.35	**1.1**	51
20	Burton	46	22	10	14	65	1.41	**1.7**	76
21	Accrington	46	14	12	20	68	1.48	**1.2**	54
22	Bristol Rovers	46	16	12	18	69	1.50	**1.3**	60
23	Rochdale	46	16	13	17	70	1.52	**1.3**	61
24	Wimbledon	46	14	11	21	76	1.65	**1.2**	53

AFC Wimbledon fans at large in Milton Keynes in the FA Cup

Clean sheets 2012-13

		P	CS	CS%
1	Cheltenham	46	19	41
2	Bradford	46	18	39
	Gillingham	46	18	39
4	Barnet	46	16	34
	Chesterfield	46	16	34
	Fleetwood	46	16	34
	Northampton	46	16	34
8	Rotherham	46	15	32
	York	46	15	32
10	Accrington	46	14	30
	Aldershot	46	14	30
	Oxford	46	14	30
	Wycombe	46	14	30
14	Exeter	46	13	28
	Port Vale	46	13	28
16	Burton	46	12	26
	Dag & Red	46	12	26
	Morecambe	46	12	26
	Southend	46	12	26
20	Rochdale	46	11	23
21	Bristol Rovers	46	10	21
22	Plymouth	46	9	19
	Torquay	46	9	19
24	Wimbledon	46	7	15

First to score 2012-13

		P	FS	FS%
1	Gillingham	46	29	63
2	Cheltenham	46	27	59
3	Wycombe	46	24	52
4	Chesterfield	46	23	50
	Northampton	46	23	50
	Oxford Utd	46	23	50
	Port Vale	46	23	50
8	Bristol Rovers	46	22	48
	Dag & Red	46	22	48
	Morecambe	46	22	48
	Rochdale	46	22	48
12	Burton	46	21	46
	Exeter	46	21	46
	Rotherham	46	21	46
15	Bradford	46	20	43
	York	46	20	43
17	Aldershot	46	19	41
	Fleetwood	46	19	41
19	Accrington	46	18	39
	Plymouth	46	18	39
	Torquay	46	18	39
22	Barnet	46	16	35
	Southend	46	16	35
24	Wimbledon	46	15	33

Top goalscorers 2012-13

	Goals
T Pope (Port Vale)	31
J Cureton (Exeter)	21
D Nardiello (Rotherham)	18
N Wells (Bradford)	18
A Akinfenwa (Northampton)	16
R Howe (Torquay)	16
B Assombalonga (Southend)	15
R Grant (Rochdale)	15
J Maghoma (Burton)	15
J Redshaw (Morecambe)	15

Port Vale's prolific Tom Pope

Record when keeping a clean sheet 2012-13

		P	W	D	L	F	GFA	PGA	Pts
1	Wimbledon	7	7	0	0	10	1.42	3.0	21
2	Burton	12	11	1	0	20	1.66	2.8	34
3	Rotherham	15	13	2	0	25	1.66	2.7	41
4	Chesterfield	16	13	3	0	24	1.5	2.6	42
	Northampton	16	13	3	0	22	1.37	2.6	42
	Oxford	14	11	3	0	23	1.64	2.6	36
	Accrington	14	11	3	0	20	1.42	2.6	36
	Wycombe	14	11	3	0	18	1.28	2.6	36
	Gillingham	18	14	4	0	23	1.27	2.6	46
10	Port Vale	13	10	3	0	26	2	2.5	33
	Exeter	13	10	3	0	23	1.76	2.5	33
12	Bristol Rovers	10	7	3	0	14	1.4	2.4	24
	Cheltenham	19	13	6	0	22	1.15	2.4	45
14	Bradford	18	12	6	0	19	1.05	2.3	42
	Southend	12	8	4	0	18	1.5	2.3	28
	Dag & Red	12	8	4	0	15	1.25	2.3	28
	Fleetwood	16	10	6	0	21	1.31	2.3	36
	Barnet	16	10	6	0	17	1.06	2.3	36
19	Morecambe	12	7	5	0	14	1.16	2.2	26
20	Aldershot	14	8	6	0	11	0.78	2.1	30
	Torquay	9	5	4	0	7	0.77	2.1	19
22	Rochdale	11	5	6	0	9	0.81	1.9	21
	Plymouth	9	4	5	0	7	0.77	1.9	17
24	York	15	6	9	0	11	0.73	1.8	27

Record when first to score 2012-13

		P	W	D	L	F	A	PGA	Pts
1	Rotherham	21	19	1	1	46	10	2.8	58
2	Port Vale	23	19	4	0	67	20	2.7	61
	Northampton	23	20	1	2	48	16	2.7	61
4	Wimbledon	15	12	3	0	27	11	2.6	39
5	Bradford	20	16	2	2	39	12	2.5	50
	Gillingham	29	23	3	3	55	22	2.5	72
	Oxford	23	18	3	2	46	16	2.5	57
	Burton	21	16	4	1	47	18	2.5	52
9	Chesterfield	23	17	5	1	45	14	2.4	56
	Exeter	21	16	3	2	47	17	2.4	51
	Accrington	18	13	4	1	34	12	2.4	43
	Fleetwood	18	13	6	0	39	13	2.4	45
	Bristol Rovers	22	16	4	2	50	26	2.4	52
14	Southend	16	11	4	1	35	13	2.3	37
15	Cheltenham	27	18	6	3	44	23	2.2	60
16	Barnet	16	10	4	2	25	10	2.1	34
	York	20	12	6	2	37	19	2.1	42
18	Morecambe	22	13	6	3	42	22	2.0	45
	Wycombe	24	14	6	4	39	25	2.0	48
	Rochdale	22	13	5	4	45	30	2.0	44
	Aldershot	19	11	5	3	31	19	2.0	38
22	Plymouth	18	10	5	3	31	19	1.9	35
	Torquay	18	10	5	3	27	18	1.9	35
	Dag & Red	22	12	6	4	39	24	1.9	42

Over 2.5 goals 2012-13

	H	A	Ov%
Rochdale	11	19	65
Rotherham	16	12	61
Exeter	11	15	57
Wimbledon	13	12	54
Oxford	10	15	54
Port Vale	14	11	54
Bristol Rovers	12	12	52
Fleetwood	13	11	52
Morecambe	11	13	52

Under 2.5 goals 2012-13

	H	A	Un%
Aldershot	13	13	57
Chesterfield	10	11	46
Barnet	14	16	65
Plymouth	15	12	59
Accrington	14	12	57
Bradford	11	11	48
Gillingham	12	11	50
York	13	12	54

Both to score 2012-13

	H	A	BS%
Rochdale	13	17	65
Torquay	19	9	61
Wimbledon	15	11	57
Dag & Red	10	15	54
Port Vale	11	14	54
Rotherham	14	11	54
Bristol Rovers, Gillingham,			52
Morecambe, Plymouth			

Rovers' promising forward signings could fire Forest into the Football League

Forest Green's claims for the upcoming season haven't been missed by bookmakers but the Gloucestershire side rate the most likely winners of the Football Conference, writes Danny Hayes.

Dave Hockday's side finished only tenth last season, some 15 points adrift of the play-offs, but there were times when they looked like potential title challengers.

They set the early pace, which included a 5-0 win at eventual play-off winners Newport County, only to tail off from February when they recorded just two victories from their final 14 games.

However, Hockday has been quick to strengthen his squad and the signings of forward duo Andy Mangan and Danny Wright signal the club's intent. Mangan enjoyed a good spell at Forest Green between 2008 and 2010 and has subsequently been a key figure in successful Wrexham and Fleetwood sides at this level.

Meanwhile, Wright's decision to swap Wrexham, who have reached the play-offs for the past two years, for Rovers suggests Hockday is serious about sustaining a title challenge this year.

They had the third-best defence in the league last season and with those new signings adding to the forward threat already posed by last year's top scorer James Norwood, **Forest Green** look well placed to push hard for a place in the Football League. Even at 9-2 with Coral, they're worth a bet.

Luton are vying for favouritism with the bookies but that's been the case for the past four seasons and the Hatters are priced up more on reputation than their quality.

The current Luton squad arguably looks weaker than it was 12 months ago and, having finished 13 points adrift of the play-offs last term, it would require all of manager John Still's experience and nous at this level for the side to challenge for top spot. A play-off place looks the best they can hope for.

Kidderminster deserve plenty of respect for their performance last season. After a dismal start they went on to win 25 of their final 29 league games and were desperately unfortunate to bump into a similarly inspired Mansfield side.

However, they lost both legs of their play-off semi-final clash with Wrexham and, having lost key midfielders James Vincent and Keith Briggs, it will be extremely tough for them to match last season's exploits.

The other two beaten play-off sides from last season, Wrexham and **Grimsby**, are again prominent in the betting, although it's the latter who look better placed for a title challenge in 2013-14.

No side lost fewer games than the Mariners last season and if they can turn a few more of their 14 draws into wins, Grimsby will go close. The return from injury of key striker Liam Hearn, who missed seven months last season, could be a crucial factor and William Hill's 5-1 for promotion looks fair.

Cash-strapped Wrexham, however, may find that they have missed their chance. Their consistency at this level has to be admired but the Welsh outfit finished 18 points off their 2011-12 total last term and, having again lost key men over the summer, they will do well to match their 2012-13 tally of 80 points.

Clubs dropping from the Football League tend to find the transition difficult and Barnet and Aldershot are unlikely to be any different.

The Shots have been dealt the additional blow of beginning the season with a ten-point deduction for entering administration,

WESTERN THERMAL STAND

The New Lawn Stadium could be hosting Football League action in 2014-15

so fifth-tier safety will be their first priority.

Barnet are better placed. Edgar Davids may not have envisaged himself managing in the Conference but he has shown his commitment to Barnet's cause and may be able to lure a better calibre of player to Underhill than the Bees would normally attract.

Cambridge have undertaken a huge overhaul of their playing squad over the summer and will be play-off contenders if they gel quickly but if there is to be a surprise package then Chester look the side.

It was only three years ago that Chester City were being wound up but that already seems a distant memory after Chester FC secured back-to-back promotions, including taking the Conference North title with a record haul of 107 points last term. However, they have decided to stay part-time and, at this level, it will leave them vulnerable over the course of a long campaign.

The other promoted sides, Halifax,

Welling and Salisbury all look capable of going well at this level and that means the struggling survivors from 2012-13 may not be quite so lucky this time around.

Hyde, Southport, Nuneaton and Tamworth are all likely to be in the relegation mix but, at a slightly bigger 9-4 (BetVictor), **Alfreton** look the value pick for the drop.

The Reds finished in a very respectable 13th place last term following promotion but they've gone part-time over the summer and Alfreton's small squad is sure to struggle.

Further down the football pyramid, **Sutton United** finished their Conference South campaign strongly last season and look ready to step up this term. Take the 15-2 available about their title chances with either BetFred or Coral.

In the Conference North, **Harrogate** have made some shrewd signings and their title prospects look better than their price of 20-1 (BetVictor) suggests – back them each way.

Blue Toon to call the tune in basement division

A ll the talk over the summer in Scotland has been about restructuring but the amalgamation of the SPL and SFL has little effect on those looking to bet on who might win the respective divisions, writes Ian Wilkerson.

What effect, if any, the new arrangements will have is not yet clear but once again punters are presented with a top division with the hottest favourite in European football.

And, given that allowing Rangers back into the top flight was not on the agenda, you would need a van load of used tenners to make any serious money on Celtic retaining their title.

Their admirable progress to the knockout rounds of the Champions League, which included a famous group-stage victory over Barcelona, didn't stop the Bhoys claiming their prize, although their domestic dominance was not as complete as some would have envisaged when the Gers were sent packing to Division Three.

But the conundrum for punters is once again who will provide them with the toughest challenge and, after last season, that picture looks cloudier than ever.

Teams thought likely to struggle, like St Johnstone and Inverness, found themselves battling it out for Europa League football, while Aberdeen and Hearts again failed to reach the top six, with Hearts falling into financial meltdown.

A dramatic improvement is required there and the Jambos' priority will simply be their survival after going into administration – they will kick off the new season with a 15-point penalty to overcome.

Dundee United endured a poor campaign where they squeezed into the top half, but they will be weaker after strikers Jon Daly and Johnny Russell upped sticks to Rangers and Derby.

While the return of David Goodwillie on loan is a boost, it could still take time for them to recover.

So, at this stage, last year's runners-up **Motherwell** could be worth an interest in the betting without Celtic, but it's difficult to be confident and it make take a few weeks for the likely candidates to emerge, even though Stuart McCall's decision to stay at Fir Park rather than join his old club Sheffield United has to be a good sign.

The competition to gain access to the top division should be keenly fought.

Expect **Dundee** to put up a decent fight. They were ill-prepared for the SPL last season after their late invite and the injustice they feel about Hearts' administration penalty being applied to the new campaign could provide huge motivation.

It will be interesting to see how Falkirk get on under rookie boss Gary Holt, but the team to really look out for are **Hamilton**.

The Accies finished strongly last year with six wins in their final eight matches and they could receive a sizeable chunk of any transfer fee should former midfielder James McCarthy leave Wigan.

Rangers will have one familiar venue to visit in Division Two after cash-strapped Dunfermline fell into the third tier and the Gers should have another comfortable campaign as they attempt to climb back up the league.

But look out for **Brechin** to provide them with their toughest test. City got their campaign off to a miserable start last year with six defeats in their first eight games, but they did well to finish third and could go one better.

Many would point to the fact that Queen's Park benefited from two bumper gates against the Gers at Hampden Park last season as a reason why they can push to Division Three glory. The Spiders should be in the mix but they won just five home games last season and finished weakly, so preference is for **Peterhead**.

The Blue Toon finished like a train before losing in the play-offs last season and with the division's best striker in Rory McAllister, it could finally be their year.

Aberdeen

Nickname: The Dons
Colours: Red
Ground: Pittodrie (21,421)
Tel: 01224 650 400   www.afc.co.uk

The Dons have finished in the bottom half of the SPL in each of the last four seasons and that was despite striker Niall McGinn scoring 20 league goals las term.

The news that McGinn has agreed a new contract at Pittodrie is a massive boost to new manager Derek McInnes, who saw his team remain unbeaten for their final five matches of the season.

However, finishing out of top six once again in 2012-13 will be seen as a failure and other players need to start chipping in with goals for Aberdeen to make any substantial progress.

Longest run without win/loss: 5/10
High/low league position: 3/9
Clean sheets: 14 **Yellow cards:** 55 **Red cards:** 4
Average attendance: 9,611 **Players used:** 29
Leading scorer: N McGinn 20 (8,16)
Key stat: No SPL team was involved in more goalless draws than Aberdeen last season, with the Dons recording eight 0-0 results

2012-13 SPL appearances	P	G	Y	R
J Langfield	37	0	0	1
G Rae	34 (1)	3	4	0
M Reynolds	34 (1)	1	3	1
N McGinn	33 (2)	20	3	0
R Anderson	30 (1)	0	5	1
J Hayes	29 (6)	4	3	0
S Vernon	29 (6)	3	4	0
S Hughes	22 (1)	0	4	0
J Shaughnessy	22 (1)	0	4	0
I Osbourne	21 (2)	1	3	0
C Robertson	21 (2)	0	3	0
10 most regular starters				

	2012-13 H	A	Last six seasons at home P	W	D	L	OV	UN	BS	CS
Celtic	L	L L	10	1	2	7	7	3	7	0
Motherwell	D D	L	9	1	4	4	5	4	5	3
St Johnstone	W	W L	7	2	2	3	2	5	2	3
Inverness CT	L	D L	8	4	0	4	3	5	3	3
Ross County	D L	L	2	0	1	1	0	2	0	1
Dundee United	D	D L	10	4	4	2	6	4	7	1
Hibernian	W D	W D	11	6	1	4	7	4	7	2
Aberdeen										
Kilmarnock	L W	W D	11	5	3	3	4	7	3	6
Hearts	D W D	L	12	2	7	3	0	12	3	6
St Mirren	D D	W D	11	5	5	1	3	8	3	7
Partick	-	-	-	-	-	-	-	-	-	-

Season	Division	Pos	P	W	D	L	F	A	GD	Pts
2012-13	SPL	8	38	11	15	12	41	43	-2	48
2011-12	SPL	9	38	9	14	15	36	44	-8	41
2010-11	SPL	9	38	11	5	22	39	59	-20	38

Over/Under 34%/66% 12th   **Both score** 45%/55% 11th

Celtic

Nickname: The Bhoys
Colours: Green and white
Ground: Celtic Park (60,355)
Tel: 0871 226 1888   www.celticfc.net

While the Bhoys' League and Cup double was largely expected following Rangers' SPL departure, progression to the last 16 of the Champions League was a great achievement and Celtic's 2-1 win over Barcelona will live long in the memory.

It was perhaps not surprising that they took their eye of the ball in the league at times and Neil Lennon's men won just eight of the 22 league games in which they failed to score three goals.

But they had plenty in hand domestically last term and are again unlikely to receive a stiff challenge this year.

Longest run without win/loss: 3/8
High/low league position: 1/2
Clean sheets: 16 **Yellow cards:** 47 **Red cards:** 1
Average attendance: 46,917 **Players used:** 34
Leading scorer: G Hooper 19 (8,15)
Key stat: Celtic scored 24 league and cup goals in the last ten minutes of matches during their 2012-13 campaign

2012-13 SPL appearances	P	G	Y	R
F Forster	34	0	4	0
V Wanyama	31 (1)	6	9	1
K Wilson	31 (1)	0	4	0
G Hooper	30 (2)	19	1	0
E Izaguirre	29 (3)	0	2	0
E Ambrose	24 (3)	3	3	0
K Commons	25 (2)	11	1	0
J Ledley	21 (4)	7	0	0
M Lustig	21 (2)	3	1	0
B Kayal	19 (8)	0	4	0
10 most regular starters				

	2012-13 H	A	Last six seasons at home P	W	D	L	OV	UN	BS	CS
Celtic										
Motherwell	W	W L L	11	9	1	1	5	6	1	9
St Johnstone	D W	L D	8	6	1	1	3	5	2	5
Inverness CT	L W	W W	8	6	1	1	4	4	3	4
Ross County	W	D L D	1	1	0	0	1	0	0	1
Dundee United	W W	D W	12	8	4	0	8	4	8	4
Hibernian	D W	L	11	7	3	1	8	3	8	3
Aberdeen	W W	W	10	10	0	0	6	4	3	7
Kilmarnock	L W	W	9	6	2	1	5	4	4	4
Hearts	W W		12	10	2	0	7	5	3	9
St Mirren	W	W D	8	7	1	0	4	4	2	6
Partick	-	-	-	-	-	-	-	-	-	-

Season	Division	Pos	P	W	D	L	F	A	GD	Pts
2012-13	SPL	1	38	24	7	7	92	35	+57	79
2011-12	SPL	1	38	30	3	5	84	21	+63	93
2010-11	SPL	2	38	29	5	4	85	22	+63	92

Over/Under 58%/42% 5th   **Both score** 50%/50% 8th

Dundee United

Nickname: The Terrors
Colours: Orange and black
Ground: Tannadice Park (14,223)
Tel: 01382 833 166   www.dundeeunitedfc.co.uk

There's work for Jackie McNamara to do at Tannadice if he is to further boost the reputation he gained in helping Partick Thistle into the SPL.

Dundee United were hotly fancied to do well last season but they only sneaked into the top half in their final game before the split and did virtually nothing having got there.

Jon Daly, top scorer in 2011-12, has dropped two divisions to join Rangers and Johnny Russell has left for Derby, but it would not take much to improve on such a disappointing campaign.

Longest run without win/loss: 6/7
High/low league position: 6/11
Clean sheets: 11 **Yellow cards:** 47 **Red cards:** 5
Average attendance: 7,547 **Players used:** 26
Leading scorer: J Russell 13 (5, 10)
Key stat: Dundee United won just four home SPL matches last season

2012-13 SPL appearances	P	G	Y	R
R Cierzniak	38	0	2	0
W Flood	37	2	7	0
J Daly	35 (1)	10	2	0
J Rankin	35	2	5	1
S Dillon	31	0	1	0
S Armstrong	30 (6)	3	3	1
J Russell	30 (2)	13	3	1
K Watson	29	2	1	0
B Douglas	27 (1)	1	3	1
G Gunning	25	3	1	0
B McLean	25 (4)	0	4	1

10 most regular starters

	2012-13 H	A	Last six seasons at home P	W	D	L	OV	UN	BS	CS
Celtic	D L	L L L	12	2	3	7	6	6	6	1
Motherwell	L L	W W	11	5	1	5	6	5	4	5
St Johnstone	D L	D D	6	2	3	1	1	5	2	3
Inverness CT	D L	D W	8	4	2	2	5	3	4	2
Ross County	D D	W L	2	0	2	0	0	2	1	1
Dundee United										
Hibernian	W D	L	12	6	5	1	5	7	5	6
Aberdeen	D W	D	10	6	2	2	5	5	6	3
Kilmarnock	D	L W	9	3	5	1	3	6	4	4
Hearts	L W	L	11	8	1	2	6	5	4	5
St Mirren	L	W D	9	4	3	2	4	5	6	3
Partick	-	-	-	-	-	-	-	-	-	-

Season	Division	Pos	P	W	D	L	F	A	GD	Pts
2012-13	SPL	6	38	11	14	13	51	62	-11	47
2011-12	SPL	4	38	16	11	11	62	50	+12	59
2010-11	SPL	4	38	17	10	11	55	50	+5	61

Over/Under 61%/39% 3rd   **Both score** 55%/45% 6th

Heart of Midlothian

Nickname: Jambos
Colours: Claret and white
Ground: Tynecastle (17,590)
Tel: 0871 663 1874   www.heartsfc.co.uk

Last season was disastrous for Hearts on and off the pitch as the Edinburgh side finished tenth in the table before going into administration, incurring a 15-point penalty for the upcoming campaign.

The days when they were a short price for title glory are long gone and it's difficult to see them returning any time soon.

The Jambos scored just 13 away goals last season and the club's young players are set to continue to be the focus of the season. Seven teenagers made at least eight appearances last term and they're likely to be heavily involved again.

Longest run without win/loss: 6/4
High/low league position: 4/11
Clean sheets: 13 **Yellow cards:** 68 **Red cards:** 2
Average attendance: 13,163 **Players used:** 31
Leading scorer: J Sutton 8 (4,8)
Key stat: Hearts won just five of their 20 matches against teams in the bottom half of the table

2012-13 SPL appearances	P	G	Y	R
J MacDonald	38	0	0	0
A Webster	33	1	5	1
D Barr	30 (2)	1	9	0
R Stevenson	28 (1)	5	1	1
M Zaliukas	24 (1)	2	6	0
M Taouil	23 (8)	0	5	0
K McHattie	21	1	4	0
R McGowan	20	0	5	0
J Sutton	20 (15)	8	2	0
C Paterson	18 (4)	3	4	0

10 most regular starters

	2012-13 H	A	Last six seasons at home P	W	D	L	OV	UN	BS	CS
Celtic	L	L L L	10	3	2	5	5	5	4	2
Motherwell	W L	D	12	5	2	5	5	7	5	4
St Johnstone	W W	D	7	4	1	2	2	5	3	4
Inverness CT	D L	D	8	4	2	2	5	3	6	2
Ross County	D W	D	2	1	1	0	2	0	2	0
Dundee United	W	W L	11	4	4	3	4	7	4	5
Hibernian	D L	D D	11	5	3	3	2	9	2	7
Aberdeen	W D	L D	8	6	1	1	6	2	3	4
Kilmarnock	L L	L W	11	3	1	7	5	6	4	2
Hearts										
St Mirren	W W	L L	11	9	1	1	6	5	5	5
Partick	-	-	-	-	-	-	-	-	-	-

Season	Division	Pos	P	W	D	L	F	A	GD	Pts
2012-13	SPL	10	38	11	11	16	40	49	-9	44
2011-12	SPL	5	38	15	7	16	45	43	+2	52
2010-11	SPL	3	38	18	9	11	53	45	+8	63

Over/Under 42%/58% 10th   **Both score** 39%/61% 12th

Hibernian

Nickname: The Hibees
Colours: Green and white
Ground: Easter Road (20,250)
Tel: 0131 661 2159   www.hibernianfc.co.uk

Hibernian got off to a decent start last term but the fact they posted just four wins in 2013 is a concern, even if they did reach the Scottish Cup final for the second successive year.

Their efforts were spearheaded by 23-goal Leigh Griffiths but they relied on him too heavily and the Wolves loanee has now returned to his parent club.

A place in the top six will be the target this term and they finished 2012-13 well, going unbeaten after the split. However, with Pat Fenlon being criticised by some for his direct football, the heat will be on.

Longest run without win/loss: 8/6
High/low league position: 1/10
Clean sheets: 11 **Yellow cards:** 68 **Red cards:** 1
Average attendance: 10,489 **Players used:** 28
Leading scorer: L Griffiths 23 (7,18)
Key stat: Hibernian won just four of the 17 games they were drawing at half-time

2012-13 SPL appearances	P	G	Y	R
B Williams	37	0	1	0
L Griffiths	36	23	4	0
P Hanlon	34	1	4	0
J Claros	29 (5)	0	2	0
J McPake	29	2	5	1
E Doyle	28 (8)	10	2	0
P Cairney	26 (3)	2	7	0
D Wotherspoon	26 (8)	4	5	0
R McGivern	25 (2)	1	5	0
A Maybury	24 (3)	0	6	0

10 most regular starters

	2012-13		Last six seasons at home							
	H	A	P	W	D	L	OV	UN	BS	CS
Celtic	W	D L	10	3	1	6	3	7	1	3
Motherwell	L	W L	9	3	2	4	2	7	4	2
St Johnstone	W L	W	8	3	2	5	3	5	3	
Inverness CT	D L	L	8	3	3	2	3	5	5	3
Ross County	L	L L	1	0	0	1	0	1	0	0
Dundee United	W	L D	9	2	4	3	7	2	8	0
Hibernian										
Aberdeen	L D	L D	12	2	7	3	6	6	6	5
Kilmarnock	W D	D W	11	7	2	2	6	5	7	3
Hearts	D D	D W	10	1	6	3	7	7	2	
St Mirren	W D	W W	11	6	3	2	5	6	6	4
Partick	-	-	-	-	-	-	-	-	-	-

Season	Division	Pos	P	W	D	L	F	A	GD	Pts
2012-13	SPL	7	38	13	12	13	49	52	-3	51
2011-12	SPL	11	38	8	9	21	40	67	-27	33
2010-11	SPL	10	38	10	7	21	39	61	-22	37

Over/Under 61%/39% 3rd   **Both score** 55%/45% 6th

Inverness CT

Nickname: Caley
Colours: Blue and red
Ground: Caledonian Stadium (7,750)
Tel: 01463 222 880   www.ictfc.com

It looked like it was going to be a difficult season for Thistle after they failed to win any of their opening seven league games, but Terry Butcher's side recovered well and eventually missed out on a place in the Europa League by a whisker.

Despite losing the services of Gregory Tade and Jonny Hayes, they were still able to exceed expectations, with former Northampton striker Billy McKay proving to be a revelation up front.

However, they will need to be sharper at the back after conceding 60 goals during the 2012-13 campaign.

Longest run without win/loss: 7/8
High/low league position: 2/11
Clean sheets: 8 **Yellow cards:** 62 **Red cards:** 4
Average attendance: 4,038 **Players used:** 26
Leading scorer: B McKay 23 (6,15)
Key stat: Inverness lost just one of their 18 matches against teams who finished in the bottom half of the SPL

2012-13 SPL appearances	P	G	Y	R
A Doran	38	3	3	0
G Shinnie	37	0	8	0
A Shinnie	37 (1)	12	6	0
D Raven	36	0	5	1
R Draper	33 (1)	5	7	0
B McKay	33 (5)	23	0	0
J Meekings	31 (3)	0	4	0
O Tudur Jones	31 (2)	2	3	2
G Warren	31	5	6	0
R Foran	25 (3)	8	6	1

10 most regular starters

	2012-13		Last six seasons at home							
	H	A	P	W	D	L	OV	UN	BS	CS
Celtic	L L	W L	8	2	1	5	5	3	5	1
Motherwell	L W	L L	8	2	0	6	8	0	6	1
St Johnstone	D D	D L	5	1	3	1	0	5	2	2
Inverness CT										
Ross County	W W	D L	4	3	0	1	4	0	3	1
Dundee United	W D L	D	8	1	2	5	5	3	4	2
Hibernian	W	D W	9	6	1	2	3	6	3	5
Aberdeen	D W	W	9	3	1	5	5	4	4	2
Kilmarnock	D D	D	9	5	3	1	6	3	8	1
Hearts	D	D W	8	2	3	3	3	5	5	1
St Mirren	D	D L	9	4	3	2	5	4	5	4
Partick			2	1	0	1	2	0	2	0

Season	Division	Pos	P	W	D	L	F	A	GD	Pts
2012-13	SPL	4	38	13	15	10	64	60	+4	54
2011-12	SPL	10	38	10	9	19	42	60	-18	39
2010-11	SPL	7	38	14	11	13	52	44	+8	53

Over/Under 66%/34% 1st   **Both score** 71%/29% 1st

Kilmarnock

Nickname: Killie
Colours: Blue and white
Ground: Rugby Park (18,128)
Tel: 01563 545300   www.kilmarnockfc.co.uk

Killie were unlucky not to get into the top-six, losing out on the last day, and they finished the season poorly with just two wins in their final 11 SPL games.

However, the dismissal of Kenny Shiels still came as a shock as the former manager had brought several decent young players through the ranks.

His succession of touchline bans and outspoken nature did not sit well at Rugby Park and Kilmarnock won more games on their travels than at home last term. Consequently, it could be a baptism of fire for his replacement.

Longest run without win/loss: 5/5
High/low league position: 3/9
Clean sheets: 10 **Yellow cards:** 52 **Red cards:** 2
Average attendance: 4,647 **Players used:** 35
Leading scorer: Heffernan 9 (3,6) Sheridan 9 (4,6)
Key stat: Kilmarnock collected just two points from the 13 matches in which they were losing at half-time last term

2012-13 SPL appearances	P	G	Y	R
J Fowler	33 (1)	3	9	0
C Bell	30	0	1	1
J Tesselaar	25 (1)	0	2	0
M Pascali	24	3	4	1
J Dayton	23 (4)	1	3	0
P Heffernan	22 (5)	9	6	0
R O'Leary	22 (6)	1	1	0
M Nelson	21	1	2	0
Borja Perez	19 (6)	3	0	0
L Kelly	19	6	6	0
C Sheridan	19 (7)	9	0	0

10 most regular starters

	2012-13 H	A	Last six seasons at home P	W	D	L	OV	UN	BS	CS
Celtic	L	W L	10	1	1	8	8	2	6	1
Motherwell	L W	D	10	4	2	4	3	7	2	5
St Johnstone	L	L L	7	2	2	3	5	2	6	1
Inverness CT	L	D D	9	3	2	4	7	2	8	1
Ross County	W	D W	1	1	0	0	1	0	0	1
Dundee United	W L	D	10	3	3	4	6	4	8	1
Hibernian	D L	L D	9	4	3	2	5	4	8	1
Aberdeen	L D	W L	10	4	3	3	3	7	6	3
Kilmarnock										
Hearts	W L	W W	10	2	4	4	4	6	5	3
St Mirren	W D L	D	13	6	3	4	6	7	8	3
Partick	-	-	-	-	-	-	-	-	-	-

Season	Division	Pos	P	W	D	L	F	A	GD	Pts
2012-13	SPL	9	38	11	12	15	52	53	-1	45
2011-12	SPL	7	38	11	14	13	44	61	-17	47
2010-11	SPL	5	38	13	10	15	53	55	-2	49

Over/Under 55%/45% 6th   **Both score** 66%/34% 2nd

Motherwell

Nickname: The Well/The Steelmen
Colours: Amber and claret
Ground: Fir Park (13,677)
Tel: 01698 333 333   www.motherwellfc.co.uk

Motherwell had a great campaign last time out, finishing second to Celtic after finishing behind the only the Old Firm in 2011-12. A further boost for all at Fir Park came with the news that Stuart McCall turned down the opportunity to manage League 1 side Sheffield United.

There are likely to be significant changes in personnel this season, but McCall has moved early to secure the services of Ross County duo Paul Lawson and Iain Vigurs.

European football proved a great motivation last season and could do so again.

Longest run without win/loss: 4/8
High/low league position: 1/8
Clean sheets: 6 **Yellow cards:** 44 **Red cards:** 6
Average attendance: 5,362 **Players used:** 24
Leading scorer: M Higdon 26 (9,19)
Key stat: Motherwell collected a near perfect 41 points from the 15 SPL games in which they scored first

2012-13 SPL appearances	P	G	Y	R
N Law	38	6	2	0
M Higdon	37	26	3	0
K Lasley	36	1	4	1
D Randolph	36	0	1	0
T Hateley	34	3	3	0
C Humphrey	32 (1)	3	1	0
S Hammell	31	0	5	1
S Hutchinson	31	1	9	1
H Ojamaa	31 (5)	4	5	1
S Ramsden	28 (1)	0	3	0

10 most regular starters

	2012-13 H	A	Last six seasons at home P	W	D	L	OV	UN	BS	CS
Celtic	L	W W L	12	3	1	8	8	4	8	1
Motherwell										
St Johnstone	D W	W L	7	4	1	2	6	1	5	1
Inverness CT	W W	W L	9	6	2	1	7	2	5	3
Ross County	W W	D L	2	2	0	0	1	1	1	1
Dundee United	L L	W W	12	4	4	4	7	5	8	1
Hibernian	L W	W	11	6	1	4	8	3	7	3
Aberdeen	W	D D	10	6	3	1	4	6	6	3
Kilmarnock	D	W L	10	3	3	4	4	6	5	3
Hearts	D	L W	9	5	1	3	6	2	5	
St Mirren	D D	L	9	3	4	2	3	6	6	1
Partick	-	-	-	-	-	-	-	-	-	-

Season	Division	Pos	P	W	D	L	F	A	GD	Pts
2012-13	SPL	2	38	18	9	11	67	51	+16	63
2011-12	SPL	3	38	18	8	12	49	44	+5	62
2010-11	SPL	6	38	13	7	18	40	60	-20	46

Over/Under 63%/37% 2nd   **Both score** 61%/39% 3rd

Partick Thistle

Nickname: The Jags
Colours: Yellow and red
Ground: Firhill Stadium (10,915)
Tel: 0141 579 1971   www.ptfc.co.uk

Partick are back in the big time after dominating Division One for much of the 2012-13 season. They won their first six league games and never looked back, managing to negotiate the departure of Jackie McNamara and seeing the job through under Alan Archibald.

Their form at Firhill was particularly impressive as the Jags dropped just seven points on their own patch all season and were not defeated after January 12. They will have high hopes of following Ross County's lead by avoiding a relegation scrap following their SPL promotion.

Longest run without win/loss: 4/18
High/low league position: 1/3
Clean sheets: 17 **Yellow cards:** 37 **Red cards:** 6
Average attendance: 3,614 **Players used:** 28
Leading scorer: S Lawless 13 (5,10)
Key stat: Partick conceded two first-half goals in their final 16 league matches of the season

2012-13 SPL appearances	P	G	Y	R
S Bannigan	32 (1)	3	7	
C Erskine	31 (3)	11	3	0
S Lawless	30 (5)	13	2	0
S Fox	29	0	1	0
A Muirhead	29 (1)	4	2	0
C Balatoni	28 (1)	6	1	0
A Sinclair	28 (5)	1	2	0
S O'Donnell	26 (3)	2	0	0
P Paton	24	0	7	1
R Forbes	22 (5)	3	1	0
S Welsh	22 (3)	2	2	0

10 most regular starters

	2012-13		Last six seasons at home							
	H	A	P	W	D	L	OV	UN	BS	CS
Celtic			-	-	-	-	-	-	-	-
Motherwell			-	-	-	-	-	-	-	-
St Johnstone			4	1	3	0	2	2	1	3
Inverness CT			2	1	0	1	1	1	1	0
Ross County			8	1	3	4	1	7	3	1
Dundee United			-	-	-	-	-	-	-	-
Hibernian			-	-	-	-	-	-	-	-
Aberdeen			-	-	-	-	-	-	-	-
Kilmarnock			-	-	-	-	-	-	-	-
Hearts			-	-	-	-	-	-	-	-
St Mirren			-	-	-	-	-	-	-	-
Partick										

Season	Division	Pos	P	W	D	L	F	A	GD	Pts
2012-13	Division One	1	36	23	9	4	76	28	+48	78
2011-12	Division One	6	36	12	11	13	50	39	+11	47
2010-11	Division One	5	36	12	11	13	44	39	+5	47

Over/Under 58%/42% 7th   **Both score** 47%/53% 10th

Ross County

Nickname: County
Colours: Blue, red and white
Ground: Global Energy Stadium (5,800)
Tel: 01349 860860   www.rosscountyfootballclub.co.uk

Ross County were able to build on the momentum gained from storming to the Division One title and the attainment of a top-six place represented an excellent first campaign back in the SPL.

That was no mean feat after winning just two of their opening 11 games. Their home form will again have a big bearing on whether they can match that this term and County should be encouraged by losing just three times at Dingwall in the entire campaign. But they were knocked out of both cup competitions at the first hurdle and will hope to improve on that.

Longest run without win/loss: 7/11
High/low league position: 3/11
Clean sheets: 15 **Yellow cards:** 74 **Red cards:** 0
Average attendance: 4,430 **Players used:** 27
Leading scorer: R Brittain 9 (4,8)
Key stat: Ross County conceded 11 of their 48 SPL goals against in the ten minutes after half-time

2012-13 SPL appearances	P	G	Y	R
G Munro	36 (1)	2	5	0
I Vigurs	36	7	8	0
S Boyd	34 (1)	0	7	0
R Brittain	34	9	7	0
R Quinn	31	5	7	0
M Kovacevic	28 (2)	0	4	0
M Fraser	24	0	0	0
P Lawson	20 (2)	2	4	0
S Kettlewell	19 (6)	2	7	0
M Fitzpatrick	18 (2)	0	2	0
E Ikonomou	18	0	3	0

10 most regular starters

	2012-13		Last six seasons at home							
	H	A	P	W	D	L	OV	UN	BS	CS
Celtic	D W D	L	3	1	2	0	1	2	3	0
Motherwell	D W	L L	2	1	1	0	1	1	0	2
St Johnstone	L W	D D	4	1	1	2	3	1	3	1
Inverness CT	D W	L L	4	2	2	0	1	3	1	3
Ross County										
Dundee United	L W	D D	2	1	0	1	1	1	1	1
Hibernian	W W	W	2	2	0	0	1	1	1	1
Aberdeen	W	D W	1	1	0	0	1	0	1	0
Kilmarnock	D L	L	2	0	1	1	0	2	0	1
Hearts	D	D L	1	0	1	0	1	0	1	0
St Mirren	D	L W	1	0	1	0	1	0	1	0
Partick			8	2	3	3	4	4	3	3

Season	Division	Pos	P	W	D	L	F	A	GD	Pts
2012-13	SPL	5	38	13	14	11	47	48	-1	53
2011-12	Division One	1	36	22	13	1	72	32	+40	79
2010-11	Division One	8	36	9	14	13	30	34	-4	41

Over/Under 45%/55% 8th   **Both score** 50%/50% 8th

St Johnstone

Nickname: The Saints
Colours: Blue and white
Ground: McDiarmid Park (10,673)
Tel: 01738 459090 www.perthstjohnstonefc.co.uk

St Johnstone will be playing in the Europa League this season but it will be interesting to see how they develop now that manager Steve Lomas has left to take over at Championship side Millwall.

The appointment of Lomas's assistant Tommy Wright should ensure a degree of continuity, but he needs to get the side to score more goals.

No team in the top six mustered fewer than their 45, but the Saints should take a great deal of confidence from the fact they lost just two of their final 12 matches of the campaign.

Longest run without win/loss: 6/7
High/low league position: 2/10
Clean sheets: 9 **Yellow cards:** 76 **Red cards:** 6
Average attendance: 3,712 **Players used:** 27
Leading scorer: R Vine 7 (2,6) L Craig 7 (4,7) M Davidson 7 (5,7)
Key stat: St Johnstone scored just four goals before the 23rd minute of their SPL matches

2012-13 SPL appearances	P	G	Y	R
A Mannus	38	0	0	0
L Craig	37	7	8	0
F Wright	35	1	9	0
D MacKay	32	3	4	1
M Davidson	31 (1)	7	9	0
S Anderson	28 (2)	0	3	1
R Vine	28 (7)	7	6	2
S MacLean	27 (4)	5	5	0
C Millar	25 (1)	0	6	1
G Tade	25 (11)	4	0	1

10 most regular starters

	2012-13		Last six seasons at home							
	H	A	P	W	D	L	OV	UN	BS	CS
Celtic	W D	D L	6	1	1	4	3	3	3	0
Motherwell	L W	D L	7	2	1	4	4	3	3	2
St Johnstone										
Inverness CT	D W	D D	6	3	2	1	1	5	0	5
Ross County	D D	W L	4	1	3	0	2	2	3	1
Dundee United	D D	D W	8	0	4	4	3	5	4	2
Hibernian	L	L W	5	3	1	1	2	3	3	1
Aberdeen	L W	L	7	2	2	3	3	4	4	2
Kilmarnock	W W	W	6	3	1	2	2	4	1	3
Hearts	D	L L	6	3	2	1	3	3	3	2
St Mirren	W W	D	7	4	2	1	3	4	3	3
Partick			4	3	1	0	2	2	2	2

Season	Division	Pos	P	W	D	L	F	A	GD	Pts
2012-13	SPL	3	38	14	14	10	45	44	+1	56
2011-12	SPL	6	38	14	8	16	43	50	-7	50
2010-11	SPL	8	38	11	11	16	23	43	-20	44

Over/Under 39%/61% 11th **Both score** 58%/42% 5th

St Mirren

Nickname: The Saints
Colours: Black and white
Ground: St Mirren Park (8,029)
Tel: 0141 889 2558 www.saintmirren.net

St Mirren claimed the League Cup by beating Hearts in the final, which gave them their first trophy for 26 years, but the league campaign was another tale of disappointment as they had only Dundee below them in the final standings.

The Saints won just one of their final ten games and had to rely too heavily on veteran striker Steven Thompson, who ended up with 16 goals in all competitions. However, the news that Paul McGowan has signed a new one-year deal will be a big boost for manager Danny Lennon.

Longest run without win/loss: 9/4
High/low league position: 4/11
Clean sheets: 8 **Yellow cards:** 66 **Red cards:** 4
Average attendance: 4,389 **Players used:** 26
Leading scorer: S Thompson 13 (2,10)
Key stat: St Mirren led at half-time in just eight of their 38 SPL matches

2012-13 SPL appearances	P	G	Y	R
C Samson	38	0	0	0
M McAusland	35 (1)	3	9	0
S Thompson	33 (1)	13	5	0
D van Zanten	32 (2)	1	4	0
P Dummett	29 (1)	2	3	0
J Goodwin	29	1	11	2
K McLean	26 (3)	3	2	1
P McGowan	25	5	3	0
G Teale	23 (7)	0	1	0
L Mair	21 (3)	0	4	0

10 most regular starters

	2012-13		Last six seasons at home							
	H	A	P	W	D	L	OV	UN	BS	CS
Celtic	L D	L L	10	1	1	8	4	6	3	1
Motherwell	W	D D	10	2	5	3	4	6	5	3
St Johnstone	D	L L	7	0	5	2	2	5	4	2
Inverness CT	D W	D	10	3	3	4	7	3	8	1
Ross County	W L	D	2	1	0	1	2	0	2	0
Dundee United	L D	W	9	0	5	4	3	6	4	2
Hibernian	L L L	L D	10	3	3	4	3	7	5	3
Aberdeen	L D	D D	11	4	3	4	8	5	5	3
Kilmarnock	D	L D W	10	5	4	1	2	8	3	6
Hearts	W W	L L	9	3	3	3	2	7	4	3
St Mirren										
Partick			-	-	-	-	-	-	-	-

Season	Division	Pos	P	W	D	L	F	A	GD	Pts
2012-13	SPL	11	38	9	14	15	47	60	-13	41
2011-12	SPL	8	38	9	16	13	39	51	-12	43
2010-11	SPL	11	38	8	9	21	33	57	-24	33

Over/Under 53%/47% 7th **Both score** 61%/39% 3rd

Scottish Premier League stats 2012-13

Key Points do not include any deductions imposed by the league. **GFA** Goals For Average per match, **GAA** Goals Against Average per match, **PGA** Average Points Gained per match, **CS** Clean Sheet, **FS** First to Score, **Ov** Over 2.5 total goals, **Un** Under 2.5 total goals, **BS** Both teams Score

Top scorers 2012-13

		P	W	D	L	F	GFA	PGA	Pts
1	Celtic	38	24	7	7	92	2.42	2.1	79
2	Motherwell	38	18	9	11	67	1.76	1.7	63
3	Inverness CT	38	13	15	10	64	1.68	1.4	54
4	Kilmarnock	38	11	12	15	52	1.37	1.2	45
5	Dundee Utd	38	11	14	13	51	1.34	1.2	47
6	Hibernian	38	13	12	13	49	1.29	1.3	51
7	Ross County	38	13	14	11	47	1.24	1.4	53
	St Mirren	38	9	14	15	47	1.24	1.1	41
9	St Johnstone	38	14	14	10	45	1.18	1.5	56
10	Aberdeen	38	11	15	12	41	1.08	1.3	48
11	Hearts	38	11	11	16	40	1.05	1.2	44
12	Dundee	38	7	9	22	28	0.74	0.8	30

Best defence 2012-13

		P	W	D	L	A	GAA	PGA	Pts
1	Celtic	38	24	7	7	35	0.92	2.1	79
2	Aberdeen	38	11	15	12	43	1.13	1.3	48
3	St Johnstone	38	14	14	10	44	1.16	1.5	56
4	Ross County	38	13	14	11	48	1.26	1.4	53
5	Hearts	38	11	11	16	49	1.29	1.2	44
6	Motherwell	38	18	9	11	51	1.34	1.7	63
7	Hibernian	38	13	12	13	52	1.37	1.3	51
8	Kilmarnock	38	11	12	15	53	1.39	1.2	45
9	Inverness CT	38	13	15	10	60	1.58	1.4	54
	St Mirren	38	9	14	15	60	1.58	1.1	41
11	Dundee Utd	38	11	14	13	62	1.63	1.2	47
12	Dundee	38	7	9	22	66	1.74	0.8	30

Clean sheets 2012-13

		P	CS	CS%
1	Celtic	38	16	42.1
2	Ross County	38	15	39.5
3	Aberdeen	38	14	36.8
4	Hearts	38	13	34.2
5	Hibernian	38	11	28.9
	Dundee Utd	38	11	28.9
7	Kilmarnock	38	10	26.3
8	St Johnstone	38	9	23.7
9	St Mirren	38	8	21.1
	Inverness CT	38	8	21.1
11	Motherwell	38	6	15.8
12	Dundee	38	5	13.2

SPL top scorer Michael Higdon

Top goalscorers 2012-13

	Goals
M Higdon (Motherwell)	26
L Griffiths (Hibernian)	23
B McKay (Inverness CT)	23
N McGinn (Aberdeen)	20
G Hooper (Celtic)	19
J Russell (Dundee Utd)	13
S Thompson (St Mirren)	13
A Shinnie (Inverness CT)	12
K Commons (Celtic)	11
J Daly (Dundee Utd)	10
E Doyle (Hibernian)	10
J Murphy (Motherwell)	10

Record when keeping a clean sheet 2012-13

		P	W	D	L	F	GFA	PGA	Pts
1	Celtic	16	16	0	0	46	2.88	3.0	48
2	Hearts	13	9	4	0	16	1.23	2.4	31
	Kilmarnock	10	7	3	0	14	1.40	2.4	24
4	Hibernian	11	7	4	0	13	1.18	2.3	25
	Dundee Utd	11	7	4	0	13	1.18	2.3	25
	St Johnstone	9	6	3	0	8	0.89	2.3	21
7	Ross County	15	9	6	0	12	0.80	2.2	33
	Dundee	5	3	2	0	3	0.60	2.2	11
9	Inverness CT	8	4	4	0	11	1.38	2.0	16
	Motherwell	6	3	3	0	8	1.33	2.0	12
11	Aberdeen	14	6	8	0	9	0.64	1.9	26
12	St Mirren	8	3	5	0	6	0.75	1.8	14

Record when first to score 2012-13

		P	W	D	L	F	A	PGA	Pts
1	Motherwell	15	13	2	0	41	14	2.7	41
2	Aberdeen	13	10	3	0	26	10	2.5	33
3	St Johnstone	18	13	5	0	32	14	2.4	44
4	Celtic	31	22	6	3	81	25	2.3	72
5	Inverness CT	20	13	5	2	45	23	2.2	44
6	Hearts	16	10	5	1	27	11	2.2	35
7	Hibernian	16	11	2	3	32	19	2.2	35
8	Kilmarnock	18	11	5	2	38	20	2.1	38
9	St Mirren	13	8	3	2	27	16	2.1	27
10	Ross County	17	11	2	4	30	19	2.1	35
11	Dundee Utd	15	8	6	1	28	17	2.0	30
12	Dundee	13	6	6	1	17	11	1.8	24

Over 2.5 goals 2012-13

		H	A	Ov%
1	Inverness CT	12	13	66
2	Motherwell	11	13	63
3	Dundee United	12	11	61
	Hibernian	10	13	61
5	Celtic	11	11	58
6	Kilmarnock	12	9	55
7	St Mirren	10	10	53
8	Dundee	10	7	45
	Ross County	7	10	45
10	Hearts	11	5	42
11	St Johnstone	8	7	39
12	Aberdeen	4	9	34

Both to score 2012-13

		H	A	BS%
1	Inverness CT	14	13	71
2	Kilmarnock	14	11	66
3	Motherwell	12	11	61
	St Mirren	12	11	61
5	St Johnstone	11	11	58
6	Dundee United	12	9	55
	Hibernian	11	10	55
8	Celtic	7	12	50
	Ross County	9	10	50
10	Dundee	10	8	47
11	Aberdeen	5	12	45
12	Hearts	8	7	39

First to score 2012-13

		P	FS	FS%
1	Celtic	38	31	81.6
2	Inverness CT	38	20	52.6
3	Kilmarnock	38	18	47.4
	St Johnstone	38	18	47.4
5	Ross County	38	17	44.7
6	Hearts	38	16	42.1
	Hibernian	38	16	42.1
8	Dundee Utd	38	15	39.5
	Motherwell	38	15	39.5
10	Dundee	38	13	34.2
	Aberdeen	38	13	34.2
	St Mirren	38	13	34.2

Alloa Athletic

Nickname: The Wasps   **Ground:** Recreation Park
Web: www.alloaathletic.co.uk

The Wasps have made great progress under Paul Hartley and have now gained promotion twice under his stewardship.

They proved they were the second best in Division Two last season and, despite having an artificial pitch, it should be noted 11 of their 20 wins came on the road.

	2012-13 H	A	Last six seasons at home P	W	D	L	OV	UN	BS	CS
Dundee			-	-	-	-	-	-	-	-
Morton			-	-	-	-	-	-	-	-
Falkirk			-	-	-	-	-	-	-	-
Livingston			2	0	1	1	2	0	2	0
Hamilton			-	-	-	-	-	-	-	-
Raith			4	2	2	0	1	3	2	2
Dumbarton			4	0	1	3	3	1	3	1
Cowdenbeath			4	4	0	0	4	0	4	0
Queen of Sth	W L	L D	2	1	0	1	1	1	1	1
Alloa										

Season	Division	Pos	P	W	D	L	F	A	GD	Pts
2012-13	Division Two	2	36	20	7	9	62	35	+27	67
2011-12	Division Three	1	36	23	8	5	70	39	+31	77
2010-11	Division Two	9	36	9	9	18	49	71	-22	36

Over/Under 50%/50% 9th   **Both score** 53%/47% 9th

Cowdenbeath

Nickname: The Blue Brazil   **Ground:** Central Park
Web: www.cowdenbeathfc.com

The Blue Brazil continue to punch above their weight and for them to avoid the relegation play-offs should be viewed as an excellent achievement.

They won just three of their opening 20 games but just had enough in the end. However, it will be tough again this term.

	2012-13 H	A	Last six seasons at home P	W	D	L	OV	UN	BS	CS
Dundee			2	1	0	1	2	0	2	0
Morton	L D	L L	4	0	2	2	2	2	3	0
Falkirk	D W	L L	4	1	2	1	2	2	3	1
Livingston	D D	D L	2	0	2	0	1	1	2	0
Hamilton	W D	L W	2	1	1	0	0	2	1	1
Raith	D D	D W	6	1	2	3	4	2	4	1
Dumbarton	L L	W D	8	3	3	2	3	5	3	4
Cowdenbeath										
Queen of Sth			2	0	1	1	2	0	2	0
Alloa			4	0	3	1	1	3	4	0

Season	Division	Pos	P	W	D	L	F	A	GD	Pts
2012-13	Division One	8	36	8	12	16	51	65	-14	36
2011-12	Division Two	1	36	20	11	5	68	29	+39	71
2010-11	Division One	9	36	9	8	19	41	72	-31	55

Over/Under 61%/39% 6th   **Both score** 64%/36% 1st

Dumbarton

Nickname: The Sons   **Ground:** The Bet Butler Stadium
Web: www.dumbartonfootballclub.com

After failing to win any of their opening ten league games, it looked only a matter of time before Dumbarton were relegated.

But they recovered well in the spring and posted some fine results against the best teams in the second tier. They just need to perform better against fellow strugglers.

	2012-13 H	A	Last six seasons at home P	W	D	L	OV	UN	BS	CS
Dundee										
Morton	L L	L W	2	0	0	2	2	0	1	0
Falkirk	L L	W W	2	0	0	2	0	2	0	0
Livingston	L L	L W	4	0	0	4	4	0	2	0
Hamilton	D W	W L	2	1	1	0	2	0	2	0
Raith	W L	D L	2	1	0	1	2	0	2	0
Dumbarton										
Cowdenbeath	L D	W W	8	2	2	4	6	2	4	0
Queen of Sth			-	-	-	-	-	-	-	-
Alloa			4	2	1	1	4	0	4	0

Season	Division	Pos	P	W	D	L	F	A	GD	Pts
2012-13	Division One	7	36	13	4	19	58	83	-25	43
2011-12	Division Two	3	36	17	7	12	61	61	0	58
2010-11	Division Two	7	36	11	7	18	52	70	-18	40

Over/Under 81%/19% 1st   **Both score** 56%/44% 5th

Dundee

Nickname: The Dark Blues   **Ground:** Dens Park
Web: www.dundeefc.co.uk

Dundee were unfortunate to have so little time to prepare for SPL life after becoming the beneficiaries of Rangers' demotion.

Consequently, it was no great surprise that they struggled in the top tier, but they should still be able to put up a decent show now they're back in Division One.

	2012-13 H	A	Last six seasons at home P	W	D	L	OV	UN	BS	CS
Dundee										
Morton			10	6	2	2	3	7	4	4
Falkirk			4	4	0	0	2	2	2	2
Livingston			6	5	0	1	4	2	2	3
Hamilton			4	1	2	1	1	3	2	1
Raith			6	4	2	0	2	4	3	3
Dumbarton			-	-	-	-	-	-	-	-
Cowdenbeath			2	1	1	0	2	0	1	1
Queen of Sth			10	5	3	2	5	5	7	3
Alloa			-	-	-	-	-	-	-	-

Season	Division	Pos	P	W	D	L	F	A	GD	Pts
2012-13	SPL	12	38	7	9	22	28	66	-38	30
2011-12	Division One	2	36	15	10	11	53	43	+10	55
2010-11	Division One	6	36	19	12	5	54	34	+20	44

Over/Under 45%/55% 8th   **Both score** 47%/53% 10th

Falkirk

Nickname: The Bairns **Ground:** Falkirk Stadium
Web: www.falkirkfc.co.uk

The Bairns never really made much headway in the league last term despite claiming a place in the Scottish Cup semi-finals.
Gary Holt has replaced Steven Pressley as manager but the rookie boss should make them a force to be reckoned with following the installation of a plastic pitch.

	2012-13 H	A	Last six seasons at home P	W	D	L	OV	UN	BS	CS
Dundee			4	1	3	0	3	1	4	0
Morton	L W	W L	6	4	0	2	2	4	2	2
Falkirk										
Livingston	L W	L W	4	2	0	2	3	1	3	1
Hamilton	W L	D D	8	4	1	3	4	4	3	3
Raith	L D	L D	6	2	2	2	2	4	3	2
Dumbarton	L L	W W	2	0	0	2	2	0	2	0
Cowdenbeath	W W	D L	4	4	0	0	2	2	1	3
Queen of Sth			4	3	0	1	3	1	1	2
Alloa			-	-	-	-	-	-	-	-

Season	Division	Pos	P	W	D	L	F	A	GD	Pts
2012-13	Division One	3	36	15	8	13	52	48	+4	53
2011-12	Division One	3	36	13	13	10	53	48	+5	52
2010-11	Division One	3	36	17	7	12	57	41	+16	58

Over/Under 44%/56% 9th **Both score** 56%/44% 5th

Hamilton Academical

Nickname: The Accies **Ground:** New Douglas Park
Web: www.acciesfc.co.uk

Close attention will be paid to the transfer activity involving former midfielder James McCarthy as that could trigger a big sell-on clause to the Accies benefit.
They finished the season strongly with six wins from their final eight games and should hit the ground running.

	2012-13 H	A	Last six seasons at home P	W	D	L	OV	UN	BS	CS
Dundee			4	3	0	1	2	2	2	2
Morton	D W	W W	6	4	1	1	4	2	4	2
Falkirk	D D	L W	8	0	5	3	1	7	4	1
Livingston	L D	W D	6	1	3	2	2	4	5	0
Hamilton										
Raith	L W	L W	4	2	1	1	2	2	2	1
Dumbarton	L W	D L	2	1	0	1	2	0	2	0
Cowdenbeath	W L	L D	2	1	0	1	2	0	2	0
Queen of Sth			4	4	0	0	2	2	1	3
Alloa			-	-	-	-	-	-	-	-

Season	Division	Pos	P	W	D	L	F	A	GD	Pts
2012-13	Division One	5	36	14	9	13	52	45	+7	51
2011-12	Division One	4	36	14	7	15	55	56	-1	49
2010-11	SPL	12	38	5	11	22	24	59	-35	26

Over/Under 50%/50% 8th **Both score** 50%/50% 9th

Livingston

Nickname: Livi Lions **Ground:** Braidwood Stadium
Web: www.livingstonfc.co.uk

Livi never really threatened to push for promotion and had a disappointing end to the season as they won just two of their final ten matches of the campaign.
Six home wins wasn't good enough for them to challenge and that's the obvious area for improvement.

	2012-13 H	A	Last six seasons at home P	W	D	L	OV	UN	BS	CS
Dundee			6	1	1	4	3	3	4	0
Morton	D L	D L	8	3	3	2	3	5	3	3
Falkirk	W L	W L	4	1	1	2	3	1	4	0
Livingston										
Hamilton	L D	W D	6	2	1	3	3	3	1	3
Raith	W L	D W	4	2	1	1	3	1	3	1
Dumbarton	W L	W W	4	2	1	1	2	2	2	2
Cowdenbeath	D W	D D	2	1	1	0	1	1	1	1
Queen of Sth			6	2	4	0	4	2	1	1
Alloa			2	1	1	0	2	0	1	1

Season	Division	Pos	P	W	D	L	F	A	GD	Pts
2012-13	Division One	4	36	14	10	12	58	56	+2	52
2011-12	Division One	5	36	13	9	14	56	54	+2	48
2010-11	Division Two	1	36	25	7	4	79	33	+46	82

Over/Under 67%/33% 2nd **Both score** 61%/39% 2nd

Morton

Nickname: The Ton **Ground:** Cappielow Park
Web: www.gmfc.net

Ton performed well to force their way into the promotion picture and suffered only three defeats before the end of February.
The pace set by ultra-consistent Partick proved to be too strong in the end, as Morton lost five of their final seven games, but they should have learned a lot last term.

	2012-13 H	A	Last six seasons at home P	W	D	L	OV	UN	BS	CS
Dundee			10	2	1	7	4	6	4	2
Morton										
Falkirk	L W	W L	6	2	3	1	3	3	3	3
Livingston	D W	D W	8	2	4	2	7	1	8	0
Hamilton	L L	D L	6	0	0	6	2	4	2	0
Raith	W W	D L	8	3	3	2	2	6	3	4
Dumbarton	W L	W W	2	1	0	1	2	0	0	1
Cowdenbeath	W W	W D	4	3	0	1	3	1	2	2
Queen of Sth			10	1	5	4	7	3	5	2
Alloa			-	-	-	-	-	-	-	-

Season	Division	Pos	P	W	D	L	F	A	GD	Pts
2012-13	Division One	2	36	20	7	9	73	47	+26	67
2011-12	Division One	8	36	10	12	14	40	55	-15	42
2010-11	Division One	7	36	11	10	15	39	43	-4	43

Over/Under 64%/36% 5th **Both score** 58%/42% 4th

Queen of the South

Nickname: The Doonhamers **Ground:** Palmerston Park
Web: www.qosfc.com

The Doonhamers hosed up as champions of Division Two, always looking sure to bounce straight back to the second tier.

They suffered just two defeats all season but it will be interesting to see how they get on without 32-goal top scorer Nicky Clark, who has signed for Rangers.

	2012-13 H	A	Last six seasons at home P	W	D	L	OV	UN	BS	CS
Dundee			10	5	3	2	4	6	5	4
Morton			10	3	2	5	7	3	8	2
Falkirk			4	0	1	3	2	2	2	1
Livingston			6	3	1	2	3	3	2	2
Hamilton			4	2	1	1	3	1	3	1
Raith			6	2	1	3	3	3	3	2
Dumbarton			-	-	-	-	-	-	-	-
Cowdenbeath			2	1	1	0	2	0	1	1
Queen of Sth										
Alloa	W D	L W	2	1	1	0	0	2	0	2

Season	Division	Pos	P	W	D	L	F	A	GD	Pts
2012-13	Division Two	1	36	29	5	2	92	23	+69	92
2011-12	Division One	10	36	7	11	18	38	64	-26	32
2010-11	Division One	4	36	14	7	15	54	53	+1	49

Over/Under 61%/39% 6th   **Both score** 44%/56% 10th

Raith Rovers

Nickname: The Rovers **Ground:** Stark's Park
Web: www.raithrovers.net

Rovers lost just four of their 18 home games last term but struggled for goals at the end of the campaign, failing to find the net in five of their final seven matches.

They will also have to cope without top goalscorer Brian Graham who has moved to Dundee United.

	2012-13 H	A	Last six seasons at home P	W	D	L	OV	UN	BS	CS
Dundee			6	2	1	3	3	3	3	1
Morton	D W	L L	8	4	3	1	6	2	5	3
Falkirk	W D	W D	6	3	2	1	4	2	4	2
Livingston	D L	L W	4	0	1	3	1	3	0	1
Hamilton	W L	W L	4	3	0	1	2	2	2	1
Raith										
Dumbarton	D W	L W	2	1	1	0	2	0	2	0
Cowdenbeath	D L	D D	6	3	2	1	4	2	4	1
Queen of Sth			6	2	1	3	1	5	1	2
Alloa			4	4	0	0	4	0	4	0

Season	Division	Pos	P	W	D	L	F	A	GD	Pts
2012-13	Division One	6	36	11	13	12	45	48	-3	46
2011-12	Division One	7	36	11	11	14	46	49	-3	44
2010-11	Division One	2	36	17	9	10	47	35	+12	60

Over/Under 42%/58% 10th   **Both score** 53%/47% 8th

Scottish Division One stats 2012-13

Key Points do not include any deductions imposed by the league. **GFA** Goals For Average per match, **GAA** Goals Against Average per match, **PGA** Average Points Gained per match, **Ov** Over 2.5 total goals, **Un** Under 2.5 total goals, **BS** Both teams Score

Top scorers 2012-13

		P	W	D	L	F	GFA	PGA	Pts
1	Partick	36	23	9	4	76	2.11	2.2	78
2	Morton	36	20	7	9	73	2.03	1.9	67
3	Dunfermline	36	14	7	15	62	1.72	1.4	49
4	Livingston	36	14	10	12	58	1.61	1.4	52
	Dumbarton	36	13	4	19	58	1.61	1.2	43
6	Falkirk	36	15	8	13	52	1.44	1.5	53
	Hamilton	36	14	9	13	52	1.44	1.4	51
8	Cowdenbeath	36	8	12	16	51	1.42	1.0	36
9	Raith	36	11	13	12	45	1.25	1.3	46
10	Airdrieonians	36	5	7	24	41	1.14	0.6	22

Best defence 2012-13

		P	W	D	L	A	GAA	PGA	Pts
1	Partick	36	23	9	4	28	0.78	2.2	78
2	Hamilton	36	14	9	13	45	1.25	1.4	51
3	Morton	36	20	7	9	47	1.31	1.9	67
4	Falkirk	36	15	8	13	48	1.33	1.5	53
	Raith	36	11	13	12	48	1.33	1.3	46
6	Livingston	36	14	10	12	56	1.56	1.4	52
7	Dunfermline	36	14	7	15	59	1.64	1.4	49
8	Cowdenbeath	36	8	12	16	65	1.81	1.0	36
9	Dumbarton	36	13	4	19	83	2.31	1.2	43
10	Airdrieonians	36	5	7	24	89	2.47	0.6	22

Over 2.5 goals 2012-13

		H	A	Ov%
1	Dumbarton	12	17	81
2	Airdrieonians	13	11	67
	Dunfermline	11	13	67
	Livingston	14	10	67
5	Morton	10	13	64
6	Cowdenbeath	10	12	61
7	Partick	13	8	58
8	Hamilton	10	8	50
9	Falkirk	8	8	44
10	Raith	7	8	42

Both to score 2012-13

		H	A	BS%
1	Cowdenbeath	14	9	64
2	Airdrieonians	12	10	61
	Livingston	12	10	61
4	Morton	8	13	58
5	Dumbarton	9	11	56
	Dunfermline	8	12	56
	Falkirk	9	11	56
8	Raith	9	10	53
9	Hamilton	11	7	50
10	Partick	9	8	47

Top goalscorers 2012-13

	Goals
S May (Hamilton)	25
L Taylor (Falkirk)	24
B Graham (Raith)	18
I Russell (Livingston)	15
P MacDonald (Morton)	14
A Campbell (Morton)	13
S Lawless (Partick)	13
S Craig (Partick)	12
K Doohan (Partick)	12
J Lister (Dumbarton)	12

Falkirk's cup run went all
the way to the semi-final

Airdrieonians

Nickname: The Diamonds **Ground:** Excelsior Stadium
Web: www.airdriefc.com

This season is going to be a rebuilding job for Airdrie who were completely outclassed in Division One last term.

The won just five games all season and will surely be delighted if there is some stability after their year of woe. Maybe the name change will prove a good omen.

	2012-13 H	A	P	W	D	L	OV	UN	BS	CS
Dunfermline	L D	W W	6	0	3	3	3	3	5	0
Airdrieonians										
Brechin			6	2	2	2	5	1	6	0
Forfar			4	3	1	0	3	1	2	2
Arbroath			2	1	1	0	1	1	1	1
Stenhousemuir			4	2	1	1	3	1	2	1
Ayr			6	1	3	2	3	3	3	1
Stranraer			-	-	-	-	-	-	-	-
East Fife			4	1	2	1	2	2	3	1
Rangers			-	-	-	-	-	-	-	-

Season	Division	Pos	P	W	D	L	F	A	GD	Pts
2012-13	Division One	10	36	5	7	24	41	89	-48	22
2011-12	Division Two	4	36	14	10	12	68	60	+8	52
2010-11	Division Two	6	36	13	9	14	52	60	-8	48

Over/Under 67%/33% 2nd   **Both score** 61%/39% 2nd

Arbroath

Nickname: The Red Lichties **Ground:** Gayfield Park
Web: www.arbroathfc.co.uk

Gaining a draw at Celtic in the Scottish Cup was undoubtedly the highlight of the season for the Red Lichties but there was little else to smile about as they narrowly missed out on a place in the play-offs.

However, they'll be encouraged by losing just two of the last nine league games.

	2012-13 H	A	P	W	D	L	OV	UN	BS	CS
Dunfermline			-	-	-	-	-	-	-	-
Airdrieonians			2	1	1	0	2	0	2	0
Brechin	W L	L L	8	2	2	4	4	4	5	2
Forfar	D W	D W	6	2	2	2	3	3	5	0
Arbroath										
Stenhousemuir	D D	D L	8	2	4	2	3	5	3	3
Ayr	W L	L W	4	1	0	3	4	0	3	0
Stranraer	W W	D L	8	4	4	0	3	5	3	5
East Fife	W W	L W	10	3	2	5	4	6	3	3
Rangers			-	-	-	-	-	-	-	-

Season	Division	Pos	P	W	D	L	F	A	GD	Pts
2012-13	Division Two	5	36	15	7	14	47	57	-10	52
2011-12	Division Two	2	36	17	12	7	76	51	+25	63
2010-11	Division Three	1	36	20	6	10	80	61	+19	66

Over/Under 50%/50% 9th   **Both score** 56%/44% 8th

Ayr United

Nickname: The Honest Men **Ground:** Somerset Park
Web: www.ayrunitedfc.co.uk

Having been 100-30 favourites for the Division Two title, it was a dismal campaign for Ayr, who finished seventh and never really looked like battling for promotion.

However, keeping hold of top goalscorer Michael Moffat and signing Craig Malcolm from Stranraer should be welcome boosts.

	2012-13 H	A	P	W	D	L	OV	UN	BS	CS
Dunfermline			2	1	0	1	1	1	1	1
Airdrieonians			6	2	2	2	3	3	5	1
Brechin	W L	L L	8	4	1	3	5	3	4	2
Forfar	L W	L L	4	2	0	2	3	1	3	0
Arbroath	W L	L W	4	3	0	1	2	2	2	1
Stenhousemuir	D L	D L	4	2	1	1	2	2	3	1
Ayr										
Stranraer	W W	L W	4	4	0	0	4	0	3	1
East Fife	L W	W D	6	3	1	2	4	2	4	1
Rangers			-	-	-	-	-	-	-	-

Season	Division	Pos	P	W	D	L	F	A	GD	Pts
2012-13	Division Two	7	36	12	5	19	53	65	-12	41
2011-12	Division One	9	36	9	11	16	44	67	-23	38
2010-11	Division Two	2	36	18	5	13	62	55	+7	59

Over/Under 67%/33% 4th   **Both score** 67%/33% 2nd

Brechin City

Nickname: The City **Ground:** Glebe Park
Web: www.brechincity.com

City did well to finish third in Division Two after losing six of their opening eight matches and there is reason to be confident after they lost to Alloa in the play-offs.

Rangers' inclusion means the title is likely to be beyond them, but they should be challenging to be the best of the rest.

	2012-13 H	A	P	W	D	L	OV	UN	BS	CS
Dunfermline			-	-	-	-	-	-	-	-
Airdrieonians			6	3	2	1	4	2	6	0
Brechin										
Forfar	W L	L W	6	2	1	3	3	3	3	1
Arbroath	W W	L W	8	3	2	3	3	5	4	2
Stenhousemuir	W L	L D	8	5	2	1	4	4	4	4
Ayr	W W	L W	8	5	1	2	5	3	4	2
Stranraer	W D	W L	4	3	1	0	3	1	2	2
East Fife	W W	D W	10	6	0	4	8	2	7	2
Rangers			-	-	-	-	-	-	-	-

Season	Division	Pos	P	W	D	L	F	A	GD	Pts
2012-13	Division Two	3	36	19	4	13	72	59	+13	61
2011-12	Division Two	8	36	10	11	15	47	62	-15	41
2010-11	Division Two	4	36	15	12	9	63	45	+18	57

Over/Under 78%/22% 2nd   **Both score** 61%/39% 5th

Dunfermline Athletic

Nickname: The Pars **Ground:** East End Park
Web: www.dafc.co.uk

A campaign to forget. Before Christmas, the Pars looked set for an SPL return but financial problems saw them plummet and eventually get relegated after they received a 15-point administration penalty.

Keeping the club going and achieving some stability will be the aim this season.

	2012-13 H A	Last six seasons at home P	W	D	L	OV	UN	BS	CS
Dunfermline		-	-	-	-	-	-	-	-
Airdrieonians	L L W D	6	2	2	2	2	4	3	3
Brechin		-	-	-	-	-	-	-	-
Forfar		-	-	-	-	-	-	-	-
Arbroath		-	-	-	-	-	-	-	-
Stenhousemuir		-	-	-	-	-	-	-	-
Ayr		2	1	0	1	1	1	1	0
Stranraer		-	-	-	-	-	-	-	-
East Fife		-	-	-	-	-	-	-	-
Rangers		2	0	0	2	2	0	1	0

Season	Division	Pos	P	W	D	L	F	A	GD	Pts
2012-13	Division One	9	36	14	7	15	62	59	+3	34
2011-12	SPL	12	38	5	10	23	40	82	-42	25
2010-11	Division One	1	36	20	10	6	66	31	+35	70

Over/Under 67%/33% 2nd   **Both score** 56%/44% 5th

East Fife

Nickname: The Fifers **Ground:** New Bayview
Web: www.eastfifefc.info

Victory over Peterhead in the play-offs just kept East Fife in the third tier, but new local owners appear to be ambitious and should help them enjoy a better season this time.

The signing of former Hearts striker Christian Nade appears a signal of intent from new manager Willie Aitchison.

	2012-13 H A	Last six seasons at home P	W	D	L	OV	UN	BS	CS
Dunfermline		-	-	-	-	-	-	-	-
Airdrieonians		4	2	1	1	1	3	1	2
Brechin	D L L L	10	3	5	2	5	5	5	4
Forfar	W L L L	8	6	0	2	8	0	3	5
Arbroath	W L L L	10	4	3	3	6	4	7	1
Stenhousemuir	W L L L	10	4	3	3	6	4	7	2
Ayr	L D W L	6	2	1	3	5	1	4	1
Stranraer	L D W L	6	3	1	2	4	2	4	1
East Fife		-	-	-	-	-	-	-	-
Rangers		-	-	-	-	-	-	-	-

Season	Division	Pos	P	W	D	L	F	A	GD	Pts
2012-13	Division Two	9	36	8	8	20	50	65	-15	32
2011-12	Division Two	6	36	14	6	16	55	57	-2	48
2010-11	Division Two	5	36	14	10	12	77	60	+17	52

Over/Under 67%/33% 4th   **Both score** 64%/36% 4th

Forfar Athletic

Nickname: The Loons **Ground:** Station Park
Web: www.forfarathletic.co.uk

The Loons qualified for the play-offs last season but need to perform better against the stronger teams this time around.

They won just two of the 16 games they played against outfits who finished in the top half of the table and an improvement on that should help them go close again.

	2012-13 H A	Last six seasons at home P	W	D	L	OV	UN	BS	CS
Dunfermline		-	-	-	-	-	-	-	-
Airdrieonians		4	1	0	3	4	0	4	0
Brechin	W L L W	6	3	2	1	3	3	4	2
Forfar		-	-	-	-	-	-	-	-
Arbroath	D L D L	6	1	2	3	3	3	5	1
Stenhousemuir	W D W L	10	3	3	4	6	4	7	2
Ayr	W W W L	4	4	0	0	4	0	4	0
Stranraer	W W L W	6	5	1	0	2	4	2	4
East Fife	W W L W	8	4	1	3	6	2	6	1
Rangers		-	-	-	-	-	-	-	-

Season	Division	Pos	P	W	D	L	F	A	GD	Pts
2012-13	Division Two	4	36	17	3	16	67	74	-7	54
2011-12	Division Two	7	36	11	9	16	59	72	-13	42
2010-11	Division Two	3	36	17	8	11	50	48	+2	59

Over/Under 81%/19% 1st   **Both score** 72%/28% 1st

Rangers

Nickname: The Gers **Ground:** Ibrox Stadium
Web: www.rangers.co.uk

The Gers will be expected to storm to another title on their three-year SPL sabbatical and they've boosted their forward line with Jon Daly from Dundee United and Nicky Clark from Queen Of The South.

But they failed to win 11 of 36 games last term and will slip up on occasion again.

	2012-13 H A	Last six seasons at home P	W	D	L	OV	UN	BS	CS
Dunfermline		1	1	0	0	1	0	1	0
Airdrieonians		-	-	-	-	-	-	-	-
Brechin		-	-	-	-	-	-	-	-
Forfar		-	-	-	-	-	-	-	-
Arbroath		-	-	-	-	-	-	-	-
Stenhousemuir		-	-	-	-	-	-	-	-
Ayr		-	-	-	-	-	-	-	-
Stranraer		-	-	-	-	-	-	-	-
East Fife		-	-	-	-	-	-	-	-
Rangers		-	-	-	-	-	-	-	-

Season	Division	Pos	P	W	D	L	F	A	GD	Pts
2012-13	Division Three	1	36	25	8	3	87	29	+58	83
2011-12	SPL	2	38	26	5	7	77	28	+49	73
2010-11	SPL	1	38	30	3	5	88	29	+59	93

Over/Under 53%/47% 9th   **Both score** 56%/44% 8th

Stenhousemuir

Nickname: Warriors **Ground:** Ochilview Park
Web: www.stenhousemuirfc.com

Stenny had to be content with a mid-table finish but they should be boosted by a decent end to the campaign which saw them win four of their final five matches.

Experience in the form of Sean Lynch and Eddie Malone has been added to the squad and that should help them improve.

	2012-13 H	A	Last six seasons at home P	W	D	L	OV	UN	BS	CS
Dunfermline	-	-	-	-	-	-	-	-	-	-
Airdrieonians			4	1	1	2	2	2	2	1
Brechin	W D	L W	8	2	4	2	5	3	7	1
Forfar	L W	L D	10	4	1	5	5	5	3	4
Arbroath	D W	D D	8	4	2	2	4	4	3	4
Stenhousemuir										
Ayr	D W	D W	4	3	1	0	3	1	3	1
Stranraer	D L	D D	4	0	2	2	2	2	3	1
East Fife	W W	L W	10	5	3	2	4	6	6	2
Rangers	-	-	-	-	-	-	-	-	-	-

Season	Division	Pos	P	W	D	L	F	A	GD	Pts
2012-13	Division Two	6	36	12	13	11	59	59	0	49
2011-12	Division Two	5	36	15	6	15	54	49	+5	51
2010-11	Division Two	8	36	10	8	18	46	59	-13	38

Over/Under 61%/39% 6th   **Both score** 67%/33% 2nd

Stranraer

Nickname: The Blues **Ground:** Stair Park
Web: www.stranraerfc.org

With just 43 goals, Stranraer were the lowest scorers in Division Two last term and the departure of top goalscorer Craig Malcolm is a worrying development.

Alloa's Martin Grehan returns to fill the void but the Blues only secured their status on the final day last term and may struggle.

	2012-13 H	A	Last six seasons at home P	W	D	L	OV	UN	BS	CS
Dunfermline	-	-	-	-	-	-	-	-	-	-
Airdrieonians	-	-	-	-	-	-	-	-	-	-
Brechin	L W	L D	4	1	0	3	3	1	2	0
Forfar	W L	L L	6	5	0	1	4	2	2	3
Arbroath	D W	L L	8	2	3	3	5	3	6	1
Stenhousemuir	D D	D W	4	1	2	1	2	2	4	0
Ayr	W L	L L	4	1	0	3	2	2	2	1
Stranraer										
East Fife	L W	W D	6	1	0	5	3	3	2	0
Rangers	-	-	-	-	-	-	-	-	-	-

Season	Division	Pos	P	W	D	L	F	A	GD	Pts
2012-13	Division Two	8	36	10	7	19	43	71	-28	37
2011-12	Division Three	3	36	17	7	12	77	57	+20	58
2010-11	Division Three	5	36	15	12	9	72	57	+15	57

Over/Under 61%/39% 6th   **Both score** 61%/39% 5th

Scottish Division Two stats 2012-13

Key Points do not include any deductions imposed by the league. **GFA** Goals For Average per match, **GAA** Goals Against Average per match, **PGA** Average Points Gained per match, **CS** Clean Sheet, **FS** First to Score, **Ov** Over 2.5 total goals, **Un** Under 2.5 total goals, **BS** Both teams Score

Top scorers 2012-13

		P	W	D	L	F	GFA	PGA	Pts
1	Queen of Sth	36	29	5	2	92	2.56	**2.6**	92
2	Brechin	36	19	4	13	72	2.00	**1.7**	61
3	Forfar	36	17	3	16	67	1.86	**1.5**	54
4	Alloa	36	20	7	9	62	1.72	**1.9**	67
5	Stenh'semuir	36	12	13	11	59	1.64	**1.4**	49
6	Ayr	36	12	5	19	53	1.47	**1.1**	41
7	East Fife	36	8	8	20	50	1.39	**0.9**	32
8	Arbroath	36	15	7	14	47	1.31	**1.4**	52
9	Albion	36	7	3	26	45	1.25	**0.7**	24
10	Stranraer	36	10	7	19	43	1.19	**1.0**	37

Best defence 2012-13

		P	W	D	L	A	GAA	PGA	Pts
1	Queen of Sth	36	29	5	2	23	**0.64**	2.6	92
2	Alloa	36	20	7	9	35	**0.97**	1.9	67
3	Arbroath	36	15	7	14	57	**1.58**	1.4	52
4	Brechin	36	19	4	13	59	**1.64**	1.7	61
	Stenh'semuir	36	12	13	11	59	**1.64**	1.4	49
6	Ayr	36	12	5	19	65	**1.81**	1.1	41
	East Fife	36	8	8	20	65	**1.81**	0.9	32
8	Stranraer	36	10	7	19	71	**1.97**	1.0	37
9	Forfar	36	17	3	16	74	**2.06**	1.5	54
10	Albion	36	7	3	26	82	**2.28**	0.7	24

Over 2.5 goals 2012-13

		H	A	Ov%
1	Forfar	15	14	81
2	Brechin	15	13	78
3	Albion	14	11	69
4	Ayr	13	11	67
	East Fife	12	12	67
6	Queen of Sth	9	13	61
	Stenhousemuir	10	12	61
	Stranraer	9	13	61
9	Alloa	9	9	50
	Arbroath	10	8	50

Both to score 2012-13

		H	A	BS%
1	Forfar	14	12	72
2	Ayr	13	11	67
	Stenhousemuir	9	15	67
4	East Fife	11	12	64
5	Albion	11	11	61
	Brechin	11	11	61
	Stranraer	11	11	61
8	Arbroath	12	8	56
9	Alloa	10	9	53
10	Queen of Sth	7	9	44

Top goalscorers 2012-13

	Goals
N Clark (Queen of Sth)	32
J Gemmell (Stenh'semuir)	18
C Malcolm (Stranraer)	18
A Trouten (Brechin)	17
A Jackson (Brechin)	16
M Moffat (Ayr)	16
C Cawley (Alloa)	13
D Lyle (Queen of Sth)	13
D Carcary (Brechin)	12
G Reilly (Queen of Sth)	12

Rangers will boost the
Division Two attendance
figures this season

Albion Rovers

Nickname: The Wee Rovers **Ground:** Cliftonhill
Web: www.albionroversfc.com

Albion were out of their depth in Division Two last term, losing 26 of their 36 games, and must shore up their defence if they are to have a chance of an immediate return.

New manager James Ward will need a decent start to provide a vital lift to everyone at Cliftonhill.

	2012-13 H	2012-13 A	Last six seasons at home P	W	D	L	OV	UN	BS	CS
Albion			-	-	-	-	-	-	-	-
Peterhead			-	-	-	-	-	-	-	-
Queen's Park			4	2	0	2	2	2	2	1
Berwick			6	4	1	1	4	2	4	1
Elgin			8	3	2	3	5	3	6	1
Montrose			8	2	1	5	3	5	2	2
Stirling			2	0	0	2	1	1	1	0
Annan			6	2	3	1	1	5	1	4
Clyde			2	1	1	0	1	1	2	0
East Stirling			8	4	1	3	4	4	3	3

Season	Division	Pos	P	W	D	L	F	A	GD	Pts
2012-13	Division Two	10	36	7	3	26	45	82	-37	24
2011-12	Division Two	9	36	10	7	19	43	66	-23	37
2010-11	Division Three	2	36	17	10	9	56	40	+16	61

Over/Under 69%/31% 3rd **Both score** 61%/39% 5th

Annan Athletic

Nickname: Galabankies **Ground:** Galabank
Web: www.annanathleticfc.com

Jim Chapman begins his first full season at the club and the Galabankies need to improve on last season's disappointing eighth place.

They caused a massive shock when they won at Ibrox but their other efforts fell short of those giddy heights.

	2012-13 H	2012-13 A	Last six seasons at home P	W	D	L	OV	UN	BS	CS
Albion			6	1	3	2	4	2	5	1
Peterhead	W D	L L	4	2	1	1	2	2	1	2
Queen's Park	L W	D D	8	4	0	4	6	2	6	1
Berwick	W D	L W	10	1	6	3	5	5	9	0
Elgin	W D	D L	10	3	5	2	5	5	5	3
Montrose	W D	D L	10	5	3	2	7	3	8	2
Stirling	W L	L L	2	1	0	1	1	1	1	0
Annan										
Clyde	L L	L W	6	3	0	3	1	5	1	3
East Stirling	W L	D W	10	7	1	2	8	2	6	3

Season	Division	Pos	P	W	D	L	F	A	GD	Pts
2012-13	Division Three	8	36	11	10	15	54	65	-11	43
2011-12	Division Three	6	36	13	10	13	53	53	0	49
2010-11	Division Three	4	36	16	11	9	58	45	+13	59

Over/Under 69%/31% 3rd **Both score** 69%/31% 3rd

Berwick Rangers

Nickname: The Borderers **Ground:** Shielfield Park
Web: www.berwickrangersfc.co.uk

The Borderers came close to gaining promotion last term but fell to East Fife in extra-time of their play-off semi-final.

Berwick must improve their away form if they're to make a title challenge, as four wins from 18 away games isn't enough for a team with promotion aspirations.

	2012-13 H	2012-13 A	Last six seasons at home P	W	D	L	OV	UN	BS	CS
Albion			6	1	2	3	4	2	4	1
Peterhead	D L	L D	6	1	2	3	3	3	4	0
Queen's Park	W W	D L	10	5	3	2	4	6	7	3
Berwick										
Elgin	D W	L W	10	6	4	0	6	4	7	3
Montrose	L W	L W	10	4	1	5	5	5	4	3
Stirling	W W	L L	2	2	0	0	1	1	1	1
Annan	W L	L D	10	3	2	5	6	4	6	1
Clyde	W D	L L	6	3	2	1	4	2	4	1
East Stirling	W W	W W	10	5	2	3	6	4	5	3

Season	Division	Pos	P	W	D	L	F	A	GD	Pts
2012-13	Division Three	4	36	14	7	15	59	55	+4	49
2011-12	Division Three	7	36	12	12	12	61	58	+3	48
2010-11	Division Three	6	36	12	13	11	62	56	+6	49

Over/Under 61%/39% 6th **Both score** 64%/36% 6th

Clyde

Nickname: The Bully Wee **Ground:** Broadwood
Web: www.clydefc.co.uk

Jim Duffy will be looking to keep as many players from last season's squad as possible as the club's finances dictate that no new faces will be coming in.

Expect a youthful look to the Bully Wee's line-up this season as they look to improve on a disappointing ninth-place finish.

	2012-13 H	2012-13 A	Last six seasons at home P	W	D	L	OV	UN	BS	CS
Albion			2	0	0	2	1	1	1	0
Peterhead	L W	L L	6	3	0	3	2	4	2	2
Queen's Park	L L	L L	6	0	0	6	4	2	3	0
Berwick	W W	L D	6	3	1	2	5	1	5	1
Elgin	D D	L L	6	0	4	2	3	3	5	0
Montrose	L W	L W	6	3	1	2	2	4	3	3
Stirling	W L	W L	6	2	0	4	5	1	4	1
Annan	W L	W W	6	1	2	3	2	4	3	1
Clyde										
East Stirling	W W	L L	6	5	0	1	4	2	3	0

Season	Division	Pos	P	W	D	L	F	A	GD	Pts
2012-13	Division Three	9	36	12	4	20	42	66	-24	40
2011-12	Division Three	9	36	8	11	17	35	50	-15	35
2010-11	Division Three	10	36	8	8	20	37	67	-30	32

Over/Under 64%/36% 5th **Both score** 56%/44% 8th

East Stirlingshire

Nickname: The Shire **Ground:** Ochilview Park
Web: www.eaststirlingshirefc.co.uk

The Division Three whipping boys could be set for an upturn in fortunes as new manager John Coughlin has brought in experienced players like Chris Townsley, Michael Bolochoweckyj and Iain Thomson.

After losing their final ten games of 2012-13, it couldn't get much worse.

	2012-13 H	A	Last six seasons at home P	W	D	L	OV	UN	BS	CS
Albion			8	4	1	3	4	4	3	4
Peterhead	W L	L L	4	2	0	2	3	1	3	0
Queen's Park	L L	W L	8	2	0	6	4	4	3	1
Berwick	L L	L L	10	5	1	4	5	5	3	4
Elgin	L W	W L	12	6	4	2	6	6	8	3
Montrose	D L	L D	12	7	1	4	10	2	8	3
Stirling	W D	D L	2	1	1	0	1	1	2	0
Annan	D L	L W	10	4	2	4	7	3	7	2
Clyde	W W	L L	6	3	2	1	2	4	1	4
East Stirling										

Season	Division	Pos	P	W	D	L	F	A	GD	Pts
2012-13	Division Three	10	36	8	5	23	49	97	-48	29
2011-12	Division Three	10	36	6	6	24	38	88	-50	24
2010-11	Division Three	9	36	10	4	22	33	62	-29	34

Over/Under 78%/22% 1st **Both score** 69%/31% 3rd

Elgin City

Nickname: Black & Whites **Ground:** Borough Briggs
Web: www.elgincity.com

A run of one victory in 13 matches in the middle of the campaign put paid to any hopes Elgin had of making the play-offs, and they've been hit by top goalscorer Stuart Leslie and midfielder Daniel Moore signing for Highland League side Nairn County. Their chance may have gone.

	2012-13 H	A	Last six seasons at home P	W	D	L	OV	UN	BS	CS
Albion			8	3	3	2	4	4	6	1
Peterhead	W L	D W	4	2	0	2	3	1	2	1
Queen's Park	L L	D W	8	2	1	5	3	5	3	1
Berwick	W L	D L	10	5	1	4	8	2	7	2
Elgin										
Montrose	W W	D L	12	9	0	3	8	4	8	2
Stirling	W L	W D	2	1	0	1	2	0	2	0
Annan	D W	L D	10	4	2	4	6	4	6	3
Clyde	W D	D D	6	2	1	3	3	3	3	0
East Stirling	L W	W L	12	6	0	6	7	5	4	4

Season	Division	Pos	P	W	D	L	F	A	GD	Pts
2012-13	Division Three	5	36	13	10	13	67	69	-2	49
2011-12	Division Three	4	36	16	9	11	68	60	+8	57
2010-11	Division Three	7	36	13	6	17	53	63	-10	45

Over/Under 69%/31% 3rd **Both score** 78%/22% 1st

Montrose

Nickname: The Gable Endies **Ground:** Links Park
Web: www.montrosefc.co.uk

The Gable Endies lost out on a place in the play-offs by two points after failing to win any of their final six games of the season.

Just six victories from their 18 home matches last term eventually put paid to their chances but the play-offs seem a realistic aim this time around.

	2012-13 H	A	Last six seasons at home P	W	D	L	OV	UN	BS	CS
Albion			8	2	2	4	2	6	2	3
Peterhead	W L	L W	4	2	0	2	3	1	2	1
Queen's Park	D L	D W	8	1	1	6	3	5	3	6	0
Berwick	W L	W L	10	1	6	3	4	6	10	0
Elgin	D W	L L	12	6	3	3	7	5	6	4
Montrose										
Stirling	W D	W L	2	1	1	0	2	0	2	0
Annan	D W	L D	10	1	5	4	4	6	6	2
Clyde	L D	W L	6	4	1	1	5	1	4	2
East Stirling	W D	D W	12	7	1	4	8	4	5	3

Season	Division	Pos	P	W	D	L	F	A	GD	Pts
2012-13	Division Three	6	36	12	11	13	60	68	-8	47
2011-12	Division Three	8	36	11	5	20	58	75	-17	38
2010-11	Division Three	8	36	10	7	19	47	61	-14	37

Over/Under 72%/28% 2nd **Both score** 78%/22% 1st

Peterhead

Nickname: The Blue Toon **Ground:** Balmoor Stadium
Web: www.peterheadfc.co.uk

The Blue Toon had a storming end to the season, winning their last eight games to finish second behind Rangers, but eventually fell in the play-off final to East Fife.

With the best striker in the division in Rory McAllister, they have a great shout of claiming the championship.

	2012-13 H	A	Last six seasons at home P	W	D	L	OV	UN	BS	CS
Albion			-	-	-	-	-	-	-	-
Peterhead										
Queen's Park	W L	D W	8	5	2	1	2	6	4	3
Berwick	W D	D W	6	4	1	1	3	3	4	2
Elgin	D L	L W	4	1	1	2	2	2	2	1
Montrose	W L	L W	4	2	0	2	2	2	2	1
Stirling	D D	L W	6	1	5	0	2	4	5	1
Annan	W W	L D	4	3	0	1	2	2	2	2
Clyde	W W	W L	6	3	3	0	1	5	1	5
East Stirling	W W	W L	4	4	0	0	1	3	0	4

Season	Division	Pos	P	W	D	L	F	A	GD	Pts
2012-13	Division Three	2	36	17	8	11	52	28	+24	59
2011-12	Division Three	5	36	15	6	15	51	53	-2	51
2010-11	Division Two	10	36	5	11	20	47	76	-29	26

Over/Under 31%/69% 10th **Both score** 25%/75% 10th

Queen's Park

Nickname: The Spiders **Ground:** Hampden Park
Web: www.queensparkfc.co.uk

Queen's Park failed to take any momentum into the play-offs after winning just two of their last nine games of the season but the money generated from Rangers' two visits to Hampden will have boosted the coffers.

However, a record of five home victories has to be improved upon.

	2012-13 H A	Last six seasons at home P	W	D	L	OV	UN	BS	CS
Albion		4	2	0	2	1	3	1	1
Peterhead	D L L W	8	2	3	3	2	6	3	2
Queen's Park									
Berwick	D W L L	10	5	3	2	4	6	6	3
Elgin	D L W W	8	2	2	4	3	5	3	2
Montrose	D L D W	8	6	1	1	7	1	5	3
Stirling	W D W W	4	2	2	0	3	1	4	0
Annan	D D W L	8	3	4	1	4	4	3	4
Clyde	W W W W	6	5	0	1	4	2	1	4
East Stirling	L W W W	8	7	0	1	3	5	3	5

Season	Division	Pos	P	W	D	L	F	A	GD	Pts
2012-13	Division Three	3	36	16	8	12	60	54	+6	56
2011-12	Division Three	2	36	19	6	11	70	48	+22	63
2010-11	Division Three	3	36	18	5	13	57	43	+14	59

Over/Under 61%/39% 6th **Both score** 58%/42% 7th

Stirling Albion

Nickname: The Binos **Ground:** Forthbank Stadium
Web: www.stirlingalbionfc.co.uk

Recovered from losing 13 of their opening 19 matches to eventually finish seventh, and top goalscorer Jordan White has agreed to stay for another season.

If they led at half-time, they tended to get the job done, winning eight and drawing one of nine such situations last season.

	2012-13 H A	Last six seasons at home P	W	D	L	OV	UN	BS	CS
Albion		2	1	1	0	2	0	1	1
Peterhead	W L D D	6	4	1	1	2	4	2	3
Queen's Park	L L L D	4	1	0	3	4	0	2	1
Berwick	W W L L	2	2	0	0	1	1	1	1
Elgin	L D L W	2	0	1	1	1	1	2	0
Montrose	L W L D	2	1	0	1	2	0	2	0
Stirling									
Annan	W W L W	2	2	0	0	2	0	2	0
Clyde	L W L W	6	2	2	2	0	6	2	2
East Stirling	D W L D	2	1	1	0	1	1	2	0

Season	Division	Pos	P	W	D	L	F	A	GD	Pts
2012-13	Division Three	7	36	12	9	15	59	58	+1	45
2011-12	Division Two	10	36	9	7	20	46	70	-24	34
2010-11	Division One	10	36	4	8	24	32	82	-50	20

Over/Under 58%/42% 8th **Both score** 69%/31% 3rd

Peterhead are fancied in Division Three this season

Key Points do not include any deductions imposed by the league. **GFA** Goals For Average per match, **GAA** Goals Against Average per match, **PGA** Average Points Gained per match, **CS** Clean Sheet, **FS** First to Score, **Ov** Over 2.5 total goals, **Un** Under 2.5 total goals, **BS** Both teams Score

Top scorers 2012-13

		P	W	D	L	F	GFA	PGA	Pts
1	Rangers	36	25	8	3	87	2.42	2.3	83
2	Elgin City	36	13	10	13	67	1.86	1.4	49
3	Queen's Park	36	16	8	12	60	1.67	1.6	56
	Montrose	36	12	11	13	60	1.67	1.3	47
5	Berwick	36	14	7	15	59	1.64	1.4	49
	Stirling	36	12	9	15	59	1.64	1.3	45
7	Annan	36	11	10	15	54	1.50	1.2	43
8	Peterhead	36	17	8	11	52	1.44	1.6	59
9	East Stirling	36	8	5	23	49	1.36	0.8	29
10	Clyde	36	12	4	20	42	1.17	1.1	40

Best defence 2012-13

		P	W	D	L	A	GAA	PGA	Pts
1	Peterhead	36	17	8	11	28	0.78	1.6	59
2	Rangers	36	25	8	3	29	0.81	2.3	83
3	Queen's Park	36	16	8	12	54	1.50	1.6	56
4	Berwick	36	14	7	15	55	1.53	1.4	49
5	Stirling	36	12	9	15	58	1.61	1.3	45
6	Annan	36	11	10	15	65	1.81	1.2	43
7	Clyde	36	12	4	20	66	1.83	1.1	40
8	Montrose	36	12	11	13	68	1.89	1.3	47
9	Elgin City	36	13	10	13	69	1.92	1.4	49
10	East Stirling	36	8	5	23	97	2.69	0.8	29

Over 2.5 goals 2012-13

		H	A	Ov%
1	East Stirling	14	14	78
2	Montrose	13	13	72
3	Annan	11	14	69
	Elgin	16	9	69
5	Clyde	12	11	64
6	Berwick	10	12	61
	Queens Park	12	10	61
8	Stirling	9	12	58
9	Rangers	10	9	53
10	Peterhead	4	7	31

Both to score 2012-13

		H	A	BS%
1	Elgin	14	14	78
	Montrose	14	14	78
3	Annan	12	13	69
	East Stirling	12	13	69
	Stirling	12	13	69
6	Berwick	10	13	64
7	Queens Park	13	8	58
8	Clyde	12	8	56
	Rangers	9	11	56
10	Peterhead	4	5	25

Top goalscorers 2012-13

	Goals
A Little (Rangers)	22
R McAllister (Peterhead)	21
D Lavery (Berwick)	17
L McCulloch (Rangers)	17
S Leslie (Elgin)	15
D Templeton (Rangers)	15
C Gunn (Elgin)	13
J White (Stirling)	13
A Love (Annan)	12
Chaplain (Annan) Quinn (E	11
Stirling) Shankland (Queen's Pk)	

British results & tables 2012-13

Premier League — Winners & Losers

Champions	Man United
Champions League	Man City
	Chelsea
	Arsenal
Europa League	Tottenham
Relegated	Wigan
	Reading
	QPR

Championship — Winners & Losers

Champions	Cardiff
Promoted	Hull
Play-off winners	Crystal Palace
Relegated	Peterborough
	Wolves
	Bristol City

League 1 — Winners & Losers

Champions	Doncaster
Promoted	Bournemouth
Play-off winners	Yeovil
Relegated	Scunthorpe
	Bury
	Hartlepool
	Portsmouth

League 2 — Winners & Losers

Champions	Gillingham
Promoted	Rotherham
	Port Vale
Play-off winners	Bradford
Relegated	Barnet
	Aldershot

Blue Square Premier — Winners & Losers

Champions	Mansfield
Play-off winners	Newport County
Relegated	Stockport
	Barrow
	Ebbsfleet
	Telford

Blue Square North — Winners & Losers

Champions	Chester
Play-off winners	Halifax
Relegated	Corby
	Droylsden
	Hinckley

Blue Square South — Winners & Losers

Champions	Welling
Play-off winners	Salisbury
Relegated	Hornchurch
	Billericay
	Truro City

Community Shield — Winners & Losers

Winners	Man City
Finalists	Chelsea

FA Cup — Winners & Losers

Winners	Wigan
Finalists	Man City

League Cup — Winners & Losers

Winners	Swansea
Finalists	Bradford

Football League Trophy — Winners & Losers

Winners	Crewe
Finalists	Southend

FA Trophy — Winners & Losers

Winners	Wrexham
Finalists	Grimsby

SPL — Winners & Losers

Champions	Celtic
Europa League	Motherwell
	St Johnstone
Relegated	Dundee

Scottish Div One	Winners & Losers
Champions	Partick
Relegated	Dunfermline
	Airdrie United

Scottish Div Two	Winners & Losers
Champions	Queen of the South
Promoted	Alloa
Relegated	Albion

Scottish Div Three	Winners & Losers
Champions	Rangers

Scottish Cup	Winners & Losers
Winners	Celtic
Finalists	Hibernian

League Cup	Winners & Losers
Winners	St Mirren
Finalists	Hearts

Challenge Cup	Winners & Losers
Winners	Queen of the South
Finalists	Partick Thistle

Champions League	Winners & Losers
Winners	Bayern Munich
Finalists	Dortmund

Europa League	Winners & Losers
Winners	Chelsea
Finalists	Benfica

A newly retired Sir Alex Ferguson puts his bus pass to work

CHAMPIONS 20|13

20 TIMES CHAMPIONS OF ENGLAND. 13 PREMIER LEAGUE TITLES

Premier League results

	Arsenal	Aston Villa	Chelsea	Everton	Fulham	Liverpool	Man City	Man United	Newcastle	Norwich	QPR	Reading	Southampton	Stoke	Sunderland	Swansea	Tottenham	West Brom	West Ham	Wigan
Arsenal		2-1	1-2	0-0	3-3	2-2	0-2	1-1	7-3	3-1	1-0	4-1	6-1	1-0	0-0	0-2	5-2	2-0	5-1	4-1
Aston Villa	0-0		1-2	1-3	1-1	1-2	0-1	2-3	1-2	1-1	3-2	1-0	0-1	0-0	6-1	2-0	0-4	1-1	2-1	0-3
Chelsea	2-1	8-0		2-1	0-0	1-1	0-0	2-3	2-0	4-1	0-1	4-2	2-2	1-0	2-1	2-0	2-2	1-0	2-0	4-1
Everton	1-1	3-3	1-2		1-0	2-2	2-0	1-0	2-2	1-1	2-0	3-1	3-1	1-0	2-1	0-0	2-1	2-1	2-0	2-1
Fulham	0-1	1-0	0-3	2-2		1-3	1-2	0-1	2-1	5-0	3-2	2-4	1-1	1-0	1-3	1-2	0-3	3-0	3-1	1-1
Liverpool	0-2	1-3	2-2	0-0	4-0		2-2	1-2	1-1	5-0	1-0	1-0	1-0	0-0	3-0	5-0	3-2	0-2	0-0	3-0
Man City	1-1	5-0	2-0	1-1	2-0	2-2		2-3	4-0	2-3	3-1	1-0	3-2	3-0	3-0	1-0	2-1	1-0	2-1	1-0
Man United	2-1	3-0	0-1	2-0	3-2	2-1	1-2		4-3	4-0	3-1	1-0	2-1	4-2	3-1	2-1	2-3	2-0	1-0	4-0
Newcastle	0-1	1-1	3-2	1-2	1-0	0-6	1-3	0-3		1-0	1-0	1-2	4-2	2-1	0-3	1-2	2-1	2-1	0-1	3-0
Norwich	1-0	1-2	0-1	2-1	0-0	2-5	3-4	1-0	0-0		1-1	2-1	0-0	1-0	2-1	2-2	1-1	4-0	0-0	2-1
QPR	0-1	1-1	0-0	1-1	2-1	0-3	0-0	0-2	1-2	0-0		1-1	1-3	0-2	3-1	0-5	0-0	1-2	1-2	1-1
Reading	2-5	1-2	2-2	2-1	3-3	0-0	0-2	3-4	2-2	0-0	0-0		0-2	1-1	2-1	0-0	1-3	3-2	1-0	0-3
Southampton	1-1	4-1	2-1	0-0	2-2	3-1	3-1	2-3	2-0	1-1	1-2	1-0		1-1	0-1	1-1	1-2	0-3	1-1	0-2
Stoke	0-0	1-3	0-4	1-1	1-0	3-1	1-1	0-2	2-1	1-0	1-0	2-1	3-3		0-0	2-0	1-2	0-0	0-1	2-2
Sunderland	0-1	0-1	1-3	1-0	2-2	1-1	1-0	0-1	1-1	1-1	0-0	3-0	1-1	1-1		0-0	1-2	2-4	3-0	1-0
Swansea	0-2	2-2	1-1	0-3	0-3	0-0	0-0	1-1	1-0	3-4	4-1	2-2	0-0	3-1	2-2		1-2	3-1	3-0	2-1
Tottenham	2-1	2-0	2-4	2-2	0-1	2-1	3-1	1-1	2-1	1-1	2-1	3-1	1-0	0-0	1-0	1-0		1-1	3-1	0-1
West Brom	1-2	2-2	2-1	2-0	1-2	3-0	1-2	5-5	1-1	2-1	3-2	1-0	2-0	0-1	2-1	2-1	0-1		0-0	2-3
West Ham	1-3	1-0	3-1	1-2	3-0	2-3	0-0	2-2	0-0	2-1	1-1	4-2	4-1	1-1	1-1	1-0	2-3	3-1		2-0
Wigan	0-1	2-2	0-2	2-2	1-2	0-4	0-2	0-4	2-1	1-0	2-2	3-2	2-2	2-2	2-3	2-3	2-2	1-2	2-1	

Championship results

	Barnsley	Birmingham	Blackburn	Blackpool	Bolton	Brighton	Bristol City	Burnley	Cardiff	Charlton	C Palace	Derby	Huddersfield	Hull	Ipswich	Leeds	Leicester	Middlesbro'	Millwall	Nottm Forest	Peterborough	Sheff Weds	Watford	Wolves
Barnsley		1-2	1-3	1-1	2-3	2-1	1-0	1-1	1-2	0-6	1-1	1-1	0-1	2-0	1-1	2-0	2-0	1-0	2-0	1-4	0-2	0-1	1-0	2-1
Birmingham	0-5		1-1	1-1	2-1	2-2	2-0	2-2	0-1	1-1	2-2	3-1	0-1	2-3	0-1	1-0	1-1	3-2	1-1	2-1	1-0	0-0	0-4	2-3
Blackburn	2-1	1-1		1-1	1-2	1-1	2-0	1-1	1-4	1-2	1-1	2-0	1-0	1-0	1-0	0-0	2-1	1-2	0-2	3-0	2-3	1-0	1-0	0-1
Blackpool	1-2	1-1	2-0		2-2	1-1	0-0	1-0	1-2	0-2	1-0	2-1	1-3	0-0	6-0	2-1	0-0	4-1	2-1	2-2	0-1	0-0	2-2	1-2
Bolton	1-1	3-1	1-0	2-2		1-0	3-2	2-1	2-1	2-0	0-1	2-0	1-0	4-1	1-2	2-2	0-0	2-1	1-1	2-2	1-0	0-1	2-1	2-0
Brighton	5-1	0-1	1-1	6-1	1-1		2-0	1-0	0-0	0-0	3-0	2-1	4-1	1-0	1-1	2-2	1-1	0-1	2-2	0-0	1-0	3-0	1-3	2-0
Bristol City	5-3	0-1	3-5	1-1	1-2	0-0		3-4	4-2	0-2	4-1	0-2	1-3	1-2	2-1	2-3	0-4	2-0	1-1	2-0	4-2	1-1	2-0	1-4
Burnley	1-1	1-2	1-1	1-0	2-0	1-3	3-1		1-1	0-1	1-0	2-0	0-1	1-0	2-0	1-0	0-0	2-2	1-1	5-2	3-3	1-1	2-0	
Cardiff	1-1	2-1	3-0	3-0	1-1	0-2	2-1	4-0		0-0	2-1	1-1	1-0	2-1	0-0	2-1	1-1	1-0	3-0	1-2	0-1	2-1	3-1	
Charlton	0-1	1-1	1-1	2-1	3-2	2-2	4-1	0-1	5-4		0-1	1-1	1-1	0-0	1-2	2-1	2-1	1-4	0-2	0-2	2-0	1-2	1-2	2-1
Crystal Palace	0-0	0-4	2-0	2-2	0-0	3-0	2-1	4-3	3-2	2-1		3-0	1-1	4-2	5-0	2-2	2-2	4-1	2-2	1-1	3-2	2-1	2-3	3-1
Derby	2-0	3-2	1-1	4-1	1-1	0-0	3-0	1-2	1-1	3-2	0-1		3-0	1-2	0-1	3-1	2-1	3-1	1-0	1-1	3-1	2-2	5-1	0-0
Huddersfield	2-2	1-1	2-2	1-1	2-2	1-2	1-0	2-0	0-0	0-1	1-0	1-0		0-1	0-0	2-4	0-2	2-1	3-0	1-1	2-2	0-0	2-3	2-1
Hull	1-0	5-2	2-0	2-3	3-1	1-0	0-0	0-1	2-2	1-0	0-0	2-1	2-0		2-1	2-0	0-0	1-0	4-1	1-2	1-3	1-3	0-1	2-1
Ipswich	1-1	3-1	1-1	1-0	1-0	0-3	1-1	2-1	1-2	1-2	3-0	1-2	2-2	1-2		3-0	1-0	4-0	3-0	3-1	1-1	0-3	0-2	0-2
Leeds	1-0	0-1	3-3	2-0	1-0	1-2	1-0	0-1	1-1	2-1	1-2	1-2	3-1	1-1	2-1		1-0	2-1	1-0	2-1	1-1	2-1	1-6	1-0
Leicester	2-2	2-2	3-0	1-0	3-2	1-0	2-0	2-1	0-1	1-2	1-2	4-1	6-1	3-1	6-0	1-1		1-0	0-1	2-2	2-0	0-1	1-2	2-1
Middlesbrough	2-3	0-1	1-0	4-2	2-1	0-2	1-3	3-2	2-1	2-2	2-1	2-2	3-0	2-0	2-0	1-0	1-2		1-2	1-0	0-0	3-1	1-2	2-0
Millwall	1-2	3-3	1-2	0-2	2-1	1-2	2-1	0-2	0-2	0-0	0-0	2-1	4-0	0-1	0-0	1-0	1-0	3-1		0-1	1-5	1-2	1-0	0-2
Nottm Forest	0-0	2-2	0-0	1-1	1-1	2-2	1-0	2-0	3-1	2-1	2-2	0-1	6-1	1-2	1-0	4-2	2-3	0-0	1-4		2-1	1-0	0-3	3-1
Peterborough	2-1	0-2	1-4	1-4	5-4	0-0	1-2	2-2	2-1	2-2	1-2	3-0	3-1	1-1	0-0	1-2	2-1	2-3	1-2	0-1		1-0	3-2	0-2
Sheffield Weds	2-1	3-2	3-2	0-2	1-2	3-1	2-3	0-2	0-2	2-0	1-0	2-2	1-3	0-1	1-1	1-1	0-2	2-0	3-2	0-1	2-1		1-4	0-0
Watford	4-1	2-0	4-0	1-2	2-1	0-1	2-2	3-3	0-0	3-4	2-2	2-1	4-0	1-2	0-1	1-2	2-1	1-2	0-0	2-0	1-0	2-1		2-1
Wolves	3-1	1-0	1-1	1-2	2-2	3-3	2-1	1-2	1-2	1-1	1-2	1-1	1-3	1-0	0-2	2-2	2-1	3-2	0-1	1-2	0-3	1-0	1-1	

League 1 results

	Bournemouth	Brentford	Bury	Carlisle	Colchester	Coventry	Crawley	Crewe	Doncaster	Hartlepool	Leyton Orient	MK Dons	Notts County	Oldham	Portsmouth	Preston	Scunthorpe	Sheff Utd	Shrewsbury	Stevenage	Swindon	Tranmere	Walsall	Yeovil
Bournemouth		2-2	4-1	3-1	1-0	0-2	3-0	3-1	1-2	1-1	2-0	1-1	3-1	4-1	2-0	1-1	1-0	0-1	2-1	1-1	1-1	3-1	1-2	3-0
Brentford	0-0		2-2	2-1	1-0	2-1	2-1	5-1	0-1	2-2	2-2	3-2	2-1	1-0	3-2	1-0	1-0	2-0	0-0	2-0	2-1	1-2	0-0	1-3
Bury	2-2	0-0		1-1	1-2	0-2	0-2	2-2	2-0	2-1	0-2	1-4	0-2	0-1	2-0	1-2	2-1	0-2	2-2	2-0	0-1	0-1	1-1	3-2
Carlisle	2-4	2-0	2-1		0-2	1-0	0-2	0-0	1-3	3-0	1-4	1-1	0-4	3-1	4-2	1-1	1-1	1-3	2-2	2-1	2-2	0-3	0-3	3-3
Colchester	0-1	1-3	2-0	2-0		1-3	1-1	1-2	3-1	2-1	0-2	0-2	0-2	2-2	1-0	1-2	1-1	0-0	1-0	0-1	1-2	0-2	2-0	2-0
Coventry	1-0	1-1	2-2	1-2	2-2		3-1	1-2	1-0	1-0	0-1	1-1	1-2	2-1	1-1	1-1	1-2	1-1	0-1	1-2	1-2	1-0	5-1	0-1
Crawley Town	3-1	1-2	3-2	1-1	3-0	2-0		2-0	1-1	2-2	1-0	2-0	0-0	1-1	0-3	1-0	3-0	0-2	2-2	1-1	1-1	2-5	2-2	0-1
Crewe	1-2	0-2	1-0	1-0	3-2	1-0	2-0		1-2	2-1	1-1	2-1	1-2	0-2	1-2	1-0	1-0	1-0	1-1	1-2	2-1	0-0	2-0	0-1
Doncaster	0-1	2-1	2-1	0-2	1-0	1-4	0-1	0-2		3-0	2-0	0-0	0-1	1-0	1-1	1-3	4-0	2-2	1-0	1-1	1-0	1-0	1-2	1-1
Hartlepool	1-2	1-1	2-0	1-2	0-0	0-5	0-1	3-0	1-1		2-1	0-2	2-1	1-2	0-0	0-1	2-0	1-2	2-2	0-2	0-0	0-2	0-0	0-0
Leyton Orient	3-1	1-0	2-0	4-1	0-2	0-1	0-1	1-1	0-2	1-0		2-0	2-1	1-1	1-0	2-0	1-3	0-1	2-1	1-0	0-0	2-1	2-1	4-1
MK Dons	0-3	2-0	1-1	2-0	5-1	2-3	0-0	1-0	3-0	1-0	1-0		1-1	2-0	2-2	1-1	0-1	1-0	2-3	0-1	2-0	3-0	2-4	1-0
Notts County	3-3	1-2	4-1	1-0	3-1	2-2	1-1	1-1	0-2	2-0	1-1	1-2		1-0	3-0	1-0	1-1	3-2	1-2	1-0	0-1	0-1	1-1	1-2
Oldham	0-1	0-2	1-2	1-2	1-1	0-1	2-1	1-2	1-2	3-0	2-0	3-1	2-2		1-0	3-1	1-1	0-2	1-0	0-1	0-2	0-1	1-1	1-0
Portsmouth	1-1	0-1	2-0	1-1	2-3	2-0	1-2	2-0	0-1	1-3	2-3	1-1	0-2	0-1		0-0	2-1	3-0	3-1	0-0	1-2	1-0	1-2	1-2
Preston	2-0	1-1	0-0	1-1	0-0	2-2	1-2	1-3	0-3	5-0	0-0	0-0	0-2	2-0	1-1		3-0	0-1	1-2	2-0	4-1	1-0	1-3	3-2
Scunthorpe	1-2	1-1	1-2	3-1	1-0	1-2	2-1	1-2	2-3	1-2	2-1	0-3	2-2	2-2	2-1	2-3		1-1	0-0	1-0	3-1	1-3	1-1	0-4
Sheff Utd	5-3	2-2	1-1	0-0	3-0	1-2	0-2	3-3	0-0	2-3	0-0	0-0	1-1	1-1	1-0	0-0	3-0		1-0	4-1	2-0	0-0	1-0	0-2
Shrewsbury	0-3	0-0	0-0	2-1	2-2	4-1	3-0	1-0	1-2	1-1	0-2	2-2	2-2	1-0	3-2	1-0	0-1	1-2		2-1	0-1	1-1	1-0	1-3
Stevenage	0-1	1-0	2-2	1-1	0-2	1-3	1-2	2-2	1-2	1-0	0-1	0-2	2-0	1-2	2-1	1-4	1-0	4-0	1-1		0-4	1-1	3-1	0-2
Swindon	4-0	0-1	0-1	4-0	0-1	2-2	3-0	4-1	1-1	1-1	0-1	1-0	0-0	1-1	5-0	1-1	1-1	0-0	2-0	3-0		5-0	2-2	4-1
Tranmere	0-0	1-1	3-0	0-1	4-0	2-0	2-0	2-1	1-2	0-1	3-1	0-1	1-1	1-0	2-2	2-1	1-1	1-0	0-1	0-2	3-1		0-0	3-2
Walsall	3-1	2-2	1-1	1-2	1-0	4-0	2-2	2-2	0-3	1-1	1-2	1-0	1-1	3-1	2-0	3-1	1-4	1-1	3-1	1-0	0-2	2-0		2-2
Yeovil	0-1	3-0	2-1	1-3	3-1	1-1	2-2	1-0	2-1	1-0	3-0	2-1	0-0	4-1	1-2	3-1	3-0	0-1	2-1	1-3	0-2	1-0	0-0	

Bournemouth fans celebrate promotion after Eddie Howe's return to Dean Court

Bradford's supporters were spoilt with two trips to Wembley

League 2 results

	Accrington	AFC Wimbledon	Aldershot	Barnet	Bradford	Bristol Rovers	Burton	Cheltenham	Chesterfield	Dag & Red	Exeter	Fleetwood	Gillingham	Morecambe	Northampton	Oxford	Plymouth	Port Vale	Rochdale	Rotherham	Southend	Torquay	Wycombe	York
Accrington		4-0	1-0	3-2	1-1	1-0	3-3	2-2	1-0	0-2	0-3	0-3	1-1	2-0	2-4	0-3	1-1	2-0	2-3	1-2	1-1	0-0	0-2	0-1
AFC Wimbledon	1-2		1-1	0-1	2-1	3-1	1-1	1-2	1-0	2-2	2-2	2-1	0-1	2-0	1-1	0-3	1-1	2-2	1-2	0-1	0-4	0-1	2-2	3-2
Aldershot	2-0	0-1		1-0	0-2	2-2	1-2	0-1	0-1	1-0	1-2	2-0	1-1	0-0	1-2	3-2	1-2	1-3	4-2	0-3	0-2	1-0	0-0	0-2
Barnet	1-1	1-1	0-1		2-0	1-1	3-2	0-0	0-2	0-0	1-2	2-0	1-3	4-1	4-0	2-2	1-4	0-0	0-0	0-0	2-0	1-0	1-0	1-3
Bradford	2-1	5-1	1-1	3-0		4-1	1-0	3-1	0-0	1-1	0-1	1-0	0-1	3-1	1-0	1-2	1-0	0-1	2-4	0-2	2-2	1-0	1-0	1-1
Bristol Rovers	0-1	1-0	2-2	2-1	3-3		3-0	0-1	3-2	0-1	2-0	0-0	0-2	0-3	3-1	0-2	2-1	2-0	2-1	1-2	2-3	3-2	1-0	0-0
Burton	1-0	6-2	0-1	1-0	1-0	1-1		3-1	0-1	3-2	0-1	3-2	3-2	3-3	4-0	1-0	1-1	3-2	2-0	2-0	2-1	2-0	1-0	2-0
Cheltenham	0-3	2-1	1-1	1-0	0-0	1-1	1-0		1-0	2-0	3-0	2-2	1-0	2-0	1-0	2-1	2-1	1-1	0-0	3-0	1-3	2-1	4-0	1-1
Chesterfield	4-3	2-0	0-0	0-1	2-2	2-0	1-1	4-1		1-2	4-0	1-2	0-1	1-1	3-0	2-1	1-2	2-2	1-1	1-1	0-1	1-1	3-1	3-0
Dag & Red	1-1	0-1	0-0	1-0	4-3	2-4	1-1	1-0	0-1		1-1	1-0	1-2	1-2	0-1	0-1	0-0	2-3	2-1	5-0	0-3	2-2	3-0	0-1
Exeter	2-0	2-0	0-0	2-2	4-1	1-2	3-0	0-1	0-1	0-1		2-2	0-0	0-3	3-0	1-3	1-1	0-2	1-2	0-1	3-0	0-1	3-2	1-1
Fleetwood Town	1-3	1-1	4-1	2-1	2-2	0-3	0-4	1-1	1-3	2-1	0-0		2-2	1-0	1-0	3-0	3-0	2-5	0-3	1-1	0-0	0-0	0-1	0-0
Gillingham	1-0	2-2	4-0	0-1	3-1	4-0	4-1	0-0	1-1	2-1	2-3	2-2		2-1	2-0	0-1	2-1	1-2	1-2	1-0	1-0	1-0	0-1	1-1
Morecambe	0-0	3-1	2-1	4-1	0-0	1-1	0-0	0-0	2-0	2-1	0-3	0-4	1-1		1-1	1-1	2-3	1-3	3-0	2-1	1-0	0-2	0-1	2-2
Northampton	2-0	2-0	2-0	0-1	1-0	2-3	0-0	3-1	3-1	2-3	0-0	3-1	2-3	0-0		1-0	1-0	2-0	3-1	2-3	1-3	1-0	3-1	0-2
Oxford	5-0	3-2	1-1	1-0	0-2	0-2	1-1	1-0	0-1	2-3	2-4	1-2	0-0	1-1	2-1		2-1	2-1	3-0	0-4	2-0	0-0	0-1	0-2
Plymouth	0-0	1-2	0-2	2-1	0-0	1-1	1-2	2-0	0-1	0-0	1-0	2-1	2-2	2-1	3-2	0-1		1-3	3-1	0-1	1-1	1-1	0-1	2-0
Port Vale	3-0	3-0	1-1	3-0	0-0	4-0	7-1	3-2	0-2	1-1	0-2	0-2	0-2	0-1	2-2	3-0	4-0		2-2	6-2	1-2	1-1	4-1	2-2
Rochdale	0-3	0-1	1-1	2-0	0-0	2-1	0-1	4-1	1-1	2-2	2-3	0-0	1-1	1-2	0-0	2-0	1-0	2-2		1-2	4-2	1-0	4-1	2-3
Rotherham	4-1	1-0	2-0	0-2	4-0	1-3	3-0	4-2	1-0	1-2	4-1	2-1	1-2	2-1	3-1	3-1	1-0	1-2	2-3		0-3	1-0	2-3	1-1
Southend	0-1	1-3	1-2	2-2	2-2	0-0	0-1	1-2	3-0	3-1	2-1	1-1	0-1	0-1	1-2	1-0	0-2	0-0	3-1	1-1		1-1	1-0	0-0
Torquay	3-1	2-3	4-3	3-2	1-3	3-3	1-1	2-2	2-1	2-1	1-1	0-1	2-1	1-0	1-1	1-3	0-0	0-1	4-2	1-3	1-4		1-2	2-1
Wycombe	0-1	0-1	2-1	0-0	0-3	2-0	3-0	1-1	2-1	1-0	0-1	1-0	0-1	2-2	0-0	1-3	1-1	1-1	1-2	2-2	1-2	2-1		4-0
York	1-1	0-3	0-0	1-2	0-2	4-1	3-0	0-0	2-2	3-2	1-2	0-2	0-0	1-4	1-1	3-1	2-0	0-2	0-0	0-0	2-1	0-2	1-3	

Blue Square Bet Premier results

	AFC Telford Utd	Alfreton Town	Barrow	Braintree Town	Cambridge	Dartford	Ebbsfleet	Forest Green	Gateshead	Grimsby	Hereford	Hyde United	Kidderminster	Lincoln	Luton	Macclesfield	Mansfield	Newport County	Nuneaton Town	Southport	Stockport	Tamworth	Woking	Wrexham
AFC Telford Utd		0-0	1-1	3-0	1-2	0-2	2-2	1-2	0-0	1-2	0-4	1-3	0-2	1-1	0-0	0-2	2-2	2-4	0-3	1-3	2-2	3-3	1-0	0-2
Alfreton Town	1-1		4-0	1-1	1-1	3-2	3-0	2-1	3-2	0-2	0-3	5-1	1-1	0-2	3-0	1-2	0-3	4-3	0-3	3-3	2-3	3-0	0-3	1-2
Barrow	0-0	1-3		0-1	1-4	0-0	1-1	2-2	0-2	2-2	0-2	1-1	1-1	1-2	1-0	1-0	0-4	0-3	1-2	3-2	0-2	2-0	2-0	0-1
Braintree Town	3-2	2-1	2-3		0-3	0-2	3-1	3-1	2-1	2-0	0-2	2-2	1-1	0-3	2-0	0-3	2-1	1-2	2-2	1-3	0-0	2-1	1-1	1-5
Cambridge	3-3	0-3	2-1	1-0		1-2	1-1	0-0	3-0	0-0	1-3	0-1	1-3	2-1	2-2	2-0	4-1	0-0	1-3	2-0	4-1	1-1	1-0	1-4
Dartford	1-4	5-1	0-1	0-0	1-1		3-1	0-1	3-0	1-2	4-0	2-1	1-0	2-4	1-0	2-0	2-0	2-1	0-1	2-2	1-1	2-3	4-1	2-1
Ebbsfleet	1-3	0-0	2-4	0-1	2-4	2-2		0-2	3-1	1-1	1-0	3-2	1-1	1-1	1-3	0-4	3-1	1-1	1-1	4-1	0-0	1-1	2-2	1-1
Forest Green	0-0	1-1	1-1	4-1	1-1	2-3	4-1		1-0	0-1	0-1	3-1	0-1	3-0	1-2	1-1	1-2	1-2	1-0	0-1	4-1	1-2	3-1	0-0
Gateshead	1-1	2-0	0-1	1-2	0-0	2-0	2-0	1-1		1-1	3-2	3-0	2-0	1-1	5-1	2-2	4-1	0-0	0-2	2-2	1-1	0-2	2-1	0-1
Grimsby	1-0	4-2	0-3	0-0	0-1	0-2	3-1	1-0	3-0		1-1	2-0	1-3	1-1	4-1	0-1	4-1	3-0	0-0	2-2	1-2	2-0	5-1	1-0
Hereford	1-1	3-3	2-1	0-0	4-2	1-0	4-2	1-2	1-1	0-2		1-2	0-1	3-2	1-0	2-1	1-2	2-3	0-0	2-2	1-2	5-2	2-1	0-1
Hyde United	2-1	1-1	0-0	1-2	2-1	3-0	1-0	0-1	1-1	3-2	5-2		0-4	1-5	1-2	1-1	0-1	0-1	2-2	0-2	0-1	2-1	7-0	2-0
Kidderminster	1-0	3-1	2-0	2-1	3-2	5-1	3-2	0-1	1-1	0-0	0-1	3-0		3-0	0-2	3-0	2-3	3-2	1-0	2-2	4-0	4-1	2-2	2-0
Lincoln	3-2	1-2	0-0	3-0	0-0	2-1	1-1	1-2	1-1	1-4	3-2	3-2	1-0		1-2	2-3	0-1	2-4	2-1	1-0	3-3	2-1	0-2	1-2
Luton	0-1	3-0	6-1	2-3	3-2	0-2	2-0	1-1	2-2	1-1	1-1	1-2	1-2	3-0		4-1	2-3	2-2	2-0	3-1	1-0	0-0	3-1	0-0
Macclesfield	2-1	1-2	2-0	2-1	2-1	2-0	1-2	1-2	0-4	1-3	0-1	3-2	1-0	2-1	1-1		0-3	1-1	0-0	2-2	1-1	2-0	0-0	2-0
Mansfield	1-0	1-2	8-1	2-0	3-1	5-0	4-1	1-0	4-0	2-0	1-1	1-0	0-2	0-2	2-2	3-1		3-4	1-0	1-1	4-1	3-1	1-0	2-3
Newport County	2-1	2-0	0-2	1-0	6-2	0-0	1-0	0-5	3-0	1-3	1-2	2-1	5-2	4-1	2-0	4-0	2-1		0-0	2-2	2-3	1-1	2-2	1-1
Nuneaton Town	3-1	1-0	1-1	2-4	2-2	1-0	4-5	1-1	0-1	1-0	0-0	3-1	0-1	1-0	0-0	3-3	1-1	1-2		0-1	2-0	2-1	0-0	0-0
Southport	0-3	0-2	5-2	0-2	2-1	2-2	1-0	1-2	2-1	1-1	2-2	0-1	1-3	4-2	1-3	3-2	1-2	0-2	3-1		1-1	0-3	1-2	1-4
Stockport	2-2	1-0	3-1	1-3	1-1	0-1	3-1	2-1	1-2	1-2	2-3	0-2	1-0	2-0	0-1	3-4	1-3	1-0	3-2	3-4		0-1	1-2	2-3
Tamworth	0-0	1-1	1-3	1-4	1-2	3-2	0-1	2-1	2-0	0-1	2-2	2-0	0-1	1-0	1-2	0-0	0-1	1-2	2-1	2-1	1-0		2-1	0-1
Woking	5-2	1-2	3-1	1-4	2-1	1-0	1-0	2-0	2-1	0-1	1-1	2-1	2-2	1-1	3-1	5-4	1-2	1-3	6-1	2-3	1-0	2-3		2-0
Wrexham	4-1	1-1	3-0	1-1	1-0	2-2	4-1	2-1	1-1	0-0	1-2	2-0	1-2	2-4	0-0	0-0	2-1	2-0	6-1	2-2	3-1	2-2	3-1	

Newport's Lenny Pidgeley clears the ball during the first leg of their play-off semi-final

Blue Square Bet North results

	Altrincham	Bishops St	Boston Utd	Brackley	Bradford PA	Chester	Colwyn Bay	Corby	Droylsden	Gainsborough	Gloucester	Guiseley	Halifax	Harrogate T	Hinckley Utd	Histon	Oxford C	Solihull Moors	Stalybridge	Vauxhall M	Worcester	Workington
Altrincham		2-1	7-1	1-4	3-1	2-4	1-1	2-1	6-0	0-1	2-0	1-3	2-0	3-0	8-0	5-0	3-1	2-1	2-1	1-0	2-0	1-2
Bishops St	1-1		1-0	1-3	2-1	1-2	2-2	2-1	2-1	1-5	1-2	2-5	1-2	0-2	1-1	3-1	0-0	4-1	0-0	2-2	0-1	0-3
Boston Utd	2-3	1-1		3-4	0-4	3-2	1-0	1-1	5-1	2-1	4-0	1-3	1-2	1-2	1-2	6-0	3-1	2-2	2-2	0-1	1-2	1-3
Brackley	0-1	1-0	0-2		3-1	2-3	1-3	2-4	3-2	2-2	0-1	1-0	0-0	2-1	5-0	2-1	0-0	2-1	4-1	1-0	2-0	3-1
Bradford PA	2-2	2-1	2-1	0-1		0-0	1-2	2-1	5-0	0-2	2-1	1-3	1-1	1-0	4-0	0-0	1-2	1-0	1-3	2-0	2-2	1-0
Chester	2-0	4-1	1-0	0-0	1-1		2-1	2-1	5-0	3-1	2-0	4-0	2-1	2-0	3-0	2-1	2-0	0-1	4-1	2-0	4-2	1-0
Colwyn Bay	1-3	1-2	0-2	1-1	1-2	1-5		1-0	1-3	1-0	1-0	0-2	0-3	1-2	3-2	3-1	3-1	3-1	2-3	2-4	0-3	1-4
Corby	2-5	2-2	2-1	0-4	4-5	1-2	3-1		5-0	0-0	3-2	2-3	1-5	0-2	5-3	0-0	1-1	2-3	1-0	0-1	1-0	1-3
Droylsden	0-5	1-2	0-1	0-3	0-7	3-4	2-0	2-2		1-3	1-0	0-3	0-6	1-3	3-2	2-2	1-3	2-4	1-1	5-2	0-2	0-1
Gainsborough	2-4	2-2	2-2	0-1	1-1	0-2	3-1	2-2	3-0		0-1	1-2	3-0	1-1	5-0	1-0	1-2	1-1	1-2	2-1	1-0	1-1
Gloucester	0-0	5-1	1-0	1-4	1-0	0-1	2-2	0-1	4-0	1-2		2-2	1-2	0-2	4-1	1-1	0-1	1-1	4-3	1-1	4-2	0-1
Guiseley	1-1	1-2	2-1	0-2	1-0	2-1	2-2	2-1	7-1	2-0	3-1		1-1	2-0	2-4	2-1	1-0	1-0	1-0	2-1	3-3	2-0
Halifax	3-4	1-1	1-2	0-0	0-1	1-1	0-1	2-0	4-1	3-1	5-0	1-1		1-2	7-0	3-3	3-1	0-0	0-0	4-0	5-0	5-1
Harrogate T	1-2	2-2	4-2	6-1	1-1	1-3	1-2	6-1	1-1	0-0	1-0	1-2	1-1		5-0	2-0	1-3	2-4	0-0	3-1	3-1	3-1
Hinckley Utd	0-6	1-5	2-4	1-3	1-4	0-6	1-3	6-3	2-2	0-2	0-3	0-3	0-2	0-2		0-1	0-2	1-1	0-3	0-6	0-5	1-1
Histon	2-0	2-0	1-1	3-0	1-4	1-4	2-1	3-4	3-1	0-3	2-1	1-4	0-1	1-3	2-1		1-1	0-0	0-2	2-0	0-0	3-0
Oxford C	2-2	0-0	4-2	2-1	1-1	0-1	1-2	0-2	2-2	1-1	0-1	0-3	2-2	0-0	6-2	0-0		1-2	0-0	1-1	2-2	5-0
Solihull Moors	2-1	0-1	1-0	0-1	3-1	0-3	2-0	3-0	2-1	0-2	2-3	2-0	0-3	2-0	1-0	1-1	1-2		1-0	2-3	0-1	2-2
Stalybridge	2-2	3-1	0-1	0-3	2-0	2-6	3-3	1-2	0-0	1-1	4-0	1-1	1-0	1-0	4-0	2-1	2-2	0-3		0-1	0-2	1-4
Vauxhall M	2-1	2-2	4-0	0-2	1-3	0-3	1-1	1-1	4-0	1-2	1-2	2-0	1-3	0-1	2-1	2-0	2-1	2-1	0-0		1-0	1-3
Worcester	0-0	2-0	0-3	1-2	2-0	0-1	2-0	5-1	2-1	0-3	0-1	0-1	0-1	2-2	3-1	2-3	3-2	1-3	1-2	2-2		1-1
Workington	2-1	2-3	1-1	0-0	1-6	1-1	1-2	2-3	2-1	0-3	0-1	0-2	0-1	1-2	2-1	3-1	1-2	1-1	4-1	3-1	1-0	

Blue Square Bet South results

	Basingstoke	Bath City	Billericay	Boreham W	Bromley	Chelmsford	Dorchester	Dover	Eastbourne	Eastleigh	Farnborough	Havant & W	Hayes & Y	Hornchurch	Maidenhead	Salisbury	Staines	Sutton Utd	Tonbridge	Truro City	Welling	Weston S-M
Basingstoke		2-1	3-3	2-3	1-1	1-2	2-1	0-1	2-2	0-3	6-2	1-2	2-2	0-2	2-0	0-4	3-1	2-1	1-0	3-2	0-1	1-3
Bath City	1-1		2-1	0-0	0-2	2-2	2-3	1-2	2-2	1-1	3-2	2-0	2-3	3-1	3-1	0-0	0-1	0-4	3-0	1-1	1-0	1-2
Billericay	1-3	2-0		1-1	2-3	0-1	3-1	1-2	1-2	4-0	2-1	3-1	4-1	1-1	1-0	1-2	2-3	2-4	3-3	2-1	1-2	0-0
Boreham W	1-1	0-0	3-0		1-2	0-0	1-2	1-1	2-1	3-0	3-1	1-2	3-0	2-1	2-1	1-0	1-1	3-0	4-2	0-0	1-1	0-1
Bromley	1-2	1-0	0-1	1-1		2-0	2-1	0-4	0-2	3-1	1-3	1-1	0-4	4-0	3-2	1-2	0-0	0-2	1-1	4-0	0-2	0-1
Chelmsford	2-0	0-1	1-1	2-1	3-2		4-0	0-3	1-0	1-1	6-0	1-1	6-2	1-4	3-1	1-2	3-2	1-0	2-1	3-2	2-3	2-1
Dorchester	2-2	2-1	6-1	0-0	0-4	1-0		1-0	1-0	2-0	0-0	2-2	3-1	4-0	2-1	0-4	0-1	1-2	2-2	2-1	2-1	
Dover	0-5	2-0	4-1	0-1	1-0	0-1	0-0		0-0	2-0	2-2	2-2	0-1	1-0	2-0	1-3	0-1	1-1	0-1	3-2	3-2	3-1
Eastbourne	1-0	0-3	2-1	1-1	3-0	1-2	0-0	0-3		1-0	0-1	0-1	2-1	1-1	0-2	1-2	1-1	0-2	1-0	1-0	0-3	0-2
Eastleigh	1-1	3-1	5-0	1-1	3-0	1-0	3-1	1-0	3-1		3-1	2-2	3-1	1-0	4-2	1-0	4-3	1-0	4-1	3-1	1-3	3-0
Farnborough	2-1	0-1	4-3	0-3	2-0	3-1	1-1	5-2	0-1	6-2		1-1	4-1	1-1	2-1	2-1	3-1	1-3	4-1	4-1	0-3	2-1
Havant & W	4-1	2-1	5-0	1-1	1-2	1-1	4-0	1-1	2-3	0-3	0-1		2-1	5-2	2-1	2-2	3-1	3-0	2-2	1-0	0-1	0-3
Hayes & Y	2-1	2-2	4-2	0-1	1-1	3-0	1-3	2-4	1-1	2-1	3-2	1-4		1-3	1-1	2-3	4-0	0-0	3-2	1-2	2-1	2-1
Hornchurch	3-0	2-1	1-0	1-1	1-0	0-2	1-0	0-1	0-1	1-0	1-1	2-2	2-0		0-2	2-2	1-1	1-1	1-2	0-3	0-0	
Maidenhead	2-2	0-1	3-2	2-1	4-2	2-1	1-2	1-2	1-2	0-2	3-2	2-0	0-2	2-4		0-1	1-0	0-1	3-1	8-0	2-1	0-1
Salisbury	0-2	3-2	2-0	2-2	3-1	3-2	4-0	1-1	1-0	5-3	1-0	5-1	2-0	2-1	1-1		3-1	1-0	2-0	4-3	2-1	1-1
Staines	2-0	1-3	1-2	1-1	3-1	1-3	2-1	0-2	0-2	1-3	1-2	1-1	7-1	3-1	0-6	3-2		1-4	1-4	1-0	2-2	1-1
Sutton Utd	3-2	0-2	3-0	2-1	4-3	1-0	1-2	2-2	2-0	2-1	0-1	1-1	5-1	3-1	1-1	1-0	1-2		2-2	0-1	2-1	1-3
Tonbridge	0-0	3-4	1-1	4-2	0-3	0-4	0-2	2-1	1-1	3-1	2-3	1-0	1-0	2-1	1-2	1-0	1-1			3-2	1-1	0-0
Truro City	2-2	2-1	2-4	2-0	0-1	1-2	1-2	0-3	2-2	1-3	3-3	3-3	3-1	3-2	0-1	1-1	0-3	1-2	2-0		0-3	1-2
Welling	1-1	1-1	5-2	4-0	3-1	3-0	3-2	1-1	2-0	1-1	2-0	1-0	3-0	4-0	3-2	1-0	3-2	2-2	4-1	4-3		4-1
Weston S-M	5-2	1-4	1-0	2-4	3-0	3-0	2-0	0-3	3-2	2-4	1-1	2-2	1-1	1-0	1-1	0-3	1-0	1-1	2-0	0-2	2-0	

Premier League

Pos		P	W	D	L	GD	Pts
1	Man Utd	38	28	5	5	43	89
2	Man City	38	23	9	6	32	78
3	Chelsea	38	22	9	7	36	75
4	Arsenal	38	21	10	7	35	73
5	Tottenham	38	21	9	8	20	72
6	Everton	38	16	15	7	15	63
7	Liverpool	38	16	13	9	28	61
8	West Brom	38	14	7	17	-4	49
9	Swansea	38	11	13	14	-4	46
10	West Ham	38	12	10	16	-8	46
11	Norwich	38	10	14	14	-17	44
12	Fulham	38	11	10	17	-10	43
13	Stoke	38	9	15	14	-11	42
14	Southampton	38	9	14	15	-11	41
15	Aston Villa	38	10	11	17	-22	41
16	Newcastle	38	11	8	19	-23	41
17	Sunderland	38	9	12	17	-13	39
18	Wigan	38	9	9	20	-26	36
19	Reading	38	6	10	22	-30	28
20	QPR	38	4	13	21	-30	25

Premier League — home

Pos		P	W	D	L	F	A	Pts
1	Man Utd	19	16	0	3	45	19	48
2	Man City	19	14	3	2	41	15	45
3	Everton	19	12	6	1	33	17	42
4	Chelsea	19	12	5	2	41	16	41
5	Arsenal	19	11	5	3	47	23	38
6	Tottenham	19	11	5	3	29	18	38
7	Liverpool	19	9	6	4	33	16	33
8	West Ham	19	9	6	4	34	22	33
9	West Brom	19	9	4	6	32	25	31
10	Norwich	19	8	7	4	25	20	31
11	Stoke	19	7	7	5	21	22	28
12	Newcastle	19	9	1	9	24	31	28
13	Swansea	19	6	8	5	28	26	26
14	Southampton	19	6	7	6	26	24	25
15	Fulham	19	7	3	9	28	30	24
16	Sunderland	19	5	8	6	20	19	23
17	Aston Villa	19	5	5	9	23	28	20
18	Reading	19	4	8	7	23	33	20
19	Wigan	19	4	6	9	26	39	18
20	QPR	19	2	8	9	13	28	14

Premier League — away

Pos		P	W	D	L	F	A	Pts
1	Man Utd	19	12	5	2	41	24	41
2	Arsenal	19	10	5	4	25	14	35
3	Chelsea	19	10	4	5	34	23	34
4	Tottenham	19	10	4	5	37	28	34
5	Man City	19	9	6	4	25	19	33
6	Liverpool	19	7	7	5	38	27	28
7	Everton	19	4	9	6	22	23	21
8	Aston Villa	19	5	6	8	24	41	21
9	Swansea	19	5	5	9	19	25	20
10	Fulham	19	4	7	8	22	30	19
11	West Brom	19	5	3	11	21	32	18
12	Wigan	19	5	3	11	21	34	18
13	Southampton	19	3	7	9	23	36	16
14	Sunderland	19	4	4	11	21	35	16
15	Stoke	19	2	8	9	13	23	14
16	Newcastle	19	2	7	10	21	37	13
17	West Ham	19	3	4	12	11	31	13
18	Norwich	19	2	7	10	16	38	13
19	QPR	19	2	5	12	17	32	11
20	Reading	19	2	2	15	20	40	8

Championship

Pos		P	W	D	L	GD	Pts
1	Cardiff	46	25	12	9	27	87
2	Hull	46	24	7	15	9	79
3	Watford	46	23	8	15	27	77
4	Brighton	46	19	18	9	26	75
5	C Palace	46	19	15	12	11	72
6	Leicester	46	19	11	16	13	68
7	Bolton	46	18	14	14	8	68
8	Nottm Forest	46	17	16	13	4	67
9	Charlton	46	17	14	15	6	65
10	Derby	46	16	13	17	3	61
11	Burnley	46	16	13	17	2	61
12	Birmingham	46	15	16	15	-6	61
13	Leeds	46	17	10	19	-9	61
14	Ipswich	46	16	12	18	-13	60
15	Blackpool	46	14	17	15	1	59
16	Middlesbro	46	18	5	23	-9	59
17	Blackburn	46	14	16	16	-7	58
18	Sheff Wed	46	16	10	20	-8	58
19	Huddersfield	46	15	13	18	-20	58
20	Millwall	46	15	11	20	-11	56
21	Barnsley	46	14	13	19	-14	55
22	Peterborough	46	15	9	22	-9	54
23	Wolves	46	14	9	23	-14	51
24	Bristol C	46	11	8	27	-25	41

Championship — home

Pos		P	W	D	L	F	A	Pts
1	Cardiff	23	15	6	2	37	15	51
2	Bolton	23	14	6	3	37	20	48
3	C Palace	23	13	8	2	52	31	47
4	Leicester	23	13	4	6	46	23	43
5	Derby	23	12	7	4	43	22	43
6	Hull	23	13	4	6	35	22	43
7	Brighton	23	11	9	3	39	17	42
8	Middlesbro	23	13	3	7	38	27	42
9	Leeds	23	13	3	7	30	26	42
10	Watford	23	11	5	7	41	27	38
11	Nottm Forest	23	10	8	5	37	28	38
12	Blackburn	23	10	6	7	27	23	36
13	Burnley	23	9	8	6	31	22	35
14	Ipswich	23	10	5	8	34	27	35
15	Blackpool	23	8	9	6	32	24	33
16	Barnsley	23	9	5	9	26	31	32
17	Huddersfield	23	7	10	6	28	26	31
18	Sheff Wed	23	9	4	10	30	35	31
19	Charlton	23	8	6	9	32	34	30
20	Birmingham	23	7	9	7	29	34	30
21	Peterborough	23	8	5	10	34	39	29
22	Bristol C	23	8	4	11	40	44	28
23	Wolves	23	7	7	9	30	35	28
24	Millwall	23	8	4	11	24	30	28

Championship — away

Pos		P	W	D	L	F	A	Pts
1	Watford	23	12	3	8	44	31	39
2	Cardiff	23	10	6	7	35	30	36
3	Hull	23	11	3	9	26	30	36
4	Charlton	23	9	8	6	33	25	35
5	Brighton	23	8	9	6	30	26	33
6	Birmingham	23	8	7	8	34	35	31
7	Nottm Forest	23	7	8	8	26	31	29
8	Millwall	23	7	7	9	27	32	28
9	Sheff Wed	23	7	6	10	23	26	27
10	Huddersfield	23	8	3	12	25	47	27
11	Burnley	23	7	5	11	31	38	26
12	Blackpool	23	6	8	9	30	39	26
13	Leicester	23	6	7	10	25	25	25
14	Peterborough	23	7	4	12	32	36	25
15	C Palace	23	6	7	10	21	31	25
16	Ipswich	23	6	7	10	14	34	25
17	Barnsley	23	5	8	10	30	39	23
18	Wolves	23	7	2	14	25	34	23
19	Blackburn	23	4	10	9	28	39	22
20	Bolton	23	4	8	11	32	41	20
21	Leeds	23	4	7	12	27	40	19
22	Derby	23	4	6	13	22	40	18
23	Middlesbro	23	5	2	16	23	43	17
24	Bristol C	23	3	4	16	19	40	13

League 1

Pos		P	W	D	L	GD	Pts
1	Doncaster	46	25	9	12	18	84
2	Bournemouth	46	24	11	11	38	83
3	Brentford	46	21	16	9	15	79
4	Yeovil	46	23	8	15	15	77
5	Sheff Utd	46	19	18	9	14	75
6	Swindon	46	20	14	12	33	74
7	Leyton Orient	46	21	8	17	7	71
8	MK Dons	46	19	13	14	17	70
9	Walsall	46	17	17	12	7	68
10	Crawley	46	18	14	14	1	68
11	Tranmere	46	19	10	17	10	67
12	Notts Co	46	16	17	13	12	65
13	Crewe	46	18	10	18	-8	64
14	Preston	46	14	17	15	5	59
15	Coventry	46	18	11	17	7	55
16	Shrewsbury	46	13	16	17	-6	55
17	Carlisle	46	14	13	19	-21	55
18	Stevenage	46	15	9	22	-17	54
19	Oldham	46	14	9	23	-13	51
20	Colchester	46	14	9	23	-21	51
21	Scunthorpe	46	13	9	24	-24	48
22	Bury	46	9	14	23	-28	41
23	Hartlepool	46	9	14	23	-28	41
24	Portsmouth	46	10	12	24	-18	32

League 1 — home

Pos		P	W	D	L	F	A	Pts
1	Brentford	23	14	6	3	37	22	48
2	Bournemouth	23	13	6	4	43	21	45
3	Yeovil	23	13	4	6	36	22	43
4	Leyton Orient	23	13	3	7	31	20	42
5	MK Dons	23	12	5	6	35	21	41
6	Swindon	23	10	9	4	44	15	39
7	Crewe	23	12	3	8	26	22	39
8	Walsall	23	10	8	5	38	29	38
9	Tranmere	23	10	6	7	31	21	36
10	Crawley	23	9	9	5	34	27	36
11	Sheff Utd	23	8	11	4	31	21	35
12	Doncaster	23	10	5	8	26	23	35
13	Shrewsbury	23	9	7	7	29	27	34
14	Preston	23	8	9	6	31	22	33
15	Notts Co	23	9	6	8	32	26	33
16	Coventry	23	7	7	9	29	27	28
17	Oldham	23	8	4	11	25	26	28
18	Colchester	23	8	4	11	25	31	28
19	Carlisle	23	7	7	9	32	43	28
20	Scunthorpe	23	7	6	10	31	38	27
21	Portsmouth	23	7	5	11	27	27	26
22	Stevenage	23	7	5	11	26	34	26
23	Bury	23	6	6	11	24	33	24
24	Hartlepool	23	5	8	10	19	27	23

League 1 — away

Pos		P	W	D	L	F	A	Pts
1	Doncaster	23	15	4	4	36	21	49
2	Sheff Utd	23	11	7	5	25	21	40
3	Bournemouth	23	11	5	7	33	32	38
4	Coventry	23	11	4	8	37	32	37
5	Swindon	23	10	5	8	28	24	35
6	Yeovil	23	10	4	9	35	34	34
7	Notts Co	23	7	11	5	29	23	32
8	Crawley	23	9	5	9	25	31	32
9	Tranmere	23	9	4	10	27	27	31
10	Brentford	23	7	10	6	25	25	31
11	Walsall	23	7	9	7	27	29	30
12	MK Dons	23	7	8	8	27	24	29
13	Leyton Orient	23	8	5	10	24	28	29
14	Stevenage	23	8	4	11	21	30	28
15	Carlisle	23	7	6	10	24	34	27
16	Preston	23	6	8	9	23	27	26
17	Crewe	23	6	7	10	28	40	25
18	Oldham	23	6	5	12	21	33	23
19	Colchester	23	6	5	12	22	37	23
20	Shrewsbury	23	4	9	10	25	33	21
21	Scunthorpe	23	6	3	14	18	35	21
22	Hartlepool	23	4	6	13	20	40	18
23	Bury	23	3	8	12	21	40	17
24	Portsmouth	23	3	7	13	24	42	16

Deductions: Coventry, Portsmouth 10pts

League 2

Pos	P	W	D	L	GD	Pts
1 Gillingham	46	23	14	9	27	83
2 Rotherham	46	24	7	15	15	79
3 Port Vale	46	21	15	10	35	78
4 Burton	46	22	10	14	6	76
5 Cheltenham	46	20	15	11	7	75
6 Northampton	46	21	10	15	9	73
7 Bradford	46	18	15	13	11	69
8 Chesterfield	46	18	13	15	15	67
9 Oxford	46	19	8	19	-1	65
10 Exeter	46	18	10	18	1	64
11 Southend	46	16	13	17	6	61
12 Rochdale	46	16	13	17	-2	61
13 Fleetwood	46	15	15	16	-2	60
14 Bristol R	46	16	12	18	-9	60
15 Wycombe	46	17	9	20	-10	60
16 Morecambe	46	15	13	18	-6	58
17 York	46	12	19	15	-10	55
18 Accrington	46	14	12	20	-17	54
19 Torquay	46	13	14	19	-7	53
20 Wimbledon	46	14	11	21	-22	53
21 Plymouth	46	13	13	20	-9	52
22 Dag & Red	46	13	12	21	-7	51
23 Barnet	46	13	12	21	-12	51
24 Aldershot	46	11	15	20	-18	48

League 2 — home

Pos	P	W	D	L	F	A	Pts
1 Burton	23	17	3	3	49	23	54
2 Northampton	23	17	2	4	41	16	53
3 Cheltenham	23	14	7	2	34	16	49
4 Rotherham	23	14	1	8	44	29	43
5 Gillingham	23	12	5	6	37	21	41
6 Bradford	23	12	5	6	34	21	41
7 Port Vale	23	10	7	6	50	26	37
8 Bristol R	23	11	4	8	32	28	37
9 Chesterfield	23	9	8	6	39	24	35
10 Barnet	23	8	9	6	28	23	33
11 Oxford	23	9	6	8	29	27	33
12 Morecambe	23	8	9	6	28	27	33
13 Torquay	23	9	6	8	38	40	33
14 Rochdale	23	8	8	7	33	27	32
15 Wycombe	23	8	7	8	27	24	31
16 Plymouth	23	8	7	8	27	24	31
17 Fleetwood	23	7	9	7	27	32	30
18 Accrington	23	7	7	9	28	34	28
19 Exeter	23	7	6	10	29	26	27
20 Dag & Red	23	7	6	10	28	28	27
21 Southend	23	6	8	9	24	25	26
22 Wimbledon	23	6	8	9	28	34	26
23 York	23	6	8	9	25	31	26
24 Aldershot	23	7	4	12	22	30	25

League 2 — away

Pos	P	W	D	L	F	A	Pts
1 Gillingham	23	11	9	3	29	18	42
2 Port Vale	23	11	8	4	37	26	41
3 Exeter	23	11	4	8	34	36	37
4 Rotherham	23	10	6	7	30	30	36
5 Southend	23	10	5	8	37	30	35
6 Chesterfield	23	9	5	9	21	21	32
7 Oxford	23	10	2	11	31	34	32
8 Fleetwood	23	8	6	9	28	25	30
9 York	23	6	11	6	25	29	29
10 Rochdale	23	8	5	10	35	43	29
11 Wycombe	23	9	2	12	23	36	29
12 Bradford	23	6	10	7	29	31	28
13 Wimbledon	23	8	3	12	26	42	27
14 Cheltenham	23	6	9	8	24	35	26
15 Accrington	23	7	5	11	23	34	26
16 Morecambe	23	7	4	12	27	34	25
17 Dag & Red	23	6	7	10	27	34	24
18 Aldershot	23	4	11	8	20	30	23
19 Bristol R	23	5	8	10	28	41	23
20 Burton	23	5	7	11	22	42	22
21 Plymouth	23	5	6	12	21	31	21
22 Torquay	23	4	8	11	17	22	20
23 Northampton	23	4	8	11	23	39	20
24 Barnet	23	5	3	15	19	36	18

Blue Sq Premier

Pos	P	W	D	L	GD	Pts
1 Mansfield	46	30	5	11	40	95
2 Kidderminster	46	28	9	9	42	93
3 Newport Co	46	25	10	11	25	85
4 Grimsby	46	23	14	9	32	83
5 Wrexham	46	22	14	10	29	80
6 Hereford	46	19	13	14	10	70
7 Luton	46	18	13	15	8	67
8 Dartford	46	19	9	18	4	66
9 Braintree	46	19	9	18	-9	66
10 Forest Green	46	18	11	17	14	65
11 Macclesfield	46	17	12	17	-5	63
12 Woking	46	18	8	20	-8	62
13 Alfreton	46	16	12	18	-5	60
14 Cambridge U	46	15	14	17	-1	59
15 Nuneaton	46	14	15	17	-8	57
16 Lincoln	46	15	11	20	-7	56
17 Gateshead	46	13	16	17	-3	55
18 Hyde	46	16	7	23	-12	55
19 Tamworth	46	15	10	21	-14	55
20 Southport	46	14	12	20	-14	54
21 Stockport	46	13	11	22	-19	50
22 Barrow	46	12	12	22	-38	44
23 Ebbsfleet	46	8	15	23	-34	39
24 Telford	46	6	17	23	-27	35

Blue Sq Premier — home

Pos	P	W	D	L	F	A	Pts
1 Mansfield	23	17	3	3	53	17	54
2 Kidderminster	23	15	4	4	49	22	49
3 Grimsby	23	13	5	5	42	19	44
4 Newport Co	23	13	5	5	43	27	44
5 Wrexham	23	11	9	3	45	24	42
6 Woking	23	13	3	7	47	34	42
7 Dartford	23	12	4	7	41	26	40
8 Luton	23	10	7	6	43	26	37
9 Gateshead	23	9	9	5	35	22	36
10 Macclesfield	23	10	6	7	29	28	36
11 Cambridge U	23	9	7	7	33	30	34
12 Hereford	23	8	9	6	37	33	33
13 Nuneaton	23	8	9	6	29	25	33
14 Hyde	23	9	5	9	35	31	32
15 Alfreton	23	9	5	9	41	39	32
16 Lincoln	23	9	5	9	34	36	32
17 Braintree	23	9	5	9	32	40	32
18 Tamworth	23	9	4	10	25	27	31
19 Forest Green	23	8	6	9	33	24	30
20 Stockport	23	8	2	13	34	39	26
21 Ebbsfleet	23	5	11	7	31	37	26
22 Southport	23	7	4	12	32	44	25
23 Barrow	23	5	7	11	20	35	22
24 Telford	23	2	9	12	22	42	15

Blue Sq Premier — away

Pos	P	W	D	L	F	A	Pts
1 Kidderminster	23	13	5	5	33	18	44
2 Newport Co	23	12	5	6	42	33	41
3 Mansfield	23	13	2	8	39	35	41
4 Grimsby	23	10	9	4	28	19	39
5 Wrexham	23	11	5	7	29	21	38
6 Hereford	23	10	7	6	36	30	37
7 Forest Green	23	10	5	8	30	25	35
8 Braintree	23	10	4	9	31	32	34
9 Luton	23	8	6	9	27	36	30
10 Southport	23	7	8	8	40	42	29
11 Alfreton	23	7	7	9	28	35	28
12 Macclesfield	23	7	6	10	36	42	27
13 Dartford	23	7	5	11	26	37	26
14 Cambridge U	23	6	7	10	35	39	25
15 Lincoln	23	6	6	11	32	37	24
16 Tamworth	23	6	6	11	30	42	24
17 Nuneaton	23	6	6	11	26	38	24
18 Stockport	23	5	9	9	23	37	24
19 Barrow	23	6	6	11	25	44	24
20 Hyde	23	7	2	14	28	44	23
21 Telford	23	4	8	11	30	37	20
22 Woking	23	5	5	13	26	47	20
23 Gateshead	23	4	7	12	23	39	19
24 Ebbsfleet	23	3	4	16	24	52	13

Blue Square North

Pos	P	W	D	L	GD	Pts
1 Chester	42	34	5	3	71	107
2 Guiseley	42	28	7	7	38	91
3 Brackley	42	26	7	9	32	85
4 Altrincham	42	24	8	10	49	80
5 Halifax	42	21	12	9	48	75
6 Harrogate T	42	20	9	13	24	69
7 Bradford PA	42	19	9	14	23	66
8 Gainsborough	42	18	12	12	23	66
9 Solihull Moors	42	17	9	16	4	60
10 Oxford C	42	13	16	13	5	55
11 Gloucester	42	16	6	20	-9	54
12 Vauxhall M	42	15	8	19	-6	53
13 Stalybridge	42	13	13	16	-7	52
14 Workington	42	16	8	18	-8	52
15 Worcester	42	14	8	20	-5	50
16 Boston Utd	42	14	7	21	-5	49
17 Bishop's St.	42	12	13	17	-16	49
18 Colwyn Bay	42	14	7	21	-21	49
19 Histon	42	11	11	20	-24	44
20 Corby	42	12	8	22	-26	44
21 Droylsden	42	5	7	30	-81	22
22 Hinckley Utd	42	3	4	35	-106	7

Blue Square North — home

Pos	P	W	D	L	F	A	Pts
1 Chester	21	18	2	1	48	11	56
2 Altrincham	21	15	1	5	56	22	46
3 Guiseley	21	14	4	3	40	22	46
4 Brackley	21	12	3	6	36	24	39
5 Bradford PA	21	10	5	6	31	22	35
6 Halifax	21	9	7	5	49	20	34
7 Harrogate T	21	9	6	6	45	28	33
8 Solihull Moors	21	10	2	9	27	25	32
9 Vauxhall M	21	8	8	5	30	27	31
10 Histon	21	9	4	8	30	31	31
11 Gainsborough	21	7	7	7	33	28	28
12 Gloucester	21	7	6	8	33	28	27
13 Stalybridge	21	7	6	8	30	33	27
14 Oxford C	21	5	11	5	32	25	26
15 Boston Utd	21	7	4	10	41	37	25
16 Worcester	21	7	4	10	29	30	25
17 Workington	21	7	4	10	28	34	25
18 Corby	21	7	4	10	36	43	25
19 Bishop's St.	21	6	6	9	27	36	24
20 Colwyn Bay	21	7	1	13	27	44	22
21 Droylsden	21	4	3	14	25	56	15
22 Hinckley Utd	21	1	3	17	16	67	6

Blue Square North — away

Pos	P	W	D	L	F	A	Pts
1 Chester	21	16	3	2	55	21	51
2 Brackley	21	14	4	3	40	20	46
3 Guiseley	21	14	3	4	43	23	45
4 Halifax	21	12	5	4	37	18	41
5 Gainsborough	21	11	5	5	35	19	38
6 Harrogate T	21	11	3	7	27	22	36
7 Altrincham	21	9	7	5	44	29	34
8 Bradford PA	21	9	4	8	44	30	31
9 Workington	21	9	4	8	32	34	31
10 Oxford C	21	8	5	8	28	30	29
11 Solihull Moors	21	7	7	7	31	29	28
12 Colwyn Bay	21	7	6	8	30	34	27
13 Gloucester	21	9	0	12	20	34	27
14 Worcester	21	7	4	10	28	32	25
15 Stalybridge	21	6	7	8	25	29	25
16 Bishop's St.	21	6	7	8	30	37	25
17 Boston Utd	21	7	3	11	27	36	24
18 Vauxhall M	21	6	4	11	28	37	22
19 Corby	21	5	4	12	30	49	19
20 Histon	21	2	7	12	18	42	13
21 Droylsden	21	1	4	16	18	68	7
22 Hinckley Utd	21	2	1	18	21	76	7

Deductions: Solihull, Workington 4pts, Hinckley 6pts

Blue Square South

Pos		P	W	D	L	GD	Pts
1	Welling	42	26	8	8	46	86
2	Salisbury	42	25	8	9	33	82
3	Dover	42	22	10	10	25	76
4	Eastleigh	42	22	6	14	18	72
5	Chelmsford	42	22	6	14	14	72
6	Sutton Utd	42	20	10	12	17	70
7	Weston S-M.	42	19	10	13	6	67
8	Dorchester	42	19	8	15	-3	65
9	Boreham W	42	15	17	10	13	62
10	Havant & W	42	14	16	12	8	58
11	Bath City	42	15	10	17	2	55
12	Eastbourne	42	14	9	19	-10	51
13	Farnborough	42	19	7	16	1	50
14	Basingstoke	42	12	12	18	-10	48
15	Bromley	42	14	6	22	-15	48
16	Tonbridge	42	12	12	18	-21	48
17	Hayes & Y	42	13	9	20	-25	48
18	Staines	42	13	8	21	-17	47
19	Maidenhead	42	13	6	23	-4	45
20	Hornchurch	42	11	11	20	-17	44
21	Billericay	42	11	7	24	-28	40
22	Truro City	42	9	8	25	-33	25

Deductions: Truro 10pts, Farnborough 14pts, Salisbury 1pt

Blue Square South — home

Pos		P	W	D	L	F	A	Pts
1	Welling	21	16	5	0	55	20	53
2	Salisbury	21	16	4	1	48	22	52
3	Eastleigh	21	16	3	2	49	21	51
4	Chelmsford	21	14	3	4	46	27	45
5	Farnborough	21	13	3	5	47	30	42
6	Dorchester	21	12	5	4	35	24	41
7	Boreham W	21	10	7	4	33	17	37
8	Sutton Utd	21	11	4	6	37	27	37
9	Havant & W	21	10	5	6	41	27	35
10	Weston S-M.	21	10	5	6	34	30	35
11	Hayes & Y	21	9	5	7	38	35	32
12	Dover	21	9	5	7	27	24	32
13	Tonbridge	21	8	7	6	28	30	31
14	Maidenhead	21	9	2	10	37	31	29
15	Hornchurch	21	7	8	6	21	21	29
16	Billericay	21	8	4	9	37	32	28
17	Bath City	21	7	7	7	30	29	28
18	Basingstoke	21	8	4	9	34	37	28
19	Bromley	21	7	4	10	25	30	25
20	Staines	21	7	4	10	33	42	25
21	Eastbourne	21	7	3	11	18	27	24
22	Truro City	21	5	5	11	30	41	20

Blue Square South — away

Pos		P	W	D	L	F	A	Pts
1	Dover	21	13	5	3	42	20	44
2	Welling	21	10	3	8	35	24	33
3	Sutton Utd	21	9	6	6	29	22	33
4	Weston S-M.	21	9	5	7	26	24	32
5	Salisbury	21	9	4	8	32	25	31
6	Bath City	21	8	3	10	30	29	27
7	Eastbourne	21	7	6	8	25	26	27
8	Chelmsford	21	8	3	10	24	29	27
9	Boreham W	21	5	10	6	26	29	25
10	Dorchester	21	7	3	11	24	38	24
11	Havant & W	21	4	11	6	27	33	23
12	Bromley	21	7	2	12	29	39	23
13	Staines	21	6	4	11	29	37	22
14	Farnborough	21	6	4	11	29	45	22
15	Eastleigh	21	6	3	12	30	40	21
16	Basingstoke	21	4	8	9	29	36	20
17	Tonbridge	21	4	5	12	27	46	17
18	Maidenhead	21	4	4	13	27	37	16
19	Hayes & Y	21	4	4	13	26	54	16
20	Hornchurch	21	4	3	14	26	43	15
21	Truro City	21	4	3	14	27	49	15
22	Billericay	21	3	3	15	25	58	12

Scottish Premier

Pos		P	W	D	L	GD	Pts
1	Celtic	38	24	7	7	57	79
2	Motherwell	38	18	9	11	16	63
3	St Johnstone	38	14	14	10	1	56
4	Inverness CT	38	13	15	10	4	54
5	Ross County	38	13	14	11	-1	53
6	Dundee Utd	38	11	14	13	-11	47
7	Hibernian	38	13	12	13	-3	51
8	Aberdeen	38	11	15	12	-2	48
9	Kilmarnock	38	11	12	15	-1	45
10	Hearts	38	11	11	16	-9	44
11	St Mirren	38	9	14	15	-13	41
12	Dundee	38	7	9	22	-38	30

Scottish Premier — home

Pos		P	W	D	L	F	A	Pts
1	Celtic	19	15	2	2	52	14	47
2	St Johnstone	19	9	7	3	25	17	34
3	Motherwell	19	9	6	4	35	24	33
4	Ross County	19	8	8	3	22	15	32
5	Hearts	19	9	3	7	27	25	30
6	Inverness CT	19	7	8	4	35	27	29
7	Hibernian	19	7	5	7	26	22	28
8	Aberdeen	19	6	9	4	18	15	27
9	St Mirren	19	6	6	7	25	31	24
10	Dundee Utd	19	4	9	6	30	33	21
11	Kilmarnock	19	5	4	10	25	29	19
12	Dundee	19	4	4	11	17	34	16

Scottish Premier — away

Pos		P	W	D	L	F	A	Pts
1	Celtic	19	9	5	5	40	21	32
2	Motherwell	19	9	3	7	32	27	30
3	Kilmarnock	19	6	8	5	27	24	26
4	Dundee Utd	19	7	5	7	21	29	26
5	Inverness CT	19	6	7	6	29	33	25
6	Hibernian	19	6	5	8	23	30	23
7	St Johnstone	19	5	7	7	20	27	22
8	Aberdeen	19	5	6	8	23	28	21
9	Ross County	19	5	6	8	25	33	21
10	St Mirren	19	3	8	8	22	29	17
11	Hearts	19	2	8	9	13	24	14
12	Dundee	19	3	5	11	11	32	14

Scottish Div One

Pos		P	W	D	L	GD	Pts
1	Partick	36	23	9	4	48	78
2	Morton	36	20	7	9	26	67
3	Falkirk	36	15	8	13	4	53
4	Livingston	36	14	10	12	2	52
5	Hamilton	36	14	9	13	7	51
6	Raith	36	11	13	12	-6	46
7	Dumbarton	36	13	4	19	-25	43
8	Cowdenbeath	36	8	12	16	-14	36
9	Dunfermline	36	14	7	15	3	34
10	Airdrie Utd	36	5	7	24	-48	22

Deductions: Dunfermline 15pts

Scottish Div One — home

Pos		P	W	D	L	F	A	Pts
1	Partick	18	15	2	1	51	13	47
2	Morton	18	11	2	5	33	21	35
3	Raith	18	6	8	4	23	21	26
4	Falkirk	18	7	4	7	28	25	25
5	Hamilton	18	7	4	7	26	23	25
6	Livingston	18	6	5	7	31	28	23
7	Dunfermline	18	6	2	10	27	29	20
8	Cowdenbeath	18	4	8	6	30	34	20
9	Dumbarton	18	4	3	11	26	40	15
10	Airdrie Utd	18	1	5	12	19	40	8

Scottish Div One — away

Pos		P	W	D	L	F	A	Pts
1	Morton	18	9	5	4	40	26	32
2	Partick	18	8	7	3	25	15	31
3	Dunfermline	18	8	5	5	35	30	29
4	Livingston	18	8	5	5	27	28	29
5	Falkirk	18	8	4	6	24	23	28
6	Dumbarton	18	9	1	8	32	43	28
7	Hamilton	18	7	5	6	26	22	26
8	Raith	18	5	5	8	22	27	20
9	Cowdenbeath	18	4	4	10	21	31	16
10	Airdrie Utd	18	4	2	12	22	49	14

Scottish Div Two

Pos		P	W	D	L	GD	Pts
1	Queen of Sth	36	29	5	2	69	92
2	Alloa	36	20	7	9	27	67
3	Brechin	36	19	4	13	13	61
4	Forfar	36	17	3	16	-7	54
5	Arbroath	36	15	7	14	-10	52
6	Stenh'semuir	36	12	13	11	0	49
7	Ayr	36	12	5	19	-12	41
8	Stranraer	36	10	7	19	-28	37
9	East Fife	36	8	8	20	-15	32
10	Albion	36	7	3	26	-37	24

Scottish Div Two — home

Pos		P	W	D	L	F	A	Pts
1	Queen of Sth	18	15	3	0	41	9	48
2	Brechin	18	12	1	5	44	30	37
3	Forfar	18	10	2	6	39	38	32
4	Alloa	18	9	4	5	31	19	31
5	Arbroath	18	9	4	5	28	22	31
6	Stenh'semuir	18	8	5	5	27	22	29
7	Ayr	18	8	2	8	30	30	26
8	Stranraer	18	7	4	7	27	33	25
9	East Fife	18	5	4	9	25	28	19
10	Albion	18	5	2	11	28	39	17

Scottish Div Two — away

Pos		P	W	D	L	F	A	Pts
1	Queen of Sth	18	14	2	2	51	14	44
2	Alloa	18	11	3	4	31	16	36
3	Brechin	18	7	3	8	28	29	24
4	Forfar	18	7	1	10	28	36	22
5	Arbroath	18	6	3	9	19	35	21
6	Stenh'semuir	18	4	8	6	32	37	20
7	Ayr	18	4	3	11	23	35	15
8	East Fife	18	3	4	11	25	37	13
9	Stranraer	18	3	3	12	16	38	12
10	Albion	18	2	1	15	17	43	7

Scottish Div Three

Pos		P	W	D	L	GD	Pts
1	Rangers	36	25	8	3	58	83
2	Peterhead	36	17	8	11	24	59
3	Queen's Park	36	16	8	12	6	56
4	Berwick	36	14	7	15	4	49
5	Elgin City	36	13	10	13	-2	49
6	Montrose	36	12	11	13	-8	47
7	Stirling	36	12	9	15	1	45
8	Annan	36	11	10	15	-1	43
9	Clyde	36	12	4	20	-24	40
10	East Stirling	36	8	5	23	-48	29

Scottish Div Three — home

Pos		P	W	D	L	F	A	Pts
1	Rangers	18	13	3	2	44	12	42
2	Berwick	18	10	4	4	34	21	34
3	Peterhead	18	9	5	4	26	11	32
4	Stirling	18	9	3	6	38	24	30
5	Elgin City	18	9	1	8	41	40	28
6	Annan	18	7	6	5	31	26	26
7	Clyde	18	8	2	8	25	29	26
8	Montrose	18	6	7	5	34	32	25
9	Queen's Park	18	5	7	6	27	27	22
10	East Stirling	18	5	3	10	28	39	18

Scottish Div Three — away

Pos		P	W	D	L	F	A	Pts
1	Rangers	18	12	5	1	43	17	41
2	Queen's Park	18	11	1	6	33	27	34
3	Peterhead	18	8	3	7	26	17	27
4	Montrose	18	6	4	8	26	36	22
5	Elgin City	18	4	9	5	26	29	21
6	Annan	18	4	5	9	23	39	17
7	Berwick	18	4	3	11	25	34	15
8	Stirling	18	3	6	9	21	34	15
9	Clyde	18	4	2	12	17	37	14
10	East Stirling	18	3	2	13	21	58	11

West Brom were the Premier League's most profitable team to back

Premier League	£ P/L
West Brom	+9.13
Tottenham	+8.18
Man Utd	+8.11
Norwich	+7.35
Chelsea	+2.78
Swansea	-0.70
Man City	-1.24
Arsenal	-1.65
Aston Villa	-2.53
Sunderland	-2.95
Everton	-3.81
West Ham	-4.12
Fulham	-4.15
Southampton	-7.52
Wigan	-8.98
Liverpool	-9.89
Newcastle	-11.65
QPR	-13.70
Reading	-14.55
Stoke	-14.95

Championship	£ P/L
Peterborough	+19.45
Watford	+18.58
Charlton	+12.67
Hull	+11.65
C Palace	+10.56
Cardiff	+10.19
Barnsley	+7.32
Sheff Wed	+5.14
Ipswich	+4.75
Leeds	+3.60
Huddersfield	+2.94
Middlesbrough	+2.25
Burnley	+0.92
Birmingham	+0.56
Millwall	+0.54
Brighton	-0.97
Derby	-5.09
Bolton	-5.92
Nottm Forest	-6.18
Wolves	-6.91
Leicester	-8.04
Blackpool	-10.21
Bristol City	-10.88
Blackburn	-14.23

League 1	£ P/L
Yeovil	+24.20
Doncaster	+22.72
Leyton Orient	+17.34
Crewe	+12.24
Walsall	+12.14
Bournemouth	+2.95
Tranmere	+2.32
Coventry	+1.84
Brentford	+1.51
Crawley	+1.41
Carlisle	-0.30
Stevenage	-1.38
Sheff Utd	-3.55
Swindon	-3.91
Shrewsbury	-3.98
Colchester	-4.05
Notts County	-4.71
Scunthorpe	-4.93
MK Dons	-5.77
Oldham	-6.68
Hartlepool	-8.93
Preston	-10.49
Portsmouth	-11.23
Bury	-16.85

League 2	£ P/L
Burton	+14.72
Wycombe	+13.28
Exeter	+8.74
Barnet	+7.67
Oxford	+6.58
Rotherham	+6.18
Port Vale	+5.72
Northampton	+5.00
Gillingham	+4.87
AFC Wimbledon	+4.74
Morecambe	+4.20
Bristol R	+4.12
Chesterfield	+2.62
Accrington	+1.62
Cheltenham	+1.51
Rochdale	+1.37
Southend	-1.93
Dag & Red	-4.33
Plymouth	-4.45
Bradford	-5.49
Fleetwood	-9.52
Torquay	-11.13
York	-12.22
Aldershot	-13.81

SPL	£ P/L
Motherwell	+12.97
Kilmarnock	+12.48
Inverness CT	+10.14
Ross County	+6.52
Hibernian	+5.45
St Johnstone	+3.51
Dundee	-2.30
Celtic	-4.21
Dundee Utd	-10.65
Hearts	-10.80
St Mirren	-11.86
Aberdeen	-12.63

Scottish Div One	£ P/L
Dumbarton	+31.26
Morton	+6.89
Partick	+6.22
Hamilton	+5.82
Falkirk	+2.37
Dunfermline	+0.18
Livingston	-3.14
Raith	-5.99
Airdrie Utd	-7.13
Cowdenbeath	-9.68

Scottish Div Two	£ P/L
Brechin	+10.56
Alloa	+10.35
Queen of Sth	+9.37
Forfar	+4.46
Stenh'semuir	-0.50
Stranraer	-0.85
Arbroath	-3.13
Albion	-6.70
Ayr	-8.94
East Fife	-12.43

Scottish Div Three	£ P/L
Annan	+18.88
Peterhead	+10.01
Stirling	+9.17
Clyde	+4.27
East Stirling	+2.03
Montrose	-1.68
Berwick	-1.70
Queen's Park	-1.79
Elgin City	-3.14
Rangers	-5.91

Profit & loss figures based on £1 level stake to best prices

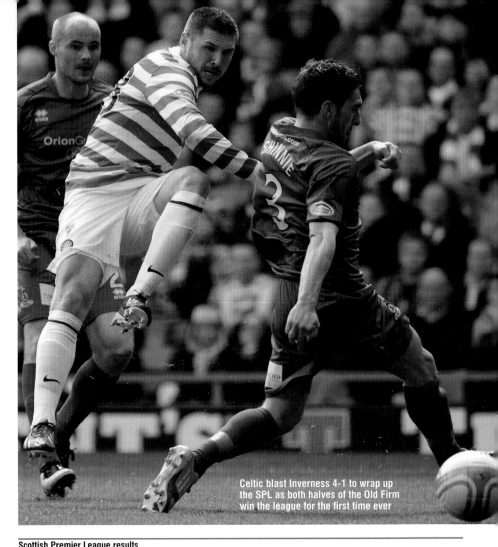

Celtic blast Inverness 4-1 to wrap up the SPL as both halves of the Old Firm win the league for the first time ever

Scottish Premier League results

	Aberdeen	Celtic	Dundee	Dundee Utd	Hearts	Hibernian	Inverness CT	Kilmarnock	Motherwell	Ross County	St Johnstone	St Mirren
Aberdeen		0-2	2-0/1-0	2-2	0-0/2-0/1-1	2-1/0-0	2-3	0-2/1-0	3-3/0-0	0-0/0-1	2-0	0-0/0-0
Celtic	1-0/4-3		2-0/5-0	4-0/6-2	1-0/4-1	2-2/3-0	0-1/4-1	0-2/4-1	1-0	4-0	1-1/4-0	2-0
Dundee	1-3/1-1	0-2		0-3	1-0/1-0	3-1	1-4/1-1	0-0/2-3	1-2/0-3	0-1/0-2	1-3/2-2	0-2/2-1
Dundee Utd	1-1/1-0	2-2/0-4	3-0/1-1		0-3/3-1	3-0/2-2	4-4	3-3	1-2/1-3	0-0/1-1	1-1/0-1	3-4
Hearts	2-0	0-4	0-1/1-0	2-1		0-0/1-2	2-2/2-3	1-3/0-3	1-0/1-2	2-2/4-2	2-0/2-0	1-0/3-0
Hibernian	0-1/0-0	1-0	3-0/1-1/1-0	2-1	1-1/0-0		2-2/1-2	2-1/2-2	2-3	0-1	2-0/1-3	2-1/3-3
Inverness CT	1-1/3-0	2-4/1-3	4-1	4-0/0-0/1-2	1-1	3-0		1-1/1-1	1-5/4-3	3-1/2-1	1-1/0-0	2-2
Kilmarnock	1-3/1-1	1-3	0-0/1-2	3-1/2-3	1-0/0-1	1-1/1-3	1-2		1-2/2-0	3-0	1-2	3-1/1-1/1-3
Motherwell	4-1	0-2/2-1/3-1	1-1	0-1/0-1	0-0	0-4/4-1	4-1/3-0	2-2		3-2/2-0	1-1/3-2	1-1/2-2
Ross County	2-1	1-1/3-2/1-1	1-1	1-2/1-0	2-2	3-2/1-0	0-0/1-0	0-0/0-1	0-0/3-0		1-2/1-0	0-0
St Johnstone	1-2/3-1	2-1/1-1	1-0	0-0/1-1	2-2	0-1	0-0/1-0	2-1/2-0	1-3/2-0	1-1/2-2		2-1/1-0
St Mirren	1-4/0-0	0-5/1-1	3-1/1-2	0-1/0-0	2-0/2-0	1-2/0-1	2-2/2-1	1-1	2-1	5-4/1-4	1-1	

Scottish Division One results

	Airdrie	Cowdenbeath	Dumbarton	Dunfermline	Falkirk	Hamilton	Livingston	Morton	Partick	Raith
Airdrie		0-3/1-1	4-1/1-2	1-2/3-3	1-4/0-1	0-4/2-2	1-3/0-2	2-3/0-4	1-1/1-2	0-0/1-2
Cowdenbeath	1-1/3-2		0-1/2-3	0-4/4-2	1-1/4-1	1-0/1-1	1-1/2-2	3-4/1-1	0-3/1-2	4-4/1-1
Dumbarton	3-4/4-1	0-3/2-2		0-2/0-1	0-2/0-2	3-3/3-1	3-4/0-3	1-5/0-3	2-0/0-0	4-2/1-2
Dunfermline	1-3/1-2	3-0/1-0	4-0/3-4		0-1/0-2	1-1/2-3	4-0/0-1	2-2/1-4	0-1/0-4	3-1/1-0
Falkirk	1-1/4-3	2-0/4-0	3-4/1-3	2-2/1-0		2-1/0-2	1-2/2-0	0-1/4-1	0-0/0-2	0-2/1-1
Hamilton	3-0/5-0	2-1/1-3	2-3/2-1	0-3/1-2	1-1/1-1		1-2/1-1	1-1/2-1	1-0/0-2	0-1/2-0
Livingston	0-2/4-1	1-1/3-0	5-0/2-3	2-1/2-2	2-1/1-2	0-3/0-0		2-2/0-2	1-2/2-2	2-1/2-3
Morton	2-0/5-2	1-0/4-2	3-0/0-3	4-2/0-1	1-2/2-0	0-1/0-2	2-2/2-1		3-1/2-2	1-0/1-0
Partick	7-0/1-0	2-1/2-1	3-0/3-0	5-1/3-3	3-1/4-1	4-0/1-0	2-0/6-1	1-2/1-0		3-2/0-0
Raith	2-0/2-0	2-2/0-1	2-2/3-2	1-3/1-1	2-1/0-0	2-0/0-2	0-0/0-2	3-3/2-1	1-1/0-0	

Scottish Division Two results

	Albion	Alloa	Arbroath	Ayr	Brechin	East Fife	Forfar	Queen of Sth	Stenh'smuir	Stranraer
Albion		0-3/1-5	4-0/0-1	2-0/1-3	1-2/3-1	0-3/1-1	2-3/1-2	0-3/0-1	4-4/4-3	2-1/2-3
Alloa	5-1/4-1		2-3/0-1	1-0/2-2	2-2/0-1	1-1/1-1	2-1/1-0	1-0/1-2	0-2/1-0	3-0/4-1
Arbroath	2-1/2-1	1-2/0-1		4-2/1-4	3-1/0-1	2-0/1-0	1-1/3-1	2-3/1-1	2-2/0-0	2-1/1-0
Ayr	2-1/5-2	0-0/0-2	2-0/0-1		3-0/1-2	2-3/2-1	2-3/2-1	2-4/1-5	1-1/1-2	2-1/2-1
Brechin	1-0/2-0	1-3/3-2	3-2/2-0	2-1/2-1		2-1/6-0	4-1/3-4	0-3/0-6	7-2/1-2	3-0/2-2
East Fife	1-2/2-0	0-1/2-1	2-1/0-1	2-3/3-3	2-2/0-3		3-0/1-2	0-0/2-3	3-2/1-2	0-1/1-1
Forfar	4-2/4-2	2-3/0-1	1-1/2-4	2-1/2-1	1-0/1-4	3-2/3-2		1-5/0-4	3-2/3-3	4-0/3-1
Queen of Sth	1-0/3-0	1-0/0-0	6-0/5-1	2-0/2-0	1-0/2-1	1-0/2-2	2-0/3-1		2-2/2-1	4-1/2-0
Stenhousemuir	1-0/0-1	0-2/1-1	2-2/1-0	1-1/4-0	3-1/3-3	3-0/2-1	0-4/2-0	1-3/2-1		0-0/1-2
Stranraer	1-1/3-2	3-2/1-2	1-1/2-0	2-0/0-1	0-2/3-2	2-6/3-1	4-1/0-3	0-2/0-5	1-1/1-1	

Scottish Division Three results

	Annan	Berwick	Clyde	East Stirling	Elgin	Montrose	Peterhead	Queens Park	Rangers	Stirling
Annan		3-2/2-2	1-3/0-1	5-2/1-2	2-0/2-2	2-1/1-1	2-1/0-0	2-3/2-0	0-0/1-3	5-2/0-1
Berwick	3-1/0-2		2-1/3-3	3-0/2-0	0-0/2-1	1-4/4-0	1-1/0-2	2-0/4-1	1-1/1-3	4-1/1-0
Clyde	2-1/2-3	2-1/2-1		2-1/2-0	2-2/1-1	1-2/1-0	0-2/2-0	0-3/2-3	0-2/1-4	2-1/1-2
East Stirling	2-2/1-2	0-1/0-3	3-0/3-0		1-4/3-2	2-2/1-2	2-1/2-4	0-2/0-2	2-6/2-4	3-1/1-1
Elgin	2-2/3-1	3-1/1-2	2-1/4-2	3-4/3-2		6-1/3-2	2-0/0-3	3-0/4-5	2-6/0-1	3-1/1-2
Montrose	0-0/5-1	3-1/1-3	2-3/3-1	3-1/2-2	2-2/4-1		2-0/0-6	1-1/1-2	2-4/0-0	3-2/2-2
Peterhead	2-0/2-0	1-0/1-1	1-0/3-0	2-0/6-0	1-1/0-1	2-0/0-1		1-0/0-2	2-2/0-1	2-2/0-0
Queens Park	2-2/2-2	1-1/2-1	1-0/4-1	1-2/5-1	1-1/0-1	2-2/1-2	0-0/0-3		0-1/1-4	2-1/2-2
Rangers	3-0/1-2	4-2/1-0	3-0/2-0	5-1/3-1	5-1/1-1	4-1/1-1	2-0/1-2	2-0/4-0		2-0/0-0
Stirling	5-1/2-1	6-3/1-0	0-1/2-0	1-1/9-1	1-4/1-1	1-3/3-1	1-0/0-1	1-2/2-3	1-0/1-1	

Rangers get a draw at Berwick's Shielfield Park

Half-time tables help to shine a light on managerial changes

Man United were first-half kings – can David Moyes keep them starting fast?

A s I write, a quarter of the Premier League sides will kick off 2013-14 under new management – Man United, Man City, Chelsea, Everton and Stoke, writes Figaro.

In addition, Sunderland's boss, Paolo Di Canio, had only been in the job a few weeks as last season ended, while many feel that Alan Pardew's position at Newcastle has been compromised by the appointment of Joe Kinnear as Director of Football.

Why give someone an eight-year contract then appoint above him someone who is best qualified to help the club's French contingent understand English swear words? Still, Mike Ashley was lampooned for replacing Chris Hughton with Alan Pardew only for the new man to take them up to fifth and into the Europa League, so not all of the owner's decisions have taken the club backwards.

There are many ways of trying to quantify the value of a manager's input and the three tables here just might help in that respect. Can we measure just how much Sir Alex Ferguson's famous hairdryer will be missed now it's been put in the attic?

As you can see from our double results table, Man United were behind at the break only three times last season but the half time blower did turn two of those games round in to wins.

But the machine was clearly switched on before kick-off as well, because the champions went in ahead at half time on 23 occasions, four more than any other team, and landed the win/win double result 50 per cent more often than anyone else – in 21 games, or 55.3 per cent.

If you had backed Man United win/win

in the double result market last term you would have made a good profit. Note how the Red Devils are nine points clear at the top of our first-half table.

Of course, United were fired up last season by the manner in which they missed out on the 2011-12 title but the speed with which they managed to take control of most games was down to the brilliance of Robin van Persie, especially in the first half of last season. Under Fergie's guidance, the dynamic Dutchman seemed to need no settling-in time, although he did, of course, learn all about breaking down Premier League defences at Arsenal and had won the golden boot in the previous season.

The biggest challenge facing David Moyes might be the way he handles the mix of United's strikers. That was a commodity he never had at Everton, where the magic was mostly conjured up in midfield – arguably United's weakest area just now.

Note how the Toffees only mustered a

half-time/full-time double results

	WW	DW	LW	WD	DD	LD	WL	DL	LL
Man Utd	21	5	2	2	3	0	0	4	1
Man City	14	8	1	1	7	1	1	2	3
Chelsea	14	5	3	5	4	0	1	3	3
Arsenal	11	10	0	0	8	2	0	2	5
Tottenham	7	11	3	0	6	3	1	5	2
Everton	10	4	2	3	9	3	2	3	2
Liverpool	11	4	1	2	7	4	0	2	7
West Brom	8	6	0	0	4	3	1	4	12
Swansea	5	5	1	0	11	2	0	5	9
West Ham	9	2	1	0	7	3	2	4	10
Fulham	9	2	1	4	4	1	0	7	10
Norwich	6	3	1	1	11	2	0	5	9
Stoke	4	5	0	4	9	2	0	5	9
Southampton	7	1	1	2	9	3	0	5	10
Aston Villa	5	5	0	4	6	1	3	4	10
Newcastle	7	4	0	3	3	2	2	7	10
Sunderland	6	3	0	3	6	3	3	4	10
Wigan	4	4	1	3	4	2	1	9	10
Reading	2	1	3	2	5	2	3	7	13
QPR	0	4	0	1	11	1	1	5	15

dismal 23 second-half goals last term, the same as Man United scored just in their home games. Moyes's replacement at Everton, Roberto Martinez, is taking over a team much closer in style to his old club than is the case with Moyes himself.

Everyone, including myself, has been making a fuss about Chelsea's chances with Jose Mourinho back in the dugout. The Portuguese peacock has nothing to prove and has inherited a squad ideally set up to make another challenge against Manchester teams in transition.

In contrast, Man City's Manuel Pellegrini is new to the Premier League and although, as I write, replacements are reportedly being lined up for Carlos Tevez, in general the form of West Ham and Man United dipped after the Argentine left them.

The biggest surprise about the second-half table is the margin by which Arsenal lead it. No team scored more home goals in the second half, no other team came close to the Gunners' remarkable away defence in the second half of their games – just a ridiculous four conceded – and no other team went through the whole season with their position in away games deteriorating in the second half in just a single game.

There's just a hint of the old Invincibles about that second half '0' in the Gunners' away defeats column. Even Per Mertesacker was looking good in the Arsenal back line back in the spring.

If any of the new signings that Arsenal fans have been promised are truly eye-catching, their long trophyless drought could end this season, especially if Jack Wilshere and Aaron Ramsey can stay fit this term and Theo Walcott and Alex Oxlade-Chamberlain continue to mature.

At the other end of the table, the key managerial point is that the three promoted clubs are managed either by newcomers at this level (Malky Mackay at Cardiff) or men who have already taken a Premier League club back down into the Championship (Steve Bruce at Hull and Ian Holloway at Crystal Palace). The Eagles have also lost their star man in Wilfried Zaha and there is unlikely to be a queue of quality players desperate to sign for those clubs.

premier league 2012-13 first-half results

Pos		P	home					away					GD	Pts	Last 5	Form
			W	D	L	F	A	W	D	L	F	A				
1	Man Utd	38	13	4	2	22	6	10	8	1	23	10	29	81	WXOWW	54
2	Chelsea	38	11	5	3	23	8	9	7	3	16	7	24	72	WOWLX	61
3	Man City	38	10	7	2	14	6	6	10	3	12	7	13	65	OWoWX	50
4	Everton	38	10	7	2	18	8	5	9	5	14	12	12	61	LWOWX	50
5	Arsenal	38	5	12	2	17	12	6	8	5	11	10	6	53	WXWXO	62
6	Liverpool	38	8	7	4	13	6	5	6	8	19	17	9	52	LWOXW	62
7	Fulham	38	9	6	4	15	8	4	7	8	8	16	-1	52	LLLXW	44
8	Aston Villa	38	5	9	5	8	11	7	6	6	14	15	-4	51	LWOWL	53
9	Newcastle	38	6	7	6	9	11	6	7	6	11	12	-3	50	WLOWO	45
10	Sunderland	38	5	7	7	8	11	7	6	6	14	14	-3	49	WLLOO	43
11	Tottenham	38	3	12	4	8	7	5	10	4	14	11	4	46	XOLXO	60
12	West Ham	38	8	7	4	17	8	3	6	10	5	12	2	46	WLOLW	48
13	Stoke	38	4	9	6	9	11	4	10	5	6	7	-3	43	WOWXO	55
14	Southampton	38	5	10	4	12	12	4	5	10	10	19	-9	42	OLOOO	41
15	Wigan	38	6	6	7	13	19	2	11	6	5	9	-10	41	XWoXW	48
16	West Brom	38	4	10	5	10	13	5	4	10	8	16	-11	41	WXLLL	45
17	Norwich	38	6	9	4	10	9	1	10	8	8	17	-8	40	OOOWX	55
18	Swansea	38	3	10	6	10	15	2	11	6	4	11	-12	36	LOLLL	43
19	Reading	38	2	6	11	7	19	5	7	7	8	11	-15	34	OOWLL	44
20	QPR	38	0	9	10	4	18	2	11	6	8	14	-20	26	LOLLL	38

premier league 2012-13 second-half results

Pos		P	home					away					GD	Pts	Last 5	Form
			W	D	L	F	A	W	D	L	F	A				
1	Arsenal	38	11	6	2	30	11	8	11	0	14	4	29	74	OOOWW	62
2	Man City	38	12	5	2	27	9	6	9	4	13	12	19	68	OOIWL	50
3	Liverpool	38	8	7	4	20	10	9	6	4	19	10	19	64	WWOWO	62
4	Tottenham	38	10	4	5	21	11	9	2	8	23	17	16	63	XWWWW	60
5	Man Utd	38	7	8	4	23	13	8	6	5	18	14	14	59	OOLXL	54
6	Chelsea	38	8	6	5	18	8	7	7	5	18	16	12	58	OWLWW	61
7	Everton	38	9	6	4	15	9	5	8	6	8	11	3	56	OOOWL	50
8	Swansea	38	9	7	3	18	11	4	9	6	15	14	8	55	OOWXL	43
9	West Brom	38	10	5	4	22	12	3	11	5	13	16	7	55	WLOLW	45
10	Southampton	38	6	8	5	14	12	5	8	6	13	17	-2	49	OLLXX	41
11	Aston Villa	38	7	6	6	15	17	4	7	8	10	26	-18	46	OWWLW	53
12	Stoke	38	7	7	5	12	11	2	8	9	7	16	-8	42	WLLX	55
13	Norwich	38	4	12	3	15	11	4	6	9	8	21	-9	42	WLLWW	55
14	Sunderland	38	7	9	3	12	8	2	6	11	7	21	-10	42	OLWXL	43
15	Wigan	38	3	8	8	13	20	7	3	9	16	24	-15	41	WLwLL	48
16	Fulham	38	4	4	11	13	22	5	9	5	14	12	-7	40	OOLLW	44
17	QPR	38	4	12	3	9	10	3	6	10	9	18	-10	39	LOOOO	38
18	West Ham	38	6	8	5	16	14	0	10	9	6	19	-11	36	OXOLX	48
19	Newcastle	38	7	5	7	15	20	1	7	11	10	25	-20	36	LLOOL	45
20	Reading	38	5	9	5	14	14	2	3	14	12	29	-17	33	LOWLX	44

Stekelenburg saves but Jesus could be summer's star buy

Dan Childs picks out the summer buys who look set to make an impact next term

**Jesus Navas (27)
Seville to Man City**
Jesus Navas showed plenty of loyalty to Seville, spending over nine years playing for the first team, but his talent has been wasted for the last couple of seasons and his switch to Man City should benefit all parties.

Seville have got a decent chunk of cash – helping them put a dent into their huge debts – and City have got themselves a classy winger, who is very similar in playing style to Samir Nasri.

The 27-year-old, who has won 28 caps for Spain, has excellent balance and control and an eye for the killer pass but his critics might suggest that a lack of goals his Achilles' heel.

Navas has never scored more than five league goals in a single campaign and he failed to find the net in 37 Primera Liga games last season.

**Modibo Diakite (26)
Lazio to Sunderland**
Paolo Di Canio promised to overhaul the Sunderland squad and seems to have taken a step in the right direction by snapping up French centre-back Modibo Diakite from Lazio.

The towering defender is yet to feature for the France national team but he is tall and physically strong and looks ideally suited to the demands of English football.

However, he missed the whole of last season with a shin injury and will need to rediscover the form he showed in 2011-12, when nailing down a regular place in the Lazio side.

Fitness-wise it looks like a gamble but Sunderland don't have the biggest budget and on the plus side, Di Canio knows Lazio inside out. He will be hoping his insider knowledge can pay dividends.

**Andre Schurrle (22)
Leverkusen to Chelsea**
Chelsea missed out on Radamel Falcao and look set to fall short in their pursuit of Edinson Cavani but their capture of Andre Schurrle could prove an inspired move.

The last time Chelsea went shopping in the German market they got their fingers burned with the expensive acquisition of Marko Marin but their deal for Schurrle is likely to have a much happier ending.

The 22-year-old is equally at home on the flank or in a central striker's position so the Blues may feel they are getting two players for the price of one.

Schurrle is yet to establish himself as a regular starter with the German national team despite winning 22 caps for the senior side but a good first season in West London could go some way towards nailing down a place in time for Brazil 2014.

**Wilfried Zaha (20)
C Palace to Man Utd**
Sir Alex Ferguson's last major piece of transfer business was to snap up Wilfried Zaha in a £15m deal and it may prove to be money well spent.

Looking at the bare statistics it would be hard to justify the size of the fee but anyone who watches Zaha at first hand will see a player with bags of ability and potential and someone who could emerge as a key man

Jesus Navas

Andre Schurrle

Modibo Diakite

Ricky van Wolfswinkel

Maarten Stekelenburg

Wilfried Zaha

for England at the World Cup finals.

Zaha sent most of the Championship season supplying the ammunition to ensure Glenn Murray ended the season as the division's top scorer but when Murray got injured at the start of the play-offs, Zaha revelled in the extra responsibility.

He destroyed Brighton in the second leg of the semi-final with two excellent goals and was the star man in the final against Watford, running the Hornets' defence ragged and winning the penalty that decided the game.

He has pace, trickery and intelligence and looks certain to be a massive hit.

Maarten Stekelenburg (30)
Roma to Fulham

Mark Schwarzer has been a key figure for Fulham in recent years and the Cottagers have taken no chances with his replacement by agreeing a deal for experienced Dutch international Maarten Stekelenburg.

A reported £4m fee was agreed and that seems good business for the Cottagers, who are acquiring a top-notch keeper with 54 international caps to his name.

Before signing for Roma in the summer of 2011 Stekelenburg spent ten seasons with Ajax and it was during his spell in Amsterdam that he worked under current Fulham boss Martin Jol.

He followed in the footsteps of Edwin van der Sar when he become Ajax's number one and is the same age (30) as Van der Sar was when he went to Craven Cottage in 2001. If their career paths continue to be closely matched, Fulham supporters will be in for a treat.

Ricky van Wolfswinkel (24)
Sporting to Norwich

Norwich have been chasing a new striker for some time and may have struck gold with their move for Dutch striker Ricky van Wolfswinkel.

The 24-year-old rose to prominence as a regular scorer for FC Utrecht and earned a big move to Sporting Lisbon in 2011.

He adapted well to Portuguese football, scoring 28 goals in 55 league appearances, and his arrival as Carrow Road will be seen as a major coup.

Norwich have been over-reliant on Grant Holt during the last two seasons and if they can get ten goals or more out of the Dutchman, they will feel much more confident of extending their stay in the top flight by at least one more year.

MONEY BACK JOY

NO.1 FOR MONEY BACKS

Ladbrokes

WE REFUNDED OVER ONE MILLION BETS DURING THE 2012/13 FOOTBALL SEASON AS A FREE BET

Sports bettors must become ever more sophisticated to stay ahead of the game

Betting has changed out of all recognition in the past 14 years or so since the market liberalised away from the archaic restrictions of old, writes Alex Deacon.

Those changes were seismic for those old enough to remember the insane concept of 9p in the pound betting tax as well as the even more ludicrous 'minimum trebles' rules and the like.

It might be hard to explain to a young family member the idea of music and video cassettes without appearing like a throwback to Victorian times, but it's even worse explaining to those too young to remember that once a upon a time it was nigh on impossible to have anything less than a treble on a football coupon, with singles largely restricted to televised live and cup games.

These are changes that, less than 20 years after their implementation, appear right up there with universal suffrage when viewed through the eyes of a long-term football punter.

But those changes are nothing alongside the incredible, transformative effect that online betting had on the traditional bookmaking industry.

We now have a wealth of betting opportunities that we couldn't have dreamed of punting on not very long ago – since the dinosaurs had roamed the earth the palette of markets was the usual high-margin fare of match odds, correct scores and the odd goalscorer market. Sports punters of every persuasion have never had it so good.

And it's not just variety. The depth of competition out there – and nowhere more than online – means you can find usually the value if you look for it. And despite a reduced margin when compared to those of the betting dark ages of the late 20th century, there remains a margin to beat, and it's that which my last 14 years or so have been dedicated to solving.

The first and most significant of those attempts, and one that is still going strong, is my weekly column in the Racing & Football Outlook that remains unique even in this enlightened age as the only regularly published set of football ratings. Over the years I've continued to develop the system and this has brought some useful tools to our readers from True Odds for all our featured matches, allowing readers an at-a-glance comparison between what the bookmakers are offering and a more objective price assessment.

My most recent innovation has been in taking those principles one step further to create forecasted league tables. At any given point in the season, they allow for an objective view of how each of the various competitions will finish and, more importantly, how that should be reflected in the various outright markets.

Whatever their sport, smart punters understand that to move forward in their betting, they must be innovative. That's why it's worth taking a copy of the RFO every Tuesday as we seek to move forward in the ever-evolving world of betting.

It remains a debatable point whether the days where information was enough to get you ahead are over but, if they aren't, then it's only a matter of time.

Yes, opinion is relevant but much less in sports betting than in racing, for example, where the increasing sophistication of both punter and bookie alike means that a winning approach requires more hard work and dedication than ever before.

League tables are one of the most deceptive tools a punter can use to make selections, showing as they do a snapshot of a competition at a specific moment in time.

In their usual format they reveal nothing of the quality of the opponents each club has faced up until that point. That's where the *Outlook Index* comes in, showing the relative strength of each side determined by the results of almost 100,000 matches and weighted by the strength of the opposition.

Detailed 60-match form is shown for every side so that trends can be identified as well as a Home and Away rating (which is calculated seperately from the main figure). Each week the Outlook prints updated *Index* ratings along with *True Odds* and analysis, including forecasted league tables, to help your betting.

Premier League Outlook Index 2012-13

	Current	1-6	7-12	13-18	19-24	25-30	31-36	37-42	43-48	49-54	55-60	Home	Away	Trend
Man Utd	938	947	956	951	947	945	939	940	949	940	941	966	918	-8
Man City	923	932	930	937	938	941	936	934	928	935	935	951	889	-6
Arsenal	920	912	902	894	896	898	905	904	912	894	903	929	904	11
Chelsea	919	908	901	906	904	911	908	898	898	902	912	953	889	10
Tottenham	916	907	906	901	895	892	892	888	899	914	918	932	881	8
Everton	894	897	888	888	885	883	890	882	872	869	869	915	827	2
Liverpool	893	886	882	875	868	866	856	866	874	893	906	929	878	9
West Ham	850	848	838	841	850	851	844	832	829	833	828	869	840	5
Newcastle	850	850	852	849	858	876	887	893	885	880	876	876	840	0
Aston Villa	848	848	837	834	844	836	838	847	853	859	861	856	869	5
Norwich	848	839	846	847	856	843	838	845	850	854	846	880	819	3
Southampton	846	851	844	838	829	821	824	831	834	820	807	870	824	2
Stoke	846	843	852	868	872	856	855	850	852	852	860	889	824	-5
Sunderland	844	846	845	856	847	852	854	854	863	861	845	886	824	-2
Swansea	843	847	855	859	856	845	845	841	846	840	832	891	817	-6
Fulham	842	846	858	852	859	871	873	874	863	863	857	872	812	-6
West Brom	841	846	856	857	868	869	864	857	854	852	850	853	844	-8
Wigan	840	841	842	840	844	853	859	860	838	827	834	862	860	0
Reading	815	816	826	830	820	833	839	854	842	836	822	870	815	-4
QPR	809	819	827	822	815	815	826	828	816	816	823	862	812	-8

Arsenal's strong finish saw their
Index Trend hit double figures

Championship Outlook Index 2012-13

	Current	1-6	7-12	13-18	19-24	25-30	31-36	37-42	43-48	49-54	55-60	Home	Away	Trend
Cardiff	825	830	834	845	836	830	827	821	816	805	806	842	813	-6
Brighton	818	808	806	800	799	798	794	802	788	798	802	852	796	9
Bolton	814	812	808	796	799	810	814	826	834	832	824	869	796	6
Hull	809	815	818	817	822	808	802	803	799	794	814	835	820	-5
Watford	809	813	820	816	807	802	791	792	799	799	784	834	821	-4
Charlton	803	795	781	790	787	794	781	780	786	775	781	822	826	10
Birmingham	798	800	798	796	797	802	805	815	822	822	823	856	806	0
Blackpool	797	792	785	788	801	803	806	822	826	816	819	839	799	5
Ipswich	794	792	782	782	783	772	766	783	793	797	792	827	801	6
Sheff Weds	793	794	788	784	763	756	768	776	781	764	748	816	802	4
Leicester	792	788	800	817	811	813	815	804	798	803	798	837	798	-5
Nottm Forest	792	799	801	785	796	798	791	784	781	778	770	841	802	-3
Crystal Palace	789	789	806	798	802	809	798	775	766	782	790	864	771	-5
Burnley	788	780	781	793	790	788	788	784	794	792	792	834	802	3
Blackburn	786	778	779	791	786	800	810	821	820	829	831	851	782	3
Barnsley	783	779	768	758	740	744	754	756	749	758	769	827	793	11
Leeds	783	780	792	786	792	783	789	785	783	788	791	824	792	-2
Derby	783	782	780	789	791	791	792	783	780	782	775	849	772	0
Peterborough	782	784	773	761	752	738	746	741	754	762	762	834	784	7
Huddersfield	780	772	771	768	772	779	780	775	758	769	773	845	789	7
Millwall	766	777	778	784	808	813	795	787	794	775	770	808	807	-10
Wolves	766	776	768	768	782	788	803	804	801	803	820	816	802	-4
Middlesbrough	761	765	778	793	812	813	813	798	799	800	808	838	775	-12
Bristol City	746	756	767	760	753	753	764	778	778	762	758	818	776	-9

League 1 Outlook Index 2012-13

	Current	1-6	7-12	13-18	19-24	25-30	31-36	37-42	43-48	49-54	55-60	Home	Away	Trend
Bournemouth	763	757	745	759	751	737	714	721	721	714	715	804	780	7
Doncaster	760	759	758	757	758	752	748	740	740	742	752	786	813	2
Brentford	747	754	754	751	758	743	729	726	729	736	722	793	733	-4
Sheff Utd	742	752	760	753	764	768	766	758	761	762	758	799	766	-9
Yeovil	740	746	744	747	720	716	708	717	715	720	721	800	750	-2
Swindon	740	746	755	758	752	740	736	731	730	737	732	793	748	-7
Walsall	739	746	743	727	708	700	716	724	708	714	708	800	746	1
Leyton Orient	739	735	731	722	712	704	701	704	694	709	720	786	762	7
MK Dons	735	735	728	728	745	752	746	750	752	747	759	778	754	2
Crawley	734	729	725	720	722	727	725	718	712	715	706	757	750	6
Notts County	733	727	733	728	736	748	748	750	742	730	728	782	752	3
Coventry	732	742	747	748	746	734	730	731	752	764	752	786	777	-8
Preston	726	724	722	712	723	727	721	716	710	709	711	794	758	4
Crewe	722	718	720	727	732	718	710	713	707	700	683	773	736	1
Carlisle	717	720	710	716	708	712	724	728	728	740	736	775	746	2
Shrewsbury	717	712	713	709	708	702	711	717	724	724	718	798	721	4
Tranmere	705	716	731	744	747	743	746	735	717	714	700	780	742	-16
Portsmouth	704	704	687	686	711	727	747	743	765	770	772	781	758	6
Scunthorpe	703	696	703	707	697	701	698	702	710	720	715	782	754	2
Oldham	702	695	692	687	697	706	713	707	704	702	713	758	750	7
Colchester	700	696	698	690	689	711	716	706	718	725	729	778	719	4
Hartlepool	698	691	697	683	667	672	688	706	712	710	713	770	751	7
Stevenage	694	700	703	720	736	754	762	756	745	729	736	725	743	-9
Bury	690	682	691	698	694	700	688	698	710	699	700	767	738	1

Stronger at home		Stronger away		Hot		Not	
Burton	110	Dunfermline	52	Peterhead	3.22%	Fleetwood	-2.42%
Celtic	96	Queen's Park	48	Dumbarton	1.75%	Exeter	-2.41%
Rangers	95	Doncaster	27	Accrington	1.66%	Tranmere	-2.27%
Crystal Palace	93	Kilmarnock	24	Barnsley	1.40%	Rangers	-1.95%
Aberdeen	89	Fleetwood	23	Charlton	1.25%	Ayr	-1.76%
Everton	88	Livingston	21	Forfar	1.25%	East Stirling	-1.74%

Dougie Freedman's Bolton have a very healthy rating

League 2 Outlook Index 2012-13

	Current	1-6	7-12	13-18	19-24	25-30	31-36	37-42	43-48	49-54	55-60	Home	Away	Trend
Rotherham	704	690	693	694	693	693	687	686	684	674	670	750	730	8
Cheltenham	700	697	697	694	699	706	700	691	686	678	693	763	718	3
Chesterfield	693	686	677	677	686	680	687	691	693	693	695	758	723	8
Burton	692	688	695	678	675	673	667	654	646	648	653	786	676	4
Bradford	691	686	673	672	684	682	677	672	662	655	663	756	713	8
Port Vale	690	695	694	710	708	700	705	693	679	673	679	726	720	-6
Gillingham	690	696	698	704	703	708	712	705	688	678	689	755	706	-5
Northampton	689	690	694	688	680	671	660	667	662	664	654	775	693	0
Oxford	682	673	680	671	673	664	668	676	687	697	699	741	713	5
Bristol Rovers	678	688	680	672	650	655	666	662	670	678	675	760	701	0
Rochdale	676	669	658	666	677	689	685	679	678	689	696	766	719	7
Wycombe	675	676	678	683	676	668	675	680	702	714	696	743	724	-2
York	674	659	663	674	679	681	685	684	676	669	669	708	711	6
Southend	670	678	688	697	703	698	692	700	696	692	697	734	728	-11
Morecambe	669	671	678	673	664	660	658	654	656	663	660	746	716	-2
Accrington	664	657	644	639	646	656	664	673	669	672	677	749	691	11
Exeter	663	678	696	692	688	684	684	700	689	688	706	733	712	-16
Plymouth	663	669	654	649	650	654	667	663	664	669	663	754	704	3
Wimbledon	662	659	659	649	641	645	644	647	657	653	660	727	700	5
Aldershot	662	665	671	665	667	662	663	681	695	691	685	710	729	-3
Fleetwood	661	677	686	699	699	700	708	712	712	723	716	683	706	-16
Torquay	660	654	649	667	685	696	703	705	710	723	716	733	701	2
Barnet	656	660	659	653	644	638	623	626	638	638	647	761	687	0
Dag & Red	645	655	657	664	672	674	664	652	663	655	648	710	702	-9

Conference Outlook Index 2012-13 2012-13

	Current	1-6	7-12	13-18	19-24	25-30	31-36	37-42	43-48	49-54	55-60	Home	Away	Trend
Kidderminster	711	702	690	676	668	647	642	632	654	655	656	722	709	15
Mansfield	708	704	700	683	674	669	672	681	685	676	661	736	698	9
Grimsby	673	663	664	678	669	662	660	650	653	660	660	694	681	5
Wrexham	673	680	688	686	681	686	692	689	689	696	702	699	688	-7
Newport County	658	660	655	656	648	644	649	636	624	619	618	682	659	1
Hereford	653	649	645	652	650	644	640	651	650	641	652	679	720	3
Luton	647	636	635	640	658	668	669	669	663	657	677	721	648	6
Nuneaton	646	636	632	621	625	620	626	637	-	-	-	680	650	11
Braintree	646	637	638	631	624	622	620	626	630	636	628	656	667	8
Dartford	639	637	632	632	639	656	662	650	-	-	-	658	649	3
Woking	634	638	630	629	616	610	614	610	614	615	618	696	633	2
Alfreton	632	625	626	626	636	632	635	631	635	633	614	654	648	4
Cambridge	630	635	638	642	644	630	633	648	647	639	643	675	647	-5
Lincoln	624	618	607	612	625	624	607	604	610	607	607	685	661	7
Gateshead	624	620	620	617	629	638	639	653	639	639	639	694	620	3
Hyde	623	632	614	626	639	632	620	626	-	-	-	665	636	-2
Macclesfield	622	626	637	634	627	629	627	633	622	634	642	711	668	-6
Forest Green	619	637	644	654	652	656	663	658	648	646	640	666	653	-16
Southport	619	616	629	639	631	630	634	638	644	656	653	628	690	-4
Stockport	613	614	610	621	615	628	628	623	628	612	610	668	664	0
Tamworth	611	611	614	614	605	607	616	612	604	612	614	682	639	0
Barrow	606	618	614	609	607	610	608	601	610	625	639	668	638	-5
Ebbsfleet	591	602	610	612	610	616	604	614	623	628	629	698	624	-10
Telford	575	575	588	600	608	626	627	623	612	608	611	634	617	-8

Scottish Premier League Outlook Index 2012-13

	Current	1-6	7-12	13-18	19-24	25-30	31-36	37-42	43-48	49-54	55-60	Home	Away	Trend
Celtic	866	865	878	879	879	887	894	904	904	904	892	930	834	-4
Motherwell	825	826	815	817	815	809	818	816	818	814	819	818	806	4
St Johnstone	813	804	797	794	796	800	784	794	804	800	802	833	790	10
Ross County	807	802	806	784	775	777	782	776	764	750	752	820	791	7
Inverness CT	799	809	806	810	806	792	779	776	784	791	782	806	800	-6
Dundee Utd	798	803	812	809	821	825	835	839	833	814	819	800	797	-7
Hibernian	782	772	777	780	782	777	767	760	758	756	762	821	790	4
Kilmarnock	778	788	797	794	793	791	790	792	791	797	801	778	802	-9
Aberdeen	778	780	781	782	787	788	776	773	776	780	768	848	759	-2
Hearts	776	780	778	796	798	793	801	808	804	808	806	816	758	-5
St Mirren	771	771	774	782	768	775	779	777	774	776	774	828	778	-1
Dundee	745	745	726	728	736	730	737	744	751	750	750	788	751	7

Scottish Division One Outlook Index 2012-13

	Current	1-6	7-12	13-18	19-24	25-30	31-36	37-42	43-48	49-54	55-60	Home	Away	Trend
Partick	758	760	751	729	734	736	727	709	711	712	714	804	735	7
Morton	722	734	738	728	722	716	700	700	699	706	704	755	754	-7
Hamilton	716	714	701	704	706	700	716	729	725	728	731	752	745	6
Falkirk	711	711	708	703	712	709	712	720	742	745	740	762	732	2
Raith	704	702	700	704	717	722	725	706	698	699	702	756	732	1
Livingston	700	708	716	720	718	706	706	715	709	717	721	727	748	-9
Dunfermline	692	693	706	731	743	750	741	742	744	748	756	716	768	-11
Dumbarton	686	675	669	667	643	634	641	642	654	646	630	703	722	12
Cowdenbeath	673	670	675	671	672	684	683	683	685	687	682	759	677	1
Airdrie Utd	636	634	647	653	657	662	666	651	637	640	635	702	693	-5

Scottish Division Two Outlook Index 2012-13

	Current	1-6	7-12	13-18	19-24	25-30	31-36	37-42	43-48	49-54	55-60	Home	Away	Trend
Queen Of Sth	717	718	717	718	710	703	690	695	694	695	702	774	734	1
Alloa	665	659	662	660	661	646	640	643	634	636	624	707	706	4
Brechin	646	646	661	650	631	613	621	630	641	647	640	710	673	-2
Forfar	641	633	625	628	633	643	635	620	620	628	628	702	674	8
Stenhousemuir	640	632	632	626	626	634	632	626	626	633	642	701	679	7
Arbroath	638	637	629	637	636	650	651	652	663	651	645	692	673	3
Ayr	624	636	642	644	655	666	674	685	690	677	677	717	673	-11
Stranraer	602	599	598	590	583	575	580	594	596	604	597	687	629	5
East Fife	602	603	616	626	628	620	633	649	642	644	646	678	664	-8
Albion	572	573	570	576	589	602	599	606	591	599	610	666	617	-1

Scottish Division Three Outlook Index 2012-13

	Current	1-6	7-12	13-18	19-24	25-30	31-36	37-42	43-48	49-54	55-60	Home	Away	Trend
Rangers	820	829	852	860	856	854	878	888	889	900	914	916	821	-16
Peterhead	621	599	584	590	590	598	602	582	577	569	562	685	682	20
Queen's Park	598	603	620	617	610	610	606	609	616	611	603	639	687	-9
Stirling	596	593	587	572	578	586	598	607	614	615	622	677	654	7
Berwick	584	586	585	576	576	578	576	574	570	580	579	685	626	1
Elgin	580	575	565	584	600	594	592	582	589	574	568	655	620	3
Annan	573	568	561	569	565	572	562	566	580	590	603	655	633	5
Montrose	569	576	575	573	574	556	547	543	535	544	544	667	625	-3
Clyde	556	558	546	551	546	544	550	542	544	554	568	656	624	3
East Stirling	518	527	543	529	528	530	517	523	527	521	523	640	580	-9

Pools draws chart 2012-13   **Key X** Score draw **0** Goalless draw. Weekend UK pools only

Pools No.	Sep	Oct	Nov	Dec	Jan	Feb	Mar	Apr	May	Jun	X	0
	18 25	1 8 15 22 29	6 13 20 27	3 10 17 24 1 8 15 22 26 29	5 12 19 26	2 9 16 23	2 9 16 23 30	6 13 20 27	4 11 18 25	1 8	X	0

```
 1  0 - - 0 - - - - - - - - - X X - X - - - - - X X - - - - - - - - - - - - X - X - - - X -  8  2
 2  - - - 0 - - X 0 - - X X - - - - 0 - - - - - - X - - - - 0 - X - 0 - X - - - 0 - X  7  7
 3  - X X - - - X - - - - - X - - - - - - X 0 - - - - X - - - X - - X - - X - - - -  8  1
 4  - - - - - - - - - - X - - - - - X - - - X - X X - 0 X - - - - 0 - - - - - - - - -  6  2
 5  - X X - 0 - - X X X - X - - - - - X 0 - - - - X X - 0 - - - 0 - 0 - X - - - - X X X - 13  5
 6  - - X - - - - X - X - - - - - - - X - - - - 0 - X 0 - X 0 - - 0 - - X - - - - - - -  7  4
 7  X 0 - 0 X - X - 0 - X X 0 - X X - - - - X - - X - - - - - - X - X 0 - - - 0 0 0 - - - - 11  8
 8  - - - X X - X - - X X X - - X X X - - 0 - - - - - - - - - - - - - - - - X X 0 X - 10  2
 9  - - X - X - - - X - 0 0 - X X - X 0 X - - - 0 - - 0 - X - - X X X - - 0 - - - 11  6
10  - X - - X X - - - - - - X - - - X - X - 0 - - - - 0 - - - - - X 0 0 X - X X 11  4
11  - - - X - - - X X - - - - X 0 X X X - - - X - - - - X 0 - - - - X X - - X - - - 12  2
12  X - - - - - - - - - - X - - - X - - - - - - - - - X - - - - - X X - - - -  6  0
13  - - - - - - - - X - X - - - - - - 0 - - X X - - - - 0 0 - 0 - X X - - - - - -  6  4
14  0 - - - - - X - - - - - - - X X - - - X - 0 - - - - - - - X - - - - -  5  2
15  - 0 - X - - 0 X - - - - - - - - - X - 0 - - - - - - - - - X - - - -  5  3
16  X - - - - X - X X - - - - - 0 - - - - X - - - - 0 - X - - 0 - 0 - -  6  4
17  - - X X X - - - - X - - - - - - X - 0 - - - - - - - - - 0 - X  8  2
18  X - - - - - - - - - X 0 - - X X - - - - - - - 0 - - - X X 0 0 X X - - X - 10  4
19  - - - X - - - - - - - - X 0 X - - X - X - X - X - - - - 0 X X - - - 10  2
20  - - - X X - - - - X X - - - - 0 - X - 0 X - X X - X - - 0 0 -  9  4
21  - X - - - - - - - - - - - - X X - 0 - - - - - - - X - - X - -  5  1
22  - X - - - - - - X X - - - - - - 0 X - X - X - - - X - 0 -  7  2
23  0 - - - X - - - X - X - X - 0 0 - - X - X - - - - 0 - 0 -  6  5
24  - - - 0 - - - X - X - - - 0 - - - X 0 - - X 0 0 - - - X - X -  6  5
25  - X - X - X - 0 - - - X - X - - 0 X - - - - - - X - - - - - X -  9  2
26  0 X - X X X - 0 - X - - X 0 - - - - - - - - - - 0 - - - - X - 10  4
27  - X - X - 0 - - - X - X - - 0 - - - X X - - - - - - - -  6  2
28  X - - X - - 0 - - X 0 X 0 - - - - - X - - - 0 - X - X - 0 -  8  5
29  0 - - - - - X - - - X - X - - X - - - X - - - 0 - - X - - 0 -  6  3
30  - - X - - - X - - - X - X - 0 0 - X - - X X - - - X - - - -  8  2
31  X - - - 0 - - - X X - - - - 0 X - - X - - - 0 - - - 0 - - - -  5  4
32  - X X - - - X - X X - - - X X 0 X - - 0 - - X - 0 - - X - - X - 11  3
33  - - - - - X - - - - X - - - - X - X - X - 0 - - - - - X X - 0 - -  7  2
34  X - X X - 0 - X - - - X X - 0 - - X - X - X - X - - 0 - X - 11  3
35  - - - - 0 - - - 0 - - - X - - - X 0 X - X - X - - - -  5  3
36  - - 0 X - - - X - 0 X - - - - - - - - - X - - - - - - -  6  2
37  - - - X 0 X - - - 0 - - X - X - 0 - 0 - - X X - - - - X - -  7  4
38  - - - - X X - X - X X - - X - - X - - 0 X 0 - - - X 0 - - 0 - - - X 10  4
39  0 X X X - - - - - - - - X - - - - - - - X - - - 0 - 0 - - X  6  3
40  - - - - X - - - - 0 - 0 X 0 - - - - X 0 - - X - X - X X - 0 X - X - 0 0 - - -  9  7
41  - - X - - - 0 - - X - - - 0 X - - - - 0 - - - - - - X - -  4  2
42  - X - - 0 X - 0 - - - 0 X 0 0 - - - - - - - - - X X - -  5  5
43  0 - - - X - - - - - X - - 0 - 0 X - X - - - - - - -  6  3
44  - - - X 0 - X - 0 - - - X 0 - - - - X - 0 X X X - - - X X X 12  4
45  - - X - - 0 - X - - X - X - 0 - 0 - - - - - X - - - 0 X 0  7  5
46  - - 0 - - 0 - X - - X - X - - - - 0 - - - - X - - - X 6  3
47  X - X - X X - - - - X - X - X - X - - X 0 - 0 - - X - - X  9  2
48  - - - X - - - - - - - - - - - - 0 - - - - - - -  1  1
49  X X 0 - - - 0 - X - X - X X - - - X - - X - - X - - - X 10  2
 X  9 11 12 9 13 10 11 6 7 9 11 7 12 9 12 8 12 11 10 5 7 8 10 9 10 9 7 6 8 4 9 8 5 8 10 8 9 10 6 6 9 9 9 53 77
 0  7 2 2 2 5 3 4 0 6 5 1 4 2 3 2 1 4 3 3 4 4 4 3 3 5 5 4 6 5 6 5 4 1 6 3 5 0 4 5 6 5 2 6 2 1 161
```

Cup results

Capital One Cup

First round
Saturday August 11

Bury .... (0) 1-2 (1) .. Middlesbro
Carlisle .... (1) 1-0 (0) ...Accrington
Cheltenham.. (0) 1-1 (1) ..... MK Dons
  AET 1-1 90 mins, MK Dons 5-3 pens
Crewe .... (4) 5-0 (0) ...Hartlepool
Doncaster .... (0) 1-1 (0) ....York
  AET 1-1 90 mins, Doncaster 4-2 pens
Hull .... (0) 1-1 (0) ...Rotherham
  AET 1-1 90 mins, Hull 7-6 pens
Leeds .... (2) 4-0 (0) . Shrewsbury
Notts Co ...... (0) 0-1 (0) ...... Bradford
  AET 0-0 90 mins
Rochdale ..... (1) 3-4 (1) ...... Barnsley
  AET 2-2 90 mins
Sheff Utd...... (0) 2-2 (1) .... Burton
  AET 1-1 90 mins, Burton 5-4 pens
Walsall......... (1) 1-0 (0) ..... Brentford
Watford........ (0) 1-0 (0) ....Wycombe
  AET 0-0 90 mins
Wolves......... (0) 1-1 (0) .....Aldershot
  AET 1-1 90 mins, Wolves 7-6 pens

Sunday August 12

Blackpool..... (0) 1-2 (1) . Morecambe

Monday August 13

Fleetwood .... (0) 0-1 (0) Nottm Forest
Oldham........ (2) 2-4 (0) ....Sheff Wed
Preston .... (2) 2-0 (0) Huddersfield

Tuesday August 14

Birmingham . (1) 5-1 (1) .... Barnet
Bristol C....... (0) 1-2 (1) ... Gillingham
Charlton....... (1) 1-1 (1)Leyton Orient
  AET 1-1 90 mins, Leyton Orient 4-3 pens
Chesterfield.. (0) 1-2 (0) ..... Tranmere
  AET 0-0 90 mins
Dag & Red ... (0) 0-1 (0) ......Coventry
Derby........... (3) 5-5 (0) ..Scunthorpe
  AET 5-5 90 mins, Scunthorpe 7-6 pens
Exeter.......... (1) 1-2 (2) ...... C Palace
Ipswich........ (1) 3-1 (1) ...... Bristol R
Millwall .... (1) 2-2 (1) .... Crawley
  AET 2-2 90 mins, Crawley 4-1 pens
Northampton (1) 2-1 (1) .... Cardiff
Oxford.......... (0) 0-0 (0)Bournemouth
  AET 0-0 90 mins, Oxford 5-3 pens
Peterborough (3) 4-0 (0) .....Southend
Plymouth ..... (1) 3-0 (0) . Portsmouth
Port Vale...... (1) 1-3 (3) ....Burnley
Stevenage.... (3) 3-1 (1)AFC Wbledon
Swindon ...... (0) 3-0 (0) ....Brighton
Torquay........ (0) 0-4 (2) ......Leicester
Yeovil........... (2) 3-0 (0) ... Colchester

Second round
Tuesday August 28

Aston Villa.... (1) 3-0 (0) ..... Tranmere
Burnley .... (1) 1-1 (0) ..... Plymouth
  AET 1-1 90 mins, Burnley 3-2 pens

Carlisle .... (0) 2-1 (1) ....Ipswich
  AET 1-1 90 mins
Coventry ...... (2) 3-2 (2) . Birmingham
  AET 2-2 90 mins
Crawley .... (0) 2-1 (1) ....Bolton
Doncaster .... (1) 3-2 (2) .... Hull
Gillingha m... (0) 0-2 (1) .. Middlesbro
Leeds .... (2) 3-0 (0) .... Oxford
Leicester...... (0) 2-4 (1) .... Burton
MK Dons...... (0) 2-1 (0) .... Blackburn
Norwich....... (1) 2-1 (1) ..Scunthorpe
Nottm Forest (0) 1-4 (3) ....Wigan
Preston .... (3) 4-1 (1) ..... C Palace
QPR............. (1) 3-0 (0) ...... Walsall
Reading .... (3) 3-2 (2)Peterborough
Sheff Wed.... (0) 1-0 (0) .... Fulham
Stevenage.... (0) 1-4 (0)Southampton
Stoke........... (0) 3-4 (2) ...... Swindon
  AET 2-2 90 mins
Sunderland .. (1) 2-0 (0) . Morecambe
Swansea...... (1) 3-1 (0) ...... Barnsley
Watford........ (0) 1-2 (0) ...... Bradford
West Ham.... (1) 2-0 (0) ....Crewe
Yeovil........... (1) 2-4 (2) .. West Brom

Wednesday August 29

Everton......... (4) 5-0 (0)Leyton Orient

Thursday August 30

Northampton (1) 1-3 (2) .... Wolves

Third round
Tuesday September 25

Bradford....... (0) 3-2 (2) .... Burton
  AET 2-2 90 mins
Chelsea........ (3) 6-0 (0) .... Wolves
Crawley .... (1) 2-3 (1) ...... Swansea
Leeds .... (1) 2-1 (0) ....Everton
MK Dons...... (0) 0-2 (0) .. Sunderland
Man City ...... (1) 2-4 (0) .. Aston Villa
  AET 2-2 90 mins
Preston .... (1) 1-3 (2) .. Middlesbro
Southampton (1) 2-0 (0) ....Sheff Wed
Swindon ...... (2) 3-1 (0) ....Burnley
West Ham.... (1) 1-4 (3) ....Wigan

Wednesday September 26

Arsenal .... (1) 6-1 (0) ......Coventry
Carlisle .... (0) 0-3 (1) ... Tottenham

Man Utd....... (1) 2-1 (0) ....Newcastle
Norwich....... (1) 1-0 (0) ....Doncaster
QPR............. (1) 2-3 (1) .... Reading
West Brom... (1) 1-2 (1) ..... Liverpool

Fourth round
Tuesday October 30

Leeds .... (1) 3-0 (0)Southampton
Reading .... (4) 5-7 (1) ....Arsenal
  AET 4-4 90 mins
Sunderland .. (0) 0-1 (1) .. Middlesbro
Swindon ...... (0) 2-3 (2) .. Aston Villa
Wigan .... (0) 0-0 (0) ...... Bradford
  AET 0-0 90 mins, Bradford 4-2 pens

Wednesday October 31

Chelsea........ (1) 5-4 (2) ...... Man Utd
  AET 3-3 90 mins
Liverpool...... (0) 1-3 (1) ..... Swansea

Quarter-finals
Tuesday December 11

Norwich....... (0) 2-1 (0) ... Tottenham
Bradford....... (1) 1-1 (0) ....Arsenal
  AET 1-1 90 mins, Bradford 3-2 pens
Norwich....... (1) 1-4 (1) .. Aston Villa

Wednesday December 12

Swansea...... (1) 1-0 (0) .. Middlesbro

Wednesday December 19

Leeds .... (1) 1-5 (0) .... Chelsea

Semi-final first legs
Tuesday January 8

Bradford....... (1) 3-1 (0) .. Aston Villa

Wednesday January 9

Chelsea........ (0) 0-2 (1) ..... Swansea

Semi-final second legs
Tuesday January 22

Aston Villa.... (1) 2-1 (0) ...... Bradford

Wednesday January 23

Swansea...... (0) 0-0 (0) .... Chelsea

Final
Sunday February 24

Bradford....... (0) 0-5 (2) ..... Swansea
SCORERS Swansea: Dyer (16, 47) Michu
(40) de Guzman (pen 59, 90) CARDS
Bradford: Duke ▀ Swansea: Ki ▀

Swansea's Nathan Dyer with his medal and man of the match award

FA Cup

First round proper

Friday November 2

Cambridge C (0) 0-0 (0) ..... MK Dons

Saturday November 3

AFC Fylde .... (0) 1-4 (2) ...Accrington
Aldershot ..... (0) 2-1 (1) ....Hendon
Barnet.......... (0) 0-2 (0) .... Oxford
Bishop's St. . (1) 1-2 (0) Hastings Utd
Boreham W.. (0) 0-2 (2) ..... Brentford
Bournemouth(1) 4-0 (0) ...Dag & Red
Bristol R....... (1) 1-2 (0) ... Sheff Utd
Bury .... (1) 1-0 (0) .... Exeter
Carlisle .... (1) 4-2 (0) ..... Ebbsfleet
Chelmsford .. (1) 3-1 (0) ... Colchester
Cheltenham.. (1) 3-0 (0) .... Yate
Chesterfield.. (3) 6-1 (0) ...Hartlepool
Coventry ...... (1) 3-0 (0) .... Arlesey
Crewe .... (2) 4-1 (1) ....Wycombe
Doncaster .... (2) 3-1 (0) . Bradford PA
Fleetwood .... (3) 3-0 (0) ......Bromley
Forest Green (1) 2-3 (2) ......Port Vale
Gillingham.... (0) 4-0 (0) ...Scunthorpe
Guiseley....... (2) 2-2 (1) .... Barrow
Hereford ...... (2) 3-1 (1) . Shrewsbury
Kidderminster(0)0-2 (0) ....Oldham
Lincoln......... (1) 1-1 (0) .... Walsall
Luton .... (0) 1-1 (1) ....Nuneaton
Mansfield ..... (0) 0-0 (0) ....Slough
Met. Police... (0) 1-2 (1) .... Crawley
Morecambe . (1) 1-1 (0) ..... Rochdale
Northampton (0) 1-1 (1) ...... Bradford
Portsmouth.. (0) 0-2 (1) ...... Notts Co
Preston........ (2) 3-0 (0) ....Yeovil
Rotherham... (1) 3-2 (0) ....Stevenage
Southend ..... (1) 3-0 (0) .... Stockport
Swindon ...... (0) 0-2 (0) Macclesfield
Torquay........ (0) 0-1 (1) . Harrogate T
Wrexham ..... (1) 2-4 (1) ......Alfreton
York............. (0) 1-1 (0) AFC Wbledon

Sunday November 4

Burton .... (0) 3-3 (2) ...Altrincham
Dorchester... (0) 1-0 (0) .....Plymouth

Tuesday November 13

Barrow......... (0) 1-0 (0) ...... Guiseley
Braintree ...... (0) 0-3 (1) ..... Tranmere

Wednesday November 14

Gloucester ... (0) 0-2 (0)Leyton Orient

First round replays

Monday November 12

AFC W'bledon(1)4-3(1) ....York
AET 2-2 after 90 mins

Tuesday November 13

Bradford....... (1) 3-3 (1)Northampton
AET 2-2 90 mins, Bradford 4-2 pens
MK Dons...... (3) 6-1 (0) Cambridge C
Nuneaton ..... (0) 0-2 (1) ....Luton
Rochdale ..... (0) 0-1 (1) . Morecambe
Slough .... (0) 1-1 (1) .....Mansfield
AET 1-1 90 mins, Mansfield 4-1 pens

Walsall......... (0) 2-3 (0) .... Lincoln
AET 1-1 90 mins

Thursday November 15

Altrincham ... (0) 0-2 (0) ....Burton

Second round

Friday November 30

Bradford....... (0) 1-1 (1) ..... Brentford

Saturday December 1

Accrington ... (1) 3-3 (1) .... Oxford
Bury .... (1) 1-1 (1) .....Southend
Carlisle .... (0) 1-3 (2)Bournemouth
Coventry...... (1) 2-1 (0) . Morecambe
Crawley .... (2) 3-0 (0) ..Chelmsford
Crewe.......... (0) 0-1 (1) ....Burton
Fleetwood .... (1) 2-3 (2) .....Aldershot
Harrogate T.. (1) 1-1 (0) Hastings Utd
Lincoln......... (1) 3-3 (1) .....Mansfield
Luton .... (1) 2-1 (0) ...Dorchester
Oldham........ (1) 3-1 (1) ....Doncaster
Preston........ (2) 2-0 (0) ...Gillingham
Rotherham... (1) 1-1 (1) ...... Notts Co
Sheff Utd...... (0) 2-1 (1) ......Port Vale
Tranmere ..... (1) 2-1 (1) . Chesterfield

Sunday December 2

Alfreton........ (1) 2-4 (3)Leyton Orient
MK Dons...... (1) 2-1 (0)AFC Wbledon

Monday December 3

Cheltenham.. (1) 1-1 (1) ...... Hereford

Tuesday December 18

Barrow......... (1) 1-1 (1) Macclesfield

Second round replays

Tuesday December 11

Hereford ..... (0) 1-2 (1) . Cheltenham
AET 1-1 90 mins

Southend ..... (0) 1-1 (0) .... Bury
AET 1-1 90 mins, Southend 3-2 pens

Wednesday December 12

Mansfield..... (1) 2-1 (1) .... Lincoln

Thursday December 13

Hastings Utd (0) 1-1 (0) . Harrogate T
AET 1-1 90 mins, Hastings Utd 5-4 pens

Tuesday December 18

Notts Co ...... (0) 0-3 (3) ...Rotherham
Oxford.......... (0) 2-0 (0) ...Accrington
Brentford...... (1) 4-2 (1) ..... Bradford
AET 1-1 90 mins

Saturday December 29

Macclesfield. (2) 4-1 (1) .... Barrow

Third round

Saturday January 5

Aldershot ..... (2) 3-1 (0) ...Rotherham
Aston Villa.... (0) 2-1 (1) ....Ipswich
Barnsley ...... (0) 1-0 (0) ......Burnley
Blackburn .... (1) 2-0 (0) ..... Bristol C
Bolton.......... (1) 2-2 (0) .. Sunderland
Brighton....... (1) 2-0 (0) ....Newcastle
C Palace ...... (0) 0-0 (0) ....Stoke
Charlton....... (0) 0-1 (1) Huddersfield
Crawley .... (1) 1-3 (2) ...... Reading
Derby........... (1) 5-0 (0) ..... Tranmere
Fulham......... (0) 1-1 (0) .... Blackpool
Hull............... (0) 1-1 (0)Leyton Orient
Leeds........... (0) 1-1 (1) .Birmingham
Leicester...... (2) 2-0 (0) ....Burton
Luton .... (0) 1-0 (0) .... Wolves
Macclesfield. (0) 2-1 (0) .... Cardiff
Man City ...... (2) 3-0 (0) .... Watford
Middlesbro... (1) 4-1 (0) Hastings Utd
Millwall........ (1) 1-0 (0) ......Preston
Nottm Forest (1) 2-3 (0) ....Oldham

Oxford.........(0) 0-3 (1).....Sheff Utd
Peterborough(0) 0-3 (2).......Norwich
QPR.............(0) 1-1 (0)..West Brom
Sheff Wed....(0) 0-0 (0).....MK Dons
Southampton(1) 1-5 (2).......Chelsea
Southend.....(1) 2-2 (2).....Brentford
Tottenham...(3) 3-0 (0)......Coventry
West Ham...(1) 2-2 (1)......Man Utd
Wigan..........(0) 1-1 (1)Bournemouth

Sunday January 6

Mansfield.....(0) 1-2 (1).....Liverpool
Swansea......(0) 2-2 (0)........Arsenal

Monday January 7

Cheltenham..(0) 1-5 (2).......Everton

Third round replays
Tuesday January 15

Birmingham.(1) 1-2 (0).........Leeds
Blackpool.....(0) 1-2 (0).......Fulham
AET 1-1 90 mins
Bournemouth(0) 0-1 (1).........Wigan
Brentford......(1) 2-1 (0).....Southend
Leyton Orient(0) 1-2 (1).............Hull
AET 1-1 90 mins
MK Dons......(1) 2-0 (0)....Sheff Wed
Stoke...........(0) 4-1 (0)......C Palace
AET 1-1 after 90 mins
Sunderland ..(0) 0-2 (0)..........Bolton
West Brom...(0) 0-1 (0)............QPR

Wednesday January 16

Arsenal ....(0) 1-0 (0)...Swansea
Man Utd.......(1) 1-0 (0)....West Ham

Fourth round
Friday January 25

Millwall ....(1) 2-1 (1)...Aston Villa

Saturday January 26

Bolton..........(1) 1-2 (1)........Everton

Ben Watson's winner restores
some romance to the FA Cup

Brighton.......(1) 2-3 (1)........Arsenal
Derby...........(0) 0-3 (1).....Blackburn
Huddersfield.(0) 1-1 (0).....Leicester
Hull..............(0) 0-1 (0).....Barnsley
Macclesfield.(0) 0-1 (1).........Wigan
Man Utd.......(1) 4-1 (0)........Fulham
Middlesbro..(0) 2-1 (0).....Aldershot
Norwich........(0) 0-1 (0)........Luton
QPR.............(0) 2-4 (2)....MK Dons
Reading ....(2) 4-0 (0).....Sheff Utd
Stoke...........(0) 0-1 (0).....Man City

Sunday January 27

Brentford......(1) 2-2 (0).......Chelsea
Leeds ....(1) 2-1 (0)....Tottenham
Oldham........(2) 3-2 (1).....Liverpool

Fourth round replay
Tuesday February 12

Leicester......(1) 1-2 (1) Huddersfield

Fourth round replay
Sunday February 17

Chelsea........(0) 4-0 (0)....Brentford

Fifth round
Saturday February 16

Arsenal ....(0) 0-1 (0)....Blackburn
Luton ....(0) 0-3 (2).......Millwall
MK Dons......(0) 1-3 (2).....Barnsley
Oldham........(1) 2-2 (1)......Everton

Sunday February 17

Huddersfield.(0) 1-4 (2).........Wigan
Man City ......(2) 4-0 (0).........Leeds

Monday February 18

Man Utd.......(0) 2-1 (0).......Reading

Tuesday February 26

Middlesbro...(0) 0-2 (0).......Chelsea

Fifth round replay
Tuesday February 26

Everton........(2) 3-1 (0)........Oldham

Sixth round
Saturday March 9

Everton ....(0) 0-3 (3)..........Wigan
Man City ......(3) 5-0 (0)......Barnsley

Sunday March 10

Man Utd.......(2) 2-2 (0).......Chelsea
Millwall ....(0) 0-0 (0)....Blackburn

Sixth round replays
Wednesday March 13

Blackburn ....(0) 0-1 (1)........Millwall

Monday April 1

Chelsea........(0) 1-0 (0)......Man Utd

Semi-finals
Saturday April 13

Millwall ....(0) 0-2 (1)..........Wigan

Sunday April 14

Chelsea........(0) 1-2 (1)......Man City

Final
Saturday May 11

Man City ......(0) 0-1 (0)..........Wigan
SCORERS Wigan: Watson (90)
CARDS Man City: Zabaleta ▼▼ Nastasic ▼
Barry ▼ **Wigan:** Robles ▼

Johnstone's Paint Trophy

Northern Area first round
Tuesday September 4

Accrington ..... 0-2 ....Morecambe
Carlisle .... 1-1 ....Preston
Chesterfield.... 2-1 ....Oldham
Coventry........ 0-0 ....Burton
Port Vale........ 2-0 ....Tranmere
Rochdale .... 2-2 ....Fleetwood
Rotherham..... 0-1 ....York
Scunthorpe .... 1-2 ....Notts Co

Southern Area first round
Tuesday September 4

Bristol R.......... 0-3 ....Yeovil
Crawley .... 3-2 ......Gillingham
Dag & Red ..... 3-2 ....Stevenage
Exeter .... 0-0 ....Aldershot
Northampton.. 1-0 ....MK Dons
Portsmouth.... 2-2 ....Bournemouth
Southend 2-1   AFC W'bledon

Wednesday September 5

Oxford............ 1-0 ....Swindon

Northern Area second round
Tuesday October 9

Doncaster ...... 1-0 ....Chesterfield
Hartlepool...... 0-0 ....Bradford
Morecambe ... 2-4 ....Preston
Rochdale .... 1-1 ....Bury
Shrewsbury ... 1-2 ....Crewe
Walsall........... 2-2 ....Port Vale
York .... 0-4 ....Coventry

Wednesday October 17

Notts Co .... 1-4 ....Sheff Utd

Southern Area second round
Tuesday October 9

Brentford........ 1-0 ....Crawley
Cheltenham.... 2-4 ....Oxford
Leyton Orient . 1-0 ....Barnet
Northampton.. 2-1 ......Colchester
Plymouth .... 2-1 ....Aldershot
Portsmouth.... 1-3 ......Wycombe
Southend .... 2-0 ......Dag & Red

Tuesday October 16

Torquay.......... 2-2 ....Yeovil

Northern Area quarter-finals
Tuesday December 18

Bury .... 3-3 ....Preston
Coventry........ 1-1 ......Sheff Utd
Crewe............. 1-1 ....Doncaster
Port Vale........ 0-2 ....Bradford

Southern Area quarter-finals
Tuesday December 4

Plymouth .... 1-1 ....Oxford
Southend .... 2-1 ....Brentford
Yeovil............. 2-0 ......Wycombe

Wednesday December 5

Northampton.. 0-3 ..Leyton Orient

Northern Area semi-finals
Thursday January 10
Coventry .... 3-2 .... Preston
Tuesday January 15
Crewe .... 4-1 .... Bradford
Southern Area semi-finals
Tuesday January 8
Leyton Orient . 1-0 .... Yeovil
Oxford .... 3-3 .... Southend
Northern Area final
Tuesday February 5
Coventry .... 0-3 .... Crewe
Wednesday February 20
Crewe .... 0-2 .... Coventry
Southern Area Final
Tuesday February 5
Leyton Orient . 0-1 .... Southend
Wednesday February 20
Southend .... 2-2 .. Leyton Orient
Final
Sunday April 7
Crewe .... 2-0 .... Southend

FA Trophy

First round
Friday November 23
Gateshead...... 2-0 ... Macclesfield
Saturday November 24
Alfreton.......... 1-3 Kidderminster
Billericay........ 0-3 .. Cambridge U
Boston Utd..... 1-1 .. Skelmersdale
Bromley .... 1-1 .... Boreham W
Chesham .... 2-1 ....Bath City
Corby............ 3-2 ..... Hayes & Y
Ebbsfleet........ 0-1 ...... Hereford
Forest Green .. 2-1 ......AFC Totton
Gainsborough 2-0 .... Harrogate T
Grimsby......... 0-0 ....Buxton
Guiseley......... 3-1 .... Brackley
Halifax .... 5-2 ...... Altrincham
Hampton & R . 1-1 .....Chelmsford
Hednesford .... 1-2 Solihull Moors
Hyde.............. 1-1 .... Barrow
Kingstonian.... 0-4 ....Dartford
Maidstone...... 2-0 .... Salisbury
Mansfield....... 1-1 .... Matlock
Stafford.......... 0-4 ...... Southport
Stockport....... 6-0 ....Ossett Town
Tamworth ...... 3-1 .... Lincoln
Telford........... 1-0 ...... Nuneaton
Welling........... 2-0 .... Newport Co
Woking .... 7-0 ... Farnborough
Worksop .... 0-1 .... King's Lynn
Wrexham .... 5-0 Rushall Olympic
First round replays
Monday November 26
Boreham W .... 0-2 ....Bromley

Tuesday November 27
Dorchester..... 2-2 ....Luton
Merthyr.......... 1-2 ...... Tonbridge
Wednesday November 28
Buxton .... 0-1 .... Grimsby
Monday December 10
Chelmsford .... 3-2 ..Hampton & R
Second round
Saturday December 15
Bromley .... 1-0 Kidderminster
Cambridge U.. 0-1 ..... Gateshead
Chesham .... 1-5 .... Barrow
Dartford .... 3-0 ...... Tonbridge
Forest Green .. 1-2 Gainsborough
Grimsby......... 4-0 .... Havant & W
Hereford .... 0-3 .....Chelmsford
King's Lynn.... 3-1 .... Telford
Matlock.......... 1-2 ....Luton
Skelmersdale . 2-0 .... Guiseley
Stockport....... 1-1 ...... Southport
Tamworth ...... 1-1 .... Corby
Woking .... 0-1 .... Welling
Wrexham .... 3-2 Solihull Moors
Tuesday December 18
Halifax .... 2-1 ..... Maidstone
Second round replays
Tuesday December 18
Southport ...... 3-1 .... Stockport
Wednesday December 19
Corby............ 2-4 ......Tamworth
Third round
Saturday January 12
Dartford .... 4-2 ....Bromley
Gainsborough 2-1 ...... Tamworth
Halifax .... 3-0 .....Chelmsford
King's Lynn.... 0-2 ...... Southport
Luton .... 2-0 ..Skelmersdale
Sutton Utd..... 0-5 ....Wrexham
Welling........... 1-2 .... Grimsby
Tuesday January 29
Gateshead...... 2-3 .... Barrow
Quarter-finals
Tuesday December 4
Braintree .... 1-2 .... Havant & W
Luton .... 3-1 .....Dorchester
Maidenhead .... 0-1 ..... Sutton Utd
Oxford C .... 1-0 ....Bishop's St.
Saturday January 26
Southport ...... 1-3 ....Wrexham
Tuesday 29 January 29
Grimsby......... 3-0 ....Luton
Wednesday January 30
Halifax .... 1-1 ....Dartford
Tuesday February 5
Gainsborough 2-0 .... Barrow
Quarter-final replay
Wednesday February 6
Dartford .... 3-2 .... Halifax

Semi-finals
Saturday February 16
Grimsby......... 3-0 ....Dartford
Wrexham .... 3-1 Gainsborough
Saturday 23February 23
Dartford .... 0-0 .... Grimsby
Gainsborough 2-1 ....Wrexham
Final
Sunday March 24
Wrexham .... 1-1 .... Grimsby

Scottish Challenge Cup

First round
Saturday July 28
Annan............ 1-0 .....Livingston
Berwick .... 2-2 .. Queen's Park
Clyde .... 0-1 ....Partick
Cowdenbeath . 1-1 ....Alloa
Dumbarton .... 0-1 ...Queen of Sth
East Stirling.... 3-1 .... Ayr
Elgin City .... 5-7 .... Arbroath
Falkirk .... 3-0 ....Stirling
Forfar............. 3-2 ....Dunfermline
Hamilton .... 0-1 ...... Airdrie Utd
Montrose .... 4-2 Inverurie Locos
Morton .... 2-0 ....Albion
Peterhead ...... 1-2 ...... East Fife
Stranraer........ 1-2 .. Stenh'semuir
Wick Academy 2-4 ....Raith
Sunday July 29
Brechin .... 1-2 ....Rangers
Second round
Tuesday August 14
Annan............ 0-3 .. Stenh'semuir
Arbroath......... 3-2 .... Forfar
Cowdenbeath . 3-0 .... East Fife
East Stirling.... 3-0 ...... Airdrie Utd
Morton .... 1-2 ...Queen of Sth
Queen's Park.. 4-5 ....Partick
Raith.............. 5-2 ....Montrose
Tuesday August 21
Falkirk .... 0-1 ....Rangers
Quarter-finals
Sunday September 9
Arbroath......... 1-0 .. Stenh'semuir
East Stirling.... 1-2 ..Cowdenbeath
Partick........... 3-0 ....Raith
Tuesday September 18
Rangers .... 2-2 ...Queen of Sth
Semi-finals
Sunday October 14
Cowdenbeath . 0-1 ....Partick
Queen of Sth.. 2-1 .... Arbroath
Final
Sunday April 7
Queen of Sth.. 1-1 ....Partick
AET. Queen of Sth 6-5 pens

"Gives all the info needed. Great for tips too. Recommended."

APP STORE REVIEW-MARCH 26, 2013

RACING POST MOBILE APP

The Racing Post App. The five-star betting app.

★★★★★* 7,714 REVIEWS

*Five stars from 7,714 reviews - April 2, 2013
18+ Please gamble responsibly www.gambleaware.co.uk

Scottish League Cup

First round
Tuesday July 31
Peterhead .... (0) 0-0 (0) ....Dundee
AET 0-0 after 90 mins, Dundee 4-1 pens
Saturday August 4
Ayr .... (0) 6-1 (0) ....Clyde
Dumbarton .. (1) 2-0 (0) ....Albion
Falkirk .... (0) 2-0 (0) ..... Elgin City
Forfar........... (0) 0-2 (2) ....Partick
Hamilton ...... (0) 2-0 (0) ....Annan
Montrose ..... (2) 2-1 (0)Cowdenbeath
Queen of Sth (1) 5-2 (0) ....Alloa
Queen's Park (0) 3-2 (0) ... Airdrie Utd
AET 2-2 after 90 mins
Raith............ (1) 4-3 (1) .... Berwick
Stenh'semuir (1) 4-0 (0) ....Brechin
Stranraer...... (0) 0-8 (3) ....Livingston
Sunday August 5
East Stirling.. (1) 1-5 (3) .... Morton
Tuesday August 7
Rangers .... (2) 4-0 (0) ...... East Fife

Second round
Wednesday August 22
Morton .... (0) 0-2 (0) .....Aberdeen
AET 0-0 after 90 mins
Tuesday August 28
Dunfermline . (2) 3-0 (0) .....Montrose
Hamilton ...... (0) 1-0 (0) ....Partick
AET 0-0 after 90 mins
Kilmarnock .. (0) 1-2 (2) Stenh'semuir
Livingston .... (1) 3-2 (1) .. Dumbarton
AET 1-1 after 90 mins
Queen of Sth (2) 2-0 (0) .....Hibernian
Ross County (0) 1-4 (2) ....Raith
Wednesday August 29
Arbroath....... (0) 0-2 (1) Inverness CT
Queen's Park (1) 2-1 (1) ....Dundee
St Mirren...... (4) 5-1 (1) .... Ayr

Third round
Tuesday September 25
Celtic .... (2) 4-1 (1) ....Raith
Hearts .... (1) 3-1 (0) ....Livingston
Queen of Sth (0) 0-1 (1) ..Dundee Utd
St Johnstone (2) 4-1 (1) Queen's Park
St Mirren...... (0) 1-0 (0) ......Hamilton
Stenh'semuir (1) 1-1 (1) Inverness CT
AET 1-1 after 90 mins, Inverness 6-5 pens
Wednesday September 26
Dunfermline . (0) 0-1 (0) .....Aberdeen
Rangers .... (0) 2-0 (0) .. Motherwell

Quarter-finals
Tuesday October 30
Aberdeen ..... (1) 2-2 (1) ..... St Mirren
AET 2-2 after 90 mins, St Mirren 4-2 pens
Celtic .... (3) 5-0 (0) St Johnstone
Wednesday October 31
Dundee Utd.. (1) 1-1 (1) .... Hearts
AET 1-1 after 90 mins, Hearts 5-4 pens
Rangers .... (0) 0-3 (1) Inverness CT

Semi-finals
Saturday January 26
Inverness CT (0) 1-1 (0) .... Hearts
AET 1-1 after 90 mins, Hearts 5-4 pens
Sunday January 27
St Mirren...... (1) 3-2 (1) ....Celtic

Final
Sunday March 17
St Mirren...... (1) 3-2 (1) .... Hearts
SCORERS St Mirren: Goncalves (36)
Thompson (46) Newton (66) **Hearts:**
Stevenson (10, 85)

Scottish Cup

First round
Threave Rovers	0-1	Vale of Leithen
Huntly	2-2	.. Wigtown & B
Bon Accord....	1-1	....Edinburgh C
Irvine Meadow	4-0	Gala Fairydean
Edinburgh U...	1-2	..... St Cuthbert
Formartine Utd	3-2	Brora Rangers
Civil Service ...	4-0	........Newton S
Spartans........	0-2	Wick Academy
Glasgow U.....	0-2	.... Selkirk
Clachnacuddin	2-1	...Lossiemouth
Fraserburgh....	4-0	.....Coldstream
Whitehill Welfare	2-4	Inverurie Locos
Buckie Thistle	0-0	...........Rothes
Hermes........	1-4	....Deveronvale
Preston Athletic	0-2	...Nairn County
Turriff Utd.......	6-1	..... Burntisland
Bonnyrigg.....	2-1	.... Girvan
Hawick Royal	2-4	........Golspie S

First round replays
Saturday September 1
Wigtown & B..	0-2	............Huntly
Edinburgh City	4-1	.... Bon Accord
Rothes...........	0-4	Buckie Thistle

Second round
Saturday September 29
Cove Rangers	7-0	........Golspie S
Fraserburgh....	1-2	.... East Stirling
Forres M........	0-1	.........Rangers
Clachnacuddin	4-2	.....Formartine
Civil Service ...	1-2	.... Turriff U
Montrose	1-3	....Edinburgh C
Buckie Thistle	0-0	.............Annan
Berwick	1-0	Wick Academy
Selkirk...........	1-1	Vale of Leithen
Inverurie Locos	4-3	............Huntly
Deveronvale ..	3-2	...... Peterhead
Elgin City	3-1	..... St Cuthbert
Dalbeattie Star	0-5	............Stirling
Queen's Park..	3-0	Irvine Meadow
Stirling U........	0-1	....Bonnyrigg
Clyde.............	3-3	...Nairn County

Second round replays
Saturday October 6
Vale of Leithen	5-1	.... Selkirk
Annan............	1-2	Buckie Thistle
Nairn County..	3-2	............Clyde

Third round
Saturday November 3
Airdrie Utd....	(1) 2-2 (1)	............Raith
Albion	(1) 1-1 (0)	.... Morton
Ayr	(0) 2-1 (1)	Clachnacuddin
Brechin	(0) 2-2 (1)	....Bonnyrigg
Buckie Thistle(0)0-1 (1)		..... Turriff U
Cowdenbeath(3) 8-1 (1)		Vale of Leithen
Dumbarton ..	(2) 4-1 (1)	. East Stirling
Edinburgh C.	(0) 0-2 (1)	Queen of Sth
Elgin City	(2) 5-1 (0)	...... East Fife
Forfar...........	(3) 3-3 (0)	Nairn County
Inverurie Locos(0) 3-3 (2)		...... Arbroath
Partick	(2) 2-1 (0)	Cove Rangers
Rangers	(3) 7-0 (0)	...........Alloa
Stenh'semuir	(0) 1-1 (1)	.... Berwick
Stirling	(0) 0-1 (0)	.Deveronvale
Stranraer......	(0) 1-1 (0)	Queen's Park

Third round replays
Saturday November 10
Arbroath.......	(2) 3-1 (0)	Inverurie Locos
Bonnyrigg	(0) 0-6 (4)	........Brechin

Gary Hooper open the scoring for Celtic in the Scottish Cup final

Nairn County (0) 2-3 (1) .... Forfar
Queen's Park (0) 0-4 (1) . East Stirling
Tuesday November 13
Berwick .... (1) 2-5 (1) Stenh'semuir
Morton .... (0) 3-0 (0) .... Albion
Raith .... (2) 4-3 (2) ... Airdrie Utd
  AET 3-3 after 90 mins
Fourth round
Saturday December 1
Aberdeen ..... (0) 1-1 (0) .. Motherwell
Celtic .... (1) 1-1 (0) ...... Arbroath
Forfar........... (0) 2-1 (1) .... Ayr
Kilmarnock .. (1) 2-1 (0) Queen of Sth
Livingston .... (0) 0-2 (2) ....Dundee
Partick .... (0) 0-1 (1) . Dunfermline
Raith .... (0) 2-1 (0) .Deveronvale
Ross County (0) 3-3 (1) Inverness CT
St Mirren...... (2) 2-0 (0) ....Brechin
Stenh'semuir (0) 0-1 (1) ....Falkirk
Stranraer...... (0) 0-5 (3) ..Dundee Utd
Turriff U .... (1) 1-1 (1) .... Morton
Sunday December 2
Hibernian ..... (0) 1-0 (0) .... Hearts

Rangers .... (1) 3-0 (0) ..... Elgin City
Monday December 17
Cowdenbeath(0) 0-3 (0) St Johnstone
Dumbarton .. (0) 1-3 (2) ......Hamilton

Fourth round replays
Tuesday December 11
Inverness CT (1) 2-1 (1) Ross County
Motherwell... (0) 1-2 (0) ..... Aberdeen
Wednesday December 12
Arbroath....... (0) 0-1 (1) ....Celtic
Monday December 17
Morton .... (2) 6-0 (0) .... Turriff U
Fifth round
Saturday February 2
Dundee Utd.. (2) 3-0 (0) ....Rangers
Dunfermline . (0) 0-2 (0) ......Hamilton
Falkirk .... (1) 4-1 (1) .... Forfar
Kilmarnock .. (0) 2-0 (0) Inverness CT
St Mirren...... (2) 2-0 (0) St Johnstone
Sunday February 3
Dundee .... (1) 5-1 (1) .... Morton

Hibernian ..... (0) 1-0 (0) .....Aberdeen
Raith .... (0) 0-3 (0) ....Celtic
Quarter-finals
Saturday March 2
Hamilton ...... (0) 1-2 (1) ....Falkirk
St Mirren...... (1) 1-2 (2) ....Celtic
Sunday March 3
Dundee .... (1) 1-2 (2) ..Dundee Utd
Kilmarnock .. (1) 2-4 (2) .....Hibernian
Semi-finals
Saturday April 13
Hibernian ..... (0) 4-3 (3) ....Falkirk
  AET 3-3 after 90 mins
Sunday April 14
Dundee Utd.. (2) 3-4 (2) ....Celtic
  AET 3-3 after 90 mins
Final
Sunday May 26
Hibernian ..... (0) 0-3 (2) ....Celtic
SCORERS Celtic: Hooper (8, 31) Ledley
(80) CARDS Hibernian: Claros ☞ Griffiths ☞
Celtic: Brown ☞

Punters should focus on Europe's drop zone

The Premier League title race may be one of the most appetising in recent years but the bookies are confident that our European neighbours are likely to be dining out on more of the same in their domestic campaigns, writes Derek Guldberg.

But that's no reason to stay out of the kitchen and there are still plenty of tasty bets to be had across the continent.

A quick glance at the outright markets in Europe's major leagues shows layers are pretty clear about where they think the power lies in Europe. In Germany, Bayern Munich are a best price of 2-9 to repeat last season's Bundesliga walkover while the Spanish market is predictably dominated by Barcelona and Real Madrid, at 3-4 and 11-8 respectively. In France, Paris Saint-Germain are 1-2 to retain the Ligue 1 title while Juventus are no bigger than 21-20 to land their third Scudetto in a row in Serie A.

And it's hard to pick a fight with these opening prices, because the sides in question are all currently dominating their respective divisions.

Bayern Munich won their league by 25 points last term, losing just once in the Bundesliga, and when they lifted the Champions League trophy and German Cup the Bavarian giants became the first German side to secure a treble.

And they achieved all this in advance of employing ex-Barcelona boss Pep Guardiola, so one-way traffic looks likely for the foreseeable future.

In France, PSG have spent a fortune assembling a highly talented squad that was good enough to hold Barcelona home and away in the quarter-finals of last season's Champions League and the Paris outfit bagged their first Ligue 1 title since 1994.

Manager Carlo Ancelotti has also moved on but it's hard to see another French outfit keeping up with PSG. After all, led by Zlatan Ibrahimovic, they scored more goals and conceded fewer than any other team in Ligue 1 last term.

And although Ancelotti's replacement, Laurent Blanc, was only appointed after a string of bigger names had said "non", Blanc did steer Bordeaux to the title in 2009 and the quarter-finals of the Champions League the following year before a disappointing spell in charge of the French national team.

As usual, Spain's Primera Liga looks to be a straight fight between Barcelona and Real Madrid. Much has been made of the Catalan crew's under performance last term, but the reality is simple enough. Barcelona scored in every league game on their way to their fourth title in five seasons, and equalled the highest points tally ever achieved in La Liga.

Real Madrid may strip fitter for saying adios to Jose Mourinho, having finished 2012-13 trophyless under the Special One, but, either way, it's between these two age-old adversaries once again in Spain.

In Italy, Juve wrapped up the title with four games to go, losing just five games all season in Serie A. That wasn't quite as impressive as 2011-12, when the Bianconeri went undefeated throughout the entire league campaign, but they still finished nine points ahead of their nearest rivals Napoli.

Rafa Benitez has since taken over at the side who finished second to the Old Lady, but she is likely to take all the beating again.

But if this air of predictability makes you feel like giving European football a wide berth, there's plenty of action to be had – it's just that you need to travel to the other end of the table and focus on the relegation markets.

In France, teams promoted from Ligue 2 struggle to find their feet in the top flight with at least one of the clubs going up having been relegated the following season in each of the last five years.

Monaco are surely safe – with the finances of Russian owner Dmitry Rybolovlev at their disposal and the tax advantage that being based in the Principality offers prospective new signings, they are second favourites

Torino could be waving goodbye to Serie A

for the title – which leaves Guingamp and Nantes looking likely to struggle. Both are Evens for the drop.

Bastia and Reims are more interesting though – in three of the last five seasons one of the two remaining promoted sides has only survived for a further 12 months. **Reims** avoided the drop last term despite scoring just one more goal than rock-bottom Brest and, at 2-1, they look vulnerable.

The Italian top flight shares the same dynamics as Le Championnat. In the last five seasons, one team coming up from Serie B has gone back down with immediate effect, and another has followed suit the next year in three of the last five seasons.

That means **Torino** and Sampdoria, promoted two years ago, could be staring down the barrel, and the former are good value to drop out at 7-2. No side drew more games in Serie A last term – a few more defeats and Torino are toast.

In Spain, it's subtly different. Just like France and Italy, one side that's gone up usually goes straight back down again but, importantly, the rest do well once they've established a foothold in Primera Liga.

In the last five seasons, none of the survivors from year one has been relegated the following season, which bodes well for Celta Vigo and Valladolid, despite the cramped prices about either side going down. **Osasuna** look likely to suffer instead.

It's the Bundesliga that really stands out as a graveyard for recently promoted

teams though. They've had a torrid time in recent years. The Bundesliga has a relegation play-off but since 2009-10, seven sides have made the jump from the second tier with only two remaining in the top flight. Four went straight back down, while Kaiserslautern held out for another 12 months before dropping back into Bundesliga 2.

If this trend continues, that leaves us with two clubs to focus on out of this post 2010 pool – Eintracht Frankfurt and **Augsburg**. The former had a super campaign last year – they were never out of the top six – but Augsburg struggled badly, avoiding a relegation play-off by a whisker. Augsburg are 3-1 to finish in the bottom two, and that's a cracking price.

The Dutch Eredivisie went to **Ajax** for the third time in a row, and it's difficult to see beyond them again this season – the Amsterdam outfit lost just two games in the league last season and, at 6-5, they look nailed on for the major honours once again.

The Portuguese title went to the wire though. Porto made it three on the trot, but only pinched the championship from **Benfica** by a solitary point, who also suffered heartbreak in the Portuguese Cup final and at the hands of Chelsea in the Europa League.

If the Eagles can bounce back from that triple whammy, they could prove hard to hold back this time and at around the even-money mark, are worth doubling up with Ajax to exact their revenge.

Almeria

Ground: Juegos Mediterraneos   www.udalmeriasad.com

	2012-13 H	A	Last six seasons at home P	W	D	L	OV	UN	BS	CS
Barcelona			4	0	2	2	3	1	2	0
Real Madrid			4	1	2	1	1	3	3	1
Atl Madrid			4	1	3	0	1	3	2	2
Sociedad			1	0	1	0	1	0	1	0
Valencia			4	0	1	3	4	0	2	0
Malaga			3	2	1	0	0	3	1	2
Betis			2	1	1	0	0	2	1	1
Vallecano			-	-	-	-	-	-	-	-
Sevilla			4	1	0	3	1	3	1	1
Getafe			4	2	0	2	2	2	2	1
Levante			2	1	0	1	1	1	1	0
Ath Bilbao			4	1	1	2	3	1	4	0
Espanyol			4	2	0	2	2	2	1	1
Valladolid			4	2	2	0	1	3	2	2
Granada			-	-	-	-	-	-	-	-
Osasuna			4	4	0	0	2	2	2	2
Celta			1	1	0	0	0	1	0	1
Elche	W	L	2	1	0	1	1	1	1	0
Villarreal	D	L	5	3	2	0	2	3	2	3
Almeria										

Season	Division	Pos	P	W	D	L	F	A	GD	Pts
2012-13	Liga Segunda	3	42	22	8	12	72	50	+22	74
2011-12	Liga Segunda	7	42	18	16	8	63	43	+20	70
2010-11	Primera Liga	20	38	6	12	20	36	70	-34	30

Over/Under 57%/43% 3rd   **Both score** 52%/48% 5th

Athletic Bilbao

Ground: San Mames   www.athletic-club.net

	2012-13 H	A	Last six seasons at home P	W	D	L	OV	UN	BS	CS
Barcelona	D	L	6	0	4	2	3	3	5	0
Real Madrid	L	L	6	1	0	5	4	2	1	1
Atl Madrid	W	L	6	3	0	3	4	2	2	3
Sociedad	L	L	3	2	0	1	2	1	2	1
Valencia	W	L	6	3	0	3	5	1	4	1
Malaga	D	L	5	2	3	0	2	3	3	2
Betis	L	D	4	1	1	2	2	2	2	2
Vallecano	L	D	2	0	1	1	1	1	2	0
Sevilla	W	L	6	4	0	2	3	3	2	3
Getafe	L	L	6	2	2	2	3	3	2	3
Levante	L	L	4	3	0	1	2	2	1	2
Ath Bilbao										
Espanyol	L	D	6	3	2	1	3	3	3	2
Valladolid	W	D	4	4	0	0	0	4	0	4
Granada	W	W	2	1	0	1	0	2	0	1
Osasuna	W	W	6	5	1	0	1	5	1	5
Celta	W	D	1	1	0	0	0	1	0	1
Elche			-	-	-	-	-	-	-	-
Villarreal			5	1	1	3	3	2	4	0
Almeria			4	2	1	1	2	2	3	1

Season	Division	Pos	P	W	D	L	F	A	GD	Pts
2012-13	Primera Liga	12	38	12	9	17	44	65	-21	45
2011-12	Primera Liga	10	38	12	13	13	49	52	-3	49
2010-11	Primera Liga	6	38	18	4	16	59	55	+4	58

Over/Under 55%/45% 6th   **Both score** 55%/45% 9th

Atletico Madrid

Ground: Vicente Calderon   www.clubatleticodemadrid.com

	2012-13 H	A	Last six seasons at home P	W	D	L	OV	UN	BS	CS
Barcelona	L	L	6	3	0	3	6	0	6	0
Real Madrid	L	L	6	0	0	6	5	1	5	0
Atl Madrid										
Sociedad	L	W	3	1	1	1	1	2	1	1
Valencia	D	L	6	3	2	1	2	4	3	3
Malaga	W	D	5	3	0	2	4	1	2	1
Betis	W	W	4	2	0	2	1	3	1	2
Vallecano	W	L	2	2	0	0	2	0	2	0
Sevilla	W	W	6	3	2	1	4	2	3	2
Getafe	W	D	6	4	1	1	2	4	1	4
Levante	W	D	4	4	0	0	3	1	2	2
Ath Bilbao	W	L	6	3	0	3	4	2	3	2
Espanyol	W	W	6	4	0	2	5	1	4	2
Valladolid	W	W	4	3	0	1	4	0	4	0
Granada	W	W	2	2	0	0	1	0	2	0
Osasuna	W	W	6	4	1	1	3	3	2	4
Celta	W	W	1	1	0	0	0	1	0	1
Elche			-	-	-	-	-	-	-	-
Villarreal			5	3	0	2	5	0	4	1
Almeria			4	2	2	0	3	1	3	1

Season	Division	Pos	P	W	D	L	F	A	GD	Pts
2012-13	Primera Liga	3	38	23	7	8	65	31	+34	76
2011-12	Primera Liga	5	38	15	11	12	53	46	+7	56
2010-11	Primera Liga	7	38	17	7	14	62	53	+9	58

Over/Under 45%/55% 16th   **Both score** 37%/63% 18th

Barcelona

Ground: Camp Nou   www.fcbarcelona.cat

	2012-13 H	A	Last six seasons at home P	W	D	L	OV	UN	BS	CS
Barcelona										
Real Madrid	D	L	6	3	1	2	3	3	2	3
Atl Madrid	W	W	6	6	0	0	6	0	3	3
Sociedad	W	L	3	3	0	0	3	0	2	1
Valencia	W	D	6	6	0	0	5	1	2	4
Malaga	W	W	5	5	0	0	5	0	4	1
Betis	W	W	4	4	0	0	4	0	3	1
Vallecano	W	W	2	2	0	0	2	0	1	1
Sevilla	W	W	6	5	1	0	5	1	2	4
Getafe	W	W	6	4	2	0	4	2	4	2
Levante	W	W	4	4	0	0	3	1	2	2
Ath Bilbao	W	D	6	6	0	0	4	2	4	2
Espanyol	W	W	6	4	1	1	3	3	1	5
Valladolid	W	W	4	4	0	0	4	0	2	2
Granada	W	W	2	2	0	0	1	1	1	1
Osasuna	W	W	6	5	0	1	4	1	4	1
Celta	W	D	1	1	0	0	1	0	1	0
Elche			-	-	-	-	-	-	-	-
Villarreal			5	2	2	1	4	1	4	1
Almeria			4	4	0	0	2	2	1	3

Season	Division	Pos	P	W	D	L	F	A	GD	Pts
2012-13	Primera Liga	1	38	32	4	2	115	40	+75	100
2011-12	Primera Liga	2	38	28	7	3	114	29	+85	91
2010-11	Primera Liga	1	38	30	6	2	95	21	+74	96

Over/Under 84%/16% 1st   **Both score** 74%/26% 1st

Betis

Ground: Benito Villamarin   www.realbetisbalompie.es

	2012-13 H	A	P	W	D	L	OV	UN	BS	CS
Barcelona	L	L	4	1	2	1	4	0	4	0
Real Madrid	W	L	4	2	0	2	3	1	3	1
Atl Madrid	L	L	4	0	1	3	2	2	2	0
Sociedad	W	D	3	2	0	1	1	2	1	2
Valencia	W	L	4	2	0	2	3	1	3	1
Malaga	W	L	3	1	1	1	2	1	1	2
Betis										
Vallecano	L	L	4	2	0	2	3	1	2	1
Sevilla	D	L	4	0	3	1	1	3	2	1
Getafe	D	W	4	1	3	0	2	2	3	1
Levante	W	D	4	2	0	2	1	3	0	2
Ath Bilbao	D	W	4	1	1	2	2	2	3	0
Espanyol	W	L	4	1	3	0	1	3	3	1
Valladolid	D	W	4	1	3	0	1	3	3	1
Granada	L	W	3	1	0	2	3	0	3	0
Osasuna	W	D	4	2	1	1	2	2	1	2
Celta	W	W	3	1	2	0	0	3	2	1
Elche			2	0	0	2	2	0	1	0
Villarreal			3	1	1	1	2	1	2	0
Almeria			2	2	0	0	1	1	1	1

Season	Division	Pos	P	W	D	L	F	A	GD	Pts
2012-13	Primera Liga	7	38	16	8	14	57	56	+1	56
2011-12	Primera Liga	13	38	13	8	17	47	56	-9	47
2010-11	Liga Segunda	1	42	25	8	9	85	44	+41	83

Over/Under 55%/45% 6th   **Both score** 50%/50% 12th

Celta Vigo

Ground: Balaidos   www.celtavigo.net

	2012-13 H	A	P	W	D	L	OV	UN	BS	CS
Barcelona	D	L	1	0	1	0	1	0	1	0
Real Madrid	L	L	1	0	0	1	1	0	1	0
Atl Madrid	L	L	1	0	0	1	1	0	1	0
Sociedad	D	L	4	0	3	1	0	4	2	1
Valencia	L	L	1	0	0	1	0	1	0	0
Malaga	L	D	2	0	0	2	1	1	1	0
Betis	L	L	3	0	2	1	0	3	2	0
Vallecano	L	L	4	0	3	1	0	4	0	3
Sevilla	W	L	1	1	0	0	0	1	0	1
Getafe	W	L	1	1	0	0	0	1	0	0
Levante	D	W	3	0	3	0	1	2	3	0
Ath Bilbao	D	L	1	0	1	0	0	1	1	0
Espanyol	W	L	1	1	0	0	0	1	0	1
Valladolid	W	W	3	1	1	1	2	1	3	0
Granada	W	L	2	1	1	0	1	1	2	0
Osasuna	W	L	1	1	0	0	0	1	0	1
Celta										
Elche			5	1	3	1	5	0	5	0
Villarreal			-	-	-	-	-	-	-	-
Almeria			1	1	0	0	1	0	1	0

Season	Division	Pos	P	W	D	L	F	A	GD	Pts
2012-13	Primera Liga	17	38	10	7	21	37	52	-15	37
2011-12	Liga Segunda	2	42	26	7	9	83	37	+46	85
2010-11	Liga Segunda	6	42	17	16	9	62	43	+19	67

Over/Under 39%/61% 19th   **Both score** 55%/45% 9th

Elche

Ground: Estadio Martinez Valero   www.elchecf.es

	2012-13 H	A	P	W	D	L	OV	UN	BS	CS
Barcelona			-	-	-	-	-	-	-	-
Real Madrid			-	-	-	-	-	-	-	-
Atl Madrid			-	-	-	-	-	-	-	-
Sociedad			3	1	1	1	2	1	2	1
Valencia			-	-	-	-	-	-	-	-
Malaga			1	1	0	0	0	1	0	1
Betis			2	1	0	1	1	0	1	0
Vallecano			3	1	2	0	1	2	2	1
Sevilla			-	-	-	-	-	-	-	-
Getafe			-	-	-	-	-	-	-	-
Levante			2	0	1	1	0	2	0	1
Ath Bilbao			-	-	-	-	-	-	-	-
Espanyol			-	-	-	-	-	-	-	-
Valladolid			2	0	1	1	2	0	2	0
Granada			1	0	1	0	0	1	0	1
Osasuna			-	-	-	-	-	-	-	-
Celta			5	2	1	2	1	4	2	2
Elche										
Villarreal	W	W	1	1	0	0	0	1	0	1
Almeria	W	L	2	1	0	1	1	1	1	1

Season	Division	Pos	P	W	D	L	F	A	GD	Pts
2012-13	Liga Segunda	1	42	23	13	6	54	27	+27	82
2011-12	Liga Segunda	11	42	17	6	19	56	58	-2	57
2010-11	Liga Segunda	4	42	18	15	9	55	42	+13	69

Over/Under 36%/64% 20th   **Both score** 40%/60% 19th

Espanyol

Ground: Cornella-El Prat   www.rcdespanyol.com

	2012-13 H	A	P	W	D	L	OV	UN	BS	CS
Barcelona	L	L	6	0	3	3	2	4	4	1
Real Madrid	D	D	6	1	1	4	3	3	2	0
Atl Madrid	L	L	6	2	1	3	4	2	3	1
Sociedad	D	W	3	1	2	0	3	0	3	0
Valencia	D	L	6	3	2	1	4	2	2	3
Malaga	D	L	5	3	1	1	3	2	2	3
Betis	W	L	4	3	0	1	1	3	1	3
Vallecano	W	L	2	2	0	0	2	0	2	0
Sevilla	D	L	6	1	2	3	3	3	4	1
Getafe	L	W	6	3	1	2	1	5	2	2
Levante	W	L	4	3	0	1	3	1	3	1
Ath Bilbao	D	W	6	5	1	0	4	2	4	2
Espanyol										
Valladolid	D	D	4	1	2	1	0	4	1	2
Granada	L	D	2	1	0	1	1	1	0	1
Osasuna	L	W	6	3	0	3	3	3	2	2
Celta	W	L	1	1	0	0	0	1	0	1
Elche			-	-	-	-	-	-	-	-
Villarreal			5	1	3	1	1	4	0	4
Almeria			4	2	1	1	2	2	2	2

Season	Division	Pos	P	W	D	L	F	A	GD	Pts
2012-13	Primera Liga	13	38	11	11	16	43	52	-9	44
2011-12	Primera Liga	14	38	12	10	16	46	56	-10	46
2010-11	Primera Liga	8	38	15	4	19	46	55	-9	49

Over/Under 42%/58% 18th   **Both score** 37%/63% 18th

Getafe

Ground: Coliseum Alfonso Perez   www.getafecf.com

	2012-13 H	A	Last six seasons at home P	W	D	L	OV	UN	BS	CS
Barcelona	L	L	6	2	0	4	2	4	2	2
Real Madrid	W	L	6	2	0	4	4	2	4	0
Atl Madrid	D	L	6	2	3	1	2	4	4	2
Sociedad	W	D	3	2	0	1	2	1	1	1
Valencia	L	L	6	2	1	3	4	2	3	1
Malaga	W	L	5	2	0	3	3	2	3	1
Betis	L	D	4	1	2	1	1	3	2	2
Vallecano	L	L	2	0	0	2	1	1	1	0
Sevilla	D	L	6	4	1	1	3	3	4	1
Getafe										
Levante	L	D	4	2	1	1	2	2	3	0
Ath Bilbao	W	W	6	3	3	0	1	5	2	4
Espanyol	L	W	6	0	3	3	1	5	4	0
Valladolid	W	L	4	3	0	1	2	2	1	2
Granada	D	L	2	1	1	0	1	1	1	1
Osasuna	D	L	6	3	2	1	3	3	3	2
Celta	W	L	1	1	0	0	1	0	1	0
Elche	-	-	-	-	-	-	-	-	-	-
Villarreal			5	2	1	2	3	2	2	3
Almeria			4	2	2	0	3	1	3	1

Season	Division	Pos	P	W	D	L	F	A	GD	Pts
2012-13	Primera Liga	10	38	13	8	17	43	57	-14	47
2011-12	Primera Liga	11	38	12	11	15	40	51	-11	47
2010-11	Primera Liga	16	38	12	8	18	49	60	-11	44

Over/Under 50%/50% 13th   **Both score** 58%/42% 7th

Granada

Ground: Nuevo Los Carmenes   www.granadacf.es

	2012-13 H	A	Last six seasons at home P	W	D	L	OV	UN	BS	CS
Barcelona	L	L	2	0	0	2	1	1	1	0
Real Madrid	W	L	2	1	0	1	1	1	1	1
Atl Madrid	L	L	2	0	1	1	0	2	0	1
Sociedad	D	D	2	1	1	0	1	1	1	1
Valencia	L	L	2	0	0	2	1	1	1	0
Malaga	W	L	2	2	0	0	1	1	1	1
Betis	L	W	3	1	0	2	2	1	1	1
Vallecano	W	L	3	1	1	1	1	2	2	1
Sevilla	D	L	2	0	1	1	1	1	1	0
Getafe	W	D	2	2	0	0	0	2	0	2
Levante	D	L	2	1	1	0	1	1	1	0
Ath Bilbao	L	L	2	0	1	1	2	0	2	0
Espanyol	D	W	2	1	1	0	1	1	1	1
Valladolid	D	L	2	0	1	1	0	2	1	0
Granada										
Osasuna	W	W	2	1	1	0	1	1	1	1
Celta	W	L	2	1	1	0	1	1	2	0
Elche			1	0	1	0	1	0	1	0
Villarreal			1	1	0	0	0	1	0	1
Almeria			-	-	-	-	-	-	-	-

Season	Division	Pos	P	W	D	L	F	A	GD	Pts
2012-13	Primera Liga	15	38	11	9	18	37	54	-17	42
2011-12	Primera Liga	17	38	12	6	20	35	56	-21	42
2010-11	Liga Segunda	5	42	18	14	10	71	47	+24	68

Over/Under 53%/47% 9th   **Both score** 47%/53% 15th

Levante

Ground: Ciutat de Valencia   www.levanteud.com

	2012-13 H	A	Last six seasons at home P	W	D	L	OV	UN	BS	CS
Barcelona	L	L	4	0	1	3	3	1	3	0
Real Madrid	L	L	4	1	1	2	1	3	1	2
Atl Madrid	D	L	4	2	1	1	0	4	1	2
Sociedad	W	D	5	4	0	1	2	3	2	1
Valencia	W	D	4	1	0	3	1	3	1	1
Malaga	L	L	3	2	0	1	3	0	2	1
Betis	D	L	4	3	1	0	2	2	3	1
Vallecano	L	L	4	2	0	2	1	3	1	1
Sevilla	W	D	4	2	0	2	1	3	1	2
Getafe	D	W	4	2	1	1	2	2	2	2
Levante										
Ath Bilbao	W	W	4	2	0	2	4	0	3	1
Espanyol	W	L	4	3	1	0	2	2	3	1
Valladolid	W	L	2	1	0	1	2	0	1	0
Granada	W	D	2	2	0	0	2	0	2	0
Osasuna	L	L	4	2	0	2	2	2	2	0
Celta	L	D	3	1	0	2	1	2	1	1
Elche			2	2	0	0	1	1	1	1
Villarreal			3	1	0	2	2	1	2	1
Almeria			2	2	0	0	1	1	0	2

Season	Division	Pos	P	W	D	L	F	A	GD	Pts
2012-13	Primera Liga	11	38	12	10	16	40	57	-17	46
2011-12	Primera Liga	6	38	16	7	15	54	50	+4	55
2010-11	Primera Liga	14	38	12	9	17	41	52	-11	45

Over/Under 45%/55% 16th   **Both score** 47%/53% 15th

Malaga

Ground: La Rosaleda   www.malagacf.es

	2012-13 H	A	Last six seasons at home P	W	D	L	OV	UN	BS	CS
Barcelona	L	L	5	0	0	5	4	1	4	0
Real Madrid	W	L	5	1	1	3	3	2	3	0
Atl Madrid	D	L	5	1	3	1	2	3	1	3
Sociedad	L	L	4	0	1	3	2	2	3	0
Valencia	W	L	5	2	0	3	2	3	1	2
Malaga										
Betis	W	L	3	1	1	1	1	2	1	1
Vallecano	L	W	2	1	0	1	2	0	2	0
Sevilla	D	W	5	1	2	2	4	1	4	1
Getafe	W	L	5	4	1	0	4	1	4	1
Levante	W	W	3	3	0	0	1	2	1	2
Ath Bilbao	W	D	5	2	3	0	0	5	2	3
Espanyol	L	D	5	4	0	1	3	2	2	2
Valladolid	D	L	3	2	1	0	2	1	2	1
Granada	W	W	2	2	0	0	2	0	0	2
Osasuna	W	D	5	2	2	1	1	4	3	1
Celta	D	W	2	0	2	0	0	2	2	0
Elche			1	1	0	0	0	1	0	1
Villarreal			4	2	1	1	3	1	3	1
Almeria			3	2	0	1	3	0	3	0

Season	Division	Pos	P	W	D	L	F	A	GD	Pts
2012-13	Primera Liga	6	38	16	9	13	53	50	+3	57
2011-12	Primera Liga	4	38	17	7	14	54	53	+1	58
2010-11	Primera Liga	11	38	13	7	18	54	68	-14	46

Over/Under 53%/47% 9th   **Both score** 53%/47% 11th

Osasuna

Ground: El Sadar www.osasuna.es

	2012-13 H	A	Last six seasons at home P	W	D	L	OV	UN	BS	CS
Barcelona	L	L	6	1	2	3	4	2	4	1
Real Madrid	D	L	6	2	2	2	3	3	3	3
Atl Madrid	L	L	6	2	1	3	3	3	2	2
Sociedad	D	D	3	2	1	0	1	2	1	2
Valencia	L	L	6	2	2	2	1	5	2	3
Malaga	D	L	5	1	3	1	3	2	3	2
Betis	D	L	4	1	1	2	1	3	1	1
Vallecano	W	D	2	1	1	0	0	2	0	2
Sevilla	W	L	6	2	3	1	2	4	3	2
Getafe	W	D	6	2	3	1	1	5	1	4
Levante	W	W	4	3	1	0	2	2	2	2
Ath Bilbao	L	L	6	3	1	2	3	3	3	2
Espanyol	L	W	6	4	0	2	2	4	1	4
Valladolid	L	W	4	0	3	1	2	2	3	0
Granada	L	L	2	1	0	1	2	0	2	0
Osasuna										
Celta	W	L	1	1	0	0	0	1	0	1
Elche			-	-	-	-	-	-	-	-
Villarreal			5	3	2	0	2	3	4	1
Almeria			4	3	1	0	2	2	2	2

Season	Division	Pos	P	W	D	L	F	A	GD	Pts
2012-13	Primera Liga	16	38	10	9	19	33	50	-17	39
2011-12	Primera Liga	7	38	13	15	10	44	61	-17	54
2010-11	Primera Liga	9	38	13	8	17	45	46	-1	47

Over/Under 39%/61% 19th **Both score** 37%/63% 18th

Real Madrid

Ground: Santiago Bernabeu www.realmadrid.com

	2012-13 H	A	Last six seasons at home P	W	D	L	OV	UN	BS	CS
Barcelona	W	D	6	2	1	3	4	2	5	0
Real Madrid										
Atl Madrid	W	W	6	5	1	0	3	3	4	2
Sociedad	W	D	3	3	0	0	3	0	3	0
Valencia	D	W	6	3	2	1	1	5	2	4
Malaga	W	L	5	4	1	0	3	2	3	2
Betis	W	L	4	4	0	0	3	1	3	1
Vallecano	W	W	2	2	0	0	1	1	1	1
Sevilla	W	L	6	5	0	1	5	1	4	2
Getafe	W	L	6	5	0	1	4	2	2	3
Levante	W	W	4	4	0	0	3	1	3	1
Ath Bilbao	W	W	6	6	0	0	6	0	5	1
Espanyol	D	D	6	4	2	0	6	0	3	3
Valladolid	W	W	4	4	0	0	3	1	2	2
Granada	W	L	2	2	0	0	2	0	1	1
Osasuna	W	D	6	6	0	0	4	2	4	2
Celta	W	W	1	1	0	0	1	0	1	0
Elche			-	-	-	-	-	-	-	-
Villarreal			5	5	0	0	4	1	3	2
Almeria			4	4	0	0	4	0	3	1

Season	Division	Pos	P	W	D	L	F	A	GD	Pts
2012-13	Primera Liga	2	38	26	7	5	103	42	+61	85
2011-12	Primera Liga	1	38	32	4	2	121	32	+89	100
2010-11	Primera Liga	2	38	29	5	4	102	33	+69	92

Over/Under 71%/29% 2nd **Both score** 63%/37% 3rd

Sevilla

Ground: Ramon Sanchez Pizjuan www.sevillafc.es

	2012-13 H	A	Last six seasons at home P	W	D	L	OV	UN	BS	CS
Barcelona	L	L	6	0	2	4	3	3	4	0
Real Madrid	W	L	6	3	0	3	4	2	4	2
Atl Madrid	L	L	6	3	1	2	3	4	4	1
Sociedad	L	L	3	2	0	1	2	1	2	1
Valencia	W	L	6	5	1	0	3	3	2	4
Malaga	L	D	5	1	2	2	2	3	2	1
Betis	W	D	4	2	0	2	4	0	3	1
Vallecano	W	D	2	2	0	0	2	0	2	0
Sevilla										
Getafe	W	D	6	3	0	3	5	1	4	1
Levante	D	L	4	2	2	0	2	2	3	1
Ath Bilbao	W	L	6	4	1	1	5	1	4	2
Espanyol	W	D	6	2	2	2	3	3	2	4
Valladolid	L	D	4	2	1	1	2	2	3	1
Granada	W	D	2	1	0	1	2	0	1	1
Osasuna	W	L	6	5	1	0	1	5	2	4
Celta	W	L	1	1	0	0	1	0	1	0
Elche			-	-	-	-	-	-	-	-
Villarreal			5	4	0	1	3	2	3	2
Almeria			4	2	0	2	3	1	3	1

Season	Division	Pos	P	W	D	L	F	A	GD	Pts
2012-13	Primera Liga	9	38	14	8	16	58	54	+4	50
2011-12	Primera Liga	9	38	13	11	14	48	47	+1	50
2010-11	Primera Liga	5	38	17	7	14	62	61	+1	58

Over/Under 63%/37% 3rd **Both score** 61%/39% 6th

Sociedad

Ground: Anoeta www.realsociedad.com

	2012-13 H	A	Last six seasons at home P	W	D	L	OV	UN	BS	CS
Barcelona	W	L	3	2	1	0	3	0	3	0
Real Madrid	D	L	3	0	1	2	2	1	2	0
Atl Madrid	L	W	3	0	3	2	1	1	0
Sociedad										
Valencia	W	W	3	2	0	1	2	1	2	1
Malaga	W	W	4	3	0	1	2	2	2	1
Betis	D	L	3	1	2	0	1	2	2	1
Vallecano	W	W	4	3	1	0	2	2	1	3
Sevilla	W	W	3	2	0	1	2	1	2	1
Getafe	D	D	3	0	3	0	0	3	2	1
Levante	D	L	5	1	3	1	2	3	5	0
Ath Bilbao	W	W	3	2	0	1	1	2	2	0
Espanyol	L	D	3	1	1	1	0	3	0	2
Valladolid	W	D	1	1	0	0	1	0	1	0
Granada	D	D	2	1	1	0	1	1	1	1
Osasuna	D	D	3	1	2	0	0	3	0	3
Celta	W	D	4	2	2	0	2	2	3	1
Elche			3	1	1	1	2	1	1
Villarreal			2	1	1	0	0	2	1	1
Almeria			1	1	0	0	1	0	1	1

Season	Division	Pos	P	W	D	L	F	A	GD	Pts
2012-13	Primera Liga	4	38	18	12	8	70	49	+21	66
2011-12	Primera Liga	12	38	12	11	15	46	52	-6	47
2010-11	Primera Liga	15	38	14	3	21	49	66	-17	45

Over/Under 58%/42% 5th **Both score** 63%/37% 3rd

Valencia

Ground: Mestalla www.valenciafc.com

	2012-13 H	A	P	W	D	L	OV	UN	BS	CS
Barcelona	D	L	6	0	4	2	3	3	3	1
Real Madrid	L	D	6	1	0	5	6	0	4	1
Atl Madrid	W	D	6	4	2	0	3	3	4	2
Sociedad	L	L	3	1	0	2	2	1	1	1
Valencia										
Malaga	W	L	5	4	1	0	2	3	3	2
Betis	W	L	4	4	0	0	4	0	2	2
Vallecano	L	W	2	1	0	1	1	1	1	0
Sevilla	W	L	6	3	0	3	3	3	3	2
Getafe	W	W	6	6	0	0	5	1	5	1
Levante	D	L	4	0	4	0	1	3	2	2
Ath Bilbao	W	L	6	4	1	1	3	3	3	2
Espanyol	W	D	6	5	0	1	5	1	5	1
Valladolid	W	D	4	3	0	1	3	1	3	1
Granada	W	W	2	2	0	0	2	0	2	2
Osasuna	W	W	6	5	1	0	5	1	1	5
Celta	W	W	1	1	0	0	1	0	1	0
Elche	-	-	-	-	-	-	-	-	-	-
Villarreal			5	3	1	1	4	1	2	2
Almeria			4	3	0	1	2	2	2	1

Season	Division	Pos	P	W	D	L	F	A	GD	Pts
2012-13	Primera Liga	5	38	19	8	11	67	54	+13	65
2011-12	Primera Liga	3	38	17	10	11	59	44	+15	61
2010-11	Primera Liga	3	38	21	8	9	64	44	+20	71

Over/Under 53%/47% 9th **Both score** 50%/50% 12th

Valladolid

Ground: Nuevo Jose Zorrilla www.realvallodolid.es

	2012-13 H	A	P	W	D	L	OV	UN	BS	CS
Barcelona	L	L	4	0	1	3	2	2	2	0
Real Madrid	L	L	4	1	1	2	2	2	3	1
Atl Madrid	L	L	4	1	1	2	3	1	2	0
Sociedad	D	L	1	0	1	0	1	0	1	0
Valencia	D	L	4	0	1	3	1	3	2	0
Malaga	D	L	3	0	2	1	1	2	3	0
Betis	L	D	4	1	1	2	1	3	1	2
Vallecano	W	W	2	1	1	0	2	0	2	0
Sevilla	D	W	4	2	2	0	2	2	3	1
Getafe	L	L	4	2	2	0	1	3	1	3
Levante	W	L	2	2	0	0	2	0	2	0
Ath Bilbao	D	L	4	1	2	1	4	0	4	0
Espanyol	D	D	4	1	3	0	1	3	3	1
Valladolid										
Granada	W	D	2	1	0	1	1	1	1	1
Osasuna	L	W	4	0	2	2	2	2	2	2
Celta	L	L	3	1	0	2	2	1	2	0
Elche			2	2	0	0	1	1	1	1
Villarreal			3	1	1	0	3	0	2	2
Almeria			4	2	2	0	4	2	2	2

Season	Division	Pos	P	W	D	L	F	A	GD	Pts
2012-13	Primera Liga	14	38	11	10	17	49	58	-9	43
2011-12	Liga Segunda	3	42	23	13	6	69	37	+32	82
2010-11	Liga Segunda	7	42	19	9	14	65	51	+14	66

Over/Under 55%/45% 6th **Both score** 66%/34% 2nd

Vallecano

Ground: Estadio de Vallecano www.rayovallecano.es

	2012-13 H	A	P	W	D	L	OV	UN	BS	CS
Barcelona	L	L	2	0	0	2	2	0	0	0
Real Madrid	L	L	2	0	0	2	0	2	0	0
Atl Madrid	W	L	2	1	0	1	1	1	1	0
Sociedad	L	L	4	2	1	1	3	1	2	1
Valencia	L	W	2	0	0	2	2	0	1	0
Malaga	L	W	2	1	0	1	1	1	1	1
Betis	W	W	4	3	1	0	3	1	1	3
Vallecano										
Sevilla	D	L	2	1	1	0	1	1	1	1
Getafe	W	W	2	2	0	0	1	1	1	1
Levante	W	W	4	1	2	1	2	2	1	3
Ath Bilbao	D	W	2	0	1	1	2	0	2	0
Espanyol	W	L	2	1	0	1	0	2	0	1
Valladolid	L	L	2	1	0	1	2	0	1	1
Granada	W	L	3	2	1	0	0	3	1	2
Osasuna	D	L	2	1	0	1	2	0	1	1
Celta	W	W	4	2	0	2	4	0	4	0
Elche			3	0	0	3	2	1	2	0
Villarreal			1	0	0	1	0	1	0	0
Almeria	-	-	-	-	-	-	-	-	-	-

Season	Division	Pos	P	W	D	L	F	A	GD	Pts
2012-13	Primera Liga	8	38	16	5	17	50	66	-16	53
2011-12	Primera Liga	15	38	13	4	21	53	73	-20	43
2010-11	Liga Segunda	2	42	23	10	9	73	48	+25	79

Over/Under 63%/37% 3rd **Both score** 50%/50% 12th

Villarreal

Ground: El Madrigal www.villarrealcf.es

	2012-13 H	A	P	W	D	L	OV	UN	BS	CS
Barcelona			5	1	1	3	3	2	3	1
Real Madrid			5	1	1	3	3	2	3	0
Atl Madrid			5	3	1	1	3	2	2	2
Sociedad			2	1	0	1	1	1	2	0
Valencia			5	3	2	0	3	2	3	2
Malaga			4	2	1	1	2	2	3	0
Betis			3	2	0	1	1	2	1	1
Vallecano			1	1	0	0	1	0	1	0
Sevilla			5	3	1	1	4	1	4	1
Getafe			5	3	1	1	4	1	4	1
Levante			3	1	0	2	2	1	0	1
Ath Bilbao			5	4	1	0	3	2	3	2
Espanyol			5	3	2	0	1	4	0	5
Valladolid			3	2	0	1	2	1	1	1
Granada			1	1	0	0	1	0	1	0
Osasuna			5	1	3	1	4	1	3	1
Celta			-	-	-	-	-	-	-	-
Elche	L	L	1	0	0	1	1	0	1	0
Villarreal										
Almeria	W	D	5	3	2	0	1	4	3	2

Season	Division	Pos	P	W	D	L	F	A	GD	Pts
2012-13	Liga Segunda	2	42	21	14	7	68	38	+30	77
2011-12	Primera Liga	18	38	9	14	15	39	53	-14	41
2010-11	Primera Liga	4	38	18	8	12	54	44	+10	62

Over/Under 40%/60% 16th **Both score** 48%/52% 10th

Atalanta

Ground: Atleti Azzurri d'Italia   www.atalanta.it

	2012-13 H	A	P	W	D	L	OV	UN	BS	CS
Juventus	L	L	5	0	0	5	3	2	2	0
Napoli	W	L	5	3	1	1	2	3	3	1
Milan	L	W	5	1	1	3	1	4	2	0
Fiorentina	L	L	5	2	1	2	3	2	3	1
Udinese	D	L	5	1	4	0	1	4	1	4
Roma	L	L	5	2	0	3	5	0	4	1
Lazio	L	L	5	3	0	2	2	3	1	2
Catania	D	L	5	1	4	0	0	5	1	4
Inter	W	W	5	2	2	1	2	3	4	0
Parma	W	L	4	3	1	0	2	2	3	1
Cagliari	D	D	5	3	2	0	2	3	2	1
Chievo	D	L	4	1	1	2	1	3	1	1
Bologna	D	L	4	1	2	1	0	4	2	1
Sampdoria	D	W	4	2	1	1	2	2	2	1
Atalanta										
Torino	L	L	4	2	1	1	3	1	3	1
Genoa	L	D	5	2	1	2	0	5	1	2
Sassuolo			1	1	0	0	0	1	0	1
Hellas Verona			-	-	-	-	-	-	-	-
Livorno			3	2	0	1	2	1	1	1

Season	Division	Pos	P	W	D	L	F	A	GD	Pts
2012-13	Serie A	15	38	11	9	18	39	56	-17	40
2011-12	Serie A	12	38	13	13	12	41	43	-2	46
2010-11	Serie B	1	42	22	13	7	61	35	+26	79

Over/Under 45%/55% 12th   **Both score** 55%/45% 5th

Bologna

Ground: Renato Dall'Ara   www.bolognafc.it

	2012-13 H	A	P	W	D	L	OV	UN	BS	CS
Juventus	L	L	5	0	2	3	2	3	3	1
Napoli	L	W	5	2	0	3	2	3	1	1
Milan	L	L	5	0	2	3	4	1	3	1
Fiorentina	W	L	5	2	2	1	2	3	4	1
Udinese	D	D	5	2	1	2	4	1	4	0
Roma	D	W	5	0	2	3	1	4	2	0
Lazio	D	L	5	2	1	2	3	2	3	1
Catania	W	L	5	4	1	0	2	3	2	3
Inter	L	W	5	0	1	4	4	1	4	1
Parma	L	W	4	1	2	1	2	2	2	2
Cagliari	W	L	5	2	1	2	2	3	1	2
Chievo	W	L	6	3	2	1	4	2	3	2
Bologna										
Sampdoria	D	L	4	1	3	0	1	3	3	1
Atalanta	W	D	4	2	1	1	3	1	3	0
Torino	D	L	2	1	1	0	2	0	2	0
Genoa	D	L	5	2	2	1	2	3	3	2
Sassuolo			-	-	-	-	-	-	-	-
Hellas Verona			-	-	-	-	-	-	-	-
Livorno			1	1	0	0	0	1	0	1

Season	Division	Pos	P	W	D	L	F	A	GD	Pts
2012-13	Serie A	13	38	11	11	16	46	52	-6	44
2011-12	Serie A	9	38	13	12	13	41	43	-2	51
2010-11	Serie A	16	38	11	12	15	35	52	-17	42

Over/Under 47%/53% 10th   **Both score** 47%/53% 15th

Cagliari

Ground: Is Arenas   www.cagliaricalcio.net

	2012-13 H	A	P	W	D	L	OV	UN	BS	CS
Juventus	L	D	6	1	0	5	3	3	3	1
Napoli	L	L	6	2	2	2	2	4	2	2
Milan	D	L	6	0	2	4	2	4	3	1
Fiorentina	W	L	6	3	2	1	4	2	4	2
Udinese	L	L	6	1	2	3	2	4	1	2
Roma	L	W	6	2	3	1	5	1	5	0
Lazio	W	L	6	3	0	3	2	4	1	3
Catania	D	D	6	3	3	0	3	3	2	4
Inter	W	D	6	2	1	3	3	3	3	1
Parma	L	L	5	1	3	1	0	5	2	2
Cagliari										
Chievo	L	D	5	2	1	2	2	3	2	2
Bologna	W	L	5	3	2	0	1	4	3	2
Sampdoria	W	W	5	3	1	1	2	3	1	3
Atalanta	D	D	5	3	1	1	1	4	1	3
Torino	W	W	5	2	3	1	0	2	1	1
Genoa	W	L	6	4	0	2	4	2	3	1
Sassuolo			-	-	-	-	-	-	-	-
Hellas Verona			-	-	-	-	-	-	-	-
Livorno			2	1	1	0	1	1	0	2

Season	Division	Pos	P	W	D	L	F	A	GD	Pts
2012-13	Serie A	11	38	12	11	15	43	55	-12	47
2011-12	Serie A	15	38	10	13	15	37	46	-9	43
2010-11	Serie A	14	38	12	9	17	44	51	-7	45

Over/Under 42%/58% 16th   **Both score** 53%/47% 8th

Catania

Ground: Angelo Massimino   www.ilcalciocatania.it

	2012-13 H	A	P	W	D	L	OV	UN	BS	CS
Juventus	L	L	6	0	3	3	2	4	5	0
Napoli	D	L	6	3	3	0	3	3	3	3
Milan	L	L	6	0	2	4	1	5	3	0
Fiorentina	W	L	6	3	1	2	5	1	3	1
Udinese	W	D	6	3	1	2	5	2	2	
Roma	W	D	6	3	0	2	4	5	1	
Lazio	W	L	6	4	1	1	2	4	2	4
Catania										
Inter	L	L	6	2	0	4	4	2	4	0
Parma	W	W	5	3	2	0	2	3	2	3
Cagliari	D	D	6	4	1	1	3	3	3	2
Chievo	W	D	5	2	1	2	3	2	4	1
Bologna	W	L	5	2	1	2	1	4	2	2
Sampdoria	W	D	5	4	0	1	2	3	2	3
Atalanta	W	D	5	3	1	1	2	3	2	3
Torino	D	D	3	1	1	2	1	2	1	1
Genoa	W	W	6	5	1	0	3	3	2	4
Sassuolo			-	-	-	-	-	-	-	-
Hellas Verona			-	-	-	-	-	-	-	-
Livorno			2	1	0	1	0	2	0	1

Season	Division	Pos	P	W	D	L	F	A	GD	Pts
2012-13	Serie A	8	38	15	11	12	50	46	+4	56
2011-12	Serie A	11	38	11	15	12	47	52	-5	48
2010-11	Serie A	13	38	12	10	16	40	52	-12	46

Over/Under 53%/47% 6th   **Both score** 50%/50% 11th

Chievo

Ground: Marc'Antonio Bentegodi   www.chievoverona.tv

	2012-13 H	A	Last six seasons at home P	W	D	L	OV	UN	BS	CS
Juventus	L	L	5	1	2	2	1	4	2	2
Napoli	W	L	5	4	0	1	2	3	2	3
Milan	L	L	5	0	0	5	2	3	2	0
Fiorentina	D	L	5	2	1	2	1	4	2	1
Udinese	D	L	5	0	3	2	2	3	3	1
Roma	W	W	5	1	2	2	1	4	1	2
Lazio	L	W	5	0	0	5	4	1	3	0
Catania	D	L	5	2	3	0	2	3	4	1
Inter	L	L	5	1	1	3	2	3	2	0
Parma	D	L	4	0	3	1	1	3	2	2
Cagliari	D	W	5	2	3	0	1	4	2	3
Chievo										
Bologna	W	L	6	2	3	1	0	6	2	3
Sampdoria	W	L	4	1	2	1	2	2	3	1
Atalanta	W	D	4	1	3	0	0	4	2	2
Torino	D	L	2	0	2	0	0	2	2	0
Genoa	L	W	5	2	1	2	2	3	2	1
Sassuolo			-	-	-	-	-	-	-	-
Hellas Verona			-	-	-	-	-	-	-	-
Livorno			1	1	0	0	0	1	0	1

Season	Division	Pos	P	W	D	L	F	A	GD	Pts
2012-13	Serie A	12	38	12	9	17	37	52	-15	45
2011-12	Serie A	10	38	12	13	13	35	45	-10	49
2010-11	Serie A	11	38	11	13	14	38	40	-2	46

Over/Under 34%/66% 19th   **Both score** 42%/58% 18th

Fiorentina

Ground: Artemio Franchi   www.violachannel.tv

	2012-13 H	A	Last six seasons at home P	W	D	L	OV	UN	BS	CS
Juventus	D	L	6	0	4	2	2	4	3	2
Napoli	D	L	6	2	2	2	2	4	3	1
Milan	D	W	6	0	2	4	3	3	3	1
Fiorentina										
Udinese	W	L	6	5	0	1	6	0	6	0
Roma	L	L	6	2	2	2	4	2	3	1
Lazio	W	W	6	3	1	2	2	4	2	4
Catania	W	L	6	5	1	0	4	2	3	3
Inter	W	L	6	1	3	2	3	3	3	2
Parma	W	D	5	4	0	1	3	2	2	3
Cagliari	W	L	6	5	1	0	3	3	3	3
Chievo	W		5	3	0	2	3	2	3	1
Bologna	W	L	5	3	1	1	1	4	2	3
Sampdoria	D		5	2	3	0	2	3	2	3
Atalanta	W	W	5	3	2	0	4	1	4	1
Torino	W	D	3	3	0	0	2	1	2	1
Genoa	W	W	6	6	0	0	3	3	2	4
Sassuolo			-	-	-	-	-	-	-	-
Hellas Verona			-	-	-	-	-	-	-	-
Livorno			2	2	0	0	1	1	1	1

Season	Division	Pos	P	W	D	L	F	A	GD	Pts
2012-13	Serie A	4	38	21	7	10	72	44	+28	70
2011-12	Serie A	13	38	11	13	14	37	43	-6	46
2010-11	Serie A	9	38	12	15	11	49	44	+5	51

Over/Under 58%/42% 1st   **Both score** 61%/39% 2nd

Genoa

Ground: Luigi Ferraris   www.genoafc.it

	2012-13 H	A	Last six seasons at home P	W	D	L	OV	UN	BS	CS
Juventus	L	D	6	1	2	3	3	3	3	1
Napoli	L	L	6	4	0	2	4	2	4	1
Milan	L	L	6	2	1	3	1	5	1	2
Fiorentina	L	L	6	1	4	1	3	3	4	1
Udinese	W	D	6	5	0	1	4	2	3	3
Roma	L	L	6	4	0	2	5	1	5	0
Lazio	W	W	6	2	1	3	3	3	3	1
Catania	L	L	6	4	1	1	2	4	2	0
Inter	D	D	6	0	2	4	1	5	1	1
Parma	D	D	5	2	3	0	3	2	4	1
Cagliari	W	L	6	5	0	1	3	3	3	2
Chievo	L	W	6	1	1	3	2	3	1	0
Bologna	W	D	5	3	1	1	2	3	3	2
Sampdoria	D	L	5	3	1	1	3	2	3	1
Atalanta	D	W	5	2	3	0	2	3	4	1
Torino	D	D	3	2	1	0	2	1	1	2
Genoa										
Sassuolo			-	-	-	-	-	-	-	-
Hellas Verona			-	-	-	-	-	-	-	-
Livorno			2	0	2	0	0	2	2	0

Season	Division	Pos	P	W	D	L	F	A	GD	Pts
2012-13	Serie A	17	38	8	14	16	38	52	-14	38
2011-12	Serie A	17	38	11	9	18	50	69	-19	42
2010-11	Serie A	10	38	14	9	15	45	47	-2	51

Over/Under 32%/68% 20th   **Both score** 50%/50% 11th

Hellas Verona

Ground: Marc'Antonio Bentegodi   www.hellasverona.it

	2012-13 H	A	Last six seasons at home P	W	D	L	OV	UN	BS	CS
Juventus			-	-	-	-	-	-	-	-
Napoli			-	-	-	-	-	-	-	-
Milan			-	-	-	-	-	-	-	-
Fiorentina			-	-	-	-	-	-	-	-
Udinese			-	-	-	-	-	-	-	-
Roma			-	-	-	-	-	-	-	-
Lazio			-	-	-	-	-	-	-	-
Catania			-	-	-	-	-	-	-	-
Inter			-	-	-	-	-	-	-	-
Parma			-	-	-	-	-	-	-	-
Cagliari			-	-	-	-	-	-	-	-
Chievo			-	-	-	-	-	-	-	-
Bologna			-	-	-	-	-	-	-	-
Sampdoria			1	0	1	0	0	1	1	0
Atalanta			-	-	-	-	-	-	-	-
Torino			1	0	0	1	1	0	1	0
Genoa			-	-	-	-	-	-	-	-
Sassuolo	W	D	2	2	0	0	0	2	0	2
Hellas Verona										
Livorno	D	W	2	1	1	0	0	2	1	1

Season	Division	Pos	P	W	D	L	F	A	GD	Pts
2012-13	Serie B	2	42	23	13	6	67	32	+35	82
2011-12	Serie B	4	42	23	9	10	60	41	+19	78
2010-11	l3	6	34	12	14	8	42	30	+12	50

Over/Under 33%/67% 21st   **Both score** 45%/55% 21st

Inter

Ground: San Siro — www.inter.it

2012-13	H	A	P	W	D	L	OV	UN	BS	CS
Juventus	L	W	6	2	1	3	3	3	3	3
Napoli	W	L	6	5	0	1	6	0	5	0
Milan	D	W	6	4	1	1	3	3	4	1
Fiorentina	W	L	6	6	0	0	2	4	2	4
Udinese	L	L	6	3	1	2	3	3	4	1
Roma	L	D	6	1	4	1	3	3	5	1
Lazio	L	L	6	5	0	1	4	2	3	3
Catania	W	W	6	5	1	0	4	2	4	2
Inter										
Parma	W	L	5	5	0	0	3	2	2	3
Cagliari	D	L	6	4	2	0	4	2	4	2
Chievo	W	W	5	5	0	0	3	2	3	2
Bologna	L	W	5	3	0	2	4	1	2	1
Sampdoria	W	W	5	3	2	0	2	3	2	3
Atalanta	L	L	5	3	1	1	4	1	4	1
Torino	D	W	3	1	2	0	2	1	2	1
Genoa	D	D	6	3	3	0	3	3	4	2
Sassuolo			-	-	-	-	-	-	-	-
Hellas Verona			-	-	-	-	-	-	-	-
Livorno			2	2	0	0	1	1	0	2

Season	Division	Pos	P	W	D	L	F	A	GD	Pts
2012-13	Serie A	9	38	16	6	16	55	57	-2	54
2011-12	Serie A	6	38	17	7	14	58	55	+3	58
2010-11	Serie A	2	38	23	7	8	69	42+27		76

Over/Under 53%/47% 6th **Both score** 55%/45% 5th

Juventus

Ground: Juventus Stadium — www.juventus.com

2012-13	H	A	P	W	D	L	OV	UN	BS	CS
Juventus										
Napoli	W	D	6	4	1	1	3	3	2	4
Milan	W	L	6	4	0	2	3	3	2	2
Fiorentina	W	D	6	3	2	1	2	4	4	2
Udinese	W	W	6	4	0	2	3	3	2	3
Roma	W	L	6	4	1	1	3	3	3	3
Lazio	D	W	6	4	2	0	3	3	4	2
Catania	W	W	6	2	3	1	3	3	5	1
Inter	L	W	6	3	2	1	2	4	4	2
Parma	W	D	5	3	0	2	4	1	3	2
Cagliari	D	W	6	2	3	1	2	4	5	1
Chievo	W	W	5	2	3	0	2	3	3	2
Bologna	W	W	5	2	2	1	2	3	4	0
Sampdoria	L	L	5	1	3	1	3	2	4	1
Atalanta	W	W	5	4	1	0	4	1	3	2
Torino	W	W	3	2	1	0	1	2	0	3
Genoa	D	W	6	4	2	0	4	2	5	1
Sassuolo			-	-	-	-	-	-	-	-
Hellas Verona			-	-	-	-	-	-	-	-
Livorno			2	2	0	0	1	1	1	1

Season	Division	Pos	P	W	D	L	F	A	GD	Pts
2012-13	Serie A	1	38	27	6	5	71	24+47		87
2011-12	Serie A	1	38	23	15	0	68	20+48		84
2010-11	Serie A	7	38	15	13	10	57	47+10		58

Over/Under 45%/55% 12th **Both score** 45%/55% 17th

Lazio

Ground: Olimpico — www.sslazio.it

2012-13	H	A	P	W	D	L	OV	UN	BS	CS
Juventus	L	D	6	0	1	5	1	5	2	0
Napoli	D	L	6	3	2	1	2	4	4	1
Milan	W	L	6	2	1	3	4	2	4	1
Fiorentina	L	L	6	3	1	2	1	5	1	3
Udinese	W	L	6	3	1	2	5	1	4	1
Roma	W	D	6	4	0	2	5	1	5	0
Lazio										
Catania	W	L	6	3	2	1	1	5	3	2
Inter	W	W	6	3	1	2	3	3	3	1
Parma	W	D	5	4	0	1	2	3	2	3
Cagliari	W	L	6	4	0	2	4	2	4	1
Chievo	L	W	5	0	3	2	1	4	2	1
Bologna	W	D	5	3	1	1	3	2	2	3
Sampdoria	W	W	5	4	1	0	1	4	2	3
Atalanta	W	W	5	4	0	1	4	0	4	0
Torino	D	L	3	0	3	0	1	2	3	0
Genoa	L	L	6	2	1	3	3	3	4	1
Sassuolo			-	-	-	-	-	-	-	-
Hellas Verona			-	-	-	-	-	-	-	-
Livorno			2	2	0	0	1	1	1	1

Season	Division	Pos	P	W	D	L	F	A	GD	Pts
2012-13	Serie A	7	38	18	7	13	51	42	+9	61
2011-12	Serie A	4	38	18	8	12	56	47	+9	62
2010-11	Serie A	5	38	20	6	12	55	39+16		66

Over/Under 47%/53% 10th **Both score** 34%/66% 20th

Livorno

Ground: Stadio Armando Picchi — www.livornocalcio.it

2012-13	H	A	P	W	D	L	OV	UN	BS	CS
Juventus			2	0	1	1	1	1	2	0
Napoli			2	0	0	2	1	1	1	0
Milan			2	0	1	1	1	1	1	1
Fiorentina			2	0	0	2	1	1	0	0
Udinese			2	0	1	1	0	2	0	1
Roma			2	0	2	0	1	1	2	0
Lazio			2	0	0	2	1	1	1	0
Catania			2	2	0	0	1	1	1	1
Inter			2	0	1	1	1	1	1	0
Parma			3	1	2	0	2	1	3	0
Cagliari			2	0	1	1	1	1	1	1
Chievo			1	0	0	1	0	1	0	0
Bologna			1	0	0	1	0	1	0	0
Sampdoria			3	2	1	0	2	1	2	1
Atalanta			3	2	1	0	2	2	2	1
Torino			3	1	0	2	1	2	1	0
Genoa			2	1	1	0	1	1	2	0
Sassuolo	W	L	4	2	1	1	3	1	2	1
Hellas Verona	L	D	2	0	0	2	0	2	0	0
Livorno										

Season	Division	Pos	P	W	D	L	F	A	GD	Pts
2012-13	Serie B	3	42	23	11	8	77	47+30		80
2011-12	Serie B	17	42	12	12	18	49	49	0	48
2010-11	Serie B	7	42	15	14	13	49	46	+3	51

Over/Under 60%/40% 1st **Both score** 60%/40% 3rd

Milan
Ground: San Siro www.acmilan.com

	2012-13 H	2012-13 A	P	W	D	L	OV	UN	BS	CS
Juventus	W	L	6	2	3	1	2	4	3	3
Napoli	D	D	6	3	3	0	2	4	3	3
Milan										
Fiorentina	L	D	6	3	1	2	2	4	3	3
Udinese	W	L	6	4	2	0	5	1	6	0
Roma	D	L	6	2	1	3	3	3	3	1
Lazio	W	L	6	2	4	0	3	3	4	2
Catania	W	W	6	3	3	0	3	3	4	2
Inter	L	D	6	3	0	3	3	3	1	2
Parma	W	D	5	4	1	0	3	2	3	2
Cagliari	W	D	6	6	0	0	4	2	3	3
Chievo	W	W	5	5	0	0	3	2	2	3
Bologna	W	W	5	3	1	1	2	3	3	2
Sampdoria	L	D	5	3	0	2	4	1	1	3
Atalanta	L	W	5	3	0	2	3	2	2	2
Torino	W	W	3	2	1	0	1	2	1	2
Genoa	W	W	6	5	1	0	1	5	2	4
Sassuolo			-	-	-	-	-	-	-	-
Hellas Verona			-	-	-	-	-	-	-	-
Livorno			2	0	2	0	0	2	2	0

Season	Division	Pos	P	W	D	L	F	A	GD	Pts
2012-13	Serie A	3	38	21	9	8	67	39	+28	72
2011-12	Serie A	2	38	24	8	6	74	33	+41	80
2010-11	Serie A	1	38	24	10	4	65	24	+41	82

Over/Under 53%/47% 6th   **Both score** 58%/42% 3rd

Napoli
Ground: San Paolo www.ssnapoli.it

	2012-13 H	2012-13 A	P	W	D	L	OV	UN	BS	CS
Juventus	D	L	6	4	2	0	5	1	5	1
Napoli										
Milan	D	D	6	2	3	1	5	1	5	1
Fiorentina	W	D	6	3	2	1	3	3	3	3
Udinese	W	D	6	3	2	1	4	2	4	2
Roma	W	L	6	2	1	3	4	2	3	1
Lazio	W	D	6	2	3	1	3	3	2	3
Catania	W	D	6	5	1	0	1	5	1	5
Inter	W	L	6	4	2	0	1	5	2	4
Parma	W	W	5	3	0	2	3	2	3	2
Cagliari	W	W	6	3	2	1	4	2	4	1
Chievo	W	L	5	4	0	1	2	3	1	4
Bologna	L	W	5	2	2	1	3	2	5	0
Sampdoria	D	W	5	4	1	0	1	4	0	5
Atalanta	W	L	5	3	1	1	2	3	2	3
Torino	D	W	3	0	2	1	1	2	3	0
Genoa	W	W	6	3	1	2	2	4	2	3
Sassuolo			-	-	-	-	-	-	-	-
Hellas Verona			-	-	-	-	-	-	-	-
Livorno			2	2	0	0	1	1	1	1

Season	Division	Pos	P	W	D	L	F	A	GD	Pts
2012-13	Serie A	2	38	23	9	6	73	36	+37	78
2011-12	Serie A	5	38	16	13	9	66	46	+20	61
2010-11	Serie A	3	38	21	7	10	59	39	+20	70

Over/Under 55%/45% 4th   **Both score** 55%/45% 5th

Parma

Ground: Ennio Tardini www.fcparma.com

	2012-13 H	2012-13 A	P	W	D	L	OV	UN	BS	CS
Juventus	D	L	5	1	3	1	2	3	3	2
Napoli	L	L	5	0	1	4	4	1	5	0
Milan	D	L	5	1	2	2	0	5	1	2
Fiorentina	D	L	5	0	4	1	2	3	5	0
Udinese	L	D	5	3	1	1	2	3	1	3
Roma	W	L	5	1	1	3	3	2	2	1
Lazio	D	L	5	1	3	1	2	3	3	1
Catania	L	L	5	2	2	1	4	1	4	1
Inter	W	L	5	3	1	1	4	2	2	2
Parma										
Cagliari	W	W	5	2	1	2	3	2	3	1
Chievo	W	D	4	3	1	0	1	3	1	3
Bologna	L	W	4	2	1	1	3	1	2	2
Sampdoria	W	L	4	3	0	1	2	2	2	2
Atalanta	W	L	4	2	0	2	2	2	2	2
Torino	W	W	2	2	0	0	1	1	1	1
Genoa	D	D	5	2	2	1	2	3	3	2
Sassuolo			1	0	1	0	0	1	1	0
Hellas Verona			-	-	-	-	-	-	-	-
Livorno			3	2	1	0	2	1	2	1

Season	Division	Pos	P	W	D	L	F	A	GD	Pts
2012-13	Serie A	10	38	13	10	15	45	46	-1	49
2011-12	Serie A	8	38	15	11	12	54	53	+1	56
2010-11	Serie A	12	38	11	13	14	39	47	-8	46

Over/Under 45%/55% 12th   **Both score** 53%/47% 8th

Roma

Ground: Olimpico www.asroma.it

	2012-13 H	2012-13 A	P	W	D	L	OV	UN	BS	CS
Juventus	W	L	6	1	2	3	3	3	4	1
Napoli	W	L	6	2	3	1	4	2	5	0
Milan	W	D	6	2	3	1	4	2	4	2
Fiorentina	W	W	6	5	0	1	4	2	4	2
Udinese	L	D	6	4	1	1	4	2	5	1
Roma										
Lazio	D	L	6	4	1	1	2	4	3	3
Catania	D	L	6	4	2	0	4	2	4	2
Inter	D	W	6	3	1	2	4	2	3	2
Parma	W	L	5	4	1	0	2	3	1	4
Cagliari	L	W	6	4	0	2	5	1	4	2
Chievo	L	L	5	3	1	1	0	5	0	4
Bologna	L	D	5	2	2	1	4	1	5	0
Sampdoria	D	W	5	3	1	1	2	3	3	2
Atalanta	W	W	5	5	0	0	3	2	3	2
Torino	W	W	3	3	0	0	2	1	2	1
Genoa	W	W	6	6	0	0	5	1	3	3
Sassuolo			-	-	-	-	-	-	-	-
Hellas Verona			-	-	-	-	-	-	-	-
Livorno			2	0	1	1	0	2	1	0

Season	Division	Pos	P	W	D	L	F	A	GD	Pts
2012-13	Serie A	6	38	18	8	12	71	56	+15	62
2011-12	Serie A	7	38	16	8	14	60	54	+6	56
2010-11	Serie A	6	38	18	9	11	59	52	+7	63

Over/Under 58%/42% 1st   **Both score** 66%/34% 1st

Sampdoria

Ground: Luigi Ferraris   www.sampdoria.it

	2012-13 H	2012-13 A	P	W	D	L	OV	UN	BS	CS
Juventus	W	W	5	2	3	0	2	3	2	3
Napoli	L	D	5	2	1	2	2	3	2	2
Milan	D	W	5	2	2	1	3	2	3	1
Fiorentina	L	D	5	2	1	2	3	2	2	1
Udinese	L	L	5	2	2	1	3	2	2	2
Roma	W	D	5	2	2	1	4	1	3	1
Lazio	L	L	5	3	1	1	2	3	2	2
Catania	D	L	5	2	3	0	2	3	3	2
Inter	L	L	5	1	2	2	0	5	2	1
Parma	W	L	4	2	1	1	1	3	1	2
Cagliari	L	L	5	0	3	2	1	4	3	0
Chievo	W	L	4	2	2	0	1	3	2	2
Bologna	W	D	4	4	0	0	2	2	2	2
Sampdoria										
Atalanta	L	D	4	3	0	1	2	2	1	3
Torino	D	D	4	1	2	1	2	2	3	1
Genoa	W	D	5	2	1	2	1	4	1	2
Sassuolo			1	0	1	0	0	1	1	0
Hellas Verona			1	1	0	0	0	1	0	1
Livorno			3	2	1	0	0	3	1	2

Season	Division	Pos	P	W	D	L	F	A	GD	Pts
2012-13	Serie A	14	38	11	10	17	43	51	-8	42
2011-12	Serie B	6	42	17	16	9	53	34	+19	67
2010-11	Serie A	18	38	8	12	18	33	49	-16	36

Over/Under 45%/55% 12th   **Both score** 53%/47% 8th

Sassuolo

Ground: Alberto Braglia   www.sassuolocalcio.it

	2012-13 H	2012-13 A	P	W	D	L	OV	UN	BS	CS
Juventus			-	-	-	-	-	-	-	-
Napoli			-	-	-	-	-	-	-	-
Milan			-	-	-	-	-	-	-	-
Fiorentina			-	-	-	-	-	-	-	-
Udinese			-	-	-	-	-	-	-	-
Roma			-	-	-	-	-	-	-	-
Lazio			-	-	-	-	-	-	-	-
Catania			-	-	-	-	-	-	-	-
Inter			-	-	-	-	-	-	-	-
Parma			1	0	1	0	1	0	1	0
Cagliari			-	-	-	-	-	-	-	-
Chievo			-	-	-	-	-	-	-	-
Bologna			-	-	-	-	-	-	-	-
Sampdoria			1	0	1	0	0	1	0	1
Atalanta			1	0	0	1	0	1	0	0
Torino			3	0	1	2	2	1	2	1
Genoa			-	-	-	-	-	-	-	-
Sassuolo										
Hellas Verona	D	L	2	1	1	0	0	2	1	1
Livorno	W	L	4	3	0	1	2	2	2	2

Season	Division	Pos	P	W	D	L	F	A	GD	Pts
2012-13	Serie B	1	42	25	10	7	78	40	+38	85
2011-12	Serie B	3	42	22	14	6	57	33	+24	80
2010-11	Serie B	16	42	13	12	17	42	46	-4	51

Over/Under 50%/50% 6th   **Both score** 55%/45% 10th

Torino

Ground: Olimpico di Torino   www.torino.it

	2012-13 H	2012-13 A	P	W	D	L	OV	UN	BS	CS
Juventus	L	L	3	0	0	3	0	3	0	0
Napoli	L	D	3	2	0	1	2	1	2	1
Milan	L	L	3	0	1	2	2	1	2	0
Fiorentina	D	L	3	0	1	2	2	1	2	0
Udinese	D	L	3	1	1	1	0	3	0	2
Roma	L	L	3	0	1	2	1	2	1	1
Lazio	W	D	3	1	1	1	1	2	1	2
Catania	D	D	3	1	2	0	2	1	3	0
Inter	L	D	3	0	0	3	1	2	1	0
Parma		L	2	0	1	1	2	0	2	0
Cagliari	L	L	3	1	0	2	0	3	0	1
Chievo	W	D	2	1	1	0	0	2	1	1
Bologna	W	D	2	1	1	0	0	2	1	1
Sampdoria	D	D	4	2	1	1	2	2	2	2
Atalanta	W	W	4	3	0	1	3	1	3	1
Torino										
Genoa	D	D	3	0	2	1	1	2	2	1
Sassuolo			3	1	0	2	2	1	1	1
Hellas Verona			1	0	0	1	1	0	1	0
Livorno			3	1	0	2	1	2	1	1

Season	Division	Pos	P	W	D	L	F	A	GD	Pts
2012-13	Serie A	16	38	8	16	14	46	55	-9	39
2011-12	Serie B	2	42	24	11	7	57	28	+29	83
2010-11	Serie B	8	42	15	13	14	49	48	+1	58

Over/Under 42%/58% 16th   **Both score** 50%/50% 11th

Udinese

Ground: Friuli   www.udinese.it

	2012-13 H	2012-13 A	P	W	D	L	OV	UN	BS	CS
Juventus	L	L	6	2	1	3	5	1	3	2
Napoli	D	L	6	2	3	1	4	2	3	2
Milan	W	L	6	3	1	2	3	3	3	2
Fiorentina	W	L	6	5	0	1	4	2	4	1
Udinese										
Roma	D	W	6	3	1	2	4	2	5	1
Lazio	W	L	6	3	0	3	3	4	2	2
Catania	D	L	6	4	2	0	4	2	5	1
Inter	W	W	6	2	1	3	4	2	3	2
Parma	W	D	5	2	2	1	4	1	4	0
Cagliari	W	W	6	3	2	1	3	3	4	1
Chievo	W	D	5	3	1	1	2	3	2	2
Bologna	D	D	5	2	3	0	0	5	2	3
Sampdoria	W	W	5	3	1	1	3	2	4	1
Atalanta	W	D	5	3	1	1	2	3	2	3
Torino	W	D	3	3	0	0	1	2	1	2
Genoa	D	L	6	2	2	2	2	4	2	3
Sassuolo			-	-	-	-	-	-	-	-
Hellas Verona			-	-	-	-	-	-	-	-
Livorno			2	2	0	0	0	2	0	2

Season	Division	Pos	P	W	D	L	F	A	GD	Pts
2012-13	Serie A	5	38	18	12	8	59	45	+14	66
2011-12	Serie A	3	38	18	10	10	52	35	+17	64
2010-11	Serie A	4	38	20	6	12	65	43	+22	66

Over/Under 58%/42% 1st   **Both score** 58%/42% 3rd

Ajaccio

Ground: Stade Francois Coty   www.ac-ajaccio.com

	2012-13 H	A	Last six seasons at home P	W	D	L	OV	UN	BS	CS
Paris SG	D	D	2	0	1	1	1	1	1	1
Marseille	L	D	2	1	0	1	0	2	0	1
Lyon	W	L	2	1	1	0	1	1	2	0
Nice	L	W	2	0	1	1	0	2	1	0
St Etienne	D	L	2	0	2	0	0	2	1	1
Lille	L	L	2	0	0	2	2	0	2	0
Bordeaux	W	D	2	1	0	1	0	2	0	1
Lorient	W	D	2	1	1	0	0	2	1	1
Montpellier	W	L	4	2	0	2	4	0	3	0
Toulouse	L	W	2	0	0	2	1	1	1	0
Valenciennes	D	L	2	1	1	0	1	1	2	0
Bastia	D	L	4	0	2	2	1	3	2	1
Rennes	L	D	2	1	0	1	1	1	1	1
Reims	W	D	4	3	1	0	2	2	1	3
Sochaux	L	D	2	1	0	1	1	1	1	0
Evian TG	W	D	3	2	1	0	0	3	1	2
Ajaccio										
Monaco			-	-	-	-	-	-	-	-
Guingamp			3	1	1	1	1	2	2	0
Nantes			3	2	0	1	3	0	3	0

Season	Division	Pos	P	W	D	L	F	A	GD	Pts
2012-13	Ligue 1	17	38	9	15	14	39	51	-12	40
2011-12	Ligue 1	16	38	9	14	15	40	61	-21	41
2010-11	Ligue 2	2	38	17	13	8	45	37	+8	64

Over/Under 32%/68% 18th   **Both score** 45%/55% 12th

Bastia

Ground: Stade Armand Cesari   www.sc-bastia.net

	2012-13 H	A	Last six seasons at home P	W	D	L	OV	UN	BS	CS
Paris SG	L	L	1	0	0	1	1	0	0	0
Marseille	L	L	1	0	0	1	1	0	1	0
Lyon	W	L	1	1	0	0	1	0	1	0
Nice	L	D	1	0	0	1	0	1	0	0
St Etienne	L	L	1	0	0	1	1	0	0	0
Lille	L	D	1	0	0	1	1	0	1	0
Bordeaux	W	L	1	1	0	0	1	0	1	0
Lorient	W	L	1	1	0	0	1	0	1	0
Montpellier	W	L	3	2	1	0	1	2	2	1
Toulouse	D	D	1	0	1	0	0	1	0	1
Valenciennes	L	W	1	0	0	1	1	0	1	0
Bastia										
Rennes	L	L	1	0	0	1	0	1	0	0
Reims	W	W	4	2	1	1	3	1	3	1
Sochaux	D	W	1	0	1	0	0	1	0	1
Evian TG	D	L	1	0	1	0	0	1	0	1
Ajaccio	W	D	4	3	0	1	1	3	1	2
Monaco			1	0	1	0	0	1	1	0
Guingamp			4	2	1	1	2	2	2	1
Nantes			3	1	1	1	2	2	2	0

Season	Division	Pos	P	W	D	L	F	A	GD	Pts
2012-13	Ligue 1	12	38	13	8	17	50	66	-16	47
2011-12	Ligue 2	1	38	21	8	9	61	36	+25	71
2010-11	National	1	40	27	10	3	81	24	+57	91

Over/Under 71%/29% 1st   **Both score** 53%/47% 8th

Bordeaux

Ground: Stade Chaban-Delmas   www.girondins.com

	2012-13 H	A	Last six seasons at home P	W	D	L	OV	UN	BS	CS
Paris SG	L	D	6	4	1	1	2	4	1	4
Marseille	W	L	6	2	4	0	2	4	5	1
Lyon	L	W	6	3	1	2	3	3	2	3
Nice	D	W	6	3	2	1	3	3	3	3
St Etienne	D	D	6	3	2	1	2	4	3	3
Lille	D	L	6	1	5	0	2	4	5	1
Bordeaux										
Lorient	D	W	6	4	2	0	2	4	3	3
Montpellier	W	L	4	2	2	0	2	2	3	1
Toulouse	W	L	6	5	0	1	3	3	3	3
Valenciennes	W	D	6	4	1	1	3		4	1
Bastia	W	L	1	1	0	0	0	1	0	1
Rennes	W	W	6	4	2	0	1	5	1	5
Reims	D	D	1	0	1	0	0	1	0	1
Sochaux	D	D	6	4	1	1	3	3	1	4
Evian TG	W	W	2	1	1	0	1	1	1	1
Ajaccio	D	L	2	0	2	0	1	1	2	0
Monaco			4	3	0	1	1	3	1	2
Guingamp			-	-	-	-	-	-	-	-
Nantes			1	1	0	0	0	1	0	1

Season	Division	Pos	P	W	D	L	F	A	GD	Pts
2012-13	Ligue 1	7	38	13	16	9	40	34	+6	55
2011-12	Ligue 1	5	38	16	13	9	53	41	+12	61
2010-11	Ligue 1	7	38	12	15	11	43	42	+1	51

Over/Under 29%/71% 20th   **Both score** 37%/63% 18th

Evian TG

Ground: Parc des Sports   www.etgfc.com

	2012-13 H	A	Last six seasons at home P	W	D	L	OV	UN	BS	CS
Paris SG	L	L	2	0	1	1	1	1	1	0
Marseille	D	L	2	1	1	0	0	2	1	1
Lyon	D	L	2	0	1	1	1	1	2	0
Nice	W	L	2	2	0	0	1	1	0	2
St Etienne	D	L	2	0	1	1	2	0	2	0
Lille	L	W	2	0	0	2	1	1	0	0
Bordeaux	L	L	2	0	1	1	1	1	1	1
Lorient	D	L	2	1	1	0	1	1	2	0
Montpellier	L	W	2	1	0	1	1	1	1	0
Toulouse	L	D	2	1	0	1	2	0	1	0
Valenciennes	W	D	2	2	0	0	1	1	1	1
Bastia	W	D	1	1	0	0	1	0	0	1
Evian TG										
Ajaccio	D	L	3	1	2	0	1	2	3	0
Monaco			-	-	-	-	-	-	-	-
Guingamp			-	-	-	-	-	-	-	-
Nantes			1	1	0	0	1	0	0	1

Season	Division	Pos	P	W	D	L	F	A	GD	Pts
2012-13	Ligue 1	16	38	10	10	18	46	53	-7	40
2011-12	Ligue 1	9	38	13	11	14	54	55	-1	50
2010-11	Ligue 2	1	38	18	13	7	63	41	+22	67

Over/Under 47%/53% 7th   **Both score** 50%/50% 10th

Guingamp

Ground: Stade du Roudourou www.eaguingamp.com

	2012-13 H	A	P	W	D	L	OV	UN	BS	CS
Paris SG	-	-	-	-	-	-	-	-	-	-
Marseille	-	-	-	-	-	-	-	-	-	-
Lyon		-	-	-	-	-	-	-	-	-
Nice		-	-	-	-	-	-	-	-	-
St Etienne		-	-	-	-	-	-	-	-	-
Lille										
Bordeaux		-	-	-	-	-	-	-	-	-
Lorient		-	-	-	-	-	-	-	-	-
Montpellier			2	0	0	2	0	2	0	0
Toulouse		-	-	-	-	-	-	-	-	-
Valenciennes		-	-	-	-	-	-	-	-	-
Bastia			4	1	2	1	1	3	3	0
Rennes		-	-	-	-	-	-	-	-	-
Reims			3	1	0	2	2	1	2	0
Sochaux		-	-	-	-	-	-	-	-	-
Evian TG		-	-	-	-	-	-	-	-	-
Ajaccio			3	1	2	0	1	2	2	1
Monaco	L	D	2	1	0	1	2	0	1	
Guingamp										
Nantes	W	D	4	3	1	0	1	3	1	3

Season	Division	Pos	P	W	D	L	F	A	GD	Pts
2012-13	Ligue 2	2	38	20	10	8	63	38	+25	70
2011-12	Ligue 2	7	38	15	10	13	46	43	+3	55
2010-11	National	3	40	23	11	6	87	36	+51	80

Over/Under 50%/50% 4th   **Both score** 53%/47% 10th

Lille

Ground: Grand Stade Lille Metropole www.losc.fr

	2012-13 H	A	P	W	D	L	OV	UN	BS	CS
Paris SG	L	L	6	2	3	1	3	3	3	3
Marseille	D	L	6	2	2	2	4	2	5	1
Lyon	D	W	6	3	2	1	2	4	4	1
Nice	L	D	6	0	5	1	1	5	5	0
St Etienne	D	W	6	4	2	0	4	2	2	4
Lille										
Bordeaux	W	D	6	3	2	1	3	3	5	1
Lorient	W	L	6	2	3	1	3	3	4	2
Montpellier	W	D	4	3	0	1	3	1	3	0
Toulouse	W	L	6	4	2	0	2	4	4	2
Valenciennes	W	W	6	6	0	0	5	1	2	4
Bastia	D	W	1	0	1	0	0	1	0	1
Rennes	W	L	6	5	1	0	2	4	2	4
Reims	W	D	1	1	0	0	1	0	0	1
Sochaux	D	D	6	3	3	0	3	3	4	2
Evian TG	L	W	2	0	1	1	1	1	2	0
Ajaccio	W	W	2	2	0	0	1	1	1	1
Monaco			4	3	0	1	3	1	2	1
Guingamp			-	-	-	-	-	-	-	-
Nantes			1	1	0	0	0	1	0	1

Season	Division	Pos	P	W	D	L	F	A	GD	Pts
2012-13	Ligue 1	6	38	16	14	8	59	40	+19	62
2011-12	Ligue 1	3	38	21	11	6	72	39	+33	74
2010-11	Ligue 1	1	38	21	13	4	68	36	+32	76

Over/Under 45%/55% 14th   **Both score** 61%/39% 2nd

Lorient

Ground: Stade du Moustoir www.fclweb.fr

	2012-13 H	A	P	W	D	L	OV	UN	BS	CS
Paris SG	L	D	6	1	2	3	2	4	4	1
Marseille	L	W	6	1	1	4	5	1	5	0
Lyon	D	L	6	2	2	2	4	3	2	
Nice	D	D	6	2	2	2	2	4	3	2
St Etienne	W	W	6	4	2	0	4	2	3	3
Lille	W	L	6	3	2	1	2	4	4	1
Bordeaux	L	D	6	3	1	2	3	3	3	2
Lorient										
Montpellier	W	L	4	2	2	0	3	1	3	1
Toulouse	W	W	6	3	3	0	0	6	1	5
Valenciennes	D	L	6	3	2	1	3	3	5	1
Bastia	W	L	1	1	0	0	1	0	1	0
Rennes	D	W	6	1	2	3	2	4	3	1
Reims	D	L	1	0	1	0	1	0	1	0
Sochaux	W	L	6	3	2	1	2	4	4	2
Evian TG	W	D	2	1	0	1	1	1	1	0
Ajaccio	D	L	2	1	1	0	1	1	1	1
Monaco			4	2	2	0	3	1	4	0
Guingamp			-	-	-	-	-	-	-	-
Nantes			1	1	0	0	1	0	0	1

Season	Division	Pos	P	W	D	L	F	A	GD	Pts
2012-13	Ligue 1	8	38	14	11	13	57	58	-1	53
2011-12	Ligue 1	17	38	9	12	17	35	49	-14	39
2010-11	Ligue 1	11	38	12	13	13	46	48	-2	49

Over/Under 55%/45% 2nd   **Both score** 58%/42% 4th

Lyon

Ground: Stade de Gerland www.olweb.fr

	2012-13 H	A	P	W	D	L	OV	UN	BS	CS
Paris SG	L	L	6	2	3	1	4	2	4	1
Marseille	D	W	6	2	3	1	3	3	3	3
Lyon										
Nice	W	D	6	4	1	1	3	3	2	4
St Etienne	D	W	6	2	3	1	0	6	3	2
Lille	L	D	6	2	3	1	4	2	6	0
Bordeaux	W	W	6	3	1	2	3	3	3	1
Lorient	W	D	6	5	1	0	3	3	3	3
Montpellier	W	W	4	3	0	1	3	1	3	1
Toulouse	W	W	6	6	0	0	5	1	4	2
Valenciennes	W	W	6	4	2	0	2	4	3	1
Bastia	W	L	1	1	0	0	1	0	1	0
Rennes	W	W	6	1	4	1	1	5	5	1
Reims	W	W	1	1	0	0	1	0	0	1
Sochaux	W	D	6	4	0	2	4	2	4	1
Evian TG	D	D	2	1	1	0	1	1	1	1
Ajaccio	W	L	2	1	1	0	0	2	1	1
Monaco			4	2	2	0	3	1	2	2
Guingamp			-	-	-	-	-	-	-	-
Nantes			1	1	0	0	1	0	0	1

Season	Division	Pos	P	W	D	L	F	A	GD	Pts
2012-13	Ligue 1	3	38	19	10	9	61	38	+23	67
2011-12	Ligue 1	4	38	19	7	12	64	51	+13	64
2010-11	Ligue 1	3	38	17	13	8	61	40	+21	64

Over/Under 45%/55% 14th   **Both score** 53%/47% 8th

Marseille

Ground: Stade Velodrome   www.om.net

	2012-13 H	A	Last six seasons at home P	W	D	L	OV	UN	BS	CS
Paris SG	[D]	[L]	6	4	1	1	5	1	4	2
Marseille										
Lyon	[L]	[D]	6	2	2	2	5	1	6	0
Nice	[D]	[W]	6	4	1	1	4	2	4	1
St Etienne	[W]	[L]	6	5	1	0	2	4	2	4
Lille	[W]	[D]	6	3	1	2	3	3	3	3
Bordeaux	[W]	[L]	6	3	2	1	2	4	2	4
Lorient	[L]	[W]	6	2	2	2	3	3	3	2
Montpellier	[W]	[W]	4	3	0	1	4	0	3	1
Toulouse	[W]	[W]	6	1	3	2	4	2	5	0
Valenciennes	[W]	[L]	6	3	3	0	3	4	2	
Bastia	[W]	[W]	1	1	0	0	1	0	1	0
Rennes	[W]	[D]	6	3	2	1	3	3	2	3
Reims	[D]	[W]	1	0	1	0	0	1	0	1
Sochaux	[W]	[L]	6	4	1	1	4	2	3	2
Evian TG	[W]	[D]	2	2	0	0	0	2	0	2
Ajaccio	[D]	[W]	2	1	1	0	0	2	0	2
Monaco			4	1	2	1	2	2	2	2
Guingamp			-	-	-	-	-	-	-	-
Nantes			1	1	0	0	0	1	0	1

Season	Division	Pos	P	W	D	L	F	A	GD	Pts
2012-13	Ligue 1	2	38	21	8	9	42	36	+6	71
2011-12	Ligue 1	10	38	12	12	14	45	41	+4	48
2010-11	Ligue 1	2	38	18	14	6	62	39	+23	68

Over/Under 37%/63% 17th   **Both score** 37%/63% 18th

Monaco

Ground: Stade Louis II   www.asm-fc.com

	2012-13 H	A	Last six seasons at home P	W	D	L	OV	UN	BS	CS
Paris SG			4	2	1	1	1	3	2	2
Marseille			4	0	1	3	2	2	2	1
Lyon			4	0	1	3	1	3	1	0
Nice			4	1	2	1	2	2	4	0
St Etienne			4	0	2	2	2	2	3	0
Lille			4	1	1	2	1	3	0	2
Bordeaux			4	0	2	2	3	1	2	1
Lorient			4	4	0	0	1	3	1	3
Montpellier			2	1	1	0	1	1	0	2
Toulouse			4	2	1	1	1	3	1	2
Valenciennes			4	1	2	1	1	3	2	1
Bastia			1	0	0	1	0	1	0	0
Rennes			4	3	0	1	2	2	2	2
Reims			1	0	0	1	1	0	1	0
Sochaux			4	3	1	0	1	3	2	2
Evian TG			-	-	-	-	-	-	-	-
Ajaccio			-	-	-	-	-	-	-	-
Monaco										
Guingamp	[D]	[W]	2	1	1	0	1	1	1	1
Nantes	[L]	[D]	3	1	0	2	2	1	2	0

Season	Division	Pos	P	W	D	L	F	A	GD	Pts
2012-13	Ligue 2	1	38	21	13	4	64	33	+31	76
2011-12	Ligue 2	8	38	13	13	12	41	48	-7	52
2010-11	Ligue 1	18	38	9	17	12	36	40	-4	44

Over/Under 47%/53% 8th   **Both score** 55%/45% 7th

Montpellier

Ground: Stade de la Mosson   www.mhscfoot.com

	2012-13 H	A	Last six seasons at home P	W	D	L	OV	UN	BS	CS
Paris SG	[D]	[L]	4	0	3	1	1	3	3	0
Marseille	[L]	[L]	4	2	0	2	1	3	1	2
Lyon	[L]	[L]	4	1	0	3	2	2	2	1
Nice	[W]	[L]	4	3	1	0	1	3	2	2
St Etienne	[D]	[L]	4	2	1	1	2	2	3	1
Lille	[D]	[L]	4	3	1	0	0	4	0	4
Bordeaux	[W]	[L]	4	3	0	1	0	4	0	3
Lorient	[W]	[L]	4	4	0	0	3	1	2	2
Montpellier										
Toulouse	[D]	[L]	4	1	3	0	0	4	3	1
Valenciennes	[W]	[D]	4	4	0	0	3	1	3	1
Bastia	[W]	[L]	3	3	0	0	3	0	2	1
Rennes	[W]	[L]	4	3	0	1	2	2	1	2
Reims	[W]	[L]	3	1	2	0	2	1	2	1
Sochaux	[W]	[W]	4	4	0	0	1	3	1	3
Evian TG	[L]	[W]	2	0	1	1	2	0	2	0
Ajaccio	[W]	[L]	4	4	0	0	3	1	1	3
Monaco			2	0	1	1	0	2	0	1
Guingamp			2	0	2	0	0	2	0	2
Nantes			1	0	1	0	0	1	0	1

Season	Division	Pos	P	W	D	L	F	A	GD	Pts
2012-13	Ligue 1	9	38	15	7	16	54	51	+3	52
2011-12	Ligue 1	1	38	25	7	6	68	34	+34	82
2010-11	Ligue 1	14	38	12	11	15	32	43	-11	47

Over/Under 50%/50% 3rd   **Both score** 61%/39% 2nd

Nantes

Ground: Beaujoire-Louis Fonteneau   www.fcnantes.com

	2012-13 H	A	Last six seasons at home P	W	D	L	OV	UN	BS	CS
Paris SG			1	0	0	1	1	0	1	0
Marseille			1	0	1	0	0	1	1	0
Lyon			1	1	0	0	1	0	1	0
Nice			1	1	0	0	1	0	1	0
St Etienne			1	1	0	0	0	1	0	1
Lille			1	0	0	1	0	1	0	0
Bordeaux			1	0	0	1	1	0	1	0
Lorient			1	0	1	0	0	1	1	0
Montpellier			1	0	1	0	0	1	1	0
Toulouse			1	0	1	0	0	1	1	0
Valenciennes			1	1	0	0	0	1	0	1
Bastia			3	2	0	1	1	2	1	1
Rennes			1	0	1	0	0	1	1	0
Reims			3	2	1	0	1	2	1	2
Sochaux			1	0	1	0	0	1	1	0
Evian TG			1	0	0	1	0	1	0	0
Ajaccio			3	3	0	0	1	2	1	2
Monaco	[D]	[W]	3	1	2	0	1	2	2	1
Guingamp	[D]	[L]	4	1	2	1	1	3	2	1
Nantes										

Season	Division	Pos	P	W	D	L	F	A	GD	Pts
2012-13	Ligue 2	3	38	19	12	7	54	29	+25	69
2011-12	Ligue 2	9	38	14	9	15	51	42	+9	55
2010-11	Ligue 2	13	38	11	14	13	38	40	-2	44

Over/Under 37%/63% 14th   **Both score** 47%/53% 14th

Nice

Ground: Stade du Ray   www.ogcnice.com

	2012-13 H	A	P	W	D	L	OV	UN	BS	CS
Paris SG	W	L	6	4	1	1	3	3	2	3
Marseille	L	D	6	1	1	4	1	5	2	1
Lyon	D	L	6	1	3	2	4	2	5	1
Nice										
St Etienne	D	L	6	3	2	1	3	3	4	1
Lille	D	W	6	0	3	3	1	5	2	1
Bordeaux	L	D	6	2	3	1	3	3	4	1
Lorient	D	D	6	4	1	1	1	5	2	4
Montpellier	W	L	4	1	0	3	1	3	0	1
Toulouse	W	W	6	3	2	1	0	6	2	3
Valenciennes	W	D	6	5	1	0	2	4	1	5
Bastia	D	W	1	0	1	0	1	0	1	0
Rennes	W	W	6	2	2	2	1	5	3	2
Reims	W	L	1	1	0	0	0	1	0	0
Sochaux	W	W	6	2	4	0	1	5	2	4
Evian TG	W	L	2	1	1	0	1	1	2	0
Ajaccio	L	W	2	1	0	1	1	1	0	1
Monaco			4	1	1	2	2	2	2	1
Guingamp			-	-	-	-	-	-	-	-
Nantes			1	1	0	0	1	0	1	0

Season	Division	Pos	P	W	D	L	F	A	GD	Pts
2012-13	Ligue 1	4	38	18	10	10	57	46	+11	64
2011-12	Ligue 1	13	38	10	12	16	39	46	-7	42
2010-11	Ligue 1	17	38	11	13	14	33	48	-15	46

Over/Under 47%/53% 7th   **Both score** 45%/55% 12th

Paris Saint-Germain

Ground: Parc des Princes   www.psg.fr

	2012-13 H	A	P	W	D	L	OV	UN	BS	CS
Paris SG										
Marseille	W	D	6	3	1	2	4	2	4	1
Lyon	W	W	6	4	1	1	1	5	2	4
Nice	W	L	6	3	1	2	4	2	3	2
St Etienne	L	D	6	4	1	1	4	2	4	2
Lille	W	W	6	3	3	0	2	4	2	4
Bordeaux	D	W	6	2	2	2	2	4	3	2
Lorient	D	W	6	1	2	3	4	2	3	1
Montpellier	W	D	4	1	2	1	3	1	3	1
Toulouse	W	W	6	4	0	2	3	3	3	2
Valenciennes	D	W	6	2	4	0	4	2	6	0
Bastia	W	W	1	1	0	0	1	0	1	0
Rennes	L	W	6	1	2	3	3	3	3	2
Reims	W	L	1	1	0	0	0	1	0	1
Sochaux	W	L	6	5	1	0	4	2	4	2
Evian TG	W	W	2	2	0	0	2	0	1	1
Ajaccio	D	D	2	1	1	0	1	1	1	1
Monaco			4	0	3	1	1	3	2	1
Guingamp			-	-	-	-	-	-	-	-
Nantes			1	1	0	0	0	1	0	1

Season	Division	Pos	P	W	D	L	F	A	GD	Pts
2012-13	Ligue 1	1	38	25	8	5	69	23	+46	83
2011-12	Ligue 1	2	38	21	10	5	75	41	+34	79
2010-11	Ligue 1	4	38	15	15	8	56	41	+15	60

Over/Under 50%/50% 3rd   **Both score** 37%/63% 18th

Reims

Ground: Auguste-Delaune II   www.stade-de-reims.com

	2012-13 H	A	P	W	D	L	OV	UN	BS	CS
Paris SG	W	L	1	1	0	0	0	1	0	1
Marseille	L	D	1	0	0	1	0	1	0	0
Lyon	W	L	1	1	0	0	0	1	0	1
Nice	W	L	1	1	0	0	1	0	1	0
St Etienne	D	D	1	0	1	0	0	1	1	0
Lille	D	L	1	0	1	0	0	1	1	0
Bordeaux	D	D	1	0	1	0	0	1	0	1
Lorient	W	D	1	1	0	0	0	1	0	1
Montpellier	W	L	3	2	0	1	3	0	2	0
Toulouse	D	D	1	0	1	0	0	1	1	0
Valenciennes	L	L	1	0	0	1	0	1	0	0
Bastia	L	L	4	2	0	2	2	2	2	2
Rennes	W	L	1	1	0	0	0	1	0	1
Reims										
Sochaux	W	L	1	1	0	0	0	1	0	1
Evian TG	L	D	2	0	0	2	2	0	2	0
Ajaccio	D	L	4	0	3	1	1	3	3	1
Monaco			1	1	0	0	0	1	0	1
Guingamp			3	2	1	0	2	1	2	1
Nantes			3	2	1	0	3	0	3	0

Season	Division	Pos	P	W	D	L	F	A	GD	Pts
2012-13	Ligue 1	14	38	10	13	15	33	42	-9	43
2011-12	Ligue 2	2	38	18	11	9	54	37	+17	65
2010-11	Ligue 2	10	38	12	13	13	53	51	+2	49

Over/Under 32%/68% 18th   **Both score** 42%/58% 17th

Rennes

Ground: Route de Lorient   www.staderennais.com

	2012-13 H	A	P	W	D	L	OV	UN	BS	CS
Paris SG	L	W	6	4	1	1	0	6	1	4
Marseille	D	L	6	1	3	2	4	2	5	0
Lyon	L	L	6	1	2	3	4	2	3	1
Nice	L	L	6	3	2	1	3	3	3	2
St Etienne	D	L	6	3	3	0	1	5	2	4
Lille	W	L	6	2	3	1	3	3	5	1
Bordeaux	L	L	6	2	1	3	2	4	2	2
Lorient	W	D	6	4	0	2	3	3	3	3
Montpellier	W	L	4	2	0	2	2	2	1	1
Toulouse	W	D	6	4	1	1	3	3	3	2
Valenciennes	W	L	6	3	2	1	1	5	1	4
Bastia	W	W	1	1	0	0	1	0	1	0
Rennes										
Reims	W	L	1	1	0	0	1	0	1	0
Sochaux	D	L	6	3	1	2	3	3	3	2
Evian TG	L	L	2	1	0	1	1	1	1	0
Ajaccio	D	W	2	1	1	0	1	1	2	0
Monaco			4	3	0	1	1	3	1	2
Guingamp			-	-	-	-	-	-	-	-
Nantes			1	0	1	0	0	1	0	1

Season	Division	Pos	P	W	D	L	F	A	GD	Pts
2012-13	Ligue 1	13	38	13	7	18	48	59	-11	46
2011-12	Ligue 1	6	38	17	9	12	53	44	+9	60
2010-11	Ligue 1	6	38	15	11	12	38	35	+3	56

Over/Under 47%/53% 7th   **Both score** 47%/53% 11th

Sochaux

Ground: Stade Auguste Bonal   www.fcsochaux.fr

	2012-13 H	A	P	W	D	L	OV	UN	BS	CS
Paris SG	W	L	6	2	1	3	4	2	5	0
Marseille	W	L	6	4	0	2	3	3	3	2
Lyon	D	W	6	1	1	4	3	3	3	0
Nice	L	L	6	5	0	1	1	5	0	5
St Etienne	L	W	6	3	1	2	3	3	4	1
Lille	D	D	6	1	4	1	1	5	4	1
Bordeaux	D	D	6	0	3	3	3	3	3	1
Lorient	W	L	6	3	3	0	0	6	3	3
Montpellier	L	L	4	0	1	3	2	2	2	1
Toulouse	L	L	6	2	0	4	4	2	3	2
Valenciennes	D	L	6	2	3	1	2	4	5	1
Bastia	L	D	1	0	0	1	1	0	1	0
Rennes	L	D	6	3	1	2	3	3	2	3
Reims	W	L	1	1	0	0	0	1	0	1
Sochaux										
Evian TG	W	L	2	1	1	0	1	1	2	0
Ajaccio	D	W	2	0	1	1	0	2	0	1
Monaco			4	3	0	1	3	1	0	3
Guingamp			-	-	-	-	-	-	-	-
Nantes			1	1	0	0	1	0	1	0

Season	Division	Pos	P	W	D	L	F	A	GD	Pts
2012-13	Ligue 1	15	38	10	11	17	41	57	-16	41
2011-12	Ligue 1	14	38	11	9	18	40	60	-20	42
2010-11	Ligue 1	5	38	17	7	14	60	43	+17	58

Over/Under 47%/53% 7th   **Both score** 55%/45% 6th

Saint-Etienne

Ground: Stade Geoffroy-Guichard   www.asse.fr

	2012-13 H	A	P	W	D	L	OV	UN	BS	CS
Paris SG	D	W	6	1	3	2	1	5	2	2
Marseille	W	L	6	2	3	1	1	5	1	4
Lyon	L	D	6	0	1	5	1	5	2	0
Nice	W	D	6	1	1	4	2	4	1	2
St Etienne										
Lille	L	D	6	1	2	3	4	2	5	1
Bordeaux	D	D	6	1	4	1	3	3	4	2
Lorient	L	L	6	2	0	4	3	3	3	1
Montpellier	W	D	4	3	1	0	2	2	2	2
Toulouse	D	L	6	1	4	1	3	3	4	1
Valenciennes	W	D	6	4	1	1	2	4	2	3
Bastia	W	W	1	1	0	0	1	0	0	1
Rennes	W	D	6	3	1	2	3	3	1	4
Reims	D	D	1	0	1	0	0	1	0	1
Sochaux	L	W	6	4	1	1	2	4	2	3
Evian TG	W	D	2	1	0	1	0	2	0	1
Ajaccio	W	D	2	2	0	0	2	0	2	0
Monaco			4	3	1	0	2	2	1	3
Guingamp			-	-	-	-	-	-	-	-
Nantes			1	1	0	0	1	0	1	0

Season	Division	Pos	P	W	D	L	F	A	GD	Pts
2012-13	Ligue 1	5	38	16	15	7	60	32	+28	63
2011-12	Ligue 1	7	38	16	9	13	49	45	+4	57
2010-11	Ligue 1	10	38	12	13	13	46	47	-1	49

Over/Under 47%/53% 7th   **Both score** 45%/55% 12th

Toulouse

Ground: Stadium Municipal   www.tfc.info

	2012-13 H	A	P	W	D	L	OV	UN	BS	CS
Paris SG	L	L	6	2	1	3	3	3	3	1
Marseille	L	L	6	0	4	2	0	6	1	3
Lyon	W	L	6	4	0	2	2	4	0	6
Nice	L	L	6	0	4	2	4	4	4	1
St Etienne	W	D	6	3	0	3	3	3	3	0
Lille	W	L	6	2	3	1	1	5	2	3
Bordeaux	D	L	6	3	1	2	3	3	2	3
Lorient	L	L	6	1	3	2	1	5	2	2
Montpellier	W	D	4	1	0	3	0	4	0	1
Toulouse										
Valenciennes	D	D	6	2	3	1	2	4	2	3
Bastia	D	D	1	0	1	0	0	1	0	1
Rennes	D	L	6	2	3	1	3	3	3	3
Reims	D	D	1	0	1	0	0	1	1	0
Sochaux	W	W	6	4	0	2	2	4	2	3
Evian TG	D	W	2	1	1	0	1	1	1	1
Ajaccio	L	W	2	0	0	2	1	1	1	0
Monaco			4	1	3	0	0	4	0	4
Guingamp			-	-	-	-	-	-	-	-
Nantes			1	1	0	0	0	1	0	1

Season	Division	Pos	P	W	D	L	F	A	GD	Pts
2012-13	Ligue 1	10	38	13	12	13	49	47	+2	51
2011-12	Ligue 1	8	38	15	11	12	37	34	+3	56
2010-11	Ligue 1	8	38	14	8	16	38	36	+2	50

Over/Under 45%/55% 14th   **Both score** 45%/55% 12th

Valenciennes

Ground: Stade du Hainaut   www.va-fc.com

	2012-13 H	A	P	W	D	L	OV	UN	BS	CS
Paris SG	L	D	6	1	1	4	5	1	4	1
Marseille	W	L	6	4	1	1	5	1	6	0
Lyon	L	L	6	3	1	2	3	3	3	2
Nice	D	L	6	4	1	1	3	3	3	3
St Etienne	D	L	6	3	2	1	1	5	2	4
Lille	L	L	6	2	3	1	1	5	2	4
Bordeaux	D	L	6	2	2	2	4	2	4	2
Lorient	W	D	6	4	2	0	3	3	2	4
Montpellier	D	L	4	1	2	1	0	4	2	1
Toulouse	D	D	6	3	1	2	3	3	3	2
Valenciennes										
Bastia	L	W	1	0	0	1	1	0	1	0
Rennes	W	L	6	4	1	1	2	4	1	4
Reims	W	W	1	1	0	0	0	1	0	1
Sochaux	W	D	6	3	3	0	4	2	5	1
Evian TG	W	L	2	1	0	1	2	0	1	1
Ajaccio	W	D	2	1	0	1	2	0	1	1
Monaco			4	3	1	0	2	2	2	2
Guingamp			-	-	-	-	-	-	-	-
Nantes			1	0	1	0	0	1	1	0

Season	Division	Pos	P	W	D	L	F	A	GD	Pts
2012-13	Ligue 1	11	38	12	12	14	49	53	-4	48
2011-12	Ligue 1	12	38	12	7	19	40	50	-10	43
2010-11	Ligue 1	12	38	10	18	10	45	41	+4	48

Over/Under 47%/53% 7th   **Both score** 55%/45% 6th

Augsburg

Ground: SGL arena   www.fcaugsburg.de

	2012-13 H	A	Last six seasons at home P	W	D	L	OV	UN	BS	CS
Bayern Munich	L	L	2	0	0	2	1	1	1	0
Dortmund	L	L	2	0	1	1	1	1	1	1
Leverkusen	L	L	2	0	0	2	2	0	2	0
Schalke	D	L	2	0	2	0	0	2	1	1
Freiburg	D	L	4	0	3	1	2	2	4	0
Ein Frankfurt	W	L	1	1	0	0	0	1	0	1
Hamburg	L	W	2	1	0	1	0	2	0	1
M'gladbach	D	L	3	1	1	1	0	3	1	1
Hannover	L	L	2	0	1	1	0	2	0	1
Nurnberg	L	D	3	0	2	1	1	2	1	2
Wolfsburg	D	D	2	1	1	0	0	2	0	2
Stuttgart	W	L	2	1	0	1	2	0	1	1
Mainz	D	L	4	2	1	1	2	2	3	0
Werder Bremen	W	W	2	1	1	0	1	1	2	0
Augsburg										
Hoffenheim	W	D	3	1	1	1	2	1	2	0
Hertha			2	1	1	0	1	1	1	1
Braunschweig			-	-	-	-	-	-	-	-

Season	Division	Pos	P	W	D	L	F	A	GD	Pts
2012-13	Bundesliga	15	34	8	9	17	33	51	-18	33
2011-12	Bundesliga	14	34	8	14	12	36	49	-13	38
2010-11	2.Bundesliga	2	34	19	8	7	58	27	+31	65

Over/Under 41%/59% 15th   **Both score** 50%/50% 14th

Bayern Munich

Ground: Allianz Arena   www.fcbayern.de

	2012-13 H	A	Last six seasons at home P	W	D	L	OV	UN	BS	CS
Bayern Munich										
Dortmund	D	D	6	3	1	2	4	2	4	1
Leverkusen	L	W	6	4	1	1	5	1	4	2
Schalke	W	W	6	3	2	1	2	4	3	2
Freiburg	W	W	4	4	0	0	3	1	2	2
Ein Frankfurt	W	W	5	4	1	0	3	2	2	3
Hamburg	W	W	6	4	2	0	4	2	3	3
M'gladbach	D	W	5	3	1	1	2	3	3	1
Hannover	W	W	6	6	0	0	6	0	2	4
Nurnberg	W	D	5	5	0	0	5	0	1	4
Wolfsburg	W	W	6	6	0	0	5	1	3	3
Stuttgart	W	W	6	5	0	1	5	1	5	1
Mainz	W	W	4	2	1	1	3	1	2	2
Werder Bremen	W	W	6	2	3	1	3	3	5	1
Augsburg	W	W	2	2	0	0	2	0	1	1
Hoffenheim	W	W	5	5	0	0	3	2	2	3
Hertha			4	4	0	0	4	0	3	1
Braunschweig			-	-	-	-	-	-	-	-

Season	Division	Pos	P	W	D	L	F	A	GD	Pts
2012-13	Bundesliga	1	34	29	4	1	98	18	+80	91
2011-12	Bundesliga	2	34	23	4	7	77	22	+55	73
2010-11	Bundesliga	3	34	19	8	7	81	40	+41	65

Over/Under 53%/47% 10th   **Both score** 38%/62% 18th

Braunschweig

Ground: Eintracht-Stadion   www.eintracht.com

	2012-13 H	A	Last six seasons at home P	W	D	L	OV	UN	BS	CS
Bayern Munich			-	-	-	-	-	-	-	-
Dortmund			-	-	-	-	-	-	-	-
Leverkusen			-	-	-	-	-	-	-	-
Schalke			-	-	-	-	-	-	-	-
Freiburg			-	-	-	-	-	-	-	-
Ein Frankfurt			1	0	0	1	1	0	0	0
Hamburg			-	-	-	-	-	-	-	-
M'gladbach			-	-	-	-	-	-	-	-
Hannover			-	-	-	-	-	-	-	-
Nurnberg			-	-	-	-	-	-	-	-
Wolfsburg			-	-	-	-	-	-	-	-
Stuttgart			-	-	-	-	-	-	-	-
Mainz			-	-	-	-	-	-	-	-
Werder Bremen			-	-	-	-	-	-	-	-
Augsburg			-	-	-	-	-	-	-	-
Hoffenheim			-	-	-	-	-	-	-	-
Hertha	D	L	1	0	1	0	0	1	1	0
Braunschweig										

Season	Division	Pos	P	W	D	L	F	A	GD	Pts
2012-13	2.Bundesliga	2	34	19	10	5	52	34	+18	67
2011-12	2.Bundesliga	8	34	10	15	9	37	35	+2	45
2010-11	3.Liga	1	38	26	7	5	81	22	+59	85

Over/Under 50%/50% 9th   **Both score** 56%/44% 6th

Dortmund

Ground: Westfalenstadion   www.bvb.de

	2012-13 H	A	Last six seasons at home P	W	D	L	OV	UN	BS	CS
Bayern Munich	D	D	6	2	3	1	1	5	3	3
Dortmund										
Leverkusen	W	W	6	4	1	1	3	3	2	3
Schalke	L	L	6	1	2	3	3	3	3	2
Freiburg	W	W	4	4	0	0	3	1	1	3
Ein Frankfurt	W	D	5	3	1	1	4	1	3	2
Hamburg	L	L	6	4	0	2	3	3	2	3
M'gladbach	W	D	5	5	0	0	4	1	2	3
Hannover	W	D	6	4	1	1	5	1	6	0
Nurnberg	W	D	5	4	1	0	2	3	0	5
Wolfsburg	L	D	6	2	2	2	3	3	4	2
Stuttgart	D	W	6	2	4	0	3	3	4	2
Mainz	W	W	4	2	2	0	1	3	2	2
Werder Bremen	W	W	6	6	0	0	3	3	2	4
Augsburg	W	W	2	2	0	0	2	0	1	1
Hoffenheim	L	W	5	1	3	1	2	4	1	4
Hertha			4	1	2	1	1	3	3	1
Braunschweig			-	-	-	-	-	-	-	-

Season	Division	Pos	P	W	D	L	F	A	GD	Pts
2012-13	Bundesliga	2	34	19	9	6	81	42	+39	66
2011-12	Bundesliga	1	34	25	6	3	80	25	+55	81
2010-11	Bundesliga	1	34	23	6	5	67	22	+45	75

Over/Under 74%/26% 1st   **Both score** 76%/24% 1st

Eintracht Frankfurt

Ground: Commerzbank-Arena   www.eintracht.de

	2012-13 H	A	Last six seasons at home P	W	D	L	OV	UN	BS	CS
Bayern Munich	L	L	5	1	1	3	3	2	4	0
Dortmund	D	L	5	1	3	1	1	4	3	1
Leverkusen	W	L	5	3	0	2	4	1	3	0
Schalke	W	D	5	1	2	2	3	2	3	2
Freiburg	W	D	3	2	0	1	2	1	2	0
Ein Frankfurt										
Hamburg	W	W	5	2	1	2	4	1	5	0
M'gladbach	L	L	4	1	0	3	2	2	2	0
Hannover	W	D	5	3	1	1	4	1	2	2
Nurnberg	D	W	4	1	2	1	1	3	2	2
Wolfsburg	D	W	5	1	2	2	4	1	4	0
Stuttgart	L	L	5	0	1	4	4	1	3	0
Mainz	L	D	3	2	0	1	2	1	2	1
Werder Bremen	W	D	5	3	1	1	2	3	2	2
Augsburg	W	L	1	1	0	0	1	0	1	0
Hoffenheim	W	W	4	1	1	2	3	1	3	0
Hertha			3	1	1	1	2	1	1	
Braunschweig			1	1	0	0	1	0	1	0

Season	Division	Pos	P	W	D	L	F	A	GD	Pts
2012-13	Bundesliga	6	34	14	9	11	49	46	+3	51
2011-12	2.Bundesliga	2	34	20	8	6	76	33	+43	68
2010-11	Bundesliga	17	34	9	7	18	31	49	-18	34

Over/Under 56%/44% 9th   **Both score** 56%/44% 8th

Freiburg

Ground: Dreisamstadion   www.scfreiburg.com

	2012-13 H	A	Last six seasons at home P	W	D	L	OV	UN	BS	CS
Bayern Munich	L	L	4	0	1	3	2	2	2	1
Dortmund	L	L	4	1	0	3	3	1	3	0
Leverkusen	D	L	4	0	1	3	1	3	0	1
Schalke	L	W	4	1	1	2	3	1	3	1
Freiburg										
Ein Frankfurt	D	L	3	0	2	1	0	3	0	2
Hamburg	W	W	4	1	2	1	1	3	2	2
M'gladbach	W	D	5	4	0	1	3	2	1	4
Hannover	W	W	4	1	1	2	3	1	4	0
Nurnberg	W	D	5	2	2	1	3	2	3	1
Wolfsburg	L	W	4	3	0	1	3	1	2	2
Stuttgart	W	L	4	2	0	2	3	1	2	1
Mainz	D	D	6	2	2	2	1	5	3	2
Werder Bremen	L	W	4	0	1	3	4	0	3	0
Augsburg	W	W	4	4	0	0	0	4	0	4
Hoffenheim	W	L	5	3	1	1	3	2	3	1
Hertha			2	0	1	1	2	0	1	0
Braunschweig			-	-	-	-	-	-	-	-

Season	Division	Pos	P	W	D	L	F	A	GD	Pts
2012-13	Bundesliga	5	34	14	9	11	45	40	+5	51
2011-12	Bundesliga	12	34	10	10	14	45	61	-16	40
2010-11	Bundesliga	9	34	13	5	16	41	50	-9	44

Over/Under 44%/56% 14th   **Both score** 50%/50% 14th

Hamburg

Ground: Volksparkstadion   www.hsv.de

	2012-13 H	A	Last six seasons at home P	W	D	L	OV	UN	BS	CS
Bayern Munich	L	L	6	2	3	1	1	5	2	3
Dortmund	W	W	6	4	1	1	4	2	5	1
Leverkusen	L	L	6	2	2	2	2	4	3	2
Schalke	W	L	6	2	2	2	4	2	4	1
Freiburg	L	D	4	1	0	3	1	3	1	1
Ein Frankfurt	L	L	5	3	1	1	1	4	1	3
Hamburg										
M'gladbach	W	D	5	2	1	2	1	4	2	2
Hannover	W	L	6	3	3	0	1	5	2	4
Nurnberg	L	D	5	3	1	1	4	1	4	3
Wolfsburg	D	D	6	0	4	2	3	3	6	0
Stuttgart	L	W	6	4	0	2	4	2	3	1
Mainz	W	W	4	1	1	2	1	3	1	2
Werder Bremen	W	L	6	4	0	2	5	1	4	1
Augsburg	L	W	2	0	1	1	0	2	1	0
Hoffenheim	W	W	5	4	1	0	1	4	1	4
Hertha			4	2	2	0	2	2	3	1
Braunschweig			-	-	-	-	-	-	-	-

Season	Division	Pos	P	W	D	L	F	A	GD	Pts
2012-13	Bundesliga	7	34	14	6	14	42	53	-11	48
2011-12	Bundesliga	15	34	8	12	14	35	57	-22	36
2010-11	Bundesliga	8	34	12	9	13	46	52	-6	45

Over/Under 41%/59% 15th   **Both score** 47%/53% 16th

Hannover

Ground: AWD-Arena   www.hannover96.de

	2012-13 H	A	Last six seasons at home P	W	D	L	OV	UN	BS	CS
Bayern Munich	L	L	6	3	0	3	5	1	3	1
Dortmund	D	L	6	2	3	1	4	2	5	0
Leverkusen	W	L	6	2	3	1	3	3	2	3
Schalke	D	L	6	2	2	2	4	2	4	1
Freiburg	L	L	4	2	1	1	3	1	4	0
Ein Frankfurt	D	L	5	3	2	0	3	2	4	1
Hamburg	W	L	6	3	2	1	4	2	4	1
M'gladbach	L	L	5	3	0	2	4	1	4	0
Hannover										
Nurnberg	W	D	5	4	0	1	4	1	4	1
Wolfsburg	W	W	6	3	1	2	3	3	2	2
Stuttgart	D	W	6	3	3	0	3	3	3	3
Mainz	W	L	4	1	3	0	1	3	3	1
Werder Bremen	W	L	6	4	1	1	5	1	6	0
Augsburg	W	W	2	1	1	0	1	1	1	1
Hoffenheim	W	L	5	3	0	2	2	3	2	2
Hertha			4	1	2	1	2	2	2	1
Braunschweig			-	-	-	-	-	-	-	-

Season	Division	Pos	P	W	D	L	F	A	GD	Pts
2012-13	Bundesliga	9	34	13	6	15	60	62	-2	45
2011-12	Bundesliga	7	34	12	12	10	41	45	-4	48
2010-11	Bundesliga	4	34	19	3	12	49	45	+4	60

Over/Under 71%/29% 3rd   **Both score** 65%/35% 3rd

Hertha Berlin

Ground: Olympiastadion   www.herthabsc.de

2012-13	H	A	P	W	D	L	OV	UN	BS	CS
Bayern Munich			4	1	1	2	3	1	2	1
Dortmund			4	1	1	2	2	2	2	1
Leverkusen			4	1	2	1	3	1	2	1
Schalke			4	0	1	3	2	2	2	1
Freiburg			2	0	0	2	2	0	1	0
Ein Frankfurt			3	1	0	2	3	0	2	0
Hamburg			4	1	1	2	3	1	3	1
M'gladbach			3	1	1	1	2	1	2	1
Hannover			4	3	0	1	1	3	0	3
Nurnberg			3	1	0	2	1	2	1	1
Wolfsburg			4	1	2	1	3	1	3	1
Stuttgart			4	3	0	1	2	2	2	1
Mainz			2	0	2	0	0	2	1	1
Werder Bremen			4	2	0	2	3	1	3	1
Augsburg			2	1	1	0	2	0	2	0
Hoffenheim			3	2	0	1	1	2	1	1
Hertha										
Braunschweig	W	D	1	1	0	0	1	0	0	1

Season	Division	Pos	P	W	D	L	F	A	GD	Pts
2012-13	2.Bundesliga	1	34	22	10	2	65	28	+37	76
2011-12	Bundesliga	16	34	7	10	17	38	64	-26	31
2010-11	2.Bundesliga	1	34	23	5	6	69	28	+41	74

Over/Under 50%/50% 9th   **Both score** 56%/44% 6th

Hoffenheim

Ground: Rhein-Neckar Arena   www.achtzehn99.de

2012-13	H	A	P	W	D	L	OV	UN	BS	CS
Bayern Munich	L	L	5	0	3	2	2	3	3	1
Dortmund	L	W	5	3	0	2	3	2	3	2
Leverkusen	L	L	5	0	1	4	4	1	3	0
Schalke	W	L	5	2	3	0	1	4	3	2
Freiburg	W	L	5	2	2	1	1	4	3	1
Ein Frankfurt	L	L	4	2	1	1	2	2	2	1
Hamburg	L	L	5	3	1	1	4	1	2	3
M'gladbach	D	L	6	4	2	0	3	3	3	3
Hannover	W	L	5	3	2	0	4	1	3	2
Nurnberg	W	L	4	2	1	1	3	1	3	1
Wolfsburg	L	D	5	2	0	3	5	0	5	0
Stuttgart	L	W	5	0	2	3	2	3	3	1
Mainz	D	L	5	1	2	2	1	4	2	2
Werder Bremen	L	D	5	1	1	3	3	2	3	1
Augsburg	D	L	3	1	2	0	1	2	1	2
Hoffenheim										
Hertha			3	1	1	1	1	2	2	0
Braunschweig			-	-	-	-	-	-	-	-

Season	Division	Pos	P	W	D	L	F	A	GD	Pts
2012-13	Bundesliga	16	34	8	7	19	42	67	-25	31
2011-12	Bundesliga	11	34	10	11	13	41	47	-6	41
2010-11	Bundesliga	11	34	11	10	13	50	50	0	43

Over/Under 74%/26% 1st   **Both score** 56%/44% 8th

Leverkusen

Ground: BayArena   www.bayer04.de

2012-13	H	A	P	W	D	L	OV	UN	BS	CS
Bayern Munich	L	W	6	1	2	3	1	5	3	1
Dortmund	L	L	6	0	3	3	4	2	5	1
Leverkusen										
Schalke	W	D	6	4	0	2	1	5	1	3
Freiburg	W	D	4	2	1	1	2	2	2	1
Ein Frankfurt	W	L	5	3	1	1	3	2	3	1
Hamburg	W	W	6	2	3	1	4	2	5	1
M'gladbach	D	D	5	2	1	2	4	1	4	1
Hannover	W	L	6	6	0	0	3	3	1	5
Nurnberg	W	W	5	3	1	1	3	2	1	3
Wolfsburg	D	L	6	4	2	0	4	2	4	2
Stuttgart	W	D	6	4	1	1	6	0	4	2
Mainz	D	L	4	2	1	1	3	1	3	0
Werder Bremen	W	W	6	2	3	1	1	5	2	3
Augsburg	W	W	2	2	0	0	2	0	2	0
Hoffenheim	W	W	5	5	0	0	3	2	2	3
Hertha			4	0	2	2	2	2	3	0
Braunschweig			-	-	-	-	-	-	-	-

Season	Division	Pos	P	W	D	L	F	A	GD	Pts
2012-13	Bundesliga	3	34	19	8	7	65	39	+26	65
2011-12	Bundesliga	5	34	15	9	10	52	44	+8	54
2010-11	Bundesliga	2	34	20	8	6	64	44	+20	68

Over/Under 65%/35% 5th   **Both score** 62%/38% 4th

Mainz

Ground: Coface Arena   www.mainz05.de

2012-13	H	A	P	W	D	L	OV	UN	BS	CS
Bayern Munich	L	L	4	2	0	2	4	0	3	0
Dortmund	L	L	4	1	0	3	2	2	2	1
Leverkusen	W	D	4	2	1	1	3	1	2	1
Schalke	D	L	4	0	2	2	2	2	2	1
Freiburg	D	D	6	2	3	1	3	3	4	2
Ein Frankfurt	D	W	3	1	2	0	2	1	1	2
Hamburg	L	L	4	0	2	2	1	3	2	1
M'gladbach	L	L	5	3	0	2	3	2	2	2
Hannover	W	D	4	2	1	1	3	2	1	
Nurnberg	W	L	5	5	0	0	3	2	2	3
Wolfsburg	D	W	4	0	2	2	0	4	1	1
Stuttgart	W	D	4	3	1	0	2	2	3	1
Mainz										
Werder Bremen	D	L	4	0	2	2	2	2	4	0
Augsburg	W	D	4	1	2	1	0	4	2	1
Hoffenheim	W	D	5	3	1	1	4	1	3	1
Hertha			2	1	0	1	2	0	2	0
Braunschweig			-	-	-	-	-	-	-	-

Season	Division	Pos	P	W	D	L	F	A	GD	Pts
2012-13	Bundesliga	13	34	10	12	12	42	44	-2	42
2011-12	Bundesliga	13	34	9	12	13	47	51	-4	39
2010-11	Bundesliga	5	34	18	4	12	52	39	+13	58

Over/Under 53%/47% 10th   **Both score** 56%/44% 8th

Monchengladbach

Ground: Borussia-Park www.borussia.de

	2012-13 H	A	Last six seasons at home P	W	D	L	OV	UN	BS	CS
Bayern Munich	L	D	5	1	3	1	4	1	5	0
Dortmund	D	L	5	1	3	1	0	5	3	1
Leverkusen	D	D	5	0	3	2	4	1	5	0
Schalke	L	D	5	4	0	1	2	3	1	3
Freiburg	D	L	5	1	3	1	1	4	3	2
Ein Frankfurt	W	W	4	2	0	2	2	2	1	2
Hamburg	D	L	5	2	2	1	3	2	4	1
M'gladbach										
Hannover	W	W	5	4	0	1	4	1	4	1
Nurnberg	L	L	4	2	1	1	2	2	3	1
Wolfsburg	W	L	5	2	1	2	3	2	3	1
Stuttgart	L	L	5	0	2	3	3	2	4	1
Mainz	W	W	5	3	0	2	1	4	1	3
Werder Bremen	D	L	5	3	1	1	4	1	4	1
Augsburg	W	D	3	2	1	0	1	2	1	2
Hoffenheim	W	D	6	2	2	2	3	3	4	2
Hertha			3	1	1	1	1	2	1	1
Braunschweig			-	-	-	-	-	-	-	-

Season	Division	Pos	P	W	D	L	F	A	GD	Pts
2012-13	Bundesliga	8	34	12	11	11	45	49	-4	47
2011-12	Bundesliga	4	34	17	9	8	49	24	+25	60
2010-11	Bundesliga	16	34	10	6	18	48	65	-17	36

Over/Under 41%/59% 15th   **Both score** 56%/44% 8th

Nurnberg

Ground: Frankenstadion www.fcn.de

	2012-13 H	A	Last six seasons at home P	W	D	L	OV	UN	BS	CS
Bayern Munich	D	L	5	0	4	1	0	5	4	0
Dortmund	D	L	5	1	1	3	1	4	2	1
Leverkusen	L	L	5	2	0	3	3	2	3	1
Schalke	W	L	5	3	0	2	4	1	3	1
Freiburg	D	L	5	1	1	3	2	3	3	1
Ein Frankfurt	L	D	4	2	1	1	3	1	3	1
Hamburg	D	W	5	1	3	1	1	4	2	2
M'gladbach	W	W	4	3	0	1	1	3	1	2
Hannover	D	L	5	1	2	2	4	1	4	0
Nurnberg										
Wolfsburg	W	D	5	3	0	2	2	3	2	2
Stuttgart	L	D	5	1	1	3	3	2	3	0
Mainz	W	W	5	2	3	0	2	3	2	3
Werder Bremen	W	D	5	1	2	2	3	2	4	0
Augsburg	D	W	3	2	1	0	2	1	2	2
Hoffenheim	W	L	4	1	1	2	2	2	2	1
Hertha			3	3	0	0	2	1	1	2
Braunschweig			-	-	-	-	-	-	-	-

Season	Division	Pos	P	W	D	L	F	A	GD	Pts
2012-13	Bundesliga	10	34	11	11	12	39	47	-8	44
2011-12	Bundesliga	10	34	12	6	16	38	49	-11	42
2010-11	Bundesliga	6	34	13	8	13	47	45	+2	47

Over/Under 50%/50% 12th   **Both score** 56%/44% 8th

Schalke

Ground: Veltins-Arena www.schalke04.de

	2012-13 H	A	Last six seasons at home P	W	D	L	OV	UN	BS	CS
Bayern Munich	L	L	6	1	0	5	2	4	2	1
Dortmund	W	W	6	3	1	2	5	1	6	0
Leverkusen	D	L	6	1	3	2	3	3	4	1
Schalke										
Freiburg	L	W	4	2	0	2	2	2	2	1
Ein Frankfurt	D	L	5	4	1	0	1	4	2	3
Hamburg	W	W	6	2	2	2	4	2	5	0
M'gladbach	D	W	5	3	2	0	3	2	4	1
Hannover	W	W	6	4	1	1	4	2	3	3
Nurnberg	W	L	5	4	1	0	2	3	2	3
Wolfsburg	W	W	6	3	1	2	5	1	3	3
Stuttgart	L	L	6	3	1	2	6	0	6	0
Mainz	W	D	4	2	1	1	2	2	2	2
Werder Bremen	W	W	6	4	1	1	3	3	2	3
Augsburg	W	D	2	2	0	0	2	0	2	0
Hoffenheim	W	L	5	3	0	2	3	2	2	2
Hertha			4	4	0	0	1	3	0	4
Braunschweig			-	-	-	-	-	-	-	-

Season	Division	Pos	P	W	D	L	F	A	GD	Pts
2012-13	Bundesliga	4	34	16	7	11	58	50	+8	55
2011-12	Bundesliga	3	34	20	4	10	74	44	+30	64
2010-11	Bundesliga	14	34	11	7	16	38	44	-6	40

Over/Under 71%/29% 3rd   **Both score** 62%/38% 4th

Stuttgart

Ground: Mercedes-Benz Arena www.vfb.de

	2012-13 H	A	Last six seasons at home P	W	D	L	OV	UN	BS	CS
Bayern Munich	L	L	6	1	2	3	4	2	4	1
Dortmund	L	D	6	2	1	3	5	1	6	0
Leverkusen	D	W	6	2	1	3	3	3	3	1
Schalke	W	W	6	4	1	1	4	2	3	3
Freiburg	W	L	4	3	0	1	3	1	3	0
Ein Frankfurt	W	W	5	4	0	1	4	1	4	1
Hamburg	L	W	6	3	0	3	3	3	2	3
M'gladbach	W	W	5	4	0	1	3	2	1	3
Hannover	L	D	6	4	0	2	3	3	2	3
Nurnberg	D	W	5	2	2	1	3	2	3	2
Wolfsburg	L	L	6	4	1	1	4	2	5	0
Stuttgart										
Mainz	D	L	4	2	2	0	3	1	3	1
Werder Bremen	L	L	6	4	0	2	5	1	4	1
Augsburg	W	L	2	2	0	0	2	0	2	0
Hoffenheim	L	W	5	2	2	1	3	2	3	1
Hertha			4	2	1	1	2	2	2	2
Braunschweig			-	-	-	-	-	-	-	-

Season	Division	Pos	P	W	D	L	F	A	GD	Pts
2012-13	Bundesliga	12	34	12	7	15	37	55	-18	43
2011-12	Bundesliga	6	34	15	8	11	63	46	+17	53
2010-11	Bundesliga	12	34	12	6	16	60	59	+1	42

Over/Under 59%/41% 7th   **Both score** 53%/47% 13th

Werder Bremen

Ground: Weserstadion   www.werder.de

	2012-13 H	A	P	W	D	L	OV	UN	BS	CS
			Last six seasons at home							
Bayern Munich	L	L	6	0	1	5	4	2	3	1
Dortmund	L	L	6	2	2	2	2	4	2	2
Leverkusen	L	L	6	1	3	2	4	2	5	0
Schalke	L	L	6	1	2	3	2	4	4	0
Freiburg	L	W	4	3	0	1	4	0	3	1
Ein Frankfurt	D	L	5	2	2	1	3	2	3	2
Hamburg	W	L	6	5	1	0	2	4	3	3
M'gladbach	W	D	5	2	3	0	3	2	3	2
Hannover	W	L	6	4	2	0	3	3	3	3
Nurnberg	D	L	5	2	1	2	2	3	3	1
Wolfsburg	L	D	6	2	1	3	4	2	3	0
Stuttgart	D	W	6	3	3	0	4	2	4	2
Mainz	W	D	4	2	0	2	3	1	1	1
Werder Bremen										
Augsburg	L	L	2	0	1	1	0	2	1	0
Hoffenheim	D	W	5	3	2	0	3	2	4	1
Hertha			4	4	0	0	4	0	4	0
Braunschweig			-	-	-	-	-	-	-	-

Season	Division	Pos	P	W	D	L	F	A	GD	Pts
2012-13	Bundesliga	14	34	8	10	16	50	66	-16	34
2011-12	Bundesliga	9	34	11	9	14	49	58	-9	42
2010-11	Bundesliga	13	34	10	11	13	47	61	-14	41

Over/Under 65%/35% 5th   **Both score** 74%/26% 2nd

Wolfsburg

Ground: Volkswagen Arena   www.vfl-wolfsburg.de

	2012-13 H	A	P	W	D	L	OV	UN	BS	CS
			Last six seasons at home							
Bayern Munich	L	L	6	1	2	3	2	4	3	1
Dortmund	D	W	6	2	1	3	6	0	3	2
Leverkusen	W	D	6	3	0	3	6	0	6	0
Schalke	L	L	6	3	2	1	5	1	6	0
Freiburg	L	W	4	2	1	1	3	1	3	0
Ein Frankfurt	L	D	5	1	3	1	3	2	4	0
Hamburg	D	D	6	2	2	2	3	3	4	1
M'gladbach	W	L	5	4	1	0	4	1	3	2
Hannover	L	L	6	5	0	1	5	0	4	1
Nurnberg	D	L	5	2	1	2	5	0	5	0
Wolfsburg										
Stuttgart	W	W	6	6	0	0	2	4	1	5
Mainz	L	D	4	0	2	2	3	1	3	0
Werder Bremen	D	W	6	2	3	1	3	3	5	1
Augsburg	D	D	2	0	1	1	1	2		0
Hoffenheim	D	W	5	2	2	1	5	0	3	2
Hertha			4	1	1	2	3	1	3	1
Braunschweig			-	-	-	-	-	-	-	-

Season	Division	Pos	P	W	D	L	F	A	GD	Pts
2012-13	Bundesliga	11	34	10	13	11	47	52	-5	43
2011-12	Bundesliga	8	34	13	5	16	47	60	-13	44
2010-11	Bundesliga	15	34	9	11	14	43	48	-5	38

Over/Under 47%/53% 13th   **Both score** 59%/41% 6th

Bayern Munich celebrate an historic treble as Jupp Heynckes signs off in style

		2008-09	2009-10	2010-11	2011-12	2012-13	Pts	Prev pos	Change	Prev Pts	Change
1	Spain	13.312	17.928	18.214	20.857	17.714	**88.025**	2	**+1**	84.186	**+3.839**
2	England	15.000	17.928	18.357	15.250	16.428	**82.963**	1	-1	84.410	-1.447
3	Germany	12.687	18.083	15.666	15.250	17.928	**79.614**	3	=	75.186	**+4.428**
4	Italy	11.375	15.428	11.571	11.357	14.416	**64.147**	4	=	59.981	**+4.166**
5	Portugal	6.785	10.000	18.800	11.833	11.750	**59.168**	5	=	55.346	**+3.822**
6	France	11.000	15.000	10.750	10.500	11.750	**59.000**	6	=	54.178	**+4.822**
7	Ukraine	16.625	5.800	10.083	7.750	9.500	**49.758**	9	**+2**	45.133	**+4.625**
8	Russia	9.750	6.166	10.916	9.750	9.750	**46.332**	7	-1	47.832	-1.500
9	Netherlands	6.333	9.416	11.166	13.600	4.214	**44.729**	8	-1	45.515	-0.786
10	Turkey	7.000	7.600	4.600	5.100	10.200	**34.500**	11	**+1**	34.050	**+0.450**
11	Belgium	4.500	8.700	4.600	10.100	6.500	**34.400**	12	**+1**	32.400	**+2.000**
12	Greece	6.500	7.900	7.600	7.600	4.400	**34.000**	10	-2	37.100	-3.100
13	Switzerland	2.900	5.750	5.900	6.000	8.375	**28.925**	14	**+1**	26.800	**+2.125**
14	Cyprus	6.333	4.250	3.125	9.125	4.000	**26.833**	16	**+2**	25.499	**+1.334**
15	Denmark	8.200	4.400	6.700	3.100	3.300	**25.700**	13	-2	27.525	-1.825
16	Austria	2.250	9.375	4.375	7.125	2.250	**25.375**	15	-1	26.325	-0.950
17	Czech Rep	2.375	4.100	3.500	5.250	8.500	**23.725**	19	**+2**	20.350	**+3.375**
18	Romania	2.642	6.083	3.166	4.333	6.800	**23.024**	22	**+4**	18.824	**+4.200**
19	Israel	1.750	7.250	4.625	6.000	3.250	**22.875**	17	-2	22.000	**+0.875**
20	Belarus	4.000	3.375	5.875	3.125	4.500	**20.875**	23	**+3**	18.208	**+2.667**
21	Poland	5.000	2.125	4.500	6.625	2.500	**20.750**	20	-1	19.916	**+0.834**
22	Croatia	4.333	3.000	4.125	3.750	4.375	**19.583**	21	-1	18.874	**+0.709**
23	Sweden	2.500	2.500	2.600	2.900	5.125	**15.625**	24	**+1**	15.900	-0.275
24	Scotland	1.875	2.666	3.600	2.750	4.300	**15.191**	18	-6	21.141	-5.950
25	Serbia	3.000	3.000	3.500	2.125	3.000	**14.625**	27	**+2**	14.250	**+0.375**
26	Slovakia	4.833	2.500	3.000	2.375	1.500	**14.208**	25	-1	14.874	-0.666
27	Norway	2.500	2.100	2.375	2.300	4.900	**14.175**	26	-1	14.675	-0.500
28	Bulgaria	2.250	3.125	4.625	1.500	0.750	**12.250**	28	=	14.250	-2.000
29	Hungary	1.000	2.750	2.750	2.250	3.000	**11.750**	29	=	9.750	**+2.000**
30	Slovenia	1.333	1.375	1.500	2.250	3.250	**9.708**	34	**+4**	7.124	**+2.584**
31	Georgia	1.166	1.750	1.875	2.875	1.500	**9.166**	31	=	8.666	**+0.500**
32	Azerbaijan	0.666	1.500	2.000	1.375	3.000	**8.541**	37	**+5**	6.207	**+2.334**
33	Finland	1.833	1.375	1.800	1.500	2.000	**8.508**	30	-3	9.133	-0.625
34	Bosnia-Hz	1.833	1.750	1.875	1.125	1.250	**7.833**	32	-2	8.416	-0.583
35	Moldova	0.666	2.125	2.125	0.500	2.250	**7.666**	36	**+1**	6.749	**+0.917**
36	Rep of Ireland	2.500	1.375	1.000	1.500	1.000	**7.375**	33	-3	7.375	=
37	Lithuania	2.500	1.250	0.625	1.000	1.125	**6.500**	35	-2	6.875	-0.375
38	Kazakhstan	0.833	1.250	0.875	1.625	1.375	**5.958**	40	**+2**	5.333	**+0.625**
39	Latvia	1.166	2.250	0.500	0.625	1.250	**5.791**	38	-1	5.874	-0.083
40	Iceland	1.166	1.250	0.375	1.375	1.250	**5.416**	41	**+1**	5.332	**+0.084**
41	Montenegro	0.500	1.125	1.750	0.500	1.375	**5.250**	42	**+1**	4.375	**+0.875**
42	Macedonia	0.500	0.500	1.375	1.625	1.250	**5.250**	39	-3	5.666	-0.416
43	Albania	0.666	1.000	0.875	0.875	0.750	**4.166**	44	**+1**	3.916	**+0.250**
44	Malta	0.000	0.750	1.500	0.833	0.875	**3.958**	45	**+1**	3.083	**+0.875**
45	Liechtenstein	0.000	1.000	0.500	2.000	0.000	**3.500**	43	-2	4.000	-0.500
46	Luxembourg	0.000	0.250	0.625	1.125	1.375	**3.375**	49	**+3**	2.333	**+1.042**
47	N Ireland	0.333	0.125	1.125	0.500	1.000	**3.083**	48	**+1**	2.583	**+0.500**
48	Wales	0.333	0.250	0.875	0.625	0.500	**2.583**	46	-2	2.749	-0.166
49	Estonia	0.333	0.875	0.250	0.375	0.375	**2.208**	47	-2	2.666	-0.458
50	Armenia	0.000	0.500	0.250	0.125	0.875	**1.750**	50	=	2.208	-0.458
51	Faroe Islands	0.333	0.000	0.250	0.500	0.500	**1.583**	51	=	1.416	**+0.167**
52	San Marino	0.000	0.500	0.166	0.000	0.000	**0.666**	53	**+1**	0.916	-0.250
53	Andorra	0.000	0.500	0.000	0.000	0.000	**0.500**	52	-1	1.000	-0.500

Uefa's country coefficients are calculated using the performances of each FA's clubs in the last five Europa League/Uefa Cup and Champions League seasons and are used to determine the number of places allocated to each country and seedings in Uefa's club tournaments.

Teams are awarded two points for a win and one for a draw – half that in qualifying and play-off rounds – with an extra point awarded for each round from the last 16 of the Champions League onwards or the quarter-finals of the Europa League. Four additional points are awarded for

reaching the group stage of the Champions League and a further four for qualifying for the knockout rounds.

The country coefficient is the sum of the average points for each nation in each of the last five seasons. So, England's teams have averaged 15, 17.928, 18.357, 15.250 and 16.428 points over the last five seasons. Add them together and you get 82.963, England's country coefficient.

Domestic league tables for the top-rated associations are shown on the facing page.

Spain

Pos	Team	P	Home					Away					GD	Pts
			W	D	L	F	A	W	D	L	F	A		
1	Barcelona	38	18	1	0	63	15	14	3	2	52	25	75	100
2	Real Madrid	38	17	2	0	67	21	9	5	5	36	21	61	85
3	Atl Madrid	38	14	2	3	42	12	9	5	5	23	19	34	76
4	Sociedad	38	10	7	2	41	22	8	5	6	29	27	21	66
5	Valencia	38	13	3	3	42	25	6	5	8	25	29	13	65
6	Malaga	38	10	5	4	33	18	6	4	9	20	32	3	57
7	Real Betis	38	9	5	5	28	18	7	3	9	29	38	1	56
8	R. Vallecano	38	9	3	7	27	29	7	2	10	23	37	-16	53
9	Seville	38	13	1	5	41	21	1	7	11	17	33	4	50
10	Getafe	38	9	4	6	25	23	4	4	11	18	34	-14	47
11	Levante	38	8	4	7	25	26	4	6	9	15	31	-17	46
12	Ath Bilbao	38	8	3	8	22	27	4	6	9	22	38	-21	45
13	Espanyol	38	6	7	6	25	28	5	4	10	18	24	-9	44
14	Valladolid	38	7	6	6	29	26	4	4	11	20	32	-9	43
15	Granada	38	6	6	7	21	21	5	3	11	16	33	-17	42
16	Osasuna	38	7	5	7	15	14	3	4	12	18	36	-17	39
17	Celta Vigo	38	7	6	6	23	21	3	1	15	14	31	-15	37
18	Mallorca	38	7	5	7	26	30	2	4	13	17	42	-29	36
19	Deportivo	38	6	5	8	23	26	2	6	11	24	44	-23	35
20	Zaragoza	38	5	4	10	23	27	4	3	12	14	35	-25	34

Neymar signs for Barcelona

Germany

Pos	Team	P	Home					Away					GD	Pts
			W	D	L	F	A	W	D	L	F	A		
1	B Munich	34	14	2	1	56	11	15	2	0	42	7	80	91
2	B Dortmund	34	10	3	4	40	19	9	6	2	41	23	39	66
3	B Leverkusen	34	12	3	2	36	15	7	5	5	29	24	26	65
4	Schalke	34	10	3	4	35	22	6	4	7	23	28	8	55
5	Freiburg	34	8	4	5	25	18	6	5	6	20	22	5	51
6	E. Frankfurt	34	9	4	4	32	23	5	5	7	17	23	3	51
7	Hamburg	34	8	2	7	18	18	6	4	7	24	35	-11	48
8	M'gladbach	34	8	5	4	27	20	4	6	7	18	29	-4	47
9	Hannover	34	9	5	3	34	23	4	1	12	26	39	-2	45
10	Nuremberg	34	7	6	4	24	19	4	5	8	15	28	-8	44
11	Wolfsburg	34	3	8	6	21	30	7	5	5	26	22	-5	43
12	Stuttgart	34	5	4	8	20	28	7	3	7	17	27	-18	43
13	Mainz	34	7	5	5	22	19	3	7	7	20	25	-2	42
14	W Bremen	34	5	5	7	23	30	3	5	9	27	36	-16	34
15	Augsburg	34	5	5	7	19	22	3	4	10	14	29	-18	33
16	Hoffenheim	34	5	4	8	21	30	3	3	11	21	37	-25	31
17	F Dusseldorf	34	5	6	6	24	28	2	3	12	15	29	-18	30
18	Greuther Furth	34	0	4	13	10	36	4	5	8	16	24	-34	21

Italy

Pos	Team	P	Home					Away					GD	Pts
			W	D	L	F	A	W	D	L	F	A		
1	Juventus	38	14	3	2	36	10	13	3	3	35	14	47	87
2	Napoli	38	14	4	1	44	18	9	5	5	29	18	37	78
3	Milan	38	13	2	4	33	16	8	7	4	34	24	28	72
4	Fiorentina	38	13	4	2	40	19	8	3	8	32	25	28	70
5	Udinese	38	11	7	1	31	16	7	5	7	28	29	14	66
6	Roma	38	10	5	4	40	24	8	3	8	31	32	15	62
7	Lazio	38	13	2	4	35	16	5	5	9	16	26	9	61
8	Catania	38	12	4	3	31	15	3	7	9	19	31	4	56
9	Inter	38	8	4	7	30	31	8	2	9	26	24	-2	54
10	Parma	38	9	6	4	28	18	4	4	11	17	28	-1	49
11	Cagliari	38	8	4	7	24	24	4	7	8	19	31	-12	47
12	Chievo	38	6	8	5	18	16	6	1	12	19	36	-15	45
13	Bologna	38	6	8	5	30	24	5	3	11	16	28	-6	44
14	Sampdoria	38	3	8	8	25	22	3	7	9	18	29	-8	42
15	Atalanta	38	6	6	7	19	24	5	3	11	20	32	-17	40
16	Torino	38	6	6	7	23	26	2	10	7	23	29	-9	39
17	Genoa	38	5	7	7	26	30	3	7	9	12	22	-14	38
18	Palermo	38	5	7	7	24	26	1	7	11	10	28	-20	32
19	Siena	38	6	5	8	16	19	3	4	12	10	38	-21	30
20	Pescara	38	4	1	14	15	42	2	3	14	12	42	-57	22

Portugal

Pos	Team	P	Home					Away					GD	Pts
			W	D	L	F	A	W	D	L	F	A		
1	Porto	30	14	1	0	38	5	10	5	0	32	9	56	78
2	Benfica	30	12	3	0	42	9	12	2	1	35	11	57	77
3	P Ferreira	30	8	5	2	20	13	6	7	2	22	16	13	54
4	Braga	30	9	1	5	34	23	7	3	5	26	21	16	52
5	Estoril	30	9	2	4	31	18	4	4	7	16	19	10	45
6	Rio Ave	30	5	4	6	14	17	7	2	6	21	25	-7	42
7	Sporting	30	7	4	4	16	14	4	5	6	20	22	0	42
8	Nacional	30	6	5	4	26	25	5	2	8	19	26	-6	40
9	Guimaraes	30	6	4	5	18	22	5	3	7	18	25	-11	40
10	Maritimo	30	4	8	3	14	14	5	3	7	20	31	-11	38
11	Academica	30	4	5	6	22	27	2	5	8	11	18	-12	28
12	Setubal	30	6	1	8	18	25	1	4	10	12	30	-25	26
13	Gil Vicente	30	4	3	8	18	24	2	4	9	13	30	-23	25
14	Olhanense	30	3	4	8	13	20	2	6	7	13	22	-16	25
15	Moreirense	30	3	5	7	16	24	2	4	9	14	27	-21	24
16	Beira Mar	30	3	6	6	21	26	2	2	11	14	29	-20	23

France

Pos	Team	P	Home					Away					GD	Pts
			W	D	L	F	A	W	D	L	F	A		
1	Paris SG	38	13	4	2	34	10	12	4	3	35	13	46	83
2	Marseille	38	12	4	3	25	18	9	4	6	17	18	6	71
3	Lyon	38	11	4	4	34	17	8	6	5	27	21	23	67
4	Nice	38	11	5	3	35	17	7	5	7	22	29	11	64
5	St Etienne	38	11	4	4	36	13	5	11	3	24	19	28	63
6	Lille	38	9	7	3	32	16	7	7	5	27	24	19	62
7	Bordeaux	38	8	8	3	22	19	5	8	6	18	15	6	55
8	Lorient	38	10	6	3	38	25	4	5	10	19	33	-1	53
9	Montpellier	38	11	5	3	33	14	4	2	13	21	37	3	52
10	Toulouse	38	7	7	5	30	26	6	5	8	19	21	2	51
11	Valenciennes	38	9	6	4	32	21	3	6	10	17	32	-4	48
12	Bastia	38	9	3	7	30	26	4	5	10	20	40	-16	47
13	Rennes	38	6	5	8	23	27	7	2	10	25	32	-11	46
14	Reims	38	8	7	4	20	13	2	6	11	13	29	-9	43
15	Sochaux	38	6	5	8	25	26	4	6	9	16	31	-16	41
16	Evian	38	6	7	6	31	25	4	3	12	15	28	-7	40
17	Ajaccio	38	7	5	7	19	20	2	10	7	20	31	-12	40
18	Nancy	38	5	5	9	17	26	4	6	9	21	32	-20	38
19	Troyes	38	6	8	5	25	24	2	5	12	18	37	-18	37
20	Brest	38	5	3	11	17	26	3	2	14	15	36	-30	29

Deductions: Ajaccio 2pts

Ukraine

Pos	Team	P	Home					Away					GD	Pts
			W	D	L	F	A	W	D	L	F	A		
1	Shakhtar	30	14	1	0	48	7	11	3	1	34	11	64	79
2	Metalist	30	12	1	2	31	10	8	5	2	28	15	34	66
3	Dyn Kyiv	30	12	1	2	30	9	8	1	6	25	14	32	62
4	Dnipro	30	10	2	3	35	10	5	6	4	19	17	27	56
5	Metalurh Donetsk	30	8	5	2	28	12	6	2	7	17	23	10	49
6	Chornomorets	30	6	5	4	18	18	6	2	7	14	18	-4	43
7	Kryvbas	30	8	4	3	25	12	4	3	8	11	29	-5	43
8	Arsenal Kyiv	30	6	4	5	20	14	4	5	6	14	27	-7	39
9	Illichivets	30	6	4	5	12	10	4	4	7	18	22	-2	38
10	Zorya	30	6	3	6	22	24	4	4	7	10	19	-11	37
11	Tavriya	30	7	2	6	18	17	3	3	9	9	29	-19	32
12	Vorskla	30	6	5	4	19	14	2	4	9	12	22	-5	31
13	Volyn	30	4	5	6	14	21	3	3	9	12	24	-19	29
14	Karpaty	30	6	3	6	24	19	1	3	11	13	33	-15	27
15	Hoverla	30	4	5	6	17	23	1	2	12	12	34	-28	22
16	M Zaporizhya	30	1	5	9	9	31	0	3	12	3	33	-52	11

Russia

Pos	Team	P	Home					Away					GD	Pts
			W	D	L	F	A	W	D	L	F	A		
1	CSKA Moscow	30	11	2	2	23	9	9	2	4	26	16	24	64
2	Zenit	30	10	3	2	26	9	8	5	2	27	16	28	62
3	Anzhi	30	10	5	0	30	15	5	3	7	15	19	11	53
4	Spartak Moscow	30	9	3	3	26	18	6	3	6	25	21	12	51
5	Kuban Krasnodar	30	8	6	1	27	13	6	3	6	21	15	20	51
6	Rubin Kazan	30	10	2	3	21	8	5	3	7	18	19	12	50
7	Dinamo Moscow	30	8	4	3	20	14	6	3	6	21	20	7	48
8	Terek Grozny	30	9	2	4	21	17	5	4	6	17	23	-2	48
9	Lok Moscow	30	6	3	6	21	16	6	5	4	18	15	3	43
10	Krasnodar	30	10	1	4	28	12	2	5	8	17	27	6	42
11	Amkar Perm	30	6	4	5	22	22	5	3	7	12	26	-17	40
12	Volga	30	2	6	7	12	22	5	2	8	16	24	-18	29
13	Rostov	30	6	3	6	20	20	1	5	9	10	21	-11	29
14	Krylya Sovetov	30	3	3	9	14	27	4	7	7	17	25	-21	28
15	Mordovia S	30	3	8	4	17	27	2	1	12	13	30	-27	20
16	Alaniya	30	4	3	8	17	28	3	0	12	16	30	-27	19

First qualifying round first leg
Tuesday July 3 2012
Dudelange..... 7-0 ...... Tre Penne
Valletta......... 8-0 .... Lusitans
Linfield......... 0-0 .... B36

First qualifying round second leg
Tuesday July 10 2012
B36 .... 0-0 .... Linfield
  Agg: 0-0 Linfield 4-3 pens
Lusitans........ 0-1 .... Valletta
  Agg: 0-9
Tre Penne...... 0-4 ..... Dudelange
  Agg: 0-11

Second qualifying round first leg
Tuesday July 17 2012
Ulisses.......... 0-1 .... Sheriff
Flora .... 0-2 .... Basel
HJK .... 7-0 ....KR
Neftci............ 3-0 ....Zestafoni
Dudelange...... 1-0 .... Salzburg
Liberec .... 1-0 ....Shakhter
Zilina............. 1-0 Kiryat Shmona
TNS .... 0-0 .... Helsingborg
Skenderbeu.... 1-0 ....Debrecen
Valletta.......... 1-4 .... Partizan
Shamrock ...... 0-0 .... Ekranas

Wednesday July 18 2012
BATE............. 3-2 ....Vardar
AEL .... 3-0 .... Linfield
Ludogorets .... 1-1 ......Din Zagreb
Maribor......... 4-1 ..... Zeljeznicar
Buducnost ..... 0-2 .... Slask
Molde .... 3-0 ....Ventspils

Second qualifying round second leg
Tuesday July 24 2012
Shakhter .... 1-1 .... Liberec
  Agg: 1-2. Liberec win extra time
Ventspils........ 1-1 ....Molde
  Agg: 1-4
Salzburg .... 4-3 ..... Dudelange
  Agg: 4-4 Dudelange away goals
Kiryat Shmona 2-0 .... Zilina
  Agg: 2-1
Ekranas.......... 2-1 ......Shamrock
  Agg: 2-1
Zestafoni........ 2-2 .... Neftci
  Agg: 2-5
Sheriff............ 1-0 .... Ulisses
  Agg: 2-0
Basel .... 3-0 ....Flora
  Agg: 5-0
Debrecen .... 3-0 .... Skenderbeu
  Agg: 3-1
Partizan .... 3-1 .... Valletta
  Agg: 7-2
Zeljeznicar...... 1-2 ....Maribor
  Agg: 2-6
KR .... 1-2 ....HJK
  Agg: 1-9

Wednesday July 25 2012
Helsingborg ... 3-0 ....TNS
  Agg: 3-0

Vardar............ 0-0 .... BATE
  Agg: 2-3
Linfield.......... 0-0 .... AEL
  Agg: 0-3
Din Zagreb ..... 3-2 ..... Ludogorets
  Agg: 4-3
Slask .... 0-1 ......Buducnost
  Agg: 2-1

Third qualifying round first leg
Tuesday July 31 2012
Dyn Kiev .... 2-1 ......Feyenoord
Motherwell..... 0-2 Panathinaikos

Wednesday August 1 2012
BATE............. 1-1 ....Debrecen
Kiryat Shmona 4-0 .... Neftci
Sheriff............ 0-1 ......Din Zagreb
Molde .... 0-1 .... Basel
AEL .... 1-0 ....Partizan
Copenhagen... 0-0 ... Club Brugge
Maribor......... 4-1 ...... Dudelange
Anderlecht ..... 5-0 .... Ekranas
Slask .... 0-3 ....Helsingborg
CFR Cluj .... 1-0 .... Liberec
Celtic .... 2-1 .... HJK
Fenerbahce .... 1-1 .... Vaslui

Third qualifying round second leg
Tuesday August 7 2012
Feyenoord...... 0-1 ....Dyn Kiev
  Agg: 1-3
Debrecen .... 0-2 .... BATE
  Agg: 1-3

Wednesday August 8 2012
Dudelange...... 0-1 ....Maribor
  Agg: 1-5
Helsingborg ... 3-1 .... Slask
  Agg: 6-1
Neftci............ 2-2 Kiryat Shmona
  Agg: 2-6
HJK .... 0-2 ....Celtic
  Agg: 1-4
Liberec .... 1-2 .... CFR Cluj
  Agg: 1-3
Ekranas.......... 0-6 ...... Anderlecht
  Agg: 0-11
Basel .... 1-1 ....Molde
  Agg: 2-1
Vaslui............ 1-4 .....Fenerbahce
  Agg: 2-5
Club Brugge... 2-3 ... Copenhagen
  Agg: 2-3
Panathinaikos. 3-0 ..... Motherwell
  Agg: 5-0
Partizan .... 0-1 .... AEL
  Agg: 0-2
Din Zagreb ..... 4-0 .... Sheriff
  Agg: 5-0

Play-offs first leg
Tuesday August 21 2012
Spartak M...... 2-1 ......Fenerbahce
B M'gladbach.. 1-3 ......Dyn Kiev
Copenhagen... 1-0 .... Lille
Basel .... 1-2 .... CFR Cluj
Helsingborg ... 0-2 ....Celtic

Wednesday August 22 2012
BATE............. 2-0 Kiryat Shmona
AEL .... 2-1 ...... Anderlecht
Din Zagreb ..... 2-1 ....Maribor
Braga............. 1-1 ....Udinese
Malaga........... 2-0 Panathinaikos

Play-offs second leg
Tuesday August 28 2012
Kiryat Shmona 1-1 .... BATE
  Agg: 1-3
Anderlecht ..... 2-0 .... AEL
  Agg: 3-2
Maribor.......... 0-1 ......Din Zagreb
  Agg: 1-3
Udinese .... 1-1 .... Braga
  Agg: 2-2
  Braga 5-4 pens
Panathinaikos. 0-0 .... Malaga
  Agg: 0-2

Wednesday August 29 2012
CFR Cluj .... 1-0 ....Basel
  Agg: 3-1
Celtic .... 2-0 ....Helsingborg
  Agg: 4-0
Fenerbahce .... 1-1 ......Spartak M
  Agg: 2-3
Dyn Kiev .... 1-2 B M'gladbach
  Agg: 4-3
Lille................ 2-0 ... Copenhagen
  Agg: 2-1 AET

Group A

	P	W	D	L	F	A	GD	Pts
1 PSG	6	5	0	1	14	3	11	15
2 Porto	6	4	1	1	10	4	6	13
3 Dyn Kiev	6	1	2	3	6	10	-4	5
4 Din Zagreb	6	0	1	5	1	14	-13	1

Tuesday September 4 2012
Paris St-G .... (3) 4-1 (0)Dynamo Kiev
Din Zagreb ... (0) 0-2 (1) ....Porto

Wednesday October 3 2012
Dyn Kiev ...... (2) 2-0 (0) ...Din Zagreb
Porto .... (0) 1-0 (0) ....Paris St-G

Wednesday October 24 2012
Din Zagreb ... (0) 0-2 (2) ....Paris St-G
Porto .... (2) 3-2 (1)Dynamo Kiev

Tuesday November 6 2012
Dynamo Kiev (0) 0-0 (0) ....Porto
Paris St-G .... (1) 4-0 (0) ...Din Zagreb

Wednesday November 21 2012
Dynamo Kiev (0) 0-2 (1) ....Paris St-G
Porto .... (1) 3-0 (0) ...Din Zagreb

Tuesday December 4 2012
Din Zagreb ... (0) 1-1 (1)Dynamo Kiev
Paris St-G .... (1) 2-1 (1) ....Porto

Group B

	P	W	D	L	F	A	GD	Pts
1 Schalke	6	3	3	0	10	6	4	12
2 Arsenal	6	3	1	2	10	8	2	10
3 Olympiacos	6	3	0	3	9	9	0	9
4 Montpellier	6	0	2	4	6	12	-6	2

Tuesday September 18 2012
Montpellier... (1) 1-2 (2) ....Arsenal
Olympiacos.. (0) 1-2 (1) .... Schalke

Wednesday October 3 2012
Arsenal .... (1) 3-1 (1) . Olympiacos
Schalke........ (1) 2-2 (1) ...Montpellier
Wednesday October 24 2012
Arsenal .... (0) 0-2 (0) ...... Schalke
Montpellier... (0) 1-2 (0) . Olympiacos
Tuesday November 6 2012
Olympiacos.. (1) 3-1 (0) ...Montpellier
Schalke........ (1) 2-2 (2) ....Arsenal
Wednesday November 21 2012
Arsenal .... (0) 2-0 (0) ...Montpellier
Schalke........ (0) 1-0 (0) . Olympiacos
Tuesday December 4 2012
Montpellier... (0) 1-1 (0) ...... Schalke
Olympiacos.. (0) 2-1 (1) ....Arsenal

Group C

	P	W	D	L	F	A	GD	Pts
1 Malaga	6	3	3	0	12	5	7	12
2 AC Milan	6	2	2	2	7	6	1	8
3 Zenit	6	2	1	3	6	9	-3	7
4 Anderlecht	6	1	2	3	4	9	-5	5

Tuesday September 18 2012
Malaga......... (2) 3-0 (0) ....Zenit
AC Milan..... (0) 0-0 (0) ... Anderlecht
Wednesday October 3 2012
Anderlecht ... (0) 0-3 (1) .... Malaga
Zenit .... (1) 2-3 (2) .....AC Milan
Wednesday October 24 2012
Malaga......... (0) 1-0 (0) .....AC Milan
Zenit .... (0) 1-0 (0) ... Anderlecht
Tuesday November 6 2012
Anderlecht ... (0) 1-0 (0) ....Zenit
AC Milan..... (0) 1-1 (1) .... Malaga
Wednesday November 21 2012
Anderlecht ... (0) 1-3 (0) .....AC Milan
Zenit .... (0) 2-2 (2) ...... Malaga
Tuesday December 4 2012
Malaga......... (1) 2-2 (0) ... Anderlecht
AC Milan...... (0) 0-1 (1) ....Zenit

Group D

	P	W	D	L	F	A	GD	Pts
1 B Dortmund	6	4	2	0	11	5	6	14
2 Real Madrid	6	3	2	1	15	9	6	11
3 Ajax	6	1	1	4	8	16	-8	4
4 Man City	6	0	3	3	7	11	-4	3

Tuesday September 18 2012
B Dortmund. (0) 1-0 (0) ....Ajax
Real Madrid . (0) 3-2 (0) .....Man City
Wednesday October 3 2012
Ajax .... (0) 1-4 (1) . Real Madrid
Man City ...... (0) 1-1 (0) .B Dortmund
Wednesday October 24 2012
Ajax .... (1) 3-1 (1) ...Man City
B Dortmund. (1) 2-1 (1) . Real Madrid
Tuesday November 6 2012
Man City ...... (1) 2-2 (2) ....Ajax
Real Madrid . (1) 2-2 (2) .B Dortmund
Wednesday November 21 2012
Ajax .... (0) 1-4 (3) .B Dortmund
Man City ...... (1) 1-1 (0) . Real Madrid

Tuesday December 4 2012
B Dortmund . (0) 1-0 (0) ......Man City
Real Madrid . (2) 4-1 (0) ....Ajax

Group E

	P	W	D	L	F	A	GD	Pts
1 Juventus	6	3	3	0	12	4	8	12
2 Shakhtar	6	3	1	2	12	8	4	10
3 Chelsea	6	3	1	2	16	10	6	10
4 Nordsjaelland	6	0	1	5	4	22	-18	1

Wednesday September 19 2012
Chelsea........ (2) 2-2 (1) ......Juventus
Shakhtar ...... (1) 2-0 (0)Nordsjaelland
Tuesday October 2 2012
Juventus ...... (1) 1-1 (1) ......Shakhtar
Nordsjaelland(0) 0-4 (1) .... Chelsea
Tuesday October 23 2012
Nordsjaelland(0) 1-1 (0) ......Juventus
Shakhtar ...... (1) 2-1 (1) .... Chelsea
Wednesday November 7 2012
Chelsea........ (2) 3-2 (1) ......Shakhtar
Juventus ...... (3) 4-0 (0)Nordsjaelland
Tuesday November 20 2012
Juventus ...... (1) 3-0 (0) ...... Chelsea
Nordsjaelland(2) 2-5 (2) ......Shakhtar
Wednesday December 5 2012
Chelsea........ (2) 6-1 (0)Nordsjaelland
Shakhtar ...... (0) 0-1 (0) ......Juventus

Group F

	P	W	D	L	F	A	GD	Pts
1 B Munich	6	4	1	1	15	7	8	13
2 Valencia	6	4	1	1	12	5	7	13
3 BATE	6	2	0	4	9	15	-6	6
4 Lille	6	1	0	5	4	13	-9	3

Wednesday September 19 2012
B Munich ..... (1) 2-1 (0) ....Valencia
Lille.............. (0) 1-3 (3) .... BATE
Tuesday October 2 2012
BATE............ (1) 3-1 (0) .....B Munich
Valencia .... (1) 2-0 (0) .... Lille
Tuesday October 23 2012
BATE Borisov(0) 0-3 (1) ....Valencia
Lille.............. (0) 0-1 (1) .....B Munich
Wednesday November 7 2012
B Munich ..... (5) 6-1 (0) .... Lille
Valencia .... (2) 4-2 (0) .... BATE
Tuesday November 20 2012
BATE............ (0) 0-2 (2) .... Lille
Valencia .... (0) 1-0 (0) .....B Munich
Wednesday December 5 2012
Lille.............. (0) 0-1 (1) ......Valencia
B Munich ..... (1) 4-1 (0) .... BATE

Group G

	P	W	D	L	F	A	GD	Pts
1 Barcelona	6	4	1	1	11	5	6	13
2 Celtic	6	3	1	2	9	8	1	10
3 Benfica	6	2	2	2	5	0	0	8
4 Spartak M	6	1	0	5	7	14	-7	3

Wednesday September 19 2012
Barcelona .... (1) 3-2 (1) ....Spartak M
Celtic .... (0) 0-0 (0) .... Benfica

Tuesday October 2 2012
Benfica .... (0) 0-2 (1) .... Barcelona
Spartak M.... (1) 2-3 (1) .... Celtic
Tuesday October 23 2012
Barcelona .... (1) 2-1 (1) .... Celtic
Spartak M ... (2) 2-1 (1) .... Benfica
Wednesday November 7 2012
Benfica .... (0) 2-0 (0) ...Spartak M
Celtic .... (1) 2-1 (0) .... Barcelona
Tuesday November 20 2012
Benfica .... (1) 2-1 (1) .... Celtic
Spartak M ... (0) 0-3 (3) .... Barcelona
Wednesday December 5 2012
Barcelona .... (0) 0-0 (0) .... Benfica
Celtic .... (1) 2-1 (1) ....Spartak M

Group H

	P	W	D	L	F	A	GD	Pts
1 Man Utd	6	4	0	2	9	6	3	12
2 Galatasaray	6	3	1	2	7	6	1	10
3 CFR Cluj	6	3	1	2	9	7	2	10
4 Braga	6	1	0	5	7	13	-6	3

Wednesday September 19 2012
Braga........... (0) 0-2 (2) ..... CFR Cluj
Man Utd....... (1) 1-0 (0) . Galatasaray
Tuesday October 2 2012
CFR Cluj ...... (1) 1-2 (1) ...... Man Utd
Galatasaray.. (0) 0-2 (1) .... Braga
Tuesday October 23 2012
Galatasaray.. (0) 1-1 (1) ..... CFR Cluj
Man Utd....... (1) 3-2 (2) .... Braga
Wednesday November 7 2012
Braga........... (0) 1-3 (0) ...... Man Utd
CFR Cluj ...... (1) 1-3 (1) . Galatasaray
Tuesday November 20 2012
CFR Cluj ...... (3) 3-1 (1) .... Braga
Galatasaray.. (0) 1-0 (0) ...... Man Utd
Wednesday December 5 2012
Man Utd....... (0) 0-1 (0) ...... CFR Cluj
Braga .... (1) 1-2 (0) . Galatasaray

Round of 16 first leg
Tuesday February 12 2013
Celtic .... (0) 0-3 (1) ......Juventus
Valencia .... (0) 1-2 (2) ....Paris St-G
Wednesday February 13 2013
Real Madrid . (1) 1-1 (1) ... Man Utd
Shakhtar ...... (1) 2-2 (1) .B Dortmund
Tuesday February 19 2013
Arsenal .... (0) 1-3 (2) ....B Munich
Porto .... (0) 1-0 (0) .... Malaga
Wednesday February 20 2013
AC Milan...... (0) 2-0 (0) ... Barcelona
Galatasaray.. (1) 1-1 (1) .... Schalke

Round of 16 second leg
Tuesday March 5 2013
B Dortmund . (2) 3-0 (0) ......Shakhtar
Agg: 5-2
Man Utd....... (0) 1-2 (0) . Real Madrid
Agg: 2-3

Wednesday March 6 2013
Juventus ...... (1) 2-0 (0) ....Celtic
　　Agg: 5-0
Paris St-G .... (0) 1-1 (0) ....Valencia
　　Agg: 3-2
Tuesday March 12 2013
Barcelona .... (2) 4-0 (0) ......AC Milan
　　Agg: 4-2
Schalke........ (1) 2-3 (2) . Galatasaray
　　Agg: 3-4
Wednesday March 13 2013
B Munich ..... (0) 0-2 (1) ....Arsenal
　　Agg: 3-3 Bayern away goals
Malaga......... (1) 2-0 (0) ....Porto
　　Agg: 2-1

Quarter-finals first leg
Tuesday April 2 2013
B Munich ..... (1) 2-0 (0) ......Juventus
Paris St-G .... (0) 2-2 (1) .... Barcelona
Wednesday April 3 2013
Malaga......... (0) 0-0 (0) .B Dortmund
Real Madrid . (2) 3-0 (0) . Galatasaray

Quarter-finals second leg
Tuesday April 9 2013
B Dortmund . (1) 3-2 (1) .... Malaga
　　Agg: 3-2
Galatasaray .. (0) 3-2 (1) . Real Madrid
　　Agg: 3-5
Wednesday April 10 2013
Barcelona .... (0) 1-1 (0) .... Paris St-G
　　Agg: 3-3 Barcelona away goals
Juventus ...... (0) 0-2 (0) .....B Munich
　　Agg: 0-4

Semi-finals first leg
Tuesday April 23 2013
B Munich ..... (1) 4-0 (0) .... Barcelona
Wednesday April 24 2013
B Dortmund . (1) 4-1 (1) . Real Madrid

Semi-finals second leg
Tuesday April 30 2013
Real Madrid . (0) 2-0 (0) .B Dortmund
　　Agg: 3-4
Wednesday May 1 2013
Barcelona .... (0) 0-3 (0) .....B Munich
　　Agg: 0-7

Final
Saturday May 25 2013
B Dortmund . (0) 1-2 (0) .....B Munich
POS 39/61 SH ON 7/10 SH OFF 2/4 CRN 6/8
SCORERS B Dortmund: Gundogan (pen 68)
B Munich: Mandzukic (60) Robben (89)
CARDS B Dortmund: Grosskreutz ▰
B Munich: Dante ▰ Ribery ▰

Europa League

First qualifying round first leg
Tuesday July 3 2012
Vikingur .... 0-6 .... Gomel
Shkendija....... 0-0 ......Portadown
Thursday July 5 2012
Xazar .... 2-2 ....Kalju
Jagodina........ 0-1 ....Ordabasy

Mario Gomez scores the first goal of Bayern's 7-0 aggregate demolition of Barcelona in the semi-finals

Trans	0-5	...... Inter Baku
KuPS	2-1	.............Llanelli
Renova	4-0	.........Libertas
Levadia..........	1-0	.... Siauliai
Pyunik	0-3	...............Zeta
JJK	2-0	.... Stabaek
Rudar Pljevlja.	0-1	...........Shirak
Baku	0-0	.... Mura
Elfsborg	8-0	.... Floriana
Suduva	0-1	.... Daugava
Differdange	3-0	................NSI
Dacia	1-0	..............Celje
Birkirkara	2-2	Metalurg Skopje
Torpedo Kutaisi	1-1	...........Aktobe
Tirana	2-0	Grevenmacher
Santa Coloma .	0-1	.... Osijek
Sarajevo	5-2	..... Hibernians
Twente	6-0	.. UE S Coloma
O Ljubljana.....	3-0	Jeunesse Esch
Lech	2-0	...........Zhetysu
EB/Streymur ..	3-1	..... Gandzasar
MTK	1-1	...........Senica
Cefn Druids....	0-0	.... MYPA

Flamurtari	0-1	..........Honved
La Fiorita........	0-2	.....Liepajas M
Teuta..............	0-3	... M Rustavi
Bangor...........	0-0	...........Zimbru
St Patrick's	1-0	.... IBV
Bohemians.....	0-0	.... Thor
Cliftonville......	1-0	...........Kalmar
Crusaders......	0-3	.....Rosenborg
Borac.............	2-2	....Celik Niksic
FH	2-1	Eschen/Mauren

First qualifying round second leg
Tuesday July 10 2012
Floriana.......... 0-4 ....Elfsborg
　　Agg: 0-12
Grevenmacher 0-0 ....Tirana
　　Agg: 0-2
Kalju .... 0-2 Xazar Lankaran
　　Agg: 2-4
Portadown ..... 2-1 ....Shkendija
　　Agg: 2-1
Thursday July 12 2012
Zhetysu.......... 1-1 ....Lech
　　Agg: 1-3

Ordabasy....... 0-0 ....Jagodina
Agg: 1-0
M Rustavi...... 6-1 .... Teuta
Agg: 9-1
Shirak........... 1-1 ..Rudar Pljevlja
Agg: 2-1
Aktobe.......... 1-0 Torpedo Kutaisi
Agg: 2-1
Metalurg Skopje 0-0 .... Birkirkara
Agg: 2-2 Metalurg Skopje away goals
Gandzasar...... 2-0 ...EB/Streymur
Agg: 3-3 Gandzasar away goals
Celik Niksic.... 1-1 .... Borac
Agg: 3-3 Celik Niksic away goals
Gomel........... 4-0 .... Vikingur
Agg: 10-0
Liepajas M..... 4-0 .... La Fiorita
Agg: 6-0
Jeunesse Esch... 0-3 ..... O Ljubljana
Agg: 0-6
Siauliai.......... 2-1 ....Levadia
Agg: 2-2 Levadia away goals
Daugava........ 2-3 ....Suduva
Agg: 3-3 Suduva away goals
Inter Baku...... 2-0 .... Trans

Agg: 7-0
Zimbru........... 2-1 .... Bangor
Agg: 2-1
MYPA............ 5-0 .... Cefn Druids
Agg: 5-0
Stabaek .... 3-2 ....JJK
Agg: 3-4
Rosenborg..... 1-0 ....Crusaders
Agg: 4-0
Kalmar........... 4-0 ......Cliftonville
Agg: 4-1
Senica .... 2-1 .... MTK
Agg: 3-2
UE S Coloma . 0-3 ....Twente
Agg: 0-9
Llanelli.......... 1-1 ....KuPS
Agg: 2-3
NSI................ 0-3 .....Differdange
Agg: 0-6
Hibernians..... 4-4 .... Sarajevo
Agg: 6-9
Eschen/Mauren 0-1 .... FH
Agg: 1-3
Zeta .... 1-2 .... Pyunik
Agg: 4-2

Celje............. 0-1 ....Dacia
Agg: 0-2
Mura............. 2-0 ....Baku
Agg: 2-0
Osijek .... 3-1 Santa Coloma
Agg: 4-1
Honved......... 2-0 ....Flamurtari
Agg: 3-0
Libertas........ 0-4 ....Renova
Agg: 0-8
Thor.............. 5-1 .... Bohemians
Agg: 5-1
IBV .... 2-1 .... St Patrick's
Agg: 2-2 St Patrick's away goals

Second qualifying round first leg
Thursday July 19 2012

Xazar............. 1-1 ....Lech
Naftan........... 3-4 Crvena Zvezda
Milsami......... 4-2 ....Aktobe
Liepajas M.... 2-2 .... Legia
Anzhi............ 1-0 ....Honved
Lok Plovdiv.... 4-4 ....Vitesse
Renova .... 0-2 .... Gomel
Levadia......... 1-3 .....Anorthosis
M Rustavi...... 1-3 .... Plzen
Inter Baku...... 1-1 ....Asteras
JJK............... 3-2 ....Zeta
O Ljubljana..... 0-0 ....Tromso
Differdange.... 0-1 .... Gent
Shakhtyor...... 1-1 .... Ried
Bnei Yehuda... 2-0 ....Shirak
Rosenborg..... 2-2 ....Ordabasy
Sp Trnava...... 3-1 ....Sligo
Levski........... 1-0 .... Sarajevo
APOEL.......... 2-0 .... Senica
Ruch........... 3-1 Metalurg Skopje
AGF.............. 1-2 ....Dila
M Boleslav.... 3-0 .... Thor
AIK............... 1-1 .... FH
Eskisehirspor . 2-0 .. St Johnstone
Tirana .... 1-1 .. Aalesund
M Donetsk..... 7-0 ....Celik Niksic
S Koprivnica... 6-0 .....Portadown
Dacia............ 1-0 ....Elfsborg
Zalgiris.......... 1-1 .... Admira
Young Boys.... 1-0 ....Zimbru
R Bucharest... 3-1 .... MYPA
Servette........ 2-0 ..... Gandzasar
Twente.......... 1-1 ..... Inter Turku
M Netanya..... 1-2 ....KuPS
Osijek .... 1-3 ....Kalmar
Mura............. 0-0 ....CSKA Sofia
S Bratislava.... 1-1 ....Videoton
Vojvodina...... 1-1 .... Siduva
Hajduk Split... 2-0 ....Skonto
Siroki Brijeg ... 1-1 ..... St Patrick's

Second qualifying round second leg
Thursday July 26 2012

Shirak........... 0-1 ....Bnei Yehuda
Agg: 0-3
Ordabasy...... 1-2 ......Rosenborg
Agg: 3-4
Dila.............. 3-1 ....AGF
Agg: 5-2
M Skopje...... 0-3 .... Ruch
Agg: 1-6

Gandzasar...... 1-3 ....Servette
Agg: 1-5
Celik Niksic .... 2-4 ......M Donetsk
Agg: 2-11
KuPS .... 0-1 ......M Netanya
Agg: 2-2 KuPS away goals
Aktobe .... 3-0 .... Milsami
Agg: 5-4
Gomel............ 0-1 ....Renova
Agg: 2-1
Inter Turku...... 0-5 ....Twente
Agg: 1-6
Elfsborg .... 2-0 ....Dacia
Agg: 2-1
Honved .... 0-4 ....Anzhi
Agg: 0-5
MYPA............ 0-2 ....R Bucharest
Agg: 1-5
Suduva .... 0-4 .....Vojvodina
Agg: 1-5
Aalesund........ 5-0 ....Tirana
Agg: 6-1
Anorthosis ..... 3-0 ....Levadia
Agg: 6-1
CSKA Sofia .... 1-1 .... Mura
Agg: 1-1 Mura away goals
Asteras .... 1-1 ......Inter Baku
Agg: 2-2 Asteras 4-2 pens
Kalmar.......... 3-0 ....Osijek
Agg: 6-1
Ried.............. 0-0 ......Shakhtyor
Agg: 1-1 Ried away goals
Tromso .... 1-0 ..... O Ljubljana
Agg: 1-0 AET
Zimbru .... 1-0 .... Young Boys
Agg: 1-1 Young Boys 4-1 pens
Gent............. 3-2 .....Differdange
Agg: 4-2
Senica .... 0-1 ....APOEL
Agg: 0-3
Plzen .... 2-0 ......M Rustavi
Agg: 5-1
Sligo .... 1-1 ...... Sp Trnava
Agg: 2-4
Vitesse.......... 3-1 .....Lok Plovdiv
Agg: 7-5
Zeta .... 1-0 ....JJK
Agg: 3-3 Zeta away goals
Lech .... 1-0 Xazar Lankaran
Agg: 2-1
Skonto .... 1-0 .... Hajduk Split
Agg: 1-2
Crvena Zvezda 3-3 .... Naftan
Agg: 7-6
Legia .... 5-1 .....Liepajas M
Agg: 7-3
Videoton .... 0-0 ... S Bratislava
Agg: 1-1 Videoton away goals
St Patrick's .... 1-1 .... Siroki Brijeg
Agg: 3-2 St Patrick's win extra time
St Johnstone.. 1-1 ..Eskisehirspor
Agg: 1-3
Portadown ..... 2-4 ... S Koprivnica
Agg: 2-10
Sarajevo .... 3-1 ....Levski
Agg: 3-2
Admira........... 5-1 ...... Zalgiris
Agg: 6-2
Thor.............. 0-1 .....M Boleslav
Agg: 0-4
FH .... 0-1 ....AIK
Agg: 1-2

Third qualifying round first leg
Thursday August 2 2012
Anzhi .... 2-0 .... Vitesse
KuPS .... 1-0 ......Bursaspor
Arsenal Kiev... 0-3 (f) .... Mura
Match forfeited
Dila.............. 0-1 ....Anorthosis
Bnei Yehuda... 0-2 ....PAOK
Ruch............. 0-2 ....Plzen
APOEL .... 2-1 .... Aalesund
Tromso .... 1-1 ......M Donetsk
Kalmar.......... 1-0 .... Young Boys
AIK .... 3-0 ....Lech
Ried.............. 2-1 .... Legia
Heerenveen .... 4-0 ....R Bucharest
Twente .... 2-0 .....M Boleslav
Steaua .... 0-1 ...... Sp Trnava
Servette .... 1-1 .....Rosenberg
Asteras .... 1-1 ....Maritimo
Gomel............ 0-1 .... Liverpool
Genk.............. 2-1 ....Aktobe
Horsens......... 1-1 ....Elfsborg
Crvena Zvezda 0-0 ....Omonia
Videoton .... 1-0 .... Gent
Dundee Utd.... 2-2 ... Din Moscow
Eskisehirspor . 1-1 ....Marseille
St Patrick's .... 0-3 ....Hannover
Hajduk Split.... 0-3 ...... Inter Milan
Vojvodina....... 2-1 .. Rapid Vienna
Ath Bilbao ...... 3-1 ... S Koprivnica
Sarajevo .... 2-1 ....Zeta
Admira........... 0-2 .... Sparta

Third qualifying round second leg
Thursday August 9 2012
Omonia.......... 0-0 Crvena Zvezda
Agg: 0-0 Crvena Zvezda 6-5 pens
Din Moscow .. 5-0 .....Dundee Utd
Agg: 7-2
Elfsborg .... 2-3 ....Horsens
Agg: 3-4
Aktobe .... 1-2 ....Genk
Agg: 2-4
S Koprivnica... 2-1 ......Ath Bilbao
Agg: 3-4
Legia .... 3-1 .... Ried
Agg: 4-3
Rosenborg .... 0-0 ....Servette
Agg: 1-1 Rosenborg away goals
M Donetsk .... 0-1 ....Tromso
Agg: 1-2
M Boleslav ..... 0-2 ....Twente
Agg: 0-4
Aalesund........ 0-1 ....APOEL
Agg: 1-3
Anorthosis ..... 0-3 ....Dila
Match abandoned
Young Boys.... 3-0 ....Kalmar
Agg: 3-1
Sp Trnava ..... 0-3 ....Steaua
Agg: 1-3
Gent............. 0-3 ....Videoton
Agg: 0-4
Lech .... 1-0 ....AIK
Agg: 1-3
Zeta .... 1-0 .... Sarajevo
Agg: 2-2 Zeta away goals
Sparta .... 2-2 .... Admira
Agg: 4-2

Mura............ 0-2 ... Arsenal Kiev
Agg: 3-2
Vitesse.......... 0-2 ....Anzhi
Agg: 0-4
Plzen .... 5-0 .... Ruch
Agg: 7-0
PAOK............ 4-1 ....Bnei Yehuda
Agg: 6-1
R Bucharest... 1-0 .... Heerenveen
Agg: 1-4
Hannover .... 2-0 ... St Patrick's
Agg: 5-0
Bursaspor...... 6-0 ....KuPS
Agg: 6-1
Marseille........ 3-0 ..Eskisehirspor
Agg: 4-1
Inter Milan..... 0-2 ... Hajduk Split
Agg: 3-2
Maritimo .... 0-0 ....Asteras
Agg: 1-1 Maritimo away goals
Liverpool........ 3-0 .... Gomel
Agg: 4-0
Rapid Vienna.. 2-0 .....Vojvodina
Agg: 3-2

Play-offs first leg
Thursday August 23 2012
Anzhi .... 1-0 .... AZ
Neftci............ 1-1 ....APOEL
Tromso .... 3-2 .... Partizan
Ekranas......... 0-2 .... Steaua
Liberec .... 2-2 .... Dnipro
AIK .... 0-1 ... CSKA Moscow
Legia .... 1-1 .....Rosenborg
Atromitos....... 1-1 ......Newcastle
Molde .... 2-0 .... Heerenveen
Sheriff........... 1-2 ....Marseille
Bursaspor...... 3-1 ....Twente
Din Bucharest 0-2 .... Metalist
Luzern .... 2-1 ....Genk
Trabzonspor... 0-0 ....Videoton
Dudelange...... 1-3 ...... H Tel-Aviv
Feyenoord...... 2-2 .... Sparta
Midtjylland..... 0-3 ... Young Boys
Debrecen ...... 0-3 ... Club Brugge
Lokeren .... 2-1 .... Plzen
PAOK............ 2-1 .. Rapid Vienna
Vaslui............ 0-2 ... Inter Milan
Hearts .... 0-1 ... Liverpool
Slask .... 3-5 ......Hannover
Motherwell..... 0-2 .... Levante
Crvena Zvezda 0-0 ...... Bordeaux
Ath Bilbao ...... 6-0 ....HJK
Maritimo .... 1-0 ....Dila
Mura............ 0-2 .... Lazio
Horsens......... 1-1 ...... Sporting
Zeta .... 0-5 ....PSV

Wednesday August 22 2012
Stuttgart .... 2-0 ... Din Moscow

Play-offs second leg
Thursday August 30 2012
Dila.............. 0-2 ....Maritimo
Agg: 0-3
Dnipro........... 4-2 .... Liberec
Agg: 6-4
CSKA Moscow 0-2 ....AIK
Agg: 1-2
Rosenborg ..... 2-1 .... Legia
Agg: 3-2

PSV .... 9-0 .... Zeta
Agg: 14-0
Heerenveen.... 1-2 ....Molde
Agg: 1-4
APOEL .... 1-3 .... Neftci
Agg: 2-4
HJK .... 3-3 ....Ath Bilbao
Agg: 3-9
H Tel-Aviv ...... 4-0 ...... Dudelange
Agg: 7-1
Sparta .... 2-0 ....Feyenoord
Agg: 4-2
Young Boys.... 0-2 ...Midtjylland
Agg: 3-2
Steaua .... 3-0 .... Ekranas
Agg: 5-0
Genk.............. 2-0 ....Luzern
Agg: 3-2
Metalist.......... 2-1   Din Bucharest
Agg: 4-1
Plzen .... 1-0 ...... Lokeren
Agg: 2-2 Plzen away goals
Bordeaux .... 3-2 Crvena Zvezda
Agg: 3-2
Club Brugge... 4-1 ....Debrecen
Agg: 7-1
Marseille........ 0-0 .... Sheriff
Agg: 2-1
Videoton .... 0-0 ....Trabzonspor
Agg: 0-0 Videoton 4-2 pens
Partizan .... 1-0 ....Tromso
Agg: 3-3 Partizan away goals
Inter Milan...... 2-2 .... Vaslui
Agg: 4-2
Levante........... 1-0 ..... Motherwell
Agg: 3-0
Hannover .... 5-1 ....Slask
Agg: 10-4
Rapid Vienna.. 3-0 ....PAOK
Agg: 4-2
Lazio.............. 3-1 .... Mura
Agg: 5-1
Twente........... 4-1 ....Bursaspor
Agg: 5-4 Twente win extra time
AZ.................. 0-5 ....Anzhi
Agg: 0-6
Newcastle...... 1-0 .... Atromitos
Agg: 2-1
Liverpool........ 1-1 .... Hearts
Agg: 2-1
Sporting......... 5-0 ....Horsens
Agg: 6-1

Tuesday August 28 2012
Din Moscow .. 1-1 .... Stuttgart
Agg: 1-3

Group A

	P	W	D	L	F	A	GD	Pts
1 Liverpool	6	3	1	2	11	9	2	10
2 Anzhi	6	3	1	2	7	5	2	10
3 Young Boys	6	3	1	2	14	13	1	10
4 Udinese	6	1	1	4	7	12	-5	4

Thursday September 20
Udinese .... (0) 1-1 (1) ....Anzhi
Young Boys.. (1) 3-5 (2) ..... Liverpool
Thursday October 4
Anzhi .... (0) 2-0 (0) . Young Boys
Liverpool...... (1) 2-3 (0) .... Udinese
Thursday October 25
Liverpool... (0) 1-0 (0) ....Anzhi
Young Boys.. (1) 3-1 (0) .... Udinese

Thursday November 8
Anzhi .... (1) 1-0 (0) ..... Liverpool
Udinese .... (0) 2-3 (1) . Young Boys
Thursday November 22
Anzhi .... (0) 2-0 (0) .... Udinese
Liverpool...... (1) 2-2 (0) . Young Boys
Thursday December 6
Udinese .... (0) 0-1 (1) ..... Liverpool
Young Boys.. (1) 3-1 (1) ....Anzhi

Group B

	P	W	D	L	F	A	GD	Pts
1 Plzen	6	4	1	1	11	4	7	13
2 Atl Madrid	6	4	0	2	7	4	3	12
3 Academica	6	1	2	3	6	9	-3	5
4 H Tel Aviv	6	1	1	4	4	11	-7	4

Thursday September 20
H Tel Aviv..... (0) 0-3 (2) ...Atl Madrid
Plzen .... (0) 3-1 (1) .. Academica
Thursday October 4
Academica... (0) 1-1 (0) .... H Tel Aviv
Atl Madrid .... (0) 1-0 (0) .... Plzen
Thursday October 25
Atl Madrid .... (0) 2-1 (0) .. Academica
H Tel Aviv..... (1) 1-2 (1) .... Plzen
Thursday November 8
Academica... (1) 2-0 (0) ....Atl Madrid
Plzen .... (2) 4-0 (0) .... H Tel Aviv
Thursday November 22
Academica... (0) 1-1 (0) .... Plzen
Atl Madrid .... (1) 1-0 (0) .... H Tel Aviv
Thursday December 6
H Tel Aviv..... (0) 2-0 (0) .. Academica
Plzen .... (1) 1-0 (0) ....Atl Madrid

Group C

	P	W	D	L	F	A	GD	Pts
1 Fenerbahce	6	4	1	1	10	7	3	13
2 M'gladbach	6	3	2	1	11	6	5	11
3 Marseille	6	1	2	3	9	11	-2	5
4 AEL Limassol	6	1	1	4	4	10	-6	4

Thursday September 20
AEL Limassol(0) 0-0 (0) ..M'gladbach
Fenerbahce .. (1) 2-2 (0) ......Marseille
Thursday October 4
M'gladbach.. (1) 2-4 (2) ..Fenerbahce
Marseille ...... (1) 5-1 (1)AEL Limassol
Thursday October 25
AEL Limassol(0) 0-1 (1) ..Fenerbahce
M'gladbach.. (1) 2-0 (0) ......Marseille
Thursday November 8
Fenerbahce .. (2) 2-0 (0)AEL Limassol
Marseille ...... (2) 2-1 (1) ..M'gladbach
Thursday November 22
M'gladbach.. (0) 2-0 (0)AEL Limassol
Marseille ...... (0) 0-1 (1) ..Fenerbahce
Thursday December 6
AEL Limassol(1) 3-0 (0) ......Marseille
Fenerbahce .. (0) 0-3 (2) ..M'gladbach

Group D

	P	W	D	L	F	A	GD	Pts
1 Bordeaux	6	4	1	1	10	5	5	13
2 Newcastle	6	2	3	1	7	5	2	9
3 Maritimo	6	1	3	2	4	6	-2	6
4 Club Brugge	6	1	1	4	6	11	-5	4

Thursday September 20
Bordeaux ..... (2) 4-0 (0) Club Brugge
Maritimo ...... (0) 0-0 (0) ...Newcastle
Thursday October 4
Club Brugge. (0) 2-0 (0) ......Maritimo
Newcastle.... (2) 3-0 (0) ..... Bordeaux
Thursday October 25
Maritimo ...... (1) 1-1 (1) ..... Bordeaux
Newcastle.... (0) 1-0 (0) Club Brugge
Thursday November 8
Club Brugge. (0) 2-2 (2) ....Newcastle
Bordeaux ..... (1) 1-0 (0) ......Maritimo
Thursday November 22
Club Brugge. (0) 1-2 (2) ...... Bordeaux
Newcastle.... (1) 1-1 (1) ......Maritimo
Thursday December 6
Bordeaux ..... (1) 2-0 (0) ....Newcastle
Maritimo ...... (1) 2-1 (0) Club Brugge

Group E

	P	W	D	L	F	A	GD	Pts
1 Steaua	6	3	2	1	9	9	0	11
2 Stuttgart	6	2	2	2	9	6	3	8
3 Copenhagen	6	2	2	2	5	6	-1	8
4 Molde	6	2	0	4	6	8	-2	6

Thursday September 20
Copenhagen. (1) 2-1 (1) .... Molde
Stuttgart ...... (1) 2-2 (1) ....Steaua
Thursday October 4
Molde .... (0) 2-0 (0) ...... Stuttgart
Steaua .... (0) 1-0 (0) Copenhagen
Thursday October 25
Steaua .... (2) 2-0 (0) .... Molde
Stuttgart ...... (0) 0-0 (0) Copenhagen
Thursday November 8
Copenhagen. (0) 0-2 (0) ...... Stuttgart
Molde .... (0) 1-2 (2) ....Steaua
Thursday November 22
Molde .... (0) 1-2 (1) Copenhagen
Steaua .... (0) 1-5 (4) ..... Stuttgart
Thursday December 6
Copenhagen. (0) 1-1 (0) ....Steaua
Stuttgart ...... (0) 0-1 (1) .... Molde

Group F

	P	W	D	L	F	A	GD	Pts
1 Dnipro	6	5	0	1	16	8	8	15
2 Napoli	6	3	0	3	12	12	0	9
3 PSV	6	2	1	3	8	7	1	7
4 AIK	6	1	1	4	5	14	-9	4

Thursday September 20
Dnipro.......... (0) 2-0 (0) ....PSV
Napoli .... (1) 4-0 (0) ....AIK
Thursday October 4
AIK .... (2) 2-3 (0) ..... Dnipro
PSV .... (2) 3-0 (0) ......Napoli
Thursday October 25
Dnipro.......... (2) 3-1 (0) ......Napoli
PSV .... (0) 1-1 (0) ......AIK
Thursday November 8
AIK .... (1) 1-0 (0) ......PSV
Napoli .... (1) 4-2 (1) ...... Dnipro

Thursday November 22
AIK ....(1) 1-2 (1) ....Napoli
PSV ....(1) 1-2 (1) .... Dnipro
Thursday December 6
Dnipro.........(2) 4-0 (0) ....AIK
Napoli.........(1) 1-3 (2) ....PSV

Group G

	P	W	D	L	F	A	GD	Pts
1 Genk	6	3	3	0	9	4	5	12
2 Basel	6	2	3	1	7	4	3	9
3 Videoton	6	2	0	4	6	8	-2	6
4 Sporting	6	1	2	3	4	10	-6	5

Thursday September 20
Genk...........(1) 3-0 (0) ......Videoton
Sporting.......(0) 0-0 (0) ....Basel
Thursday October 4
Basel ....(0) 2-2 (2) ....Genk
Videoton ......(3) 3-0 (0) ..... Sporting
Thursday October 25
Genk...........(1) 2-1 (1) ..... Sporting
Videoton ......(2) 2-1 (0) ....Basel
Thursday November 8
Basel ....(0) 1-0 (0) ......Videoton
Sporting.......(0) 1-1 (0) ....Genk
Thursday November 22
Basel ....(1) 3-0 (0) ...... Sporting
Videoton ......(0) 0-1 (1) ....Genk
Thursday December 6
Genk...........(0) 0-0 (0) ....Basel
Friday December 7
Sporting.......(0) 2-1 (0) .....Videoton

Group H

	P	W	D	L	F	A	GD	Pts
1 Rubin	6	4	2	0	10	3	7	14
2 Inter	6	3	2	1	11	9	2	11
3 Partizan	6	0	3	3	8	8	-5	3
4 Neftci	6	0	3	3	4	8	-4	3

Thursday September 20
Inter.............(1) 2-2 (1) ....Rubin
Partizan ......(0) 0-0 (0) ....Neftci
Thursday October 4
Neftci...........(0) 1-3 (3) ....Inter
Rubin...........(1) 2-0 (0) ....Partizan
Thursday October 25
Inter.............(0) 1-0 (0) ....Partizan
Rubin...........(1) 1-0 (0) ....Neftci
Thursday November 8
Neftci...........(0) 0-1 (1) ....Rubin
Partizan ......(0) 1-3 (0) ....Inter
Thursday November 22
Neftchi Baku (1) 1-1 (0) ......Partizan
Rubin...........(1) 3-0 (0) ....Inter
Thursday December 6
Inter.............(1) 2-2 (1) ....Neftci
Partizan ......(0) 1-1 (0) ....Rubin

Group I

	P	W	D	L	F	A	GD	Pts
1 Lyon	6	5	1	0	14	8	6	16
2 Sparta	6	2	3	1	9	6	3	9
3 Ath Bilbao	6	1	2	3	7	9	-2	5
4 Kiryat Shmona	6	0	2	4	6	13	-7	2

Thursday September 20
Ath Bilbao ....(1) 1-1 (1) ....Kiryat S
Lyon ....(0) 2-1 (0) ....Sparta
Thursday October 4
Ironi Kiryat S (1) 3-4 (3) ....Lyon
Sparta ....(2) 3-1 (0) ....Ath Bilbao
Thursday October 25
Lyon ....(0) 2-1 (0) ....Ath Bilbao
Sparta ....(3) 3-1 (0) Ironi Kiryat S
Thursday November 8
Ath Bilbao ....(0) 2-3 (2) ....Lyon
Ironi Kiryat S (1) 1-1 (1) ....Sparta
Thursday November 22
Sparta ....(0) 1-1 (0) ....Lyon
Wednesday November 28
Ironi Kiryat S (0) 0-2 (1) ....Ath Bilbao
Thursday December 6
Ath Bilbao ....(0) 0-0 (0) ....Sparta
Lyon ....(1) 2-0 (0) Ironi Kiryat S

Group J

	P	W	D	L	F	A	GD	Pts
1 Lazio	6	3	3	0	9	2	7	12
2 Tottenham	6	2	4	0	8	4	4	10
3 Panathinaikos	6	1	2	3	4	11	-7	5
4 Maribor	6	1	1	4	6	10	-4	4

Thursday September 20
Maribor........(1) 3-0 (0)Panathinaikos
Tottenham....(0) 0-0 (0) .... Lazio
Thursday October 4
Lazio............(0) 1-0 (0) ....Maribor
Panathinaikos(0)1-1 (1) ... Tottenham
Thursday October 25
Maribor........(1) 1-1 (0) ... Tottenham
Panathinaikos(0)1-1 (1) ....Lazio
Thursday November 8
Lazio............(2) 3-0 (0)Panathinaikos
Tottenham....(1) 3-1 (1) ....Maribor
Thursday November 22
Lazio............(0) 0-0 (0) ... Tottenham
Panathinaikos(0)1-0 (0) ....Maribor
Thursday December 6
Maribor........(0) 1-4 (3) ....Lazio
Tottenham....(1) 3-1 (0)Panathinaikos

Group K

	P	W	D	L	F	A	GD	Pts
1 Metalist	6	4	1	1	9	3	6	13
2 B Leverkusen	6	4	1	1	9	2	7	13
3 Rosenborg	6	2	0	4	7	10	-3	6
4 Rapid Vienna	6	1	0	5	4	14	-10	3

Thursday September 20
B Leverkusen(0) 0-0 (0) .... Metalist
Rapid Vienna (0) 1-2 (1) ...Rosenborg
Thursday October 4
Metalist........(0) 2-0 (0) Rapid Vienna
Rosenborg ... (0) 0-1 (1)B Leverkusen
Thursday October 25
Rapid Vienna (0) 0-4 (1)B Leverkusen
Rosenborg ... (0) 1-2 (0) .... Metalist
Thursday November 8
B Leverkusen(1) 3-0 (0) Rapid Vienna
Metalist........(1) 3-1 (1) ...Rosenborg

Thursday November 22
Metalist........(0) 2-0 (0)B Leverkusen
Rosenborg ... (1) 3-2 (0) Rapid Vienna
Thursday December 6
B Leverkusen(0) 1-0 (0) ...Rosenborg
Rapid Vienna (1) 1-0 (0) .... Metalist

Group L

	P	W	D	L	F	A	GD	Pts
1 Hannover	6	3	3	0	11	8	3	12
2 Levante	6	3	2	1	10	5	5	11
3 Helsingborgs	6	1	1	4	9	12	-3	4
4 Twente	6	0	4	2	5	10	-5	4

Thursday September 20
Levante........(1) 1-0 (0)Helsingborgs
Twente ....(1) 2-2 (0) .....Hannover
Thursday October 4
Hannover .....(1) 2-1 (1) .... Levante
Helsingborgs (2) 2-2 (0) ....Twente
Thursday October 25
Helsingborgs (0) 1-2 (1) .....Hannover
Levante........(0) 3-0 (0) ....Twente
Thursday November 8
Hannover .....(1) 3-2 (0)Helsingborgs
Twente ....(0) 0-0 (0) .... Levante
Thursday November 22
Hannover .....(0) 0-0 (0) ....Twente
Helsingborgs (0) 1-3 (2) ..... Levante
Thursday December 6
Levante........(0) 2-2 (2) .....Hannover
Twente ....(0) 1-3 (2)Helsingborgs

Last 32 first leg

Thursday February 14
Ajax ....(1) 2-0 (0) ....Steaua
Anzhi ....(1) 3-1 (1) .....Hannover
Atl Madrid .... (0) 0-2 (1) ....Rubin
B Leverkusen(0) 0-1 (0) ....Benfica
BATE Borisov(0) 0-0 (0) ..Fenerbahce
Basel ....(1) 2-0 (0) .... Dnipro
Dynamo Kiev (1) 1-1 (1) ....Bordeaux
Inter ....(1) 2-0 (0) ..... CFR Cluj
Levante........(2) 3-0 (0) . Olympiacos
M'gladbach.. (1) 3-3 (3) ....Lazio
Napoli...........(0) 0-3 (1) ....Plzen
Newcastle.... (0) 0-0 (0) .... Metalist
Sparta ....(0) 0-1 (0) ...... Chelsea
Stuttgart ...... (1) 1-1 (0) ....Genk
Tottenham.... (1) 2-1 (0) ....Lyon
Zenit ....(0) 2-0 (0) ..... Liverpool

Last 32 second leg

Thursday February 21
Benfica ....(0) 1-1 (1) ..B Leverkusen
Agg: 3-1
Bordeaux .....(1) 1-0 (0)Dynamo Kiev
Agg: 2-1
CFR Cluj ......(0) 0-3 (2) ....Inter
Agg: 0-5
Chelsea........(0) 1-1 (1) ....Sparta
Agg: 2-1
Dnipro...........(0) 1-1 (0) ....Basel
Agg: 1-3
Fenerbahce .. (1) 1-0 (0) ....BATE
Agg: 1-0

Branislav Ivanovic heads home Chelsea's 90th-minute Europa League final winner

Genk............ (0) 0-2 (1) ...... Stuttgart
Agg: 1-3

Hannover ..... (0) 1-1 (0) .... Anzhi
Agg: 2-4

Lazio............ (2) 2-0 (0) ..M'gladbach
Agg: 5-3

Liverpool...... (2) 3-1 (1) .... Zenit
Agg: 3-3 Zenit away goals

Lyon .... (1) 1-1 (0) ... Tottenham
Agg: 2-3

Metalist........ (0) 0-1 (0) ....Newcastle
Agg: 0-1

Olympiacos.. (0) 0-1 (1) .... Levante
Agg: 0-4

Rubin........... (0) 0-1 (0) ....Atl Madrid
Agg: 2-1

Steaua .... (1) 2-0 (0) .... Ajax
AET 2-0 90 mins Steaua 4-2 pens

Plzen .... (0) 2-0 (0) .... Napoli
Agg: 5-0

Last 16 first leg
Thursday March 7

Anzhi .... (0) 0-0 (0) ....Newcastle
Basel .... (0) 2-0 (0) .... Zenit
Benfica .... (1) 1-0 (0) ..... Bordeaux
Levante........ (0) 0-0 (0) .... Rubin
Steaua .... (1) 1-0 (0) .... Chelsea
Stuttgart ...... (0) 0-2 (1) .... Lazio

Tottenham.... (2) 3-0 (0) ....Inter
Plzen .... (0) 0-1 (0) ..Fenerbahce

Last 16 second leg
Thursday March 14

Bordeaux ..... (0) 2-3 (1) .... Benfica
Agg: 2-4

Chelsea........ (1) 3-1 (1) .... Steaua
Agg: 3-2

Fenerbahce .. (1) 1-1 (0) .... Plzen
Agg: 2-1

Inter............. (1) 4-1 (0) ... Tottenham
AET 3-0 90 Agg: 4-4 Tottenham away goals

Lazio............ (2) 3-1 (0) ...... Stuttgart
Agg: 5-1

Newcastle.... (0) 1-0 (0) .... Anzhi
Agg: 1-0

Rubin........... (0) 2-0 (0) .... Levante
AET 0-0 90 mins Agg: 2-0

Zenit .... (1) 1-0 (0) .... Basel
Agg: 1-2

Quarter-finals first leg
Thursday April 4

Benfica .... (1) 3-1 (1) ....Newcastle
Chelsea........ (2) 3-1 (1) .... Rubin
Fenerbahce .. (1) 2-0 (0) .... Lazio
Tottenham.... (1) 2-2 (2) .... Basel

Quarter-finals second leg
Thursday April 11

Basel .... (1) 2-2 (1) ... Tottenham
AET 2-2 90 mins, Agg: 4-4 Basel 4-1 pens

Lazio............ (0) 1-1 (0) ..Fenerbahce
Agg: 1-3

Newcastle.... (0) 1-1 (0) .... Benfica
Agg: 2-4

Rubin........... (0) 3-2 (1) .... Chelsea
Agg: 4-5

Semi-finals first leg
Thursday April 25

Basel .... (0) 1-2 (1) .... Chelsea
Fenerbahce .. (1) 1-0 (0) .... Benfica

Semi-finals second leg
Thursday May 2

Benfica .... (2) 3-1 (1) ..Fenerbahce
Agg: 3-2

Chelsea........ (0) 3-1 (1) .... Basel
Agg: 5-2

Final
Wednesday May 15

Benfica .... (0) 1-2 (0) .... Chelsea
POS 58/42 SH ON 3/5 SH OFF 7/4 CRN 4/4
SCORERS Benfica: Cardozo (pen 68)
Chelsea: Torres (59) Ivanovic (90)
CARDS Benfica: Garay ▮ Luisao ▮
Chelsea: Oscar ▮

World Cup qualifying results & fixtures

Europe

How it works 53 participating teams, 13 qualify **Round 1** 53 teams, 8 groups of 6, 1 group of 5, round-robin home-and-away format. 9 group winners qualify, 8 best group runners-up advance **Round 2** 8 teams, 4 two-legged knockout ties, winners qualify for World Cup

Group A

	P	W	D	L	F	A	GD	Pts
1 Belgium	7	6	1	0	13	2	11	19
2 Croatia	7	5	1	1	10	4	6	16
3 Serbia	7	2	1	4	9	9	0	7
4 Wales	6	2	0	4	6	14	-8	6
5 Scotland	7	1	2	4	4	9	-5	5
6 Macedonia	6	1	1	4	3	7	-4	4

Friday September 7 2012
Croatia......... (0) 1-0 (0) ...Macedonia
Wales .... (0) 0-2 (1) .... Belgium
Saturday September 8 2012
Scotland ...... (0) 0-0 (0) ....Serbia
Tuesday September 11 2012
Belgium .... (1) 1-1 (1) ....Croatia
Scotland ...... (1) 1-1 (1) ...Macedonia
Serbia .... (3) 6-1 (1) .... Wales
Friday October 12 2012
Macedonia... (1) 1-2 (1) ....Croatia
Serbia .... (0) 0-3 (1) ...... Belgium
Wales .... (0) 2-1 (1) ..... Scotland
Tuesday October 16 2012
Belgium .... (0) 2-0 (0) ..... Scotland
Croatia......... (1) 2-0 (0) .... Wales
Macedonia... (0) 1-0 (0) ....Serbia
Friday March 22 2013
Croatia......... (2) 2-0 (0) ....Serbia
Macedonia... (0) 0-2 (1) ...... Belgium
Scotland ...... (1) 1-2 (0) .... Wales
Tuesday March 26 2013
Belgium .... (0) 1-0 (0) ...Macedonia
Serbia .... (0) 2-0 (0) ..... Scotland
Wales .... (1) 1-2 (0) ....Croatia
Friday June 7 2013
Belgium .... (1) 2-1 (0) ....Serbia
Croatia......... (0) 0-1 (1) ..... Scotland
Friday September 6 2013
Macedonia..... v .... Wales
Scotland ...... v .... Belgium
Serbia............ v ....Croatia
Wednesday October 9 2013
Macedonia..... v .... Scotland
Wales .... v ....Serbia
Friday October 11 2013
Croatia......... v .... Belgium
Wales .... v ......Macedonia

Tuesday October 15 2013
Belgium .... v .... Wales
Serbia............ v ......Macedonia
Scotland .... v ....Croatia

Group B

	P	W	D	L	F	A	GD	Pts
1 Italy	6	4	2	0	12	4	8	14
2 Bulgaria	6	2	4	0	11	4	7	10
3 Czech Rep	6	2	3	1	6	4	2	9
4 Armenia	6	2	0	4	6	8	-2	6
5 Denmark	6	1	3	2	6	9	-3	6
6 Malta	6	1	0	5	2	14	-12	3

Friday September 7 2012
Bulgaria .... (1) 2-2 (2) .... Italy
Malta .... (0) 0-1 (0) ......Armenia
Saturday September 8 2012
Denmark...... (0) 0-0 (0) ... Czech Rep
Tuesday September 11 2012
Bulgaria .... (1) 1-0 (0) ......Armenia
Italy .... (1) 2-0 (0) .... Malta
Friday October 12 2012
Armenia....... (1) 1-3 (1) .... Italy
Bulgaria .... (1) 1-1 (1) .....Denmark
Czech Rep ... (1) 3-1 (1) .... Malta
Tuesday October 16 2012
Czech Rep ... (0) 0-0 (0) .... Bulgaria
Italy .... (2) 3-1 (1) .....Denmark
Friday March 22 2013
Bulgaria .... (2) 6-0 (0) .... Malta
Czech Rep ... (0) 0-3 (0) .....Denmark
Tuesday March 26 2013
Armenia....... (0) 0-3 (0) ... Czech Rep
Denmark...... (0) 1-1 (0) .... Bulgaria
Malta .... (0) 0-2 (2) .... Italy
Friday June 7 2013
Armenia....... (0) 0-1 (1) .... Malta
Czech Rep ... (0) 0-0 (0) .... Italy
Tuesday June 11 2013
Denmark...... (0) 0-4 (2) ......Armenia
Friday September 6 2013
Czech Rep ..... v ....Armenia
Italy .... v .... Bulgaria
Malta .... v ....Denmark
Wednesday October 9 2013
Armenia......... v ....Denmark
Malta .... v .... Bulgaria
Italy .... v .... Czech Rep
Friday October 11 2013
Malta .... v ..... Czech Rep
Denmark......... v .... Italy
Armenia.......... v .... Bulgaria
Tuesday October 15 2013
Bulgaria .... v ..... Czech Rep
Denmark......... v .... Malta
Italy .... v ....Armenia

Group C

	P	W	D	L	F	A	GD	Pts
1 Germany	6	5	1	0	22	7	15	16
2 Austria	6	3	2	1	15	5	10	11
3 Sweden	6	3	2	1	11	7	4	11
4 Rep of Ireland	6	3	2	1	12	10	2	11
5 Kazakhstan	6	0	1	5	2	15	-13	1
6 Faroe Islands	6	0	0	6	2	20	-18	0

Friday September 7 2012
Germany...... (1) 3-0 (0) Faroe Islands
Kazakhstan .. (1) 1-2 (0)Rep of Ireland
Tuesday September 11 2012
Austria......... (0) 1-2 (1) ..... Germany
Sweden .... (1) 2-0 (0) .. Kazakhstan
Friday October 12 2012
Faroe Islands (0) 1-2 (0) .... Sweden
Kazakhstan .. (0) 0-0 (0) ....Austria
Rep of Ireland(0)1-6 (2) ..... Germany
Tuesday October 16 2012
Austria......... (1) 4-0 (0) .. Kazakhstan
Faroe Islands (0) 1-4 (0)Rep of Ireland
Germany...... (3) 4-4 (0) .... Sweden
Friday March 22 2013
Austria......... (3) 6-0 (0)Faroe Islands
Kazakhstan .. (0) 0-3 (2) ..... Germany
Sweden .... (0) 0-0 (0)Rep of Ireland
Tuesday March 26 2013
Germany...... (3) 4-1 (0) .. Kazakhstan
Rep of Ireland(2)2-2 (1) ....Austria
Friday June 7 2013
Austria......... (2) 2-1 (0) ..... Sweden
Rep of Ireland(1)3-0 (0)Faroe Islands
Tuesday June 11 2013
Sweden .... (1) 2-0 (0)Faroe Islands
Friday September 6 2013
Germany........ v ....Austria
Rep of Ireland ... v .... Sweden
Kazakhstan .... v .. Faroe Islands
Wednesday October 9 2013
Kazakhstan .... v .... Sweden
Austria........... v ..... Rep of Ireland
Faroe Islands . v .... Germany
Friday October 11 2013
Sweden .... v ....Austria
Faroe Islands . v ..... Kazakhstan
Germany........ v ..... Rep of Ireland
Tuesday October 15 2013
Faroe Islands . v ....Austria
Sweden .... v .... Germany
Rep of Ireland ... v .....Kazakhstan

Group D

	P	W	D	L	F	A	GD	Pts
1 Netherlands	6	6	0	0	20	2	18	18
2 Hungary	6	3	2	1	13	8	5	11
3 Romania	6	3	1	2	10	0	10	10
4 Turkey	6	2	1	3	7	7	0	7
5 Estonia	6	2	0	4	3	9	-6	6
6 Andorra	6	0	0	6	0	17	-17	0

Friday September 7 2012
Andorra ...... (0) 0-5 (2) ...... Hungary
Estonia .... (0) 0-2 (0) ......Romania
Netherlands.. (1) 2-0 (0) .... Turkey
Tuesday September 11 2012
Hungary....... (1) 1-4 (2) . Netherlands
Romania ...... (2) 4-0 (0) .... Andorra
Turkey.......... (1) 3-0 (0) .... Estonia
Friday October 12 2012
Estonia .... (0) 0-1 (0) ...... Hungary
Netherlands.. (2) 3-0 (0) .... Andorra
Turkey.......... (0) 0-1 (1) ......Romania
Tuesday October 16 2012
Andorra ...... (0) 0-1 (0) ...... Estonia
Hungary....... (1) 3-1 (1) .... Turkey
Romania ...... (1) 1-4 (3) . Netherlands
Friday March 22 2013
Andorra ...... (0) 0-2 (2) .... Turkey
Hungary....... (1) 2-2 (0) ......Romania
Netherlands.. (0) 3-0 (0) .... Estonia
Tuesday March 26 2013
Estonia .... (1) 2-0 (0) .... Andorra
Netherlands.. (1) 4-0 (0) ......Romania
Turkey.......... (0) 1-1 (0) ...... Hungary
Friday September 6 2013
Romania .... v .... Hungary
Estonia .... v .... Netherlands
Turkey............ v .... Andorra
Wednesday October 9 2013
Romania .... v .... Turkey
Hungary........ v .... Estonia
Andorra .... v .... Netherlands
Friday October 11 2013
Estonia .... v .... Turkey
Andorra .... v ....Romania
Netherlands.... v .... Hungary
Tuesday October 15 2013
Turkey............ v .... Netherlands
Romania .... v .... Estonia
Hungary........ v .... Andorra

Group E

		P	W	D	L	F	A	GD	Pts
1	Switzerland	6	4	2	0	8	1	7	14
2	Albania	6	3	1	2	7	6	1	10
3	Iceland	6	3	0	3	8	9	-1	9
4	Norway	6	2	2	2	7	7	0	8
5	Slovenia	6	2	0	4	8	10	-2	6
6	Cyprus	6	1	1	4	4	9	-5	4

Friday September 7 2012
Albania .... (1) 3-1 (1) .... Cyprus
Iceland........ (1) 2-0 (0) .... Norway
Slovenia....... (0) 0-2 (1) ..Switzerland
Tuesday September 11 2012
Cyprus........ (0) 1-0 (0) .... Iceland
Norway....... (1) 2-1 (1) ...... Slovenia
Switzerland .. (1) 2-0 (0) ...... Albania
Friday October 12 2012
Albania .... (1) 1-2 (1) .... Iceland
Slovenia....... (1) 2-1 (0) .... Cyprus
Switzerland .. (0) 1-1 (0) ...... Norway

Tuesday October 16 2012
Albania .... (1) 1-0 (0) ...... Slovenia
Cyprus......... (1) 1-3 (1) .... Norway
Iceland......... (0) 0-2 (0) ..Switzerland
Friday March 22 2013
Norway........ (0) 0-1 (0) .... Albania
Slovenia....... (1) 1-2 (0) .... Iceland
Saturday March 23 2013
Cyprus......... (0) 0-0 (0) ..Switzerland
Friday June 7 2013
Albania .... (1) 1-1 (0) .... Norway
Iceland......... (2) 2-4 (2) ...... Slovenia
Saturday June 8 2013
Switzerland .. (0) 1-0 (0) .... Cyprus
Friday September 6 2013
Switzerland .... v .... Iceland
Slovenia........ v .... Albania
Norway......... v .... Cyprus
Wednesday October 9 2013
Norway......... v .....Switzerland
Cyprus.......... v .... Slovenia
Iceland........... v .... Albania
Friday October 11 2013
Albania .... v .....Switzerland
Slovenia........ v .... Norway
Iceland........... v .... Cyprus
Tuesday October 15 2013
Norway......... v .... Iceland
Cyprus.......... v .... Albania
Switzerland .... v .... Slovenia

Group F

		P	W	D	L	F	A	GD	Pts
1	Portugal	7	4	2	1	12	6	6	14
2	Russia	5	4	0	1	8	1	7	12
3	Israel	6	3	2	1	15	8	7	11
4	Azerbaijan	7	0	4	3	3	9	-6	4
5	N Ireland	5	0	3	2	3	7	-4	3
6	Luxembourg	6	0	3	3	3	13	-10	3

Friday September 7 2012
Azerbaijan.... (0) 1-1 (0) .... Israel
Luxembourg. (1) 1-2 (1) ....Portugal
Russia .... (1) 2-0 (0) ......N Ireland
Tuesday September 11 2012
Israel .... (0) 0-4 (2) ....Russia
N Ireland ...... (1) 1-1 (0) Luxembourg
Portugal........ (1) 3-0 (0) ....Azerbaijan
Friday October 12 2012
Luxembourg. (0) 0-6 (3) .... Israel
Russia .... (1) 1-0 (0) ......Portugal
Tuesday October 16 2012
Israel .... (2) 3-0 (0) ...... Luxembourg
Portugal........ (0) 1-1 (1) ......N Ireland
Russia .... (0) 1-0 (0) ....Azerbaijan
Wednesday November 14 2012
N Ireland ...... (0) 1-1 (1) ....Azerbaijan
Friday March 22 2013
Israel .... (2) 3-3 (1) ......Portugal
Luxembourg. (0) 0-0 (0) ....Azerbaijan
Tuesday March 26 2013
Azerbaijan.... (0) 0-2 (0) ......Portugal

N Ireland ...... (0) 0-2 (0) .... Israel
Friday June 7 2013
Azerbaijan.... (0) 1-1 (0) Luxembourg
Portugal....... (1) 1-0 (0) .... Russia
Wednesday August 14 2013
N Ireland .... v .... Russia
Friday September 6 2013
Israel .... v ......Azerbaijan
Russia .... v ... Luxembourg
N Ireland .... v ....Portugal
Wednesday October 9 2013
Russia .... v .... Israel
Luxembourg... v ....N Ireland
Friday October 11 2013
Portugal........ v .... Israel
Luxembourg... v .... Russia
Azerbaijan...... v ....N Ireland
Tuesday October 15 2013
Israel .... v ....N Ireland
Portugal........ v ... Luxembourg
Azerbaijan...... v .... Russia

Group G

		P	W	D	L	F	A	GD	Pts
1	Bosnia-Hz	6	5	1	0	23	3	20	16
2	Greece	6	4	1	1	7	4	3	13
3	Slovakia	6	2	3	1	7	5	2	9
4	Lithuania	6	1	2	3	4	8	-4	5
5	Latvia	6	1	1	4	6	14	-8	4
6	Liechtenstein	6	0	2	4	3	16	-13	2

Friday September 7 2012
Latvia.......... (1) 1-2 (0) ....Greece
Liechtenstein (0) 1-8 (4) ....Bosnia-Hz
Lithuania...... (1) 1-1 (1) ....Slovakia
Tuesday September 11 2012
Bosnia-Hz.... (2) 4-1 (1) .... Latvia
Greece......... (0) 2-0 (0) ......Lithuania
Slovakia....... (1) 2-0 (0)Liechtenstein
Friday October 12 2012
Greece......... (0) 0-0 (0) ....Bosnia-Hz
Liechtenstein (0) 0-2 (0) ......Lithuania
Slovakia....... (2) 2-1 (0) .... Latvia
Tuesday October 16 2012
Bosnia-Hz.... (3) 3-0 (0) ......Lithuania
Latvia........... (1) 2-0 (0)Liechtenstein
Slovakia....... (0) 0-1 (0) ....Greece
Friday March 22 2013
Bosnia-Hz.... (2) 3-1 (0) ....Greece
Liechtenstein (1) 1-1 (1) .... Latvia
Slovakia....... (1) 1-1 (1) .....Lithuania
Friday June 7 2013
Latvia.......... (0) 0-5 (0) ....Bosnia-Hz
Liechtenstein (1) 1-1 (0) ....Slovakia
Lithuania...... (0) 0-1 (1) ....Greece
Friday September 6 2013
Liechtenstein.. v ....Greece
Bosnia-Hz..... v ....Slovakia
Latvia............ v ....Lithuania
Wednesday October 9 2013
Greece.......... v .... Latvia
Slovakia......... v ......Bosnia-Hz

Lithuania....... v .. Liechtenstein
Friday October 11 2013
Lithuania....... v .... Latvia
Greece.......... v ....Slovakia
Bosnia-Hz...... v .. Liechtenstein
Tuesday October 15 2013
Latvia............. v ....Slovakia
Lithuania....... v ......Bosnia-Hz
Greece.......... v .. Liechtenstein

Group H

	P	W	D	L	F	A	GD	Pts
1 Montenegro	7	4	2	1	14	7	7	14
2 England	6	3	3	0	21	3	18	12
3 Ukraine	6	3	2	1	10	4	6	11
4 Poland	6	2	3	1	12	7	5	9
5 Moldova	7	1	2	4	4	11	-7	5
6 San Marino	6	0	0	6	0	29	-29	0

Friday September 7 2012
Moldova....... (0) 0-5 (3) .... England
Montenegro . (2) 2-2 (1) ....Poland
Tuesday September 11 2012
England ...... (0) 1-1 (1) ....Ukraine
Poland .... (1) 2-0 (0) ...... Moldova
San Marino .. (0) 0-6 (2) . Montenegro
Friday October 12 2012
England .... (2) 5-0 (0) ..San Marino
Moldova....... (0) 0-0 (0) ....Ukraine
Tuesday October 16 2012
San Marino .. (0) 0-2 (0) ...... Moldova
Ukraine .... (0) 0-1 (1) . Montenegro
Wednesday October 17 2012
Poland .... (0) 1-1 (1) .... England
Wednesday November 14 2012
Montenegro . (2) 3-0 (0) ..San Marino
Friday March 22 2013
Moldova....... (0) 0-1 (0) . Montenegro
Poland .... (1) 1-3 (3) ....Ukraine
San Marino .. (0) 0-8 (5) .... England
Tuesday March 26 2013
Montenegro . (0) 1-1 (1) .... England
Poland .... (2) 5-0 (0) ..San Marino
Ukraine .... (0) 2-1 (0) ...... Moldova
Friday June 7 2013
Moldova....... (1) 1-1 (1) ....Poland
Montenegro . (0) 0-4 (0) ....Ukraine
Friday September 6 2013
Poland .... v .... Montenegro
Ukraine .... v ....San Marino
England .... v .... Moldova
Wednesday October 9 2013
Ukraine .... v .... England
San Marino .... v ....Poland
Friday October 11 2013
Ukraine .... v ....Poland
Moldova......... v .....San Marino
England .... v .... Montenegro
Tuesday October 15 2013
Montenegro ... v .... Moldova
San Marino .... v ....Ukraine
England .... v ....Poland

Group I

	P	W	D	L	F	A	GD	Pts
1 Spain	5	3	2	0	8	2	6	11
2 France	5	3	1	1	8	4	4	10
3 Finland	5	1	3	1	4	4	0	6
4 Georgia	5	1	1	3	3	7	-4	4
5 Belarus	6	1	1	4	4	10	-6	4

Friday September 7 2012
Finland........ (0) 0-1 (1) .... France
Georgia....... (0) 1-0 (0) ....Belarus
Tuesday September 11 2012
France .... (0) 3-1 (0) ....Belarus
Georgia....... (0) 0-1 (0) ....Spain
Friday October 12 2012
Belarus .... (0) 0-4 (2) ....Spain
Finland......... (0) 1-1 (0) ....Georgia
Tuesday October 16 2012
Belarus .... (2) 2-0 (0) ....Georgia
Spain .... (1) 1-1 (0) .... France
Friday March 22 2013
France .... (1) 3-1 (0) ....Georgia
Spain .... (0) 1-1 (0) .... Finland
Tuesday March 26 2013
France .... (0) 0-1 (0) ....Spain
Friday June 7 2013
Finland......... (0) 1-0 (0) ....Belarus
Tuesday June 11 2013
Belarus .... (0) 1-1 (1) .... Finland
Friday September 6 2013
Finland.......... v ....Spain
Georgia......... v .... France
Wednesday October 9 2013
Georgia......... v .... Finland
Belarus .... v .... France
Friday October 11 2013
Spain .... v ....Belarus
Tuesday October 15 2013
Spain .... v ....Georgia
France .... v .... Finland

Africa

How it works 52 participating teams, 5 qualify. **Round 1** 24 teams, 12 two-legged knockout ties **Round 2** 40 teams, 10 round-robin home-and-away groups of 4. Group winners advance **Round 3** 10 teams, 5 two-legged knockout ties, winners qualify for World Cup

Round 1

Friday November 11 2011
Sao Tome .... (0) 0-5 (3) .... Congo
Djibouti .... (0) 0-4 (1) ......Namibia
Comoros...... (0) 0-1 (0) Mozambique
Eritrea.......... (1) 1-1 (0) ....Rwanda
Swaziland .... (0) 1-3 (2) ...DR Congo
Eq Guinea .... (1) 2-0 (0) .Madagascar
Chad............ (1) 1-2 (1) ...... Tanzania
Guinea-Biss . (1) 1-1 (1) ....Togo
Seychelles ... (0) 0-3 (1) ....Kenya

Lesotho .... (0) 1-0 (0) .... Burundi
Saturday November 12 2011
Somalia ...... (0) 0-0 (0) .... Ethiopia
Tuesday November 15 2011
Burundi....... (1) 2-2 (2) .... Lesotho
Agg: 2-3
Rwanda .... (1) 3-1 (0) ....Eritrea
Agg: 4-2
Congo.......... (0) 1-1 (0) .... Sao Tome
Agg: 6-1
DR Congo.... (1) 5-1 (0) .... Swaziland
Agg: 8-2
Togo .... (1) 1-0 (0) . Guinea-Biss
Agg: 2-1
Madagascar. (0) 2-1 (1) ....Eq Guinea
Agg: 3-2
Kenya .... (3) 4-0 (0) .... Seychelles
Agg: 7-0
Tanzania....... (0) 0-1 (0) .... Chad
Agg: 2-2
Mozambique (2) 4-1 (0) ..... Comoros
Agg: 5-1
Namibia .... (2) 4-0 (0) ....Djibouti
Agg: 8-0
Wednesday November 16 2011
Ethiopia........ (1) 5-0 (0) .... Somalia
Agg: 5-0

Round 2

Group A

	P	W	D	L	F	A	GD	Pts
1 Ethiopia	5	4	1	0	8	3	5	13
2 South Africa	5	2	2	1	8	4	4	8
3 Botswana	5	1	1	3	5	8	-3	4
4 Central Af Rep	5	1	0	4	4	10	-6	3

Saturday June 2 2012
C African Rep(1)2-0 (0) .... Botswana
Sunday June 3 2012
S Africa........ (0) 1-1 (1) .... Ethiopia
Saturday June 9 2012
Botswana..... (1) 1-1 (1) .... S Africa
Sunday June 10 2012
Ethiopia........ (1) 2-0 (0)C African Rep
Saturday March 23 2013
S Africa........ (1) 2-0 (0)C African Rep
Sunday March 24 2013
Ethiopia........ (0) 1-0 (0) .... Botswana
Saturday June 8 2013
Botswana..... (0) 1-2 (2) .... Ethiopia
C African Rep(0)0-3 (2) .... S Africa
Saturday June 15 2013
Botswana..... (1) 3-2 (1)C African Rep
Saturday June 16 2013
Ethiopia....... (1) 2-1 (1) .... S Africa
Friday September 6 2013
S Africa.......... v .... Botswana
C African Rep. v .... Ethiopia

Group B

	P	W	D	L	F	A	GD	Pts
1 Tunisia	5	3	2	0	10	6	4	11
2 Cape Verde	5	2	0	3	8	9	-1	6
3 Sierra Leone	5	1	2	2	7	8	-1	5
4 Eq Guinea	5	1	2	2	9	11	-2	5

Saturday June 2 2012
Sierra Leone (2) 2-1 (0) .. Cape Verde
Tunisia .... (0) 3-1 (1) .... Eq Guinea
Saturday June 9 2012
Cape Verde .. (1) 1-2 (1) .... Tunisia
Eq Guinea .... (2) 2-2 (2) Sierra Leone
Saturday March 23 2013
Tunisia .... (0) 2-1 (0) Sierra Leone
Sunday March 24 2013
Eq Guinea .... (2) 4-3 (2) .. Cape Verde
Saturday June 8 2013
Sierra Leone (1) 2-2 (0) .... Tunisia
Cape Verde .. (1) 2-1 (0) .... Eq Guinea
Saturday June 15 2013
Cape Verde .. (1) 1-0 (0) Sierra Leone
Saturday June 16 2013
Eq Guinea .... (1) 1-1 (0) .... Tunisia
Friday September 6 2013
Sierra Leone ..   v   ..... Eq Guinea
Tunisia   v   ..... Cape Verde

Group C
	P	W	D	L	F	A	GD	Pts
1 Ivory Coast	5	4	1	0	14	4	10	13
2 Morocco	5	2	2	1	8	7	1	8
3 Tanzania	5	2	0	3	8	10	-2	6
4 Gambia	5	0	1	4	2	11	-9	1

Saturday June 2 2012
Gambia .... (1) 1-1 (0) ...... Morocco
Ivory Coast .. (1) 2-0 (0) ...... Tanzania
Saturday June 9 2012
Morocco ...... (1) 2-2 (1) .. Ivory Coast
Sunday June 10 2012
Tanzania....... (0) 2-1 (1) .... Gambia
Saturday March 23 2013
Ivory Coast .. (0) 3-0 (0) .... Gambia
Sunday March 24 2013
Tanzania....... (0) 3-1 (0) ...... Morocco
Saturday June 8 2013
Gambia .... (0) 0-3 (1) .. Ivory Coast
Morocco ...... (1) 2-1 (0) ...... Tanzania
Saturday June 15 2013
Morocco ...... (1) 2-0 (0) .... Gambia
Saturday June 16 2013
Tanzania....... (2) 2-4 (3) .. Ivory Coast
Friday September 6 2013
Gambia   v   .... Tanzania
Ivory Coast   v   .... Morocco

Group D
	P	W	D	L	F	A	GD	Pts
1 Ghana	5	4	0	1	16	2	14	12
2 Zambia	5	3	2	0	10	2	8	11
3 Sudan	5	0	2	3	2	11	-9	2
4 Lesotho	5	0	2	3	1	14	-13	2

Friday June 1 2012
Ghana .... (3) 7-0 (0) .... Lesotho
Saturday June 2 2012
Sudan   0-3   .... Zambia
Match awarded

Saturday June 9 2012
Zambia......... (1) 1-0 (0) .... Ghana
Sunday June 10 2012
Lesotho ...... (0) 0-0 (0) .... Sudan
Sunday March 24 2013
Ghana .... (2) 4-0 (0) .... Sudan
Lesotho ...... (0) 1-1 (0) .... Zambia
Friday June 7 2013
Sudan .... (1) 1-3 (1) .... Ghana
Saturday June 8 2013
Zambia......... (1) 4-0 (0) .... Lesotho
Saturday June 15 2013
Zambia......... (0) 1-1 (0) .... Sudan
Saturday June 16 2013
Lesotho ...... (0) 0-2 (1) .... Ghana
Friday September 6 2013
Ghana   v   .... Zambia
Sudan   v   .... Lesotho

Group E
	P	W	D	L	F	A	GD	Pts
1 Congo	5	3	1	1	5	1	4	10
2 Burkina Faso	5	3	0	2	6	4	2	9
3 Gabon	5	2	1	2	5	5	0	7
4 Niger	5	1	0	4	4	10	-6	3

Saturday June 2 2012
Burkina Faso ..   0-3   .... Congo
Match awarded

Sunday June 3 2012
Niger.............   3-0   .... Gabon
Match awarded

Saturday June 9 2012
Congo.......... (0) 1-0 (0) .... Niger
Gabon.......... (0) 1-0 (0) Burkina Faso
Saturday March 23 2013
Burkina Faso (2) 4-0 (0) .... Niger
Congo.......... (0) 1-0 (0) .... Gabon
Saturday June 8 2013
Gabon.......... (0) 0-0 (0) .... Congo
Sunday June 9 2013
Niger........... (0) 0-1 (0) Burkina Faso
Saturday June 15 2013
Congo.......... (0) 0-1 (1) Burkina Faso
Gabon.......... (1) 4-1 (1) .... Niger
Friday September 6 2013
Burkina Faso ..   v   .... Gabon
Niger.............   v   .... Congo

Group F
	P	W	D	L	F	A	GD	Pts
1 Nigeria	5	2	3	0	5	3	2	9
2 Malawi	5	1	4	0	4	3	1	7
3 Namibia	5	1	2	2	4	-1	5	5
4 Kenya	5	0	3	2	3	5	-2	3

Saturday June 2 2012
Kenya .... (0) 0-0 (0) .... Malawi
Sunday June 3 2012
Nigeria .... (0) 1-0 (0) ...... Namibia
Saturday June 9 2012
Malawi......... (0) 1-1 (0) .... Nigeria
Namibia ...... (0) 1-0 (0) .... Kenya

Saturday June 9 2012
Zambia......... (1) 1-0 (0) .... Ghana
Sunday June 10 2012
Lesotho ...... (0) 0-0 (0) .... Sudan
Sunday March 24 2013
Ghana .... (2) 4-0 (0) .... Sudan
Lesotho ...... (0) 1-1 (0) .... Zambia
Friday June 7 2013
Sudan .... (1) 1-3 (1) .... Ghana
Saturday June 8 2013
Zambia......... (1) 4-0 (0) .... Lesotho
Saturday June 15 2013
Zambia......... (0) 1-1 (0) .... Sudan
Saturday June 16 2013
Lesotho ...... (0) 0-2 (1) .... Ghana
Friday September 6 2013
Ghana   v   .... Zambia
Sudan   v   .... Lesotho

Saturday March 23 2013
Namibia .... (0) 0-1 (0) .... Malawi
Nigeria .... (0) 1-1 (1) .... Kenya
Wednesday June 5 2013
Kenya .... (0) 0-1 (0) ...... Nigeria
Malawi......... (0) 0-0 (0) ...... Namibia
Thursday June 12 2013
Malawi......... (0) 2-2 (0) .... Kenya
Namibia ...... (0) 1-1 (0) .... Nigeria
Friday September 6 2013
Kenya   v   .... Namibia
Nigeria   v   .... Malawi

Group G
	P	W	D	L	F	A	GD	Pts
1 Egypt	5	5	0	0	12	5	7	15
2 Guinea	5	3	1	1	10	4	6	10
3 Mozambique	5	0	2	3	1	9	-8	2
4 Zimbabwe	5	0	1	4	3	8	-5	1

Friday June 1 2012
Egypt.......... (0) 2-0 (0) Mozambique
Sunday June 3 2012
Zimbabwe.... (0) 0-1 (1) .... Guinea
Sunday June 10 2012
Mozambique (0) 0-0 (0) ....Zimbabwe
Guinea .... (1) 2-3 (0) .... Egypt
Sunday March 24 2013
Mozambique (0) 0-0 (0) .... Guinea
Tuesday March 26 2013
Egypt.......... (0) 2-1 (0) ....Zimbabwe
Sunday June 9 2013
Guinea .... (3) 6-1 (1) Mozambique
Zimbabwe.... (1) 2-4 (2) .... Egypt
Saturday June 16 2013
Mozambique (0) 0-1 (1) .... Egypt
Guinea .... (1) 1-0 (0) ....Zimbabwe
Friday September 6 2013
Egypt.............   v   ....Guinea
Zimbabwe......   v   ...Mozambique

Group H
	P	W	D	L	F	A	GD	Pts
1 Algeria	5	4	0	1	12	4	8	12
2 Mali	5	2	2	1	7	6	1	8
3 Benin	5	1	2	2	6	9	-3	5
4 Rwanda	5	0	2	3	3	9	-6	2

Saturday June 2 2012
Algeria .... (2) 4-0 (0) .... Rwanda
Sunday June 3 2012
Benin .... (1) 1-0 (0) .... Mali
Sunday June 10 2012
Rwanda .... (0) 1-1 (0) .... Benin
Mali .... (1) 2-1 (1) .... Algeria
Sunday March 24 2013
Rwanda .... (1) 1-2 (0) .... Mali
Tuesday March 26 2013
Algeria .... (1) 3-1 (1) .... Benin
Sunday June 9 2013
Benin .... (1) 1-3 (2) .... Algeria
Mali .... (0) 1-1 (1) .... Rwanda

Saturday June 16 2013
Mali .... (1) 2-2 (2) ....Benin
Rwanda ...... (0) 0-1 (0) ....Algeria
Friday September 6 2013
Algeria .... v ....Mali
Benin .... v ....Rwanda

Group I

	P	W	D	L	F	A	GD	Pts
1 Libya	5	2	3	0	5	2	3	9
2 Cameroon	5	2	1	2	4	5	-1	7
3 Congo DR	5	1	3	1	2	1	1	6
4 Togo	5	1	1	3	4	7	-3	4

Saturday June 2 2012
Cameroon.... (0) 1-0 (0) ....DR Congo
Sunday June 3 2012
Togo .... (1) 1-1 (1) .... Libya
Sunday June 10 2012
DR Congo.... (1) 2-0 (0) .... Togo
Libya .... (1) 2-1 (1) ....Cameroon
Saturday March 23 2013
Cameroon.... (1) 2-1 (1) .... Togo
Sunday March 24 2013
DR Congo.... (0) 0-0 (0) .... Libya
Friday June 7 2013
Libya .... (0) 0-0 (0) ....DR Congo
Sunday June 9 2013
Togo .... (1) 2-0 (0) ....Cameroon
Friday June 14 2013
Libya .... (2) 2-0 (0) .... Togo
Saturday June 16 2013
DR Congo.... (0) 0-0 (0) ....Cameroon
Friday September 6 2013
Cameroon...... v ....Libya
Togo .... v ....DR Congo

Group J

	P	W	D	L	F	A	GD	Pts
1 Senegal	5	2	3	0	8	4	4	9
2 Uganda	5	2	1	5	5	0		8
3 Angola	5	0	4	1	4	5	-1	4
4 Liberia	5	1	1	3	3	6	-3	4

Saturday June 2 2012
Senegal........ (1) 3-1 (1) .... Liberia
Sunday June 3 2012
Angola .... (1) 1-1 (0) ....Uganda
Saturday June 9 2012
Uganda........ (0) 1-1 (1) .... Senegal
Sunday June 10 2012
Liberia .... (0) 0-0 (0) ....Angola
Saturday March 23 2013
Senegal........ (1) 1-1 (0) ....Angola
Sunday March 24 2013
Liberia .... (1) 2-0 (0) ....Uganda
Saturday June 8 2013
Angola .... (0) 1-1 (1) .... Senegal
Uganda........ (1) 1-0 (0) .... Liberia
Saturday June 15 2013
Uganda........ (0) 2-1 (0) ....Angola

Saturday June 16 2013
Liberia .... (0) 0-2 (1) .... Senegal
Friday September 6 2013
Angola .... v ....Liberia
Senegal......... v ....Uganda

Asia

How it works 43 participating teams, 4.5 qualify. **Round 1** 16 teams, 8 two-legged knockout ties **Round 2** 30 teams, 15 two-legged knockout ties **Round 3** 20 teams, 5 round-robin home-and-away groups of 4. Group winners and runners-up advance **Round 4** 10 teams, 2 round-robin home-and-away groups of 5. Group winners qualify for World Cup. Third-placed advance **Round 5** 2 teams, 1 two-legged knockout tie. Winners qualify for intercontinental play-off against South America

Round 1
Wednesday June 29 2011
Cambodia .... (0) 4-2 (1) ....Laos
Nepal........... (1) 2-1 (0) . Timor-Leste
Afghanistan.. (0) 0-2 (1) ......Palestine
Sri Lanka ..... (1) 1-1 (0) ...Philippines
Bangladesh.. (2) 3-0 (0) ....Pakistan
Mongolia...... (0) 1-0 (0) ......Myanmar
Vietnam .... (3) 6-0 (0) ....Macau
Malaysia ...... (1) 2-1 (0)Chinese Taipei
Saturday July 2 2011
Timor-Leste . (0) 0-5 (1) ....Nepal
Agg: 1-7
Sunday July 3 2011
Myanmar ..... (0) 2-0 (0) ..... Mongolia
Agg: 2-1
Philippines ... (2) 4-0 (0) ..... Sri Lanka
Agg: 5-1
Palestine ...... (1) 1-1 (0) . Afghanistan
Agg: 3-1
Laos .... (2) 6-2 (1) ....Cambodia
AET Agg: 8-6
Macau .... (0) 1-7 (4) ....Vietnam
Agg: 1-13
Chinese Taipei(2)3-2(2) ......Malaysia
Agg: 4-4
Pakistan....... (0) 0-0 (1) ..Bangladesh
Agg: 0-3

Round 2
Saturday July 23 2011
China PR...... (1) 7-2 (2) ....Laos
Lebanon....... (2) 4-0 (0) ..Bangladesh
Thailand....... (1) 1-0 (0) ......Palestine
Turkmenistan(1) 1-1 (1) .....Indonesia
Iraq.............. (1) 2-0 (0) .... Yemen
Jordan .... (4) 9-0 (0) ....Nepal
Syria............. 0-3 .... Tajikistan
Match awarded
Uzbekistan ... (1) 4-0 (0) ...Kyrgyzstan
Qatar .... (1) 3-0 (0) .... Vietnam

Oman............. 3-0 ....Myanmar
Singapore .... (4) 5-3 (1) ......Malaysia
Kuwait .... (1) 3-0 (0) ...Philippines
Iran............... (1) 4-0 (0) ......Maldives
UAE .... (2) 3-0 (0) ....India
Saudi Arabia (2) 3-0 (0) .. Hong Kong
Thursday July 28 2011
Nepal........... (0) 1-1 (0) ....Jordan
Agg: 1-10
Myanmar .... A-A .... Oman
Match abandoned Agg: 0-4
Tajikistan........ 3-0 ....Syria
Match awarded Agg: 6-0
Laos .... (0) 1-6 (2) ..... China PR
Agg: 3-13
Palestine ...... (1) 2-2 (1) ...... Thailand
Agg: 2-3
Bangladesh.. (0) 2-0 (0) ...... Lebanon
Agg: 2-4
Kyrgyzstan ... (0) 0-3 (0) ...Uzbekistan
Agg: 0-7
Indonesia ..... (3) 4-3 (0)Turkmenistan
Agg: 5-4
India .... (0) 2-2 (1) ....UAE
Agg: 2-5
Philippines ... (1) 1-2 (0) .... Kuwait
Agg: 1-5
Vietnam .... (0) 2-1 (1) .... Qatar
Agg: 2-4
Yemen .... (0) 0-0 (0) ....Iraq
Agg: 0-2
Hong Kong... (0) 0-5 (1) Saudi Arabia
Agg: 0-8
Malaysia ...... (0) 1-1 (0) .... Singapore
Agg: 4-6
Maldives ...... (0) 0-1 (1) ....Iran
Agg: 0-5

Round 3

Group A

	P	W	D	L	F	A	GD	Pts
1 Iraq	6	5	0	1	14	4	10	15
2 Jordan	6	4	0	2	11	7	4	12
3 China PR	6	3	0	3	10	6	4	9
4 Singapore	6	0	0	6	2	20	-18	0

Friday September 2 2011
China PR...... (0) 2-1 (1) ....Singapore
Iraq.............. (0) 0-2 (1) ....Jordan
Tuesday September 6 2011
Jordan .... (0) 2-1 (0) ..... China PR
Singapore .... (0) 0-2 (0) ....Iraq
Tuesday October 11 2011
China PR....... (0) 0-1 (1) ....Iraq
Singapore .... (0) 0-3 (1) ....Jordan
Friday November 11 2011
Iraq.............. (0) 1-0 (0) ..... China PR
Jordan .... (1) 2-0 (0) ....Singapore
Tuesday November 15 2011
Jordan .... (1) 1-3 (0) ....Iraq
Singapore .... (0) 0-4 (1) ..... China PR
Wednesday February 29 2012
China PR...... (1) 3-1 (0) ....Singapore
Iraq.............. (4) 7-1 (1) ....Jordan

Group B

	P	W	D	L	F	A	GD	Pts
1 S Korea	6	4	1	1	14	4	10	13
2 Lebanon	6	3	1	2	10	14	-4	10
3 Kuwait	6	2	2	2	8	9	-1	8
4 UAE	6	1	0	5	9	14	-5	3

Friday September 2 2011
S Korea........ (2) 6-0 (0) ..... Lebanon
UAE .... (0) 2-3 (1) .... Kuwait
Tuesday September 6 2011
Kuwait .... (0) 1-1 (1) .... S Korea
Lebanon....... (1) 3-1 (1) .... UAE
Tuesday October 11 2011
Lebanon....... (1) 2-2 (0) .... Kuwait
S Korea........ (0) 2-1 (0) .... UAE
Friday November 11 2011
Kuwait .... (0) 0-1 (0) ...... Lebanon
UAE .... (0) 0-2 (0) .... S Korea
Tuesday November 15 2011
Kuwait .... (0) 2-1 (1) .... UAE
Lebanon....... (2) 2-1 (1) ...... S Korea
Wednesday February 29 2012
S Korea........ (0) 2-0 (0) .... Kuwait
UAE .... (2) 4-2 (2) ..... Lebanon

Group C

	P	W	D	L	F	A	GD	Pts
1 Uzbekistan	6	5	1	0	8	1	7	16
2 Japan	6	3	1	2	14	3	11	10
3 N Korea	6	2	1	3	3	4	-1	7
4 Tajikistan	6	0	1	5	1	18	-17	1

Friday September 2 2011
Japan........... (0) 1-0 (0) .... N Korea
Tajikistan...... (0) 0-1 (0) ... Uzbekistan
Tuesday September 6 2011
N Korea........ (1) 1-0 (0) ..... Tajikistan
Uzbekistan ... (1) 1-1 (0) .... Japan
Tuesday October 11 2011
Japan........... (4) 8-0 (0) ..... Tajikistan
N Korea........ (0) 0-1 (1) ...Uzbekistan
Friday November 11 2011
Tajikistan...... (0) 0-4 (1) .... Japan
Uzbekistan ... (0) 1-0 (0) .... N Korea
Tuesday November 15 2011
N Korea........ (0) 1-0 (0) .... Japan
Uzbekistan ... (1) 3-0 (0) ..... Tajikistan
Wednesday February 29 2012
Japan........... (0) 0-1 (0) ...Uzbekistan
Tajikistan...... (0) 1-1 (0) .... N Korea

Group D

	P	W	D	L	F	A	GD	Pts
1 Australia	6	5	0	1	13	5	8	15
2 Oman	6	2	2	2	3	6	-3	8
3 Saudi Arabia	6	1	3	2	6	7	-1	6
4 Thailand	6	1	1	4	4	8	-4	4

Friday September 2 2011
Australia ...... (0) 2-1 (1) ...... Thailand
Oman........... (0) 0-0 (0) Saudi Arabia
Tuesday September 6 2011
Saudi Arabia (0) 1-3 (1) ...... Australia
Thailand....... (2) 3-0 (0) .... Oman

Tuesday October 11 2011
Australia ...... (1) 3-0 (0) .... Oman
Thailand....... (0) 0-0 (0) Saudi Arabia
Friday November 11 2011
Oman........... (1) 1-0 (0) ...... Australia
Saudi Arabia (0) 3-0 (0) ...... Thailand
Tuesday November 15 2011
Saudi Arabia (0) 0-0 (0) .... Oman
Thailand....... (0) 0-1 (0) ..... Australia
Wednesday February 29 2012
Australia ...... (1) 4-2 (2) Saudi Arabia
Oman........... (1) 2-0 (0) ..... Thailand

Group E

	P	W	D	L	F	A	GD	Pts
1 Iran	6	3	3	0	17	5	12	12
2 Qatar	6	2	4	0	10	5	5	10
3 Bahrain	6	2	3	1	13	7	6	9
4 Indonesia	6	0	0	6	3	26	-23	0

Friday September 2 2011
Bahrain .... (0) 0-0 (0) .... Qatar
Iran .... (0) 3-0 (0) .....Indonesia
Tuesday September 6 2011
Indonesia ..... (0) 0-2 (1) ....Bahrain
Qatar .... (0) 1-1 (0) ....Iran
Tuesday October 11 2011
Indonesia ..... (2) 2-3 (2) .... Qatar
Iran .... (3) 6-0 (0) ....Bahrain
Friday November 11 2011
Bahrain .... (1) 1-1 (0) ....Iran
Qatar .... (2) 4-0 (0) ...Indonesia
Tuesday November 15 2011
Indonesia ..... (1) 1-4 (3) ....Iran
Qatar .... (0) 0-0 (0) ....Bahrain
Wednesday February 29 2012
Bahrain .... (4)10-0(0).....Indonesia
Iran .... (1) 2-2 (1) .... Qatar

Round 4

Group A

	P	W	D	L	F	A	GD	Pts
1 Iran	8	5	1	2	8	2	6	16
2 S Korea	8	4	2	2	13	7	6	14
3 Uzbekistan	8	4	2	2	11	6	5	14
4 Qatar	8	2	1	5	5	13	-8	7
5 Lebanon	8	1	2	5	3	12	-9	5

Sunday June 3 2012
Lebanon....... (0) 0-1 (0) .... Qatar
Uzbekistan ... (0) 0-1 (0) ....Iran
Friday June 8 2012
Lebanon....... (1) 1-1 (1) ...Uzbekistan
Qatar .... (1) 1-4 (1) .... S Korea
Tuesday June 12 2012
Iran .... (0) 0-0 (0) .... Qatar
S Korea........ (1) 3-0 (0) ..... Lebanon
Tuesday September 11 2012
Lebanon....... (1) 1-0 (0) ....Iran
Uzbekistan ... (1) 2-2 (1) .... S Korea
Tuesday October 16 2012
Iran .... (0) 1-0 (0) .... S Korea
Qatar .... (0) 0-1 (0) ...Uzbekistan

Wednesday November 14 2012
Iran .... (0) 0-1 (0) ...Uzbekistan
Qatar .... (0) 1-0 (0) ...... Lebanon
Tuesday March 26 2013
S Korea........ (0) 2-1 (0) .... Qatar
Uzbekistan ... (0) 1-0 (0) ...... Lebanon
Tuesday June 4 2013
Lebanon....... (1) 1-1 (0) .... S Korea
Qatar .... (0) 0-1 (0) ....Iran
Tuesday June 11 2013
Iran .... (2) 4-0 (0) ...... Lebanon
S Korea........ (1) 1-0 (0) ...Uzbekistan
Tuesday June 18 2013
S Korea........ (0) 0-1 (0) ....Iran
Uzbekistan ... (0) 5-1 (1) .... Qatar

Group B

	P	W	D	L	F	A	GD	Pts
1 Japan	8	5	2	1	16	5	11	17
2 Australia	8	3	4	1	12	7	5	13
3 Jordan	8	3	1	4	7	16	-9	10
4 Oman	8	2	3	3	7	10	-3	9
5 Iraq	8	1	2	5	4	8	-4	5

Sunday June 3 2012
Japan........... (1) 3-0 (0) .... Oman
Jordan .... (1) 1-1 (1) ....Iraq
Friday June 8 2012
Japan........... (4) 6-0 (0) ....Jordan
Oman........... (0) 0-0 (0) ...... Australia
Tuesday June 12 2012
Australia ...... (0) 1-1 (0) .... Japan
Iraq .... (1) 1-1 (1) .... Oman
Tuesday September 11 2012
Japan........... (1) 1-0 (0) ....Iraq
Jordan .... (0) 2-1 (0) ...... Australia
Tuesday October 16 2012
Iraq .... (0) 1-2 (0) ...... Australia
Oman........... (0) 2-1 (0) ....Jordan
Wednesday November 14 2012
Iraq .... (0) 1-0 (0) ....Jordan
Oman........... (0) 1-2 (1) .... Japan
Tuesday March 26 2013
Australia ...... (0) 2-2 (1) .... Oman
Jordan .... (1) 2-1 (0) .... Japan
Tuesday June 4 2013
Japan........... (0) 1-1 (1) ...... Australia
Oman........... (1) 1-0 (0) ....Iraq
Tuesday June 11 2013
Australia ...... (1) 4-0 (0) ....Jordan
Iraq .... (0) 0-1 (0) .... Japan
Tuesday June 18 2013
Australia ...... (0) 1-0 (0) ....Iraq
Jordan .... (0) 1-0 (0) .... Oman

Round 5

Friday September 6 2013
Jordan   v   ......Uzbekistan
Tuesday September 10 2013
Uzbekistan   v   ....Jordan

How it works 35 participating teams, 3.5 qualify. **Round 1** 10 teams, 5 two-legged knockout ties **Round 2** 24 teams, 6 round-robin home-and-away groups of 4. Group winners advance **Round 3** 12 teams, 3 round-robin home-and-away groups of 4. Group winners and runners-up advance **Round 4** 6 teams, 1 round-robin home-and-away group of 6. Top 3 qualify for World Cup, 4th place qualifies for intercontinental play-off v Oceania

Round 1
Wednesday June 15 2011
Montserrat ... (1) 2-5 (1) .... Belize
Saturday July 2 2011
Turks/Caicos (0) 0-4 (2) ..... Bahamas
Sunday July 3 2011
US Virgin I.... (1) 2-0 (0)British Virgin I
Friday July 8 2011
Anguilla........ (0) 0-2 (2) Dominican R
Aruba .... (1) 4-2 (1) .... St Lucia
Saturday July 9 2011
Bahamas ..... (2) 6-0 (0) Turks/Caicos
Agg: 10-0
Sunday July 10 2011
British Virgin I(1)1-2 (1) ... US Virgin I
Agg: 1-4
Dominican R (3) 4-0 (0) .... Anguilla
Agg: 6-0
Tuesday July 12 2011
St Lucia .... (2) 4-2 (1) .... Aruba
AET Agg: 6-6 St Lucia 5-4 pens
Sunday July 17 2011
Belize........... (1) 3-1 (0) ...Montserrat
Agg: 8-3

Round 2
Group A
	P	W	D	L	F	A	GD	Pts
1 El Salvador	6	6	0	0	20	5	15	18
2 Dominican R	6	2	2	2	12	8	4	8
3 Suriname	6	2	1	3	5	11	-6	7
4 Cayman I	6	0	1	5	2	15	-13	1
Friday September 2 2011
El Salvador... (0) 3-2 (0) Dominican R
Suriname ..... (1) 1-0 (0) ..... Cayman I
Tuesday September 6 2011
Cayman I ..... (0) 1-4 (0) .. El Salvador
Dominican R (0) 1-1 (1) ..... Suriname
Friday October 7 2011
Cayman I ..... (0) 0-1 (0) ..... Suriname
Dominican R (0) 1-2 (1) .. El Salvador
Tuesday October 11 2011
El Salvador... (3) 4-0 (0) ..... Cayman I
Suriname ..... (0) 1-3 (1) Dominican R
Friday November 11 2011
Dominican R (2) 4-0 (0) ..... Cayman I

Suriname ..... (0) 1-3 (1) .. El Salvador
Monday November 14 2011
Cayman I ..... (0) 1-1 (1) Dominican R
Tuesday November 15 2011
El Salvador... (1) 4-0 (0) ..... Suriname

Group B
	P	W	D	L	F	A	GD	Pts
1 Guyana	6	4	1	1	9	6	3	13
2 Trin/Tobago	6	4	0	2	12	4	8	12
3 Bermuda	6	3	1	2	8	7	1	10
4 Barbados	6	0	0	6	2	14	-12	0
Friday September 2 2011
Guyana .... (1) 2-0 (0) ..... Barbados
Trin/Tobago.. (1) 1-0 (0) ......Bermuda
Tuesday September 6 2011
Barbados ..... (0) 0-2 (1) ..Trin/Tobago
Guyana .... (0) 2-1 (0) ......Bermuda
Friday October 7 2011
Barbados ..... (0) 0-2 (0) ....Guyana
Bermuda...... (0) 2-1 (0) ..Trin/Tobago
Tuesday October 11 2011
Bermuda...... (0) 1-1 (0) ....Guyana
Trin/Tobago.. (1) 4-0 (0) ..... Barbados
Friday November 11 2011
Bermuda...... (1) 2-1 (1) ..... Barbados
Guyana .... (1) 2-1 (0) ..Trin/Tobago
Monday November 14 2011
Barbados ..... (0) 1-2 (0) ......Bermuda
Tuesday November 15 2011
Trin/Tobago.... 3-0 ....Guyana

Group C
	P	W	D	L	F	A	GD	Pts
1 Panama	4	4	0	0	15	2	13	12
2 Nicaragua	4	2	0	2	5	7	-2	6
3 Dominica	4	0	0	4	0	11	-11	0
Friday September 2 2011
Dominica ..... (0) 0-2 (2) .... Nicaragua
Tuesday September 6 2011
Nicaragua .... (1) 1-2 (1) .... Panama
Friday October 7 2011
Dominica ..... (0) 0-5 (2) .... Panama
Tuesday October 11 2011
Panama .... (1) 5-1 (0) .... Nicaragua
Friday November 11 2011
Nicaragua .... (0) 1-0 (0) ..... Dominica
Tuesday November 15 2011
Panama ...... (2) 3-0 (0) ..... Dominica

Group D
	P	W	D	L	F	A	GD	Pts
1 Canada	6	4	2	0	18	1	17	14
2 Puerto Rico	6	2	3	1	8	4	4	9
3 St Kitts/Nevis	6	1	4	1	6	8	-2	7
4 St Lucia	6	0	1	5	4	23	-19	1
Friday September 2 2011
Canada .... (1) 4-1 (1) .... St Lucia
St Kitts/Nevis(0) 0-0 (0) . Puerto Rico
Tuesday September 6 2011
Puerto Rico.. (0) 0-3 (1) ....Canada
St Lucia .... (0) 2-4 (4)St Kitts/Nevis

Friday October 7 2011
Puerto Rico.. (1) 1-1 (0)St Kitts/Nevis
St Lucia .... (0) 0-7 (4) ....Canada
Tuesday October 11 2011
Canada .... (0) 0-0 (0) . Puerto Rico
St Kitts/Nevis(0) 1-1 (0) .... St Lucia
Friday November 11 2011
St Kitts/Nevis(0) 0-0 (0) ....Canada
St Lucia ...... (0) 0-4 (2) . Puerto Rico
Monday November 14 2011
Puerto Rico.. (1) 3-0 (0) .... St Lucia
Tuesday November 15 2011
Canada .... (3) 4-0 (0)St Kitts/Nevis

Group E
	P	W	D	L	F	A	GD	Pts
1 Guatemala	6	6	0	0	19	3	16	18
2 Belize	6	2	1	3	9	10	-1	7
3 St Vincent/G	6	1	2	3	4	12	-8	5
4 Grenada	6	1	1	4	7	14	-7	4
Friday September 2 2011
Grenada .... (0) 0-3 (2) .... Belize
Guatemala ... (2) 4-0 (0) St Vincent/G
Tuesday September 6 2011
Belize........... (0) 1-2 (1) ... Guatemala
Thursday September 18 2011
St Vincent/G. (1) 2-1 (0) ....Grenada
Friday October 7 2011
Belize........... (0) 1-4 (2) ......Grenada
St Vincent/G. (0) 0-3 (1) ... Guatemala
Tuesday October 11 2011
Guatemala ... (1) 3-1 (1) .... Belize
Saturday October 15 2011
Grenada .... (0) 1-1 (0) St Vincent/G
Friday November 11 2011
Belize........... (1) 1-1 (1) St Vincent/G
Guatemala ... (3) 3-0 (0) ......Grenada
Tuesday November 15 2011
Grenada ...... (1) 1-4 (0) ... Guatemala
St Vincent/G. (0) 0-2 (0) .... Belize

Group F
	P	W	D	L	F	A	GD	Pts
1 Antigua/Barb	6	5	0	1	28	5	23	15
2 Haiti	6	4	1	1	21	6	15	13
3 Curacao	6	2	1	3	15	15	0	7
4 US Virgin I	6	0	0	6	2	40	-38	0
Friday September 2 2011
Antigua/Barb (2) 5-2 (1) ......Curacao
Haiti............. (3) 6-0 (0) ... US Virgin I
Tuesday September 6 2011
Curacao....... (2) 2-4 (1) ....Haiti
US Virgin I.... (0) 1-8 (2) Antigua/Barb
Friday October 7 2011
Curacao......... 0-3 ...Antigua/Barb
Match awarded
US Virgin I.... (0) 0-7 (2) ....Haiti
Tuesday October 11 2011
Antigua/Barb (5)10-0(0)... US Virgin I
Haiti............. (1) 2-2 (2) ....Curacao

Friday November 11 2011
Antigua/Barb (0) 1-0 (0) ....Haiti
US Virgin I.... (0) 0-3 (3) ......Curacao
Tuesday November 15 2011
Curacao...... (2) 6-1 (0) ... US Virgin I
Haiti............. (0) 2-1 (1) Antigua/Barb

Round 3

Group A

	P	W	D	L	F	A	GD	Pts
1 USA	6	4	1	1	11	6	5	13
2 Jamaica	6	3	1	2	9	6	3	10
3 Guatemala	6	3	1	2	9	8	1	10
4 Antigua/Barb	6	0	1	5	4	13	-9	1

Friday June 8 2012
Jamaica...... (1) 2-1 (0) ... Guatemala
USA............. (2) 3-1 (0) Antigua/Barb
Tuesday June 12 2012
Antigua/Barb (0) 0-0 (0) ....Jamaica
Guatemala ... (0) 1-1 (1) ....USA
Friday September 7 2012
Guatemala ... (0) 3-1 (1) Antigua/Barb
Jamaica...... (1) 2-1 (1) ....USA
Tuesday September 11 2012
Antigua/Barb (0) 0-1 (1) ... Guatemala
USA............. (0) 1-0 (0) ....Jamaica
Friday October 12 2012
Antigua/Barb (1) 1-2 (1) ....USA
Guatemala ... (1) 2-1 (0) ....Jamaica
Tuesday October 16 2012
Jamaica...... (2) 4-1 (0) Antigua/Barb
USA............. (3) 3-1 (1) ... Guatemala

Group B

	P	W	D	L	F	A	GD	Pts
1 Mexico	6	6	0	0	15	2	13	18
2 Costa Rica	6	3	1	2	14	5	9	10
3 El Salvador	6	1	2	3	8	11	-3	5
4 Guyana	6	0	1	5	5	24	-19	1

Friday June 8 2012
Costa Rica ... (2) 2-2 (1) .. El Salvador
Mexico......... (2) 3-1 (0) ....Guyana
Tuesday June 12 2012
El Salvador... (0) 1-2 (0) .... Mexico
Guyana .... (0) 0-4 (2) ...Costa Rica
Friday September 7 2012
Costa Rica... (0) 0-2 (1) .... Mexico
El Salvador... (2) 2-2 (1) ....Guyana
Tuesday September 11 2012
Guyana .... (1) 2-3 (1) .. El Salvador
Mexico......... (0) 1-0 (0) ...Costa Rica
Friday October 12 2012
El Salvador... (0) 0-1 (1) ...Costa Rica
Guyana .... (0) 0-5 (0) .... Mexico
Tuesday October 16 2012
Costa Rica... (2) 7-0 (0) ....Guyana
Mexico......... (0) 2-0 (0) .. El Salvador

Group C

	P	W	D	L	F	A	GD	Pts
1 Honduras	6	3	2	1	12	3	9	11
2 Panama	6	3	2	1	6	2	4	11
3 Canada	6	3	1	2	6	10	-4	10
4 Cuba	6	0	1	5	1	10	-9	1

Friday June 8 2012
Cuba............ (0) 0-1 (0) ....Canada
Honduras..... (0) 0-2 (0) .... Panama
Tuesday June 12 2012
Canada .... (0) 0-0 (0) .....Honduras
Panama ...... (0) 1-0 (0) .... Cuba
Friday September 7 2012
Canada .... (0) 1-0 (0) ...... Panama
Cuba............ (0) 0-3 (1) .....Honduras
Tuesday September 11 2012
Honduras..... (1) 1-0 (0) .... Cuba
Panama .... (1) 2-0 (0) ....Canada
Friday October 12 2012
Canada .... (1) 3-0 (0) .... Cuba
Panama ...... (0) 0-0 (0) .....Honduras
Tuesday October 16 2012
Cuba............ (1) 1-1 (0) ...... Panama
Honduras..... (4) 8-1 (0) ....Canada

Round 4

Standings

	P	W	D	L	F	A	GD	Pts
1 USA	6	4	1	1	7	3	4	13
2 Costa Rica	6	3	2	1	7	3	4	11
3 Mexico	6	1	5	0	3	2	1	8
4 Honduras	6	2	1	3	6	7	-1	7
5 Panama	6	1	3	2	5	7	-2	6
6 Jamaica	6	0	2	4	2	8	-6	2

Wednesday February 6 2013
Honduras..... (1) 2-1 (1) ....USA
Mexico......... (0) 0-0 (0) ....Jamaica
Panama .... (2) 2-2 (1) ...Costa Rica
Friday March 22 2013
Honduras..... (0) 2-2 (1) ...... Mexico
USA............. (1) 1-0 (0) ...Costa Rica
Jamaica...... (1) 1-1 (0) ...... Panama
Tuesday March 26 2013
Costa Rica ... (1) 2-0 (0) ....Jamaica
Mexico......... (0) 0-0 (0) ....USA
Panama .... (0) 2-0 (0) ...Honduras
Tuesday June 4 2013
Jamaica...... (0) 0-1 (0) ...... Mexico
Friday June 7 2013
Costa Rica ... (1) 1-0 (0) .....Honduras
Jamaica...... (0) 1-2 (1) ....USA
Panama .... (0) 0-0 (0) ...... Mexico
Tuesday June 11 2013
Honduras..... (1) 2-0 (0) ....Jamaica
Mexico......... (0) 0-0 (0) ...Costa Rica
USA............. (1) 2-0 (0) ...... Panama
Tuesday June 18 2013
USA............. (0) 1-0 (0) .....Honduras
Costa Rica ... (0) 2-0 (0) ...... Panama
Friday September 6 2013
Mexico.......... v ....Honduras
Panama .... v ....Jamaica
Costa Rica ... v ....USA
Saturday September 10 2013
USA............. v .... Mexico
Honduras....... v ....Panama
Jamaica......... v .....Costa Rica

Friday October 11 2013
Mexico.......... v ....Panama
Honduras....... v ......Costa Rica
USA............... v ....Jamaica
Tuesday October 15 2013
Jamaica........ v ....Honduras
Panama .... v ....USA
Costa Rica..... v .... Mexico

Oceania

How it works 11 participating teams, 0.5 qualify. **Round 1** 1 round-robin group of 4 contested in Samoa. Winners advance **Round 2** Group stage of OFC Nations Cup. 2 round-robin groups of 4 contested in Fiji, winners and runners-up advance **Round 3** 1 round-robin, home-and-away group of 4. Winners advance to intercontinental play-off against Concacaf

Round 1

Standings

	P	W	D	L	F	A	GD	Pts
1 Samoa	3	2	1	0	5	3	2	7
2 Tonga	3	1	1	1	4	4	0	4
3 Am Samoa	3	1	1	1	3	3	0	4
4 Cook I	3	0	1	2	4	6	-2	1

Tuesday November 22 2011
Am Samoa... (1) 2-1 (0) .... Tonga
Cook I......... (1) 2-3 (2) ....Samoa
Thursday November 24 2011
Am Samoa... (1) 1-1 (0) ....Cook I
Samoa........ (1) 1-1 (0) .... Tonga
Saturday November 26 2011
Tonga .... (1) 2-1 (1) ....Cook I
Samoa......... (0) 1-0 (0) .. Am Samoa

Round 2

Group A

	P	W	D	L	F	A	GD	Pts
1 Tahiti	3	3	0	0	18	5	13	9
2 New Caledonia	3	2	0	1	17	6	11	6
3 Vanuatu	3	1	0	2	8	9	-1	3
4 Samoa	3	0	0	3	1	24	-23	0

Friday June 1 2012
Samoa......... (0)1-10(4).......... Tahiti
Vanuatu ...... (0) 2-5 (1) .. N Caledonia
Sunday June 3 2012
Vanuatu ...... (2) 5-0 (0) ....Samoa
Tahiti............ (3) 4-3 (0) .N Caledonia
Tuesday June 5 2012
N Caledonia . (6) 9-0 (0) ....Samoa
Tahiti............ (2) 4-1 (0) ....Vanuatu

Group B

	P	W	D	L	F	A	GD	Pts
1 New Zealand	3	2	1	0	4	2	2	7
2 Solomon I	3	1	2	0	2	1	1	5
3 Fiji	3	0	2	1	1	2	-1	2
4 Papua NG	3	0	1	2	2	4	-2	1

Saturday June 2 2012
Fiji .... (0) 0-1 (1) New Zealand
Solomon I .... (1) 1-0 (0) .... Papua NG
Monday June 4 2012
Papua NG..... (0) 1-2 (1) New Zealand
Fiji .... (0) 0-0 (0) ....Solomon I
Wednesday June 6 2012
Papua NG..... (0) 1-1 (1) .... Fiji
New Zealand (1) 1-1 (0) ....Solomon I

Round 3

Standings

	P	W	D	L	F	A	GD	Pts
1 New Zealand	6	6	0	0	17	2	15	18
2 New Caledonia	6	4	0	2	17	6	11	12
3 Tahiti	6	1	0	5	2	12	-10	3
4 Solomon I	6	1	0	5	5	21	-16	3

Friday September 7 2012
Solomon I .... (1) 2-0 (0) .... Tahiti
N Caledonia . (0) 0-2 (1) New Zealand
Tuesday September 11 2012
New Zealand (2) 6-1 (0) ....Solomon I
Tahiti............ (0) 0-4 (0) . N Caledonia
Friday October 12 2012
Solomon I .... (1) 2-6 (2) . N Caledonia
Tahiti............ (0) 0-2 (1) New Zealand
Tuesday October 16 2012
N Caledonia . (4) 5-0 (0) ....Solomon I
New Zealand (1) 3-0 (0) .... Tahiti
Friday March 22 2013
New Zealand (1) 2-1 (0) . N Caledonia
Tahiti............ (1) 2-0 (0) ....Solomon I
Tuesday March 26 2013
Solomon I .... (0) 0-2 (1) New Zealand
N Caledonia . (0) 1-0 (0) .... Tahiti

South America

How it works 9 participating teams,
4.5 qualify plus Brazil as hosts.
1 round-robin, home-and-away group
of 9. Top 4 qualify for World Cup, 5th
team advances to intercontinental
play-off against Asia

Standings

	P	W	D	L	F	A	GD	Pts
1 Argentina	13	7	5	1	25	9	16	26
2 Colombia	12	7	2	3	21	7	14	23
3 Ecuador	12	6	3	3	17	12	5	21
4 Chile	13	7	0	6	21	21	0	21
5 Uruguay	12	4	4	4	18	21	-3	16
6 Venezuela	13	4	4	5	10	14	-4	16
7 Peru	12	4	2	6	12	17	-5	14
8 Bolivia	13	2	4	7	15	24	-9	10
9 Paraguay	12	2	2	8	9	23	-14	8

Friday October 7 2011
Ecuador .... (2) 2-0 (0) .... Venezuela
Uruguay........ (3) 4-2 (1) .... Bolivia
Argentina ..... (2) 4-1 (0) ....Chile
Peru............. (0) 2-0 (0) ..... Paraguay
Tuesday October 11 2011
Bolivia.......... (0) 1-2 (0) .....Colombia
Paraguay ..... (0) 1-1 (0) ...... Uruguay

Chile .... (2) 4-2 (0) .... Peru
Venezuela .... (0) 1-0 (0) .....Argentina
Friday November 11 2011
Argentina ..... (0) 1-1 (0) .... Bolivia
Colombia ..... (1) 1-1 (0) .... Venezuela
Uruguay........ (2) 4-0 (0) ....Chile
Paraguay ..... (0) 2-1 (0) ......Ecuador
Tuesday November 15 2011
Colombia ..... (1) 1-2 (0) .....Argentina
Ecuador .... (0) 2-0 (0) .... Peru
Venezuela .... (1) 1-0 (0) .... Bolivia
Chile .... (1) 2-0 (0) ..... Paraguay
Saturday June 2 2012
Uruguay........ (1) 1-1 (0) .... Venezuela
Bolivia.......... (0) 0-2 (1) ....Chile
Argentina ..... (3) 4-0 (0) ......Ecuador
Sunday June 3 2012
Peru............. (0) 0-1 (0) .....Colombia
Saturday June 9 2012
Bolivia.......... (1) 3-1 (0) .... Paraguay
Venezuela .... (0) 0-2 (0) ....Chile
Sunday June 10 2012
Uruguay........ (2) 4-2 (1) .... Peru
Ecuador .... (0) 1-0 (0) .....Colombia
Friday September 7 2012
Colombia ..... (1) 4-0 (0) ...... Uruguay
Ecuador .... (0) 1-0 (0) .... Bolivia
Argentina ..... (2) 3-1 (1) ..... Paraguay
Peru............. (0) 2-1 (1) .... Venezuela
Tuesday September 11 2012
Chile .... (1) 1-3 (0) .....Colombia
Uruguay........ (0) 1-1 (1) ....Ecuador
Paraguay ..... (0) 0-2 (1) .... Venezuela
Peru............. (1) 1-1 (1) .....Argentina
Friday October 12 2012
Colombia ..... (0) 2-0 (0) ..... Paraguay
Ecuador .... (1) 3-1 (1) ....Chile
Bolivia.......... (0) 1-1 (1) .... Peru
Argentina ..... (0) 3-0 (0) ...... Uruguay
Tuesday October 16 2012
Bolivia.......... (2) 4-1 (0) ...... Uruguay
Venezuela .... (1) 1-1 (1) ....Ecuador
Paraguay ..... (0) 1-0 (0) .... Peru
Chile .... (0) 1-2 (1) .....Argentina
Friday March 22 2013
Colombia ..... (1) 5-0 (0) .... Bolivia
Uruguay........ (0) 1-1 (0) ..... Paraguay
Argentina ..... (2) 3-0 (0) ..... Venezuela
Peru............. (0) 1-0 (0) ....Chile
Tuesday March 26 2013
Ecuador .... (1) 4-1 (0) ..... Paraguay
Bolivia.......... (1) 1-1 (1) .....Argentina
Venezuela .... (1) 1-0 (0) .....Colombia
Chile .... (1) 2-0 (0) ...... Uruguay
Friday June 7 2013
Bolivia.......... (0) 1-1 (0) .... Venezuela
Argentina ..... (0) 0-0 (0) .....Colombia
Paraguay ..... (0) 1-2 (1) ....Chile
Peru............. (1) 1-0 (0) ....Ecuador
Tuesday June 11 2013
Colombia .... (2) 2-0 (0) .... Peru

Ecuador .... (1) 1-1 (1) .....Argentina
Venezuela .... (0) 0-1 (1) ...... Uruguay
Chile .... (2) 3-1 (1) .... Bolivia
Friday September 6 2013
Colombia .... v ....Ecuador
Chile .... v ...... Venezuela
Peru............... v .... Uruguay
Paraguay .... v .... Bolivia
Tuesday September 10 2013
Bolivia............ v ....Ecuador
Paraguay .... v ....Argentina
Uruguay.......... v ......Colombia
Venezuela ...... v .... Peru
Friday October 11 2013
Colombia .... v ....Chile
Venezuela ...... v ...... Paraguay
Argentina .... v .... Peru
Ecuador .... v ...... Uruguay
Tuesday October 15 2013
Chile .... v ....Ecuador
Peru............... v .... Bolivia
Paraguay .... v ....Colombia
Uruguay.......... v ....Argentina

Play-offs

Friday November 15 2013
World Cup 2014 qualifying play-offs
(Uefa & intercontinental), first legs
Tuesday November 19 2013
World Cup 2014 qualifying play-offs
(Uefa & intercontinental), second legs

World Cup finals

Friday December 6 2013
Group-stage draw
Thursday June 12 2014
Group stage begins
Thursday June 26 2014
Group stage ends
Saturday June 28 2014
Round of 16 begins
Tuesday July 1 2014
Round of 16 ends
Friday July 4 2014
Quarter-finals begin
Saturday July 5 2014
Quarter-finals end
Tuesday July 8 2014
First semi-final
Wednesday July 9 2014
Second semi-final
Saturday July 12 2014
Third-place match
Sunday July 13 2014
World Cup final

**Facing page: Neymar lifts the
Confederations Cup after Brazil
beat Spain 3-0 in the Maracana**

Fixtures 2013-14

Alongside each fixture are the results for the corresponding league match over the last six seasons. The most recent result – 2012-13 – is on the right. For English clubs, the results cover the Premier League, the Championship, League 1, League 2 and the Conference. For Scottish clubs the results cover the Scottish Premier League and Divisions One, Two and Three.

Where Scottish clubs have met more than once in the same season, each result is separated by an oblique stroke with the most recent to the right. The Scottish Premier League will split into top- and bottom-six sections later in the season. These fixtures cover the period until that split.

Please note that television coverage and weather conditions will cause alterations to the fixture list.

	2007-08	2008-09	2009-10	2010-11	2011-12	2012-13
Friday August 2nd, 2013						
League 1						
Sheffield United v Notts County	-	-	-	-	2-1	1-1
Saturday August 3rd, 2013						
Championship						
Barnsley v Wigan	-	-	-	-	-	-
Birmingham v Watford	-	3-2	-	-	3-0	0-4
Bournemouth v Charlton	-	-	-	2-2	0-1	-
Burnley v Bolton	-	-	1-1	-	-	2-0
Doncaster v Blackpool	-	0-0	3-3	-	1-3	-
Leeds v Brighton	0-0	3-1	1-1	-	1-2	1-2
Middlesbrough v Leicester	-	-	0-1	3-3	0-0	1-2
Millwall v Yeovil	2-1	1-1	0-0	-	-	-
Nottm Forest v Huddersfield	2-1	-	-	-	-	6-1
QPR v Sheffield Weds	0-0	3-2	1-1	-	-	-
Reading v Ipswich	-	0-1	1-1	1-0	1-0	-
League 1						
Bristol City v Bradford	-	-	-	-	-	-
Carlisle v Leyton Orient	1-0	1-3	2-2	0-1	4-1	1-4
Crawley v Coventry	-	-	-	-	-	2-0
Crewe v Rotherham	-	-	2-3	0-1	1-2	-
Gillingham v Colchester	-	-	0-0	-	-	-
Peterborough v Swindon	-	2-2	-	5-4	-	-
Port Vale v Brentford	-	0-3	-	-	-	-
Preston v Wolves	2-1	1-3	-	-	-	-
Shrewsbury v MK Dons	3-3	-	-	-	-	2-2
Stevenage v Oldham	-	-	-	-	1-0	1-2
Walsall v Tranmere	2-1	0-1	2-1	1-4	0-1	2-0
League 2						
Bury v Chesterfield	0-1	1-2	2-1	1-1	1-1	-
Cheltenham v Burton	-	-	0-1	2-1	2-0	1-0
Exeter v Bristol Rovers	-	-	1-0	2-2	-	1-2
Fleetwood v Dag & Red	-	-	-	-	-	2-1
Newport County v Accrington	-	-	-	-	-	-
Portsmouth v Oxford	-	-	-	-	-	-
Rochdale v Hartlepool	-	-	-	0-0	1-3	-
Scunthorpe v Mansfield	-	-	-	-	-	-
Southend v Plymouth	-	-	-	-	2-0	0-2
Torquay v AFC Wimbledon	-	-	-	-	4-0	2-3
Wycombe v Morecambe	2-0	1-1	-	2-0	-	2-2
York v Northampton	-	-	-	-	-	1-1

Results cover matches from Premier League to Conference and Scottish Premier League to Division Three

	2007-08	2008-09	2009-10	2010-11	2011-12	2012-13
Scottish Premier League						
Aberdeen v Kilmarnock	2-1	1-0/0-0	1-0/1-2	0-1/5-0	2-2/0-0	0-2/1-0
Celtic v Ross County	-	-	-	-	-	4-0
Inverness CT v St Mirren	1-0/0-0	1-2/2-1	-	1-2/1-0	2-1/0-0	2-2
Partick v Dundee United	-	-	-	-	-	-
St Johnstone v Hearts	-	-	2-2/1-0	0-2	2-0/2-1	2-2

Sunday August 4th, 2013

	2007-08	2008-09	2009-10	2010-11	2011-12	2012-13
Championship						
Derby v Blackburn	1-2	-	-	-	-	1-1
Scottish Premier League						
Hibernian v Motherwell	1-0/0-2	0-1/1-1	2-0	2-1	0-1/1-1	2-3

Saturday August 10th, 2013

	2007-08	2008-09	2009-10	2010-11	2011-12	2012-13
Championship						
Blackburn v Nottm Forest	-	-	-	-	-	3-0
Blackpool v Barnsley	1-1	1-0	1-2	-	1-1	1-2
Bolton v Reading	3-0	-	-	-	-	-
Brighton v Derby	-	-	-	-	2-0	2-1
Charlton v Middlesbrough	-	-	-	-	-	1-4
Huddersfield v QPR	-	-	-	-	-	-
Ipswich v Millwall	-	-	-	2-0	0-3	3-0
Sheffield Weds v Burnley	0-2	4-1	-	-	-	0-2
Watford v Bournemouth	-	-	-	-	-	-
Yeovil v Birmingham	-	-	-	-	-	-
League 1						
Bradford v Carlisle	-	-	-	-	-	-
Brentford v Sheffield United	-	-	-	-	0-2	2-0
Colchester v Port Vale	-	-	-	-	-	-
Coventry v Bristol City	0-3	0-3	1-1	1-4	1-0	-
Leyton Orient v Shrewsbury	-	-	-	-	-	2-1
MK Dons v Crewe	-	2-2	-	-	-	1-0
Notts County v Peterborough	0-1	-	-	0-1	-	-
Oldham v Walsall	0-2	3-2	1-0	1-1	2-1	1-1
Rotherham v Preston	-	-	-	-	-	-
Swindon v Stevenage	-	-	-	-	-	3-0
Tranmere v Crawley	-	-	-	-	-	2-0
Wolves v Gillingham	-	-	-	-	-	-
League 2						
Accrington v Portsmouth	-	-	-	-	-	-
AFC Wimbledon v Wycombe	-	-	-	-	-	2-2
Bristol Rovers v Scunthorpe	-	1-2	-	-	-	-
Burton v Rochdale	-	-	1-0	-	-	3-2
Chesterfield v Cheltenham	-	-	1-0	3-0	-	4-1
Dag & Red v York	-	-	-	-	-	0-1
Hartlepool v Southend	4-3	3-0	3-0	-	-	-
Mansfield v Exeter	-	-	-	-	-	-
Morecambe v Torquay	-	-	2-0	2-1	1-2	0-2
Northampton v Newport County	-	-	-	-	-	-
Oxford v Bury	-	-	-	1-2	-	-
Plymouth v Fleetwood	-	-	-	-	-	2-1
Conference						
Barnet v Chester	3-1	3-1	-	-	-	-
Cambridge v Halifax	2-2	-	-	-	-	-
Dartford v Alfreton	-	-	-	-	-	5-1

Results cover matches from Premier League to Conference and Scottish Premier League to Division Three

	2007-08	2008-09	2009-10	2010-11	2011-12	2012-13
Forest Green v Hyde	-	-	-	-	-	3-1
Grimsby v Aldershot	-	1-0	1-2	-	-	-
Hereford v Braintree	-	-	-	-	-	0-0
Kidderminster v Gateshead	-	-	3-2	2-1	2-3	1-1
Macclesfield v Nuneaton	-	-	-	-	-	0-0
Salisbury v Tamworth	-	-	1-0	-	-	-
Southport v Luton	-	-	-	2-1	3-3	1-3
Woking v Lincoln	-	-	-	-	-	1-1
Wrexham v Welling	-	-	-	-	-	-
Scottish Premier League						
Dundee United v Inverness CT	0-1	2-1/1-1	-	0-4/1-0	3-1/3-0	4-4
Hearts v Hibernian	0-1/1-0	0-0/0-1	0-0/2-1	1-0	2-0/2-0	0-0/1-2
Kilmarnock v St Johnstone	-	-	2-1/3-2/1-2	1-1	1-2/0-0	1-2
Ross County v Partick	-	1-0/0-2	2-2/1-2	0-2/0-0	2-2/3-0	-
Scottish Division One						
Alloa v Livingston	-	-	-	2-2/1-3	-	-
Dumbarton v Falkirk	-	-	-	-	-	0-2/0-2
Morton v Cowdenbeath	-	-	-	1-2/3-0	-	1-0/4-2
Queen of Sth v Dundee	2-1/1-0	3-1/0-1	2-0/1-1	1-2/3-0	0-0/1-1	-
Raith v Hamilton	-	-	-	-	3-2/2-1	2-0/0-2
Scottish Division Two						
Arbroath v Ayr	-	0-3/1-3	-	-	-	4-2/1-4
East Fife v Dunfermline	-	-	-	-	-	-
Forfar v Airdrieonians	-	-	-	1-2/1-2	3-2/2-3	-
Rangers v Brechin	-	-	-	-	-	-
Stenhousemuir v Stranraer	1-4/1-1	-	-	-	-	0-0/1-2
Scottish Division Three						
Clyde v Berwick	-	-	-	1-4/2-0	1-4/2-2	2-1/2-1
Elgin v Albion	3-2/1-1	1-6/1-0	0-2/3-1	2-2/1-1	-	-
Montrose v Stirling	-	-	-	-	-	3-2/2-2
Peterhead v Annan	-	-	-	-	2-3/3-2	2-0/2-0
Queen's Park v East Stirling	-	-	1-0/2-0	2-0/2-0	2-0/5-1	1-2/5-1

Sunday August 11th, 2013

	2007-08	2008-09	2009-10	2010-11	2011-12	2012-13
Championship						
Leicester v Leeds	-	1-0	-	2-2	0-1	1-1
Scottish Premier League						
Motherwell v Aberdeen	3-0/2-1	0-1/1-1	1-1	1-1/2-1	1-0/1-0	4-1

Tuesday August 13th, 2013

	2007-08	2008-09	2009-10	2010-11	2011-12	2012-13
Conference						
Aldershot v Dartford	-	-	-	-	-	-
Alfreton v Kidderminster	-	-	-	-	0-2	1-1
Braintree v Woking	-	-	-	-	-	1-1
Chester v Hereford	1-1	-	-	-	-	-
Gateshead v Grimsby	-	-	-	0-0	1-0	1-1
Halifax v Wrexham	-	-	-	-	-	-
Hyde v Southport	-	-	-	-	-	0-2
Lincoln v Macclesfield	3-1	1-0	0-0	2-1	-	2-3
Luton v Salisbury	-	-	4-0	-	-	-
Nuneaton v Forest Green	-	-	-	-	-	1-1
Tamworth v Barnet	-	-	-	-	-	-
Welling v Cambridge	-	-	-	-	-	-

Results cover matches from Premier League to Conference and Scottish Premier League to Division Three

Saturday August 17th, 2013

Premier League

	2007-08	2008-09	2009-10	2010-11	2011-12	2012-13
Arsenal v Aston Villa	1-1	0-2	3-0	1-2	3-0	2-1
Chelsea v Hull	-	0-0	2-1	-	-	-
Crystal Palace v Tottenham	-	-	-	-	-	-
Liverpool v Stoke	-	0-0	4-0	2-0	0-0	0-0
Man City v Newcastle	3-1	2-1	-	2-1	3-1	4-0
Norwich v Everton	-	-	-	-	2-2	2-1
Sunderland v Fulham	1-1	1-0	0-0	0-3	0-0	2-2
Swansea v Man United	-	-	-	-	0-1	1-1
West Brom v Southampton	1-1	-	-	-	-	2-0
West Ham v Cardiff	-	-	-	-	0-1	-

Championship

Barnsley v Charlton	3-0	0-0	-	-	-	0-6
Birmingham v Brighton	-	-	-	-	0-0	2-2
Bournemouth v Wigan	-	-	-	-	-	-
Burnley v Yeovil	-	-	-	-	-	-
Derby v Leicester	-	-	1-0	0-2	0-1	2-1
Doncaster v Blackburn	-	-	-	-	-	-
Leeds v Sheffield Weds	-	-	-	-	-	2-1
Middlesbrough v Blackpool	-	-	0-3	-	2-2	4-2
Millwall v Huddersfield	1-2	2-1	3-1	-	-	4-0
Nottm Forest v Bolton	-	-	-	-	-	1-1
QPR v Ipswich	1-1	1-3	1-2	2-0	-	-
Reading v Watford	-	4-0	1-1	1-1	0-2	-

League 1

Bristol City v Wolves	0-0	2-2	-	-	-	1-4
Carlisle v Coventry	-	-	-	-	-	1-0
Crawley v Rotherham	-	-	-	-	3-0	-
Crewe v Tranmere	4-3	2-1	-	-	-	0-0
Gillingham v Brentford	-	1-1	0-1	-	-	-
Peterborough v Oldham	-	2-2	-	5-2	-	-
Port Vale v Bradford	-	0-2	2-1	2-1	3-2	0-0
Preston v MK Dons	-	-	-	-	1-1	0-0
Sheffield United v Colchester	2-2	-	-	-	3-0	3-0
Shrewsbury v Swindon	-	-	-	-	2-1	0-1
Stevenage v Leyton Orient	-	-	-	-	0-1	0-1
Walsall v Notts County	-	-	-	0-3	0-1	1-1

League 2

Bury v Accrington	2-1	1-0	0-2	3-0	-	-
Cheltenham v Plymouth	-	-	-	-	2-1	2-1
Exeter v AFC Wimbledon	-	-	-	-	-	2-0
Fleetwood v Burton	-	-	-	-	-	0-4
Newport County v Bristol Rovers	-	-	-	-	-	-
Portsmouth v Morecambe	-	-	-	-	-	-
Rochdale v Chesterfield	0-1	2-1	2-3	-	1-1	1-1
Scunthorpe v Dag & Red	-	-	-	-	-	-
Southend v Northampton	1-1	1-0	-	1-1	2-2	1-2
Torquay v Oxford	3-2	1-1	-	3-4	0-0	1-3
Wycombe v Mansfield	1-2	-	-	-	-	-
York v Hartlepool	-	-	-	-	-	-

Conference

Aldershot v Cambridge	0-0	-	-	-	-	-
Alfreton v Salisbury	-	-	-	-	-	-
Braintree v Kidderminster	-	-	-	-	1-4	1-1

Results cover matches from Premier League to Conference and Scottish Premier League to Division Three

	2007-08	2008-09	2009-10	2010-11	2011-12	2012-13
Chester v Woking	-	-	-	-	-	-
Gateshead v Barnet	-	-	-	-	-	-
Halifax v Dartford	-	-	-	-	-	-
Hyde v Hereford	-	-	-	-	-	5-2
Lincoln v Forest Green	-	-	-	-	1-1	1-2
Luton v Macclesfield	-	1-0	-	-	-	4-1
Nuneaton v Southport	-	-	-	-	-	0-1
Tamworth v Wrexham	-	-	2-1	1-1	1-2	0-1
Welling v Grimsby	-	-	-	-	-	-
Scottish Premier League						
Aberdeen v Celtic	1-3/1-5	4-2/1-3	1-3/4-4	0-3	0-1/1-1	0-2
Hibernian v Dundee United	2-2	2-1/1-2	1-1/2-4	2-2	3-3/0-2	2-1
Inverness CT v Motherwell	0-3	1-2/1-2	-	1-2/3-0	2-3	1-5/4-3
Partick v Hearts	-	-	-	-	-	-
St Johnstone v Ross County	-	2-1/0-0	-	-	-	1-1/2-2
St Mirren v Kilmarnock	0-0/1-0	0-0/1-1	1-0/1-0	0-2	3-0/4-2	1-1
Scottish Division One						
Cowdenbeath v Raith	1-0/1-4	-	-	1-2/0-3	-	4-4/1-1
Dundee v Alloa	-	-	-	-	-	-
Falkirk v Morton	-	-	-	2-1/1-0	1-0/0-2	0-1/4-1
Hamilton v Dumbarton	-	-	-	-	-	2-3/2-1
Livingston v Queen of Sth	2-2/1-0	2-0/2-2	-	-	2-2/2-2	-
Scottish Division Two						
Airdrieonians v Stenhousemuir	-	-	-	1-0/2-2	5-2/0-3	-
Ayr v Forfar	-	-	-	0-1/3-1	-	2-3/2-1
Brechin v East Fife	-	2-1/2-1	3-2/1-0	1-3/2-3	0-2/1-3	2-1/6-0
Dunfermline v Arbroath	-	-	-	-	-	-
Stranraer v Rangers	-	-	-	-	-	-
Scottish Division Three						
Albion v Clyde	-	-	-	3-1/1-1	-	-
Annan v Montrose	-	1-2/2-1	2-0/0-0	2-2/2-1	2-1/1-2	2-1/1-1
Berwick v Queen's Park	1-1/1-4	-	1-0/1-1	1-1/3-1	2-0/1-4	2-0/4-1
East Stirling v Elgin	3-1/0-0	5-2/1-0	1-1/2-0	0-2/2-1	1-1/2-2	1-4/3-2
Stirling v Peterhead	-	0-0/2-1	2-1/2-0	-	-	1-0/0-1

Tuesday August 20th, 2013

Championship

Wigan v Doncaster	-	-	-	-	-	-

Friday August 23rd, 2013

League 1

Wolves v Crawley	-	-	-	-	-	-

Saturday August 24th, 2013

Premier League

	2007-08	2008-09	2009-10	2010-11	2011-12	2012-13
Aston Villa v Liverpool	1-2	0-0	0-1	1-0	0-2	1-2
Cardiff v Man City	-	-	-	-	-	-
Everton v West Brom	-	2-0	-	1-4	2-0	2-1
Fulham v Arsenal	0-3	1-0	0-1	2-2	2-1	0-1
Hull v Norwich	2-1	-	-	1-1	-	-
Man United v Chelsea	2-0	3-0	1-2	2-1	3-1	0-1
Newcastle v West Ham	3-1	2-2	-	5-0	-	0-1
Southampton v Sunderland	-	-	-	-	-	0-1
Stoke v Crystal Palace	1-2	-	-	-	-	-
Tottenham v Swansea	-	-	-	-	3-1	1-0

Results cover matches from Premier League to Conference and Scottish Premier League to Division Three

	2007-08	2008-09	2009-10	2010-11	2011-12	2012-13
Championship						
Blackburn v Barnsley	-	-	-	-	-	2-1
Blackpool v Reading	-	2-2	2-0	-	1-0	-
Bolton v QPR	-	-	-	-	2-1	-
Brighton v Burnley	-	-	-	-	0-1	1-0
Charlton v Doncaster	-	1-2	-	-	-	-
Huddersfield v Bournemouth	1-0	-	-	2-2	0-1	-
Ipswich v Leeds	-	-	-	2-1	2-1	3-0
Leicester v Birmingham	-	-	-	-	3-1	2-2
Sheffield Weds v Millwall	-	-	-	-	-	3-2
Watford v Nottm Forest	-	2-1	0-0	1-1	0-1	2-0
Wigan v Middlesbrough	1-0	0-1	-	-	-	-
Yeovil v Derby	-	-	-	-	-	-
League 1						
Bradford v Sheffield United	-	-	-	-	-	-
Brentford v Walsall	-	-	1-1	1-2	0-0	0-0
Colchester v Carlisle	-	5-0	2-1	1-1	1-1	2-0
Coventry v Preston	2-1	0-0	1-1	1-2	-	1-1
Leyton Orient v Crewe	0-1	1-0	-	-	-	1-1
MK Dons v Bristol City	-	-	-	-	-	-
Notts County v Stevenage	-	-	-	-	1-0	1-2
Oldham v Port Vale	1-1	-	-	-	-	-
Rotherham v Shrewsbury	2-0	1-2	1-1	1-3	1-1	-
Swindon v Gillingham	5-0	-	3-1	-	2-0	-
Tranmere v Peterborough	-	1-1	-	1-0	-	-
League 2						
Accrington v Cheltenham	-	-	4-0	2-4	0-1	2-2
AFC Wimbledon v Scunthorpe	-	-	-	-	-	-
Bristol Rovers v York	-	-	-	-	-	0-0
Burton v Bury	-	-	0-0	1-3	-	-
Chesterfield v Southend	-	-	-	2-1	-	0-1
Dag & Red v Newport County	-	-	-	-	-	-
Hartlepool v Fleetwood	-	-	-	-	-	-
Mansfield v Portsmouth	-	-	-	-	-	-
Morecambe v Exeter	-	1-1	-	-	-	0-3
Northampton v Torquay	-	-	0-0	2-2	0-0	1-0
Oxford v Wycombe	-	-	-	2-2	-	0-1
Plymouth v Rochdale	-	-	-	0-1	-	3-1
Conference						
Barnet v Nuneaton	-	-	-	-	-	-
Cambridge v Lincoln	-	-	-	-	2-0	2-1
Dartford v Braintree	-	-	-	-	-	0-0
Forest Green v Luton	-	-	0-1	0-1	3-0	1-2
Grimsby v Alfreton	-	-	-	-	5-2	4-2
Hereford v Tamworth	-	-	-	-	-	5-2
Kidderminster v Chester	-	-	-	-	-	-
Macclesfield v Halifax	-	-	-	-	-	-
Salisbury v Aldershot	0-4	-	-	-	-	-
Southport v Gateshead	-	-	-	5-1	1-3	2-1
Woking v Welling	-	-	-	-	-	-
Wrexham v Hyde	-	-	-	-	-	2-0
Scottish Premier League						
Celtic v Inverness CT	5-0/2-1	1-0	-	2-2	2-0/1-0	0-1/4-1
Dundee United v St Johnstone	-	-	3-3	1-0/2-0	0-0	1-1/0-1
Hearts v Aberdeen	4-1	1-1/2-1	0-3	5-0	3-0/3-0	2-0
Kilmarnock v Hibernian	2-1	1-0/1-1	1-1	2-1	4-1/1-3	1-1/1-3

Results cover matches from Premier League to Conference and Scottish Premier League to Division Three

	2007-08	2008-09	2009-10	2010-11	2011-12	2012-13
Motherwell v Partick	-	-	-	-	-	-
Ross County v St Mirren	-	-	-	-	-	0-0
Scottish Division One						
Alloa v Cowdenbeath	3-2/3-2	-	2-1/3-1	-	-	-
Dumbarton v Morton	-	-	-	-	-	1-5/0-3
Hamilton v Queen of Sth	1-0/1-0	-	-	-	3-1/3-0	-
Livingston v Falkirk	-	-	-	-	1-1/1-2	2-1/1-2
Raith v Dundee	-	-	2-2/1-0	1-2/2-1	0-1/0-1	-
Scottish Division Two						
Airdrieonians v Rangers	-	-	-	-	-	-
Brechin v Forfar	-	-	-	0-0/0-1	0-1/2-1	4-1/3-4
East Fife v Arbroath	0-2/2-1	3-2/0-0	1-1/3-1	-	2-2/1-3	2-1/0-1
Stenhousemuir v Dunfermline	-	-	-	-	-	-
Stranraer v Ayr	-	1-3/1-4	-	-	-	2-0/0-1
Scottish Division Three						
Annan v Albion	-	2-4/1-1	0-0/1-2	4-1/2-2	-	-
Clyde v Queen's Park	-	-	-	2-3/0-2	0-2/1-2	0-3/2-3
Montrose v Berwick	-	1-1/1-1	1-3/1-1	1-1/1-1	3-5/1-1	3-1/1-3
Peterhead v Elgin	-	-	-	-	1-3/3-0	1-1/0-1
Stirling v East Stirling	-	-	-	-	-	1-1/9-1

Monday August 26th, 2013

	2007-08	2008-09	2009-10	2010-11	2011-12	2012-13
Conference						
Aldershot v Woking	2-1	-	-	-	-	-
Alfreton v Hereford	-	-	-	-	-	0-3
Braintree v Barnet	-	-	-	-	-	-
Chester v Forest Green	-	-	-	-	-	-
Gateshead v Macclesfield	-	-	-	-	-	2-2
Halifax v Southport	-	-	-	-	-	-
Hyde v Grimsby	-	-	-	-	-	3-2
Lincoln v Wrexham	2-4	-	-	-	1-2	1-2
Luton v Cambridge	-	-	2-2	2-0	0-1	3-2
Nuneaton v Kidderminster	-	-	-	-	-	0-1
Tamworth v Dartford	-	-	-	-	-	3-2
Welling v Salisbury	-	-	-	-	-	-

Saturday August 31st, 2013

	2007-08	2008-09	2009-10	2010-11	2011-12	2012-13
Premier League						
Arsenal v Tottenham	2-1	4-4	3-0	2-3	5-2	5-2
Cardiff v Everton	-	-	-	-	-	-
Chelsea v Aston Villa	4-4	2-0	7-1	3-3	1-3	8-0
Crystal Palace v Sunderland	-	-	-	-	-	-
Liverpool v Man United	0-1	2-1	2-0	3-1	1-1	1-2
Man City v Hull	-	5-1	1-1	-	-	-
Newcastle v Fulham	2-0	0-1	-	0-0	2-1	1-0
Norwich v Southampton	2-1	2-2	0-2	-	-	0-0
West Brom v Swansea	-	-	0-1	-	1-2	2-1
West Ham v Stoke	-	2-1	0-1	3-0	-	1-1
Championship						
Barnsley v Huddersfield	-	-	-	-	-	0-1
Birmingham v Ipswich	-	2-1	-	-	2-1	0-1
Blackburn v Bolton	4-1	2-2	3-0	1-0	1-2	1-2
Blackpool v Watford	1-1	0-2	3-2	-	0-0	2-2
Brighton v Millwall	3-0	4-1	0-1	-	2-2	2-2
Charlton v Leicester	2-0	-	-	-	-	2-1

Results cover matches from Premier League to Conference and Scottish Premier League to Division Three

	2007-08	2008-09	2009-10	2010-11	2011-12	2012-13
Derby v Burnley	-	1-1	-	2-4	1-2	1-2
Doncaster v Bournemouth	1-2	-	-	-	-	0-1
Leeds v QPR	-	-	-	2-0	-	-
Middlesbrough v Sheffield Weds	-	-	1-0	-	-	3-1
Wigan v Nottm Forest	-	-	-	-	-	-
Yeovil v Reading	-	-	-	-	-	-
League 1						
Brentford v Carlisle	-	-	3-1	2-1	4-0	2-1
Colchester v Leyton Orient	-	1-0	1-0	3-2	1-1	2-1
Gillingham v Bristol City	-	-	-	-	-	-
Notts County v Rotherham	0-1	0-3	1-0	-	-	-
Oldham v Tranmere	3-1	0-2	0-0	0-0	1-0	0-1
Peterborough v Crawley	-	-	-	-	-	-
Port Vale v Wolves	-	-	-	-	-	-
Sheffield United v MK Dons	-	-	-	-	2-1	0-0
Shrewsbury v Coventry	-	-	-	-	-	4-1
Stevenage v Bradford	-	-	-	2-1	-	-
Swindon v Crewe	1-1	0-0	-	-	3-0	4-1
Walsall v Preston	-	-	-	-	1-0	3-1
League 2						
Accrington v Burton	-	-	0-2	3-1	2-1	3-3
AFC Wimbledon v Fleetwood	-	-	-	1-0	-	2-1
Bristol Rovers v Northampton	1-1	1-0	-	-	2-1	3-1
Bury v Cheltenham	-	-	0-1	2-3	-	-
Exeter v York	1-1	-	-	-	-	1-1
Mansfield v Dag & Red	0-1	-	-	-	-	-
Morecambe v Plymouth	-	-	-	-	2-2	2-3
Oxford v Rochdale	-	-	-	-	-	3-0
Portsmouth v Chesterfield	-	-	-	-	-	-
Scunthorpe v Newport County	-	-	-	-	-	-
Torquay v Hartlepool	-	-	-	-	-	-
Wycombe v Southend	-	-	1-1	3-1	-	1-2
Conference						
Barnet v Hyde	-	-	-	-	-	-
Cambridge v Tamworth	-	-	2-0	3-3	0-1	1-1
Dartford v Lincoln	-	-	-	-	-	2-4
Forest Green v Alfreton	-	-	-	-	4-1	1-1
Grimsby v Nuneaton	-	-	-	-	-	0-0
Hereford v Welling	-	-	-	-	-	-
Kidderminster v Luton	-	-	1-2	3-3	1-2	0-2
Macclesfield v Braintree	-	-	-	-	-	2-1
Salisbury v Halifax	1-0	-	-	-	-	-
Southport v Aldershot	-	-	-	-	-	-
Woking v Gateshead	-	-	-	-	-	2-1
Wrexham v Chester	2-2	-	-	-	-	-
Scottish Premier League						
Aberdeen v St Johnstone	-	-	2-1/1-3	0-1/0-2	0-0/0-0	2-0
Dundee United v Celtic	0-2/0-1	1-1/2-2	2-1/0-2	1-2/1-3	0-1/1-0	2-2/0-4
Hibernian v Ross County	-	-	-	-	-	0-1
Inverness CT v Hearts	2-1/0-3	0-1	-	1-3/1-1	1-1/1-0	1-1
Motherwell v Kilmarnock	1-2/1-0	0-2/1-2	3-1/1-0	0-1/1-1	0-0	2-2
St Mirren v Partick	-	-	-	-	-	-
Scottish Division One						
Cowdenbeath v Dumbarton	-	2-0/0-0	2-1/0-0	-	0-0/4-1	0-1/2-3
Dundee v Livingston	4-1/2-0	0-3/4-1	-	-	3-0/1-0	-

Results cover matches from Premier League to Conference and Scottish Premier League to Division Three

	2007-08	2008-09	2009-10	2010-11	2011-12	2012-13
Falkirk v Hamilton	-	4-1/1-2	2-0/0-1	-	0-0/3-0	2-1/0-2
Morton v Raith	-	-	5-0/1-1	0-1/0-0	1-1/1-3	1-0/1-0
Queen of Sth v Alloa	-	-	-	-	-	1-0/0-0
Scottish Division Two						
Arbroath v Brechin	-	1-2/0-0	1-4/1-0	-	1-1/2-3	3-1/0-1
Ayr v Airdrieonians	1-1/1-2	-	1-1/1-4	1-0/3-1	-	-
Dunfermline v Stranraer	-	-	-	-	-	-
Forfar v Stenhousemuir	0-1/1-2	1-0/4-4	-	1-1/2-0	2-3/1-2	3-2/3-3
Rangers v East Fife	-	-	-	-	-	-
Scottish Division Three						
Albion v Montrose	1-3/0-3	0-1/0-1	0-0/1-0	3-1/0-2	-	-
Berwick v Annan	-	3-0/1-1	2-1/0-2	2-2/2-3	0-1/1-3	3-1/0-2
East Stirling v Peterhead	-	-	-	-	0-2/6-3	2-1/2-4
Elgin v Clyde	-	-	-	0-1/0-1	0-3/1-1	2-1/4-2
Queen's Park v Stirling	-	1-1/3-1	-	-	-	2-1/2-2

Saturday September 7th, 2013

	2007-08	2008-09	2009-10	2010-11	2011-12	2012-13
League 1						
Bradford v Brentford	1-2	1-1	-	-	-	-
Bristol City v Shrewsbury	-	-	-	-	-	-
Carlisle v Port Vale	3-2	-	-	-	-	-
Coventry v Colchester	1-0	-	-	-	-	2-2
Crawley v Gillingham	-	-	-	-	1-2	-
Crewe v Peterborough	-	1-1	-	-	-	-
Leyton Orient v Notts County	-	-	-	2-0	0-3	2-1
MK Dons v Swindon	-	1-2	2-1	2-1	-	2-0
Rotherham v Sheffield United	-	-	-	-	-	-
Tranmere v Stevenage	-	-	-	-	3-0	3-1
Wolves v Walsall	-	-	-	-	-	-
League 2						
Burton v Oxford	1-2	0-1	-	0-0	1-1	4-0
Cheltenham v Portsmouth	-	-	-	-	-	-
Chesterfield v Accrington	4-2	1-1	1-0	5-2	-	4-3
Dag & Red v Exeter	-	1-2	-	1-1	-	1-1
Fleetwood v Torquay	-	-	-	-	-	0-0
Hartlepool v Wycombe	-	-	1-1	-	1-3	-
Newport County v Mansfield	-	-	-	1-0	1-0	2-0
Northampton v Scunthorpe	-	3-3	-	-	-	-
Plymouth v Bristol Rovers	-	-	-	3-1	1-1	1-1
Rochdale v Bury	1-2	1-1	3-0	-	3-0	-
Southend v Morecambe	-	-	-	2-3	1-1	0-1
York v AFC Wimbledon	-	-	5-0	4-1	-	0-3
Conference						
Aldershot v Macclesfield	-	1-1	0-0	0-0	1-2	-
Alfreton v Woking	-	-	-	-	-	0-3
Braintree v Forest Green	-	-	-	-	1-5	3-1
Chester v Dartford	-	-	-	-	-	-
Gateshead v Hereford	-	-	-	-	-	3-2
Halifax v Barnet	-	-	-	-	-	-
Hyde v Cambridge	-	-	-	-	-	2-1
Lincoln v Salisbury	-	-	-	-	-	-
Luton v Grimsby	-	2-1	-	1-0	1-1	1-1
Nuneaton v Wrexham	-	-	-	-	-	0-0
Tamworth v Southport	-	-	-	0-1	2-2	2-1
Welling v Kidderminster	-	-	-	-	-	-

Results cover matches from Premier League to Conference and Scottish Premier League to Division Three

Monday September 9th, 2013

League 1

	2007-08	2008-09	2009-10	2010-11	2011-12	2012-13
Preston v Oldham	-	-	-	-	3-3	2-0

Saturday September 14th, 2013

Premier League

	2007-08	2008-09	2009-10	2010-11	2011-12	2012-13
Aston Villa v Newcastle	4-1	1-0	-	1-0	1-1	1-2
Everton v Chelsea	0-1	0-0	2-1	1-0	2-0	1-2
Fulham v West Brom	-	2-0	-	3-0	1-1	3-0
Hull v Cardiff	2-2	-	-	0-2	2-1	2-2
Man United v Crystal Palace	-	-	-	-	-	-
Southampton v West Ham	-	-	-	-	1-0	1-1
Stoke v Man City	-	1-0	1-1	1-1	1-1	1-1
Sunderland v Arsenal	0-1	1-1	1-0	1-1	1-2	0-1
Swansea v Liverpool	-	-	-	-	1-0	0-0
Tottenham v Norwich	-	-	-	-	1-2	1-1

Championship

	2007-08	2008-09	2009-10	2010-11	2011-12	2012-13
Bolton v Leeds	-	-	-	-	-	2-2
Bournemouth v Blackpool	-	-	-	-	-	-
Burnley v Blackburn	-	-	0-1	-	-	1-1
Huddersfield v Doncaster	2-2	-	-	-	-	-
Ipswich v Middlesbrough	-	-	1-1	3-3	1-1	4-0
Leicester v Wigan	-	-	-	-	-	-
Millwall v Derby	-	-	-	2-0	0-0	2-1
Nottm Forest v Barnsley	-	1-0	1-0	2-2	0-0	0-0
QPR v Birmingham	-	1-0	-	-	-	-
Reading v Brighton	-	-	-	-	3-0	-
Sheffield Weds v Yeovil	-	-	-	2-2	2-1	-
Watford v Charlton	1-1	1-0	-	-	-	3-4

League 1

	2007-08	2008-09	2009-10	2010-11	2011-12	2012-13
Bradford v Colchester	-	-	-	-	-	-
Bristol City v Peterborough	-	-	1-1	-	1-2	4-2
Carlisle v Sheffield United	-	-	-	-	3-2	1-3
Coventry v Gillingham	-	-	-	-	-	-
Crawley v Shrewsbury	-	-	-	-	2-1	2-2
Crewe v Walsall	0-0	2-1	-	-	-	2-0
Leyton Orient v Port Vale	3-1	-	-	-	-	-
MK Dons v Notts County	3-0	-	-	2-1	3-0	1-1
Preston v Stevenage	-	-	-	-	0-0	2-0
Rotherham v Oldham	-	-	-	-	-	-
Tranmere v Brentford	-	-	1-0	0-3	2-2	1-1
Wolves v Swindon	-	-	-	-	-	-

League 2

	2007-08	2008-09	2009-10	2010-11	2011-12	2012-13
Burton v Portsmouth	-	-	-	-	-	-
Cheltenham v Oxford	-	-	-	1-1	0-0	2-1
Chesterfield v AFC Wimbledon	-	-	-	-	-	2-0
Dag & Red v Bristol Rovers	-	-	-	0-3	4-0	2-4
Fleetwood v Bury	-	-	-	-	-	-
Hartlepool v Accrington	-	-	-	-	-	-
Newport County v Morecambe	-	-	-	-	-	-
Northampton v Exeter	-	-	-	-	-	3-0
Plymouth v Wycombe	-	-	-	-	-	0-1
Rochdale v Torquay	-	-	2-1	-	-	1-0
Southend v Scunthorpe	-	2-0	-	-	-	-
York v Mansfield	-	1-1	3-0	2-1	2-2	-

Results cover matches from Premier League to Conference and Scottish Premier League to Division Three

	2007-08	2008-09	2009-10	2010-11	2011-12	2012-13
Conference						
Barnet v Lincoln	5-2	3-2	1-2	4-2	-	-
Cambridge v Gateshead	-	-	3-0	5-0	0-1	3-0
Dartford v Nuneaton	-	-	-	-	-	0-1
Forest Green v Halifax	2-0	-	-	-	-	-
Grimsby v Braintree	-	-	-	-	1-1	3-0
Hereford v Aldershot	-	-	2-0	2-2	0-2	-
Kidderminster v Hyde	-	-	-	-	-	3-0
Macclesfield v Alfreton	-	-	-	-	-	1-2
Salisbury v Chester	-	-	-	-	-	-
Southport v Welling	-	-	-	-	-	-
Woking v Tamworth	-	-	-	-	-	2-3
Wrexham v Luton	-	-	3-0	1-0	2-0	0-0
Scottish Premier League						
Hearts v Celtic	1-1	0-2/1-1	2-1/1-2	2-0/0-3	2-0/0-4	0-4
Kilmarnock v Inverness CT	2-2/4-1	1-2/1-0	-	1-2/1-1	3-6/4-3	1-2
Partick v Aberdeen	-	-	-	-	-	-
Ross County v Dundee United	-	-	-	-	-	1-2/1-0
St Johnstone v Hibernian	-	-	5-1	2-0/1-1	3-1	0-1
St Mirren v Motherwell	0-1/3-1	0-0/1-3	3-3/0-0	1-1	0-1/0-0	2-1
Scottish Division One						
Alloa v Dumbarton	-	-	1-3/1-2	0-0/2-3	-	-
Cowdenbeath v Falkirk	-	-	-	0-0/1-2	-	1-1/4-1
Dundee v Hamilton	1-0/1-1	-	-	-	0-1/2-2	-
Livingston v Morton	4-0/6-1	1-0/0-2	-	-	1-1/0-0	2-2/0-2
Queen of Sth v Raith	-	-	1-1/3-0	1-3/0-2	1-3/1-0	-
Scottish Division Two						
Airdrieonians v Stranraer	-	-	-	-	-	-
Brechin v Dunfermline	-	-	-	-	-	-
East Fife v Forfar	3-0/3-0	-	-	1-3/3-0	4-3/4-0	3-0/1-2
Rangers v Arbroath	-	-	-	-	-	-
Stenhousemuir v Ayr	-	-	-	3-1/2-1	-	1-1/4-0
Scottish Division Three						
Albion v Berwick	-	2-0/2-1	2-1/4-1	2-2/0-1	-	-
Clyde v East Stirling	-	-	-	1-2/2-0	7-1/3-0	2-1/2-0
Elgin v Montrose	0-2/2-1	1-2/1-0	0-1/5-2	3-2/1-0	3-1/2-1	6-1/3-2
Peterhead v Queen's Park	1-0/1-0	4-1/1-1	-	-	1-1/2-1	1-0/0-2
Stirling v Annan	-	-	-	-	-	5-1/2-1

Tuesday September 17th, 2013

	2007-08	2008-09	2009-10	2010-11	2011-12	2012-13
Championship						
Bolton v Derby	1-0	-	-	-	-	2-0
Bournemouth v Barnsley	-	-	-	-	-	-
Burnley v Birmingham	-	1-1	2-1	-	1-3	1-2
Huddersfield v Charlton	-	-	1-1	3-1	1-0	0-1
Ipswich v Yeovil	-	-	-	-	-	-
Leicester v Blackburn	-	-	-	-	-	3-0
Millwall v Blackpool	-	-	-	-	2-2	0-2
Nottm Forest v Middlesbrough	-	-	1-0	1-0	2-0	0-0
QPR v Brighton	-	-	-	-	-	-
Reading v Leeds	-	-	-	0-0	2-0	-
Sheffield Weds v Wigan	-	-	-	-	-	-
Watford v Doncaster	-	1-1	1-1	2-2	4-1	-

Results cover matches from Premier League to Conference and Scottish Premier League to Division Three

	2007-08	2008-09	2009-10	2010-11	2011-12	2012-13
Conference						
Aldershot v Barnet	-	1-1	4-0	1-0	4-1	1-0
Alfreton v Cambridge	-	-	-	-	2-1	1-1
Chester v Macclesfield	0-0	0-2	-	-	-	-
Gateshead v Wrexham	-	-	1-0	0-1	1-4	0-1
Halifax v Grimsby	-	-	-	-	-	-
Hyde v Woking	-	-	-	-	-	7-0
Lincoln v Southport	-	-	-	-	2-0	1-0
Luton v Dartford	-	-	-	-	-	0-2
Nuneaton v Hereford	-	-	-	-	-	0-0
Salisbury v Braintree	-	-	-	-	-	-
Tamworth v Kidderminster	-	-	2-1	2-2	0-0	0-1
Welling v Forest Green	-	-	-	-	-	-

Saturday September 21st, 2013

	2007-08	2008-09	2009-10	2010-11	2011-12	2012-13
Premier League						
Arsenal v Stoke	-	4-1	2-0	1-0	3-1	1-0
Cardiff v Tottenham	-	-	-	-	-	-
Chelsea v Fulham	0-0	3-1	2-1	1-0	1-1	0-0
Crystal Palace v Swansea	-	2-0	0-1	0-3	-	-
Liverpool v Southampton	-	-	-	-	-	1-0
Man City v Man United	1-0	0-1	0-1	0-0	1-0	2-3
Newcastle v Hull	-	1-2	-	-	-	-
Norwich v Aston Villa	-	-	-	-	2-0	1-2
West Brom v Sunderland	-	3-0	-	1-0	4-0	2-1
West Ham v Everton	0-2	1-3	1-2	1-1	-	1-2
Championship						
Barnsley v Watford	3-2	2-1	1-0	0-0	1-1	1-0
Birmingham v Sheffield Weds	-	3-1	-	-	-	0-0
Blackburn v Huddersfield	-	-	-	-	-	1-0
Blackpool v Leicester	2-1	-	1-2	-	3-3	0-0
Brighton v Bolton	-	-	-	-	-	1-1
Charlton v Millwall	-	-	4-4	-	-	0-2
Derby v Reading	0-4	0-2	2-1	1-2	0-1	-
Doncaster v Nottm Forest	1-0	0-0	1-0	1-1	0-1	-
Leeds v Burnley	-	-	-	1-0	2-1	1-0
Middlesbrough v Bournemouth	-	-	-	-	-	-
Wigan v Ipswich	-	-	-	-	-	-
Yeovil v QPR	-	-	-	-	-	-
League 1						
Brentford v Leyton Orient	-	-	1-0	2-1	5-0	2-2
Colchester v Crawley	-	-	-	-	-	1-1
Gillingham v Bradford	-	0-2	-	2-0	0-0	3-1
Notts County v Tranmere	-	-	-	0-1	3-2	0-1
Oldham v Crewe	3-2	1-1	-	-	-	1-2
Peterborough v MK Dons	1-2	0-0	-	2-1	-	-
Port Vale v Coventry	-	-	-	-	-	-
Sheffield United v Preston	1-1	1-0	1-0	1-0	2-1	0-0
Shrewsbury v Wolves	-	-	-	-	-	-
Stevenage v Carlisle	-	-	-	-	1-0	1-1
Swindon v Bristol City	-	-	-	-	-	-
Walsall v Rotherham	-	-	-	-	-	-
League 2						
Accrington v Rochdale	1-2	1-3	2-4	-	-	2-3
AFC Wimbledon v Burton	-	-	-	-	4-0	1-1
Bristol Rovers v Hartlepool	0-0	4-1	2-0	0-0	-	-

Results cover matches from Premier League to Conference and Scottish Premier League to Division Three

	2007-08	2008-09	2009-10	2010-11	2011-12	2012-13
Bury v Southend	-	-	-	1-0	-	-
Exeter v Newport County	-	-	-	-	-	-
Mansfield v Northampton	-	-	-	-	-	-
Morecambe v Dag & Red	1-0	1-2	1-0	-	1-2	2-1
Oxford v Chesterfield	-	-	-	0-0	-	0-1
Portsmouth v Fleetwood	-	-	-	-	-	-
Scunthorpe v Plymouth	1-0	-	2-1	-	-	-
Torquay v Cheltenham	-	-	3-0	2-1	2-2	2-2
Wycombe v York	-	-	-	-	-	4-0

Conference

	2007-08	2008-09	2009-10	2010-11	2011-12	2012-13
Aldershot v Wrexham	-	-	-	-	-	-
Alfreton v Barnet	-	-	-	-	-	-
Braintree v Southport	-	-	-	-	0-0	1-3
Cambridge v Forest Green	2-0	0-1	7-0	1-1	1-1	0-0
Chester v Grimsby	0-2	1-1	-	-	-	-
Dartford v Kidderminster	-	-	-	-	-	1-0
Halifax v Hereford	-	-	-	-	-	-
Hyde v Welling	-	-	-	-	-	-
Luton v Lincoln	-	3-2	-	-	1-0	3-0
Macclesfield v Woking	-	-	-	-	-	0-0
Nuneaton v Salisbury	-	-	-	-	-	-
Tamworth v Gateshead	-	-	1-0	1-1	1-1	2-0

Scottish Premier League

	2007-08	2008-09	2009-10	2010-11	2011-12	2012-13
Aberdeen v Inverness CT	1-0	0-2/1-0	-	1-2/1-0	2-1/0-1	2-3
Celtic v St Johnstone	-	-	5-2/3-0	2-0	0-1/2-0/1-0	1-1/4-0
Dundee United v Motherwell	1-0/2-0	0-4	0-1/3-0	2-0/4-0	1-3/1-1	1-2/1-3
Hibernian v St Mirren	0-1/2-0	2-0	2-1/2-1	2-0/1-1	1-2/0-0	2-1/3-3
Partick v Kilmarnock	-	-	-	-	-	-
Ross County v Hearts	-	-	-	-	-	2-2

Scottish Division One

	2007-08	2008-09	2009-10	2010-11	2011-12	2012-13
Dumbarton v Livingston	-	-	-	1-2/0-3	-	3-4/0-3
Falkirk v Dundee	-	-	-	3-3/2-2	2-1/1-1	-
Hamilton v Cowdenbeath	-	-	-	-	-	2-1/1-3
Morton v Queen of Sth	0-1/0-3	0-0/2-2	1-2/3-3	2-0/0-4	2-2/2-2	-
Raith v Alloa	2-1/3-2	4-1/3-1	-	-	-	-

Scottish Division Two

	2007-08	2008-09	2009-10	2010-11	2011-12	2012-13
Arbroath v Stenhousemuir	2-2/1-0	-	0-3/1-1	-	1-0/0-2	2-2/0-0
Ayr v Brechin	2-1/0-3	1-1/4-2	-	0-2/2-0	-	3-0/1-2
Dunfermline v Airdrieonians	-	0-0/1-1	2-0/2-0	-	-	1-3/1-2
Forfar v Rangers	-	-	-	-	-	-
Stranraer v East Fife	0-2/0-2	0-4/0-1	-	-	-	2-6/3-1

Scottish Division Three

	2007-08	2008-09	2009-10	2010-11	2011-12	2012-13
Annan v Clyde	-	-	-	0-2/1-0	1-0/1-0	1-3/0-1
Berwick v Stirling	-	-	-	-	-	4-1/1-0
East Stirling v Albion	4-5/3-0	1-0/0-1	2-0/3-1	0-0/1-2	-	-
Montrose v Peterhead	-	-	-	-	2-1/1-3	2-0/0-6
Queen's Park v Elgin	-	-	0-3/0-1	1-1/1-0	6-0/1-3	1-1/0-1

Tuesday September 24th, 2013

Conference

	2007-08	2008-09	2009-10	2010-11	2011-12	2012-13
Barnet v Macclesfield	2-2	1-3	1-2	1-0	2-1	-
Cambridge v Nuneaton	-	-	-	-	-	1-3
Forest Green v Tamworth	-	-	3-4	4-0	3-1	1-2
Gateshead v Chester	-	-	-	-	-	-
Grimsby v Dartford	-	-	-	-	-	0-2

Results cover matches from Premier League to Conference and Scottish Premier League to Division Three

	2007-08	2008-09	2009-10	2010-11	2011-12	2012-13
Hereford v Lincoln	3-1	-	2-0	0-1	-	3-2
Kidderminster v Halifax	1-0	-	-	-	-	-
Salisbury v Hyde	-	-	-	-	-	-
Southport v Alfreton	-	-	-	-	2-1	0-2
Welling v Aldershot	-	-	-	-	-	-
Woking v Luton	-	-	-	-	-	3-1
Wrexham v Braintree	-	-	-	-	5-1	1-1

Saturday September 28th, 2013

Premier League

	2007-08	2008-09	2009-10	2010-11	2011-12	2012-13
Aston Villa v Man City	1-1	4-2	1-1	1-0	0-1	0-1
Everton v Newcastle	3-1	2-2	-	0-1	3-1	2-2
Fulham v Cardiff	-	-	-	-	-	-
Hull v West Ham	-	1-0	3-3	-	0-2	-
Man United v West Brom	-	4-0	-	2-2	2-0	2-0
Southampton v Crystal Palace	1-4	1-0	-	-	2-0	-
Stoke v Norwich	2-1	-	-	-	1-0	1-0
Sunderland v Liverpool	0-2	0-1	1-0	0-2	1-0	1-1
Swansea v Arsenal	-	-	-	-	3-2	0-2
Tottenham v Chelsea	4-4	1-0	2-1	1-1	1-1	2-4

Championship

	2007-08	2008-09	2009-10	2010-11	2011-12	2012-13
Bolton v Yeovil	-	-	-	-	-	-
Bournemouth v Blackburn	-	-	-	-	-	-
Burnley v Charlton	1-0	2-1	-	-	-	0-1
Huddersfield v Blackpool	-	-	-	-	-	1-1
Ipswich v Brighton	-	-	-	-	3-1	0-3
Leicester v Barnsley	2-0	-	1-0	4-1	1-2	2-2
Millwall v Leeds	0-2	3-1	2-1	3-2	0-1	1-0
Nottm Forest v Derby	-	1-3	3-2	5-2	1-2	0-1
QPR v Middlesbrough	-	-	1-5	3-0	-	-
Reading v Birmingham	2-1	1-2	-	-	1-0	-
Sheffield Weds v Doncaster	-	1-0	0-2	-	-	-
Watford v Wigan	-	-	-	-	-	-

League 1

	2007-08	2008-09	2009-10	2010-11	2011-12	2012-13
Bradford v Shrewsbury	4-2	0-0	1-3	1-2	3-1	-
Bristol City v Colchester	1-1	-	-	-	-	-
Carlisle v Notts County	-	-	-	1-0	0-3	0-4
Coventry v Brentford	-	-	-	-	-	1-1
Crawley v Oldham	-	-	-	-	-	1-1
Crewe v Gillingham	2-3	-	-	1-1	1-2	-
Leyton Orient v Walsall	1-0	0-1	2-0	0-0	1-1	2-1
MK Dons v Stevenage	-	-	-	-	1-0	0-1
Preston v Swindon	-	-	-	-	-	4-1
Rotherham v Peterborough	3-1	-	-	-	-	-
Tranmere v Port Vale	2-0	-	-	-	-	-
Wolves v Sheffield United	0-0	1-1	-	-	-	-

League 2

	2007-08	2008-09	2009-10	2010-11	2011-12	2012-13
Burton v Scunthorpe	-	-	-	-	-	-
Cheltenham v AFC Wimbledon	-	-	-	-	0-0	2-1
Chesterfield v Mansfield	2-0	-	-	-	-	-
Dag & Red v Bury	1-1	1-3	3-1	-	-	-
Fleetwood v Exeter	-	-	-	-	-	0-0
Hartlepool v Oxford	-	-	-	-	-	-
Newport County v Torquay	-	-	-	-	-	-
Northampton v Morecambe	-	-	2-0	3-3	0-2	3-0
Plymouth v Accrington	-	-	-	-	2-2	0-0
Rochdale v Wycombe	0-1	0-1	-	-	2-1	4-1

Results cover matches from Premier League to Conference and Scottish Premier League to Division Three

	2007-08	2008-09	2009-10	2010-11	2011-12	2012-13
Southend v Bristol Rovers	0-1	1-0	2-1	-	1-1	0-0
York v Portsmouth	-	-	-	-	-	-

Conference						
Barnet v Salisbury	-	-	-	-	-	-
Braintree v Alfreton	-	-	-	-	1-2	2-1
Dartford v Southport	-	-	-	-	-	2-2
Forest Green v Gateshead	-	-	1-0	1-1	2-1	1-0
Grimsby v Tamworth	-	-	-	2-2	0-0	2-0
Halifax v Chester	-	-	-	-	-	-
Hereford v Luton	-	-	-	-	-	1-0
Kidderminster v Aldershot	1-2	-	-	-	-	-
Lincoln v Hyde	-	-	-	-	-	3-2
Macclesfield v Welling	-	-	-	-	-	-
Woking v Nuneaton	-	-	-	-	-	6-1
Wrexham v Cambridge	-	2-0	2-2	1-0	1-1	1-0

Scottish Premier League						
Hearts v Dundee United	1-3/1-0	0-0/3-0	0-0/0-0	1-1/2-1	0-1/0-2	2-1
Inverness CT v Hibernian	2-0	1-1/2-0	-	4-2/2-0	0-1/2-3/2-0	3-0
Kilmarnock v Celtic	1-2	1-3/1-2	1-0	1-2/0-4/0-2	3-3/0-6	1-3
Motherwell v Ross County	-	-	-	-	-	3-2/2-0
St Johnstone v Partick	2-1/2-0	3-0/1-1	-	-	-	-
St Mirren v Aberdeen	0-1	0-1/1-1	1-0/0-1	2-1/3-2	1-0/1-1	1-4/0-0

Scottish Division One						
Alloa v Hamilton	-	-	-	-	-	-
Dundee v Morton	2-1/2-0	1-0/0-0	1-0/3-1	2-1/1-1	0-1/0-1	-
Livingston v Cowdenbeath	-	-	-	-	-	1-1/3-0
Queen of Sth v Dumbarton	-	-	-	-	-	-
Raith v Falkirk	-	-	-	2-1/1-2	1-0/2-2	2-1/0-0

Scottish Division Two						
Arbroath v Forfar	3-4/1-1	-	-	-	4-1/0-1	1-1/3-1
Brechin v Stranraer	-	1-0/2-1	-	-	-	3-0/2-2
Dunfermline v Ayr	-	-	3-1/0-1	-	-	-
East Fife v Airdrieonians	-	-	-	3-3/0-1	2-0/2-0	-
Rangers v Stenhousemuir	-	-	-	-	-	-

Scottish Division Three						
Albion v Peterhead	-	-	-	-	-	-
Clyde v Montrose	-	-	-	2-0/1-1	1-0/1-2	1-2/1-0
East Stirling v Berwick	-	1-0/0-4	1-0/3-2	0-0/1-0	1-3/2-1	0-1/0-3
Elgin v Stirling	-	-	-	-	-	3-1/1-2
Queen's Park v Annan	-	-	0-0/3-2	3-0/0-1	0-0/2-0	2-2/2-2

Tuesday October 1st, 2013

Championship						
Barnsley v Reading	-	0-1	1-3	0-1	0-4	-
Birmingham v Millwall	-	-	-	-	3-0	1-1
Blackburn v Watford	-	-	-	-	-	1-0
Blackpool v Bolton	-	-	-	4-3	-	2-2
Brighton v Sheffield Weds	-	-	-	2-0	-	3-0
Charlton v Nottm Forest	-	0-2	-	-	-	0-2
Derby v Ipswich	-	0-1	1-3	1-2	0-0	0-1
Doncaster v Burnley	-	2-1	-	1-0	1-2	-
Leeds v Bournemouth	2-0	-	-	-	-	-
Middlesbrough v Huddersfield	-	-	-	-	-	3-0
Wigan v QPR	-	-	-	-	2-0	2-2
Yeovil v Leicester	-	0-2	-	-	-	-

Results cover matches from Premier League to Conference and Scottish Premier League to Division Three

Saturday October 5th, 2013

Premier League	2007-08	2008-09	2009-10	2010-11	2011-12	2012-13
Cardiff v Newcastle	-	-	0-1	-	-	-
Fulham v Stoke	-	1-0	0-1	2-0	2-1	1-0
Hull v Aston Villa	-	0-1	0-2	-	-	-
Liverpool v Crystal Palace	-	-	-	-	-	-
Man City v Everton	0-2	0-1	0-2	1-2	2-0	1-1
Norwich v Chelsea	-	-	-	-	0-0	0-1
Southampton v Swansea	-	2-2	-	-	-	1-1
Sunderland v Man United	0-4	1-2	0-1	0-0	0-1	0-1
Tottenham v West Ham	4-0	1-0	2-0	0-0	-	3-1
West Brom v Arsenal	-	1-3	-	2-2	2-3	1-2

Championship	2007-08	2008-09	2009-10	2010-11	2011-12	2012-13
Birmingham v Bolton	1-0	-	1-2	2-1	-	2-1
Bournemouth v Millwall	2-0	-	-	-	-	-
Brighton v Nottm Forest	0-2	-	-	-	1-0	0-0
Burnley v Reading	-	1-0	-	0-4	0-1	-
Charlton v Blackpool	4-1	2-2	-	-	-	2-1
Derby v Leeds	-	-	-	2-1	1-0	3-1
Doncaster v Leicester	-	-	0-1	1-1	2-1	-
Huddersfield v Watford	-	-	-	-	-	2-3
Middlesbrough v Yeovil	-	-	-	-	-	-
QPR v Barnsley	2-0	2-1	5-2	4-0	-	-
Sheffield Weds v Ipswich	1-2	0-0	0-1	-	-	1-1
Wigan v Blackburn	5-3	3-0	1-1	4-3	3-3	-

League 1	2007-08	2008-09	2009-10	2010-11	2011-12	2012-13
Brentford v Rotherham	1-1	0-0	-	-	-	-
Colchester v Wolves	0-1	-	-	-	-	-
Gillingham v MK Dons	-	-	2-2	-	-	-
Notts County v Crewe	-	-	2-0	-	-	1-1
Oldham v Leyton Orient	2-0	1-1	2-0	1-1	0-1	2-0
Peterborough v Preston	-	-	0-1	-	-	-
Port Vale v Bristol City	-	-	-	-	-	-
Sheffield United v Crawley	-	-	-	-	-	0-2
Shrewsbury v Carlisle	-	-	-	-	-	2-1
Stevenage v Coventry	-	-	-	-	-	1-3
Swindon v Tranmere	1-0	3-1	3-0	0-0	-	5-0
Walsall v Bradford	-	-	-	-	-	-

League 2	2007-08	2008-09	2009-10	2010-11	2011-12	2012-13
Accrington v Dag & Red	1-0	0-0	0-1	-	3-0	0-2
AFC Wimbledon v Northampton	-	-	-	-	0-3	1-1
Bristol Rovers v Fleetwood	-	-	-	-	-	0-0
Bury v Newport County	-	-	-	-	-	-
Exeter v Plymouth	-	-	-	1-0	-	1-1
Mansfield v Hartlepool	-	-	-	-	-	-
Morecambe v Chesterfield	1-1	2-2	0-1	1-1	-	2-0
Oxford v Southend	-	-	-	0-2	0-2	2-0
Portsmouth v Rochdale	-	-	-	-	-	-
Scunthorpe v Cheltenham	-	3-0	-	-	-	-
Torquay v York	0-0	1-1	-	-	-	2-1
Wycombe v Burton	-	-	-	4-1	-	3-0

Conference	2007-08	2008-09	2009-10	2010-11	2011-12	2012-13
Aldershot v Grimsby	-	2-2	1-1	-	-	-
Alfreton v Forest Green	-	-	-	-	1-6	2-1
Cambridge v Hereford	-	-	-	-	-	1-3

Results cover matches from Premier League to Conference and Scottish Premier League to Division Three

	2007-08	2008-09	2009-10	2010-11	2011-12	2012-13
Chester v Kidderminster	-	-	-	-	-	-
Gateshead v Dartford	-	-	-	-	-	2-0
Hyde v Braintree	-	-	-	-	-	1-2
Luton v Halifax	-	-	-	-	-	-
Nuneaton v Lincoln	-	-	-	-	-	1-0
Salisbury v Wrexham	-	1-4	1-1	-	-	-
Southport v Woking	-	-	-	-	-	1-2
Tamworth v Macclesfield	-	-	-	-	-	0-0
Welling v Barnet	-	-	-	-	-	-

Scottish Premier League						
Celtic v Motherwell	3-0/0-1	2-0	0-0/2-1/4-0	1-0/4-0	4-0/1-0	1-0
Dundee United v Kilmarnock	2-0	0-2/0-0	0-0	1-1/4-2	1-1/4-0	3-3
Hearts v St Mirren	0-1/3-2	2-1/1-1	1-0	3-0/3-2	2-0/5-2	1-0/3-0
Partick v Hibernian	-	-	-	-	-	-
Ross County v Aberdeen	-	-	-	-	-	2-1
St Johnstone v Inverness CT	-	-	-	1-0/0-3	2-0/0-0	0-0/1-0

Scottish Division One						
Cowdenbeath v Dundee	-	-	-	2-1/1-3	-	-
Dumbarton v Raith	-	-	-	-	-	4-2/1-2
Falkirk v Queen of Sth	-	-	-	3-1/0-3	1-0/3-0	-
Hamilton v Livingston	1-1/3-1	-	-	-	1-1/0-1	1-2/1-1
Morton v Alloa	-	-	-	-	-	-

Scottish Division Two						
Airdrieonians v Brechin	2-1/1-2	-	-	1-1/2-2	2-3/4-1	-
Ayr v Rangers	-	-	-	-	-	-
Forfar v Dunfermline	-	-	-	-	-	-
Stenhousemuir v East Fife	2-1/0-1	-	1-1/1-1	1-1/0-2	2-1/1-0	3-0/2-1
Stranraer v Arbroath	1-1/0-3	2-2/1-5	-	4-1/3-4	-	1-1/2-0

Tuesday October 8th, 2013

Conference						
Aldershot v Luton	-	2-1	-	-	-	-
Alfreton v Chester	-	-	-	-	-	-
Braintree v Welling	-	-	-	-	-	-
Dartford v Salisbury	-	-	-	-	-	-
Grimsby v Cambridge	-	-	-	1-1	2-1	0-1
Halifax v Nuneaton	-	-	-	-	-	-
Hyde v Gateshead	-	-	-	-	-	1-1
Kidderminster v Forest Green	1-0	1-1	2-1	1-0	1-0	0-1
Lincoln v Tamworth	-	-	-	-	4-0	2-1
Macclesfield v Hereford	0-1	-	3-1	1-1	2-2	0-1
Woking v Barnet	-	-	-	-	-	-
Wrexham v Southport	-	-	-	2-1	2-0	2-2

Saturday October 12th, 2013

League 1						
Bradford v Tranmere	-	-	-	-	-	-
Bristol City v Crawley	-	-	-	-	-	-
Carlisle v Wolves	-	-	-	-	-	-
Colchester v Walsall	-	0-2	2-1	2-0	1-0	2-0
Coventry v Sheffield United	0-1	1-2	3-2	0-0	-	1-1
Leyton Orient v MK Dons	-	1-2	1-2	2-2	0-3	2-0
Notts County v Oldham	-	-	-	0-2	1-0	1-0
Port Vale v Peterborough	-	-	-	-	-	-
Preston v Crewe	-	-	-	-	-	1-3
Rotherham v Swindon	-	-	-	-	1-2	-

Results cover matches from Premier League to Conference and Scottish Premier League to Division Three

	2007-08	2008-09	2009-10	2010-11	2011-12	2012-13
Shrewsbury v Gillingham	-	7-0	-	0-0	2-0	-
Stevenage v Brentford	-	-	-	-	2-1	1-0
League 2						
AFC Wimbledon v Accrington	-	-	-	-	0-2	1-2
Burton v Southend	-	-	-	3-1	0-2	2-0
Bury v Morecambe	2-1	2-1	0-0	1-0	-	-
Dag & Red v Cheltenham	-	-	0-2	-	0-5	1-0
Exeter v Hartlepool	-	-	3-1	1-2	0-0	-
Fleetwood v Chesterfield	-	-	-	-	-	1-3
Mansfield v Bristol Rovers	-	-	-	-	-	-
Oxford v Northampton	-	-	-	3-1	2-0	2-1
Plymouth v Portsmouth	-	-	-	-	-	-
Rochdale v Newport County	-	-	-	-	-	-
Wycombe v Torquay	-	-	-	1-3	-	2-1
York v Scunthorpe	-	-	-	-	-	-
Conference						
Barnet v Wrexham	3-2	-	-	-	-	-
Chester v Cambridge	-	-	-	-	-	-
Forest Green v Macclesfield	-	-	-	-	-	1-1
Gateshead v Alfreton	-	-	-	-	2-0	2-0
Hereford v Dartford	-	-	-	-	-	1-0
Lincoln v Aldershot	-	0-2	1-0	0-3	-	-
Luton v Hyde	-	-	-	-	-	1-2
Nuneaton v Braintree	-	-	-	-	-	2-4
Salisbury v Grimsby	-	-	-	-	-	-
Southport v Kidderminster	-	-	-	2-2	1-2	1-3
Welling v Tamworth	-	-	-	-	-	-
Woking v Halifax	1-0	-	-	-	-	-
Scottish Division One						
Alloa v Falkirk	-	-	-	-	-	-
Dumbarton v Dundee	-	-	-	-	-	-
Morton v Hamilton	0-2/1-3	-	-	-	0-2/1-2	0-1/0-2
Queen of Sth v Cowdenbeath	-	-	-	3-0/2-2	-	-
Raith v Livingston	-	-	-	-	0-1/0-3	0-0/0-2
Scottish Division Two						
Arbroath v Airdrieonians	-	-	-	-	3-1/2-2	-
East Fife v Ayr	-	3-0/0-1	-	2-3/3-2	-	2-3/3-3
Forfar v Stranraer	1-1/1-0	-	1-0/2-0	-	-	4-0/3-1
Rangers v Dunfermline	-	-	-	-	2-1	-
Stenhousemuir v Brechin	-	-	1-1/1-2	0-0/1-3	1-1/2-1	3-1/3-3
Scottish Division Three						
Annan v East Stirling	-	2-1/4-0	0-1/1-0	3-1/2-1	3-0/2-2	5-2/1-2
Berwick v Elgin	-	1-1/2-1	2-0/2-1	6-2/4-0	1-1/3-3	0-0/2-1
Montrose v Queen's Park	-	-	1-2/1-2	1-2/0-2	0-1/3-1	1-1/1-2
Peterhead v Clyde	-	-	2-0/0-0	-	0-0/1-1	1-0/3-0
Stirling v Albion	-	-	-	-	2-2/3-0	-
Saturday October 19th, 2013						
Premier League						
Arsenal v Norwich	-	-	-	-	3-3	3-1
Aston Villa v Tottenham	2-1	1-2	1-1	1-2	1-1	0-4
Chelsea v Cardiff	-	-	-	-	-	-
Crystal Palace v Fulham	-	-	-	-	-	-
Everton v Hull	-	2-0	5-1	-	-	-
Man United v Southampton	-	-	-	-	-	2-1

Results cover matches from Premier League to Conference and Scottish Premier League to Division Three

	2007-08	2008-09	2009-10	2010-11	2011-12	2012-13
Newcastle v Liverpool	0-3	1-5	-	3-1	2-0	0-6
Stoke v West Brom	3-1	1-0	-	1-1	1-2	0-0
Swansea v Sunderland	-	-	-	-	0-0	2-2
West Ham v Man City	0-2	1-0	1-1	1-3	-	0-0
Championship						
Barnsley v Middlesbrough	-	-	2-1	2-0	1-3	1-0
Blackburn v Charlton	-	-	-	-	-	1-2
Blackpool v Wigan	-	-	-	1-3	-	-
Bolton v Sheffield Weds	-	-	-	-	-	0-1
Ipswich v Burnley	0-0	1-1	-	1-1	1-0	2-1
Leeds v Birmingham	-	-	-	-	1-4	0-1
Leicester v Huddersfield	-	4-2	-	-	-	6-1
Millwall v QPR	-	-	-	2-0	-	-
Nottm Forest v Bournemouth	0-0	-	-	-	-	-
Reading v Doncaster	-	2-1	0-0	4-3	2-0	-
Watford v Derby	-	3-1	0-1	3-0	0-1	2-1
Yeovil v Brighton	2-1	1-1	2-2	0-1	-	-
League 1						
Brentford v Colchester	-	-	1-0	1-1	1-1	1-0
Crawley v Bradford	-	-	-	-	3-1	-
Crewe v Bristol City	-	-	-	-	-	-
Gillingham v Preston	-	-	-	-	-	-
MK Dons v Rotherham	1-1	-	-	-	-	-
Oldham v Carlisle	2-0	0-0	2-0	0-1	2-1	1-2
Peterborough v Shrewsbury	2-1	-	-	-	-	-
Sheffield United v Port Vale	-	-	-	-	-	-
Swindon v Notts County	-	-	-	1-2	-	0-0
Tranmere v Leyton Orient	1-1	0-0	2-1	1-2	2-0	3-1
Walsall v Stevenage	-	-	-	-	1-1	1-0
Wolves v Coventry	1-0	2-1	-	-	-	-
League 2						
Accrington v Oxford	-	-	-	0-0	0-2	0-3
Bristol Rovers v Wycombe	-	-	2-3	-	-	1-0
Cheltenham v Rochdale	-	-	1-4	-	-	0-0
Chesterfield v Burton	-	-	5-2	1-2	-	1-1
Hartlepool v Plymouth	-	-	-	2-0	-	-
Morecambe v AFC Wimbledon	-	-	-	-	1-2	3-1
Newport County v York	-	-	-	4-0	2-1	-
Northampton v Dag & Red	-	-	1-0	-	2-1	3-1
Portsmouth v Bury	-	-	-	-	-	2-0
Scunthorpe v Exeter	-	-	-	-	1-0	-
Southend v Fleetwood	-	-	-	-	-	1-1
Torquay v Mansfield	-	2-0	-	-	-	-
Conference						
Aldershot v Alfreton	-	-	-	-	-	-
Braintree v Chester	-	-	-	-	-	-
Cambridge v Salisbury	1-1	4-0	3-1	-	-	-
Dartford v Hyde	-	-	-	-	-	2-1
Grimsby v Forest Green	-	-	-	1-1	2-1	1-0
Halifax v Welling	-	-	-	-	-	-
Hereford v Barnet	1-2	-	2-1	1-2	1-0	-
Kidderminster v Lincoln	-	-	-	-	1-1	3-0
Macclesfield v Southport	-	-	-	-	-	2-2
Nuneaton v Gateshead	-	-	-	-	-	0-1
Tamworth v Luton	-	-	1-1	3-1	1-3	1-2

Results cover matches from Premier League to Conference and Scottish Premier League to Division Three

	2007-08	2008-09	2009-10	2010-11	2011-12	2012-13
Wrexham v Woking	-	1-1	-	-	-	3-1
Scottish Premier League						
Aberdeen v Dundee United	2-0/2-1	0-1/2-2	0-2/2-2	1-1	3-1/3-1	2-2
Hibernian v Celtic	3-2/0-2	2-0/0-0	0-1/0-1	0-3	0-2/0-5	1-0
Inverness CT v Partick	-	-	2-3/2-1	-	-	-
Kilmarnock v Ross County	-	-	-	-	-	3-0
Motherwell v Hearts	0-2/0-1	1-0	1-0/3-1	1-2	1-0/3-0	0-0
St Mirren v St Johnstone	-	-	1-1/1-1	1-2/0-0	0-0/0-3	1-1
Scottish Division One						
Cowdenbeath v Morton	-	-	-	2-2/0-2	-	3-4/1-1
Dundee v Queen of Sth	2-1/2-3	2-0/2-3	0-0/1-1	1-0/2-1	2-1/1-1	-
Falkirk v Dumbarton	-	-	-	-	-	3-4/1-3
Hamilton v Raith	-	-	-	-	2-2/2-1	0-1/2-0
Livingston v Alloa	-	-	-	3-3/4-0	-	-
Scottish Division Two						
Airdrieonians v Forfar	-	-	-	2-0/3-1	4-4/3-0	-
Ayr v Arbroath	-	2-1/2-1	-	-	-	2-0/0-1
Brechin v Rangers	-	-	-	-	-	-
Dunfermline v East Fife	-	-	-	-	-	-
Stranraer v Stenhousemuir	2-3/3-1	-	-	-	-	1-1/1-1
Scottish Division Three						
Albion v Elgin	3-4/1-1	2-1/0-3	1-1/1-2	3-1/2-0	-	-
Annan v Peterhead	-	-	-	-	2-0/0-3	2-1/0-0
Berwick v Clyde	-	-	-	2-1/1-1	0-2/3-0	2-1/3-3
East Stirling v Queen's Park	-	-	1-0/0-3	0-1/3-2	1-3/1-2	0-2/0-2
Stirling v Montrose	-	-	-	-	-	1-3/3-1

Tuesday October 22nd, 2013

	2007-08	2008-09	2009-10	2010-11	2011-12	2012-13
League 1						
Bristol City v Brentford	-	-	-	-	-	-
Coventry v Leyton Orient	-	-	-	-	-	0-1
Crawley v Port Vale	-	-	-	-	3-2	-
Crewe v Stevenage	-	-	-	0-1	-	1-2
Gillingham v Notts County	-	2-2	-	-	-	-
MK Dons v Carlisle	-	3-1	3-4	3-2	1-2	2-0
Peterborough v Sheffield United	-	-	1-0	-	-	-
Preston v Bradford	-	-	-	-	-	-
Rotherham v Tranmere	-	-	-	-	-	-
Shrewsbury v Colchester	-	-	-	-	-	2-2
Swindon v Walsall	0-3	3-2	1-1	0-0	-	2-2
Wolves v Oldham	-	-	-	-	-	-
League 2						
Accrington v Bristol Rovers	-	-	-	-	2-1	1-0
Burton v Torquay	3-1	0-1	0-2	3-3	1-4	2-1
Bury v Mansfield	2-0	-	-	-	-	-
Cheltenham v Morecambe	-	-	2-0	1-1	1-2	2-0
Chesterfield v York	-	-	-	-	-	3-0
Fleetwood v Scunthorpe	-	-	-	-	-	-
Hartlepool v AFC Wimbledon	-	-	-	-	-	-
Oxford v Exeter	2-2	-	-	-	-	2-4
Plymouth v Newport County	-	-	-	-	-	-
Portsmouth v Wycombe	-	-	-	-	-	-
Rochdale v Northampton	-	-	1-0	-	-	0-0
Southend v Dag & Red	-	-	-	-	1-1	3-1

Results cover matches from Premier League to Conference and Scottish Premier League to Division Three

	2007-08	2008-09	2009-10	2010-11	2011-12	2012-13

Saturday October 26th, 2013

Premier League

	2007-08	2008-09	2009-10	2010-11	2011-12	2012-13
Aston Villa v Everton	2-0	3-3	2-2	1-0	1-1	1-3
Chelsea v Man City	6-0	1-0	2-4	2-0	2-1	0-0
Crystal Palace v Arsenal	-	-	-	-	-	-
Liverpool v West Brom	-	3-0	-	1-0	0-1	0-2
Man United v Stoke	-	5-0	4-0	2-1	2-0	4-2
Norwich v Cardiff	1-2	2-0	-	1-1	-	-
Southampton v Fulham	-	-	-	-	-	2-2
Sunderland v Newcastle	1-1	2-1	-	1-1	0-1	1-1
Swansea v West Ham	-	-	-	-	-	3-0
Tottenham v Hull	-	0-1	0-0	-	-	-

Championship

	2007-08	2008-09	2009-10	2010-11	2011-12	2012-13
Barnsley v Sheffield Weds	0-0	2-1	1-2	-	-	0-1
Blackpool v Blackburn	-	-	-	1-2	-	2-0
Bolton v Ipswich	-	-	-	-	-	1-2
Brighton v Watford	-	-	-	-	2-2	1-3
Burnley v QPR	0-2	1-0	-	0-0	-	-
Charlton v Wigan	-	-	-	-	-	-
Derby v Birmingham	1-2	1-1	-	-	2-1	3-2
Huddersfield v Leeds	1-0	1-0	2-2	-	-	2-4
Leicester v Bournemouth	-	-	-	-	-	-
Middlesbrough v Doncaster	-	-	2-0	3-0	0-0	-
Reading v Millwall	-	-	-	2-1	2-2	-
Yeovil v Nottm Forest	0-3	-	-	-	-	-

League 1

	2007-08	2008-09	2009-10	2010-11	2011-12	2012-13
Bradford v Wolves	-	-	-	-	-	-
Brentford v Shrewsbury	1-1	1-1	-	-	-	0-0
Carlisle v Bristol City	-	-	-	-	-	-
Colchester v Peterborough	-	0-1	-	2-1	-	-
Leyton Orient v Rotherham	-	-	-	-	-	-
Notts County v Preston	-	-	-	-	0-0	0-1
Oldham v Swindon	2-2	0-0	2-2	2-0	-	0-2
Port Vale v Gillingham	2-1	1-3	-	0-0	2-1	0-2
Sheffield United v Crewe	-	-	-	-	-	3-3
Stevenage v Crawley	3-1	1-1	2-0	-	-	1-2
Tranmere v MK Dons	-	1-1	0-1	4-2	0-2	0-1
Walsall v Coventry	-	-	-	-	-	4-0

League 2

	2007-08	2008-09	2009-10	2010-11	2011-12	2012-13
AFC Wimbledon v Oxford	-	-	0-1	-	0-2	0-3
Bristol Rovers v Chesterfield	-	-	-	-	-	3-2
Dag & Red v Rochdale	1-1	3-2	1-2	0-1	-	2-1
Exeter v Burton	1-4	-	-	-	-	3-0
Mansfield v Plymouth	-	-	-	-	-	-
Morecambe v Accrington	0-1	1-1	1-2	1-2	1-2	0-0
Newport County v Southend	-	-	-	-	-	-
Northampton v Cheltenham	2-1	4-2	2-1	1-1	2-3	2-3
Scunthorpe v Hartlepool	-	3-0	-	-	0-2	1-2
Torquay v Portsmouth	-	-	-	-	-	-
Wycombe v Bury	1-0	2-1	-	1-0	0-2	-
York v Fleetwood	-	-	-	1-0	0-1	0-2

Scottish Premier League

	2007-08	2008-09	2009-10	2010-11	2011-12	2012-13
Dundee United v St Mirren	2-0/1-1	2-0/3-2	3-2	1-2	1-1/0-0	3-4
Hibernian v Aberdeen	3-3/3-1	2-2/0-0	2-0/2-2	1-2/1-3	0-0/0-0	0-1/0-0
Kilmarnock v Hearts	3-1/0-0	0-2	1-2	1-2/2-2	0-0/1-1	1-0/0-1

Results cover matches from Premier League to Conference and Scottish Premier League to Division Three

	2007-08	2008-09	2009-10	2010-11	2011-12	2012-13
Partick v Celtic	-	-	-	-	-	-
Ross County v Inverness CT	-	-	2-1/0-0	-	-	0-0/1-0
St Johnstone v Motherwell	-	-	2-2/1-2	0-2/1-0	0-3	1-3/2-0

Scottish Division One

	2007-08	2008-09	2009-10	2010-11	2011-12	2012-13
Alloa v Queen of Sth	-	-	-	-	-	1-0/1-2
Dumbarton v Cowdenbeath	-	2-1/1-1	0-3/2-1	-	0-4/0-2	0-3/2-2
Hamilton v Falkirk	-	1-1/0-1	0-0/2-2	-	0-1/0-1	1-1/1-1
Livingston v Dundee	0-2/1-1	1-2/0-1	-	-	4-2/2-3	-
Raith v Morton	-	-	3-0/1-2	1-0/2-2	1-1/5-0	3-3/2-1

Scottish Division Two

	2007-08	2008-09	2009-10	2010-11	2011-12	2012-13
Airdrieonians v Ayr	0-0/0-2	-	3-1/1-1	2-2/0-5	-	-
Brechin v Arbroath	-	3-1/0-1	0-0/0-2	-	2-3/1-1	3-2/2-0
East Fife v Rangers	-	-	-	-	-	-
Stenhousemuir v Forfar	4-0/2-0	1-1/0-1	-	3-0/0-1	2-3/1-2	0-4/2-0
Stranraer v Dunfermline	-	-	-	-	-	-

Scottish Division Three

	2007-08	2008-09	2009-10	2010-11	2011-12	2012-13
Clyde v Stirling	1-3/3-0	-	0-1/1-2	-	-	2-1/1-2
Elgin v Annan	-	1-2/0-1	1-1/1-0	2-0/2-3	3-0/1-2	2-2/3-1
Montrose v East Stirling	3-1/2-0	3-0/0-2	0-3/0-1	0-2/3-0	2-1/3-1	3-1/2-2
Peterhead v Berwick	4-3/9-2	-	-	-	1-0/1-2	1-0/1-1
Queen's Park v Albion	-	-	0-1/1-0	0-1/2-1	-	-

Saturday November 2nd, 2013

Premier League

	2007-08	2008-09	2009-10	2010-11	2011-12	2012-13
Arsenal v Liverpool	1-1	1-1	1-0	1-1	0-2	2-2
Cardiff v Swansea	-	2-2	2-1	0-1	-	-
Everton v Tottenham	0-0	0-0	2-2	2-1	1-0	2-1
Fulham v Man United	0-3	2-0	3-0	2-2	0-5	0-1
Hull v Sunderland	-	1-4	0-1	-	-	-
Man City v Norwich	-	-	-	-	5-1	2-3
Newcastle v Chelsea	0-2	0-2	-	1-1	0-3	3-2
Stoke v Southampton	3-2	-	-	-	-	3-3
West Brom v Crystal Palace	1-1	-	0-1	-	-	-
West Ham v Aston Villa	2-2	0-1	2-1	1-2	-	1-0

Championship

	2007-08	2008-09	2009-10	2010-11	2011-12	2012-13
Birmingham v Charlton	-	3-2	-	-	-	1-1
Blackburn v Middlesbrough	1-1	1-1	-	-	-	1-2
Bournemouth v Bolton	-	-	-	-	-	-
Doncaster v Brighton	0-0	-	-	-	1-1	-
Ipswich v Barnsley	0-0	3-0	1-0	1-3	1-0	1-1
Leeds v Yeovil	1-0	4-0	4-0	-	-	-
Millwall v Burnley	-	-	-	1-1	0-1	0-2
Nottm Forest v Blackpool	-	0-0	0-1	-	0-0	1-1
QPR v Derby	-	0-2	1-1	0-0	-	-
Sheffield Weds v Reading	-	1-2	0-2	-	-	-
Watford v Leicester	1-0	-	3-3	3-2	3-2	2-1
Wigan v Huddersfield	-	-	-	-	-	-

League 1

	2007-08	2008-09	2009-10	2010-11	2011-12	2012-13
Bristol City v Oldham	-	-	-	-	-	-
Coventry v Notts County	-	-	-	-	-	1-2
Crawley v Brentford	-	-	-	-	-	1-2
Crewe v Bradford	-	-	0-1	2-1	1-0	-
Gillingham v Carlisle	0-0	-	0-0	-	-	-
MK Dons v Walsall	-	0-1	1-0	1-1	0-1	2-4
Peterborough v Leyton Orient	-	3-0	-	2-2	-	-

Results cover matches from Premier League to Conference and Scottish Premier League to Division Three

	2007-08	2008-09	2009-10	2010-11	2011-12	2012-13
Preston v Tranmere	-	-	-	-	2-1	1-0
Rotherham v Colchester	-	-	-	-	-	-
Shrewsbury v Sheffield United	-	-	-	-	-	1-2
Swindon v Port Vale	6-0	-	-	-	5-0	-
Wolves v Stevenage	-	-	-	-	-	-

League 2						
Accrington v Wycombe	0-2	0-1	-	1-1	-	0-2
Burton v Morecambe	-	-	5-2	3-2	3-2	3-2
Bury v Torquay	-	-	0-3	1-2	-	-
Cheltenham v York	-	-	-	-	-	1-1
Chesterfield v Scunthorpe	-	-	-	-	1-4	-
Fleetwood v Newport County	-	-	-	1-1	1-4	-
Hartlepool v Dag & Red	-	-	-	0-1	-	-
Oxford v Bristol Rovers	-	-	-	-	3-0	0-2
Plymouth v Northampton	-	-	-	-	4-1	3-2
Portsmouth v Exeter	-	-	-	-	-	-
Rochdale v AFC Wimbledon	-	-	-	-	-	0-1
Southend v Mansfield	-	-	-	-	-	-

Conference						
Alfreton v Halifax	-	-	-	-	-	-
Barnet v Kidderminster	-	-	-	-	-	-
Chester v Aldershot	-	0-1	-	-	-	-
Forest Green v Dartford	-	-	-	-	-	2-3
Gateshead v Luton	-	-	0-1	1-0	0-0	5-1
Hyde v Nuneaton	-	-	-	-	-	2-2
Macclesfield v Wrexham	3-2	-	-	-	-	2-0
Salisbury v Hereford	-	-	-	-	-	-
Southport v Cambridge	-	-	-	1-1	1-0	2-1
Tamworth v Braintree	-	-	-	-	1-0	1-4
Welling v Lincoln	-	-	-	-	-	-
Woking v Grimsby	-	-	-	-	-	0-1

Scottish Premier League						
Aberdeen v Partick	-	-	-	-	-	-
Celtic v Dundee United	3-0/0-0	2-2/2-1	1-1/1-0	1-1/4-1	5-1/2-1	4-0/6-2
Hearts v St Johnstone	-	-	1-2	1-1/1-0	1-2/2-0	2-0/2-0
Inverness CT v Kilmarnock	3-1/3-0	3-1/2-1	-	1-3	2-1/1-1	1-1/1-1
Motherwell v Hibernian	2-1/1-0	1-4	1-3/1-0/6-6	2-3/2-0	4-3	0-4/4-1
St Mirren v Ross County	-	-	-	-	-	5-4/1-4

Saturday November 9th, 2013

Premier League						
Aston Villa v Cardiff	-	-	-	-	-	-
Chelsea v West Brom	-	2-0	-	6-0	2-1	1-0
Crystal Palace v Everton	-	-	-	-	-	-
Liverpool v Fulham	2-0	0-0	0-0	1-0	0-1	4-0
Man United v Arsenal	2-1	0-0	2-1	1-0	8-2	2-1
Norwich v West Ham	-	-	-	-	-	0-0
Southampton v Hull	4-0	-	-	-	2-1	-
Sunderland v Man City	1-2	0-3	1-1	1-0	1-0	1-0
Swansea v Stoke	-	-	-	-	2-0	3-1
Tottenham v Newcastle	1-4	1-0	-	2-0	5-0	2-1

Championship						
Barnsley v Doncaster	-	4-1	0-1	2-2	2-0	-
Blackpool v Ipswich	1-1	0-1	1-0	-	2-0	6-0
Bolton v Millwall	-	-	-	-	-	1-1
Brighton v Blackburn	-	-	-	-	-	1-1

Results cover matches from Premier League to Conference and Scottish Premier League to Division Three

	2007-08	2008-09	2009-10	2010-11	2011-12	2012-13
Burnley v Bournemouth	-	-	-	-	-	-
Charlton v Leeds	-	-	1-0	-	-	2-1
Derby v Sheffield Weds	-	3-0	3-0	-	-	2-2
Huddersfield v Birmingham	-	-	-	-	-	1-1
Leicester v Nottm Forest	-	-	3-0	1-0	0-0	2-2
Middlesbrough v Watford	-	-	0-1	2-1	1-0	1-2
Reading v QPR	-	0-0	1-0	0-1	-	0-0
Yeovil v Wigan	-	-	-	-	-	-

Conference						
Aldershot v Braintree	-	-	-	-	-	-
Cambridge v Macclesfield	-	-	-	-	-	2-0
Dartford v Barnet	-	-	-	-	-	-
Grimsby v Welling	-	-	-	-	-	-
Hereford v Halifax	-	-	-	-	-	-
Hyde v Chester	-	-	-	-	-	-
Kidderminster v Woking	1-1	3-0	-	-	-	2-2
Lincoln v Gateshead	-	-	-	-	1-0	1-1
Luton v Southport	-	-	-	6-0	5-1	3-1
Nuneaton v Alfreton	-	-	-	-	-	1-0
Salisbury v Forest Green	0-0	2-2	1-3	-	-	-
Wrexham v Tamworth	-	-	0-0	4-2	3-0	2-2

Scottish Premier League						
Aberdeen v Hearts	1-1/0-1	1-0/0-0	1-1/0-1	0-1/0-0	0-0	0-0/2-0/1-1
Hibernian v Inverness CT	1-0/2-0	1-2	-	1-1/2-0	1-1	2-2/1-2
Motherwell v Dundee United	5-3/2-2	1-1/2-1	2-2/2-3	2-1/2-1	0-0/0-2	0-1/0-1
Partick v St Mirren	-	-	-	-	-	-
Ross County v Celtic	-	-	-	-	-	1-1/3-2/1-1
St Johnstone v Kilmarnock	-	-	0-1	0-3/0-0	2-0	2-1/2-0

Scottish Division One						
Cowdenbeath v Alloa	1-4/1-1	-	1-1/1-1	-	-	-
Dundee v Raith	-	-	2-1/2-0	0-0/2-1	1-0/1-1	-
Falkirk v Livingston	-	-	-	-	4-3/2-5	1-2/2-0
Morton v Dumbarton	-	-	-	-	-	3-0/0-3
Queen of Sth v Hamilton	2-1/2-2	-	-	-	1-0/1-2	-

Scottish Division Two						
Arbroath v East Fife	2-3/0-1	0-1/0-2	0-1/2-2	-	3-0/2-2	2-0/1-0
Ayr v Stranraer	-	3-2/5-0	-	-	-	2-1/2-1
Dunfermline v Stenhousemuir	-	-	-	-	-	-
Forfar v Brechin	-	-	-	1-1/2-1	0-0/4-1	1-0/1-4
Rangers v Airdrieonians	-	-	-	-	-	-

Scottish Division Three						
Albion v Annan	-	0-1/2-1	0-0/1-0	0-0/0-0	-	-
Berwick v Montrose	-	3-2/0-1	2-0/0-2	1-0/0-1	1-2/2-2	1-4/4-0
East Stirling v Stirling	-	-	-	-	-	3-1/1-1
Elgin v Peterhead	-	-	-	-	6-1/1-2	2-0/0-3
Queen's Park v Clyde	-	-	-	0-1/4-0	3-0/3-0	1-0/4-1

Tuesday November 12th, 2013

Conference						
Barnet v Welling	-	-	-	-	-	-
Braintree v Luton	-	-	-	-	3-1	2-0
Cambridge v Aldershot	1-1	-	-	-	-	-
Forest Green v Nuneaton	-	-	-	-	-	1-0
Halifax v Hyde	-	-	-	-	-	-
Hereford v Chester	2-2	-	-	-	-	-

Results cover matches from Premier League to Conference and Scottish Premier League to Division Three

	2007-08	2008-09	2009-10	2010-11	2011-12	2012-13
Macclesfield v Kidderminster	-	-	-	-	-	1-0
Southport v Lincoln	-	-	-	-	2-2	4-2
Tamworth v Alfreton	-	-	-	-	2-2	1-1
Woking v Dartford	-	-	-	-	-	1-0
Wrexham v Gateshead	-	-	0-0	2-7	2-1	1-1

Saturday November 16th, 2013

League 1

	2007-08	2008-09	2009-10	2010-11	2011-12	2012-13
Bradford v Coventry	-	-	-	-	-	-
Brentford v Crewe	-	-	-	-	-	5-1
Carlisle v Crawley	-	-	-	-	-	0-2
Colchester v Swindon	-	3-2	3-0	2-1	-	0-1
Leyton Orient v Preston	-	-	-	-	2-1	2-0
Notts County v Wolves	-	-	-	-	-	-
Oldham v MK Dons	-	2-0	2-1	1-2	2-1	3-1
Port Vale v Shrewsbury	-	1-1	1-1	1-0	2-3	-
Sheffield United v Gillingham	-	-	-	-	-	-
Stevenage v Rotherham	-	-	-	3-0	-	-
Tranmere v Bristol City	-	-	-	-	-	-
Walsall v Peterborough	-	1-2	-	1-3	-	-

League 2

	2007-08	2008-09	2009-10	2010-11	2011-12	2012-13
AFC Wimbledon v Portsmouth	-	-	-	-	-	-
Bristol Rovers v Bury	-	-	-	-	-	-
Dag & Red v Burton	-	-	2-1	-	1-1	1-1
Exeter v Southend	-	-	1-0	-	-	3-0
Mansfield v Oxford	-	1-3	2-1	-	-	-
Morecambe v Rochdale	1-1	1-1	3-3	-	-	3-0
Newport County v Hartlepool	-	-	-	-	-	-
Northampton v Fleetwood	-	-	-	-	-	3-1
Scunthorpe v Accrington	-	-	-	-	-	-
Torquay v Chesterfield	-	-	2-0	0-0	-	2-1
Wycombe v Cheltenham	-	-	-	2-1	-	1-1
York v Plymouth	-	-	-	-	-	2-0

Conference

	2007-08	2008-09	2009-10	2010-11	2011-12	2012-13
Alfreton v Braintree	-	-	-	-	0-1	1-1
Barnet v Cambridge	-	-	-	-	-	-
Chester v Luton	-	2-2	-	-	-	-
Forest Green v Lincoln	-	-	-	-	0-2	3-0
Gateshead v Salisbury	-	-	2-1	-	-	-
Halifax v Aldershot	0-0	-	-	-	-	-
Kidderminster v Wrexham	-	1-0	2-0	1-0	0-1	2-0
Macclesfield v Dartford	-	-	-	-	-	2-0
Southport v Hereford	-	-	-	-	-	2-2
Tamworth v Grimsby	-	-	-	2-1	1-1	0-1
Welling v Nuneaton	-	-	-	-	-	-
Woking v Hyde	-	-	-	-	-	2-1

Scottish Division One

	2007-08	2008-09	2009-10	2010-11	2011-12	2012-13
Alloa v Raith	2-1/2-0	1-1/0-0	-	-	-	-
Cowdenbeath v Hamilton	-	-	-	-	-	1-0/1-1
Dundee v Falkirk	-	-	-	2-0/1-0	4-2/3-1	-
Livingston v Dumbarton	-	-	-	2-0/1-1	-	5-0/2-3
Queen of Sth v Morton	1-3/0-0	1-4/1-1	2-3/1-2	2-0/1-4	4-1/2-1	-

Scottish Division Two

	2007-08	2008-09	2009-10	2010-11	2011-12	2012-13
Airdrieonians v Dunfermline	-	1-3/1-1	1-1/0-1	-	-	1-2/3-3
Brechin v Ayr	2-2/5-1	0-1/1-0	-	0-3/1-0	-	2-1/2-1
East Fife v Stranraer	3-1/2-1	1-2/4-0	-	-	-	0-1/1-1

Results cover matches from Premier League to Conference and Scottish Premier League to Division Three

	2007-08	2008-09	2009-10	2010-11	2011-12	2012-13
Rangers v Forfar	-	-	-	-	-	-
Stenhousemuir v Arbroath	1-0/0-3	-	3-0/1-1	-	2-0/1-3	2-2/1-0

Scottish Division Three						
Annan v Berwick	-	1-2/1-1	1-1/0-1	1-1/2-3	2-2/1-1	3-2/2-2
Clyde v Elgin	-	-	-	1-1/3-3	1-2/0-2	2-2/1-1
Montrose v Albion	0-1/2-1	1-2/1-0	0-0/0-0	0-2/0-2	-	-
Peterhead v East Stirling	-	-	-	-	1-0/2-0	2-0/6-0
Stirling v Queen's Park	-	0-3/4-0	-	-	-	1-2/2-3

Tuesday November 19th, 2013

Conference						
Dartford v Wrexham	-	-	-	-	-	2-1
Lincoln v Alfreton	-	-	-	-	0-1	1-2

Saturday November 23rd, 2013

Premier League						
Arsenal v Southampton	-	-	-	-	-	6-1
Cardiff v Man United	-	-	-	-	-	-
Everton v Liverpool	1-2	0-2	0-2	2-0	0-2	2-2
Fulham v Swansea	-	-	-	-	0-3	1-2
Hull v Crystal Palace	2-1	-	-	1-1	0-1	0-0
Man City v Tottenham	2-1	1-2	0-1	1-0	3-2	2-1
Newcastle v Norwich	-	-	-	-	1-0	1-0
Stoke v Sunderland	-	1-0	1-0	3-2	0-1	0-0
West Brom v Aston Villa	-	1-2	-	2-1	0-0	2-2
West Ham v Chelsea	0-4	0-1	1-1	1-3	-	3-1

Championship						
Birmingham v Blackpool	-	0-1	-	2-0	3-0	1-1
Blackburn v Reading	4-2	-	-	-	-	-
Bournemouth v Derby	-	-	-	-	-	-
Doncaster v Yeovil	1-2	-	-	-	-	1-1
Ipswich v Leicester	3-1	-	0-0	3-0	1-2	1-0
Leeds v Middlesbrough	-	-	-	1-1	0-1	2-1
Millwall v Barnsley	-	-	-	2-0	0-0	1-2
Nottm Forest v Burnley	-	1-2	-	2-0	0-2	2-0
QPR v Charlton	1-0	2-1	-	-	-	-
Sheffield Weds v Huddersfield	-	-	-	0-2	4-4	1-3
Watford v Bolton	-	-	-	-	-	2-1
Wigan v Brighton	-	-	-	-	-	-

League 1						
Bristol City v Sheffield United	2-0	0-0	2-3	3-0	-	-
Coventry v Tranmere	-	-	-	-	-	1-0
Crawley v Walsall	-	-	-	-	-	2-2
Crewe v Port Vale	0-2	-	1-2	2-1	1-1	-
Gillingham v Oldham	0-0	-	1-0	-	-	-
MK Dons v Bradford	2-1	-	-	-	-	-
Peterborough v Stevenage	-	-	-	-	-	-
Preston v Colchester	0-3	-	-	-	2-4	0-0
Rotherham v Carlisle	-	-	-	-	-	-
Shrewsbury v Notts County	0-0	3-2	0-1	-	-	2-2
Swindon v Leyton Orient	1-1	0-1	3-2	2-2	-	0-1
Wolves v Brentford	-	-	-	-	-	-

League 2						
Accrington v Torquay	-	-	4-2	1-0	3-1	0-0
Burton v Bristol Rovers	-	-	-	-	2-1	1-1

Results cover matches from Premier League to Conference and Scottish Premier League to Division Three

	2007-08	2008-09	2009-10	2010-11	2011-12	2012-13
Bury v AFC Wimbledon	-	-	-	-	-	-
Cheltenham v Newport County	-	-	-	-	-	-
Chesterfield v Wycombe	2-0	0-1		4-1	4-0	3-1
Fleetwood v Mansfield	-	-	-	3-0	2-0	-
Hartlepool v Northampton	0-1	2-0		-	-	-
Oxford v Morecambe	-	-	-	4-0	1-2	1-1
Plymouth v Dag & Red	-	-	-	2-1	0-0	0-0
Portsmouth v Scunthorpe	-	-	-	2-0	-	2-1
Rochdale v Exeter	-	2-2	-	0-1	3-2	2-3
Southend v York	-	-	-	-	-	0-0

Conference

	2007-08	2008-09	2009-10	2010-11	2011-12	2012-13
Aldershot v Southport	-	-	-	-	-	-
Braintree v Halifax	-	-	-	-	-	-
Cambridge v Woking	1-0	4-1	-	-		1-0
Dartford v Gateshead	-	-	-	-	-	3-0
Grimsby v Barnet	4-1	0-1	2-0		-	-
Hyde v Alfreton	-	-	-	-	-	1-1
Kidderminster v Tamworth	-	-	0-0	2-2	2-0	4-1
Lincoln v Hereford	2-1	-	3-1	3-1	-	3-2
Luton v Welling	-	-	-	-	-	-
Nuneaton v Chester	-	-	-	-	-	-
Salisbury v Macclesfield	-	-	-	-	-	-
Wrexham v Forest Green	-	1-1	1-0	2-1	1-2	2-1

Scottish Premier League

	2007-08	2008-09	2009-10	2010-11	2011-12	2012-13
Celtic v Aberdeen	3-0/1-0	3-2/2-0	3-0	9-0/1-0	2-1	1-0/4-3
Dundee United v Partick	-	-	-	-	-	-
Hearts v Ross County	-	-	-	-	-	2-2/4-2
Inverness CT v St Johnstone	-	-	-	1-1/2-0	0-1	1-1/0-0
Kilmarnock v Motherwell	0-1	1-0/0-0	0-3	0-1/3-1	0-0/2-0	1-2/2-0
St Mirren v Hibernian	2-1	0-0/1-1	1-1	1-0/0-1	2-3/1-0	1-2/0-1

Scottish Division One

	2007-08	2008-09	2009-10	2010-11	2011-12	2012-13
Dumbarton v Alloa	-	-	1-3/3-1	4-1/2-2	-	-
Falkirk v Cowdenbeath	-	-	-	5-1/2-0	-	2-0/4-0
Hamilton v Dundee	2-0/1-0	-	-	-	1-6/3-1	-
Morton v Livingston	2-2/1-1	1-2/2-2	-	-	2-1/1-3	2-2/2-1
Raith v Queen of Sth	-	-	1-0/0-0	0-1/0-1	0-2/3-1	-

Scottish Division Two

	2007-08	2008-09	2009-10	2010-11	2011-12	2012-13
Arbroath v Rangers	-	-	-	-	-	-
Ayr v Stenhousemuir	-	-	-	2-0/4-3	-	1-1/1-2
Dunfermline v Brechin	-	-	-	-	-	-
Forfar v East Fife	0-2/2-3	-	-	3-2/0-0	3-2/1-4	3-2/3-2
Stranraer v Airdrieonians	-	-	-	-	-	-

Scottish Division Three

	2007-08	2008-09	2009-10	2010-11	2011-12	2012-13
Annan v Stirling	-	-	-	-	-	5-2/0-1
Berwick v Albion	-	0-3/1-1	2-0/1-2	1-6/2-2	-	-
East Stirling v Clyde	-	-	-	0-0/2-0	1-1/0-1	3-0/3-0
Montrose v Elgin	0-0/3-2	1-0/3-1	1-1/0-4	0-1/1-0	3-0/2-3	2-2/4-1
Queen's Park v Peterhead	1-1/2-0	0-1/2-1	-	-	1-1/0-1	0-0/0-3

Tuesday November 26th, 2013

League 1

	2007-08	2008-09	2009-10	2010-11	2011-12	2012-13
Bradford v Notts County	3-0	2-1	0-0	-	-	-
Brentford v Peterborough	1-2	-	-	2-1	-	-
Bristol City v Leyton Orient	-	-	-	-	-	-
Carlisle v Crewe	1-0	4-2	-	-	-	0-0

Results cover matches from Premier League to Conference and Scottish Premier League to Division Three

	2007-08	2008-09	2009-10	2010-11	2011-12	2012-13
Colchester v MK Dons	-	0-3	2-0	1-3	1-5	0-2
Coventry v Rotherham	-	-	-	-	-	-
Crawley v Swindon	-	-	-	-	0-3	1-1
Gillingham v Stevenage	-	-	-	1-0	-	-
Port Vale v Preston	-	-	-	-	-	-
Sheffield United v Walsall	-	-	-	-	3-2	1-0
Shrewsbury v Oldham	-	-	-	-	-	1-0
Wolves v Tranmere	-	-	-	-	-	-
League 2						
Accrington v Fleetwood	-	-	-	-	-	0-3
AFC Wimbledon v Dag & Red	-	-	-	-	2-1	2-2
Burton v Mansfield	-	1-0	-	-	-	-
Bury v Hartlepool	-	-	-	-	1-2	2-1
Cheltenham v Bristol Rovers	1-0	2-1	-	-	0-2	1-1
Chesterfield v Northampton	-	-	1-0	2-1	-	3-0
Morecambe v York	-	-	-	-	-	2-2
Oxford v Newport County	-	-	-	-	-	-
Portsmouth v Southend	-	-	-	-	-	-
Rochdale v Scunthorpe	-	-	-	-	1-0	-
Torquay v Plymouth	-	-	-	-	3-1	0-0
Wycombe v Exeter	-	1-1	2-2	-	3-1	0-1

Saturday November 30th, 2013

	2007-08	2008-09	2009-10	2010-11	2011-12	2012-13
Premier League						
Aston Villa v Sunderland	0-1	2-1	1-1	0-1	0-0	6-1
Cardiff v Arsenal	-	-	-	-	-	-
Chelsea v Southampton	-	-	-	-	-	2-2
Everton v Stoke	-	3-1	1-1	1-0	0-1	1-0
Hull v Liverpool	-	1-3	0-0	-	-	-
Man City v Swansea	-	-	-	-	4-0	1-0
Newcastle v West Brom	-	2-1	2-2	3-3	2-3	2-1
Norwich v Crystal Palace	1-0	1-2	-	1-2	-	-
Tottenham v Man United	1-1	0-0	1-3	0-0	1-3	1-1
West Ham v Fulham	2-1	3-1	2-2	1-1	-	3-0
Championship						
Barnsley v Birmingham	-	1-1	-	-	1-3	1-2
Blackburn v Leeds	-	-	-	-	-	0-0
Blackpool v Sheffield Weds	2-1	0-2	1-2	-	-	0-0
Bournemouth v Brighton	0-2	-	-	1-0	-	-
Charlton v Ipswich	3-1	2-1	-	-	-	1-2
Doncaster v QPR	-	2-0	2-0	0-1	-	-
Huddersfield v Burnley	-	-	-	-	-	2-0
Leicester v Millwall	-	0-1	-	4-2	0-3	0-1
Middlesbrough v Bolton	0-1	1-3	-	-	-	2-1
Nottm Forest v Reading	-	0-0	2-1	3-4	1-0	-
Watford v Yeovil	-	-	-	-	-	-
Wigan v Derby	2-0	-	-	-	-	-
League 1						
Crewe v Crawley	-	-	-	-	1-1	2-0
Leyton Orient v Sheffield United	-	-	-	-	1-1	0-1
MK Dons v Coventry	-	-	-	-	-	2-3
Notts County v Brentford	1-1	1-1	-	1-1	1-1	1-2
Oldham v Bradford	-	-	-	-	-	-
Peterborough v Wolves	-	-	-	-	-	0-2
Preston v Bristol City	0-0	2-0	2-2	0-4	-	-
Rotherham v Gillingham	-	2-0	-	0-1	3-0	1-2

Results cover matches from Premier League to Conference and Scottish Premier League to Division Three

	2007-08	2008-09	2009-10	2010-11	2011-12	2012-13
Stevenage v Shrewsbury	-	-	-	1-1	-	1-1
Swindon v Carlisle	2-2	1-1	2-0	0-1	-	4-0
Tranmere v Colchester	-	3-4	1-1	1-0	0-0	4-0
Walsall v Port Vale	0-0	-	-	-	-	-

League 2						
Bristol Rovers v AFC Wimbledon	-	-	-	-	1-0	1-0
Dag & Red v Wycombe	2-2	0-1	-	-	-	3-0
Exeter v Bury	-	0-0	-	-	3-2	-
Fleetwood v Oxford	-	-	-	-	-	3-0
Hartlepool v Portsmouth	-	-	-	-	-	0-0
Mansfield v Morecambe	1-2	-	-	-	-	-
Newport County v Chesterfield	-	-	-	-	-	-
Northampton v Accrington	-	-	4-0	0-0	0-0	2-0
Plymouth v Burton	-	-	-	-	2-1	1-2
Scunthorpe v Torquay	-	-	-	-	-	-
Southend v Cheltenham	2-2	2-0	-	1-2	4-0	1-2
York v Rochdale	-	-	-	-	-	0-0

Scottish Division Three						
Albion v East Stirling	2-3/2-2	0-2/0-2	3-0/2-1	1-0/2-0	-	-
Clyde v Annan	-	-	-	0-2/0-2	0-0/1-1	2-1/2-3
Elgin v Queen's Park	-	-	0-1/0-1	4-2/0-1	2-0/1-1	0-4/3-5
Peterhead v Montrose	-	-	-	-	2-3/2-1	2-0/0-1
Stirling v Berwick	-	-	-	-	-	6-3/1-0

Tuesday December 3rd, 2013

Premier League						
Arsenal v Hull	-	1-2	3-0	-	-	-
Crystal Palace v West Ham	-	-	-	-	2-2	-
Liverpool v Norwich	-	-	-	-	1-1	5-0
Man United v Everton	2-1	1-0	3-0	1-0	4-4	2-0
Southampton v Aston Villa	-	-	-	-	-	4-1
Stoke v Cardiff	2-1	-	-	-	-	-
Sunderland v Chelsea	0-1	2-3	1-3	2-4	1-2	1-3
Swansea v Newcastle	-	-	1-1	-	0-2	1-0
West Brom v Man City	-	2-1	-	0-2	0-0	1-2

Championship						
Birmingham v Doncaster	-	1-0	-	-	2-1	-
Bolton v Huddersfield	-	-	-	-	-	1-0
Brighton v Barnsley	-	-	-	-	2-0	5-1
Burnley v Watford	2-2	3-2	-	3-2	2-2	1-1
Derby v Middlesbrough	0-1	-	2-2	3-1	0-1	3-1
Ipswich v Blackburn	-	-	-	-	-	1-1
Leeds v Wigan	-	-	-	-	-	-
Millwall v Nottm Forest	2-2	-	-	0-0	2-0	0-1
QPR v Bournemouth	-	-	-	-	-	-
Reading v Charlton	-	2-2	-	-	-	-
Sheffield Weds v Leicester	0-2	-	2-0	-	-	0-2
Yeovil v Blackpool	-	-	-	-	-	-

Wednesday December 4th, 2013

Premier League						
Fulham v Tottenham	3-3	2-1	0-0	1-2	1-3	0-3

Saturday December 7th, 2013

Premier League						
Arsenal v Everton	1-0	3-1	2-2	2-1	1-0	0-0
Crystal Palace v Cardiff	0-0	0-2	1-2	1-0	1-2	3-2

Results cover matches from Premier League to Conference and Scottish Premier League to Division Three

	2007-08	2008-09	2009-10	2010-11	2011-12	2012-13
Fulham v Aston Villa	2-1	3-1	0-2	1-1	0-0	1-0
Liverpool v West Ham	4-0	0-0	3-0	3-0	-	0-0
Man United v Newcastle	6-0	1-1	-	3-0	1-1	4-3
Southampton v Man City	-	-	-	-	-	3-1
Stoke v Chelsea	-	0-2	1-2	1-1	0-0	0-4
Sunderland v Tottenham	1-0	1-1	3-1	1-2	0-0	1-2
Swansea v Hull	-	-	-	1-1	-	-
West Brom v Norwich	2-0	-	-	-	1-2	2-1
Championship						
Birmingham v Middlesbrough	3-0	-	-	-	3-0	3-2
Bolton v Doncaster	-	-	-	-	-	-
Brighton v Leicester	-	3-2	-	-	1-0	1-1
Burnley v Barnsley	2-1	1-2	-	3-0	2-0	1-1
Derby v Blackpool	-	4-1	0-2	-	2-1	4-1
Ipswich v Huddersfield	-	-	-	-	-	2-2
Leeds v Watford	-	-	-	2-2	0-2	1-6
Millwall v Wigan	-	-	-	-	-	-
QPR v Blackburn	-	-	-	-	1-1	-
Reading v Bournemouth	-	-	-	-	-	-
Sheffield Weds v Nottm Forest	-	1-0	1-1	-	-	0-1
Yeovil v Charlton	-	-	1-1	0-1	2-3	-
Conference						
Alfreton v Luton	-	-	-	-	0-0	3-0
Barnet v Dartford	-	-	-	-	-	-
Chester v Braintree	-	-	-	-	-	-
Forest Green v Grimsby	-	-	-	3-3	0-1	0-1
Gateshead v Aldershot	-	-	-	-	-	-
Halifax v Salisbury	1-1	-	-	-	-	-
Hereford v Nuneaton	-	-	-	-	-	0-0
Macclesfield v Lincoln	1-2	1-2	0-1	1-1	-	2-1
Southport v Wrexham	-	-	-	0-1	0-0	1-4
Tamworth v Cambridge	-	-	0-0	1-1	2-2	1-2
Welling v Hyde	-	-	-	-	-	-
Woking v Kidderminster	3-0	1-5	-	-	-	2-2
Scottish Premier League						
Dundee United v Hearts	4-1	3-0/0-1	2-0/1-0	2-0/2-1	1-0/2-2	0-3/3-1
Hibernian v Partick	-	-	-	-	-	-
Motherwell v Celtic	1-4/1-2	2-4/1-1	2-3	0-1/2-0	1-2/0-3	0-2/2-1/3-1
Ross County v Kilmarnock	-	-	-	-	-	0-0/0-1
St Johnstone v Aberdeen	-	-	1-0/1-1	0-1/0-0	1-2	1-2/3-1
St Mirren v Inverness CT	2-1/1-1	2-0/1-2	-	1-2/3-3	1-2/0-1	2-2/2-1
Scottish Division One						
Cowdenbeath v Livingston	-	-	-	-	-	1-1/2-2
Dumbarton v Queen of Sth	-	-	-	-	-	-
Falkirk v Raith	-	-	-	0-0/2-1	2-0/2-3	0-2/1-1
Hamilton v Alloa	-	-	-	-	-	-
Morton v Dundee	0-2/1-2	2-0/2-0	0-1/2-2	0-1/1-3	1-2/0-2	-
Scottish Division Two						
Arbroath v Stranraer	2-2/0-0	1-0/2-0	-	0-0/2-2	-	2-1/1-0
Brechin v Airdrieonians	4-2/2-1	-	-	3-1/1-2	1-1/1-1	-
Dunfermline v Forfar	-	-	-	-	-	-
East Fife v Stenhousemuir	7-0/0-1	-	2-1/1-1	6-0/1-1	1-3/1-1	3-2/1-2
Rangers v Ayr	-	-	-	-	-	-
Scottish Division Three						
Albion v Stirling	-	-	-	-	0-1/1-2	-

Results cover matches from Premier League to Conference and Scottish Premier League to Division Three

	2007-08	2008-09	2009-10	2010-11	2011-12	2012-13
Clyde v Peterhead	-	-	1-3/3-1	-	2-0/0-1	0-2/2-0
East Stirling v Annan	-	2-1/1-1	1-3/3-1	1-5/2-0	1-0/0-4	2-2/1-2
Elgin v Berwick	-	0-2/2-0	3-3/1-5	1-2/3-2	4-1/4-0	3-1/1-2
Queen's Park v Montrose	-	-	3-2/3-0	1-0/4-1	3-1/5-0	2-2/1-2

Saturday December 14th, 2013

Premier League						
Aston Villa v Man United	1-4	0-0	1-1	2-2	0-1	2-3
Cardiff v West Brom	0-0	-	1-1	-	-	-
Chelsea v Crystal Palace	-	-	-	-	-	-
Everton v Fulham	3-0	1-0	2-1	2-1	4-0	1-0
Hull v Stoke	1-1	1-2	2-1	-	-	-
Man City v Arsenal	1-3	3-0	4-2	0-3	1-0	1-1
Newcastle v Southampton	-	-	-	-	-	4-2
Norwich v Swansea	-	2-3	-	2-0	3-1	2-2
Tottenham v Liverpool	0-2	2-1	2-1	2-1	4-0	2-1
West Ham v Sunderland	3-1	2-0	1-0	0-3	-	1-1

Championship						
Barnsley v Yeovil	-	-	-	-	-	-
Blackburn v Millwall	-	-	-	-	-	0-2
Blackpool v QPR	1-0	0-3	2-2	-	-	-
Bournemouth v Birmingham	-	-	-	-	-	-
Charlton v Derby	-	2-2	-	-	-	1-1
Doncaster v Leeds	0-1	-	-	0-0	0-3	-
Huddersfield v Reading	-	-	-	-	-	-
Leicester v Burnley	0-1	-	-	4-0	0-0	2-1
Middlesbrough v Brighton	-	-	-	-	1-0	0-2
Nottm Forest v Ipswich	-	1-1	3-0	2-0	3-2	1-0
Watford v Sheffield Weds	2-1	2-2	4-1	-	-	2-1
Wigan v Bolton	1-0	0-0	0-0	1-1	1-3	-

League 1						
Bradford v Leyton Orient	-	-	-	-	-	-
Brentford v Oldham	-	-	1-1	1-3	2-0	1-0
Bristol City v Rotherham	-	-	-	-	-	-
Carlisle v Tranmere	0-1	1-2	3-0	2-0	0-0	0-3
Colchester v Notts County	-	-	-	2-1	4-2	0-2
Coventry v Crewe	-	-	-	-	-	1-2
Crawley v Preston	-	-	-	-	-	1-0
Gillingham v Peterborough	-	-	-	-	-	-
Port Vale v Stevenage	-	-	-	1-3	-	-
Sheffield United v Swindon	-	-	-	-	-	2-0
Shrewsbury v Walsall	-	-	-	-	-	1-0
Wolves v MK Dons	-	-	-	-	-	-

League 2						
Accrington v Exeter	-	2-1	-	-	-	0-3
AFC Wimbledon v Mansfield	-	-	2-0	2-1	-	-
Burton v York	4-3	2-1	-	-	-	3-1
Bury v Northampton	-	-	2-2	1-1	-	-
Cheltenham v Hartlepool	1-1	2-0	-	-	-	-
Chesterfield v Plymouth	-	-	-	-	-	1-2
Morecambe v Bristol Rovers	-	-	-	-	2-3	1-1
Oxford v Dag & Red	-	-	-	-	2-1	2-3
Portsmouth v Newport County	-	-	-	-	-	-
Rochdale v Fleetwood	-	-	-	-	-	0-0
Torquay v Southend	-	-	-	1-1	0-0	1-4
Wycombe v Scunthorpe	-	-	-	-	1-1	-

Results cover matches from Premier League to Conference and Scottish Premier League to Division Three

	2007-08	2008-09	2009-10	2010-11	2011-12	2012-13
Conference						
Barnet v Aldershot	-	0-3	3-0	1-2	2-1	0-1
Cambridge v Luton	-	-	3-4	0-0	1-1	2-2
Dartford v Halifax	-	-	-	-	-	-
Forest Green v Braintree	-	-	-	-	0-2	4-1
Gateshead v Welling	-	-	-	-	-	-
Kidderminster v Alfreton	-	-	-	-	3-1	3-1
Lincoln v Nuneaton	-	-	-	-	-	2-1
Macclesfield v Salisbury	-	-	-	-	-	-
Southport v Grimsby	-	-	-	2-2	1-2	1-1
Tamworth v Hyde	-	-	-	-	-	2-0
Woking v Chester	-	-	-	-	-	-
Wrexham v Hereford	0-2	-	-	-	-	1-2
Scottish Premier League						
Aberdeen v St Mirren	4-0/1-1	2-0	1-0/2-1	2-0/0-1	2-2/0-0	0-0/0-0
Celtic v Hibernian	1-1/2-0	4-2/3-1	1-2/3-2	2-1/3-1	0-0	2-2/3-0
Hearts v Inverness CT	2-3/1-0	1-0/3-2	-	1-1	2-1	2-2/2-3
Kilmarnock v Dundee United	2-1/1-2	2-0	0-2/4-4	1-2/1-1	1-1	3-1/2-3
Partick v St Johnstone	2-2/0-0	4-0/0-0	-	-	-	-
Ross County v Motherwell	-	-	-	-	-	0-0/3-0
Scottish Division One						
Alloa v Morton	-	-	-	-	-	-
Dundee v Cowdenbeath	-	-	-	3-0/2-2	-	-
Livingston v Hamilton	2-0/1-3	-	-	-	1-0/0-4	0-3/0-0
Queen of Sth v Falkirk	-	-	-	1-5/0-1	1-5/0-0	-
Raith v Dumbarton	-	-	-	-	-	2-2/3-2
Scottish Division Two						
Airdrieonians v East Fife	-	-	-	1-1/2-2	1-3/2-0	-
Ayr v Dunfermline	-	-	1-0/1-2	-	-	-
Forfar v Arbroath	1-3/1-0	-	-	-	1-1/2-4	1-1/2-4
Stenhousemuir v Rangers	-	-	-	-	-	-
Stranraer v Brechin	-	1-2/0-3	-	-	-	0-2/3-2
Scottish Division Three						
Annan v Queen's Park	-	-	3-1/0-2	2-1/1-2	5-2/2-3	2-3/2-0
Berwick v East Stirling	-	2-1/1-2	0-1/2-2	3-0/1-1	4-2/0-2	3-0/2-0
Montrose v Clyde	-	-	-	8-1/3-1	4-0/5-0	2-3/1-1
Peterhead v Albion	-	-	-	-	-	-
Stirling v Elgin	-	-	-	-	-	1-4/1-1

Saturday December 21st, 2013

	2007-08	2008-09	2009-10	2010-11	2011-12	2012-13
Premier League						
Arsenal v Chelsea	1-0	1-4	0-3	3-1	0-0	1-2
Crystal Palace v Newcastle	-	-	0-2	-	-	-
Fulham v Man City	3-3	1-1	1-2	1-4	2-2	1-2
Liverpool v Cardiff	-	-	-	-	-	-
Man United v West Ham	4-1	2-0	3-0	3-0	-	1-0
Southampton v Tottenham	-	-	-	-	-	1-2
Stoke v Aston Villa	-	3-2	0-0	2-1	0-0	1-3
Sunderland v Norwich	-	-	-	-	3-0	1-1
Swansea v Everton	-	-	-	-	0-2	0-3
West Brom v Hull	1-2	0-3	-	-	-	-
Championship						
Birmingham v Nottm Forest	-	2-0	-	-	1-2	2-1
Bolton v Charlton	-	-	-	-	-	2-0

Results cover matches from Premier League to Conference and Scottish Premier League to Division Three

	2007-08	2008-09	2009-10	2010-11	2011-12	2012-13
Brighton v Huddersfield	1-1	0-1	0-0	2-3	-	4-1
Burnley v Blackpool	2-2	2-0	-	-	3-1	1-0
Derby v Doncaster	-	0-1	0-2	1-3	3-0	-
Ipswich v Watford	1-2	0-0	1-1	0-3	1-2	0-2
Leeds v Barnsley	-	-	-	3-3	1-2	1-0
Millwall v Middlesbrough	-	-	-	2-3	1-3	3-1
QPR v Leicester	3-1	-	1-2	1-0	-	-
Reading v Wigan	2-1	-	-	-	-	0-3
Sheffield Weds v Bournemouth	-	-	-	1-1	3-0	-
Yeovil v Blackburn	-	-	-	-	-	-
League 1						
Crewe v Shrewsbury	-	-	0-3	1-2	1-1	1-1
Leyton Orient v Crawley	-	-	-	-	-	0-1
MK Dons v Port Vale	-	-	-	-	-	-
Notts County v Bristol City	-	-	-	-	-	-
Oldham v Colchester	-	0-1	2-2	0-0	1-1	1-1
Peterborough v Bradford	2-1	-	-	-	-	-
Preston v Brentford	-	-	-	-	1-3	1-1
Rotherham v Wolves	-	-	-	-	-	-
Stevenage v Sheffield United	-	-	-	-	2-1	4-0
Swindon v Coventry	-	-	-	-	-	2-2
Tranmere v Gillingham	2-0	-	4-2	-	-	-
Walsall v Carlisle	1-1	2-1	2-2	2-1	1-1	1-2
League 2						
Bristol Rovers v Portsmouth	-	-	-	-	-	-
Dag & Red v Torquay	-	-	5-3	-	1-1	2-2
Exeter v Chesterfield	-	1-6	-	-	2-1	0-1
Fleetwood v Cheltenham	-	-	-	-	-	1-1
Hartlepool v Burton	-	-	-	-	-	-
Mansfield v Accrington	1-2	-	-	-	-	-
Newport County v AFC Wimbledon	-	-	-	3-3	-	-
Northampton v Wycombe	-	-	-	1-1	-	3-1
Plymouth v Bury	-	-	-	-	-	-
Scunthorpe v Morecambe	-	-	-	-	-	-
Southend v Rochdale	-	-	-	-	-	3-1
York v Oxford	0-1	0-0	1-1	-	-	3-1
Conference						
Aldershot v Tamworth	-	-	-	-	-	-
Alfreton v Dartford	-	-	-	-	-	3-2
Braintree v Macclesfield	-	-	-	-	-	0-3
Chester v Lincoln	1-2	0-2	-	-	-	-
Grimsby v Kidderminster	-	-	-	3-3	1-2	1-3
Halifax v Forest Green	1-1	-	-	-	-	-
Hereford v Cambridge	-	-	-	-	-	4-2
Hyde v Barnet	-	-	-	-	-	-
Luton v Gateshead	-	-	2-1	2-2	5-1	2-2
Nuneaton v Woking	-	-	-	-	-	0-0
Salisbury v Southport	-	-	-	-	-	-
Welling v Wrexham	-	-	-	-	-	-
Scottish Premier League						
Celtic v Hearts	5-0/3-0	1-1/0-0	2-1/2-0	3-0/4-0	1-0/5-0	1-0/4-1
Dundee United v Ross County	-	-	-	-	-	0-0/1-1
Hibernian v St Johnstone	-	-	3-0/1-1	0-0/1-2	3-2/2-3	2-0/1-3
Inverness CT v Aberdeen	1-2/3-4	0-3	-	2-0/0-2	2-1/0-2	1-1/3-0
Kilmarnock v Partick	-	-	-	-	-	-
Motherwell v St Mirren	1-1	2-1/0-2	2-0	3-1/0-1	1-1	1-1/2-2

Results cover matches from Premier League to Conference and Scottish Premier League to Division Three

Thursday December 26th, 2013

Premier League

	2007-08	2008-09	2009-10	2010-11	2011-12	2012-13
Aston Villa v Crystal Palace	-	-	-	-	-	-
Cardiff v Southampton	1-0	2-1	-	-	2-1	-
Chelsea v Swansea	-	-	-	-	4-1	2-0
Everton v Sunderland	7-1	3-0	2-0	2-0	4-0	2-1
Hull v Man United	-	0-1	1-3	-	-	-
Man City v Liverpool	0-0	2-3	0-0	3-0	3-0	2-2
Newcastle v Stoke	-	2-2	-	1-2	3-0	2-1
Norwich v Fulham	-	-	-	-	1-1	0-0
Tottenham v West Brom	-	1-0	-	2-2	1-0	1-1
West Ham v Arsenal	0-1	0-2	2-2	0-3	-	1-3

Championship

	2007-08	2008-09	2009-10	2010-11	2011-12	2012-13
Barnsley v Bolton	-	-	-	-	-	2-3
Blackburn v Sheffield Weds	-	-	-	-	-	1-0
Blackpool v Leeds	-	-	-	-	1-0	2-1
Bournemouth v Yeovil	2-0	-	-	2-0	0-0	3-0
Charlton v Brighton	-	-	1-2	0-4	-	2-2
Doncaster v Ipswich	-	1-0	3-3	0-6	2-3	-
Huddersfield v Derby	-	-	-	-	-	1-0
Leicester v Reading	-	-	1-2	1-2	0-2	-
Middlesbrough v Burnley	-	-	-	2-1	0-2	3-2
Nottm Forest v QPR	-	2-2	5-0	0-0	-	-
Watford v Millwall	-	-	-	1-0	2-1	0-0
Wigan v Birmingham	2-0	-	2-3	2-1	-	-

League 1

	2007-08	2008-09	2009-10	2010-11	2011-12	2012-13
Bradford v Rotherham	3-2	3-0	2-4	2-1	2-3	0-2
Brentford v Swindon	-	-	2-3	0-1	-	2-1
Bristol City v Walsall	-	-	-	-	-	-
Carlisle v Preston	-	-	-	-	0-0	1-1
Colchester v Stevenage	-	-	-	-	1-6	1-0
Coventry v Peterborough	-	-	3-2	-	2-2	-
Crawley v MK Dons	-	-	-	-	-	2-0
Gillingham v Leyton Orient	3-1	-	1-1	-	-	-
Port Vale v Notts County	-	1-2	2-1	-	-	-
Sheffield United v Oldham	-	-	-	-	2-3	1-1
Shrewsbury v Tranmere	-	-	-	-	-	1-1
Wolves v Crewe	-	-	-	-	-	-

League 2

	2007-08	2008-09	2009-10	2010-11	2011-12	2012-13
Accrington v York	-	-	-	-	-	0-1
AFC Wimbledon v Southend	-	-	-	-	1-4	0-4
Burton v Northampton	-	-	3-2	1-1	0-1	3-3
Bury v Scunthorpe	-	-	-	-	0-0	2-1
Cheltenham v Exeter	-	-	-	-	-	3-0
Chesterfield v Hartlepool	-	-	-	-	2-3	-
Morecambe v Fleetwood	-	-	-	-	-	0-4
Oxford v Plymouth	-	-	-	-	5-1	2-1
Portsmouth v Dag & Red	-	-	-	-	-	-
Rochdale v Mansfield	1-0	-	-	-	-	-
Torquay v Bristol Rovers	-	-	-	-	2-2	3-3
Wycombe v Newport County	-	-	-	-	-	-

Conference

	2007-08	2008-09	2009-10	2010-11	2011-12	2012-13
Barnet v Luton	-	1-1	-	-	-	-
Cambridge v Braintree	-	-	-	-	2-0	1-0
Dartford v Welling	-	-	-	-	-	-

Results cover matches from Premier League to Conference and Scottish Premier League to Division Three

	2007-08	2008-09	2009-10	2010-11	2011-12	2012-13
Forest Green v Aldershot	2-3	-	-	-	-	-
Gateshead v Halifax	-	-	-	-	-	-
Kidderminster v Hereford	-	-	-	-	-	0-1
Lincoln v Grimsby	1-2	1-1	0-0	-	1-2	1-4
Macclesfield v Hyde	-	-	-	-	-	3-2
Southport v Chester	-	-	-	-	-	-
Tamworth v Nuneaton	-	-	-	-	-	2-1
Woking v Salisbury	3-2	1-0	-	-	-	-
Wrexham v Alfreton	-	-	-	-	0-1	1-1

Scottish Premier League						
Aberdeen v Motherwell	1-2/1-1	2-0	0-0/0-3	1-2	1-2	3-3/0-0
Hearts v Kilmarnock	1-1/0-2	1-2/3-1	1-0/1-0	0-3/0-2	0-1	1-3/0-3
Partick v Inverness CT	-	-	2-1/0-1	-	-	-
Ross County v Hibernian	-	-	-	-	-	3-2/1-0
St Johnstone v Celtic	-	-	1-4	0-3/0-1	0-2	2-1/1-1
St Mirren v Dundee United	0-3	0-2	0-0/1-2	1-1/1-1	2-2	0-1/0-0

Scottish Division One						
Alloa v Dundee	-	-	-	-	-	-
Dumbarton v Hamilton	-	-	-	-	-	3-3/3-1
Morton v Falkirk	-	-	-	0-0/2-2	3-2/0-0	1-2/2-0
Queen of Sth v Livingston	1-0/1-0	6-1/3-3	-	-	0-2/0-4	-
Raith v Cowdenbeath	2-0/3-2	-	-	2-1/2-2	-	2-2/0-1

Scottish Division Two						
Arbroath v Dunfermline	-	-	-	-	-	-
East Fife v Brechin	-	0-0/2-1	2-0/2-0	1-3/0-0	1-1/2-2	2-2/0-3
Forfar v Ayr	-	-	-	4-1/3-2	-	2-1/2-1
Rangers v Stranraer	-	-	-	-	-	-
Stenhousemuir v Airdrieonians	-	-	-	1-3/1-0	1-1/0-3	-

Scottish Division Three						
Clyde v Albion	-	-	-	1-2/0-1	-	-
Elgin v East Stirling	6-0/3-0	0-4/0-2	1-2/0-1	0-2/2-0	2-0/3-1	3-4/3-2
Montrose v Annan	-	1-1/0-3	0-0/1-2	1-1/0-1	2-3/1-1	0-0/5-1
Peterhead v Stirling	-	1-1/1-1	3-2/1-1	-	-	2-2/0-0
Queen's Park v Berwick	1-0/3-1	-	2-0/2-3	0-2/1-0	1-1/2-2	1-1/2-1

Saturday December 28th, 2013

Premier League						
Aston Villa v Swansea	-	-	-	-	0-2	2-0
Cardiff v Sunderland	-	-	-	-	-	-
Chelsea v Liverpool	0-0	0-1	2-0	0-1	1-2	1-1
Everton v Southampton	-	-	-	-	-	3-1
Hull v Fulham	-	2-1	2-0	-	-	-
Man City v Crystal Palace	-	-	-	-	-	-
Newcastle v Arsenal	1-1	1-3	-	4-4	0-0	0-1
Norwich v Man United	-	-	-	-	1-2	1-0
Tottenham v Stoke	-	3-1	0-1	3-2	1-1	0-0
West Ham v West Brom	-	0-0	-	2-2	-	3-1

Conference						
Aldershot v Welling	-	-	-	-	-	-
Alfreton v Southport	-	-	-	-	0-0	3-3
Braintree v Tamworth	-	-	-	-	3-1	2-1
Chester v Gateshead	-	-	-	-	-	-
Dartford v Woking	-	-	-	-	-	4-1
Grimsby v Macclesfield	1-1	0-0	1-1	-	-	0-1
Halifax v Lincoln	-	-	-	-	-	-

Results cover matches from Premier League to Conference and Scottish Premier League to Division Three

	2007-08	2008-09	2009-10	2010-11	2011-12	2012-13
Hereford v Forest Green	-	-	-	-	-	1-2
Hyde v Wrexham	-	-	-	-	-	2-0
Luton v Kidderminster	-	-	3-1	1-1	1-0	1-2
Nuneaton v Cambridge	-	-	-	-	-	2-2
Salisbury v Barnet	-	-	-	-	-	-
Scottish Division One						
Cowdenbeath v Queen of Sth	-	-	-	1-3/2-2	-	-
Dundee v Dumbarton	-	-	-	-	-	-
Falkirk v Alloa	-	-	-	-	-	-
Hamilton v Morton	1-0/3-0	-	-	-	1-2/4-3	1-1/2-1
Livingston v Raith	-	-	-	-	1-1/4-0	2-1/2-3
Scottish Division Two						
Airdrieonians v Arbroath	-	-	-	-	3-3/2-0	-
Ayr v East Fife	-	4-2/2-0	-	0-4/1-1	-	2-3/2-1
Brechin v Stenhousemuir	-	-	1-0/2-2	0-0/3-1	2-0/1-0	7-2/1-2
Dunfermline v Rangers	-	-	-	-	0-4/1-4	-
Stranraer v Forfar	3-0/2-1	-	1-0/2-0	-	-	4-1/0-3
Scottish Division Three						
Albion v Queen's Park	-	-	0-1/1-0	2-1/1-2	-	-
Annan v Elgin	-	5-0/6-0	0-2/3-3	0-1/2-2	1-1/1-1	2-0/2-2
Berwick v Peterhead	1-2/2-2	-	-	-	2-1/0-1	1-1/0-2
East Stirling v Montrose	0-3/3-1	5-0/2-1	1-0/2-3	2-1/1-2	1-0/3-1	2-2/1-2
Stirling v Clyde	0-2/1-1	-	1-1/1-0	-	-	0-1/2-0

Sunday December 29th, 2013

Championship						
Barnsley v Derby	-	2-0	0-0	1-1	3-2	1-1
Blackburn v Birmingham	2-1	-	2-1	1-1	-	1-1
Blackpool v Brighton	-	-	-	-	3-1	1-1
Bournemouth v Ipswich	-	-	-	-	-	-
Charlton v Sheffield Weds	3-2	1-2	-	1-0	1-1	1-2
Doncaster v Millwall	0-0	-	-	2-1	0-3	-
Huddersfield v Yeovil	1-0	0-0	2-1	4-2	2-0	-
Leicester v Bolton	-	-	-	-	-	3-2
Middlesbrough v Reading	0-1	-	1-1	3-1	0-2	-
Nottm Forest v Leeds	1-2	-	-	1-1	0-4	4-2
Watford v QPR	2-4	3-0	3-1	0-2	-	-
Wigan v Burnley	-	-	1-0	-	-	-
League 1						
Bradford v Swindon	-	-	-	-	0-0	-
Brentford v MK Dons	0-3	-	3-3	0-2	3-3	3-2
Bristol City v Stevenage	-	-	-	-	-	-
Carlisle v Peterborough	-	3-3	-	0-1	-	-
Colchester v Crewe	-	0-1	-	-	-	1-2
Coventry v Oldham	-	-	-	-	-	2-1
Crawley v Notts County	-	-	-	-	-	0-0
Gillingham v Walsall	2-1	-	0-0	-	-	-
Port Vale v Rotherham	-	0-0	1-2	1-0	2-0	6-2
Sheffield United v Tranmere	-	-	-	-	1-1	0-0
Shrewsbury v Preston	-	-	-	-	-	1-0
Wolves v Leyton Orient	-	-	-	-	-	-
League 2						
Accrington v Southend	-	-	-	3-1	1-2	1-1
AFC Wimbledon v Plymouth	-	-	-	-	1-2	1-1
Burton v Newport County	-	-	-	-	-	-

Results cover matches from Premier League to Conference and Scottish Premier League to Division Three

	2007-08	2008-09	2009-10	2010-11	2011-12	2012-13
Bury v York	-	-	-	-	-	-
Cheltenham v Mansfield	-	-	-	-	-	-
Chesterfield v Dag & Red	1-1	1-1	2-2	-	-	1-2
Morecambe v Hartlepool	-	-	-	-	-	-
Oxford v Scunthorpe	-	-	-	-	-	-
Portsmouth v Northampton	-	-	-	-	-	-
Rochdale v Bristol Rovers	-	-	-	3-1	-	2-1
Torquay v Exeter	1-0	-	-	-	-	1-1
Wycombe v Fleetwood	-	-	-	-	-	1-0

Scottish Premier League						
Aberdeen v Ross County	-	-	-	-	-	0-0/0-1
Hibernian v Kilmarnock	4-1/2-0	2-4	1-0/1-0	2-1/2-1	1-1/0-1	2-1/2-2
Inverness CT v Celtic	3-2	1-2/0-0	-	0-1/3-2	0-2	2-4/1-3
Partick v Motherwell	-	-	-	-	-	-
St Johnstone v Dundee United	-	-	2-3/0-1	0-0	3-3/1-5/0-2	0-0/1-1
St Mirren v Hearts	1-3/1-1	0-1	2-1/1-1	0-2	0-0	2-0/2-0

Wednesday January 1st, 2014

Premier League						
Arsenal v Cardiff	-	-	-	-	-	-
Crystal Palace v Norwich	1-1	3-1	-	0-0	-	-
Fulham v West Ham	0-1	1-2	3-2	1-3	-	3-1
Liverpool v Hull	-	2-2	6-1	-	-	-
Man United v Tottenham	1-0	5-2	3-1	2-0	3-0	2-3
Southampton v Chelsea	-	-	-	-	-	2-1
Stoke v Everton	-	2-3	0-0	2-0	1-1	1-1
Sunderland v Aston Villa	1-1	1-2	0-2	1-0	2-2	0-1
Swansea v Man City	-	-	-	-	1-0	0-0
West Brom v Newcastle	-	2-3	1-1	3-1	1-3	1-1

Championship						
Birmingham v Barnsley	-	2-0	-	-	1-1	0-5
Bolton v Middlesbrough	0-0	4-1	-	-	-	2-1
Brighton v Bournemouth	3-2	-	-	1-1	-	-
Burnley v Huddersfield	-	-	-	-	-	0-1
Derby v Wigan	0-1	-	-	-	-	-
Ipswich v Charlton	2-0	1-1	-	-	-	1-2
Leeds v Blackburn	-	-	-	-	-	3-3
Millwall v Leicester	-	0-1	-	2-0	2-1	1-0
QPR v Doncaster	-	2-0	2-1	3-0	-	-
Reading v Nottm Forest	-	0-1	0-0	1-1	1-0	-
Sheffield Weds v Blackpool	2-1	1-1	2-0	-	-	0-2
Yeovil v Watford	-	-	-	-	-	-

League 1						
Crewe v Carlisle	0-1	1-2	-	-	-	1-0
Leyton Orient v Bristol City	-	-	-	-	-	-
MK Dons v Colchester	-	1-1	2-1	1-1	1-0	5-1
Notts County v Bradford	1-3	3-1	5-0	-	-	-
Oldham v Shrewsbury	-	-	-	-	-	1-0
Peterborough v Brentford	7-0	-	-	2-1	-	-
Preston v Port Vale	-	-	-	-	-	-
Rotherham v Coventry	-	-	-	-	-	-
Stevenage v Gillingham	-	-	-	2-2	-	-
Swindon v Crawley	-	-	-	-	3-0	3-0
Tranmere v Wolves	-	-	-	-	-	-
Walsall v Sheffield United	-	-	-	-	3-2	1-1

Results cover matches from Premier League to Conference and Scottish Premier League to Division Three

	2007-08	2008-09	2009-10	2010-11	2011-12	2012-13
League 2						
Bristol Rovers v Cheltenham	2-0	3-2	-	-	1-3	0-1
Dag & Red v AFC Wimbledon	-	-	-	-	0-2	0-1
Exeter v Wycombe	-	1-0	1-1	-	1-3	3-2
Fleetwood v Accrington	-	-	-	-	-	1-3
Hartlepool v Bury	-	-	-	-	3-0	2-0
Mansfield v Burton	-	0-2	-	-	-	-
Newport County v Oxford	-	-	-	-	-	-
Northampton v Chesterfield	-	-	0-0	1-2	-	0-0
Plymouth v Torquay	-	-	-	-	1-2	1-1
Scunthorpe v Rochdale	-	-	-	-	1-0	-
Southend v Portsmouth	-	-	-	-	-	-
York v Morecambe	-	-	-	-	-	1-4
Conference						
Aldershot v Forest Green	0-1	-	-	-	-	-
Alfreton v Wrexham	-	-	-	-	1-4	1-2
Braintree v Cambridge	-	-	-	-	3-2	0-3
Chester v Southport	-	-	-	-	-	-
Grimsby v Lincoln	1-0	5-1	2-2	-	3-1	1-1
Halifax v Gateshead	-	-	-	-	-	-
Hereford v Kidderminster	-	-	-	-	-	0-1
Hyde v Macclesfield	-	-	-	-	-	1-1
Luton v Barnet	-	3-1	-	-	-	-
Nuneaton v Tamworth	-	-	-	-	-	2-1
Salisbury v Woking	2-1	1-0	-	-	-	-
Welling v Dartford	-	-	-	-	-	-
Scottish Premier League						
Celtic v Partick	-	-	-	-	-	-
Dundee United v Aberdeen	1-0/3-0	2-1/1-1	0-1	3-1/3-1	1-2	1-1/1-0
Hibernian v Hearts	1-1	1-1/1-0	1-1/1-2	0-2/2-2	1-3	1-1/0-0
Inverness CT v Ross County	-	-	1-3/3-0	-	-	3-1/2-1
Kilmarnock v St Mirren	0-0/1-0	0-1/2-1	1-2/1-1	2-1/2-0	2-1/0-2	3-1/1-1/1-3
Motherwell v St Johnstone	-	-	1-3	4-0	0-3/3-2/5-1	1-1/3-2

Thursday January 2nd, 2014

	2007-08	2008-09	2009-10	2010-11	2011-12	2012-13
Scottish Division One						
Alloa v Cowdenbeath	3-2/3-2	-	2-1/3-1	-	-	-
Dumbarton v Morton	-	-	-	-	-	1-5/0-3
Hamilton v Queen of Sth	1-0/1-0	-	-	-	3-1/3-0	-
Livingston v Falkirk	-	-	-	-	1-1/1-2	2-1/1-2
Raith v Dundee	-	-	2-2/1-0	1-2/2-1	0-1/0-1	-
Scottish Division Two						
Airdrieonians v Rangers	-	-	-	-	-	-
Brechin v Forfar	-	-	-	0-0/0-1	0-1/2-1	4-1/3-4
East Fife v Arbroath	0-2/2-1	3-2/0-0	1-1/3-1	-	2-2/1-3	2-1/0-1
Stenhousemuir v Dunfermline	-	-	-	-	-	-
Stranraer v Ayr	-	1-3/1-4	-	-	-	2-0/0-1
Scottish Division Three						
Annan v Albion	-	2-4/1-1	0-0/1-2	4-1/2-2	-	-
Clyde v Queen's Park	-	-	-	2-3/0-2	0-2/1-2	0-3/2-3
Montrose v Berwick	-	1-1/1-1	1-3/1-1	1-1/1-1	3-5/1-1	3-1/1-3
Peterhead v Elgin	-	-	-	-	1-3/3-0	1-1/0-1
Stirling v East Stirling	-	-	-	-	-	1-1/9-1

Results cover matches from Premier League to Conference and Scottish Premier League to Division Three

Saturday January 4th, 2014

League 1

	2007-08	2008-09	2009-10	2010-11	2011-12	2012-13
Bristol City v Coventry	2-1	2-0	1-1	1-2	3-1	-
Carlisle v Bradford	-	-	-	-	-	-
Crawley v Tranmere	-	-	-	-	-	2-5
Crewe v MK Dons	-	2-2	-	-	-	2-1
Gillingham v Wolves	-	-	-	-	-	-
Peterborough v Notts County	0-0	-	-	2-3	-	-
Port Vale v Colchester	-	-	-	-	-	-
Preston v Rotherham	-	-	-	-	-	-
Sheffield United v Brentford	-	-	-	-	2-0	2-2
Shrewsbury v Leyton Orient	-	-	-	-	-	0-2
Stevenage v Swindon	-	-	-	-	-	0-4
Walsall v Oldham	0-3	1-2	3-0	1-1	0-1	3-1

League 2

	2007-08	2008-09	2009-10	2010-11	2011-12	2012-13
Bury v Oxford	-	-	-	3-0	-	-
Cheltenham v Chesterfield	-	-	0-1	0-3	-	1-0
Exeter v Mansfield	-	-	-	-	-	-
Fleetwood v Plymouth	-	-	-	-	-	3-0
Newport County v Northampton	-	-	-	-	-	-
Portsmouth v Accrington	-	-	-	-	-	-
Rochdale v Burton	-	-	1-2	-	-	0-1
Scunthorpe v Bristol Rovers	-	0-2	-	-	-	-
Southend v Hartlepool	2-1	3-2	3-2	-	-	-
Torquay v Morecambe	-	-	2-2	3-1	1-1	1-0
Wycombe v AFC Wimbledon	-	-	-	-	-	0-1
York v Dag & Red	-	-	-	-	-	3-2

Conference

	2007-08	2008-09	2009-10	2010-11	2011-12	2012-13
Barnet v Alfreton	-	-	-	-	-	-
Cambridge v Grimsby	-	-	-	1-1	0-1	0-0
Forest Green v Salisbury	0-3	1-2	3-1	-	-	-
Gateshead v Hyde	-	-	-	-	-	3-0
Kidderminster v Dartford	-	-	-	-	-	5-1
Lincoln v Luton	-	0-0	-	-	1-1	1-2
Macclesfield v Chester	1-2	3-1	-	-	-	-
Southport v Nuneaton	-	-	-	-	-	3-1
Tamworth v Halifax	-	-	-	-	-	-
Welling v Braintree	-	-	-	-	-	-
Woking v Hereford	-	-	-	-	-	1-1
Wrexham v Aldershot	-	-	-	-	-	-

Scottish Premier League

	2007-08	2008-09	2009-10	2010-11	2011-12	2012-13
Dundee United v Hibernian	0-0/1-1/1-1	2-0/2-2	1-0/0-2	1-0/3-0	3-1	3-0/2-2
Hearts v Partick	-	-	-	-	-	-
Kilmarnock v Aberdeen	0-1/3-1	1-2	1-1/2-0	2-0	2-0/1-1	1-3/1-1
Motherwell v Inverness CT	2-1/3-1	3-2/2-2	-	0-0	3-0/0-1	4-1/3-0
Ross County v St Johnstone	-	1-2/2-2	-	-	-	1-2/1-0
St Mirren v Celtic	1-5/0-1	1-3	0-2/4-0	0-1	0-2/0-2	0-5/1-1

Saturday January 11th, 2014

Premier League

	2007-08	2008-09	2009-10	2010-11	2011-12	2012-13
Aston Villa v Arsenal	1-2	2-2	0-0	2-4	1-2	0-0
Cardiff v West Ham	-	-	-	-	0-2	-
Everton v Norwich	-	-	-	-	1-1	1-1
Fulham v Sunderland	1-3	0-0	1-0	0-0	2-1	1-3
Hull v Chelsea	-	0-3	1-1	-	-	-
Man United v Swansea	-	-	-	-	2-0	2-1

Results cover matches from Premier League to Conference and Scottish Premier League to Division Three

	2007-08	2008-09	2009-10	2010-11	2011-12	2012-13
Newcastle v Man City	0-2	2-2	-	1-3	0-2	1-3
Southampton v West Brom	3-2	-	-	-	-	0-3
Stoke v Liverpool	-	0-0	1-1	2-0	1-0	3-1
Tottenham v Crystal Palace	-	-	-	-	-	-
Championship						
Blackburn v Doncaster	-	-	-	-	-	-
Blackpool v Middlesbrough	-	-	2-0	-	3-0	4-1
Bolton v Nottm Forest	-	-	-	-	-	2-2
Brighton v Birmingham	-	-	-	-	1-1	0-1
Charlton v Barnsley	1-1	1-3	-	-	-	0-1
Huddersfield v Millwall	1-0	1-2	1-0	-	-	3-0
Ipswich v QPR	0-0	2-0	3-0	0-3	-	-
Leicester v Derby	-	-	0-0	2-0	4-0	4-1
Sheffield Weds v Leeds	-	-	-	-	-	1-1
Watford v Reading	-	2-2	3-0	1-1	1-2	-
Wigan v Bournemouth	-	-	-	-	-	-
Yeovil v Burnley	-	-	-	-	-	-
League 1						
Bradford v Bristol City	-	-	-	-	-	-
Brentford v Port Vale	-	2-0	-	-	-	-
Colchester v Gillingham	-	-	2-1	-	-	-
Coventry v Crawley	-	-	-	-	-	3-1
Leyton Orient v Carlisle	0-3	0-0	2-2	0-0	1-2	4-1
MK Dons v Shrewsbury	3-0	-	-	-	-	2-3
Notts County v Sheffield United	-	-	-	-	2-5	1-1
Oldham v Stevenage	-	-	-	-	1-1	0-1
Rotherham v Crewe	-	-	0-0	3-1	1-1	-
Swindon v Peterborough	-	2-2	-	1-1	-	-
Tranmere v Walsall	0-0	2-1	2-3	3-3	2-1	0-0
Wolves v Preston	1-0	1-3	-	-	-	-
League 2						
Accrington v Newport County	-	-	-	-	-	-
AFC Wimbledon v Torquay	-	-	-	-	2-0	0-1
Bristol Rovers v Exeter	-	-	1-0	0-2	-	2-0
Burton v Cheltenham	-	-	5-6	2-0	0-2	3-1
Chesterfield v Bury	3-1	1-3	1-0	2-3	1-0	-
Dag & Red v Fleetwood	-	-	-	-	-	1-0
Hartlepool v Rochdale	-	-	-	0-2	2-0	-
Mansfield v Scunthorpe	-	-	-	-	-	-
Morecambe v Wycombe	0-1	0-0	-	0-3	-	0-1
Northampton v York	-	-	-	-	-	0-2
Oxford v Portsmouth	-	-	-	-	-	-
Plymouth v Southend	-	-	-	-	2-2	1-1
Conference						
Barnet v Grimsby	0-3	3-3	3-0	-	-	-
Cambridge v Alfreton	-	-	-	-	3-0	0-3
Dartford v Aldershot	-	-	-	-	-	-
Forest Green v Hereford	-	-	-	-	-	0-1
Gateshead v Nuneaton	-	-	-	-	-	0-2
Kidderminster v Salisbury	1-2	3-2	0-1	-	-	-
Lincoln v Welling	-	-	-	-	-	-
Macclesfield v Luton	-	2-1	-	-	-	1-1
Southport v Hyde	-	-	-	-	-	0-1
Tamworth v Chester	-	-	-	-	-	-
Woking v Braintree	-	-	-	-	-	1-4
Wrexham v Halifax	-	-	-	-	-	-

Results cover matches from Premier League to Conference and Scottish Premier League to Division Three

	2007-08	2008-09	2009-10	2010-11	2011-12	2012-13
Scottish Premier League						
Aberdeen v Hibernian	3-1/2-1	1-2/2-1	0-2	4-2/0-1	1-0/1-2	2-1/0-0
Celtic v Kilmarnock	0-0/1-0	3-0	3-0/3-1	1-1	2-1	0-2/4-1
Hearts v Motherwell	1-2	3-2/2-1	1-0/0-2	0-2/0-0/3-3	2-0/0-1	1-0/1-2
Inverness CT v Dundee United	0-3/1-1	1-3	-	0-2	2-3	4-0/0-0/1-2
Partick v Ross County	-	0-1/0-2	0-0/2-1	1-1/1-1	0-1/0-1	-
St Johnstone v St Mirren	-	-	1-0/2-2	2-1/0-0	0-1	2-1/1-0
Scottish Division One						
Cowdenbeath v Dumbarton	-	2-0/0-0	2-1/0-0	-	0-0/4-1	0-1/2-3
Dundee v Livingston	4-1/2-0	0-3/4-1	-	-	3-0/1-0	-
Falkirk v Hamilton	-	4-1/1-2	2-0/0-1	-	0-0/3-0	2-1/0-2
Morton v Raith	-	-	5-0/1-1	0-1/0-0	1-1/1-3	1-0/1-0
Queen of Sth v Alloa	-	-	-	-	-	1-0/0-0
Scottish Division Two						
Arbroath v Brechin	-	1-2/0-0	1-4/1-0	-	1-1/2-3	3-1/0-1
Ayr v Airdrieonians	1-1/1-2	-	1-1/1-4	1-0/3-1	-	-
Dunfermline v Stranraer	-	-	-	-	-	-
Forfar v Stenhousemuir	0-1/1-2	1-0/4-4	-	1-1/2-0	2-3/1-2	3-2/3-3
Rangers v East Fife	-	-	-	-	-	-
Scottish Division Three						
Albion v Montrose	1-3/0-3	0-1/0-1	0-0/1-0	3-1/0-2	-	-
Berwick v Annan	-	3-0/1-1	2-1/0-2	2-2/2-3	0-1/1-3	3-1/0-2
East Stirling v Peterhead	-	-	-	-	0-2/6-3	2-1/2-4
Elgin v Clyde	-	-	-	0-1/0-1	0-3/1-1	2-1/4-2
Queen's Park v Stirling	-	1-1/3-1	-	-	-	2-1/2-2

Saturday January 18th, 2014

	2007-08	2008-09	2009-10	2010-11	2011-12	2012-13
Premier League						
Arsenal v Fulham	2-1	0-0	4-0	2-1	1-1	3-3
Chelsea v Man United	2-1	1-1	1-0	2-1	3-3	2-3
Crystal Palace v Stoke	1-3	-	-	-	-	-
Liverpool v Aston Villa	2-2	5-0	1-3	3-0	1-1	1-3
Man City v Cardiff	-	-	-	-	-	-
Norwich v Hull	1-1	-	-	0-2	-	-
Sunderland v Southampton	-	-	-	-	-	1-1
Swansea v Tottenham	-	-	-	-	1-1	1-2
West Brom v Everton	-	1-2	-	1-0	0-1	2-0
West Ham v Newcastle	2-2	3-1	-	1-2	-	0-0
Championship						
Barnsley v Blackpool	2-1	0-1	1-0	-	1-3	1-1
Birmingham v Yeovil	-	-	-	-	-	-
Bournemouth v Watford	-	-	-	-	-	-
Burnley v Sheffield Weds	1-1	2-4	-	-	-	3-3
Derby v Brighton	-	-	-	-	0-1	0-0
Doncaster v Wigan	-	-	-	-	-	-
Leeds v Leicester	-	1-1	-	1-2	1-2	1-0
Middlesbrough v Charlton	-	-	-	-	-	2-2
Millwall v Ipswich	-	-	-	2-1	4-1	0-0
Nottm Forest v Blackburn	-	-	-	-	-	0-0
QPR v Huddersfield	-	-	-	-	-	-
Reading v Bolton	0-2	-	-	-	-	-
League 1						
Bristol City v MK Dons	-	-	-	-	-	-
Carlisle v Colchester	-	0-2	2-1	4-1	1-0	0-2

Results cover matches from Premier League to Conference and Scottish Premier League to Division Three

	2007-08	2008-09	2009-10	2010-11	2011-12	2012-13
Crawley v Wolves	-	-	-	-	-	-
Crewe v Leyton Orient	0-2	0-2	-	-	-	1-1
Gillingham v Swindon	1-1	-	5-0	-	3-1	-
Peterborough v Tranmere	-	2-2	-	2-1	-	-
Port Vale v Oldham	0-3	-	-	-	-	-
Preston v Coventry	1-0	2-1	3-2	2-1	-	2-2
Sheffield United v Bradford	-	-	-	-	-	-
Shrewsbury v Rotherham	1-1	1-0	2-0	1-0	3-1	-
Stevenage v Notts County	-	-	-	-	0-2	2-0
Walsall v Brentford	-	-	2-1	3-2	0-1	2-2
League 2						
Bury v Burton	-	-	3-0	1-0	-	-
Cheltenham v Accrington	-	-	1-1	1-2	4-1	0-3
Exeter v Morecambe	-	2-2	-	-	-	0-3
Fleetwood v Hartlepool	-	-	-	-	-	-
Newport County v Dag & Red	-	-	-	-	-	-
Portsmouth v Mansfield	-	-	-	-	-	-
Rochdale v Plymouth	-	-	-	1-1	-	1-0
Scunthorpe v AFC Wimbledon	-	-	-	-	-	-
Southend v Chesterfield	-	-	-	2-3	-	3-0
Torquay v Northampton	-	-	1-0	3-0	1-0	1-1
Wycombe v Oxford	-	-	-	0-0	-	1-3
York v Bristol Rovers	-	-	-	-	-	4-1
Conference						
Aldershot v Kidderminster	2-1	-	-	-	-	-
Alfreton v Tamworth	-	-	-	-	5-2	3-0
Braintree v Lincoln	-	-	-	-	1-0	0-3
Chester v Barnet	3-0	5-1	-	-	-	-
Grimsby v Gateshead	-	-	-	2-2	2-0	3-0
Halifax v Cambridge	1-2	-	-	-	-	-
Hereford v Southport	-	-	-	-	-	2-2
Hyde v Forest Green	-	-	-	-	-	0-1
Luton v Wrexham	-	-	1-0	1-1	0-1	0-0
Nuneaton v Macclesfield	-	-	-	-	-	3-3
Salisbury v Dartford	-	-	-	-	-	-
Welling v Woking	-	-	-	-	-	-
Scottish Premier League						
Aberdeen v Inverness CT	1-0	0-2/1-0	-	1-2/1-0	2-1/0-1	2-3
Celtic v Motherwell	3-0/0-1	2-0	0-0/2-1/4-0	1-0/4-0	4-0/1-0	1-0
Hibernian v St Mirren	0-1/2-0	2-0	2-1/2-1	2-0/1-1	1-2/0-0	2-1/3-3
Partick v Kilmarnock	-	-	-	-	-	-
Ross County v Dundee United	-	-	-	-	-	1-2/1-0
St Johnstone v Hearts	-	-	2-2/1-0	0-2	2-0/2-1	2-2
Scottish Division One						
Alloa v Dumbarton	-	-	1-3/1-2	0-0/2-3	-	-
Cowdenbeath v Falkirk	-	-	-	0-0/1-2	-	1-1/4-1
Dundee v Hamilton	1-0/1-1	-	-	-	0-1/2-2	-
Livingston v Morton	4-0/6-1	1-0/0-2	-	-	1-1/0-0	2-2/0-2
Queen of Sth v Raith	-	-	1-1/3-0	1-3/0-2	1-3/1-0	-
Scottish Division Two						
Arbroath v Stenhousemuir	2-2/1-0	-	0-3/1-1	-	1-0/0-2	2-2/0-0
Ayr v Brechin	2-1/0-3	1-1/4-2	-	0-2/2-0	-	3-0/1-2
Dunfermline v Airdrieonians	-	0-0/1-1	2-0/2-0	-	-	1-3/1-2
Forfar v Rangers	-	-	-	-	-	-
Stranraer v East Fife	0-2/0-2	0-4/0-1	-	-	-	2-6/3-1

Results cover matches from Premier League to Conference and Scottish Premier League to Division Three

	2007-08	2008-09	2009-10	2010-11	2011-12	2012-13
Scottish Division Three						
Annan v Clyde	-	-	-	0-2/1-0	1-0/1-0	1-3/0-1
Berwick v Stirling	-	-	-	-	-	4-1/1-0
East Stirling v Albion	4-5/3-0	1-0/0-1	2-0/3-1	0-0/1-2	-	-
Montrose v Peterhead	-	-	-	-	2-1/1-3	2-0/0-6
Queen's Park v Elgin	-	-	0-3/0-1	1-1/1-0	6-0/1-3	1-1/0-1

Saturday January 25th, 2014

	2007-08	2008-09	2009-10	2010-11	2011-12	2012-13
Championship						
Blackburn v Derby	3-1	-	-	-	-	2-0
Blackpool v Doncaster	-	2-3	2-0	-	2-1	-
Bolton v Burnley	-	-	1-0	-	-	2-1
Brighton v Leeds	0-1	0-2	0-3	-	3-3	2-2
Charlton v Bournemouth	-	-	-	1-0	3-0	-
Huddersfield v Nottm Forest	1-1	-	-	-	-	1-1
Ipswich v Reading	-	2-0	2-1	1-3	2-3	-
Leicester v Middlesbrough	-	-	2-0	0-0	2-2	1-0
Sheffield Weds v QPR	2-1	1-0	1-2	-	-	-
Watford v Birmingham	-	0-1	-	-	2-2	2-0
Wigan v Barnsley	-	-	-	-	-	-
Yeovil v Millwall	0-1	2-0	1-1	-	-	-
League 1						
Bradford v Port Vale	-	0-1	0-0	0-2	1-1	0-1
Brentford v Gillingham	-	1-1	4-0	-	-	-
Colchester v Sheffield United	2-2	-	-	-	1-1	1-1
Coventry v Carlisle	-	-	-	-	-	1-2
Leyton Orient v Stevenage	-	-	-	-	0-0	0-1
MK Dons v Preston	-	-	-	-	0-1	1-1
Notts County v Walsall	-	-	-	1-1	2-1	0-1
Oldham v Peterborough	-	1-2	-	0-5	-	-
Rotherham v Crawley	-	-	-	-	1-2	-
Swindon v Shrewsbury	-	-	-	-	2-1	2-0
Tranmere v Crewe	1-1	2-0	-	-	-	2-1
Wolves v Bristol City	1-1	2-0	-	-	-	2-1
League 2						
Accrington v Bury	0-2	1-2	2-4	1-0	-	-
AFC Wimbledon v Exeter	-	-	-	-	-	2-2
Bristol Rovers v Newport County	-	-	-	-	-	-
Burton v Fleetwood	-	-	-	-	-	0-1
Chesterfield v Rochdale	3-4	3-0	2-0	-	2-1	1-1
Dag & Red v Scunthorpe	-	-	-	-	-	-
Hartlepool v York	-	-	-	-	-	-
Mansfield v Wycombe	0-4	-	-	-	-	-
Morecambe v Portsmouth	-	-	-	-	-	-
Northampton v Southend	0-1	2-3	-	2-1	2-5	3-3
Oxford v Torquay	3-3	0-2	-	0-2	2-2	0-0
Plymouth v Cheltenham	-	-	-	-	1-2	2-0
Conference						
Aldershot v Halifax	1-0	-	-	-	-	-
Barnet v Southport	-	-	-	-	-	-
Braintree v Gateshead	-	-	-	-	3-1	2-1
Dartford v Cambridge	-	-	-	-	-	1-1
Forest Green v Chester	-	-	-	-	-	-
Hereford v Salisbury	-	-	-	-	-	-
Hyde v Tamworth	-	-	-	-	-	2-1

Results cover matches from Premier League to Conference and Scottish Premier League to Division Three

	2007-08	2008-09	2009-10	2010-11	2011-12	2012-13
Kidderminster v Macclesfield	-	-	-	-	-	3-0
Lincoln v Woking	-	-	-	-	-	0-2
Luton v Nuneaton	-	-	-	-	-	2-0
Welling v Alfreton	-	-	-	-	-	-
Wrexham v Grimsby	0-0	-	-	2-0	2-2	0-0
Scottish Premier League						
Dundee United v St Johnstone	-	-	3-3	1-0/2-0	0-0	1-1/0-1
Hibernian v Celtic	3-2/0-2	2-0/0-0	0-1/0-1	0-3	0-2/0-5	1-0
Kilmarnock v Inverness CT	2-2/4-1	1-2/1-0	-	1-2/1-1	3-6/4-3	1-2
Motherwell v Aberdeen	3-0/2-1	0-1/1-1	1-1	1-1/2-1	1-0/1-0	4-1
Ross County v Hearts	-	-	-	-	-	2-2
St Mirren v Partick	-	-	-	-	-	-
Scottish Division One						
Dumbarton v Livingston	-	-	-	1-2/0-3	-	3-4/0-3
Falkirk v Dundee	-	-	-	3-3/2-2	2-1/1-1	-
Hamilton v Cowdenbeath	-	-	-	-	-	2-1/1-3
Morton v Queen of Sth	0-1/0-3	0-0/2-2	1-2/3-3	2-0/0-4	2-2/2-2	-
Raith v Alloa	2-1/3-2	4-1/3-1	-	-	-	-
Scottish Division Two						
Airdrieonians v Stranraer	-	-	-	-	-	-
Brechin v Dunfermline	-	-	-	-	-	-
East Fife v Forfar	3-0/3-0	-	-	1-3/3-0	4-3/4-0	3-0/1-2
Rangers v Arbroath	-	-	-	-	-	-
Stenhousemuir v Ayr	-	-	-	3-1/2-1	-	1-1/4-0
Scottish Division Three						
Albion v Berwick	-	2-0/2-1	2-1/4-1	2-2/0-1	-	-
Clyde v East Stirling	-	-	-	1-2/2-0	7-1/3-0	2-1/2-0
Elgin v Montrose	0-2/2-1	1-2/1-0	0-1/5-2	3-2/1-0	3-1/2-1	6-1/3-2
Peterhead v Queen's Park	1-0/1-0	4-1/1-1	-	-	1-1/2-1	1-0/0-2
Stirling v Annan	-	-	-	-	-	5-1/2-1

Tuesday January 28th, 2014

	2007-08	2008-09	2009-10	2010-11	2011-12	2012-13
Premier League						
Aston Villa v West Brom	-	2-1	-	2-1	1-2	1-1
Crystal Palace v Hull	1-1	-	-	0-0	0-0	4-2
Liverpool v Everton	1-0	1-1	1-0	2-2	3-0	0-0
Man United v Cardiff	-	-	-	-	-	-
Norwich v Newcastle	-	-	-	-	4-2	0-0
Southampton v Arsenal	-	-	-	-	-	1-1
Sunderland v Stoke	-	2-0	0-0	2-0	4-0	1-1
Swansea v Fulham	-	-	-	-	2-0	0-3
Championship						
Barnsley v Blackburn	-	-	-	-	-	1-3
Birmingham v Leicester	-	-	-	-	2-0	1-1
Bournemouth v Huddersfield	0-1	-	-	1-1	2-0	-
Burnley v Brighton	-	-	-	-	1-0	1-3
Derby v Yeovil	-	-	-	-	-	-
Doncaster v Charlton	-	0-1	-	-	-	-
Leeds v Ipswich	-	-	-	0-0	3-1	2-0
Middlesbrough v Wigan	1-0	0-0	-	-	-	-
Millwall v Sheffield Weds	-	-	-	-	-	1-2
QPR v Bolton	-	-	-	-	0-4	-
Reading v Blackpool	-	1-0	2-1	-	3-1	-

Results cover matches from Premier League to Conference and Scottish Premier League to Division Three

	2007-08	2008-09	2009-10	2010-11	2011-12	2012-13
League 1						
Bradford v Preston	-	-	-	-	-	-
Brentford v Bristol City	-	-	-	-	-	-
Carlisle v MK Dons	-	3-2	5-0	4-1	1-3	1-1
Colchester v Shrewsbury	-	-	-	-	-	0-0
Leyton Orient v Coventry	-	-	-	-	-	0-1
Notts County v Gillingham	-	0-1	-	-	-	-
Oldham v Wolves	-	-	-	-	-	-
Port Vale v Crawley	-	-	-	-	2-2	-
Sheffield United v Peterborough	-	-	1-0	-	-	-
Stevenage v Crewe	-	-	-	1-1	-	2-2
Tranmere v Rotherham	-	-	-	-	-	-
Walsall v Swindon	2-2	2-1	1-1	1-2	-	0-2
League 2						
AFC Wimbledon v Hartlepool	-	-	-	-	-	-
Bristol Rovers v Accrington	-	-	-	-	5-1	0-1
Dag & Red v Southend	-	-	-	-	2-3	0-3
Exeter v Oxford	2-0	-	-	-	-	1-3
Mansfield v Bury	1-1	-	-	-	-	-
Morecambe v Cheltenham	-	-	1-0	1-1	3-1	0-0
Newport County v Plymouth	-	-	-	-	-	-
Northampton v Rochdale	-	-	1-2	-	-	3-1
Scunthorpe v Fleetwood	-	-	-	-	-	-
Torquay v Burton	1-2	2-1	2-3	1-0	2-2	1-1
Wycombe v Portsmouth	-	-	-	-	-	-
York v Chesterfield	-	-	-	-	-	2-2
Conference						
Salisbury v Nuneaton	-	-	-	-	-	-

Wednesday January 29th, 2014

	2007-08	2008-09	2009-10	2010-11	2011-12	2012-13
Premier League						
Chelsea v West Ham	1-0	1-1	4-1	3-0	-	2-0
Tottenham v Man City	2-1	2-1	3-0	0-0	1-5	3-1
Championship						
Nottm Forest v Watford	-	3-2	2-4	1-0	1-1	0-3

Saturday February 1st, 2014

	2007-08	2008-09	2009-10	2010-11	2011-12	2012-13
Premier League						
Arsenal v Crystal Palace	-	-	-	-	-	-
Cardiff v Norwich	1-2	2-2	-	3-1	-	-
Everton v Aston Villa	2-2	2-3	1-1	2-2	2-2	3-3
Fulham v Southampton	-	-	-	-	-	1-1
Hull v Tottenham	-	1-2	1-5	-	-	-
Man City v Chelsea	0-2	1-3	2-1	1-0	2-1	2-0
Newcastle v Sunderland	2-0	1-1	-	5-1	1-1	0-3
Stoke v Man United	-	0-1	0-2	1-2	1-1	0-2
West Brom v Liverpool	-	0-2	-	2-1	0-2	3-0
West Ham v Swansea	-	-	-	-	-	1-0
Championship						
Birmingham v Derby	1-1	1-0	-	-	2-2	3-1
Blackburn v Blackpool	-	-	-	2-2	-	1-1
Bournemouth v Leicester	-	-	-	-	-	-
Doncaster v Middlesbrough	-	-	1-4	2-1	1-3	-
Ipswich v Bolton	-	-	-	-	-	1-0
Leeds v Huddersfield	4-0	1-2	2-2	-	-	1-2
Millwall v Reading	-	-	-	0-0	1-2	-

Results cover matches from Premier League to Conference and Scottish Premier League to Division Three

	2007-08	2008-09	2009-10	2010-11	2011-12	2012-13
Nottm Forest v Yeovil	3-2	-	-	-	-	-
QPR v Burnley	2-4	1-2	-	1-1	-	-
Sheffield Weds v Barnsley	1-0	0-1	2-2	-	-	2-1
Watford v Brighton	-	-	-	-	1-0	0-1
Wigan v Charlton	-	-	-	-	-	-
League 1						
Bristol City v Carlisle	-	-	-	-	-	-
Coventry v Walsall	-	-	-	-	-	5-1
Crawley v Stevenage	2-1	0-2	0-3	-	-	1-1
Crewe v Sheffield United	-	-	-	-	-	1-0
Gillingham v Port Vale	1-2	1-0	-	3-0	1-1	1-2
MK Dons v Tranmere	-	1-0	1-0	2-0	3-0	3-0
Peterborough v Colchester	-	2-1	-	1-1	-	-
Preston v Notts County	-	-	-	-	2-0	0-0
Rotherham v Leyton Orient	-	-	-	-	-	-
Shrewsbury v Brentford	0-1	1-3	-	-	-	0-0
Swindon v Oldham	3-0	2-0	4-2	0-2	-	1-1
Wolves v Bradford	-	-	-	-	-	-
League 2						
Accrington v Morecambe	3-2	1-0	3-2	1-1	1-1	2-0
Burton v Exeter	4-4	-	-	-	-	4-2
Bury v Wycombe	2-2	0-0	-	1-3	1-4	-
Cheltenham v Northampton	1-1	0-1	2-2	1-0	2-2	1-0
Chesterfield v Bristol Rovers	-	-	-	-	-	2-0
Fleetwood v York	-	-	-	2-1	0-0	0-0
Hartlepool v Scunthorpe	-	2-3	-	-	1-2	2-0
Oxford v AFC Wimbledon	-	-	2-0	-	1-0	3-2
Plymouth v Mansfield	-	-	-	-	-	-
Portsmouth v Torquay	-	-	-	-	-	-
Rochdale v Dag & Red	1-0	0-2	3-1	3-2	-	2-2
Southend v Newport County	-	-	-	-	-	-
Conference						
Alfreton v Hyde	-	-	-	-	-	5-1
Cambridge v Wrexham	-	2-0	2-0	1-3	1-1	1-4
Chester v Welling	-	-	-	-	-	-
Dartford v Luton	-	-	-	-	-	1-0
Gateshead v Kidderminster	-	-	0-2	2-2	2-1	2-0
Grimsby v Hereford	2-1	-	1-0	-	-	1-1
Lincoln v Halifax	-	-	-	-	-	-
Macclesfield v Barnet	3-0	2-1	1-1	1-1	0-0	-
Nuneaton v Aldershot	-	-	-	-	-	-
Southport v Braintree	-	-	-	-	0-4	0-2
Tamworth v Salisbury	-	-	2-0	-	-	-
Woking v Forest Green	1-1	0-1	-	-	-	2-0
Scottish Premier League						
Aberdeen v Celtic	1-3/1-5	4-2/1-3	1-3/4-4	0-3	0-1/1-1	0-2
Hearts v St Mirren	0-1/3-2	2-1/1-1	1-0	3-0/3-2	2-0/5-2	1-0/3-0
Inverness CT v Hibernian	2-0	1-1/2-0	-	4-2/2-0	0-1/2-3/2-0	3-0
Kilmarnock v Ross County	-	-	-	-	-	3-0
Partick v Dundee United	-	-	-	-	-	-
St Johnstone v Motherwell	-	-	2-2/1-2	0-2/1-0	0-3	1-3/2-0
Scottish Division One						
Cowdenbeath v Raith	1-0/1-4	-	-	1-2/0-3	-	4-4/1-1
Dundee v Alloa	-	-	-	-	-	-
Falkirk v Morton	-	-	-	2-1/1-0	1-0/0-2	0-1/4-1
Hamilton v Dumbarton	-	-	-	-	-	2-3/2-1

Results cover matches from Premier League to Conference and Scottish Premier League to Division Three

	2007-08	2008-09	2009-10	2010-11	2011-12	2012-13
Livingston v Queen of Sth	2-2/1-0	2-0/2-2	-	-	2-2/2-2	-
Scottish Division Two						
Arbroath v Ayr	-	0-3/1-3	-	-	-	4-2/1-4
East Fife v Dunfermline	-	-	-	-	-	-
Forfar v Airdrieonians	-	-	-	1-2/1-2	3-2/2-3	-
Rangers v Brechin	-	-	-	-	-	-
Stenhousemuir v Stranraer	1-4/1-1	-	-	-	-	0-0/1-2
Scottish Division Three						
Clyde v Berwick	-	-	-	1-4/2-0	1-4/2-2	2-1/2-1
Elgin v Albion	3-2/1-1	1-6/1-0	0-2/3-1	2-2/1-1	-	-
Montrose v Stirling	-	-	-	-	-	3-2/2-2
Peterhead v Annan	-	-	-	-	2-3/3-2	2-0/2-0
Queen's Park v East Stirling	-	-	1-0/2-0	2-0/2-0	2-0/5-1	1-2/5-1

Saturday February 8th, 2014

	2007-08	2008-09	2009-10	2010-11	2011-12	2012-13
Premier League						
Aston Villa v West Ham	1-0	1-1	0-0	3-0	-	2-1
Chelsea v Newcastle	2-1	0-0	-	2-2	0-2	2-0
Crystal Palace v West Brom	1-1	-	1-1	-	-	-
Liverpool v Arsenal	1-1	4-4	1-2	1-1	1-2	0-2
Man United v Fulham	2-0	3-0	3-0	2-0	1-0	3-2
Norwich v Man City	-	-	-	-	1-6	3-4
Southampton v Stoke	3-2	-	-	-	-	1-1
Sunderland v Hull	-	1-0	4-1	-	-	-
Swansea v Cardiff	-	2-2	3-2	0-1	-	-
Tottenham v Everton	1-3	0-1	2-1	1-1	2-0	2-2
Championship						
Barnsley v Ipswich	4-1	1-2	2-1	1-1	3-5	1-1
Blackpool v Nottm Forest	-	1-1	3-1	-	1-2	2-2
Bolton v Bournemouth	-	-	-	-	-	-
Brighton v Doncaster	1-0	-	-	-	2-1	-
Burnley v Millwall	-	-	-	0-3	1-3	2-2
Charlton v Birmingham	-	0-0	-	-	-	1-1
Derby v QPR	-	0-2	2-4	2-2	-	-
Huddersfield v Wigan	-	-	-	-	-	-
Leicester v Watford	4-1	-	4-1	4-2	2-0	1-2
Middlesbrough v Blackburn	1-2	0-0	-	-	-	1-0
Reading v Sheffield Weds	-	6-0	5-0	-	-	-
Yeovil v Leeds	0-1	1-1	1-2	-	-	-
League 1						
Bradford v Crewe	-	-	2-3	1-5	3-0	-
Brentford v Crawley	-	-	-	-	-	2-1
Carlisle v Gillingham	2-0	-	2-0	-	-	-
Colchester v Rotherham	-	-	-	-	-	-
Leyton Orient v Peterborough	-	2-3	-	2-1	-	-
Notts County v Coventry	-	-	-	-	-	2-2
Oldham v Bristol City	-	-	-	-	-	-
Port Vale v Swindon	2-1	-	-	-	0-2	-
Sheffield United v Shrewsbury	-	-	-	-	-	1-0
Stevenage v Wolves	-	-	-	-	-	-
Tranmere v Preston	-	-	-	-	2-1	1-1
Walsall v MK Dons	-	0-3	2-1	1-2	0-2	1-0
League 2						
AFC Wimbledon v Rochdale	-	-	-	-	-	1-2
Bristol Rovers v Oxford	-	-	-	-	0-0	0-2

Results cover matches from Premier League to Conference and Scottish Premier League to Division Three

	2007-08	2008-09	2009-10	2010-11	2011-12	2012-13
Dag & Red v Hartlepool	-	-	-	1-1	-	-
Exeter v Portsmouth	-	-	-	-	-	-
Mansfield v Southend	-	-	-	-	-	-
Morecambe v Burton	-	-	3-2	2-1	2-2	0-0
Newport County v Fleetwood	-	-	-	1-3	0-1	-
Northampton v Plymouth	-	-	-	-	0-0	1-0
Scunthorpe v Chesterfield	-	-	-	-	2-2	-
Torquay v Bury	-	-	1-1	3-4	-	-
Wycombe v Accrington	0-1	2-1	-	1-2	-	0-1
York v Cheltenham	-	-	-	-	-	0-0

Conference						
Aldershot v Chester	-	2-2	-	-	-	-
Braintree v Nuneaton	-	-	-	-	-	2-2
Forest Green v Barnet	-	-	-	-	-	-
Grimsby v Southport	-	-	-	1-1	0-1	2-2
Halifax v Woking	1-0	-	-	-	-	-
Hereford v Macclesfield	0-1	-	0-2	2-2	0-4	2-1
Hyde v Lincoln	-	-	-	-	-	1-5
Kidderminster v Cambridge	1-0	1-3	1-0	0-0	0-0	3-2
Luton v Tamworth	-	-	2-1	2-0	3-0	0-0
Salisbury v Alfreton	-	-	-	-	-	-
Welling v Gateshead	-	-	-	-	-	-
Wrexham v Dartford	-	-	-	-	-	2-2

Scottish Division Two						
Airdrieonians v Stenhousemuir	-	-	-	1-0/2-2	5-2/0-3	-
Ayr v Forfar	-	-	-	0-1/3-1	-	2-3/2-1
Brechin v East Fife	-	2-1/2-1	3-2/1-0	1-3/2-3	0-2/1-3	2-1/6-0
Dunfermline v Arbroath	-	-	-	-	-	-
Stranraer v Rangers	-	-	-	-	-	-

Scottish Division Three						
Albion v Clyde	-	-	-	3-1/1-1	-	-
Annan v Montrose	-	1-2/2-1	2-0/0-0	2-2/2-1	2-1/1-2	2-1/1-1
Berwick v Queen's Park	1-1/1-4	-	1-0/1-1	1-1/3-1	2-0/1-4	2-0/4-1
East Stirling v Elgin	3-1/0-0	5-2/1-0	1-1/2-0	0-2/2-1	1-1/2-2	1-4/3-2
Stirling v Peterhead	-	0-0/2-1	2-1/2-0	-	-	1-0/0-1

Tuesday February 11th, 2014

Premier League						
Arsenal v Man United	2-2	2-1	1-3	1-0	1-2	1-1
Cardiff v Aston Villa	-	-	-	-	-	-
Hull v Southampton	5-0	-	-	-	0-2	-
Stoke v Swansea	-	-	-	-	2-0	2-0
West Brom v Chelsea	-	0-3	-	1-3	1-0	2-1
West Ham v Norwich	-	-	-	-	-	2-1

Wednesday February 12th, 2014

Premier League						
Everton v Crystal Palace	-	-	-	-	-	-
Fulham v Liverpool	0-2	0-1	3-1	2-5	1-0	1-3
Man City v Sunderland	1-0	1-0	4-3	5-0	3-3	3-0
Newcastle v Tottenham	3-1	2-1	-	1-1	2-2	2-1

Saturday February 15th, 2014

Championship						
Birmingham v Huddersfield	-	-	-	-	-	0-1
Blackburn v Brighton	-	-	-	-	-	1-1

Results cover matches from Premier League to Conference and Scottish Premier League to Division Three

	2007-08	2008-09	2009-10	2010-11	2011-12	2012-13
Bournemouth v Burnley	-	-	-	-	-	-
Doncaster v Barnsley	-	0-1	0-1	0-2	2-0	-
Ipswich v Blackpool	2-1	1-1	3-1	-	2-2	1-0
Leeds v Charlton	-	-	0-0	-	-	1-1
Millwall v Bolton	-	-	-	-	-	2-1
Nottm Forest v Leicester	-	-	5-1	3-2	2-2	2-3
QPR v Reading	-	0-0	4-1	3-1	-	1-1
Sheffield Weds v Derby	-	0-1	0-0	-	-	2-2
Watford v Middlesbrough	-	-	1-1	3-1	2-1	1-2
Wigan v Yeovil	-	-	-	-	-	-
League 1						
Bristol City v Tranmere	-	-	-	-	-	-
Coventry v Bradford	-	-	-	-	-	-
Crawley v Carlisle	-	-	-	-	-	1-1
Crewe v Brentford	-	-	-	-	-	0-2
Gillingham v Sheffield United	-	-	-	-	-	-
MK Dons v Oldham	-	6-2	0-0	0-0	5-0	2-0
Peterborough v Walsall	-	1-0	-	4-1	-	-
Preston v Leyton Orient	-	-	-	-	0-2	0-0
Rotherham v Stevenage	-	-	-	1-1	-	-
Shrewsbury v Port Vale	-	1-2	0-1	2-2	1-0	-
Swindon v Colchester	-	1-3	1-1	2-1	-	0-1
Wolves v Notts County	-	-	-	-	-	-
League 2						
Accrington v Scunthorpe	-	-	-	-	-	-
Burton v Dag & Red	-	-	0-1	-	1-1	3-2
Bury v Bristol Rovers	-	-	-	-	-	-
Cheltenham v Wycombe	-	-	-	1-2	-	4-0
Chesterfield v Torquay	-	-	1-0	1-0	-	1-1
Fleetwood v Northampton	-	-	-	-	-	1-0
Hartlepool v Newport County	-	-	-	-	-	-
Oxford v Mansfield	-	1-0	2-0	-	-	-
Plymouth v York	-	-	-	-	-	2-0
Portsmouth v AFC Wimbledon	-	-	-	-	-	-
Rochdale v Morecambe	1-0	1-1	4-1	-	-	1-2
Southend v Exeter	-	-	0-0	-	-	2-1
Conference						
Alfreton v Aldershot	-	-	-	-	-	-
Barnet v Tamworth	-	-	-	-	-	-
Braintree v Wrexham	-	-	-	-	0-0	1-5
Cambridge v Welling	-	-	-	-	-	-
Chester v Halifax	-	-	-	-	-	-
Dartford v Grimsby	-	-	-	-	-	1-2
Gateshead v Woking	-	-	-	-	-	2-1
Lincoln v Kidderminster	-	-	-	-	0-1	1-0
Luton v Hereford	-	-	-	-	-	1-1
Macclesfield v Forest Green	-	-	-	-	-	1-2
Nuneaton v Hyde	-	-	-	-	-	3-1
Southport v Salisbury	-	-	-	-	-	-
Scottish Premier League						
Celtic v St Johnstone	-	-	5-2/3-0	2-0	0-1/2-0/1-0	1-1/4-0
Dundee United v Kilmarnock	2-0	0-2/0-0	0-0	1-1/4-2	1-1/4-0	3-3
Hibernian v Ross County	-	-	-	-	-	0-1
Inverness CT v Hearts	2-1/0-3	0-1	-	1-3/1-1	1-1/1-0	1-1
Motherwell v Partick	-	-	-	-	-	-
St Mirren v Aberdeen	0-1	0-1/1-1	1-0/0-1	2-1/3-2	1-0/1-1	1-4/0-0

Results cover matches from Premier League to Conference and Scottish Premier League to Division Three

	2007-08	2008-09	2009-10	2010-11	2011-12	2012-13
Scottish Division One						
Alloa v Livingston	-	-	-	2-2/1-3	-	-
Dumbarton v Falkirk	-	-	-	-	-	0-2/0-2
Morton v Cowdenbeath	-	-	-	1-2/3-0	-	1-0/4-2
Queen of Sth v Dundee	2-1/1-0	3-1/0-1	2-0/1-1	1-2/3-0	0-0/1-1	-
Raith v Hamilton	-	-	-	-	3-2/2-1	2-0/0-2
Scottish Division Two						
Airdrieonians v Brechin	2-1/1-2	-	-	1-1/2-2	2-3/4-1	-
Ayr v Rangers	-	-	-	-	-	-
Forfar v Dunfermline	-	-	-	-	-	-
Stenhousemuir v East Fife	2-1/0-1	-	1-1/1-1	1-1/0-2	2-1/1-0	3-0/2-1
Stranraer v Arbroath	1-1/0-3	2-2/1-5	-	4-1/3-4	-	1-1/2-0
Scottish Division Three						
Annan v East Stirling	-	2-1/4-0	0-1/1-0	3-1/2-1	3-0/2-2	5-2/1-2
Berwick v Elgin	-	1-1/2-1	2-0/2-1	6-2/4-0	1-1/3-3	0-0/2-1
Montrose v Queen's Park	-	-	1-2/1-2	1-2/0-2	0-1/3-1	1-1/1-2
Peterhead v Clyde	-	-	2-0/0-0	-	0-0/1-1	1-0/3-0
Stirling v Albion	-	-	-	-	2-2/3-0	-

Tuesday February 18th, 2014

	2007-08	2008-09	2009-10	2010-11	2011-12	2012-13
Conference						
Halifax v Braintree	-	-	-	-	-	-

Saturday February 22nd, 2014

	2007-08	2008-09	2009-10	2010-11	2011-12	2012-13
Premier League						
Arsenal v Sunderland	3-2	0-0	2-0	0-0	2-1	0-0
Cardiff v Hull	1-0	-	-	2-0	0-3	2-1
Chelsea v Everton	1-1	0-0	3-3	1-1	3-1	2-1
Crystal Palace v Man United	-	-	-	-	-	-
Liverpool v Swansea	-	-	-	-	0-0	5-0
Man City v Stoke	-	3-0	2-0	3-0	3-0	3-0
Newcastle v Aston Villa	0-0	2-0	-	6-0	2-1	1-1
Norwich v Tottenham	-	-	-	-	0-2	1-1
West Brom v Fulham	-	1-0	-	2-1	0-0	1-2
West Ham v Southampton	-	-	-	-	1-1	4-1
Championship						
Barnsley v Millwall	-	-	-	1-0	1-3	2-0
Blackpool v Birmingham	-	2-0	-	1-2	2-2	1-1
Bolton v Watford	-	-	-	-	-	2-1
Brighton v Wigan	-	-	-	-	-	-
Burnley v Nottm Forest	-	5-0	-	1-0	5-1	1-1
Charlton v QPR	0-1	2-2	-	-	-	-
Derby v Bournemouth	-	-	-	-	-	-
Huddersfield v Sheffield Weds	-	-	-	1-0	0-2	0-0
Leicester v Ipswich	2-0	-	1-1	4-2	1-1	6-0
Middlesbrough v Leeds	-	-	-	1-2	0-2	1-0
Reading v Blackburn	0-0	-	-	-	-	-
Yeovil v Doncaster	2-1	-	-	-	-	2-1
League 1						
Bradford v MK Dons	1-2	-	-	-	-	-
Brentford v Wolves	-	-	-	-	-	-
Carlisle v Rotherham	-	-	-	-	-	-
Colchester v Preston	2-1	-	-	-	3-0	1-0
Leyton Orient v Swindon	2-1	1-2	0-0	3-0	-	0-0
Notts County v Shrewsbury	2-1	2-2	1-1	-	-	3-2

Results cover matches from Premier League to Conference and Scottish Premier League to Division Three

	2007-08	2008-09	2009-10	2010-11	2011-12	2012-13
Oldham v Gillingham	2-1	-	1-0	-	-	-
Port Vale v Crewe	0-1	-	0-1	2-1	1-1	-
Sheffield United v Bristol City	2-1	3-0	2-0	3-2	-	-
Stevenage v Peterborough	-	-	-	-	-	-
Tranmere v Coventry	-	-	-	-	-	2-0
Walsall v Crawley	-	-	-	-	-	2-2
League 2						
AFC Wimbledon v Bury	-	-	-	-	-	-
Bristol Rovers v Burton	-	-	-	-	7-1	3-0
Dag & Red v Plymouth	-	-	-	0-1	2-3	0-0
Exeter v Rochdale	-	4-1	-	1-0	3-1	1-2
Mansfield v Fleetwood	-	-	-	2-5	1-1	-
Morecambe v Oxford	-	-	-	0-3	0-0	1-1
Newport County v Cheltenham	-	-	-	-	-	-
Northampton v Hartlepool	1-1	1-0	-	-	-	-
Scunthorpe v Portsmouth	-	-	-	1-1	-	2-1
Torquay v Accrington	-	-	2-1	0-0	1-0	3-1
Wycombe v Chesterfield	1-0	1-1	-	1-2	3-2	2-1
York v Southend	-	-	-	-	-	2-1
Conference						
Alfreton v Gateshead	-	-	-	-	1-1	3-2
Dartford v Hereford	-	-	-	-	-	4-0
Forest Green v Southport	-	-	-	0-0	2-3	0-1
Grimsby v Halifax	-	-	-	-	-	-
Hyde v Aldershot	-	-	-	-	-	-
Kidderminster v Braintree	-	-	-	-	5-4	2-1
Lincoln v Chester	0-1	1-1	-	-	-	-
Nuneaton v Luton	-	-	-	-	-	0-0
Salisbury v Cambridge	0-2	1-2	2-1	-	-	-
Tamworth v Welling	-	-	-	-	-	-
Woking v Macclesfield	-	-	-	-	-	5-4
Wrexham v Barnet	0-2	-	-	-	-	-
Scottish Premier League						
Dundee United v Motherwell	1-0/2-0	0-4	0-1/3-0	2-0/4-0	1-3/1-1	1-2/1-3
Hearts v Celtic	1-1	0-2/1-1	2-1/1-2	2-0/0-3	2-0/0-4	0-4
Kilmarnock v Hibernian	2-1	1-0/1-1	1-1	2-1	4-1/1-3	1-1/1-3
Partick v Aberdeen	-	-	-	-	-	-
Ross County v St Mirren	-	-	-	-	-	0-0
St Johnstone v Inverness CT	-	-	-	1-0/0-3	2-0/0-0	0-0/1-0
Scottish Division One						
Cowdenbeath v Dundee	-	-	-	2-1/1-3	-	-
Dumbarton v Raith	-	-	-	-	-	4-2/1-2
Falkirk v Queen of Sth	-	-	-	3-1/0-3	1-0/3-0	-
Hamilton v Livingston	1-1/3-1	-	-	-	1-1/0-1	1-2/1-1
Morton v Alloa	-	-	-	-	-	-
Scottish Division Two						
Arbroath v Forfar	3-4/1-1	-	-	-	4-1/0-1	1-1/3-1
Brechin v Stranraer	-	1-0/2-1	-	-	-	3-0/2-2
Dunfermline v Ayr	-	-	3-1/0-1	-	-	-
East Fife v Airdrieonians	-	-	-	3-3/0-1	2-0/2-0	-
Rangers v Stenhousemuir	-	-	-	-	-	-
Scottish Division Three						
Albion v Peterhead	-	-	-	-	-	-
Clyde v Montrose	-	-	-	2-0/1-1	1-0/1-2	1-2/1-0

Results cover matches from Premier League to Conference and Scottish Premier League to Division Three

	2007-08	2008-09	2009-10	2010-11	2011-12	2012-13
East Stirling v Berwick	-	1-0/0-4	1-0/3-2	0-0/1-0	1-3/2-1	0-1/0-3
Elgin v Stirling	-	-	-	-	-	3-1/1-2
Queen's Park v Annan	-	-	0-0/3-2	3-0/0-1	0-0/2-0	2-2/2-2

Saturday March 1st, 2014

Premier League

	2007-08	2008-09	2009-10	2010-11	2011-12	2012-13
Aston Villa v Norwich	-	-	-	-	3-2	1-1
Everton v West Ham	1-1	3-1	2-2	2-2	-	2-0
Fulham v Chelsea	1-2	2-2	0-2	0-0	1-1	0-3
Hull v Newcastle	-	1-1	-	-	-	-
Man United v Man City	1-2	2-0	4-3	2-1	1-6	1-2
Southampton v Liverpool	-	-	-	-	-	3-1
Stoke v Arsenal	-	2-1	1-3	3-1	1-1	0-0
Sunderland v West Brom	-	4-0	-	2-3	2-2	2-4
Swansea v Crystal Palace	-	1-3	0-0	3-0	-	-
Tottenham v Cardiff	-	-	-	-	-	-

Championship

	2007-08	2008-09	2009-10	2010-11	2011-12	2012-13
Bolton v Blackburn	1-2	0-0	0-2	2-1	2-1	1-0
Bournemouth v Doncaster	0-2	-	-	-	-	1-2
Burnley v Derby	-	3-0	-	2-1	0-0	2-0
Huddersfield v Barnsley	-	-	-	-	-	2-2
Ipswich v Birmingham	-	0-1	-	-	1-1	3-1
Leicester v Charlton	1-1	-	-	-	-	1-2
Millwall v Brighton	3-0	0-1	1-1	-	1-1	1-2
Nottm Forest v Wigan	-	-	-	-	-	-
QPR v Leeds	-	-	-	1-2	-	-
Reading v Yeovil	-	-	-	-	-	-
Sheffield Weds v Middlesbrough	-	-	1-3	-	-	2-0
Watford v Blackpool	1-1	3-4	2-2	-	0-2	1-2

League 1

	2007-08	2008-09	2009-10	2010-11	2011-12	2012-13
Bradford v Stevenage	-	-	-	1-0	-	-
Bristol City v Gillingham	-	-	-	-	-	-
Carlisle v Brentford	-	-	1-3	2-0	2-2	2-0
Coventry v Shrewsbury	-	-	-	-	-	0-1
Crawley v Peterborough	-	-	-	-	-	-
Crewe v Swindon	0-0	1-0	-	-	2-0	2-1
Leyton Orient v Colchester	-	2-1	0-1	4-2	0-1	0-2
MK Dons v Sheffield United	-	-	-	-	1-0	1-0
Preston v Walsall	-	-	-	-	0-0	1-3
Rotherham v Notts County	1-1	2-1	0-0	-	-	-
Tranmere v Oldham	0-1	0-1	0-1	1-2	1-0	1-0
Wolves v Port Vale	-	-	-	-	-	-

League 2

	2007-08	2008-09	2009-10	2010-11	2011-12	2012-13
Burton v Accrington	-	-	0-2	1-1	0-2	1-0
Cheltenham v Bury	-	-	5-2	0-2	-	-
Chesterfield v Portsmouth	-	-	-	-	-	-
Dag & Red v Mansfield	2-0	-	-	-	-	-
Fleetwood v AFC Wimbledon	-	-	-	1-1	-	1-1
Hartlepool v Torquay	-	-	-	-	-	-
Newport County v Scunthorpe	-	-	-	-	-	-
Northampton v Bristol Rovers	0-1	0-0	-	-	3-2	1-0
Plymouth v Morecambe	-	-	-	-	1-1	2-1
Rochdale v Oxford	-	-	-	-	-	2-0
Southend v Wycombe	-	-	1-1	3-2	-	1-0
York v Exeter	3-2	-	-	-	-	1-2

Results cover matches from Premier League to Conference and Scottish Premier League to Division Three

	2007-08	2008-09	2009-10	2010-11	2011-12	2012-13
Conference						
Aldershot v Lincoln	-	2-0	3-1	2-2	-	-
Barnet v Woking	-	-	-	-	-	-
Braintree v Hyde	-	-	-	-	-	2-2
Cambridge v Kidderminster	0-3	2-1	2-0	1-2	1-2	1-3
Chester v Nuneaton	-	-	-	-	-	-
Gateshead v Forest Green	-	-	3-1	1-1	1-0	1-1
Grimsby v Salisbury	-	-	-	-	-	-
Halifax v Tamworth	-	-	-	-	-	-
Hereford v Wrexham	2-0	-	-	-	-	0-1
Luton v Alfreton	-	-	-	-	1-0	3-0
Southport v Dartford	-	-	-	-	-	2-2
Welling v Macclesfield	-	-	-	-	-	-
Scottish Premier League						
Aberdeen v St Johnstone	-	-	2-1/1-3	0-1/0-2	0-0/0-0	2-0
Celtic v Inverness CT	5-0/2-1	1-0	-	2-2	2-0/1-0	0-1/4-1
Hibernian v Dundee United	2-2	2-1/1-2	1-1/2-4	2-2	3-3/0-2	2-1
Motherwell v Hearts	0-2/0-1	1-0	1-0/3-1	1-2	1-0/3-0	0-0
Ross County v Partick	-	1-0/0-2	2-2/1-2	0-2/0-0	2-2/3-0	-
St Mirren v Kilmarnock	0-0/1-0	0-0/1-1	1-0/1-0	0-2	3-0/4-2	1-1
Scottish Division One						
Alloa v Hamilton	-	-	-	-	-	-
Dundee v Morton	2-1/2-0	1-0/0-0	1-0/3-1	2-1/1-1	0-1/0-1	-
Livingston v Cowdenbeath	-	-	-	-	-	1-1/3-0
Queen of Sth v Dumbarton	-	-	-	-	-	-
Raith v Falkirk	-	-	-	2-1/1-2	1-0/2-2	2-1/0-0
Scottish Division Two						
Airdrieonians v Ayr	0-0/0-2	-	3-1/1-1	2-2/0-5	-	-
Brechin v Arbroath	-	3-1/0-1	0-0/0-2	-	2-3/1-1	3-2/2-0
East Fife v Rangers	-	-	-	-	-	-
Stenhousemuir v Forfar	4-0/2-0	1-1/0-1	-	3-0/0-1	2-3/1-2	0-4/2-0
Stranraer v Dunfermline	-	-	-	-	-	-
Scottish Division Three						
Annan v Berwick	-	1-2/1-1	1-1/0-1	1-1/2-3	2-2/1-1	3-2/2-2
Clyde v Elgin	-	-	-	1-1/3-3	1-2/0-2	2-2/1-1
Montrose v Albion	0-1/2-1	1-2/1-0	0-0/0-0	0-2/0-2	-	-
Peterhead v East Stirling	-	-	-	-	1-0/2-0	2-0/6-0
Stirling v Queen's Park	-	0-3/4-0	-	-	-	1-2/2-3

Saturday March 8th, 2014

	2007-08	2008-09	2009-10	2010-11	2011-12	2012-13
Premier League						
Arsenal v Swansea	-	-	-	-	1-0	0-2
Cardiff v Fulham	-	-	-	-	-	-
Chelsea v Tottenham	2-0	1-1	3-0	2-1	0-0	2-2
Crystal Palace v Southampton	1-1	3-0	-	-	0-2	-
Liverpool v Sunderland	3-0	2-0	3-0	2-2	1-1	3-0
Man City v Aston Villa	1-0	2-0	3-1	4-0	4-1	5-0
Newcastle v Everton	3-2	0-0	-	1-2	2-1	1-2
Norwich v Stoke	0-1	-	-	-	1-1	1-0
West Brom v Man United	-	0-5	-	1-2	1-2	5-5
West Ham v Hull	-	2-0	3-0	-	2-1	-
Championship						
Barnsley v Nottm Forest	-	1-1	2-1	3-1	1-1	1-4
Birmingham v QPR	-	1-0	-	-	-	-

Results cover matches from Premier League to Conference and Scottish Premier League to Division Three

	2007-08	2008-09	2009-10	2010-11	2011-12	2012-13
Blackburn v Burnley	-	-	3-2	-	-	1-1
Blackpool v Bournemouth	-	-	-	-	-	-
Brighton v Reading	-	-	-	-	0-1	-
Charlton v Watford	2-2	2-3	-	-	-	1-2
Derby v Millwall	-	-	-	0-0	3-0	1-0
Doncaster v Huddersfield	2-0	-	-	-	-	-
Leeds v Bolton	-	-	-	-	-	1-0
Middlesbrough v Ipswich	-	-	3-1	1-3	0-0	2-0
Wigan v Leicester	-	-	-	-	-	-
Yeovil v Sheffield Weds	-	-	-	0-2	2-3	-
League 1						
Brentford v Bradford	2-2	2-1	-	-	-	-
Colchester v Coventry	1-5	-	-	-	-	1-3
Gillingham v Crawley	-	-	-	-	0-1	-
Notts County v Leyton Orient	-	-	-	3-2	1-2	1-1
Oldham v Preston	-	-	-	-	1-1	3-1
Peterborough v Crewe	-	4-2	-	-	-	-
Port Vale v Carlisle	1-1	-	-	-	-	-
Sheffield United v Rotherham	-	-	-	-	-	-
Shrewsbury v Bristol City	-	-	-	-	-	-
Stevenage v Tranmere	-	-	-	-	2-1	1-1
Swindon v MK Dons	-	1-1	0-0	0-1	-	1-0
Walsall v Wolves	-	-	-	-	-	-
League 2						
Accrington v Chesterfield	2-1	1-0	2-0	2-2	-	1-0
AFC Wimbledon v York	-	-	0-1	1-0	-	3-2
Bristol Rovers v Plymouth	-	-	-	2-3	2-3	2-1
Bury v Rochdale	1-1	2-1	1-0	-	2-4	-
Exeter v Dag & Red	-	2-1	-	2-1	-	0-1
Mansfield v Newport County	-	-	-	3-3	5-0	3-4
Morecambe v Southend	-	-	-	2-1	1-0	1-0
Oxford v Burton	0-3	2-1	-	3-0	2-2	1-1
Portsmouth v Cheltenham	-	-	-	-	-	-
Scunthorpe v Northampton	-	4-4	-	-	-	-
Torquay v Fleetwood	-	-	-	-	-	0-1
Wycombe v Hartlepool	-	-	2-0	-	5-0	-
Conference						
Alfreton v Lincoln	-	-	-	-	1-3	0-2
Barnet v Gateshead	-	-	-	-	-	-
Braintree v Hereford	-	-	-	-	-	0-2
Dartford v Chester	-	-	-	-	-	-
Forest Green v Cambridge	3-1	2-2	1-1	1-1	2-1	1-1
Hyde v Halifax	-	-	-	-	-	-
Macclesfield v Grimsby	1-2	1-0	0-0	-	-	1-3
Nuneaton v Welling	-	-	-	-	-	-
Salisbury v Luton	-	-	1-1	-	-	-
Tamworth v Aldershot	-	-	-	-	-	-
Woking v Southport	-	-	-	-	-	2-3
Wrexham v Kidderminster	-	0-1	2-2	2-2	2-0	1-2
Scottish Division One						
Cowdenbeath v Alloa	1-4/1-1	-	1-1/1-1	-	-	-
Dundee v Raith	-	-	2-1/2-0	0-0/2-1	1-0/1-1	-
Falkirk v Livingston	-	-	-	-	4-3/2-5	1-2/2-0
Morton v Dumbarton	-	-	-	-	-	3-0/0-3
Queen of Sth v Hamilton	2-1/2-2	-	-	-	1-0/1-2	-

Results cover matches from Premier League to Conference and Scottish Premier League to Division Three

	2007-08	2008-09	2009-10	2010-11	2011-12	2012-13
Scottish Division Two						
Arbroath v East Fife	2-3/0-1	0-1/0-2	0-1/2-2	-	3-0/2-2	2-0/1-0
Ayr v Stranraer	-	3-2/5-0	-	-	-	2-1/2-1
Dunfermline v Stenhousemuir	-	-	-	-	-	-
Forfar v Brechin	-	-	-	1-1/2-1	0-0/4-1	1-0/1-4
Rangers v Airdrieonians	-	-	-	-	-	-
Scottish Division Three						
Albion v Annan	-	0-1/2-1	0-0/1-0	0-0/0-0	-	-
Berwick v Montrose	-	3-2/0-1	2-0/0-2	1-0/0-1	1-2/2-2	1-4/4-0
East Stirling v Stirling	-	-	-	-	-	3-1/1-1
Elgin v Peterhead	-	-	-	-	6-1/1-2	2-0/0-3
Queen's Park v Clyde	-	-	-	0-1/4-0	3-0/3-0	1-0/4-1

Tuesday March 11th, 2014

	2007-08	2008-09	2009-10	2010-11	2011-12	2012-13
Championship						
Barnsley v Leicester	0-1	-	1-0	0-2	1-1	2-0
Birmingham v Burnley	-	1-1	2-1	-	2-1	2-2
Blackburn v Bournemouth	-	-	-	-	-	-
Blackpool v Millwall	-	-	-	-	1-0	2-1
Brighton v QPR	-	-	-	-	-	-
Charlton v Huddersfield	-	-	2-1	0-1	2-0	1-1
Derby v Bolton	1-1	-	-	-	-	1-1
Doncaster v Watford	-	1-2	2-1	1-1	0-0	-
Leeds v Reading	-	-	-	0-0	0-1	-
Middlesbrough v Nottm Forest	-	-	1-1	1-1	2-1	1-0
Wigan v Sheffield Weds	-	-	-	-	-	-
Yeovil v Ipswich	-	-	-	-	-	-
League 1						
Brentford v Tranmere	-	-	2-1	2-1	0-2	1-2
Colchester v Bradford	-	-	-	-	-	-
Gillingham v Coventry	-	-	-	-	-	-
Notts County v MK Dons	1-2	-	-	2-0	1-1	1-2
Oldham v Rotherham	-	-	-	-	-	-
Peterborough v Bristol City	-	-	0-1	-	3-0	1-2
Port Vale v Leyton Orient	2-1	-	-	-	-	-
Sheffield United v Carlisle	-	-	-	-	1-0	0-0
Shrewsbury v Crawley	-	-	-	-	2-1	3-0
Stevenage v Preston	-	-	-	-	1-1	1-4
Swindon v Wolves	-	-	-	-	-	-
Walsall v Crewe	1-1	1-1	-	-	-	2-2
League 2						
Accrington v Hartlepool	-	-	-	-	-	-
AFC Wimbledon v Chesterfield	-	-	-	-	-	1-0
Bristol Rovers v Dag & Red	-	-	-	0-2	2-0	0-1
Bury v Fleetwood	-	-	-	-	-	-
Exeter v Northampton	-	-	-	-	-	3-0
Mansfield v York	-	1-0	0-1	5-0	1-1	-
Morecambe v Newport County	-	-	-	-	-	-
Oxford v Cheltenham	-	-	-	1-1	1-3	1-0
Portsmouth v Burton	-	-	-	-	-	-
Scunthorpe v Southend	-	1-1	-	-	-	-
Torquay v Rochdale	-	-	5-0	-	-	4-2
Wycombe v Plymouth	-	-	-	-	-	1-1

Saturday March 15th, 2014

	2007-08	2008-09	2009-10	2010-11	2011-12	2012-13
Premier League						
Aston Villa v Chelsea	2-0	0-1	2-1	0-0	2-4	1-2

Results cover matches from Premier League to Conference and Scottish Premier League to Division Three

	2007-08	2008-09	2009-10	2010-11	2011-12	2012-13
Everton v Cardiff	-	-	-	-	-	-
Fulham v Newcastle	0-1	2-1	-	1-0	5-2	2-1
Hull v Man City	-	2-2	2-1	-	-	-
Man United v Liverpool	3-0	1-4	2-1	3-2	2-1	2-1
Southampton v Norwich	0-1	2-0	2-2	-	-	1-1
Stoke v West Ham	-	0-1	2-1	1-1	-	0-1
Sunderland v Crystal Palace	-	-	-	-	-	-
Swansea v West Brom	-	-	0-2	-	3-0	3-1
Tottenham v Arsenal	1-3	0-0	2-1	3-3	2-1	2-1
Championship						
Bolton v Brighton	-	-	-	-	-	1-0
Bournemouth v Middlesbrough	-	-	-	-	-	-
Burnley v Leeds	-	-	-	2-3	1-2	1-0
Huddersfield v Blackburn	-	-	-	-	-	2-2
Ipswich v Wigan	-	-	-	-	-	-
Leicester v Blackpool	0-1	-	2-1	-	2-0	1-0
Millwall v Charlton	-	-	4-0	-	-	0-0
Nottm Forest v Doncaster	0-0	2-4	4-1	0-0	1-2	-
QPR v Yeovil	-	-	-	-	-	-
Reading v Derby	1-0	3-0	4-1	2-1	2-2	-
Sheffield Weds v Birmingham	-	1-1	-	-	-	3-2
Watford v Barnsley	0-3	1-1	1-0	1-0	2-1	4-1
League 1						
Bradford v Gillingham	-	2-2	-	1-0	2-2	0-1
Bristol City v Swindon	-	-	-	-	-	-
Carlisle v Stevenage	-	-	-	-	1-0	2-1
Coventry v Port Vale	-	-	-	-	-	-
Crawley v Colchester	-	-	-	-	-	3-0
Crewe v Oldham	1-4	0-3	-	-	-	0-2
Leyton Orient v Brentford	-	-	2-1	1-0	2-0	1-0
MK Dons v Peterborough	1-1	1-2	-	1-0	-	-
Preston v Sheffield United	3-1	0-0	2-1	3-1	2-4	0-1
Rotherham v Walsall	-	-	-	-	-	-
Tranmere v Notts County	-	-	-	0-1	1-1	1-1
Wolves v Shrewsbury	-	-	-	-	-	-
League 2						
Burton v AFC Wimbledon	-	-	-	-	3-2	6-2
Cheltenham v Torquay	-	-	1-1	2-2	0-1	2-1
Chesterfield v Oxford	-	-	-	1-2	-	2-1
Dag & Red v Morecambe	2-0	0-2	1-1	-	1-2	1-2
Fleetwood v Portsmouth	-	-	-	-	-	-
Hartlepool v Bristol Rovers	1-0	1-1	1-2	2-2	-	-
Newport County v Exeter	-	-	-	-	-	-
Northampton v Mansfield	-	-	-	-	-	-
Plymouth v Scunthorpe	3-0	-	2-1	-	-	-
Rochdale v Accrington	4-1	3-1	1-2	-	-	0-3
Southend v Bury	-	-	-	1-1	-	-
York v Wycombe	-	-	-	-	-	1-3
Conference						
Aldershot v Nuneaton	-	-	-	-	-	-
Cambridge v Dartford	-	-	-	-	-	1-2
Chester v Alfreton	-	-	-	-	-	-
Grimsby v Wrexham	1-0	-	-	2-1	1-3	1-0
Hereford v Hyde	-	-	-	-	-	1-2
Kidderminster v Barnet	-	-	-	-	-	-
Lincoln v Braintree	-	-	-	-	3-3	3-0
Luton v Woking	-	-	-	-	-	3-1

Results cover matches from Premier League to Conference and Scottish Premier League to Division Three

	2007-08	2008-09	2009-10	2010-11	2011-12	2012-13
Salisbury v Gateshead	-	-	0-1	-	-	-
Southport v Macclesfield	-	-	-	-	-	3-2
Tamworth v Forest Green	-	-	0-0	2-1	0-1	2-1
Welling v Halifax	-	-	-	-	-	-
Scottish Premier League						
Dundee United v St Mirren	2-0/1-1	2-0/3-2	3-2	1-2	1-1/0-0	3-4
Hearts v Aberdeen	4-1	1-1/2-1	0-3	5-0	3-0/3-0	2-0
Inverness CT v Motherwell	0-3	1-2/1-2	-	1-2/3-0	2-3	1-5/4-3
Kilmarnock v Celtic	1-2	1-3/1-2	1-0	1-2/0-4/0-2	3-3/0-6	1-3
Partick v Hibernian	-	-	-	-	-	-
St Johnstone v Ross County	-	2-1/0-0	-	-	-	1-1/2-2
Scottish Division One						
Alloa v Queen of Sth	-	-	-	-	-	1-0/1-2
Dumbarton v Cowdenbeath	-	2-1/1-1	0-3/2-1	-	0-4/0-2	0-3/2-2
Hamilton v Falkirk	-	1-1/0-1	0-0/2-2	-	0-1/0-1	1-1/1-1
Livingston v Dundee	0-2/1-1	1-2/0-1	-	-	4-2/2-3	-
Raith v Morton	-	-	3-0/1-2	1-0/2-2	1-1/5-0	3-3/2-1
Scottish Division Two						
Arbroath v Airdrieonians	-	-	-	-	3-1/2-2	-
East Fife v Ayr	-	3-0/0-1	-	2-3/3-2	-	2-3/3-3
Forfar v Stranraer	1-1/1-0	-	1-0/2-0	-	-	4-0/3-1
Rangers v Dunfermline	-	-	-	-	2-1	-
Stenhousemuir v Brechin	-	-	1-1/1-2	0-0/1-3	1-1/2-1	3-1/3-3
Scottish Division Three						
Clyde v Stirling	1-3/3-0	-	0-1/1-2	-	-	2-1/1-2
Elgin v Annan	-	1-2/0-1	1-1/1-0	2-0/2-3	3-0/1-2	2-2/3-1
Montrose v East Stirling	3-1/2-0	3-0/0-2	0-3/0-1	0-2/3-0	2-1/3-1	3-1/2-2
Peterhead v Berwick	4-3/9-2	-	-	-	1-0/1-2	1-0/1-1
Queen's Park v Albion	-	-	0-1/1-0	0-1/2-1	-	-

Saturday March 22nd, 2014

	2007-08	2008-09	2009-10	2010-11	2011-12	2012-13
Premier League						
Aston Villa v Stoke	-	2-2	1-0	1-1	1-1	0-0
Cardiff v Liverpool	-	-	-	-	-	-
Chelsea v Arsenal	2-1	1-2	2-0	2-0	3-5	2-1
Everton v Swansea	-	-	-	-	1-0	0-0
Hull v West Brom	1-3	2-2	-	-	-	-
Man City v Fulham	2-3	1-3	2-2	1-1	3-0	2-0
Newcastle v Crystal Palace	-	-	2-0	-	-	-
Norwich v Sunderland	-	-	-	-	2-1	2-1
Tottenham v Southampton	-	-	-	-	-	1-0
West Ham v Man United	2-1	0-1	0-4	2-4	-	2-2
Championship						
Barnsley v Bournemouth	-	-	-	-	-	-
Birmingham v Reading	1-1	1-3	-	-	2-0	-
Blackburn v Leicester	-	-	-	-	-	2-1
Blackpool v Huddersfield	-	-	-	-	-	1-3
Brighton v Ipswich	-	-	-	-	3-0	1-1
Charlton v Burnley	1-3	1-1	-	-	-	0-1
Derby v Nottm Forest	-	1-1	1-0	0-1	1-0	1-1
Doncaster v Sheffield Weds	-	1-0	1-0	-	-	-
Leeds v Millwall	4-2	2-0	0-2	3-1	2-0	1-0
Middlesbrough v QPR	-	-	2-0	0-3	-	-
Wigan v Watford	-	-	-	-	-	-
Yeovil v Bolton	-	-	-	-	-	-

Results cover matches from Premier League to Conference and Scottish Premier League to Division Three

	2007-08	2008-09	2009-10	2010-11	2011-12	2012-13
League 1						
Brentford v Coventry	-	-	-	-	-	2-1
Colchester v Bristol City	1-2	-	-	-	-	-
Gillingham v Crewe	0-3	-	-	1-3	3-4	-
Notts County v Carlisle	-	-	-	0-1	2-0	1-0
Oldham v Crawley	-	-	-	-	-	2-1
Peterborough v Rotherham	3-1	-	-	-	-	-
Port Vale v Tranmere	0-0	-	-	-	-	-
Sheffield United v Wolves	3-1	1-3	-	-	-	-
Shrewsbury v Bradford	1-0	2-0	1-2	3-1	1-0	-
Stevenage v MK Dons	-	-	-	-	4-2	0-2
Swindon v Preston	-	-	-	-	-	1-1
Walsall v Leyton Orient	0-0	0-2	2-2	0-2	1-0	1-2
League 2						
Accrington v Plymouth	-	-	-	-	0-4	1-1
AFC Wimbledon v Cheltenham	-	-	-	-	4-1	1-2
Bristol Rovers v Southend	1-1	4-2	4-3	-	1-0	2-3
Bury v Dag & Red	0-2	2-2	0-0	-	-	-
Exeter v Fleetwood	-	-	-	-	-	2-2
Mansfield v Chesterfield	1-3	-	-	-	-	-
Morecambe v Northampton	-	-	2-4	1-2	1-2	1-1
Oxford v Hartlepool	-	-	-	-	-	-
Portsmouth v York	-	-	-	-	-	-
Scunthorpe v Burton	-	-	-	-	-	-
Torquay v Newport County	-	-	-	-	-	-
Wycombe v Rochdale	0-1	0-1	-	-	3-0	1-2
Conference						
Barnet v Hereford	1-2	-	0-0	2-0	1-1	-
Braintree v Aldershot	-	-	-	-	-	-
Forest Green v Welling	-	-	-	-	-	-
Gateshead v Lincoln	-	-	-	-	3-3	1-1
Halifax v Alfreton	-	-	-	-	-	-
Hyde v Dartford	-	-	-	-	-	3-0
Kidderminster v Southport	-	-	-	3-4	2-0	2-2
Luton v Chester	-	1-1	-	-	-	-
Macclesfield v Tamworth	-	-	-	-	-	2-0
Nuneaton v Grimsby	-	-	-	-	-	1-0
Woking v Cambridge	0-0	0-1	-	-	-	2-1
Wrexham v Salisbury	-	1-1	1-2	-	-	-
Scottish Premier League						
Aberdeen v Kilmarnock	2-1	1-0/0-0	1-0/1-2	0-1/5-0	2-2/0-0	0-2/1-0
Celtic v St Mirren	1-1	1-0/7-0	3-1	4-0/1-0	5-0	2-0
Hearts v Dundee United	1-3/1-0	0-0/3-0	0-0/0-0	1-1/2-1	0-1/0-2	2-1
Inverness CT v Partick	-	-	2-3/2-1	-	-	-
Motherwell v Ross County	-	-	-	-	-	3-2/2-0
St Johnstone v Hibernian	-	-	5-1	2-0/1-1	3-1	0-1
Scottish Division One						
Alloa v Falkirk	-	-	-	-	-	-
Dumbarton v Dundee	-	-	-	-	-	-
Morton v Hamilton	0-2/1-3	-	-	-	0-2/1-2	0-1/0-2
Queen of Sth v Cowdenbeath	-	-	-	3-0/2-2	-	-
Raith v Livingston	-	-	-	-	0-1/0-3	0-0/0-2
Scottish Division Two						
Airdrieonians v Forfar	-	-	-	2-0/3-1	4-4/3-0	-
Ayr v Arbroath	-	2-1/2-1	-	-	-	2-0/0-1

Results cover matches from Premier League to Conference and Scottish Premier League to Division Three

	2007-08	2008-09	2009-10	2010-11	2011-12	2012-13
Brechin v Rangers	-	-	-	-	-	-
Dunfermline v East Fife	-	-	-	-	-	-
Stranraer v Stenhousemuir	2-3/3-1	-	-	-	-	1-1/1-1

Scottish Division Three

Albion v Elgin	3-4/1-1	2-1/0-3	1-1/1-2	3-1/2-0	-	-
Annan v Peterhead	-	-	-	-	2-0/0-3	2-1/0-0
Berwick v Clyde	-	-	-	2-1/1-1	0-2/3-0	2-1/3-3
East Stirling v Queen's Park	-	-	1-0/0-3	0-1/3-2	1-3/1-2	0-2/0-2
Stirling v Montrose	-	-	-	-	-	1-3/3-1

Tuesday March 25th, 2014

Championship

Bolton v Blackpool	-	-	-	2-2	-	2-2
Bournemouth v Leeds	1-3	-	-	-	-	-
Burnley v Doncaster	-	0-0	-	1-1	3-0	-
Huddersfield v Middlesbrough	-	-	-	-	-	2-1
Ipswich v Derby	-	2-0	1-0	0-2	1-0	1-2
Leicester v Yeovil	-	1-0	-	-	-	-
Millwall v Birmingham	-	-	-	-	0-6	3-3
Nottm Forest v Charlton	-	0-0	-	-	-	2-1
QPR v Wigan	-	-	-	-	3-1	1-1
Reading v Barnsley	-	0-0	1-0	3-0	1-2	-
Sheffield Weds v Brighton	-	-	-	1-0	-	3-1
Watford v Blackburn	-	-	-	-	-	4-0

League 1

Bradford v Walsall	-	-	-	-	-	-
Bristol City v Port Vale	-	-	-	-	-	-
Carlisle v Shrewsbury	-	-	-	-	-	2-2
Coventry v Stevenage	-	-	-	-	-	1-2
Crawley v Sheffield United	-	-	-	-	-	0-2
Crewe v Notts County	-	-	0-1	-	-	1-2
Leyton Orient v Oldham	1-0	2-1	1-2	1-0	1-3	1-1
MK Dons v Gillingham	-	-	2-0	-	-	-
Preston v Peterborough	-	-	2-0	-	-	-
Rotherham v Brentford	1-2	0-0	-	-	-	-
Tranmere v Swindon	2-1	1-0	1-4	0-2	-	1-3
Wolves v Colchester	1-0	-	-	-	-	-

League 2

Burton v Wycombe	-	-	-	1-2	-	2-0
Cheltenham v Scunthorpe	-	1-2	-	-	-	-
Chesterfield v Morecambe	2-2	1-2	1-1	0-2	-	1-1
Dag & Red v Accrington	1-3	0-0	3-1	-	2-1	1-1
Fleetwood v Bristol Rovers	-	-	-	-	-	0-3
Hartlepool v Mansfield	-	-	-	-	-	-
Newport County v Bury	-	-	-	-	-	-
Northampton v AFC Wimbledon	-	-	-	-	1-0	2-0
Plymouth v Exeter	-	-	-	2-0	-	1-0
Rochdale v Portsmouth	-	-	-	-	-	-
Southend v Oxford	-	-	-	2-1	2-1	1-0
York v Torquay	0-1	1-2	-	-	-	0-2

Conference

Aldershot v Gateshead	-	-	-	-	-	-
Chester v Tamworth	-	-	-	-	-	-
Grimsby v Luton	-	2-2	-	2-0	0-1	4-1

Scottish Division One

Cowdenbeath v Morton	-	-	-	2-2/0-2	-	3-4/1-1

Results cover matches from Premier League to Conference and Scottish Premier League to Division Three

	2007-08	2008-09	2009-10	2010-11	2011-12	2012-13
Dundee v Queen of Sth	2-1/2-3	2-0/2-3	0-0/1-1	1-0/2-1	2-1/1-1	-
Falkirk v Dumbarton	-	-	-	-	-	3-4/1-3
Hamilton v Raith	-	-	-	-	2-2/2-1	0-1/2-0
Livingston v Alloa	-	-	-	3-3/4-0	-	-

Wednesday March 26th, 2014

Scottish Premier League

	2007-08	2008-09	2009-10	2010-11	2011-12	2012-13
Dundee United v Inverness CT	0-1	2-1/1-1	-	0-4/1-0	3-1/3-0	4-4
Hibernian v Motherwell	1-0/0-2	0-1/1-1	2-0	2-1	0-1/1-1	2-3
Kilmarnock v Hearts	3-1/0-0	0-2	1-2	1-2/2-2	0-0/1-1	1-0/0-1
Partick v Celtic	-	-	-	-	-	-
Ross County v Aberdeen	-	-	-	-	-	2-1
St Mirren v St Johnstone	-	-	1-1/1-1	1-2/0-0	0-0/0-3	1-1

Saturday March 29th, 2014

Premier League

	2007-08	2008-09	2009-10	2010-11	2011-12	2012-13
Arsenal v Man City	1-0	2-0	0-0	0-0	1-0	0-2
Crystal Palace v Chelsea	-	-	-	-	-	-
Fulham v Everton	1-0	0-2	2-1	0-0	1-3	2-2
Liverpool v Tottenham	2-2	3-1	2-0	0-2	0-0	3-2
Man United v Aston Villa	4-0	3-2	0-1	3-1	4-0	3-0
Southampton v Newcastle	-	-	-	-	-	2-0
Stoke v Hull	1-1	1-1	2-0	-	-	-
Sunderland v West Ham	2-1	0-1	2-2	1-0	-	3-0
Swansea v Norwich	-	2-1	-	3-0	2-3	3-4
West Brom v Cardiff	3-3	-	0-2	-	-	-

Championship

	2007-08	2008-09	2009-10	2010-11	2011-12	2012-13
Birmingham v Bournemouth	-	-	-	-	-	-
Bolton v Wigan	4-1	0-1	4-0	1-1	1-2	-
Brighton v Middlesbrough	-	-	-	-	1-1	0-1
Burnley v Leicester	1-1	-	-	3-0	1-3	0-1
Derby v Charlton	-	1-0	-	-	-	3-2
Ipswich v Nottm Forest	-	2-1	1-1	0-1	1-3	3-1
Leeds v Doncaster	0-1	-	-	5-2	3-2	-
Millwall v Blackburn	-	-	-	-	-	1-2
QPR v Blackpool	3-2	1-1	1-1	-	-	-
Reading v Huddersfield	-	-	-	-	-	-
Sheffield Weds v Watford	0-1	2-0	2-1			1-4
Yeovil v Barnsley	-	-	-	-	-	-

League 1

	2007-08	2008-09	2009-10	2010-11	2011-12	2012-13
Crewe v Coventry	-	-	-	-	-	1-0
Leyton Orient v Bradford	-	-	-	-	-	-
MK Dons v Wolves	-	-	-	-	-	-
Notts County v Colchester	-	-	-	2-0	4-1	3-1
Oldham v Brentford	-	-	2-3	2-1	0-2	0-2
Peterborough v Gillingham	-	-	-	-	-	-
Preston v Crawley	-	-	-	-	-	1-2
Rotherham v Bristol City	-	-	-	-	-	-
Stevenage v Port Vale	-	-	-	1-0	-	-
Swindon v Sheffield United	-	-	-	-	-	0-0
Tranmere v Carlisle	2-0	4-1	0-0	2-1	1-2	0-1
Walsall v Shrewsbury	-	-	-	-	-	3-1

League 2

	2007-08	2008-09	2009-10	2010-11	2011-12	2012-13
Bristol Rovers v Morecambe	-	-	-	-	2-1	0-3
Dag & Red v Oxford	-	-	-	-	0-1	0-1
Exeter v Accrington	-	2-1	-	-	-	2-0
Fleetwood v Rochdale	-	-	-	-	-	0-3

Results cover matches from Premier League to Conference and Scottish Premier League to Division Three

	2007-08	2008-09	2009-10	2010-11	2011-12	2012-13
Hartlepool v Cheltenham	0-2	4-1	-	-	-	-
Mansfield v AFC Wimbledon	-	-	0-1	2-5	-	-
Newport County v Portsmouth	-	-	-	-	-	-
Northampton v Bury	-	-	1-1	2-4	-	-
Plymouth v Chesterfield	-	-	-	-	-	0-1
Scunthorpe v Wycombe	-	-	-	-	4-1	-
Southend v Torquay	-	-	-	2-1	4-1	1-1
York v Burton	0-0	1-3	-	-	-	3-0

Conference

	2007-08	2008-09	2009-10	2010-11	2011-12	2012-13
Aldershot v Hyde	-	-	-	-	-	-
Alfreton v Nuneaton	-	-	-	-	-	0-3
Cambridge v Barnet	-	-	-	-	-	-
Dartford v Macclesfield	-	-	-	-	-	2-0
Gateshead v Braintree	-	-	-	-	2-2	1-2
Halifax v Luton	-	-	-	-	-	-
Hereford v Grimsby	2-0	-	0-1	-	-	0-2
Salisbury v Kidderminster	0-1	0-0	1-0	-	-	-
Southport v Forest Green	-	-	-	4-0	1-3	1-2
Tamworth v Lincoln	-	-	-	-	4-0	1-0
Welling v Chester	-	-	-	-	-	-
Woking v Wrexham	-	1-1	-	-	-	2-0

Scottish Premier League

	2007-08	2008-09	2009-10	2010-11	2011-12	2012-13
Aberdeen v Dundee United	2-0/2-1	0-1/2-2	0-2/2-2	1-1	3-1/3-1	2-2
Celtic v Ross County	-	-	-	-	-	4-0
Hearts v Hibernian	0-1/1-0	0-0/0-1	0-0/2-1	1-0	2-0/2-0	0-0/1-2
Inverness CT v St Mirren	1-0/0-0	1-2/2-1	-	1-2/1-0	2-1/0-0	2-2
Motherwell v Kilmarnock	1-2/1-0	0-2/1-2	3-1/1-0	0-1/1-1	0-0	2-2
St Johnstone v Partick	2-1/2-0	3-0/1-1	-	-	-	-

Scottish Division One

	2007-08	2008-09	2009-10	2010-11	2011-12	2012-13
Alloa v Raith	2-1/2-0	1-1/0-0	-	-	-	-
Cowdenbeath v Hamilton	-	-	-	-	-	1-0/1-1
Dundee v Falkirk	-	-	-	2-0/1-0	4-2/3-1	-
Livingston v Dumbarton	-	-	-	2-0/1-1	-	5-0/2-3
Queen of Sth v Morton	1-3/0-0	1-4/1-1	2-3/1-2	2-0/1-4	4-1/2-1	-

Scottish Division Two

	2007-08	2008-09	2009-10	2010-11	2011-12	2012-13
Arbroath v Rangers	-	-	-	-	-	-
Ayr v Stenhousemuir	-	-	-	2-0/4-3	-	1-1/1-2
Dunfermline v Brechin	-	-	-	-	-	-
Forfar v East Fife	0-2/2-3	-	-	3-2/0-0	3-2/1-4	3-2/3-2
Stranraer v Airdrieonians	-	-	-	-	-	-

Scottish Division Three

	2007-08	2008-09	2009-10	2010-11	2011-12	2012-13
Annan v Stirling	-	-	-	-	-	5-2/0-1
Berwick v Albion	-	0-3/1-1	2-0/1-2	1-6/2-2	-	-
East Stirling v Clyde	-	-	-	0-0/2-0	1-1/0-1	3-0/3-0
Montrose v Elgin	0-0/3-2	1-0/3-1	1-1/0-4	0-1/1-0	3-0/2-3	2-2/4-1
Queen's Park v Peterhead	1-1/2-0	0-1/2-1	-	-	1-1/0-1	0-0/0-3

Tuesday April 1st, 2014

Conference

	2007-08	2008-09	2009-10	2010-11	2011-12	2012-13
Macclesfield v Cambridge	-	-	-	-	-	2-1

Saturday April 5th, 2014

Premier League

	2007-08	2008-09	2009-10	2010-11	2011-12	2012-13
Aston Villa v Fulham	2-1	0-0	2-0	2-2	1-0	1-1

Results cover matches from Premier League to Conference and Scottish Premier League to Division Three

	2007-08	2008-09	2009-10	2010-11	2011-12	2012-13
Cardiff v Crystal Palace	1-1	2-1	1-1	0-0	2-0	2-1
Chelsea v Stoke	-	2-1	7-0	2-0	1-0	1-0
Everton v Arsenal	1-4	1-1	1-6	1-2	0-1	1-1
Hull v Swansea	-	-	-	2-0	-	-
Man City v Southampton	-	-	-	-	-	3-2
Newcastle v Man United	1-5	1-2	-	0-0	3-0	0-3
Norwich v West Brom	1-2	-	-	-	0-1	4-0
Tottenham v Sunderland	2-0	1-2	2-0	1-1	1-0	1-0
West Ham v Liverpool	1-0	0-3	2-3	3-1	-	2-3
Championship						
Barnsley v Brighton	-	-	-	-	0-0	2-1
Blackburn v Ipswich	-	-	-	-	-	1-0
Blackpool v Yeovil	-	-	-	-	-	-
Bournemouth v QPR	-	-	-	-	-	-
Charlton v Reading	-	4-2	-	-	-	-
Doncaster v Birmingham	-	0-2	-	-	1-3	-
Huddersfield v Bolton	-	-	-	-	-	2-2
Leicester v Sheffield Weds	1-3	-	3-0	-	-	0-1
Middlesbrough v Derby	1-0	-	2-0	2-1	2-0	2-2
Nottm Forest v Millwall	2-0	-	-	1-1	3-1	1-4
Watford v Burnley	1-2	3-0	-	1-3	3-2	3-3
Wigan v Leeds	-	-	-	-	-	-
League 1						
Bradford v Oldham	-	-	-	-	-	-
Brentford v Notts County	0-0	1-1	-	1-1	0-0	2-1
Bristol City v Preston	3-0	1-1	4-2	1-1	-	-
Carlisle v Swindon	3-0	1-1	0-1	0-0	-	2-2
Colchester v Tranmere	-	0-1	1-1	3-1	4-2	1-5
Coventry v MK Dons	-	-	-	-	-	1-1
Crawley v Crewe	-	-	-	-	1-1	2-0
Gillingham v Rotherham	-	4-0	-	3-1	0-0	1-0
Port Vale v Walsall	1-1	-	-	-	-	-
Sheffield United v Leyton Orient	-	-	-	-	3-1	0-0
Shrewsbury v Stevenage	-	-	-	1-0	-	2-1
Wolves v Peterborough	-	-	-	-	-	0-3
League 2						
Accrington v Northampton	-	-	0-3	3-1	2-1	2-4
AFC Wimbledon v Bristol Rovers	-	-	-	-	2-3	3-1
Burton v Plymouth	-	-	-	-	2-1	1-0
Bury v Exeter	-	0-1	-	-	2-0	-
Cheltenham v Southend	1-1	0-0	-	0-2	3-0	1-3
Chesterfield v Newport County	-	-	-	-	-	-
Morecambe v Mansfield	3-1	-	-	-	-	-
Oxford v Fleetwood	-	-	-	-	-	1-2
Portsmouth v Hartlepool	-	-	-	-	-	1-3
Rochdale v York	-	-	-	-	-	2-3
Torquay v Scunthorpe	-	-	-	-	-	-
Wycombe v Dag & Red	0-1	2-1	-	-	-	1-0
Conference						
Alfreton v Welling	-	-	-	-	-	-
Barnet v Forest Green	-	-	-	-	-	-
Braintree v Salisbury	-	-	-	-	-	-
Cambridge v Southport	-	-	-	0-0	3-0	2-0
Chester v Hyde	-	-	-	-	-	-
Gateshead v Tamworth	-	-	1-1	3-1	1-1	0-2
Hereford v Woking	-	-	-	-	-	2-1

Results cover matches from Premier League to Conference and Scottish Premier League to Division Three

	2007-08	2008-09	2009-10	2010-11	2011-12	2012-13
Kidderminster v Grimsby	-	-	-	3-2	1-1	0-0
Lincoln v Dartford	-	-	-	-	-	2-1
Luton v Aldershot	-	3-1	-	-	-	-
Nuneaton v Halifax	-	-	-	-	-	-
Wrexham v Macclesfield	1-1	-	-	-	-	0-0
Scottish Premier League						
Dundee United v Celtic	0-2/0-1	1-1/2-2	2-1/0-2	1-2/1-3	0-1/1-0	2-2/0-4
Hibernian v Aberdeen	3-3/3-1	2-2/0-0	2-0/2-2	1-2/1-3	0-0/0-0	0-1/0-0
Kilmarnock v St Johnstone	-	-	2-1/3-2/1-2	1-1	1-2/0-0	1-2
Partick v Hearts	-	-	-	-	-	-
Ross County v Inverness CT	-	-	2-1/0-0	-	-	0-0/1-0
St Mirren v Motherwell	0-1/3-1	0-0/1-3	3-3/0-0	1-1	0-1/0-0	2-1
Scottish Division One						
Dumbarton v Alloa	-	-	1-3/3-1	4-1/2-2	-	-
Falkirk v Cowdenbeath	-	-	-	5-1/2-0	-	2-0/4-0
Hamilton v Dundee	2-0/1-0	-	-	-	1-6/3-1	-
Morton v Livingston	2-2/1-1	1-2/2-2	-	-	2-1/1-3	2-2/2-1
Raith v Queen of Sth	-	-	1-0/0-0	0-1/0-1	0-2/3-1	-
Scottish Division Two						
Airdrieonians v Dunfermline	-	1-3/1-1	1-1/0-1	-	-	1-2/3-3
Brechin v Ayr	2-2/5-1	0-1/1-0	-	0-3/1-0	-	2-1/2-1
East Fife v Stranraer	3-1/2-1	1-2/4-0	-	-	-	0-1/1-1
Rangers v Forfar	-	-	-	-	-	-
Stenhousemuir v Arbroath	1-0/0-3	-	3-0/1-1	-	2-0/1-3	2-2/1-0
Scottish Division Three						
Albion v East Stirling	2-3/2-2	0-2/0-2	3-0/2-1	1-0/2-0	-	-
Clyde v Annan	-	-	-	0-2/0-2	0-0/1-1	2-1/2-3
Elgin v Queen's Park	-	-	0-1/0-1	4-2/0-1	2-0/1-1	0-4/3-5
Peterhead v Montrose	-	-	-	-	2-3/2-1	2-0/0-1
Stirling v Berwick	-	-	-	-	-	6-3/1-0

Tuesday April 8th, 2014

	2007-08	2008-09	2009-10	2010-11	2011-12	2012-13
Championship						
Barnsley v Burnley	1-1	3-2	-	1-2	2-0	1-1
Blackburn v QPR	-	-	-	-	3-2	-
Blackpool v Derby	-	3-2	0-0	-	0-1	2-1
Bournemouth v Reading	-	-	-	-	-	-
Charlton v Yeovil	-	-	2-0	3-2	3-0	-
Doncaster v Bolton	-	-	-	-	-	-
Huddersfield v Ipswich	-	-	-	-	-	0-0
Leicester v Brighton	-	0-0	-	-	1-0	1-0
Middlesbrough v Birmingham	2-0	-	-	-	3-1	0-1
Nottm Forest v Sheffield Weds	-	2-1	2-1	-	-	1-0
Watford v Leeds	-	-	-	0-1	1-1	1-2
Wigan v Millwall	-	-	-	-	-	-
Conference						
Forest Green v Kidderminster	2-2	2-2	1-1	1-1	1-1	0-1
Grimsby v Woking	-	-	-	-	-	5-1
Hyde v Salisbury	-	-	-	-	-	-
Southport v Barnet	-	-	-	-	-	-
Welling v Hereford	-	-	-	-	-	-

Saturday April 12th, 2014

	2007-08	2008-09	2009-10	2010-11	2011-12	2012-13
Premier League						
Arsenal v West Ham	2-0	0-0	2-0	1-0	-	5-1

Results cover matches from Premier League to Conference and Scottish Premier League to Division Three

	2007-08	2008-09	2009-10	2010-11	2011-12	2012-13
Crystal Palace v Aston Villa	-	-	-	-	-	-
Fulham v Norwich	-	-	-	-	2-1	5-0
Liverpool v Man City	1-0	1-1	2-2	3-0	1-1	2-2
Man United v Hull	-	4-3	4-0	-	-	-
Southampton v Cardiff	1-0	1-0	-	-	1-1	-
Stoke v Newcastle	-	1-1	-	4-0	1-3	2-1
Sunderland v Everton	0-1	0-2	1-1	2-2	1-1	1-0
Swansea v Chelsea	-	-	-	-	1-1	1-1
West Brom v Tottenham	-	2-0	-	1-1	1-3	0-1
Championship						
Birmingham v Wigan	3-2	-	1-0	0-0	-	-
Bolton v Barnsley	-	-	-	-	-	1-1
Brighton v Charlton	-	-	0-2	1-1	-	0-0
Burnley v Middlesbrough	-	-	-	3-1	0-2	0-0
Derby v Huddersfield	-	-	-	-	-	3-0
Ipswich v Doncaster	-	1-3	1-1	3-2	2-3	-
Leeds v Blackpool	-	-	-	-	0-5	2-0
Millwall v Watford	-	-	-	1-6	0-2	1-0
QPR v Nottm Forest	-	2-1	1-1	1-1	-	-
Reading v Leicester	-	-	0-1	3-1	3-1	-
Sheffield Weds v Blackburn	-	-	-	-	-	3-2
Yeovil v Bournemouth	2-1	-	-	2-2	1-3	0-1
League 1						
Crewe v Wolves	-	-	-	-	-	-
Leyton Orient v Gillingham	0-0	-	3-1	-	-	-
MK Dons v Crawley	-	-	-	-	-	0-0
Notts County v Port Vale	-	4-2	3-1	-	-	-
Oldham v Sheffield United	-	-	-	-	0-2	0-2
Peterborough v Coventry	-	-	0-1	-	1-0	-
Preston v Carlisle	-	-	-	-	3-3	1-1
Rotherham v Bradford	1-1	0-2	1-2	0-0	3-0	4-0
Stevenage v Colchester	-	-	-	-	0-0	0-2
Swindon v Brentford	-	-	3-2	1-1	-	0-1
Tranmere v Shrewsbury	-	-	-	-	-	0-2
Walsall v Bristol City	-	-	-	-	-	-
League 2						
Bristol Rovers v Torquay	-	-	-	-	1-2	3-2
Dag & Red v Portsmouth	-	-	-	-	-	-
Exeter v Cheltenham	-	-	-	-	-	0-1
Fleetwood v Morecambe	-	-	-	-	-	1-0
Hartlepool v Chesterfield	-	-	-	-	1-2	-
Mansfield v Rochdale	0-4	-	-	-	-	-
Newport County v Wycombe	-	-	-	-	-	-
Northampton v Burton	-	-	1-1	2-3	2-3	1-0
Plymouth v Oxford	-	-	-	-	1-1	0-1
Scunthorpe v Bury	-	-	-	-	1-3	1-2
Southend v AFC Wimbledon	-	-	-	-	2-0	1-3
York v Accrington	-	-	-	-	-	1-1
Conference						
Barnet v Halifax	-	-	-	-	-	-
Cambridge v Hyde	-	-	-	-	-	0-1
Dartford v Forest Green	-	-	-	-	-	0-1
Grimsby v Chester	1-2	1-3	-	-	-	-
Hereford v Gateshead	-	-	-	-	-	1-1
Kidderminster v Welling	-	-	-	-	-	-
Luton v Braintree	-	-	-	-	3-1	2-3

Results cover matches from Premier League to Conference and Scottish Premier League to Division Three

	2007-08	2008-09	2009-10	2010-11	2011-12	2012-13
Macclesfield v Aldershot	-	4-2	1-1	2-0	0-1	-
Salisbury v Lincoln	-	-	-	-	-	-
Southport v Tamworth	-	-	-	2-1	1-1	0-3
Woking v Alfreton	-	-	-	-	-	1-2
Wrexham v Nuneaton	-	-	-	-	-	6-1

Scottish Division One						
Alloa v Morton	-	-	-	-	-	-
Dundee v Cowdenbeath	-	-	-	3-0/2-2	-	-
Livingston v Hamilton	2-0/1-3	-	-	-	1-0/0-4	0-3/0-0
Queen of Sth v Falkirk	-	-	-	1-5/0-1	1-5/0-0	-
Raith v Dumbarton	-	-	-	-	-	2-2/3-2

Scottish Division Two						
Arbroath v Stranraer	2-2/0-0	1-0/2-0	-	0-0/2-2	-	2-1/1-0
Brechin v Airdrieonians	4-2/2-1	-	-	3-1/1-2	1-1/1-1	-
Dunfermline v Forfar	-	-	-	-	-	-
East Fife v Stenhousemuir	7-0/0-1	-	2-1/1-1	6-0/1-1	1-3/1-1	3-2/1-2
Rangers v Ayr	-	-	-	-	-	-

Scottish Division Three						
Albion v Stirling	-	-	-	-	0-1/1-2	-
Clyde v Peterhead	-	-	1-3/3-1	-	2-0/0-1	0-2/2-0
East Stirling v Annan	-	2-1/1-1	1-3/3-1	1-5/2-0	1-0/0-4	2-2/1-2
Elgin v Berwick	-	0-2/2-0	3-3/1-5	1-2/3-2	4-1/4-0	3-1/1-2
Queen's Park v Montrose	-	-	3-2/3-0	1-0/4-1	3-1/5-0	2-2/1-2

Saturday April 19th, 2014

Premier League						
Aston Villa v Southampton	-	-	-	-	-	0-1
Cardiff v Stoke	0-1	-	-	-	-	-
Chelsea v Sunderland	2-0	5-0	7-2	0-3	1-0	2-1
Everton v Man United	0-1	1-1	3-1	3-3	0-1	1-0
Hull v Arsenal	-	1-3	1-2	-	-	-
Man City v West Brom	-	4-2	-	3-0	4-0	1-0
Newcastle v Swansea	-	-	3-0	-	0-0	1-2
Norwich v Liverpool	-	-	-	-	0-3	2-5
Tottenham v Fulham	5-1	0-0	2-0	1-0	2-0	0-1
West Ham v Crystal Palace	-	-	-	-	0-0	-

Championship						
Barnsley v Leeds	-	-	-	5-2	4-1	2-0
Blackburn v Yeovil	-	-	-	-	-	-
Blackpool v Burnley	3-0	0-1	-	-	4-0	1-0
Bournemouth v Sheffield Weds	-	-	-	0-0	2-0	-
Charlton v Bolton	-	-	-	-	-	3-2
Doncaster v Derby	-	2-1	2-1	2-3	1-2	-
Huddersfield v Brighton	2-1	2-2	7-1	2-1	-	1-2
Leicester v QPR	1-1	-	4-0	0-2	-	-
Middlesbrough v Millwall	-	-	-	0-1	1-1	1-2
Nottm Forest v Birmingham	-	1-1	-	-	1-3	2-2
Watford v Ipswich	2-0	2-1	2-1	2-1	2-1	0-1
Wigan v Reading	0-0	-	-	-	-	3-2

League 1						
Bradford v Peterborough	1-0	-	-	-	-	-
Brentford v Preston	-	-	-	-	1-3	1-0
Bristol City v Notts County	-	-	-	-	-	-

Results cover matches from Premier League to Conference and Scottish Premier League to Division Three

	2007-08	2008-09	2009-10	2010-11	2011-12	2012-13
Carlisle v Walsall	2-1	1-1	1-1	1-3	1-1	0-3
Colchester v Oldham	-	2-2	1-0	1-0	4-1	0-2
Coventry v Swindon	-	-	-	-	-	1-2
Crawley v Leyton Orient	-	-	-	-	-	1-0
Gillingham v Tranmere	0-2	-	0-1	-	-	-
Port Vale v MK Dons	-	-	-	-	-	-
Sheffield United v Stevenage	-	-	-	-	2-2	4-1
Shrewsbury v Crewe	-	-	2-0	0-1	2-0	1-0
Wolves v Rotherham	-	-	-	-	-	-
League 2						
Accrington v Mansfield	1-0	-	-	-	-	-
AFC Wimbledon v Newport County	-	-	-	2-2	-	-
Burton v Hartlepool	-	-	-	-	-	-
Bury v Plymouth	-	-	-	-	-	-
Cheltenham v Fleetwood	-	-	-	-	-	2-2
Chesterfield v Exeter	-	2-1	-	-	0-2	4-0
Morecambe v Scunthorpe	-	-	-	-	-	-
Oxford v York	1-1	1-0	2-1	-	-	0-0
Portsmouth v Bristol Rovers	-	-	-	-	-	-
Rochdale v Southend	-	-	-	-	-	4-2
Torquay v Dag & Red	-	-	0-0	-	1-0	2-1
Wycombe v Northampton	-	-	-	2-2	-	0-0
Conference						
Aldershot v Salisbury	2-1	-	-	-	-	-
Alfreton v Grimsby	-	-	-	-	2-5	0-2
Braintree v Dartford	-	-	-	-	-	0-2
Chester v Wrexham	0-2	-	-	-	-	-
Forest Green v Woking	2-1	0-2	-	-	-	3-1
Gateshead v Southport	-	-	-	1-0	2-3	2-2
Halifax v Macclesfield	-	-	-	-	-	-
Hyde v Kidderminster	-	-	-	-	-	0-4
Lincoln v Cambridge	-	-	-	-	0-1	0-0
Nuneaton v Barnet	-	-	-	-	-	-
Tamworth v Hereford	-	-	-	-	-	2-2
Welling v Luton	-	-	-	-	-	-
Scottish Division One						
Cowdenbeath v Livingston	-	-	-	-	-	1-1/2-2
Dumbarton v Queen of Sth	-	-	-	-	-	-
Falkirk v Raith	-	-	-	0-0/2-1	2-0/2-3	0-2/1-1
Hamilton v Alloa	-	-	-	-	-	-
Morton v Dundee	0-2/1-2	2-0/2-0	0-1/2-2	0-1/1-3	1-2/0-2	-
Scottish Division Two						
Airdrieonians v East Fife	-	-	-	1-1/2-2	1-3/2-0	-
Ayr v Dunfermline	-	-	1-0/1-2	-	-	-
Forfar v Arbroath	1-3/1-0	-	-	-	1-1/2-4	1-1/2-4
Stenhousemuir v Rangers	-	-	-	-	-	-
Stranraer v Brechin	-	1-2/0-3	-	-	-	0-2/3-2
Scottish Division Three						
Annan v Queen's Park	-	-	3-1/0-2	2-1/1-2	5-2/2-3	2-3/2-0
Berwick v East Stirling	-	2-1/1-2	0-1/2-2	3-0/1-1	4-2/0-2	3-0/2-0
Montrose v Clyde	-	-	-	8-1/3-1	4-0/5-0	2-3/1-0
Peterhead v Albion	-	-	-	-	-	-
Stirling v Elgin	-	-	-	-	-	1-4/1-1

Results cover matches from Premier League to Conference and Scottish Premier League to Division Three

Monday April 21st, 2014

Championship

	2007-08	2008-09	2009-10	2010-11	2011-12	2012-13
Birmingham v Blackburn	4-1	-	2-1	2-1	-	1-1
Bolton v Leicester	-	-	-	-	-	0-0
Brighton v Blackpool	-	-	-	-	2-2	6-1
Burnley v Wigan	-	-	1-3	-	-	-
Derby v Barnsley	-	0-0	2-3	0-0	1-1	2-0
Ipswich v Bournemouth	-	-	-	-	-	-
Leeds v Nottm Forest	1-1	-	-	4-1	3-7	2-1
Millwall v Doncaster	0-3	-	-	1-0	3-2	-
QPR v Watford	1-1	0-0	1-0	1-3	-	-
Reading v Middlesbrough	1-1	-	0-2	5-2	0-0	-
Sheffield Weds v Charlton	0-0	4-1	-	2-2	0-1	2-0
Yeovil v Huddersfield	0-2	1-0	0-1	1-1	0-1	-

League 1

	2007-08	2008-09	2009-10	2010-11	2011-12	2012-13
Crewe v Colchester	-	2-0	-	-	-	3-2
Leyton Orient v Wolves	-	-	-	-	-	-
MK Dons v Brentford	1-1	-	0-1	1-1	1-2	2-0
Notts County v Crawley	-	-	-	-	-	1-1
Oldham v Coventry	-	-	-	-	-	0-1
Peterborough v Carlisle	-	1-0	-	6-0	-	-
Preston v Shrewsbury	-	-	-	-	-	1-2
Rotherham v Port Vale	-	1-0	1-2	5-0	0-1	1-2
Stevenage v Bristol City	-	-	-	-	-	-
Swindon v Bradford	-	-	-	-	0-0	-
Tranmere v Sheffield United	-	-	-	-	1-1	0-1
Walsall v Gillingham	2-1	-	0-0	-	-	-

League 2

	2007-08	2008-09	2009-10	2010-11	2011-12	2012-13
Bristol Rovers v Rochdale	-	-	-	2-1	-	2-1
Dag & Red v Chesterfield	0-3	3-0	2-1	-	-	0-1
Exeter v Torquay	4-3	-	-	-	-	0-1
Fleetwood v Wycombe	-	-	-	-	-	0-1
Hartlepool v Morecambe	-	-	-	-	-	-
Mansfield v Cheltenham	-	-	-	-	-	-
Newport County v Burton	-	-	-	-	-	-
Northampton v Portsmouth	-	-	-	-	-	-
Plymouth v AFC Wimbledon	-	-	-	-	0-2	1-2
Scunthorpe v Oxford	-	-	-	-	-	-
Southend v Accrington	-	-	-	1-1	2-2	0-1
York v Bury	-	-	-	-	-	-

Conference

	2007-08	2008-09	2009-10	2010-11	2011-12	2012-13
Barnet v Braintree	-	-	-	-	-	-
Cambridge v Chester	-	-	-	-	-	-
Dartford v Tamworth	-	-	-	-	-	2-3
Grimsby v Hyde	-	-	-	-	-	2-0
Hereford v Alfreton	-	-	-	-	-	3-3
Kidderminster v Nuneaton	-	-	-	-	-	1-0
Luton v Forest Green	-	-	2-1	6-1	1-1	1-1
Macclesfield v Gateshead	-	-	-	-	-	0-4
Salisbury v Welling	-	-	-	-	-	-
Southport v Halifax	-	-	-	-	-	-
Woking v Aldershot	0-1	-	-	-	-	-
Wrexham v Lincoln	1-0	-	-	-	2-0	2-4

Results cover matches from Premier League to Conference and Scottish Premier League to Division Three

Saturday April 26th, 2014

Premier League

	2007-08	2008-09	2009-10	2010-11	2011-12	2012-13
Arsenal v Newcastle	3-0	3-0	-	0-1	2-1	7-3
Crystal Palace v Man City	-	-	-	-	-	-
Fulham v Hull	-	0-1	2-0	-	-	-
Liverpool v Chelsea	1-1	2-0	0-2	2-0	4-1	2-2
Man United v Norwich	-	-	-	-	2-0	4-0
Southampton v Everton	-	-	-	-	-	0-0
Stoke v Tottenham	-	2-1	1-2	1-2	2-1	1-2
Sunderland v Cardiff	-	-	-	-	-	-
Swansea v Aston Villa	-	-	-	-	0-0	2-2
West Brom v West Ham	-	3-2	-	3-3	-	0-0

Championship

	2007-08	2008-09	2009-10	2010-11	2011-12	2012-13
Birmingham v Leeds	-	-	-	-	1-0	1-0
Bournemouth v Nottm Forest	2-0	-	-	-	-	-
Brighton v Yeovil	1-2	5-0	1-0	2-0	-	-
Burnley v Ipswich	2-2	0-3	-	1-2	4-0	2-0
Charlton v Blackburn	-	-	-	-	-	1-1
Derby v Watford	-	1-0	2-0	4-1	1-2	5-1
Doncaster v Reading	-	0-1	1-2	0-3	1-1	-
Huddersfield v Leicester	-	2-3	-	-	-	0-2
Middlesbrough v Barnsley	-	-	2-1	1-1	2-0	2-3
QPR v Millwall	-	-	-	0-0	-	-
Sheffield Weds v Bolton	-	-	-	-	-	1-2
Wigan v Blackpool	-	-	-	0-4	-	-

League 1

	2007-08	2008-09	2009-10	2010-11	2011-12	2012-13
Bradford v Crawley	-	-	-	-	1-2	-
Bristol City v Crewe	-	-	-	-	-	-
Carlisle v Oldham	1-0	1-1	1-2	2-2	3-3	3-1
Colchester v Brentford	-	-	3-3	0-2	2-1	1-3
Coventry v Wolves	1-1	2-1	-	-	-	-
Leyton Orient v Tranmere	3-0	0-1	2-1	0-3	0-1	2-1
Notts County v Swindon	-	-	-	1-0	-	1-0
Port Vale v Sheffield United	-	-	-	-	-	-
Preston v Gillingham	-	-	-	-	-	-
Rotherham v MK Dons	0-1	-	-	-	-	-
Shrewsbury v Peterborough	0-2	-	-	-	-	-
Stevenage v Walsall	-	-	-	-	0-0	3-1

League 2

	2007-08	2008-09	2009-10	2010-11	2011-12	2012-13
AFC Wimbledon v Morecambe	-	-	-	-	1-1	2-0
Burton v Chesterfield	-	-	2-2	1-0	-	0-1
Bury v Portsmouth	-	-	-	-	-	2-0
Dag & Red v Northampton	-	-	0-1	-	0-1	0-1
Exeter v Scunthorpe	-	-	-	-	0-0	-
Fleetwood v Southend	-	-	-	-	-	0-0
Mansfield v Torquay	-	1-1	-	-	-	-
Oxford v Accrington	-	-	-	0-0	1-1	5-0
Plymouth v Hartlepool	-	-	-	0-1	-	-
Rochdale v Cheltenham	-	-	0-1	-	-	4-1
Wycombe v Bristol Rovers	-	-	2-1	-	-	2-0
York v Newport County	-	-	-	2-1	1-1	-

Conference

	2007-08	2008-09	2009-10	2010-11	2011-12	2012-13
Aldershot v Hereford	-	-	2-2	1-2	1-0	-
Alfreton v Macclesfield	-	-	-	-	-	1-2
Braintree v Grimsby	-	-	-	-	5-0	2-0

Results cover matches from Premier League to Conference and Scottish Premier League to Division Three

	2007-08	2008-09	2009-10	2010-11	2011-12	2012-13
Chester v Salisbury	-	-	-	-	-	-
Forest Green v Wrexham	-	2-3	0-2	3-0	1-0	0-0
Gateshead v Cambridge	-	-	2-0	2-3	1-1	0-0
Halifax v Kidderminster	1-6	-	-	-	-	-
Hyde v Luton	-	-	-	-	-	1-2
Lincoln v Barnet	4-1	2-0	1-0	1-0	-	-
Nuneaton v Dartford	-	-	-	-	-	1-0
Tamworth v Woking	-	-	-	-	-	2-1
Welling v Southport	-	-	-	-	-	-
Scottish Division One						
Alloa v Dundee	-	-	-	-	-	-
Dumbarton v Hamilton	-	-	-	-	-	3-3/3-1
Morton v Falkirk	-	-	-	0-0/2-2	3-2/0-0	1-2/2-0
Queen of Sth v Livingston	1-0/1-0	6-1/3-3	-	-	0-2/0-4	-
Raith v Cowdenbeath	2-0/3-2	-	-	2-1/2-2	-	2-2/0-1
Scottish Division Two						
Arbroath v Dunfermline	-	-	-	-	-	-
East Fife v Brechin	-	0-0/2-1	2-0/2-0	1-3/0-0	1-1/2-2	2-2/0-3
Forfar v Ayr	-	-	-	4-1/3-2	-	2-1/2-1
Rangers v Stranraer	-	-	-	-	-	-
Stenhousemuir v Airdrieonians	-	-	-	1-3/1-0	1-1/0-3	-
Scottish Division Three						
Clyde v Albion	-	-	-	1-2/0-1	-	-
Elgin v East Stirling	6-0/3-0	0-4/0-2	1-2/0-1	0-2/2-0	2-0/3-1	3-4/3-2
Montrose v Annan	-	1-1/0-3	0-0/1-2	1-1/0-1	2-3/1-1	0-0/5-1
Peterhead v Stirling	-	1-1/1-1	3-2/1-1	-	-	2-2/0-0
Queen's Park v Berwick	1-0/3-1	-	2-0/2-3	0-2/1-0	1-1/2-2	1-1/2-1

Saturday May 3rd, 2014

	2007-08	2008-09	2009-10	2010-11	2011-12	2012-13
Premier League						
Arsenal v West Brom	-	1-0	-	2-3	3-0	2-0
Aston Villa v Hull	-	1-0	3-0	-	-	-
Chelsea v Norwich	-	-	-	-	3-1	4-1
Crystal Palace v Liverpool	-	-	-	-	-	-
Everton v Man City	1-0	1-2	2-0	2-1	1-0	2-0
Man United v Sunderland	1-0	1-0	2-2	2-0	1-0	3-1
Newcastle v Cardiff	-	-	5-1	-	-	-
Stoke v Fulham	-	0-0	3-2	0-2	2-0	1-0
Swansea v Southampton	-	3-0	-	-	-	0-0
West Ham v Tottenham	1-1	0-2	1-2	1-0	-	2-3
Championship						
Barnsley v QPR	0-0	2-1	0-1	0-1	-	-
Blackburn v Wigan	3-1	2-0	2-1	2-1	0-1	-
Blackpool v Charlton	5-3	2-0	-	-	-	0-2
Bolton v Birmingham	3-0	-	2-1	2-2	-	3-1
Ipswich v Sheffield Weds	4-1	1-1	0-0	-	-	0-3
Leeds v Derby	-	-	-	1-2	0-2	1-2
Leicester v Doncaster	-	-	0-0	5-1	4-0	-
Millwall v Bournemouth	2-1	-	-	-	-	-
Nottm Forest v Brighton	0-0	-	-	-	1-1	2-2
Reading v Burnley	-	3-1	-	2-1	1-0	-
Watford v Huddersfield	-	-	-	-	-	4-0
Yeovil v Middlesbrough	-	-	-	-	-	-
League 1						
Brentford v Stevenage	-	-	-	-	0-1	2-0

Results cover matches from Premier League to Conference and Scottish Premier League to Division Three

	2007-08	2008-09	2009-10	2010-11	2011-12	2012-13
Crawley v Bristol City	-	-	-	-	-	-
Crewe v Preston	-	-	-	-	-	1-0
Gillingham v Shrewsbury	-	2-2	-	2-0	0-1	-
MK Dons v Leyton Orient	-	1-2	1-0	2-3	4-1	1-0
Oldham v Notts County	-	-	-	3-0	3-2	2-2
Peterborough v Port Vale	-	-	-	-	-	-
Sheffield United v Coventry	2-1	1-1	1-0	0-1	-	1-2
Swindon v Rotherham	-	-	-	-	3-2	-
Tranmere v Bradford	-	-	-	-	-	-
Walsall v Colchester	-	2-0	1-0	0-1	3-1	1-0
Wolves v Carlisle	-	-	-	-	-	-

League 2						
Accrington v AFC Wimbledon	-	-	-	-	2-1	4-0
Bristol Rovers v Mansfield	-	-	-	-	-	-
Cheltenham v Dag & Red	-	-	1-1	-	2-1	2-0
Chesterfield v Fleetwood	-	-	-	-	-	1-2
Hartlepool v Exeter	-	-	1-1	2-3	2-0	-
Morecambe v Bury	2-1	0-0	3-0	1-4	-	-
Newport County v Rochdale	-	-	-	-	-	-
Northampton v Oxford	-	-	-	2-1	2-1	1-0
Portsmouth v Plymouth	-	-	-	-	-	-
Scunthorpe v York	-	-	-	-	-	-
Southend v Burton	-	-	-	1-1	0-1	0-1
Torquay v Wycombe	-	-	-	0-0	-	1-2

Scottish Division One						
Cowdenbeath v Queen of Sth	-	-	-	1-3/2-2	-	-
Dundee v Dumbarton	-	-	-	-	-	-
Falkirk v Alloa	-	-	-	-	-	-
Hamilton v Morton	1-0/3-0	-	-	-	1-2/4-3	1-1/2-1
Livingston v Raith	-	-	-	-	1-1/4-0	2-1/2-3

Scottish Division Two						
Airdrieonians v Arbroath	-	-	-	-	3-3/2-0	-
Ayr v East Fife	-	4-2/2-0	-	0-4/1-1	-	2-3/2-1
Brechin v Stenhousemuir	-	-	1-0/2-2	0-0/3-1	2-0/1-0	7-2/1-2
Dunfermline v Rangers	-	-	-	-	0-4/1-4	-
Stranraer v Forfar	3-0/2-1	-	1-0/2-0	-	-	4-1/0-3

Scottish Division Three						
Albion v Queen's Park	-	-	0-1/1-0	2-1/1-2	-	-
Annan v Elgin	-	5-0/6-0	0-2/3-3	0-1/2-2	1-1/1-1	2-0/2-2
Berwick v Peterhead	1-2/2-2	-	-	-	2-1/0-1	1-1/0-2
East Stirling v Montrose	0-3/3-1	5-0/2-1	1-0/2-3	2-1/1-2	1-0/3-1	2-2/1-2
Stirling v Clyde	0-2/1-1	-	1-1/1-0	-	-	0-1/2-0

Sunday May 11th, 2014

Premier League						
Cardiff v Chelsea	-	-	-	-	-	-
Fulham v Crystal Palace	-	-	-	-	-	-
Hull v Everton	-	2-2	3-2	-	-	-
Liverpool v Newcastle	3-0	3-0	-	3-0	3-1	1-1
Man City v West Ham	1-1	3-0	3-1	2-1	-	2-1
Norwich v Arsenal	-	-	-	-	1-2	1-0
Southampton v Man United	-	-	-	-	-	2-3
Sunderland v Swansea	-	-	-	-	2-0	0-0
Tottenham v Aston Villa	4-4	1-2	0-0	2-1	2-0	2-0
West Brom v Stoke	1-1	0-2	-	0-3	0-1	0-1

Results cover matches from Premier League to Conference and Scottish Premier League to Division Three

Swansea's Michu grabs the first goal of the 2012-13 Premier League season

Correct scores 2012-13

	Prem	Chmp	Lg1	Lg2	Conf	SPL	Sct 1	Sct 2	Sct 3
1-0	41	62	64	55	44	21	11	14	10
2-0	18	39	42	34	37	15	10	13	17
2-1	41	61	36	40	41	14	12	21	14
3-0	12	17	22	24	19	10	6	6	6
3-1	18	19	24	20	24	8	4	7	9
3-2	9	14	9	16	19	4	3	9	5
4-0	5	5	6	11	5	4	4	3	2
4-1	7	10	11	13	17	7	6	5	5
4-2	4	5	1	5	4	1	4	3	2
4-3	1	1	0	3	1	2	1	1	0
0-0	35	37	38	49	41	23	8	5	8
1-1	41	64	71	64	61	30	18	14	16
2-2	27	39	37	32	32	16	12	8	15
3-3	4	5	3	5	6	3	4	3	1
4-4	0	0	0	0	0	1	1	1	0
0-1	20	40	48	56	39	14	11	13	11
0-2	13	23	35	25	26	7	14	5	7
1-2	28	52	54	38	47	15	14	12	13
0-3	10	4	8	16	13	4	8	6	4
1-3	10	10	16	16	18	11	5	3	5
2-3	11	13	7	12	14	5	6	9	5
0-4	4	3	3	4	5	3	4	2	1
1-4	0	8	5	3	7	3	2	2	5
2-4	3	1	2	4	7	1	0	2	3
3-4	3	2	0	0	3	1	5	1	1
Other	15	18	10	7	22	5	7	12	15

Home win/away win/draw percentages 2012-13

	Prem	Chmp	Lg1	Lg2	Conf	SPL	Sct 1	Sct 2	Sct 3
Home	44	45	40	41	41	39	37	49	45
Draw	28	26	27	27	25	32	24	17	22
Away	28	29	33	32	33	29	39	34	33

Over/under percentages 2012-13

	Prem	Chmp	Lg1	Lg2	Conf	SPL	Sct 1	Sct 2	Sct 3
<1.5 gls	25	25	27	29	22	25	17	18	16
>1.5 gls	75	75	73	71	78	75	83	82	84
<2.5 gls	44	48	54	51	45	48	40	36	38
>2.5 gls	56	52	46	49	55	52	60	64	62
<3.5 gls	68	72	76	73	67	67	62	61	59
>3.5 gls	32	28	24	27	33	33	38	39	41
<4.5 gls	85	86	91	88	82	86	78	73	77
>4.5 gls	15	14	9	12	18	14	22	27	23

Odds conversion

Odds-on			Odds-against	
As %	Decimal	Fractional	Decimal	As %
50.00%	2.00	Evens	2.00	50.00%
52.38%	1.91	11-10	2.10	47.62%
54.55%	1.83	6-5	2.20	45.45%
55.56%	1.80	5-4	2.25	44.44%
57.89%	1.73	11-8	2.38	42.11%
60.00%	1.67	6-4	2.50	40.00%
61.90%	1.62	13-8	2.63	38.10%
63.64%	1.57	7-4	2.75	36.36%
65.22%	1.53	15-8	2.88	34.78%
66.67%	1.50	2-1	3.00	33.33%
69.23%	1.44	9-4	3.25	30.77%
71.43%	1.40	5-2	3.50	28.57%
72.22%	1.38	13-5	3.60	27.78%
73.33%	1.36	11-4	3.75	26.67%
73.68%	1.36	14-5	3.80	26.32%
75.00%	1.33	3-1	4.00	25.00%
76.92%	1.30	10-3	4.33	23.08%
77.78%	1.29	7-2	4.50	22.22%
80.00%	1.25	4-1	5.00	20.00%
81.82%	1.22	9-2	5.50	18.18%
83.33%	1.20	5-1	6.00	16.67%
84.62%	1.18	11-2	6.50	15.38%
85.71%	1.17	6-1	7.00	14.29%
86.67%	1.15	13-2	7.50	13.33%
87.50%	1.14	7-1	8.00	12.50%
88.24%	1.13	15-2	8.50	11.76%
88.89%	1.13	8-1	9.00	11.11%

Asian handicaps

Conceding handicap		Receiving handicap		
Result of bet	Result of match	Handicap	Result of match	Result of bet
Win	Win	0	Win	Win
No bet	Draw	Scratch	Draw	No bet
Lose	Lose		Lose	Lose
Win	Win	0,0.5	Win	Win
Lose ½	Draw	0.25	Draw	Win ½
Lose	Lose		Lose	Lose
Win	Win	0.5	Win	Win
Lose	Draw		Draw	Win
Lose	Lose		Lose	Lose
Win	Win by 2+	0.5,1	Lose by 2+	Lose
Win ½	Win by 1	0.75	Lose by 1	Lose ½
Lose	Draw		Draw	Win
Lose	Lose		Win	Win
Win	Win by 2+	1	Lose by 2+	Lose
No bet	Win by 1		Lose by 1	No bet
Lose	Draw		Draw	Win
Lose	Lose		Win	Win